Qualitative Inquiry & Research Design

Fifth Edition

John dedicates this book to Uncle Jim (James W. Marshall, MD, 1915–1997), who provided love, support, and inspiration.

Cheryl dedicates this book to her dad (Richard F. Poth, MBA, 1944–2016), who instilled confidence for trying new things, lessons for guiding life choices, and encouragement for pursuing bold dreams.

Qualitative Inquiry & Research Design

Choosing Among Five Approaches

Fifth Edition

John W. Creswell
University of Michigan

Cheryl N. Poth
University of Alberta

FOR INFORMATION:

2455 Teller Road
Thousand Oaks, California 91320
E-mail: order@sagepub.com

1 Oliver's Yard
55 City Road
London EC1Y 1SP
United Kingdom

Unit No 323-333, Third Floor, F-Block
International Trade Tower
Nehru Place, New Delhi – 110 019
India

3 Church Street
#10-04 Samsung Hub
Singapore 049483

Acquisitions Editor: Leah Fargotstein

Editorial Assistant: Latoya Douse

Production Editor: Vishwajeet Mehra

Copy Editor: Taryn Bigelow

Typesetter: diacriTech

Cover Designer: Candice Harman

Marketing Manager: Victoria Velasquez

Copyright © 2025 by Sage.

All rights reserved. Except as permitted by U.S. copyright law, no part of this work may be reproduced or distributed in any form or by any means, or stored in a database or retrieval system, without permission in writing from the publisher.

All third party trademarks referenced or depicted herein are included solely for the purpose of illustration and are the property of their respective owners. Reference to these trademarks in no way indicates any relationship with, or endorsement by, the trademark owner.

ISBN: 978-1-0719-4775-3

Library of Congress Cataloging-in-Publication Data

Names: Creswell, John W., author. | Poth, Cheryl N., author.

Title: Qualitative inquiry and research design: choosing among five approaches / John W. Creswell, Cheryl N. Poth.

Description: Fifth edition. | Thousand Oaks, California: Sage, [2023] | Includes bibliographical references and index.

Identifiers: LCCN 2023051364 (print) | LCCN 2023051365 (ebook) | ISBN 9781544398396 (paperback) | ISBN 9781544398402 (epub)

Subjects: LCSH: Social sciences–Methodology. | Research–Design.

Classification: LCC H61.C73 2023 (print) | LCC H61 (ebook) | DDC 300.72/1–dc23/eng/20231213

LC record available at https://lccn.loc.gov/2023051364

LC ebook record available at https://lccn.loc.gov/2023051365

This book is printed on acid-free paper.

24 25 26 27 28 10 9 8 7 6 5 4 3 2 1

Printed in the United Kingdom by Henry Ling Limited

BRIEF CONTENTS

Preface	xv
What Is New in This Edition	xvii
About the Authors	xix
Acknowledgments	xxi
Analytic Table of Contents by Approach	xxiii
List of Tables	xxvii
List of Figures	xxix
List of Examples	xxxi
List of "Try This Now" Activities	xxxiii
Chapter 1 — Introduction to Qualitative Inquiry and Research Design	1
Chapter 2 — Philosophical Assumptions and Interpretive Frameworks	17
Chapter 3 — Designing a Qualitative Study	47
Chapter 4 — Five Qualitative Approaches to Inquiry	75
Chapter 5 — Five Different Qualitative Studies	135
Chapter 6 — Introducing and Focusing the Study	155
Chapter 7 — Data Collection	175
Chapter 8 — Data Analysis and Representation	215
Chapter 9 — Writing a Qualitative Study	257
Chapter 10 — Standards of Validation and Evaluation	285
Chapter 11 — "Turning the Story" and Conclusion	319
Appendix A - A Narrative Research Study—"Living in the Space Between Participant and Researcher as a Narrative Inquirer: Examining Ethnic Identity of Chinese Canadian Students as Conflicting Stories to Live By"	345
Elaine Chan	

Appendix B - Resilient Leadership: A Phenomenological Exploration Into How Black Women in Higher Education Leadership Navigate Cultural Adversity   365
   Nuchelle L. Chance

Appendix C - Aging With Intellectual Disabilities in Families: Navigating Ever-Changing Seas—A Theoretical Model   395
   Henrietta Trip, Lisa Whitehead, Marie Crowe, Brigit Mirfin-Veitch and Chris Daffue

Appendix D - An Ethnography—"British-Born Pakistani and Bangladeshi Young Men: Exploring Unstable Concepts of Muslim, Islamophobia and Racialization"   421
   Mairtin Mac an Ghaill and Chris Haywood

Appendix E - Learning from Error in Violence Prevention: A School Shooting as an Organizational Accident   443
   Sarah Goodrum, Jessie Slepicka, William Woodward and Beverly Kingston

Glossary   471

References   485

Index   505

DETAILED CONTENTS

Preface	xv
What Is New in This Edition	xvii
About the Authors	xix
Acknowledgments	xxi
Analytic Table of Contents by Approach	xxiii
List of Tables	xxvii
List of Figures	xxix
List of Examples	xxxi
List of "Try This Now" Activities	xxxiii

Chapter 1	**Introduction to Qualitative Inquiry and Research Design**	1
	Rationale for Our Approach to the Book	2
	Positioning Ourselves	2
	Defining Qualitative Research	4
	Distinguishing Characteristics	5
	Selection of the Five Approaches	8
	Key Book Readings	11
	Narrative Research	11
	Phenomenology	12
	Grounded Theory	12
	Ethnography	12
	Case Study	13
	Chapter Check-In	13
	Summary	13
	Chapter Key Terms	14
	Further Readings	14
Chapter 2	**Philosophical Assumptions and Interpretive Frameworks**	17
	Situating Philosophy and Interpretive Frameworks Within the Research Process	18
	Philosophical Assumptions	21
	Why Philosophy Is Important	21
	Four Philosophical Assumptions	22
	Writing Philosophical Assumptions Into Qualitative Studies	24

Interpretive Frameworks	25
Postpositivism	26
Social Constructivism	27
Transformative Frameworks	28
Postmodern Perspectives	29
Pragmatism	30
Feminist Theories	31
Critical Theory	32
Critical Race Theory	33
Postcolonial Theories	34
Queer Theory	35
Disability Theories	36
The Practice of Using Interpretive Frameworks in Qualitative Research	36
Linking Philosophy and Interpretive Frameworks in Qualitative Research	40
Chapter Check-In	43
Summary	43
Chapter Key Terms	44
Further Readings	44

Chapter 3   Designing a Qualitative Study   47

When to Use Qualitative Research	48
What a Qualitative Study Requires From Us	49
The Features of a "Good" Qualitative Study	50
The Process of Designing a Qualitative Study	53
Preliminary Considerations	53
Phases in the Research Process	54
Elements in All Phases of the Research	56
Practical Guidance for Qualitative Research Ethics	57
Ethical Situations Across the Research Process	58
The Design Structures of a Qualitative Research Plan or Proposal	66
Design Considerations Useful for Engaging Readers	66
General Writing Structures	68
Chapter Check-In	70
Summary	71
Chapter Key Terms	72
Further Readings	72

Chapter 4   Five Qualitative Approaches to Inquiry   75

Deciding Among the Five Approaches	76
Narrative Research	78
Definition of Narrative Research	78
Origins of Narrative Research	78

Defining Features of Narrative Studies	79
Types of and Variations Within Narrative Research	80
Procedures for Conducting Narrative Research	82
Challenges and Opportunities in Narrative Research	85

Phenomenological Research — 87

Definition of Phenomenological Research	87
Origins of Phenomenological Research	87
Defining Features of Phenomenology	89
Types of and Variations Within Phenomenology	90
Procedures for Conducting Phenomenological Research	91
Challenges and Opportunities in Phenomenological Research	94

Grounded Theory Research — 96

Definition of Grounded Theory Research	96
Origins of Grounded Theory Research	97
Defining Features of Grounded Theory	98
Types of and Variations Within Grounded Theory Studies	99
Procedures for Conducting Grounded Theory Research	101
Challenges and Opportunities in Grounded Theory Research	104

Ethnographic Research — 106

Definition of Ethnographic Research	106
Origins of Ethnographic Research	106
Defining Features of Ethnographies	107
Types of and Variations Within Ethnographies	108
Procedures for Conducting an Ethnography	109
Challenges and Opportunities in Ethnographic Research	112

Case Study Research — 114

Definition of Case Study Research	114
Origins of Case Study Research	115
Defining Features of Case Studies	116
Types of and Variations Within Case Studies	117
Procedures for Conducting a Case Study	118
Challenges and Opportunities in Case Study Research	121

Comparing the Five Approaches	123
Chapter Check-In	128
Summary	128
Chapter Key Terms	129
New Terms Specific to Narrative Research	129
New Terms Specific to Phenomenological Research	129
New Terms Specific to Grounded Theory Research	130
New Terms Specific to Ethnographic Research	130
New Terms Specific to Case Study Research	130
Further Readings	131

Chapter 5 Five Different Qualitative Studies — 135

- A Narrative Study (Chan, 2010; see Appendix A) — 136
- A Phenomenological Study (Chance, 2022; see Appendix B) — 139
- A Grounded Theory Study (Trip et al., 2019; see Appendix C) — 141
- An Ethnographic Study (Mac an Ghaill & Haywood, 2015; see Appendix D) — 144
- A Case Study (Goodrum et al., 2022; see Appendix E) — 147
- Differences Among the Approaches — 149
  - Selecting Your Approach — 151
- Chapter Check-In — 152
- Summary — 152
- Further Readings — 152

Chapter 6 Introducing and Focusing the Study — 155

- Interrelating the Study Problem, Purpose, and Questions Within Research — 156
- The Research Problem Statement — 157
- The Purpose Statement — 161
- The Research Questions — 165
  - The Central Question — 166
  - Subquestions — 169
- Introducing and Focusing Your Study — 172
- Chapter Check-In — 172
- Summary — 173
- Chapter Key Terms — 173
- Further Readings — 173

Chapter 7 Data Collection — 175

- The Data Collection Circle — 176
  - Ethical Considerations for Data Collection — 177
    - Institutional Review Boards — 180
  - The Site or Individual — 180
    - Self-Study Considerations — 182
  - Access and Rapport — 183
    - Letter of information — 184
    - Documenting Consent — 185
  - Purposeful Sampling Strategies — 188
    - Participants in the Sample — 189
    - Types of Sampling Strategies — 190
    - Sample Size — 192

Forms of Data	192
Interviewing	197
Observing	201
Recording Information Procedures	203
Fieldwork Issues	205
Entry and Organizational Access	205
Procedures for Participant Observations	206
Dynamics Between Interviewer and Interviewee	206
Availability of Documents and Audiovisual and Social Media Materials	207
Data Storage and Security	208
Comparing the Five Approaches in Data Collection	209
Chapter Check-In	210
Summary	211
Chapter Key Terms	211
Further Readings	211
For Guidance Related to Interviewing	212

Chapter 8 Data Analysis and Representation — 215

Three Analysis Strategies	216
The Data Analysis Spiral	218
Ethical Considerations in Data Analysis	220
Managing and Organizing the Data	221
Reading and Memoing Emergent Ideas	221
Describing and Classifying Codes Into Themes	224
Developing and Assessing Interpretations	229
Representing and Visualizing the Data	230
How to Use Computer Qualitative Data Analysis Software (QDAS)	232
Advantages and Disadvantages	233
A Sampling of Computer Software for Qualitative Data Analysis	234
ATLAS.ti (http://www.atlasti.com)	235
Dedoose (http://www.dedoose.com)	235
HyperRESEARCH (http://www.researchware.com)	235
MAXQDA (http://www.maxqda.com)	236
NVivo (http://www.qsrinternational.com)	236
Steps in Using a QDAS Program	236
Analysis Within Approaches to Inquiry	238
Narrative Research Analysis and Representation	238
Phenomenological Analysis and Representation	241
Grounded Theory Analysis and Representation	245
Ethnographic Analysis and Representation	247
Case Study Analysis and Representation	250

Comparing the Five Approaches in Data Analysis	252
Chapter Check-In	253
Summary	254
Chapter Key Terms	254
Further Readings	254

Chapter 9 Writing a Qualitative Study — 257

Ethical Considerations for Writing	258
Several Writing Strategies	259
Reflexivity and Representations in Writing	260
Audience for Our Writings	262
Encoding Our Writings	263
Quotes in Our Writings	264
Overall and Embedded Writing Strategies	265
Narrative Writing Structures	265
Overall Structures	267
Embedded Structures	269
Phenomenological Writing Structures	270
Overall Structures	270
Embedded Structures	272
Grounded Theory Writing Structures	273
Overall Structures	273
Embedded Structures	275
Ethnographic Writing Structures	276
Overall Structures	276
Embedded Structures	278
Case Study Writing Structures	279
Overall Structures	280
Embedded Structures	281
Comparing Writing Structures Across the Five Approaches	282
Chapter Check-In	283
Summary	283
Chapter Key Terms	283
Further Readings	284

Chapter 10 Standards of Validation and Evaluation — 285

Validation and Reliability in Qualitative Research	285
Perspectives on Validation Within Qualitative Research	286

Validation Strategies	291
Researcher's Lens	292
Participant's Lens	293
Reader's or Reviewer's Lens	294
Reliability Perspectives and Procedures	296
Evaluation Criteria for Qualitative Research	299
Evaluation Criteria Specific to Each of the Five Approaches	303
Narrative Research	303
Phenomenological Research	305
Grounded Theory Research	307
Ethnographic Research	311
Case Study Research	312
Comparing Evaluation Standards Across the Five Approaches	314
Chapter Check-In	316
Summary	316
Chapter Key Terms	317
Further Readings	317

Chapter 11 "Turning the Story" and Conclusion   319

Turning the Story Across the Five Approaches	320
The Original Story: "Campus Response to a Student Gunman"	320
A Case Study	333
A Narrative Study	334
A Phenomenology	335
A Grounded Theory Study	335
An Ethnography	336
Conclusion: Seven Key Takeaways	338
Study Focus	338
Interpretive Orientation	338
Language Use	339
Participant Samples	339
Analysis Strategies	339
Report Writing	340
Research Quality	340
Chapter Check-In	340
Summary	341

Appendix A - A Narrative Research Study—"Living in the Space Between Participant and Researcher as a Narrative Inquirer: Examining Ethnic Identity of Chinese Canadian Students as Conflicting Stories to Live By"   345
Elaine Chan

Appendix B – Resilient Leadership: A Phenomenological Exploration Into How Black Women in Higher Education Leadership Navigate Cultural Adversity   365
   Nuchelle L. Chance

Appendix C – Aging With Intellectual Disabilities in Families: Navigating Ever-Changing Seas—A Theoretical Model   395
   Henrietta Trip, Lisa Whitehead, Marie Crowe, Brigit Mirfin-Veitch and Chris Daffue

Appendix D – An Ethnography—"British-Born Pakistani and Bangladeshi Young Men: Exploring Unstable Concepts of Muslim, Islamophobia and Racialization"   421
   Mairtin Mac an Ghaill and Chris Haywood

Appendix E – Learning from Error in Violence Prevention: A School Shooting as an Organizational Accident   443
   Sarah Goodrum, Jessie Slepicka, William Woodward and Beverly Kingston

Glossary   471

References   485

Index   505

PREFACE

We are delighted to offer a fully updated fifth edition of this book. In this newest edition, John along with Cheryl (who joined as a coauthor on the fourth edition) offer updated examples and guidance on designing qualitative research across five approaches. The work on this book spans almost three decades with each edition reflecting evolutions in qualitative research. The primary purpose of this book is to introduce qualitative research and highlight five approaches to inquiry. In this way, readers can see options for conducting research and select the best option for their studies.

AUDIENCE

Although multiple audiences, both known and unknown, exist for any text (Fetterman, 2019), we direct this book toward academics and scholars affiliated with the social, human, and health sciences. Examples throughout the book illustrate the diversity of disciplines and fields of study including sociology, psychology, education, nursing, family medicine, allied health, urban studies, marketing, communication and journalism, educational psychology, family science and therapy, and other social and human science areas.

Our aim is to provide a useful text for those who produce scholarly qualitative research in the form of journal articles, theses, or dissertations. We have pitched the level of discussion to be suitable for upper-division students and beyond into graduate school. For graduate students writing master's theses or doctoral dissertations, we compare the five approaches in the hope that such analysis helps in establishing a rationale for the choice of a type to use. For beginning qualitative researchers, we introduce the philosophical and interpretive frameworks that shape qualitative research, followed by the basic elements in designing a qualitative study. We feel that understanding the basics of qualitative research is essential before venturing out into the specifics of one of the qualitative approaches. We begin each chapter with an overview of the topic of the chapter and then go into how the topic might be addressed within each of the five approaches. While discussing the basic elements, we suggest several books aimed at the beginning qualitative researcher that can provide a more extensive review of the basics of qualitative research (e.g., Creswell & Bàez, 2021). Such basics are necessary before delving into the five approaches. A focus on comparing the five approaches throughout this book provides an introduction for experienced researchers to approaches that build on their training and research experiences.

ORGANIZATION

Following our introduction to the book, we define qualitative research and explain our selection of the five approaches. We conclude Chapter 1 with a list of key book readings to get you ready for a discussion of the philosophical assumptions and interpretive frameworks that inform qualitative research. In Chapter 2, we explore how philosophical assumptions and interpretive frameworks might be written into a qualitative study. In Chapter 3, we review the basic elements for designing a qualitative study. We revisit the definition of and explore the reasons for using qualitative research. We describe the phases in the process of research as well as the skills needed for "good" qualitative research. In Chapter 4, we introduce each of the five approaches of inquiry: narrative research, phenomenology, grounded theory, ethnography, and case study research. The chapter includes an overview of the elements of each of the five approaches. Chapter 5 continues this discussion by presenting five published journal articles (one using each approach, with the complete articles in Appendices A–E), which provide good illustrations of each of the approaches. By reading our overview in Chapter 4 and then reviewing a journal article that illustrates the approach, you can develop a working knowledge of an approach. Choosing one of the books we recommend for the approach in this chapter and beginning a mastery of it for your research study can then expand this knowledge.

These five preliminary chapters form an introduction to the five approaches and an overview of the process of research design. They set the stage for the remaining chapters, which take up, in turn, each step in the research process: writing introductions to studies (Chapter 6), collecting data (Chapter 7), analyzing and representing data (Chapter 8), writing qualitative studies (Chapter 9), and validating and evaluating a qualitative study (Chapter 10). Throughout these design chapters, we start with the basics of qualitative research and then expand the discussion to advance and compare the five types.

As a final experience to sharpen distinctions made among the five approaches, we present Chapter 11, in which we present a gunman case study (Asmussen & Creswell, 1995), and "turn" the story from a case study into a narrative biography, a phenomenology, a grounded theory study, and an ethnography. This culminating chapter brings the reader full circle to examining the gunman case in several ways, an extension of John's 1994 Vail, Colorado, seminar experience (see Chapter 1) in looking at the same problem from diverse qualitative perspectives.

WHAT IS NEW IN THIS EDITION

In this fifth edition, we introduce new and revised content to keep pace with the evolutions in qualitative research thinking and practice. Across all the chapters, we have responded to reviewer feedback about the need for further inclusivity and diversity in our examples, references, and terminology. We have enhanced our descriptions of design topics identified as challenging for beginning qualitative researchers, such as ethical considerations and use of theory. Throughout the book we have expanded content and examples to reflect technological developments and use across the qualitative research process. A healthy respect exists for variations within each of the five approaches. We have come to understand that there is no single way to approach an ethnography, a grounded theory study, and so forth. We have selectively chosen what we believe to be the most popular approaches within each approach and to highlight books that emphasize them.

The learning features included in this book are intended to guide your learning and assist in developing the skills necessary to inform your choice of a suitable qualitative approach to inquiry for your research problem. Embedded throughout the book you will find

- **Discussion questions** that help orient you to the topics within each chapter.
- **Key chapter terms** that draw attention to new terms as they are mentioned throughout the book with definitions provided in the glossary.
- **Featured studies** that are purposefully selected to represent each of the five approaches to qualitative research are introduced in Chapter 5, revisited throughout Chapters 6–10 as a means of bridging theory with real research projects, and presented in their entirety in Appendices A to E.
- **"Try this now" activities** that extend your learning by applying understandings of material covered in the book to inform your design of qualitative research.
- **Examples** that are purposefully selected to represent diverse qualitative studies to help you navigate real-world complexities.
- **Chapter check-ins** that make you pause for a moment at the end of each chapter. Taking time to assess the extent to which you have developed the intended knowledge and skills allows you to build confidence.
- **Summaries** that recap information about topics covered in the chapter.
- **Further readings** that allow you to go and explore up-to-date literature beyond the chapters.
- **Visual organizers** that are used throughout the book to provide new information and to summarize text in a quick and accessible format using figures and tables.

ABOUT THE AUTHORS

John W. Creswell, PhD, is a Professor of Family Medicine and Senior Research Scientist of the Michigan Mixed Methods Program. He has authored numerous articles and 34 books on mixed methods research, qualitative research, and research design. While at the University of Nebraska–Lincoln, he held the Clifton Endowed Professor Chair, served as Director of the Mixed Methods Research Office, co-founded SAGE's *Journal of Mixed Methods Research*, and was an Adjunct Professor of Family Medicine at the University of Michigan and a consultant to the Veterans Administration Health Services Research Center in Ann Arbor, Michigan. He was a Senior Fulbright Scholar to South Africa in 2008 and to Thailand in 2012. In 2011, he co-led a National Institutes of Health working group on the "best practices of mixed methods research in the health sciences," served as a Visiting Professor at Harvard's School of Public Health and received an honorary doctorate from the University of Pretoria, South Africa. In 2014, he was the founding President of the Mixed Methods International Research Association. In 2015, he joined the staff of Family Medicine at the University of Michigan to Co-Direct the Michigan Mixed Methods Program. In 2017, he coauthored the American Psychological Association "standards" on qualitative and mixed methods research. The fourth edition of this book on *Qualitative Inquiry & Research Design* won the 2018 McGuffey Longevity Award from the U.S. Textbook & Academic Authors Association. During the COVID-19 pandemic, he gave virtual keynote presentations to many countries from his office in Osaka, Japan. Updates on his work can be found on his website at johnwcreswell.com.

Cheryl N. Poth, PhD, is a Professor in the Faculty of Education and faculty member of the research-intensive Centre for Research and Applied Measurement and Evaluation at the University of Alberta. In this role, she has developed and taught graduate-level research methods and program evaluation courses in addition to supervising and mentoring students, faculty, and local as well as global community members in qualitative, quantitative, and mixed methods research. She is the author of over 50 peer-reviewed journal articles, three books as well as numerous book chapters. Her work has been recognized by the American Educational Research Association with the Division D Significant Contributions to Research Methodology Award in 2023 (with Peggy Shannon-Baker) and by the Textbook & Academic Authors Association with the Most Promising New Textbook Award in 2020 and the McGuffey Longevity Award for Qualitative Research book in 2018 (with John Creswell). She served as Editor of the *SAGE Handbook of Mixed Methods Research* (2023) and as Guest Coeditor of several journal special issues, including the *International Journal of Qualitative Methods*. In addition to more than 40 invited talks and 150 conference presentations, she has led research methods workshops with diverse audiences on four continents. She served as an Advisory Board Member of the

International Institute of Qualitative Methodology (2014–2020); the President of the Mixed Methods International Research Association (2017–2018); a Research Fellow at the University of South Africa (2018–2020); a Helen Glass Scholar in the College of Nursing within the Rady Faculty of Health Sciences at the University of Manitoba (2022); and as a MERIT Visiting Professor in the Faculty of Health Sciences at McMaster University (2023–2025). In 2009, she cofounded the interdisciplinary Alberta Clinical and Community-Based Evaluation Research Team to advance innovative community–university research partnership supports for program planning and impact assessments of service delivery for individuals with complex needs. She serves as the Methodologist on several cross-disciplinary research teams and has led federally, provincially, and locally funded research projects. She is an Associate Editor of the *Journal of Mixed Methods Research* and is an editorial board member of several journals. Updates on her work can be found on her website at https://sites.google.com/ualberta.ca/cheryl-poth/.

ACKNOWLEDGMENTS

John is most thankful to the many students in his qualitative research methods classes at the University of Nebraska–Lincoln who helped to shape this book over the years. They offered suggestions, provided examples, and discussed the material in this book. Also, he benefited from capable scholars who helped to shape and form this book in the first edition: Paul Turner, Ken Robson, Dana Miller, Diane Gillespie, Gregory Schraw, Sharon Hudson, Karen Eifler, Neilida Aguilar, and Harry Wolcott. Ben Crabtree and Rich Hofmann also helped inform the first edition text significantly, encouraged him to proceed, and diligently and quickly responded to the Sage request to be first edition external reviewers. In addition, Keith Pezzoli, Kathy O'Byrne, Joanne Cooper, and Phyllis Langton served as first edition reviewers for Sage and added insight into content and structure that he could not see because of his closeness to the material.

To the reviewers for this fifth edition, we appreciate your time and effort reviewing the draft of our book. As always, John is indebted to C. Deborah Laughton, who served as his acquisition editor for the first edition; to Lisa Cuevas Shaw, who served as editor for the second edition; to Vicki Knight, who served as editor for the third edition; Helen Salmon, who served as editor for the fourth edition; and Leah Fargotstein, who served as editor for this fifth edition. Also in previous editions, members of the Office of Qualitative and Mixed Methods Research (OQMMR) at Nebraska and the Mixed Methods Program at Michigan all provided valuable input. John especially singles out professors Vicki Plano Clark and Ron Shope, who have been instrumental in refining and shaping his ideas about qualitative research through the editions.

Cheryl is grateful to John for the opportunity to join the fourth edition as coauthor and further our collaboration on the current edition. John has been an influential mentor for her thinking and writing about qualitative research. She has especially appreciated John's willingness to consider new content ideas and ways of presenting material. Also, we are both grateful to the Faculty of Education, University of Alberta, and the Department of Family Medicine, University of Michigan, and colleagues. Specific to the fifth edition, Cheryl would like to express her thanks to Winston Pei and Danae Stelau for their keen eye for detail during the finalizing of the current edition. She has also appreciated the support and sage advice of Trevor Jordan over the past 15 years.

Finally, to members of our families (for John—Mariko, David, Kasey, Johanna, and Bonny; for Cheryl—Damian, Avery, and Jasper), thanks for providing us with time to spend long hours writing and revising this book. Thank you all.

ANALYTIC TABLE OF CONTENTS BY APPROACH

NARRATIVE RESEARCH

Use of narrative approaches	9
Key books and references	11
Definition of narrative research	78
Origin of narrative research	78
Defining features of narrative studies	79
Types of narrative studies	80
Procedures for conducting narrative research	82
Challenges and opportunities in narrative research	85
Focus of narrative research	150
Featured example of a narrative study, Appendix A	345
Research problem	159
Purpose statement	163
Research questions	167
Individual or site to be studied	180
Access and rapport issues	183
Sampling strategy	190
Forms of data	192
Data analysis	238
Writing a narrative study	265
Standards of evaluation	303
Case study "turned" into a narrative study	334

PHENOMENOLOGY

Use of psychological approach	9
Key books and references	12
Definition of phenomenological research	87
Origin of phenomenological research	87

xxiii

Defining features of phenomenology	89
Types of phenomenology	90
Procedures for conducting phenomenology	91
Challenges and opportunities in phenomenology	94
Focus of phenomenology	150
Featured example of a phenomenological study, Appendix B	365
Research problem	159
Purpose statement	164
Research questions	167
Participants in a phenomenological study	180
Access issues	187
Sampling strategy	190
Forms of data	192
Data analysis	241
Writing a phenomenological study	270
Standards of evaluation	305
Case study "turned" into a phenomenology	335

GROUNDED THEORY

Use of sociological approach	9
Key books and references	12
Definition of grounded theory research	96
Origins of grounded theory research	97
Defining features of grounded theory	98
Types of grounded theory studies	99
Procedures for using grounded theory research	101
Challenges and opportunities in grounded theory research	104
Focus of grounded theory research	150
Featured example of a grounded theory study, Appendix C	395
Research problem	159
Purpose statement	164
Research questions	168
Participants in a grounded theory study	180
Access issues	187
Sampling strategy	190
Forms of data	192

Data analysis	245
Writing a grounded theory study	273
Standards of evaluation	307
Case study "turned" into a grounded theory study	335

ETHNOGRAPHY

Use of anthropological, sociological, and interpretive approaches	9
Key books and references	12
Definition of ethnographic research	106
Origin of ethnographic research	106
Defining features of ethnography	107
Types of ethnographies	108
Procedures in conducting ethnography	109
Challenges and opportunities in ethnographic research	112
Focus of ethnography	150
Featured example of an ethnography, Appendix D	421
Research problem	159
Purpose statement	164
Research questions	168
Site to be studied	180
Access and rapport issues	187
Sampling strategy	190
Forms of data	192
Data analysis	247
Writing an ethnography	276
Standards of evaluation	311
Case study "turned" into ethnography	336

CASE STUDY

Use of evaluation approach	9
Key books and references	13
Definition of case study research	114
Origin of case study research	115
Defining features of case studies	116
Types of case studies	117

Procedures for conducting a case study 118
Challenges and opportunities in case study research 121
Focus of a case study 150
Featured example of a case study, Appendix E 443
Research problem 159
Purpose statement 165
Research questions 169
Site to be studied 180
Access and rapport issues 187
Sampling strategy 190
Forms of data 192
Data analysis 250
Writing a case study 279
Standards of evaluation 312
A case study revisited before "turning" 333

LIST OF TABLES

Table 1.1	Distinguishing Characteristics of Qualitative Research	6
Table 1.2	Qualitative Approaches Mentioned by Authors and Their Disciplines/Fields	9
Table 2.1	Practical Implications of Philosophical Assumptions for Qualitative Researchers	22
Table 2.2	Comparing Major Interpretive Frameworks	37
Table 2.3	Interpretive Frameworks and Associated Philosophical Beliefs	41
Table 3.1	Ethical Issues and Addressing Them in the Phases of the Research Process	60
Table 4.1	Contrasting Foundational Considerations of Five Qualitative Approaches	124
Table 4.2	Contrasting Data Procedures of Five Qualitative Approaches	125
Table 4.3	Contrasting Research Reporting of Five Qualitative Approaches	126
Table 5.1	Defining Features of Narrative Studies as Presented in Chan (2010) and Guiding Design Questions	137
Table 5.2	Defining Features of Phenomenology as Presented in Chance (2022) and Guiding Design Questions	140
Table 5.3	Defining Features of Grounded Theory Studies as Presented in Trip et al. (2019) and Guiding Design Questions	143
Table 5.4	Defining Features of Ethnography as Presented in Mac an Ghaill and Haywood (2015) and Guiding Design Questions	145
Table 5.5	Defining Features of Case Study Research as Presented in Goodrum et al. (2022) and Guiding Design Questions	148
Table 5.6	Contrasting the Defining Features of Foundational Considerations for the Five Studies	150
Table 6.1	Words to Use in Encoding the Purpose Statement Across Five Qualitative Research Approaches	162
Table 7.1	Data Collection Activities by Five Qualitative Approaches	178
Table 7.2	Ethical Situations to Anticipate and Address by Data Collection Activity	181
Table 7.3	Types of Sampling Strategies in Qualitative Inquiry	191

Table 8.1	General Data Analysis Strategies Advanced by Select Authors	217
Table 8.2	The Data Analysis Spiral Activities, Strategies, and Outcomes	219
Table 8.3	Ethical Situations to Anticipate and Address by Data Analysis Activity	220
Table 8.4	Sample Codebook Entry for Theme "Fostering Relationships"	226
Table 8.5	Data Analysis and Representation by Five Qualitative Approaches	239
Table 9.1	Ethical Questions, Issues, and Situations in Writing a Qualitative Study	258
Table 9.2	Overall and Embedded Writing Structures Within the Five Approaches	266
Table 10.1	Perspectives and Terms Used for Validation in Qualitative Research	287
Table 10.2	Comparing the Evaluation Standards Across the Five Qualitative Approaches	315
Table 11.1	Data Collection Matrix: Type of Information by Source	324
Table 11.2	Evidence From the Case, Questions for a Campus Plan, and References	329

LIST OF FIGURES

Figure 2.1	Situating Philosophy and Interpretive Frameworks Within the Research Process	20
Figure 3.1	When to Use Qualitative Research	49
Figure 3.2	Research Quality Assessment Checklist	51
Figure 3.3	Phases in the Qualitative Research Process	55
Figure 3.4	Ethical Qualitative Research Involves an Anticipate, Mitigate, Respond, and Learn (AMRL) Cycle	59
Figure 4.1	Assessing the Fit of Five Qualitative Approaches	77
Figure 4.2	Defining Features of Narrative Studies	79
Figure 4.3	Procedures for Conducting Narrative Research	83
Figure 4.4	Defining Features of a Phenomenology	89
Figure 4.5	Procedures for Conducting Phenomenological Research	92
Figure 4.6	Defining Features of Grounded Theory Studies	98
Figure 4.7	Procedures for Conducting Grounded Theory Research	102
Figure 4.8	Defining Features of an Ethnography	107
Figure 4.9	Procedures for Conducting Ethnographic Research	110
Figure 4.10	Defining Features of Case Studies	116
Figure 4.11	Procedures for Conducting Case Study Research	119
Figure 6.1	Interrelating a Study's Research Problem, Purpose, and Questions	156
Figure 6.2	Sample Research Problem Section (Introduction) to a Study	158
Figure 7.1	Data Collection Activities	176
Figure 7.2	Sample Human Subjects Consent-to-Participate Form	186
Figure 7.3	A Compendium of Data Forms in Qualitative Research	193
Figure 7.4	Online Research Ethics Map	194
Figure 7.5	Procedures for Preparing and Conducting Interviews	198
Figure 7.6	Sample Interview Protocol or Guide	200
Figure 7.7	Procedures for Preparing for and Conducting Observations	202

Figure 7.8	Sample Observational Protocol	204
Figure 8.1	The Data Analysis Spiral	218
Figure 8.2	Sample Coding Procedures for Theme "Fostering Relationships"	225
Figure 8.3	Sample Hierarchical Tree Diagram: Layers of Analysis in the Gunman Case	231
Figure 8.4	Template for Coding a Narrative Study	240
Figure 8.5	Template for Coding a Phenomenological Study	243
Figure 8.6	Sample Visual Map of the Developing Hermeneutic Understanding of the Essence of a Lived Experience in a Phenomenology	244
Figure 8.7	Template for Coding a Grounded Theory Study	245
Figure 8.8	Sample Procedural Diagram of the Constant Comparison Analytic Process in a Grounded Theory Study	247
Figure 8.9	Sample File Organization and Visual Model Mapping in an Ethnography	249
Figure 8.10	Template for Coding an Ethnography	249
Figure 8.11	Template for Coding a Case Study (Using a Multiple or Collective Case Approach)	251
Figure 10.1	Strategies for Validation in Qualitative Research	292
Figure 10.2	Procedures for Reliability of Intercoder Agreement in Qualitative Research	297
Figure 10.3	Reprising the Features of a "Good" Qualitative Study	300
Figure 10.4	Guiding Evaluative Criteria for a Narrative Study	305
Figure 10.5	Standards for Assessing the Quality of a Phenomenology	307
Figure 10.6	Features for Evaluating a Grounded Theory Study	311
Figure 10.7	Criteria for Evaluating an Ethnography	312
Figure 10.8	Evaluative Criteria for a Case Study	314
Figure 11.1	Turning the Story Across the Five Approaches With Case Study as the Original Study	333

LIST OF EXAMPLES

Example 2.1	Descriptions of Underlying Philosophical Assumptions	24
Example 3.1	Design Ideas Useful for Engaging Readers	67
Example 4.1	Narrative Research Variations	86
Example 4.2	Phenomenological Research Variations	95
Example 4.3	Grounded Theory Research Variations	105
Example 4.4	Ethnographic Research Variations	113
Example 4.5	Case Study Research Variations	122
Example 6.1	Narrative Research Purpose Statements	163
Example 6.2	Phenomenological Research Purpose Statements	164
Example 6.3	Grounded Theory Research Purpose Statements	164
Example 6.4	Ethnographic Research Purpose Statements	164
Example 6.5	Case Study Research Purpose Statements	165
Example 6.6	Narrative Study Research Questions	167
Example 6.7	Phenomenology Research Questions	167
Example 6.8	Grounded Theory Study Research Questions	168
Example 6.9	Ethnography Research Questions	168
Example 6.10	Case Study Research Questions	169
Example 6.11	Narrative Study Research Subquestions	170
Example 6.12	Phenomenology Research Subquestions	170
Example 6.13	Grounded Theory Study Research Subquestions	171
Example 6.14	Ethnographic Research Subquestions	171
Example 6.15	Case Study Research Subquestions	171
Example 7.1	Evidence of Ethical Reviews and Approvals	183
Example 7.2	Creative Qualitative Data Collection Methods and Rationales for Their Use	195

LIST OF "TRY THIS NOW" ACTIVITIES

Try This Now 1.1	Describing Your Positionality to Qualitative Research	4
Try This Now 2.1	Unpacking Your Philosophical Assumptions as a Qualitative Researcher	24
Try This Now 2.2	Exploring Your Use of Interpretive Frameworks in Qualitative Research	40
Try This Now 3.1	Examining Your Familiarity With Key Quality Criteria of Qualitative Research	53
Try This Now 3.2	Planning for Common Ethical Issues in Your Qualitative Research	64
Try This Now 4.1	Considering the Focus of Your Qualitative Research	77
Try This Now 4.2	Locating Defining Features of a Qualitative Approach in Journal Articles	123
Try This Now 5.1	Applying the Defining Features of Narrative Research to Your Study Design	138
Try This Now 5.2	Applying the Defining Features of Phenomenology to Your Study Design	141
Try This Now 5.3	Applying the Defining Features of Grounded Theory Research to Your Study Design	144
Try This Now 5.4	Applying the Defining Features of Ethnography to Your Study Design	146
Try This Now 5.5	Applying the Defining Features of Case Study Research to Your Study Design	149
Try This Now 6.1	Identifying the Five Elements of a Research Problem Section (Introduction) in the Appendix Studies	161
Try This Now 6.2	Examining Encoding Words in the Purpose Statements of the Appendix Studies	165
Try This Now 7.1	Comparing Data Collection Activity Descriptions in the Appendix Studies	209
Try This Now 8.1	Aligning Your Qualitative Data Analysis Needs With Computer and Software Capacities	234
Try This Now 8.2	Comparing Data Analysis Descriptions in the Appendix Studies	252

Try This Now 9.1	Identifying Use of Writing Strategies in the Appendix Studies	265
Try This Now 10.1	Conveying Your Perspective on Validation in Qualitative Research	291
Try This Now 10.2	Comparing Validation Strategy Descriptions in the Appendix Studies	296
Try This Now 10.3	Assessing Intercoder Agreement in Your Coding Practice	299

1 INTRODUCTION TO QUALITATIVE INQUIRY AND RESEARCH DESIGN

> **QUESTIONS FOR DISCUSSION**
>
> - Why focus on examining five approaches to qualitative inquiry?
> - What does positioning oneself as a qualitative researcher involve?
> - What are the distinguishing characteristics of qualitative research?
> - What are the key readings for each of the five selected approaches?

The idea for this book was inspired by conversations that took place during a summer qualitative research seminar in Vail, Colorado, sponsored by the University of Denver under the able guidance of Edith King of the College of Education. At that 1994 seminar, while discussing qualitative data analysis, John began on a personal note, introducing one of his recently completed qualitative studies—a case study of a campus response to a student gun incident (Asmussen & Creswell, 1995). John knew this case might provoke some discussion and present some complex analysis issues. It involved a Midwestern university's reaction to a gunman who entered an actuarial science undergraduate class with a semiautomatic rifle and attempted to fire on students in his class. The rifle jammed and did not discharge, and the gunman fled and was captured a few miles away. Standing before the group, John chronicled the events of the case, the themes, and the lessons we learned about a university reaction to a near tragic event. Then, unplanned, Harry Wolcott of the University of Oregon, another resource person for this seminar, raised his hand and asked for the podium. He explained how *he* would approach the study as a cultural anthropologist. To John's surprise, Harry had "turned" his case study into ethnography, framing the study in an entirely new way. After Harry had concluded, Les Goodchild, then of University of Denver, discussed how he would examine the gunman case from a historical perspective. Together the three had, then, offered multiple renderings of the incident, to create surprising "turns" of the initial case study using different qualitative approaches. It was this event that sparked an idea that John had long harbored—that the design of a qualitative study is related to the specific *approach* taken to **qualitative research** (see the glossary for definitions of bold terms). John began to write the first edition of this book, guided by a single, compelling question: How does the type or approach of qualitative inquiry shape the design or procedures of a study?

This chapter will introduce you to qualitative research and the five approaches to inquiry examined in this book. We do this by describing our approach to this book including our rationale for examining five qualitative research approaches and our positioning as qualitative researchers. Then we help you begin to distinguish qualitative research by discussing our definition and nine common characteristics. Finally, alongside presenting our selection of the five qualitative approaches examined in this book, we offer key book readings for narrative research, phenomenology, grounded theory, ethnography, and case study.

RATIONALE FOR OUR APPROACH TO THE BOOK

In this book, we examine five different approaches to qualitative inquiry—narrative, phenomenology, grounded theory, ethnography, and case studies—and put them side by side to compare and contrast. Differences across the five approaches are most vividly displayed by exploring their use throughout the process of qualitative research, including the introduction to a study through its purpose and research questions, data collection, data analysis, report writing, and standards of validation and evaluation. By studying published qualitative journal articles, we can see, for example, that research questions framed from grounded theory are different from questions framed from a phenomenological study.

This combination of the different approaches and how their distinctiveness plays out in the process of research is what distinguishes this book from others on qualitative research that you may have read. Most qualitative researchers focus on only one approach—say ethnography or grounded theory—and try to convince their readers of the value of that approach. This makes sense in our highly specialized world of academia. However, students and beginning qualitative researchers need choices that fit their research problems and that suit their own interests in conducting research. We hope this book opens up the expanse of qualitative research and invites readers to examine multiple ways of engaging in the process of research. It provides qualitative researchers with options for conducting qualitative inquiry and helps them with decisions about what approach is best to use in studying their research problems. With so many books on qualitative research in general and on the various approaches of inquiry, qualitative researchers are often at a loss for understanding what options (i.e., approaches) exist and how one makes an informed choice of an option for research.

By reading this book and engaging with the learning features, we hope that you will gain a better understanding of the steps in the process of research, recognize the differences and similarities among the five qualitative **approaches to inquiry**, and apply new understandings to inform the design of qualitative research using the five approaches to inquiry.

POSITIONING OURSELVES

You need to know some information about our backgrounds in order to understand our approach to this book. The evolution of this book has been influenced by the multifaceted and dynamic contexts in which we work and live and especially by the people with whom and the communities with which we interact. This presents an opportunity for us to introduce (and model) the principle of being transparent about one's positionality when presenting research—and in our case, a rationale for our content. We write from the standpoint of conveying an understanding of the process of qualitative research (whether you want to call it the scientific method or something else), a focus on strong methods features such as extensive qualitative data collection, rigorous data analysis through multiple steps, and the use of computer programs. Moreover, this book reflects John's highlighting the structure of writing, whether the writing is a qualitative study, a poem, or creative nonfiction. An enduring interest of John's has been the *composition* of qualitative research. This compositional interest flows into how to best structure qualitative inquiry and to visualize how the structure shifts and changes given different approaches to research. For Cheryl, a persistent research interest in promoting use of findings and processes has led to her focus on providing enhanced *access* to the generation of findings in qualitative research and seeking diverse *formats* for the communication and evaluation of research.

John was trained as a quantitative researcher almost 50 years ago. By the mid-1980s, John was asked to teach the first qualitative research course at his university, and he proceeded to do so. This was followed a few years later with the writing of the first edition of this book. While John has expanded his repertoire to mixed methods research, he continually returns to his strong interest in qualitative research. Over the years, John has evolved into an applied research methodologist with a specialization in **research design**, qualitative research, and mixed methods research.

Cheryl was trained as a quantitative researcher within the biological natural sciences about 30 years ago. When working as a high school science teacher, she began to question the limitations of the quantitative evidence test scores for assessing and reporting student learning. Instead, she began to draw upon more qualitative evidence to inform her communication with students and parents. This was followed by a return to graduate school to gain expertise in qualitative research methods and eventually to engage in the emerging field of mixed methods research. As an applied researcher and program evaluator, she is committed to building research capacity through mentoring her students and collaborators in rigorous methods across a variety of organizational settings.

John's interest in structured features has often placed him in the camp of postpositivist writers in qualitative inquiry (see Denzin & Lincoln, 2005), but like most researchers, he defies easy categorization. In an article about a homeless shelter in *Qualitative Inquiry* (D. W. Miller et al., 1998), John's ethnography assumed a realist, a confessional, and an advocacy stance. Also, he is not advocating the acceptance of qualitative research in a "quantitative" world (Ely et al., 1991). Qualitative inquiry represents a legitimate mode of social and human science exploration, without apology or comparisons to quantitative research. In the same way, Cheryl draws on her experiences as a quantitative and mixed methods researcher in her qualitative work but is careful to maintain the essential characteristics of qualitative research discussed in this introductory chapter.

John also tends to be oriented toward citing numerous ideas to document articles; to incorporate the latest writings from the ever-growing, vast literature of qualitative inquiry; and to advance an applied, practical form of conducting research. John concurs with Agger (1991), who says that readers and writers can understand methodology in less technical ways, thereby affording greater access to scholars and democratizing science. We continue to seek and be influenced by our interactions with beginning and more experienced researchers who are expanding their methodological expertise in our courses, workshops, and conferences. Always before us as we write is the picture of a beginning master's or doctoral student who is learning qualitative research for the first time. Because this picture remains central in our thinking, some may say that we oversimplify the craft of research. This picture may well blur the image for a more seasoned qualitative writer—and especially one who seeks more advanced discussions and who looks for problematizing the process of research. It is important to both of us that, in this book, we provide access to learning about five qualitative research approaches in a way that stimulates the beginning of a qualitative inquiry journey.

> **TRY THIS NOW 1.1**
> **DESCRIBING YOUR POSITIONALITY TO QUALITATIVE RESEARCH**
>
> Positionality is shaped by many influences including the researcher's lived experience. What are some key aspects of your lived experiences that may influence the conduct of qualitative research for you? How would you convey these influences in a positionality statement?

DEFINING QUALITATIVE RESEARCH

We typically begin a book about qualitative research by posing a definition for it. This seemingly uncomplicated approach has become more difficult in recent years. We note that some extremely useful introductory books on qualitative research these days do not contain a definition that can be easily located (e.g., Morse & Richards, 2002; Weis & Fine, 2000). Perhaps this has less to do with the authors' decision to convey the nature of this inquiry and more to do with a reluctance to "fix" a definition. Other authors advance a definition. The evolving definition in *The SAGE Handbook of Qualitative Research* (Denzin & Lincoln, 1994, 2000, 2005, 2011b, 2018b) conveys the ever-changing nature of qualitative inquiry from social construction, to interpretivism, and then on to social justice in the world. We include the latest definition here:

> Qualitative research consists of a set of interpretive, material practices that make the world visible. These practices transform the world. They turn the world into a series of representations, including field notes, interviews, conversations, photographs, recordings, and memos to the self. At this level, qualitative research involves an interpretive, naturalistic approach to the world. This means that qualitative researchers study things in their natural settings, attempting to make sense of or interpret phenomena in terms of the meanings people bring to them. (Denzin & Lincoln, 2018a, p. 10)

Although some of the traditional approaches to qualitative research, such as the "interpretive, naturalistic approach" and "meanings," are evident in this definition, the definition also has a strong orientation toward the impact of qualitative research and its ability to transform the world.

As applied research methodologists, our working definitions of qualitative research incorporate many of the Denzin and Lincoln elements, but it provides greater emphasis on the design of research and the use of distinct approaches to inquiry (e.g., ethnography, narrative). We adopt the following definition:

> Qualitative research begins with assumptions and the use of interpretive/theoretical frameworks that inform the study of research problems addressing the meaning individuals or groups ascribe to a social or human problem. To study this problem, qualitative researchers use an emerging qualitative approach to inquiry, the collection of data in a natural setting sensitive to the people and places under study, and data analysis that is both inductive and deductive and establishes patterns or themes. The final written report or presentation includes the voices of participants, the reflexivity of the researcher, a complex description and interpretation of the problem, and its contribution to the literature or a call for change. (Creswell, 2013, p. 44)

Distinguishing Characteristics

Our rationale underlying our working definition of qualitative research emphasizes the design of research and the use of distinct approaches to inquiry (e.g., ethnography, narrative). It is helpful to move from a more general definition to specific characteristics found in qualitative research. We believe that the characteristics have evolved over time (which we can see across the editions of this book!) and they certainly do not present a definitive set of elements. Key among the shifts over time, qualitative research today involves closer attention to the interpretive nature of the research; the role of the researcher and the methods used for data collection; situating the study within the political, social, and cultural context of the research setting; and the reflexivity or "presence" of the researchers in the work they do and the accounts they present. Examine Table 1.1 for how these common characteristics have remained unchanged or evolved in some way over time and across influential introductory qualitative research books. The nine common characteristics of qualitative research are as follows and are presented in no specific order of importance:

- *Natural setting.* Qualitative researchers often collect data in the field at the site where participants experience the issue or problem under study. They do not bring individuals into a lab (a contrived situation), nor do they typically send out instruments for individuals to complete, such as in survey research. Instead, qualitative researchers gather information by talking directly to people and seeing them behave and act within their context. These interactions might occur over time face-to-face and be influenced by technology.

- *Researcher as key instrument.* Qualitative researchers collect data themselves through examining documents, observing behavior, and interviewing participants. They may use an instrument, but it is one designed by the researcher using open-ended questions.

TABLE 1.1 Distinguishing Characteristics of Qualitative Research						
Characteristics	LeCompte & Schensul (1999)	Hatch (2002)	Ravitch & Carl (2020)	Marshall, Rossman, & Blanco (2021)	Creswell & Poth (2023)	Trends Over Time/ Across Books
Conducted in a natural setting (the field)	Yes	Yes	Yes	Yes	Yes	Unchanged
Relies on the researcher as key instrument in data collection	—	Yes	Yes	—	Yes	Increased prominence
Involves using multiple methods	Yes	—	—	Yes	Yes	Increased prominence
Involves complex reasoning through inductive and deductive logic	Yes	Yes	Yes	Yes	Yes	Unchanged
Focuses on participants' multiple perspectives and meanings	Yes	Yes	Yes	—	Yes	Increased prominence
Is situated within the larger context or setting of participants or sites	Yes	—	Yes	Yes	Yes	Increased prominence
Involves an emergent and evolving design	—	Yes	Yes	Yes	Yes	Mostly unchanged
Is reflective and interpretive of researcher's background influences	—	—	Yes	Yes	Yes	Increased prominence
Presents a holistic, complex picture	—	Yes	Yes	Yes	Yes	Mostly unchanged

Note: The em-dashes represent the absence of reference to the characteristic by specific authors.

They do not tend to use or rely on questionnaires or instruments developed by other researchers. A key exception is when qualitative researchers access existing qualitative data for secondary analysis (see Chapter 7 for further information and cautions).

- *Multiple methods.* Qualitative researchers typically gather multiple forms of data, such as interviews, observations, and documents, rather than rely on a single data source. Then they review the data and make sense of it, organizing it into categories or themes that cut across all of the data sources.

- *Complex reasoning through inductive and deductive logic.* Qualitative researchers build their patterns, categories, and themes from the "bottom up" by organizing the data inductively into increasingly more abstract units of information. This inductive process involves researchers working back and forth between the themes and the database until they establish a comprehensive set of themes. It may also involve collaborating with the participants interactively so that they have a chance to shape the themes or abstractions that emerge from the process. Researchers also use deductive thinking in that they build themes that are constantly being checked against the data. The inductive–deductive logic process means that the qualitative researcher uses complex reasoning skills throughout the process of research.

- *Participants' multiple perspectives and meanings.* In the entire qualitative research process, the researchers keep a focus on learning the meaning that the participants hold about the problem or issue, not the meaning that the researchers bring to the research or writers from the literature. The participant meanings further suggest multiple perspectives on a topic and diverse views. This is why a theme developed in a qualitative report should reflect multiple perspectives of the participants in the study.

- *Context-dependent.* The research is situated within the context or setting of participants or sites. In order to report the setting in which the problem is being studied, the researcher must seek an understanding of contextual features and their influence on participants' experiences (e.g., social, political, and historical). This is essential because the particular contexts allow researchers to "understand how events, actions, and meaning are shaped by the unique circumstances in which these occur" (Maxwell, 2013, p. 30). It is important for the researcher to assume contexts are dynamic, to monitor for various changes over time, and to respond appropriately.

- *Emergent design.* The research process for qualitative researchers is emergent. This means that the initial plan for research cannot be tightly prescribed and that all phases of the process may change or shift after the researchers enter the field and begin to collect data. For example, the questions may change, the forms of data collection may be altered, and the individuals studied and the sites visited may be modified during the process of conducting the study. The key idea behind qualitative research is to learn about the problem or issue from participants and engage in the best practices to obtain that information.

- *Reflexivity.* Researchers "position themselves" in a qualitative research study. This means that researchers engage in practices that help them understand how they influence the research process and convey (i.e., in a method section, in an introduction, or in other places in a study) their background (e.g., work experiences, cultural experiences, history), how it informs their interpretation of the information in a study, and what they have to gain from the study. Wolcott (2010) said the following:

> Our readers have a right to know about us. And they do not want to know whether we played in the high school band. They want to know what prompts our interest in the topics we investigate, to whom we are reporting, and what we personally stand to gain from our study. (p. 36)

- *Complex account.* Qualitative researchers try to develop a complex picture of the problem or issue under study. This involves reporting multiple perspectives, identifying the many factors involved in a situation, and generally sketching the larger picture that emerges. Researchers are bound not by cause-and-effect relationships among factors but rather by describing the complex interactions of factors in any situation.

SELECTION OF THE FIVE APPROACHES

Those undertaking qualitative studies have a baffling number of choices of approaches. One can gain a sense of this diversity by examining several classifications or typologies. Tesch (1990) provided a classification consisting of 28 approaches organized into four branches of a flowchart, sorting out these approaches based on the central interest of the investigator. Wolcott (1992) classified approaches in a "tree" diagram with branches of the tree designating strategies for data collection. W. L. Miller and Crabtree (1992) organized 18 types according to the "domain" of human life of primary concern to the researcher, such as a focus on the individual, the social world, or the culture. In the field of education, Jacob (1987) categorized all qualitative research into "traditions," such as ecological psychology, symbolic interactionism, and holistic ethnography. Jacob's categorization provided a key framework for the first edition of this book. Lancy (1993) organized qualitative inquiry into discipline perspectives, such as anthropology, sociology, biology, cognitive psychology, and history. Denzin and Lincoln (1994, 2005, 2011b, 2018b) have organized and reorganized their types of qualitative strategies over the years.

Table 1.2 provides these and other various classifications of qualitative approaches that have surfaced. This list is not meant to be exhaustive of the possibilities; it is intended to illustrate the diversity of approaches recommended by different authors and how the disciplines might emphasize some approaches over others.

Looking closely at these classifications, we can discern that some approaches consistently appear, such as ethnography, grounded theory, phenomenology, and case studies. Also, a number of narrative-related approaches have been discussed, such as life history, autoethnography, and biography. With so many possibilities, how was the selection decision made to focus on the five approaches presented in this book?

TABLE 1.2 ■ Qualitative Approaches Mentioned by Authors and Their Disciplines/Fields

Authors	Qualitative Approaches Mentioned by the Authors			Disciplines
Jacob (1987)	• Ecological psychology • Ethnography of communication	• Holistic ethnography • Symbolic interactionism	• Cognitive anthropology	Education
Munhall & Oiler (1986)	• Phenomenology • Historical research	• Grounded theory	• Ethnography	Nursing
Lancy (1993)	• Anthropological perspectives • Case studies • Personal accounts	• Sociological perspectives • Historical inquiries	• Biological perspectives • Cognitive studies	Education
Strauss & Corbin (1990)	• Grounded theory • Life histories	• Ethnography • Conversational analysis	• Phenomenology	Sociology, nursing
Morse (1994)	• Phenomenology • Grounded theory	• Ethnography	• Ethnoscience	Nursing
Moustakas (1994)	• Ethnography • Empirical phenomenological research • Phenomenology	• Grounded theory • Heuristic research	• Hermeneutics • Transcendental	Psychology
Denzin & Lincoln (1994)	• Case studies • Ethnomethodology • Biographical	• Ethnography • Interpretative practices • Historical	• Phenomenology • Grounded theory • Clinical research	Social sciences
Miles & Huberman (1994)	Approaches to Qualitative Data Analysis • Interpretivism	• Social anthropology	• Collaborative social research	Social sciences
Slife & Williams (1995)	Categories of Qualitative Methods • Ethnography	• Phenomenology	• Studies of artifacts	Psychology

(Continued)

TABLE 1.2 ■ Qualitative Approaches Mentioned by Authors and Their Disciplines/Fields (Continued)

Authors	Qualitative Approaches Mentioned by the Authors			Disciplines
Denzin & Lincoln (2005)	• Performance, critical, and public ethnography • Grounded theory • Interpretive practices	• Life history • Case studies	• Narrative authority • Participatory action research	Social sciences
Saldaña (2011)	• Ethnography • Case study • Narrative inquiry • Evaluation research • Critical inquiry	• Grounded theory • Content analysis • Arts-based research • Action research • Autoethnography	• Phenomenology • Mixed methods research • Investigative journalism	Arts (theater)
Denzin & Lincoln (2011b, 2018b)	Research Strategies			Social sciences
	• Ethnography • Ethnomethodology • Historical method • Clinical research	• Case study • Phenomenology • Grounded theory • Action and applied research	• Ethnography, participant observation, performance • Life history, testimonio	
Mertens (2019)	Types of Qualitative Research			Education, psychology
	• Ethnographic research • Grounded theory	• Case study • Participatory action research	• Phenomenological research	
Marshall et al. (2021)	• Ethnographic approaches	• Phenomenological approaches	• Sociolinguistic approaches (e.g., critical genres)	Education

The choice of the five approaches resulted from reflecting on personal interests, selecting different approaches popular in the social science and health science literature, and electing to choose representative discipline orientations. Both of us have had personal experience with all five approaches and have advised students and participated on research teams using these qualitative approaches. Beyond these personal experiences, our reading of the qualitative literature has been ongoing and our learning continues. The five approaches discussed in this book reflect the types of qualitative research that we most frequently see in the social, behavioral, and health science literature. It is not unusual, too, for authors to state that certain approaches are most important in their field (e.g., Morse & Field, 1995). Also, we prefer approaches with systematic procedures for inquiry. The books we have chosen to illustrate each approach tend to have rigorous data collection procedures and analysis methods that are attractive to beginning researchers. The primary books chosen for each approach also represent different discipline perspectives in the social, behavioral, and health sciences. This is an attractive feature to broaden the audience for the book and to recognize the diverse disciplines that have embraced qualitative research. For example, narrative originates from the humanities and social sciences, phenomenology from psychology and philosophy, grounded theory from sociology, ethnography from anthropology and sociology, and case studies from the human and social sciences and applied areas such as evaluation research.

We recognize the possibility of including more than five approaches. We see the involvement of qualitative scholars in, for example, discourse analysis (Cheek, 2004) and in participatory action research (Ivankova, 2015). A strong possibility for adding a sixth approach in future editions might be "descriptive methods." Several authors have described this approach as a "foundational method," "thematic analysis," "descriptive analysis," or a "descriptive" approach to inquiry (Braun & Clarke, 2006; Levitt et al., 2018; Sandelowski, 2010). A descriptive method approach involves the researcher staying close to the data, using limited frameworks and interpretations, and cataloging the data into themes. It is a popular approach among qualitative health researchers. Also, recent standards from the American Psychological Association highlight "thematic analysis" as one of the qualitative designs (American Psychological Association, 2020). It can be distinguished from the "analytic traditions" found in discipline fields (Braun & Clarke, 2006, p. 78) and emphasized in this book (e.g., narrative studies, phenomenology, ethnography). We chose, however, not to include "descriptive methods" as a sixth, distinct approach because our chapters emphasize the foundational ideas (e.g., coding, themes) closely aligned with the "descriptive method."

KEY BOOK READINGS

The primary ideas that we use to discuss each approach come from select books. More specifically, we will rely heavily on two books for each approach. These are the books that we highly recommend for you to get started in learning a specific approach to qualitative inquiry. These books include classics often cited by authors, as well as new works. They also reflect diverse disciplines and perspectives. In addition, please see the essential readings for each chapter listed under the Further Readings heading at the end of each chapter.

Narrative Research

Clandinin, D. J. (2023). *Engaging in narrative inquiry* (2nd ed.). Routledge.

In this updated edition from the 2013 book, Jean Clandinin articulates her intention to "return to the question of what it is that narrative inquirers do" (2023, p. 7). The first three chapters are noteworthy for her practical guidance detailing what it means to think and act narratively. She illustrates this guidance by using updated examples.

Riessman, C. K. (2008). *Narrative methods for the human sciences*. Sage.

Catherine Riessman uses cross-disciplinary exemplars alongside detailed descriptions for four specific methods of narrative analysis (thematic, structural, dialogic/performance, and visual). A unique contribution is the discussion of visual analysis and how images can be used within qualitative research.

Phenomenology

Moustakas, C. (1994). *Phenomenological research methods*. Sage.

Clark Moustakas contributes a description of a heuristic process in phenomenological analysis. His practical instructions in the systematic interpretation of interview transcripts is helpful for extracting themes common across interviews or unique to an interview and then creating a conceptual link.

van Manen, M. (2023). *Phenomenology of practice: Meaning-giving methods in phenomenological research and writing* (2nd ed.). Routledge.

In this updated edition, Max van Manen describes the evolution of key phenomenological ideas, presents a range of methods, and discusses writing. Among the key contributions are his discussion of methodological issues and his description of a variety of phenomenological orientations.

Grounded Theory

Charmaz, K. (2014). *Constructing grounded theory* (2nd ed.). Sage.

Kathy Charmaz uses examples from varied disciplines and professions as well as reflections from scholars about doing grounded theory from a constructivist perspective. Her detailed descriptions of coding and writing processes, including guidelines and examples, provide essential practical guidance.

Corbin, J., & Strauss, A. (2015). *Basics of qualitative research: Techniques and procedures for developing grounded theory* (4th ed.). Sage.

To enrich the reader experience with viewpoints from former students and colleagues, Julie Corbin and Anselm Strauss use a pedagogical feature called Insider Insights. Of note is a summary of data analysis processes (see pp. 216–219).

Ethnography

Fetterman, D. M. (2019). *Ethnography: Step-by-step* (4th ed.). Sage.

In the fourth edition, David Fetterman expands discussions of ethnography to highlight reflexivity and the use of theory. The revised chapter on anthropological concepts further emphasizes culture and contextualization during the cyclical processes of acquiring ethnographic knowledge of human life. This, along with the updated descriptions of ethnographic equipment in Chapter 4 and the analytical strategies described in Chapter 5, make this resource required reading.

Wolcott, H. F. (2008a). *Ethnography: A way of seeing* (2nd ed.). AltaMira Press.

A good understanding of the nature of ethnography, the study of groups, and the development of an understanding of culture is provided by Harry Wolcott. In particular, his emphasis on both the artistic and common sense elements involved in fieldwork provides a unique perspective.

Case Study

Thomas, G. (2021). *How to do your case study* (3rd ed.). Sage.

Comprehensive guidance about when and how to use case studies is provided by Gary Thomas. In particular, he expands coverage of navigating ethical issues and multidisciplinary case examples in the newest edition.

Yin, R. K. (2017). *Case study research and applications: Design and methods* (6th ed.). Sage.

Robert Yin adds breadth and depth to this new edition with his emphasis on systems and procedures for generating reliable findings and valid interpretations in designs (see Chapter 2), data collection (see Chapter 4), and analysis (see Chapter 5).

CHAPTER CHECK-IN

1. Can you "see" how this book is distinguished from other books in its focus on examining five approaches to qualitative inquiry? Compare the purpose of this book with those of at least two other introductory qualitative research books; for ideas see Table 1.2.

2. Can you discern the influences of your lived experiences in your positionality statement representing your approach to qualitative research? Review your response to the Try this Now 1.1 activity.

3. Can you recognize how authors incorporate the nine distinguishing characteristics of qualitative research? Select one of the qualitative articles presented in Appendices B through F. Begin with identifying each of the characteristics advanced in this chapter (summarized in Table 1.1) as they have been applied in the journal article. Note which characteristics are easy and which are more difficult to identify.

SUMMARY

In this chapter, we introduced ourselves and this book examining five approaches to qualitative research. We began with a rationale for why examining different approaches is helpful to qualitative researchers followed by a description of our backgrounds to understand our approach to this book. We asked you to consider some of your life experiences that may influence how you approach qualitative research. We provided our definition of qualitative research as an approach to inquiry that begins with assumptions, an interpretive or theoretical lens, and the study of research problems exploring the meaning individuals or groups ascribe to a social or human problem. Nine common characteristics of qualitative research were described, including collecting data in natural settings with a sensitivity to the people under study, using inductive and deductive analysis strategies to establish patterns or themes, and developing a complex description and interpretation of the problem that provides for the voices of participants and a reflexivity of the researchers. Recent introductory textbooks underscore the characteristics embedded in this definition. We described our selection of the five approaches and the key book readings for each approach.

CHAPTER KEY TERMS

Approaches to inquiry

Research design

Qualitative research

FURTHER READINGS

The following resources are offered as additional references for this chapter. The list should not be considered exhaustive, and readers are encouraged to seek out other readings in the end-of-book reference list.

Beck, C. T. (2021). *Introduction to phenomenology*. Sage.

Cheryl Tatano Beck draws on her depth of experience to contrast interpretive and descriptive phenomenology from design to reporting specific key authors. See Chapters 5 and 7 describing the unique aspects of Clark Moustakas's modification of Adrian van Kaam's descriptive phenomenological methodology and Max van Manen's hermeneutic phenomenological approach, respectively.

Denzin, N. K., Lincoln, Y. S., Giardina, M. D., & Cannella, G. S. (2023). *The SAGE handbook of qualitative research* (6th ed.). Sage.

New topics and approaches are covered in this sixth edition, including the theoretical frames of intersectionality, critical disability research, and postcolonial and decolonized knowledge from familiar and emerging authors.

Hammersley, M., & Atkinson, P. (2019). *Ethnography: Principles in practice* (4th ed.). Routledge.

A new chapter on "ethnography in the digital world" and expanded discussions about the ethical issues involved in ethnographic research make this fourth edition an excellent resource. See Chapter 1 for features that most ethnographic work involves.

Kim, J.-H. (2015). *Understanding narrative inquiry: The crafting and analysis of stories as research*. Sage.

Jeong-Hee Kim guides readers through the narrative inquiry process with the author's own research experiences, locating narrative inquiry in the interdisciplinary context. Unique contributions include describing five genres of narrative research (see Chapter 4) and discussions of the role of theory in narrative inquiry.

Morse, J. M., Bowers, B. J., Charmaz, K., Clarke, A. E., Cobin, J., & Poor, C. J. (with Stern, P. N.). (Eds.). (2021). *Developing grounded theory: The second generation revisited* (2nd ed.). Routledge.

In this updated edition, the authors provide a succinct overview of the development of grounded theory and distinguish among Glaserian and Straussian grounded theory as well as Charmaz's constructivist grounded theory and Clarke's situational analysis.

Stake, R. (1995). *The art of case study research*. Sage.

Through his personable style, Robert Stake offers insights gained from experience along with illustrative examples. The book reads differently than a typical text, emphasizing the "art" involved in conducting a case study and the role of researcher's intuition.

2 PHILOSOPHICAL ASSUMPTIONS AND INTERPRETIVE FRAMEWORKS

> **QUESTIONS FOR DISCUSSION**
>
> - Where do philosophy and interpretive frameworks (theory) fit into the overall process of research?
> - Why is it important to understand the philosophical assumptions?
> - What four philosophical assumptions exist when you choose qualitative research?
> - How are these philosophical assumptions used and written into a qualitative study?
> - What interpretive frameworks are commonly used in qualitative research?
> - How are interpretive frameworks written into a qualitative study?
> - How are philosophical assumptions and interpretive frameworks linked in a qualitative study?

Whether we are aware of it or not, as researchers, we always bring certain beliefs and **philosophical assumptions** to our research. These philosophical assumptions come from a researcher's beliefs and values about conducting research. Sometimes they are deeply ingrained views about the types of problems that we need to study, what research questions to ask, or how we go about gathering data. These beliefs are instilled during our educational training through journal articles and books, through advice dispensed by our advisors, and through the scholarly communities we engage with at conferences and scholarly meetings. The challenge lies in becoming aware of these assumptions and beliefs and then in deciding whether we will actively incorporate them into our qualitative studies.

Often, at a less abstract level, these philosophical assumptions are *applied* through interpretive frameworks or theories in our research. These interpretive frameworks come from the literature where researchers form interpretations to explore individuals (e.g., women, or persons with disabilities) or frame approaches to conducting research (e.g., social constructivism). Interpretive frameworks or theories are more apparent in our qualitative studies than are philosophical assumptions, and researchers, often trained in the use of frameworks or theories, typically make them explicit in research studies.

Qualitative researchers have underscored the importance of not only understanding the beliefs and theories that inform our research but also actively writing about them in our reports and studies. This chapter highlights various philosophical assumptions that have occupied the minds of qualitative researchers for some years and the various interpretive and theoretical frameworks that enact these beliefs. A close tie exists between the philosophy brought to research and how one proceeds to apply a framework to inform their inquiry. Making explicit the philosophical assumptions and interpretive frameworks for a qualitative study is essential yet is not always done. Caine et al. (2022) describe a concerning trend they see

> that often makes research a technical exercise focused on methods. There is an absence of philosophical discussion, in both academia and the public realm, about the ways in which we take methodological turns as well as about the multiple ways to think about, and see, the world. (p. 3)

Qualitative researchers benefit from opportunities to reflect upon and make explicit the experiential and theoretical influences on their designs.

This chapter will help you begin to explore your philosophical assumptions and inform decisions about the influence of theories in your qualitative research. We do this by presenting a framework for understanding how both philosophy and theory fit into the large schema of the research process. Then we present details about philosophical assumptions common to qualitative researchers, consider the types of philosophical assumptions, and explore how they are often used or made explicit in qualitative studies. Finally, various interpretive frameworks are suggested that link back to philosophical assumptions with embedded commentary related to how these frameworks play out in the actual practice of research.

SITUATING PHILOSOPHY AND INTERPRETIVE FRAMEWORKS WITHIN THE RESEARCH PROCESS

To examine the influence of philosophical assumptions and interpretive frameworks in qualitative research, we restate our working definition from Chapter 1 here:

> Qualitative research begins with assumptions and the use of interpretive/theoretical frameworks that inform the study of research problems addressing the meaning individuals or groups ascribe to a social or human problem. To study this problem, qualitative researchers use an emerging qualitative approach to inquiry, the collection of data in a natural setting sensitive to the people and places under study, and data analysis that is both inductive and deductive and establishes patterns or themes. The final written report or presentation includes the voices of participants, the reflexivity of the researcher, a complex description and interpretation of the problem, and its contribution to the literature or a call for change. (Creswell, 2013, p. 44)

Notice in this definition that the *process* of research is described as flowing from philosophical assumptions to interpretive lens, and on to the procedures involved in studying social or human problems. Developing an understanding of the philosophical assumptions behind qualitative research begins with assessing where it fits within the overall process of research and considering how to write it into a study design. To help in this iterative process, we use a framework to guide understanding of how philosophical assumptions and interpretive frameworks (paradigm perspectives and theoretical orientations) are situated within and influential to the research process. It is here that adapting an overview of the process of research compiled by Denzin and Lincoln (2018a, p. 17), as shown in Figure 2.1, helps us situate philosophy and interpretative frameworks into perspective in the research process. The questions embedded within each phase help you begin to explore the philosophical assumptions you bring to research. Notice in Figure 2.1 that the phases tend to build upon each other (as indicated by the larger arrows), yet it is also possible for answers to invite a revisit of a previous phase (as indicated by the smaller arrows).

This conceptualization of the research process begins in Phase 1 with the researchers considering the **multifaceted experiences** that they bring to the inquiry, such as their personal histories, cultural assumptions, research traditions, views of themselves and others, and ethical and political beliefs. Researchers often overlook this phase, so it is helpful to have it highlighted and positioned early in the research process. In Phase 2, the researcher brings to the inquiry certain philosophical assumptions and interpretive frameworks. These are stances taken by the researcher that provide direction for the study, such as the researcher's view of reality (ontology), how the researcher knows reality (epistemology), the value-stance taken by the inquirer (axiology), and the procedures used in the study (methodology). These assumptions, in turn, are often applied in research through **paradigms** and theories (or, as we call them, interpretive frameworks). Paradigms are a "basic set of beliefs that guides action" (Guba, 1990, p. 17). These beliefs are brought to the process of research by the investigator and they may be called worldviews (Creswell & Plano Clark, 2018). **Theories or theoretical orientations**, on the other hand, are found in the literature and they provide a general explanation as to what the researcher hopes to find in a study or a lens through which to view the needs of participants and communities in a study. Granted, the difference between the philosophical assumptions, paradigms, and theoretical orientation is not always clear, but sorting out what exists at a broad philosophical level (assumptions) and what operates at a more practical level (interpretive frameworks) is a helpful heuristic.

In Phase 2, we find the philosophical and paradigm/theoretical interpretative frameworks addressed in this chapter. The following chapters in this book are devoted, then, to the Phase 3 **research strategies**, called approaches in this book, that will be enumerated as they relate to the research process. Finally, the inquirer engages in Phase 4 **methods of data collection** and analysis, followed by Phase 5, the **interpretation** and **evaluation** of the data. Taking Figure 2.1 in its entirety, we see that research involves differing levels of abstraction from the broad assessment of individual characteristics brought by the researcher through the researcher's philosophy and theory that lay the foundation for more specific approaches and methods of data collection, analysis, and interpretation. Also implicit in Figure 2.1 is the importance of having an understanding of philosophy and interpretative frameworks that inform a qualitative study.

FIGURE 2.1 ■ Situating Philosophy and Interpretive Frameworks Within the Research Process

Phase 1: The Researcher as a Multifaceted Subject

What perspectives and experiences do you bring to your research?

- Personal histories
- Cultural assumptions
- Research traditions
- Views of self and others
- The ethics and politics of research

Phase 2: Philosophical Assumptions and Interpretive Frameworks

How do your beliefs guide your actions as a researcher?

- Philosophical stances: Ontological, Epistemological, Axiological, and Methodological
- Paradigm interpretive frameworks (examples): Postpositivism, Social constructivism, Transformative frameworks, Postmodern perspectives, and Pragmatism
- Theoretical interpretive frameworks (examples): Feminist theories, Queer theory, Intersectionality theory, Critical theory, Critical race theory, and Disabilities theories

Phase 3: Research Strategies and Approaches

How do your philosophical and theoretical frameworks inform your choice of research approaches?

- Study design features and decisions
- Single and multiple case studies
- Ethnography, participant observation, performance ethnography
- Phenomenology and ethnomethodology
- Grounded theory
- Life history and testimonial
- Historical method
- Action and applied research
- Clinical research

Phase 4: Methods of Data Collection and Analysis

In what ways does your research approach influence the methods used for data collection and analysis?

- Observing
- Arts-based inquiry
- Interviewing, focus groups, and oral histories
- Artifacts, documents, and records
- Visual methods
- Autoethnography and applied ethnography
- Analyzing talk and text
- Computer-assisted technology for data management and analysis

Phase 5: The Art, Practice, and Politics of Interpretation and Evaluation

How do the methods influence decisions related to rigor, inferences, and use of findings?

- Evidence, criteria, policy, politics
- Rigor
- Writing as a method of inquiry
- Evaluation traditions

Source: Adapted from Denzin and Lincoln (2018a), Table 1.1, p. 18, and from Crotty (1998). Used with permission from Sage.

PHILOSOPHICAL ASSUMPTIONS

Why Philosophy Is Important

Philosophy refers to the use of abstract ideas and beliefs that inform our research. We can begin by thinking about why it is important to understand the philosophical assumptions that underlie qualitative research and to be able to articulate them in a research study or present them to an audience. Huff (2009) is helpful in articulating the importance of philosophy in research.

- *Philosophy provides direction for research goals and outcomes.* How we formulate our problem and research questions to study is shaped by our assumptions and, in turn, influences how we seek information to answer the questions. A cause-and-effect type of question in which certain variables are predicted to explain an outcome is different from an exploration of a single phenomenon as found in qualitative research.

- *Philosophy relates to training and research experiences.* These assumptions are deeply rooted in our training and reinforced by the scholarly community in which we work. Granted, some communities are more eclectic and borrow from many disciplines (e.g., education), while others are more narrowly focused on studying specific research problems, using particular methods, and adding certain research knowledge.

- *Philosophy informs evaluative criteria for research-related decisions.* Unquestionably, reviewers make philosophical assumptions about a study when they evaluate it. Knowing how reviewers stand on issues of epistemology is helpful to author-researchers. When the assumptions between the author and the reviewer diverge, the author's work may not receive a fair hearing, and conclusions may be drawn that it does not contribute to the literature. This unfair hearing may occur within the context of a graduate student presenting to a committee, an author submitting to a scholarly journal, or an investigator sending a proposal to a funding agency. On the reverse side, understanding the assumptions used by a reviewer may enable a researcher to resolve points of difference before they become a focal point for critique.

The question as to whether key assumptions can change and/or whether multiple philosophical assumptions can influence a given study needs to be addressed. Our stance is that assumptions can change over time and over a career, and they often do, especially after a scholar leaves the enclave of their discipline and begins to work in more of a trans- or multidisciplinary way. Whether multiple assumptions can be written into a given study is open to debate, and again, it may be related to the research experiences of the investigator, their openness to exploring differing assumptions, and the acceptability of ideas in the larger scientific community of which the investigator is a part. Looking across the four philosophical assumptions described next can be helpful for monitoring individual changes over time.

Four Philosophical Assumptions

What are the philosophical assumptions made by researchers when they undertake a qualitative study? These assumptions have been articulated throughout the past 20 years in the various editions of *The SAGE Handbook of Qualitative Research* (Denzin & Lincoln, 1994, 2000, 2005, 2011b, 2018b) as guiding the philosophical stances behind qualitative research. These stances relate beliefs about ontology (the nature of reality), epistemology (what counts as knowledge and how knowledge claims are justified), axiology (the role of values and ethics in research), and methodology (the process of research). We will next discuss each of these four categories of philosophy, detail how the philosophical assumptions might be used and written into qualitative research, and then link them to different interpretive frameworks that operate at a more specific level in the process of research (see Table 2.1).

TABLE 2.1 ■ Practical Implications of Philosophical Assumptions for Qualitative Researchers

Philosophical Assumption	Guiding Questions	Belief Characteristics	Practical Implications for Qualitative Researchers (Examples)
Ontological	What is the nature of reality?	Multiple realities can be seen through many views; researchers conduct the study with the intent to report these multiple realities.	Researchers report different perspectives as themes develop in the findings.
Epistemological	What counts as knowledge? How are knowledge claims justified?	Subjective evidence is obtained from participants; researchers attempt to lessen the distance between them and those being researched.	Researchers rely on quotes as evidence from participants as well as collaborate, spend time with participants in their natural setting, and make sense of what is shared with them.
Axiological	What is the role of values and ethics?	Research is value-laden; researchers acknowledge that biases are present in relation to their role in the study context.	Researchers openly discuss values that shape the narrative and include their own interpretations in conjunction with those of participants.
Methodological	What is the process of research? What is the language of research?	Procedures are inductive and emergent; researchers use inductive logic, study the topic within its context, and use an emerging design.	Researchers work with particulars (details) before generalizations, describe in detail the context of the study, and continually revise questions from experiences in the field.

Ontological assumptions relate the nature of reality and its characteristics. When researchers conduct qualitative research, they are embracing the idea of multiple realities. Different researchers embrace different realities, as do the individuals being studied and the readers of a qualitative study. When studying individuals, qualitative researchers conduct a study with the intent of reporting these multiple realities. Evidence of multiple realities includes the use of numerous forms of evidence through themes, using the actual words of different individuals, and presenting varying or multiple perspectives. For example, when writers compile a phenomenology, they report how individuals participating in the study view their experiences differently (Moustakas, 1994). A qualitative researcher's ontological assumptions can impact the topic they choose to study, the focus of the research questions, and the approach they select for guiding the study (Hesse-Biber, 2016).

At the core of **epistemological assumptions** is relating what counts as knowledge. Conducting a qualitative study means that researchers "study things in their natural settings, attempting to make sense of or interpret phenomena in terms of the meanings people bring to them" (Denzin & Lincoln, 2018a, p. 10). Therefore, subjective evidence is assembled based on individual views. This is how knowledge is known—through the subjective experiences of people. It becomes important, then, to conduct studies in their natural setting, where the participants live and work; these are important contexts for understanding what the participants are saying. The longer researchers know the participants and their natural setting, the more they "know what they know" from firsthand information. For example, a good ethnography requires a prolonged stay at the research site (Wolcott, 2008a). In short, qualitative researchers try to minimize the "distance" or "objective separateness" (Guba & Lincoln, 1988, p. 94) between them and those being researched to accurately represent what is shared with them.

All researchers bring values to a study, but qualitative researchers make their values known in a study. **Axiological assumptions** relate the values and ethics that characterize qualitative research. In a qualitative study, the inquirers admit the value-laden nature of the study and actively report their values and biases as well as the value-laden nature of information gathered from participants and their natural settings. We say that researchers "position themselves" by identifying their "positionality" in relation to the context and setting of the research (see Chapter 1). Among the aspects described are the researchers' social position (e.g., gender, age, race, immigration status), personal experiences, and political and professional beliefs (Berger, 2015). In an interpretive biography, for example, the researcher's presence is apparent in the text, and the author admits that the stories voiced represent an interpretation of the author as much as the subject of the study (Denzin, 1989).

The procedures of qualitative research, or its methodology, are characterized as inductive, emerging, and shaped by the researcher's experience in collecting and analyzing the data. **Methodological assumptions** relate how researchers go about their qualitative study. The logic that the qualitative researcher follows is inductive, from the ground up, rather than handed down entirely from a theory or from the perspectives of the inquirer. Sometimes the research questions change in the middle of the study to reflect better the types of questions needed to understand the research problem. In response, the data collection strategy, planned before the study, needs to be modified to accompany the new questions. During the data analysis, the researcher follows a path of analyzing the data to develop an increasingly detailed knowledge of the topic being studied.

> **TRY THIS NOW 2.1**
>
> **UNPACKING YOUR PHILOSOPHICAL ASSUMPTIONS AS A QUALITATIVE RESEARCHER**
>
> Philosophical assumptions relate beliefs about ontology (the nature of reality), epistemology (what counts as knowledge and how knowledge claims are justified), axiology (the role of values and ethics in research), and methodology (the process of research). What are some key aspects of your ontological and epistemological assumptions that may influence your work as a qualitative researcher? Use the guiding questions in Table 2.1 to get you started.

Writing Philosophical Assumptions Into Qualitative Studies

One further thought is important about philosophical assumptions. In some qualitative studies they remain hidden from view; they can be deduced, however, by the discerning reader who sees the multiple views that appear in the themes, the detailed rendering of the subjective quotes of participants, the carefully laid-out biases of the researcher, or the emerging design that evolves in ever-expanding levels of abstraction from description to themes to broad generalizations. In other studies, the philosophy is made explicit by a special section in the study—typically in the description of the characteristics of qualitative inquiry often found in the methods section. Here, the inquirer talks about ontology, epistemology, and other assumptions explicitly and details how they are exemplified in the study. The intent of this discussion is to convey the assumptions, to provide definitions for them, and to discuss how they are illustrated in the study. References to the literature about the philosophy of qualitative research round out the discussion. Sections of this nature are often found in doctoral dissertations, in journal articles reported in major qualitative journals, and in conference paper presentations where the audience may ask about the underlying philosophy of the study. While there are infinite ways for authors to go about describing their philosophical assumptions and implications for research practice, we offer three descriptions from journal articles to examine in Example 2.1.

> **EXAMPLE 2.1 DESCRIPTIONS OF UNDERLYING PHILOSOPHICAL ASSUMPTIONS**
>
> Notice how each of the four major philosophical assumptions (ontology—what is reality? epistemology—how is reality known? axiology—how are values of the research expressed? and methodology—how is the research conducted?) are made explicit in the following journal articles:

1. Healey, G. K. (2014). Inuit family understandings of sexual health and relationships in Nunavut. *Canadian Journal of Public Health, 105*(2), e133–e137. https://doi.org/10.17269/cjph.105.4189

   See the "methods" section (pp. e134-e135) in Healey (2014) for the full description of the five Inuit concepts informing the research approach for the *Piliriqatigiinniq*, the Partnership Community Health research model, calling "attention to indigenous ways of knowing and the research approaches that grow from an indigenous worldview" (p. e135), and emphasizing connections between people in all aspects of the research:

   Piliriqatigiinniq (the concept of working together for the common good); Pittiarniq (the concept of being good or kind); Inuuqatigiinniq (the concept of being respectful of others); Unikkaaqatigiinniq (the philosophy of story-telling and/or the power and meaning of story); and Iqqaumaqatigiinniq (the concept that ideas or thoughts may come into "one") (p. e135)

2. Brown, J., Sorrell, J. H., McClaren, J., & Creswell, J. W. (2006). Waiting for a liver transplant. *Qualitative Health Research, 16*(1), 119–136. fhttps://doi.org/10.1177/1049732305284011

   See the "phenomenological approach" section (p. 122) inspired by Frankl (1997) in Brown et al. (2006) for the full description and rationale of the choice of qualitative approach for the study examining the meaning that people with liver failure ascribe to the experience of waiting for a liver transplant:

   Living with ESLD [end-stage liver disease] and waiting for a transplant become experiences in and of themselves as the illness progresses and outcomes are not known. It is with this understanding that we chose phenomenology as the tradition of inquiry. (p. 122)

3. Jungnickel, K. (2014). Getting there . . . and back: How ethnographic commuting (by bicycle) shaped a study of Australian backyard technologists. *Qualitative Research, 14*(6), 640–655. https://doi.org/10.1177/1468794113481792

   See the "positioning the mobile ethnographer" section (p. 642) in Jungnickel (2014) for the full statement of the researcher positionality description for the study of Australian backyard technologists:

   Regardless of the nature of distance (physical, virtual or symbolic), movement and travel are deemed vital to the development of an authentic ethnographic presence and authoritative voice . . . In this section, I attempt, by no means exhaustively, to categorise four types of ethnographer mobility and attending issues of positionality with the aim of locating the case study and a discussion of the ethnographic commute. (p. 642)

INTERPRETIVE FRAMEWORKS

As shown in Figure 2.1, philosophical assumptions are often applied within interpretive frameworks that qualitative researchers use when they conduct a study. Thus, Denzin and Lincoln (2018a) consider the philosophical assumptions as key premises that are folded into interpretive frameworks used in qualitative research. What are these interpretive frameworks? They may be paradigms or beliefs that the researcher brings to the process of research, or they may be theories or theoretical orientations that guide the practice of research. Paradigm interpretative frameworks may be **postpositivism**, **social constructivism**, transformative, and postmodern. Theories may be **social science theories** to frame their theoretical lens in studies, such as the use of these theories in ethnography (see Chapter 4). Social science theories may be theories of leadership, attribution, political influence and control, and hundreds of other possibilities that are taught in the social science disciplines. On the other hand, the theories may be **social justice theories** seeking to bring about change or address social justice issues in our societies. John W. Creswell and his coauthor J. David Creswell (2023) state, "researchers increasingly use a theoretical standpoint in qualitative research to provide an overall orienting lens for the study questions about gender, class, and race (or other issues of marginalized groups). This lens becomes a transformative perspective to bring about change, lift the voices of underrepresented groups, and uncover largely hidden assumptions of individuals" (p. 60).

The interpretive frameworks are ever expanding, and the list in Figure 2.1 does not account for all that are popularly used in qualitative research. Other approaches that have been extensively discussed elsewhere involve the realist perspective and intersectionality. The realist perspective combines a realist ontology (the belief that a real world exists independently of our beliefs and constructions) and a constructivist epistemology (knowledge of the world is inevitably our own construction; see Maxwell, 2012).

Intersectionality helps qualitative researchers generate nuanced understandings of social relations and structural inequalities by examining how an array of socially constructed dimensions of difference shape experiences and actions (see Abrams et al., 2020; Esposito & Evans-Winters, 2021). Consequently, any discussion (including this one) can only be a partial description of possibilities, but a review of several commonly used interpretive frameworks can provide a sense of options. The participants in these interpretive, theoretically oriented projects often represent underrepresented or marginalized groups, whether those differences take the form of economic levels, gender, race/ethnicity, religion, immigrant or Indigenous status, sexual identity, disability, or geography or some intersection of these differences.

Postpositivism

Those who engage in qualitative research using a belief system grounded in postpositivism will take a scientific approach to research. They will employ a social science theoretical lens. We will use the term *postpositivism* rather than *positivism* to denote this approach because postpositivists do not believe in strict cause and effect but rather recognize that all cause and effect is a probability that may or may not occur. Postpositivism has the elements of being reductionistic, logical, empirical, cause-and-effect oriented, and deterministic based on a priori theories. We can see this approach at work among individuals with prior quantitative research training and in fields such as the health sciences in which qualitative research often plays a supportive role to quantitative research and must be couched in terms acceptable to quantitative researchers and funding agents (e.g., the a priori use of theory; see Barbour, 2000). Good overviews of postpositivist approaches are available in Phillips and Burbules (2000) and Mertens (2019).

In practice, postpositivist researchers view inquiry as a series of logically related steps, believe in multiple perspectives from participants rather than a single reality, and espouse rigorous methods of qualitative data collection and analysis. They use multiple levels of data analysis for rigor, employ computer programs to assist in their analysis, encourage the use of validity approaches, and write their qualitative studies in the form of scientific reports, with a structure resembling quantitative articles (e.g., problem, questions, data collection, results, conclusions). We see a postpositivist approach in the constructivist grounded theory study example by Churchill et al. (2007) to develop a theoretical model from the mothers' perspective of what low-income rural families with young children do for fun. In this example, researchers used the MAXQDA computer software program to systematically analyze and generate themes from a database of 368 interviews. In their methods, the researchers described several validation strategies including purposeful sampling and debriefings.

Our approaches to qualitative research have been identified as tending toward postpositivism (Denzin & Lincoln, 2005, 2011b, 2018b), as have the approaches of others (e.g., Taylor et al., 2015). We do use this belief system, although neither of us would characterize our research as entirely framed within a postpositivist qualitative orientation (e.g., see the constructivist approach in McVea et al., 1999; the social justice perspective in D. W. Miller et al., 1998; and the pragmatic approach in Henderson, 2011). This postpositivist interpretive framework is exemplified in the systematic procedures of grounded theory found in Strauss and Corbin (1990, 1998) and Corbin and Strauss (2007, 2015), the analytic data analysis steps in phenomenology (Moustakas, 1994), and the data analysis strategies of case comparisons of Yin (2017).

Social Constructivism

Social constructivism (which is often described as interpretivism, see Denzin & Lincoln, 2018b; and constructivism, see Mertens, 2019) is another paradigm or worldview. In social constructivism, individuals seek understanding of the world in which they live and work. They develop subjective meanings of their experiences—meanings directed toward certain objects or things. These meanings are varied and multiple, leading the researcher to look for the complexity of views rather than narrowing the meanings into a few categories or ideas. The goal of research, then, is to rely as much as possible on the participants' views of the situation. Often these subjective meanings are negotiated socially and historically. In other words, they are not simply imprinted on individuals but are formed through interaction with others (hence social construction) and through historical and cultural norms that operate in individuals' lives. Rather than starting with a theory (as in postpositivism), inquirers generate or inductively develop a theory or pattern of meaning. Examples of writers who have summarized this position are Burr (2015), Crotty (1998), Gergen (2023), Lincoln and Guba (2000), and Schwandt (2015).

In terms of practice, the questions become broad and general so that the participants can construct the meaning of a situation, a meaning typically forged in discussions or interactions with other persons. The more open-ended the questioning, the better, as the researcher listens carefully to what people say or do in their life setting. Thus, constructivist researchers often address the "processes" of interaction among individuals. They also focus on the specific contexts in which people live and work to understand the historical and cultural settings of the participants. Researchers recognize that their own background shapes their interpretation, and they "position themselves" in the research to acknowledge how their interpretation flows from their own personal, cultural, and historical experiences. The researcher's intent, then, is to make sense of (or interpret) the meanings others have about the world. This is why qualitative research is often called interpretive research.

The researchers make an interpretation of what they find, an interpretation shaped by their own experiences and background; for example, see study impetus described by Brown et al. (2006). In this phenomenological inquiry, the researchers identify one of the authors as a psychiatrist with responsibility "for the assessment and selection of all patients with end-stage liver disease who present as candidates for liver transplantation at a large midwestern transplant center" (Brown et al., 2006, p. 119). The nature of the relationship of one of the researchers to the research topic and context was important to disclose because of its usefulness for contributing to the data interpretation. Thus, we see the constructivist worldview manifest in phenomenological studies, in which individuals describe their experiences (Moustakas, 1994), and in the grounded theory perspective of Charmaz (2014), in which she grounds her theoretical orientation in the views or perspectives of individuals.

Transformative Frameworks

Researchers might use a **transformative framework** because the postpositivists impose structural laws and theories that do not fit marginalized individuals or groups and the constructivists do not go far enough in advocating action to help individuals. The basic tenet of this transformative framework is that knowledge is not neutral, and it reflects the power and social relationships within society; thus, the purpose of knowledge construction is to aid people to improve society (Mertens, 2003). These individuals include marginalized groups such as Indigenous groups, lesbians, gay people, bisexuals, transgender persons, and societies that need a more hopeful, positive psychology and resilience (Mertens, 2009, 2019).

Qualitative research, then, should contain an action agenda for reform that may change the lives of participants, the institutions in which they live and work, or even the researchers' lives. Mavrogordato and White (2020) describe case studies examining the role school leaders play in enacting equity policies for historically marginalized groups such as students studying English as a foreign language. The findings were used to generate a framework for helping school leaders with important implications for students, schools, and communities. The issues facing marginalized groups are of paramount importance to study—issues such as oppression, domination, suppression, alienation, and hegemony. As these issues are studied and exposed, the researchers provide a voice for these participants, raising their consciousness and improving their lives. Mertens (2021) describes the transformative framework as characterized by

- An ethical stance that promotes social inclusion and challenges oppressive structures that sustain inequality and discrimination.
- A participatory and reflective entry process into a community, designed to build trust, address power differences, and make goals and strategies more transparent.
- The dissemination of findings in ways that encourage the use of results to enhance human rights and social, economic, and environmental justice.
- A commitment to addressing the intersectionality of relevant dimensions of diversity—such as gender, disability, indigeneity, poverty status, and language—by incorporating culturally responsive, equity-focused, feminist, and indigenous approaches. (p. 3)

Other research approaches are informed by this worldview including participatory action research (Kemmis & Wilkinson, 1998), Maori research based on the principles of "by Maori, for Maori, with Maori" (L. T. Smith, 2005, 2021), and action research (Bradbury, 2015; Reason & Bradbury, 2006). In practice, the transformative framework has shaped several approaches to inquiry. Specific social issues (e.g., domination, oppression, inequity) help organize the research questions. Not wanting to further marginalize the individuals participating in the research, transformative inquirers collaborate with research participants. They may ask participants to help with designing the questions, collecting the data, analyzing it, and shaping the final report of the research. It should be noted that the level and type of community involvement will vary depending on the research context but that the relationship with participants should be reciprocal (Mertens, 2009, 2021). In this way, the "voice" of the participants becomes heard throughout the research process and the research products are meaningful for all involved. It is encouraging to see guiding research resources emerge from the perspectives of marginalized groups (e.g., Lovern & Locust, 2013; Mertens et al., 2013). The research also contains an action agenda for reform, a specific plan for addressing the injustices of the marginalized group. These practices will be seen in the ethnographic approaches to research with a social justice agenda found in Denzin and Lincoln (2018a) and in the change-oriented (Daiute & Lightfoot, 2004) and equity-seeking (Clandinin, 2023) forms of narrative research.

Postmodern Perspectives

Postmodernism (which is also described as poststructuralism, although the relationship between the terms remains under debate among scholars) might be considered a family of theories and perspectives that have something in common (Slife & Williams, 1995). Postmodernists advance a reaction to or critique of the 19th-century Enlightenment and early 20th-century emphasis on technology, rationality, reason, universals, science, and the positivist, scientific method (Bloland, 1995; Stringer, 1993). The basic concept is that knowledge claims must be set within the conditions of the world today and in the multiple perspectives of class, race, gender, and other group affiliations. These conditions are well articulated by individuals such as Foucault, Derrida, Lyotard, Giroux, and Freire (Bloland, 1995). These are negative conditions, and they show themselves in the presence of hierarchies, power and control by individuals, and the multiple meanings of language. The conditions include the importance of different discourses, the importance of marginalized people and groups (the "other"), and the presence of "metanarratives" or universals that hold true regardless of the social conditions.

As an example, Chipango (2021) adopts a postmodern perspective to examine the nature of the discourse surrounding Zimbabwe's mismatch between energy supply and demand, also known as energy poverty. From her case study drawing upon interviews and documents, Chipango (2021) concludes that "energy poverty cannot be understood outside of the political-economic discourse that constructs and interprets it" (p. 1). Also included is the need to examine texts in terms of language, their reading and writing, and bringing to the surface concealed hierarchies as well as dominations, oppositions, inconsistencies, and contradictions (Bloland, 1995; Clarke, 2005; Stringer, 1993). Postmodernism highlights the usefulness of researcher reflexivity and creativity in representing the multiple voices and perspectives that have become distinguishing characteristics in qualitative research (Christians, 2018; Clandinin, 2023). These practices are seen in Denzin's (1989) approach to "interpretive" biography, Clandinin and Connelly's (2000) approach to narrative research, and Clarke's (2005) perspective on grounded theory. Postmodernism researchers study turning points, or problematic situations in which people find themselves during transition periods (Borgatta & Borgatta, 1992). Regarding a "postmodern-influenced ethnography," J. Thomas (1993) writes that such a study might "confront the centrality of media-created realities and the influence of information technologies" (p. 25). Thomas also comments that narrative texts need to be challenged (and written), according to the postmodernists, for their "subtexts" of dominant meanings. These ways of knowing have been important for researchers who are open to uncertainty, plurality, and want to recognize the complexity inherent in their qualitative studies (O'leary, 2021).

Pragmatism

There are many forms of **pragmatism**. Individuals holding an interpretive framework based on pragmatism focus on the outcomes of the research—the actions, situations, and consequences of inquiry—rather than antecedent conditions (as in postpositivism). As a theoretical stance, pragmatism privileges practice and method over all else (Denzin & Lincoln, 2018a). There is a concern with applications—"what works"—and solutions to problems (Patton, 1990). In Hammond et al. (2022), we see their choice of in-depth interviews with 15 women who were sutured following birth as the most appropriate method for improving women's experiences of perineal suturing. Cherryholmes (1992), Murphy (1990), and Rorty (1990) provide direction for the basic ideas of pragmatism:

- Pragmatism is not committed to any one system of philosophy and reality.
- Individual researchers have a freedom of choice. They are "free" to choose the methods, techniques, and procedures of research that best meet their needs and purposes.
- Pragmatists do not see the world as an absolute unity. In a similar way, researchers look to many approaches to collecting and analyzing data rather than subscribing to only one way (e.g., multiple qualitative approaches).
- Truth is what works at the time; it is not based in a dualism between reality independent of the mind or within the mind.
- Pragmatist researchers look to the "what" and "how" of research based on its intended consequences—where they want to go with it.
- Pragmatists agree that research always occurs in social, historical, political, and other contexts.
- Pragmatists have believed in an external world independent of the mind as well as those lodged in the mind. They believe (Cherryholmes, 1992) that we need to stop asking questions about reality and the laws of nature. "They would simply like to change the subject" (Rorty, 1983, p. xiv).

In practice, the individual using pragmatism will use multiple methods of data collection to best answer the research question, will employ multiple sources of data collection, will focus on the practical implications of the research, and will emphasize the importance of conducting research that best addresses the research problem. Not surprisingly, researchers often link pragmatism with mixed methods research, in which the inquirers integrate *both* quantitative and qualitative research (Creswell, 2021; Tashakkori & Teddlie, 2003). In the discussion here of the five approaches to research, you will see this framework at work when ethnographers employ both quantitative (e.g., surveys) and qualitative data collection (LeCompte & Schensul, 1999) and when case study researchers use both quantitative and qualitative data (Luck et al., 2006; Yin, 2017).

Feminist Theories

Feminism draws on different theoretical and pragmatic orientations, different international contexts, and different dynamic developments (Olesen, 2018). Brisolara (2014) describes most feminist theories as intending to contribute to 'the promotion of greater equity, the establishment of equal rights and opportunities, and the end of oppression" (p. 4). **Feminist research approaches** center on women's diverse situations and the institutions that frame those situations. Feminist research embraces many of the tenets of postmodern and poststructuralist critiques as a challenge to the injustices of current society. In feminist research approaches, the goals are to establish collaborative and nonexploitative relationships, to place the researcher within the study to avoid objectification, and to conduct research that is transformative. Research topics may include a postcolonial thought related to forms of feminism depending on the context of nationalism, globalization, and diverse international contexts (e.g., sex workers, domestic servants); social disparities within and across nations; and specific issues such as sexual violence against women as instruments of war and the continued overrepresentation of women, women of color, and women-headed families in poverty rates. S. Harding (1990, 2012) documented the transformation of standpoint theories and their contributions to understandings about specific groups of women (e.g., lesbians, women with disabilities, women with tribal affiliations, and women of color).

The theme of domination prevails in the feminist literature as well, but the subject matter is often gender domination within a patriarchal society. One of the leading scholars of this approach, Lather (1991), comments on the essential perspectives of this framework. Feminist researchers see gender as a basic organizing principle that shapes the conditions of their lives. It is "a lens that brings into focus particular questions" (Fox-Keller, 1985, p. 6). The questions feminists pose relate to the centrality of gender in the shaping of our consciousness. Olesen (2018) notes the dominant, continuing theme in feminist research as the issue of knowledge: "Whose knowledges? Where and how obtained, by whom, from whom, and for what purposes?" (p. 152). The aim of this ideological research is to "correct both the invisibility and distortion of female experience in ways relevant to ending women's unequal social position" (Lather, 1991, p. 71). Another writer, A. J. Stewart (1994), views women as having agency, the ability to make choices and resist oppression, and she suggests that researchers need to inquire into how women understand gender, acknowledging that gender is a social construct that differs for each individual. Such essential recognition of the heterogeneity of women around the world means that relevant dimensions of diversity can be considered (Mertens, 2014) and inclusive spaces can be created (Bettcher, 2015).

Discussions indicate that the approach of finding appropriate methods for feminist research has given way to the thought that any method can be made feminist (Deem, 2002; Moss, 2007). DeVault (2018) describes several emerging lines of feminist qualitative inquiry research methods using visual (e.g., textbooks, advertisements, images) and online (e.g., blogs, social media, photo-sharing sites) techniques. In practice, a feminist researcher can use a variety of approaches and methods. Malecki et al. (2022) describe a feminist phenomenological approach employing an arts-based research technique called body mapping. Researchers used the life-sized outline of eight women to explore and visually represent how the experience of child abuse influenced the development of anorexia.

Critical work continues to address protecting Indigenous knowledge and the intersectionality of feminist research (e.g., the intersection of race, class, gender, sexuality, able-bodiedness, and age; Olesen, 2018). Olesen (2018) summarizes the current state of feminist research under a number of transformative developments (e.g., globalization, transnational feminism, and standpoint research), critical trends (e.g., endarkened, decolonizing research and intersectionality), continuing issues (e.g., destabilizing insider–outsider, troubling traditional concepts), enduring concerns (e.g., bias, reflexivity, participants' voices, ethics), influences on feminist work (e.g., the academy and publishing), and challenges of the future (e.g., the interplay of multiple factors in women's lives, hidden oppressions). Recent discussions about emergent practices integrate international perspectives (e.g., Brisolara et al., 2014; Denzin et al., 2023) and new research technologies (e.g., DeVault, 2018; Hesse-Biber, 2012).

Critical Theory

Critical theory perspectives are concerned with empowering human beings to transcend the constraints placed on them by race, class, and gender (Fay, 1987). Critical theory provides new and valuable lenses to view our world and ourselves and gain new insights (Tyson, 2023). Researchers need to acknowledge their own power, privilege, and bias; engage in dialogues; and use theory to interpret or illuminate social action (Madison, 2019). Central themes that a critical researcher might explore include the scientific study of social institutions and their transformations through interpreting the meanings of social life; the historical problems of domination, alienation, and social struggles; and a critique of society and the envisioning of new possibilities (Fay, 1987; R. A. Morrow, 1994). With the aim of uncovering the cultural factors that impeded maintaining patients' dignity in a hospital intensive care setting, Bidabadi et al. (2019) used a critical ethnographic approach to inform a culture shift in therapeutic relationships.

In research, critical theory can be defined by the configuration of methodological postures it embraces. The critical researcher might design, for example, an ethnographic study to include changes in how people think; encourage people to interact, form networks, become activists, and form action-oriented groups; and help individuals examine the conditions of their existence (Madison, 2019; J. Thomas, 1993). The end goal of the study might be social theorizing, which R. A. Morrow (1994) define as "the desire to comprehend and, in some cases, transform (through praxis) the underlying orders of social life—those social and systemic relations that constitute society" (p. 211). The investigator accomplishes this, for example, through an intensive case study or across a small number of historically comparable cases of specific actors (biographies), mediations, or systems and through "ethnographic accounts (interpretive social psychology), componential taxonomies (cognitive anthropology), and formal models (mathematical sociology)" (p. 212). In critical action research in teacher education, for example, Kincheloe (1991/2012) recommends that the "critical teacher" exposes the assumptions of existing research orientations; critiques the knowledge base; and through these critiques, reveals ideological effects on teachers, schools, and the culture's view of education. An example of a study using critical intersectionality was a review of literature seeking to understand the secondary school experiences of trans youth with the intent to address the patterns of educational disadvantage that reflect broader structures of social inequality (McBride, 2020).

The design of research within a critical theory approach, according to sociologist Agger (1991), falls into two broad categories: *methodological*, in that it affects the ways in which people write and read, and *substantive*, in the theories and topics of the investigator (e.g., theorizing about the role of the state and culture in advanced capitalism). An often-cited classic of critical theory is the ethnography from Willis (1977) of the "lads" who participated in behavior as opposition to authority, as informal groups "having a laff" (p. 29) as a form of resistance to their school. In a study of the manifestations of resistance and state regulation, R. A. Morrow (1994) highlight ways in which actors come to terms with and struggle against cultural forms that dominate them. Resistance is also the theme addressed in an ethnography of a subcultural group of youths (Haenfler, 2004).

Critical Race Theory

Critical race theory is a set of theories committed to social justice that rely on "intersectionality (i.e., the nexus of race, gender, class, etc.), a critique of liberalism, the use of critical social science, a combination of structural and poststructural analysis, the denial of neutrality in scholarship, and the incorporation of storytelling, or … 'counternarratives,' to speak back against dominant discourses" (Donnor & Ladson-Billings, 2018, p. 202). Others have described critical race theory as a "collection of activists and scholars engaged in studying and transforming the relationship among race, racism, and power" (Delgado & Stefancic, 2023, p. 2). Race and racism is deeply embedded within the framework of American society (Parker & Lynn, 2002) and has directly shaped the U.S. legal system and the ways people think about the law, racial categories, and privilege (C. Harris, 1993). Through the use of diverse research methods (e.g., observations of natural settings such as classrooms and reviews of personal and public documents), researchers seek missing voices to contribute to "dispelling notions of color-blindness and post-racial imaginings so that we can better understand and remedy the disparities that are prevalent in our society" (Donnor & Ladson-Billings, 2018, p. 209). Counternarratives are emerging as promising tool for stimulating transformative action for educational equity (R. Miller et al., 2020).

According to Chapman and Crawford (2023), critical race theory provides scholars with tools to critique and question with a goal to "move marginalized peoples by challenging stock stories and stereotypes and offering new, contextualized stories and perspectives" (p. 80), which they argue is key to achieving racial justice. Parker and Lynn (2002) advance three aims of critical race theory. The first aim presents stories about discrimination from the perspective of people of color. These may be qualitative case studies of descriptions and interviews. These cases may then be drawn together to build cases against racially biased officials or discriminatory practices. Since many stories advance White privilege through "majoritarian" master narratives, counter stories by people of color can help to shatter the complacency that may accompany such privilege and challenge the dominant discourses that serve to suppress people on the margins of society (Solorzano & Yosso, 2002). The second aim recognizes that race is a social construct, meaning that *race* is not a fixed term but one that is fluid and continually shaped by political pressures and informed by individual lived experiences. The third aim addresses other areas of difference, such as gender, class, and any inequities experienced by individuals. As Parker and Lynn (2002) comment, "in the case of Black women, race does not exist outside of gender and gender does not exist outside of race" (p. 12).

In practice, the use of critical race theory methodology means that the researcher foregrounds race and racism in all aspects of the research process; challenges the traditional research paradigms, texts, and theories used to explain the experiences of people of color; and offers transformative solutions to racial, gender, and class subordination in our societal and institutional structures. Researchers sometimes use critical race theory in concert with other frameworks—for example, disability studies (Annamma et al., 2020; Watts & Erevelles, 2004) or feminist theories (Chepp, 2015; Mendoza Aviña et al. 2023).

Postcolonial Theories

A postcolonial lens assesses how knowledge production and theories of the past and the present have been shaped by ideas and power relations of imperialism, colonialism, neocolonialism, globalization, and racism. We honor the diverse perspectives and note the lack of agreement for terminology to describe Indigenous understandings as applied to theories, approaches, and paradigms. According to Chilisa and Phatshwane (2022), **postcolonial theories** provide a lens through which to "plan and conduct a study that is without prejudices and is respectful of all groups of people, including the marginalized in our communities" (p. 225). A postcolonial lens holds great potential for diverse roles in decolonizing research practice by focusing on, for example, the role of literature and language in the construction of knowledge and how we collect, analyze, and interpret data. A key characteristic of a postcolonial lens is to bring to its center the voices of those who have been muted by the dominance of Euro-Western methodologies.

In practice, some **postcolonial theory** promotes the use of data collection interactions that invoke Indigenous worldviews; for example, by informing the type of interview questions and the analysis of that data, postcolonial theory can mitigate power relationships where the researcher can become a colonizer (Chilisa & Phatshwane, 2022). In other studies, researchers intersect postcolonial theoretical frameworks with another lens. For example, Arur and DeJaeghere (2019) describe a study using postcolonial feminist perspectives to inform their study addressing gender oppression in life skills programming. The researchers describe how over time, they "had to unlearn some of the ways of thinking that inform [their] knowledge production, and to consider what we did not know because of how [they] have framed the [interview] questions and ideas around gender relations, power and schooling" (p. 495).

Chilisa and Phatshwane (2022) describe the call by Indigenous scholars (e.g., Grande, 2000; G. H. Smith, 2000) for the inclusion of survivance in postcolonial theory. They describe the concept of survivance as going "beyond survival, endurance, and resistance to colonial domination, calling for the colonizers and the colonized to learn from each other" (p. 229). Chilisa and Mertens (2021) discuss nine principles for building relationships between the researchers and the communities and connecting with the environment: relationality, responsibility, reverence, reciprocity, respectful representation, reflexivity, responsivity, rights and regulations, and decolonization.

Queer Theory

According to Alexander (2018), **queer theory** "is a collective of intellectual speculations and challenges to the social and political constructions of sexualized and gender identity" (p. 278). de Lauretis (1991) coined the phrase "queer theory" and outlined a complete rethinking of sexuality divorced from the binaries and standards defined by heterosexual power structures. Queer theory, also referred to as LGBTQ+ (lesbian, gay, bisexual, transgender, and queer) theory (Mertens, 2019), is characterized by a variety of methods and strategies relating to individual identity (Plummer, 2011a; K. Watson, 2005). As a body of literature continuing to evolve, it explores the myriad complexities of the construct, identity, and how identities reproduce and "perform" in social forums. Queer theory intends to remap the terrain of gender, identity, and cultural studies. Milani and Borba (2022) explain, "what characterizes queer theoretical approaches is a staunch commitment to unveiling and actively opposing regimes of sexual normality" (p. 195), questioning all aspects of normality—for example, its origins, contexts, and interests—and not exclusively in the realm of sexuality and gender.

Writers also use a postmodern or poststructural orientation to critique and deconstruct dominant theories related to identity (Plummer, 2011a, 2011b; Watson, 2005). Most queer theorists work to challenge and undercut identity as singular, fixed, or normal (Watson, 2005). Queer theorists have engaged in research and/or political activities and provide important insights for informing policies and practices. One such example described by Adams et al. (2014) generated vital health service information about how to appropriately engage with men who have sex with other men but who resist being labeled as gay. Plummer (2011a) provides a concise overview of the queer theory stance including a decentering of identities; an openness, fluidity, and nonfixedness of identities; and abandonment of deviance perspectives. Queer theorists can seek to understand particular populations such as queer people of color (Johnson & Henderson, 2005) and use methods that find expression in a rereading of cultural texts. Plummer (2011a) describes cultural texts as including a wide range of formats such as films and literature; ethnographies and case studies of sexual worlds that challenge assumptions; data sources that contain multiple texts; documentaries; and projects that focus on individuals.

Disability Theories

Disability inquiry addresses the meaning of inclusion in schools and encompasses administrators, teachers, students, and parents who have children with disabilities (Mertens, 2009, 2019). Mertens (2003) recounts how disability research has moved through stages of development, from the medical model of disability (sickness and the role of the medical community in threatening it) to an environmental response to individuals with a disability. Researchers using **disability theories** as an interpretive lens focus on disability as a dimension of human difference and not from a deficit perspective. As a human difference, the meaning of disability is derived from social construction (Mertens, 2003). According to Shildrick (2020), critical disability theories intend to "unsettle entrenched ways of thinking on both sides of the putative divide between disabled and non-disabled, and to offer an analysis of how and why certain definitions are constructed and maintained" (p. 37).

Viewing individuals with disabilities as different is reflected in the research process, such as the types of questions asked, the labels applied to these individuals, the benefits of data collection for the community, the appropriateness of communication methods, and the report of data respectful of power relationships. The lead researcher for an Australian study of people with a disability described having a lived experience of disability and as working in conjunction with industry and community service partners to provide the support needed for the involvement of participants with many different disabilities (Darcy et al., 2022). Mertens et al. (2011) have also linked critical disability theory with transformative frameworks because of its use as an intersection for many sources of discrimination. Further examples of disability theory with feminist theories, postmodern perspectives, queer theory, and critical race theory provide important areas for future development (Shildrick, 2020). Also, see Kroll et al. (2007) as a resource for guiding research informed by disability theories.

THE PRACTICE OF USING INTERPRETIVE FRAMEWORKS IN QUALITATIVE RESEARCH

The practice of using interpretive frameworks in a qualitative study varies, and it depends on the framework being used and the particular researcher's approach. Each of the descriptions of the interpretive frameworks highlighted unique researcher influences, goals, and practices. Qualitative researchers have found it helpful to distinguish among the interpretive frameworks. See an overall summary in Table 2.2. Once researchers can distinguish among the interpretive frameworks, then it is easier to see how they are applied in practice. At the most fundamental level, there are differences and commonalities based on the goals of the research. Seeking an understanding of the world is different from generating solutions to real-world problems. Potential similarities among the goals should also be noted. Feminist theories, critical theory and critical race theory, queer theories, and disability theories share a general intent for researchers to call for action and document struggles. Some common elements for practicing interpretive frameworks are as follows:

- Researchers focus on understanding specific issues or topics. The problems and the research questions explored aim to allow the researcher to understand specific issues or topics—the conditions that serve to disadvantage and exclude individuals or cultures, such as hierarchy, hegemony, racism, sexism, unequal power relations, identity, or inequities in our society.

TABLE 2.2 ■ Comparing Major Interpretive Frameworks

Interpretive Frameworks	Possible Researcher Goals	Potential Researcher Influences	Examples of Researcher Practices	Example Journal Articles
Postpositivism	To discover contributors to probability within situations of cause and effect	Prior quantitative research training	Reports systematic data collection and analysis procedures followed to ensure rigor	Churchill, S. L., Plano Clark, V. L., Prochaska-Cue, M. K., Creswell, J. W., & Onta-Grzebik, L. (2007). How rural low-income families have fun: A grounded theory study. *Journal of Leisure Research, 39*(2), 271–294. https://doi.org/10.1080/00222216.2007.11950108
Social constructivism	To understand the world in which they live and work	Recognition of background as shaping interpretation	Interprets participants' constructions of meaning in their accounts	Brown, J., Sorrell, J. H., McClaren, J., & Creswell, J. W. (2006). Waiting for a liver transplant. *Qualitative Health Research, 16*(1), 119–136. https://doi.org/10.1177/1049732305284011
Transformative frameworks	To act for societal improvements	Knowledge of power and social relationships within society	Adopts an action agenda for addressing the injustices of marginalized groups	Mavrogordato, M., & White, R. S. (2020). Leveraging policy implementation for social justice: How school leaders shape educational opportunity when implementing policy for English learners. *Educational Administration Quarterly, 56*(1), 3–45. https://doi.org/10.1177/0013161X18821364
Postmodern perspectives	To change ways of thinking	Understandings of the conditions of the world today	Situates research to highlight multiplicity of perspectives	Chipango, E. F. (2021). Constructing, understanding and interpreting energy poverty in Zimbabwe: A postmodern perspective. *Energy Research & Social Science, 75,* Article 102026. https://doi.org/10.1016/j.erss.2021.102026

(Continued)

TABLE 2.2 ■ Comparing Major Interpretive Frameworks (Continued)

Interpretive Frameworks	Possible Researcher Goals	Potential Researcher Influences	Examples of Researcher Practices	Example Journal Articles
Pragmatism	To find solutions to real-world problems	Appreciation for diverse approaches to collecting and analyzing and the contexts in which research takes place	Uses the most appropriate methods for addressing the research question	Hammond, A., Priddis, H., Ormsby, S., & Dahlen, H. G. (2022). Improving women's experiences of perineal suturing: A pragmatic qualitative analysis of what is helpful and harmful. *Women and Birth, 35*(6), e598–e606. https://doi.org/10.1016/j.wombi.2022.02.008
Feminist theories	To conduct research that is transformative for women	Perspectives of power relationships and individuals' social position and how they impact women	Poses questions that relate to the centrality of gender in the shaping of our consciousness	Malecki, J. S., Rhodes, P., Ussher, J. M., & Boydell, K. (2022). A feminist phenomenological approach to the analysis of body maps: Childhood trauma and anorexia nervosa. *Health Care for Women International*. https://doi.org/10.1080/07399332.2022.2096026
Critical theory	To address areas of inequities and empower humans	Acknowledgment of own power, privilege, and bias; engagement in dialogues; and use of theory to interpret social actions	Designs research in such a way that transforms the underlying orders of social life	Bidabadi, F. S., Yazdannik, A., & Zargham-Boroujeni, A. (2019). Patient's dignity in intensive care unit: A critical ethnography. *Nursing Ethics, 26*(3), 738–752. https://doi.org/10.1177/0969733017720826
Critical race theory	To transform the relationship among race, racism, and power	Recognition of races as a social construct, and address other areas of difference	Designs research to tell counternarratives to speak back against dominant discourse	Annamma, S. A., Handy, T., Miller, A. L., & Jackson, E. (2020). Animating discipline disparities through debilitating practices: Girls of color and inequitable classroom interactions. *Teachers College Record, 122*(5), 1–46. https://doi.org/10.1177/016146812200512

Interpretive Frameworks	Possible Researcher Goals	Potential Researcher Influences	Examples of Researcher Practices	Example Journal Articles
Postcolonial theories	To assess how knowledge production and theories of the past and the present have been shaped by ideas and power relations of imperialism, colonialism, neocolonialism, globalization, and racism	Center the voices of those who have been muted by the dominance of Euro-Western methodologies	Designs research without prejudices and is respectful of all groups of people, including the marginalized in our communities	Arur, A., & DeJaeghere, J. (2019). Decolonizing life skills education for girls in Brahmanical India: A Dalitbahujan perspective. *Gender and Education, 31*(4), 490–507. https://doi.org/10.1080/09540253.2019.1594707
Queer theory	To convey the voices and experiences of individuals who have been suppressed	Understandings of need for thinking about sexual categories as open, fluid, and nonfixed	Engages in inquiry with a focus on exploring the myriad complexities of individual identity	Adams, J., Braun, V., & McCreanor, T. (2014). "Aren't labels for pickle jars, not people?" Negotiating identity and community in talk about "being gay." *American Journal of Men's Health, 8*(6), 457–469. https://doi.org/10.1177/1557988313518800
Disability theories	To address the meaning of inclusion	Recognition of disability as a dimension of human difference and not as a defect	Employs a disability interpretive lens for informing the research process	Darcy, S., Collins, J., & Stronach, M. (2022). Entrepreneurs with disability: Australian insights through a social ecology lens. *Small Enterprise Research, 30*(1), 24–48. https://doi.org/10.1080/13215906.2022.2092888

- Research procedures are sensitive to participants and context. The procedures of research, such as data collection, data analysis, representing the material to audiences, and standards of evaluation and ethics, emphasize an interpretive stance. During data collection, the researcher does not further marginalize the participants but respects the participants and the sites for research. Further, researchers provide reciprocity by giving back to those who participate in research, and they focus on the multiple individual stories and those who tell the stories. Researchers are also sensitive to power imbalances during all facets of the research process. They respect individual differences and avoid traditional aggregation of categories such as gender.

- Researchers are respectful co-constructors of knowledge. Ethical practices of the researchers recognize the importance of the subjectivity of their own lens, acknowledge the powerful position they have in the research, and admit that the participants or the co-constructors of the account between the researchers and the participants are the true owners of the information collected.

- Research is reported in diverse formats and calls for societal change. The research may be presented in traditional ways, such as journal articles, or in experimental approaches, such as theater or poetry. Using an interpretive lens may also lead to the call for action and transformation—the aims of social justice—in which the qualitative project ends with distinct steps of reform and an incitement to action.

TRY THIS NOW 2.2
EXPLORING YOUR USE OF INTERPRETIVE FRAMEWORKS IN QUALITATIVE RESEARCH

The use of theory can vary greatly in qualitative research and be influenced by the goals a researcher is trying to accomplish. What might influence the ways you use interpretive frameworks in qualitative research?

LINKING PHILOSOPHY AND INTERPRETIVE FRAMEWORKS IN QUALITATIVE RESEARCH

Although the philosophical assumptions are not always stated, the interpretive frameworks do convey different philosophical assumptions, and qualitative researchers need to be aware of this connection. A thoughtful chapter by Lincoln and colleagues (2018) makes this connection explicit. We have taken their overview of this connection and adapted it to fit the interpretive communities discussed in this chapter. As shown in Table 2.3, the philosophical assumptions of ontology, epistemology, axiology, and methodology take different forms given the interpretive framework used by the inquirer.

The use of information from Table 2.3 in a qualitative study would be to discuss the interpretive framework used in a project by weaving together the framework, discussing its central tenets, and identifying how it informs the problem to a study, the research questions, the data collection and analysis, and the interpretation. A section of this discussion would also mention

TABLE 2.3 ■ Interpretive Frameworks and Associated Philosophical Beliefs

Interpretive Frameworks	Ontological Beliefs (the nature of reality)	Epistemological Beliefs (how reality is known)	Axiological Beliefs (role of values)	Methodological Beliefs (approach to inquiry)
Postpositivism	A single reality exists beyond ourselves, "out there." The researcher may not be able to understand it or get to it because of a lack of absolutes.	Reality can only be approximated, but it is constructed through research and statistics. Interaction with research subjects is kept to a minimum. Validity comes from peers, not participants.	The researcher's biases need to be controlled and not expressed in a study.	Scientific method and writing is used. Object of research is to create new knowledge. Method is important. Deductive methods are important, such as testing of theories, specifying important variables, and making comparisons among groups.
Social constructivism	Multiple realities are constructed through our lived experiences and interactions with others.	Reality is co-constructed between the researcher and the researched and shaped by individual experiences.	Individual values are honored and are negotiated among individuals.	More of a literary style of writing is used. Use of an inductive method of emergent ideas (through consensus) is obtained through methods such as interviewing, observing, and analyzing texts.
Transformative/ postmodern/ postcolonial	Participation between researcher and communities or individuals is being studied. Often a subjective–objective reality emerges.	There are co-created findings with multiple ways of knowing.	There is respect for Indigenous values; values need to be problematized and interrogated.	Methods consist of using collaborative processes of research, encouraging political participation, questioning of methods, and highlighting issues and concerns.

(Continued)

TABLE 2.3 ■ Interpretive Frameworks and Associated Philosophical Beliefs (*Continued*)

Interpretive Frameworks	Ontological Beliefs (the nature of reality)	Epistemological Beliefs (how reality is known)	Axiological Beliefs (role of values)	Methodological Beliefs (approach to inquiry)
Pragmatism	Reality is what is useful, is practical, and "works."	Reality is known through using many tools of research that reflect both deductive (objective) evidence and inductive (subjective) evidence.	Values are discussed because of the way that knowledge reflects both the researchers' and the participants' views.	The research process involves both quantitative and qualitative approaches to data collection and analysis.
Critical, critical race, feminist, postcolonial, queer, disability theories	Reality is based on power and identity struggles. Privilege or oppression is based on race or ethnicity, class, gender, mental abilities, sexual orientation.	Reality is known through the study of social structures, freedom and oppression, power, and control. Reality can be changed through research.	Diversity of values is emphasized within the standpoint of various communities.	Start with assumptions of power and identity struggles, document them, and call for action and change.

Source: Adapted from Lincoln et al. (2018).

the philosophical assumptions (ontology, epistemology, axiology, methodology) associated with the interpretive framework. Thus, there would be two ways to discuss the interpretive framework: its nature and use in the study, and its philosophical assumptions.

As we proceed to examine the five qualitative approaches in this book, recognize that each one might use any of the interpretive frameworks. For example, if a grounded theory study were presented as a scientific paper using a postpositivist interpretive framework, the study would place major emphasis on objectivity, result in a theoretical model, report researcher's bias, and provide a systematic rendering of data analysis. On the other hand, if the intent of the qualitative narrative study was to examine a marginalized group of learners with disabilities with the aim of documenting their struggles for identity about prostheses that they wear, the researcher might use a disability interpretative framework. This framework would highlight utmost respect for their views and values and end the study with a call for a more inclusive society. We could see using any of the interpretive frameworks with any of the five approaches advanced in this book.

CHAPTER CHECK-IN

1. Can you see the differences among the associated philosophical beliefs among interpretive frameworks (postpositivism, social constructivism, transformative frameworks, postmodern perspectives, pragmatism, feminist theories, critical theory, critical race theory, postcolonial theory, queer theory, and disability theories)? Read qualitative journal articles that adopt different interpretive lenses (see Table 2.2 for examples) and identify how articles differ in their interpretive frameworks.

2. Can you identify unique elements within specific interpretive frameworks? Read one of the example qualitative journal articles listed in Table 2.2 and identify unique elements for the specific interpretive framework.

3. Can you discern the differences among interpretive frameworks when used in combinations? Examine qualitative journal articles that adopt a combination of different interpretive lenses, such as Chepp (2015) from feminist and critical race theory frameworks and Watts and Erevelles (2004) from disabilities and critical race theory frameworks. Identify examples of influence from each interpretive framework using Tables 2.2 and 2.3 in this chapter as a guide.

Chepp, V. (2015). Black feminist theory and the politics of irreverence: The case of women's rap. *Feminist Theory, 16*(2), 207–226. https://doi.org/10.1177/1464700115585705

Watts, I. E., & Erevelles, N. (2004). These deadly times: Reconceptualizing school violence by using critical race theory and disability studies. *American Journal of Educational Research, 41*, 271–299. https://doi.org/10.3102/00028312041002271

SUMMARY

This chapter began with an overview of the research process so that philosophical assumptions and interpretive frameworks could be seen as positioned at the beginning of the process and informing the procedures that follow, including the selection and use of one of the five approaches in this book. Then the philosophical assumptions of ontology, epistemology, axiology, and methodology were discussed, as were the key questions being asked for each assumption, its major characteristics, and the implication for the practice of writing a qualitative study. Furthermore, the popular interpretive frameworks (paradigm perspectives and theoretical orientations) used in qualitative research were advanced. How these interpretive frameworks are used in a qualitative study was suggested. Finally, a link was made between the philosophical assumptions and the interpretive frameworks, and a discussion followed about how to connect the two in a qualitative project.

CHAPTER KEY TERMS

Axiological assumptions
Critical race theory
Critical theory
Disability theories
Epistemological assumptions
Evaluation
Feminist research approaches
Interpretation
Methods of data collection
Multifaceted experiences
Ontological assumptions
Paradigms

Philosophical assumptions
Postmodernism
Postpositivism
Pragmatism
Queer theory
Research strategies
Social constructivism
Social justice theories
Social science theories
Theories or theoretical orientations
Transformative framework

FURTHER READINGS

The following resources are offered as foundational references for this chapter. The list should not be considered exhaustive, and readers are encouraged to seek out additional readings in the end-of-book reference list.

Brisolara, S., Seigart, D., & SenGupta, S. (Eds.). (2014). *Feminist evaluation and research: Theory and practice*. Guilford Press.

Sharon Brisolara, Denise Seigart, and Saumitra SenGupta bring together illustrative examples exploring the processes involved in feminist research. The authors uniquely situate feminist research within disciplines and international contexts.

Denzin, N. K., & Lincoln, Y. S. (Eds.). (2018). *The SAGE handbook of qualitative research* (5th ed.). Sage.

Norm Denzin and Yvonna Lincoln offer contemporary discussions about the role of guiding philosophy behind qualitative research. Specifically, we found the chapters on feminist research by Virginia Olesen and Marjorie Lyne DeVault; queer theory by Bryant Alexander; and critical race theory by Jamel Donnor and coauthor Gloria Ladson-Billings to be noteworthy.

Gergen, K. J. (2023). *An invitation to social construction: Co-creating the future* (4th ed.). Sage.

In this updated edition, Kenneth J. Gergen offers updated examples of social constructionist theory across diverse research contexts and disciplines.

Guba, E. G., & Lincoln, Y. S. (1988). Do inquiry paradigms imply inquiry methodologies? In D. M. Fetterman (Ed.), *Qualitative approaches to evaluation in education* (pp. 89–115). Praeger.

Egon Guba and Yvonna Lincoln, in offering their perspective of the relationship between paradigms and methodologies, contribute important work to these discussions.

Hesse-Biber, S. N. (2012). *Handbook of feminist research: Theory and praxis* (2nd ed.). Sage.

Sharlene Nagy Hesse-Biber provides a grounding in feminist research through discussions of current perspectives on its influence on social change and transformation as well as the new technologies that are influencing methodological approaches within the field.

Lovern, L. L., & Locust, C. (2013). *Native American communities on health and disability: Borderland dialogues*. Palgrave Macmillan.

Lavonna Lovern and Carol Locust provide a foundational resource for researchers interested in how to begin a genuine dialogue with Indigenous communities. The authors' experiences are particularly noted in the sections focused on "wellness" concepts that are respectful of disability and indigeneity.

Lynn, M., & Dixson, A. D. (Eds.). (2023). *Handbook of critical race theory in education* (2nd ed.). Routledge.

Marvin Lynn and Adrienne Dixon offer contemporary discussions about the role of critical race theory in educational research. Specifically, we found the chapters on critical race feminist praxis and scholar activism to be noteworthy.

Mertens, D. M. (2019). *Research and evaluation in education and psychology: Integrating diversity with quantitative, qualitative, and mixed methods* (5th ed.). Sage.

Donna Mertens presents a brief history and then focuses on the philosophical underpinnings of four research paradigms: postpositivism, constructivist, transformative, and pragmatic. Of particular note is her useful description of the transformative paradigm including a rationale for its emergence and description of its philosophical and theoretical basis.

Mertens, D. M. (2021). Transformative research methods to increase social impact for vulnerable groups and cultural minorities. *International Journal of Qualitative Methods, 20*, 1–9. https://doi.org/10.1177/16094069211051563

Donna Mertens provides an updated guide to conducting research using a transformative lens in a way that clearly connects theory to social impact.

Phillips, D. C., & Burbules, N. C. (2000). *Postpositivism and educational research*. Rowman & Littlefield.

Dennis Phillips and Nicholas Burbules offer an excellent description of postpositivism in practice that is a foundational read for researchers.

Slife, B. D., & Williams, R. N. (1995). *What's behind the research? Discovering hidden assumptions in the behavioral sciences*. Sage.

Brent Slife and Richard Williams explore the assumptions underpinning major theoretical approaches in the behavioral sciences. This important work has been widely cited across disciplines (e.g., psychology, education) as useful for encouraging critical thinking of theories.

Watson, N., Roulstone, A., & Thomas, C. (Eds.). (2020). *Routledge handbook of disability studies* (2nd ed.). Routledge.

The editors adopt a multidisciplinary approach to discussions about disability. We found the critical disability studies chapter by Margrit Shildrick to be an essential read.

3 DESIGNING A QUALITATIVE STUDY

QUESTIONS FOR DISCUSSION

- What types of problems are best suited for qualitative inquiry?
- What research skills are required to undertake this type of research?
- What are the features of a "good" qualitative study?
- How do researchers design a qualitative study?
- What types of ethical issues need to be anticipated during the process of qualitative research?
- What design structures are useful for a qualitative study plan or proposal

We think metaphorically of qualitative research as an intricate fabric comprising minute threads, many colors, different textures, and various blends of material. This fabric is not explained easily or simply. Like the loom on which fabric is woven, general assumptions and interpretive frameworks hold qualitative research together. To describe these frameworks, qualitative researchers use these terms—*constructivist, interpretivist, feminist, postmodernist*, and so forth. Within these assumptions and through these frameworks are approaches (or designs) to qualitative inquiry, such as narrative research, phenomenology, grounded theory, ethnography, and case studies. This field has many different individuals with different perspectives who are on their own looms creating the fabric of qualitative research. Aside from these differences, the creative artists have the common task of making a fabric. In other words, there are characteristics common to all forms of qualitative research, and the different characteristics will receive different emphases depending on the qualitative project. Not all characteristics are present in all qualitative projects, but many are.

The intent of this chapter is to provide an overview of, and introduction to, the process of designing a qualitative study so that we can see commonalities before we explore the differences across the five approaches (e.g., narrative, phenomenology, and others). We begin with a discussion of the types of research problems and issues best suited for a qualitative study. We emphasize the requirements needed to conduct this rigorous, time-consuming research as well as criteria for assessing its quality. Given that you have the essentials (the problem, the time, the criteria) to engage in this inquiry, we then sketch out the overall process involved in designing and planning a study. This process entails preliminary considerations, phases in the process, and overall elements to consider throughout the process. Within these aspects, qualitative researchers need to anticipate and plan for potential ethical issues because these issues arise during many phases of the research process. We end by suggesting design structures including considerations for engaging readers and an outline that you might use to guide the overall structure for planning or proposing a qualitative research study. The chapters to follow will then address the different types of inquiry approaches. The general design features, outlined here, will be refined for the five approaches discussed in the remainder of the book.

WHEN TO USE QUALITATIVE RESEARCH

When is it appropriate to use qualitative research? We conduct qualitative research because a problem or issue needs to be explored. This exploration is needed, in turn, because of a need to study a group or a population, identify variables that cannot be easily measured, or hear silenced voices These are all good reasons to explore a problem rather than to use predetermined information from the literature or rely on results from other research studies. We also conduct qualitative research because we need a complex, detailed understanding of the issue being explored. The focus of the exploration can be on understanding the self or the relationships of others in groups or cultures—wherever they are happening, including virtual contexts. The necessary detail can only be established by talking directly with people, going to their homes or places of work or recreation, and allowing them to tell their stories unencumbered by what we expect to find or what we have read in the literature. It is the responsibility of the researcher to create environments where participants feel comfortable and empowered to share their stories and their experiences of things that happen in their lives. Qualitative researchers are limited by what participants can and are willing to share with us.

We conduct qualitative research when we want to empower individuals to share their stories, hear their voices, and minimize the power relationships that often exist between a researcher and the participants in a study. To further deemphasize a power relationship, we may collaborate directly with participants by having them review our research questions, or by having them collaborate with us during the data analysis and interpretation phases of research. We conduct qualitative research when we want to write in a literary, flexible style that conveys stories, theatrical plays, or poems, without the restrictions of formal academic structures of writing. We conduct qualitative research because we want to understand the contexts or settings in which participants in a study address a problem or issue. We cannot always separate what people say from the place where they say it—whether this context is their home, family, or work. We use qualitative research to follow up quantitative research and help explain the mechanisms or linkages in causal theories or models. These theories provide a general picture of trends, associations, and relationships, but they do not tell us about the processes that people experience, why they responded as they did, the context in which they responded, and their deeper thoughts and behaviors that governed their responses.

We use qualitative research to develop theories when partial or inadequate theories exist for certain populations and samples, or existing theories do not adequately capture the complexity

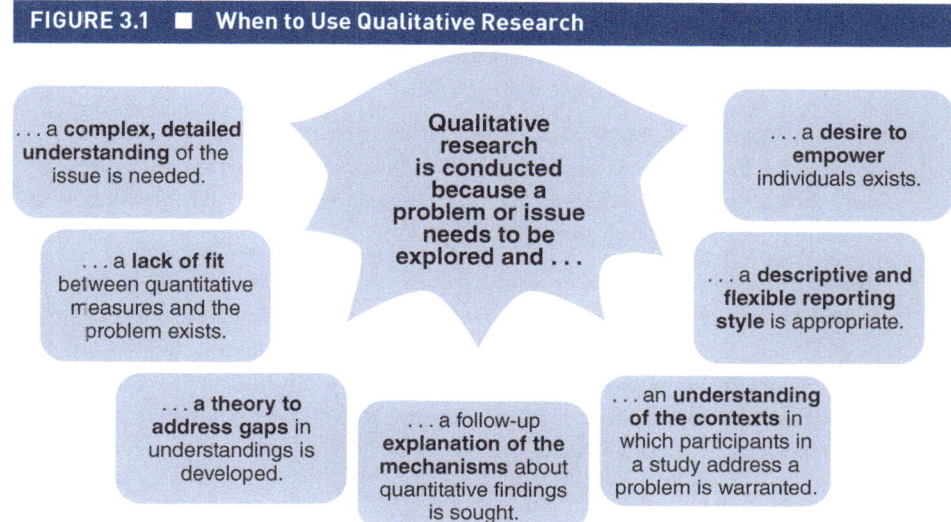

FIGURE 3.1 ■ When to Use Qualitative Research

Qualitative research is conducted because a problem or issue needs to be explored and . . .

- . . . a **complex, detailed understanding** of the issue is needed.
- . . . a **lack of fit** between quantitative measures and the problem exists.
- . . . a **theory to address gaps** in understandings is developed.
- . . . a follow-up **explanation of the mechanisms** about quantitative findings is sought.
- . . . an **understanding of the contexts** in which participants in a study address a problem is warranted.
- . . . a **descriptive and flexible reporting style** is appropriate.
- . . . a **desire to empower** individuals exists.

of the problem we are examining. We also use qualitative research because quantitative measures and statistical analyses simply do not fit the problem. Interactions among people, for example, are difficult to capture with existing measures, and these measures may not be sensitive to issues such as gender differences, race, economic status, and individual differences. To level all individuals to a statistical mean overlooks the uniqueness of individuals in our studies. Examine Figure 3.1 for a summary description of when qualitative approaches are simply a better fit for our research problem.

WHAT A QUALITATIVE STUDY REQUIRES FROM US

What does it take to engage in this form of research? To undertake qualitative research requires a strong commitment to study a problem and to its demands of time and resources. Qualitative research keeps good company with the most rigorous quantitative approaches, and it should not be viewed as an easy substitute for a "statistical" or quantitative study. Qualitative inquiry is for the researcher who is willing to do the following:

- *Commit to extensive time in the natural setting of individuals and communities* (e.g., homes, schools, workplaces). The investigator collects extensive data and labors over site issues of trying to gain access and establish rapport. Collaborating with participants takes time yet is important for developing an "insider" perspective.

- *Engage in the complex, time-consuming process of data analysis.* The investigator undertakes the ambitious task of **data management**, including sorting through large amounts of data and making sense of the data. For a multidisciplinary team of qualitative researchers, this task can be shared; for most researchers, it requires an intensive time commitment.

- *Write lengthy and descriptive passages.* The investigator presents the evidence in a way that the claims are substantiated and reflective of multiple perspectives. The incorporation of quotes to provide participants' perspectives also lengthens the study.

- *Embrace dynamic and emergent procedures.* The investigator participates in a form of social and human science research that does not follow specific procedures and is constantly changing. This might complicate telling others about study plans and how others judge the study when completed.

- *Attend to anticipated and developing ethical issues.* The investigator considers what ethical issues might surface during the study and plans how these issues need to be addressed. Additionally, new issues might emerge, which require attention and engaging in **ethical reasoning**, while undertaking the study. Ethical reasoning involves making decisions based on a careful assessment of different options in light of the facts, circumstances, and ethical issues.

THE FEATURES OF A "GOOD" QUALITATIVE STUDY

In the end, individuals such as readers, participants, graduate committees, editorial board members for journals, and reviewers of proposals for funding will apply some criteria to assess the quality of a study. Standards for assessing the quality of qualitative research are available (Howe & Eisenhardt, 1990; Lincoln, 1995; Marshall et al., 2021; Tracy, 2010, 2017). Here and in Figure 3.2 is our short list describing the features of a "good" qualitative study. You will see an emphasis on rigorous methods present in this list.

- *The researcher frames the study within the assumptions and characteristics of the qualitative approach to research.* This includes fundamental characteristics, such as an evolving design, the presentation of multiple realities, the researcher as an instrument of data collection, and a focus on participants' views—in short, all of the distinguishing characteristics for qualitative research mentioned in Table 1.1.

- *The researcher conducts an ethical study.* This involves more than simply the researcher seeking an **ethical review** and obtaining the permission of institutional review committees or boards. It means that the researcher considers and addresses all anticipated and emergent ethical issues in the study.

- *The researcher uses a recognizable approach to qualitative inquiry.* Use of a recognized approach to research, such as one of the five approaches (or others) addressed in this book, enhances the rigor and sophistication of the research design. It also provides some means to evaluate the qualitative study. Use of an approach means that the researcher identifies and defines the approach, cites studies that employ it, and follows the procedures outlined in the approach. Certainly, the approach taken in the study may not exhaustively cover all of the elements of the approach. However, for the beginning student of qualitative research, we recommend staying within one approach, learning it, becoming comfortable with it, and keeping a study concise and straightforward. Later, especially in long and complex studies, features from several approaches may be useful.

FIGURE 3.2 ■ Research Quality Assessment Checklist

Research Quality Assessment Checklist

The researcher . . .

- ☐ Frames the study within the assumptions and characteristics of the qualitative approach to research.

- ☐ Conducts an ethical study.

- ☐ Uses a recognizable approach to qualitative inquiry.

- ☐ Begins with a single focus or concept being explored.

- ☐ Employs rigorous data collection procedures.

- ☐ Includes detailed methods describing a rigorous approach to data collection, data analysis, and report writing.

- ☐ Analyzes data using multiple levels of abstraction.

- ☐ Writes persuasively so that the reader experiences "being there."

- ☐ Situates themselves within the study to reflect their history, culture, and personal experiences.

- *The researcher begins with a single focus or concept being explored.* Although examples of qualitative research show a comparison of groups or factors or themes, as in case study projects or in ethnographies, we like to begin a qualitative study focused on understanding a single concept or idea (e.g., What does it mean to be a professional? A teacher? A painter? A single mother? A homeless person?). As the study progresses, it can begin incorporating the comparison (e.g., How does the case of a professional teacher differ from that of a professional administrator?) or related factors (e.g., What explains why a painting evokes feelings?). All too often qualitative researchers advance to the comparison or the relationship analysis without first understanding their core concept or idea.

- *The researcher employs rigorous data collection procedures.* This means that the researcher collects multiple forms of data, creates a summary—perhaps in table form—of the forms of data and details about them, and spends adequate time in the field. It is not unusual for qualitative studies to include information about the specific amount of time in the field (e.g., 25 hours observing). We especially like to see unusual forms of qualitative data collection, such as using photographs, sounds, or digital text messages to elicit participant responses.

- *The researcher includes detailed methods describing a rigorous approach to data collection, data analysis, and report writing.* Rigor is seen, for example, when extensive data collection in the field occurs or when the researcher conducts multiple levels of data analysis from the narrow codes or themes to broader interrelated themes to more abstract dimensions. Rigor means, too, that the researcher validates the accuracy of the account using one or more of the procedures for validation, such as member checking, triangulating sources of data, or using a peer or external auditor of the account.

- *The researcher analyzes data using multiple levels of* **abstraction**. We like to see the active work of researchers as they move from particulars to general levels of abstraction. Often, writers present their studies in stages (e.g., multiple themes that can be combined into larger themes or perspectives) or layer their analysis from the particular to the general. The codes and themes derived from the data might show mundane, expected, and surprising ideas. Often the best qualitative studies present themes analyzed in terms of exploring the shadow side or unusual angles. In one class project, the student examined how students in a distance learning class reacted to viewing their classmates. Rather than looking at the students' reaction when the camera was on them, the researcher sought to understand what happened when the camera was *off* them. This approach led to the author taking an unusual angle—one not expected by the readers.

- *The researcher writes persuasively so that the reader experiences "being there."* The concept of *verisimilitude*, a literary term, captures our thinking (Richardson, 1994, p. 521). The writing is clear, engaging, and full of unexpected ideas. The story and findings become believable and realistic, accurately reflecting all the complexities that exist in real life and engaging the reader.

- *The researcher situates themselves within the study to reflect their history, culture, and personal experiences.* This is more than simply an **autobiography**, with the writer or the researcher talking about their background. It focuses on how individuals' culture, gender, history, and experiences shape all aspects of the qualitative project, from their choice of a question to address, how they collect data, how they make an interpretation of the situation, to what they expect to obtain from conducting the research. In some way—such as discussing their role, interweaving themselves into the text, or reflecting on the questions they have about the study—individuals position themselves in the qualitative study.

> **TRY THIS NOW 3.1**
>
> **EXAMINING YOUR FAMILIARITY WITH KEY QUALITY CRITERIA OF QUALITATIVE RESEARCH**
>
> Quality criteria relate the features of "good" qualitative studies. As you look across the list of features in Figure 3.2, which of them are new to you and which are familiar? What do you notice when you map them against the list of distinguishing characteristics of qualitative research from Chapter 1?

THE PROCESS OF DESIGNING A QUALITATIVE STUDY

There is no agreed upon structure for how to design a qualitative study. Although books on qualitative research vary in their suggestions for design, the process is very much shaped by the particular approach adopted by the researcher. You may recall from Chapter 1 that *research design* means the plan for conducting the study. Some authors believe that by reading a study, discussing the procedures, and pointing out issues that emerge, the aspiring qualitative researcher will have a sense of how to conduct this form of inquiry (see Weis & Fine, 2000). That may be true for some individuals. For others, understanding the broader issues may suffice to help design a study (see Richards & Morse, 2013) or to seek guidance from a how-to book (see Hatch, 2002). Rather than offering a how-to perspective, we consider our approach as more in line with creating options for qualitative researchers (hence, the five approaches), weighing the options given our experiences, and then letting readers make informed choices for themselves.

We can share, however, how we think about designing a qualitative study that is logically consistent across its research elements. It can be conveyed in three components: preliminary considerations that we think through prior to beginning a study, the steps we engage in during the conduct of the study, and the elements that flow through all phases of the process of research.

Preliminary Considerations

There are certain design principles that we work from when designing qualitative research studies. We find that qualitative research generally falls within the process of the scientific method, with common phases whether one is writing qualitatively or quantitatively. The scientific method can be described as including the problem, the hypotheses (or questions), the data collection, the results, and the discussion. All researchers seem to start with an issue or problem, examine the literature in some way related to the problem, pose questions, gather data and then analyze them, and write up their reports. Qualitative research fits within this structure, and we have accordingly organized the chapters in this book to reflect this process.

Qualitative research is iterative and much less stepwise than it may appear in plans and reports. As an example, the reality of how researchers identify their issue or problem is quite varied, and, unlike our description above, reading the literature can often spark an idea for a problem or issue to be explored and help researchers refine and focus their study. In other cases, study ideas come from a variety of sources including previous experiences or from those around you. Bloomberg (2022) aptly describes the continuum of emotions from frustration to excitement that researchers can experience as they search for a topic for qualitative study. She also offers the following advice: "Finding a research topic that is interesting, relevant, and worthy of your time may take substantial effort, so you should be prepared to invest your time accordingly" (Bloomberg, 2022, p. 32). We could not agree more!

We like the concept of **methodological congruence** advanced by Morse and Richards (2002) and revisited in Richards and Morse (2013)—that the purposes, questions, and methods of research are all interconnected and interrelated so that the study appears as a cohesive whole rather than as fragmented, isolated parts. With a similar goal of creating coherent and workable relationships among the key components of a research design, Maxwell (2013) advances an interactive approach to research design. When engaging in the process of designing a qualitative study, we believe that the inquirer must be mindful of the interconnectedness of the parts and the interactive design processes.

Several aspects of a qualitative project vary from study to study, and from initial discussions, we make preliminary decisions about what will be emphasized. For example, stances on the use of the literature vary widely, as does the emphasis on using an a priori theory. The literature may be fully reviewed and used to inform the questions actually asked, reviewed late in the process of research, or used solely to help document the importance of the research problem. Other options may also exist, but these possibilities point to the varied uses of literature in qualitative research. Similarly, the use of theory varies in qualitative research (Collins & Stockton, 2018). For example, cultural theories form the basic building blocks of a good qualitative ethnography (LeCompte & Schensul, 1999), whereas in grounded theory, the theories are developed or generated during the process of research (Strauss & Corbin, 1990). In health science research, we find the use of a priori theories common practice and a key element to be included in rigorous qualitative investigations (Barbour, 2000). Another consideration in qualitative research is the writing or reporting format for the qualitative project. It varies considerably from scientific-oriented approaches, to literary storytelling, and on to performances, such as theatrical plays or poems. There is no one standard or accepted structure as one typically finds in quantitative research.

Finally, we also consider background and interests and what each of us brings to research. Researchers have a personal history that situates them as inquirers. They also have an orientation to research and a sense of personal ethics and political stances that inform their research. An important starting point for inquiry is recognizing that the researchers' "position" (including their philosophical assumptions or worldviews as well as their experiences and backgrounds; see Chapter 2) influences their studies.

Phases in the Research Process

With these preliminary considerations in place, we engage in an eight-phase research process summarized in Figure 3.3 and map the chapters in this book. We begin by acknowledging the *broad assumptions* that bring us to qualitative inquiry, and the *interpretive lens* that we will use (see Chapter 2). In addition, we bring a *topic* or a substantive area of investigation, and have reviewed the literature about the topic and can confidently say that a problem or issue exists that needs to be studied (Chapter 6). This problem may be one in the real world, or it may be a deficiency or gap in the literature or past investigations on a topic, or both. Problems in qualitative research span the topics in the social, human, and health sciences, and a hallmark of qualitative research today is the deep involvement in issues of gender, culture, and marginalized groups. The topics about which we write are emotion-laden, close to people, and practical. Notice for Figure 3.3 that the phases tend to build upon each other, and yet, the phases can result in revisions to a previous phase.

To study these topics, we will ask *open-ended research questions*, listen to the participants we are studying, and shape the questions after we "explore" by talking with a few individuals. We refrain from assuming the role of the expert researcher with the "best" questions. Our questions will change and become more refined during the process of research to reflect an increased understanding of the problem. Furthermore, we will collect a *variety of sources of data* after gaining access to our site and participants. We use ethical practices to collect data, including information in the form of "words" or "images" (Chapter 7). We tend to think in terms of four basic sources of qualitative information: interviews (i.e., data generated through direct interactions),

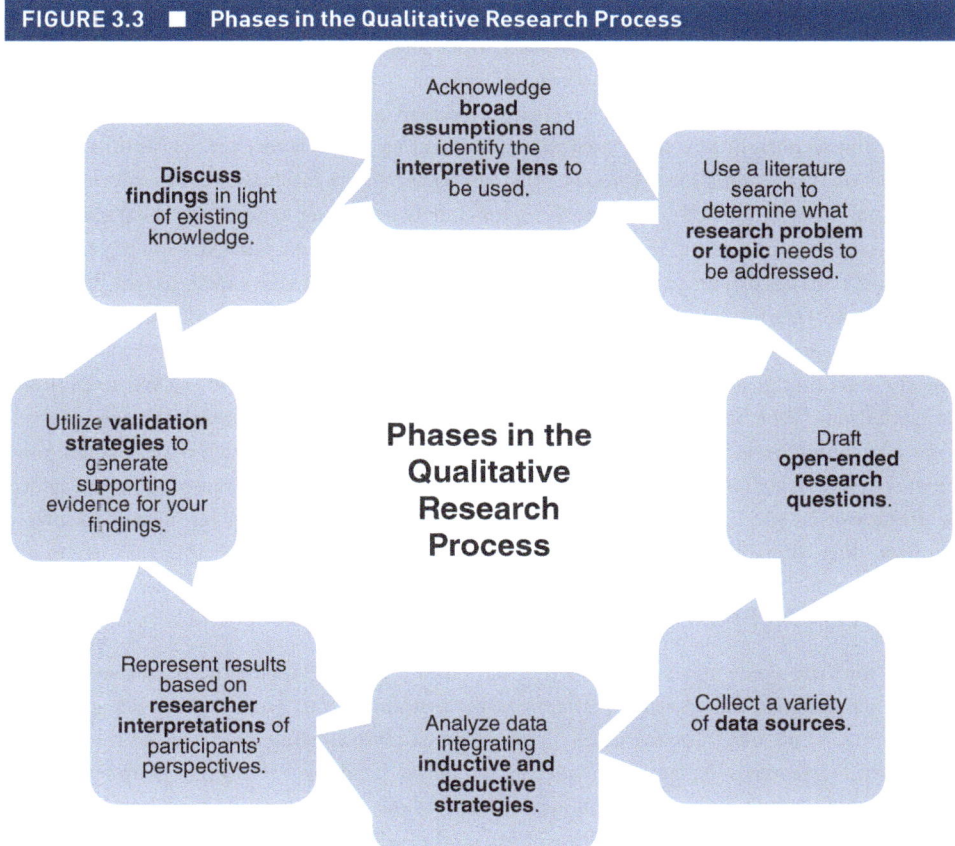

FIGURE 3.3 ■ Phases in the Qualitative Research Process

observations (i.e., data generated through passive interactions), documents (i.e., data generated from existing materials), and artifacts (i.e., data generated from audio and visual methods). Certainly, new and emergent sources (e.g., social media) have challenged this traditional categorization. Unquestionably, the backbone of qualitative research is extensive collection of data, typically from multiple sources of information. Further, we collect data using these sources based on open-ended questions without much structure and by observing and collecting documents (and artifacts) without an agenda of what we hope to find. After organizing and storing data, we analyze them by carefully masking the names of respondents, and engage in the perplexing exercise of trying to make sense of the data (Chapter 8).

To engage in meaning-making of the data, we *analyze the qualitative data* working inductively from particulars to more general perspectives, whether these perspectives are called codes, categories, themes, or dimensions. We then work deductively to gather evidence to support the themes and the interpretations. One helpful way to see this process is to recognize it as working through multiple levels of abstraction, starting with the raw data and forming broader and broader categories. Recognizing the highly interrelated set of activities of data collection, analysis, and report writing, we intermingle these stages and find ourselves collecting data, analyzing another set of data, and beginning to write the qualitative report. For example, during a case study, we find ourselves engaging in the interconnectedness processes involved in interviewing, analyzing, and writing the case study—not distinct phases in the process (Chapter 9). Also, as we write, we experiment with many forms of narrative, such as making metaphors and analogies, developing matrices and tables, and using visuals to convey simultaneously breaking down the data and reconfiguring them into new forms. Next, we might layer the analysis into increasing levels of abstractions from codes, to themes, to the interrelationship of themes, to larger conceptual models. We will *(re)present these data*, partly based on participants' perspectives and partly based on our own interpretation, never clearly escaping a personal stamp on a study. In the end, we discuss by comparing our findings with our personal views, with extant literature, and with emerging models that seem to adequately convey the essence of the findings.

At some point we ask ourselves, "Did we (I) get the story 'right'?" (Stake, 1995), knowing that there are no right stories, only multiple stories. Perhaps qualitative studies have no endings, only questions (Wolcott, 1994). We also seek to have the account resonate with the participants, to be an accurate reflection of what they said. So we engage in *validation strategies*, often multiple strategies, which include confirming or triangulating data from several sources, having our studies reviewed and corrected by the participants, and employing other researchers to review our procedures (Chapter 9).

Elements in All Phases of the Research

Throughout the slow process of collecting data and analyzing them, the narrative is being shaped—a narrative that assumes different forms from project to project. We tell a story that unfolds over time and, in some cases, presents the study following the traditional approach to scientific research (i.e., problem, question, method, findings). Throughout the different forms, we find it important to talk about our background and experiences and how they have shaped our interpretation of the findings. This might be best described by letting the voices of participants speak and carry the story through dialogue, perhaps dialogue presented in Spanish with English subtitles. The resulting qualitative research process of inquiry is considered as shifting and iterative because of engaging often in data collection, data analysis, and reporting writing (Levitt et al., 2018). Changes to procedures and even research questions are to be expected. It is also expected that qualitative researchers will be as transparent as possible in their descriptions of what has occurred and why.

Qualitative researchers find it helpful to engage in practices that help them recognize and convey their influences on the research process—**reflexivity**. Recall that this is also a key distinguishing characteristic of qualitative research described in Chapter 1. If you ever wondered why qualitative researchers engage in reflexivity, you need only to consider the wise description of May and Perry (2017):

> Reflexivity is a guard against . . . the assumption that there is an unproblematic relationship between us and the world, including social scientific practices and its products, which results in a valid and reliable representation of the world. Reflexivity also guards against the opposite view . . . that reflects a fluid world in which choices and interpretive flexibility are as numerous as the number of people on the planet. (p. 2)

It is important to note that reflexivity is not restricted to individual researchers, because groups (such as members of a research team or of an organization) together can engage in what Poth et al. (2023) called **collective reflexivity**. The advantage of collective reflexivity is the engagement of a research group that is co-constructing knowledge from and during a group research process.

Throughout all phases of the research process, we strive to be sensitive to ethical considerations. We ask our research participants to give considerable time to our projects. As researchers, it is our responsibility to assess and mitigate risks to protect participants, researchers, and society. It is also important that researchers think about giving back to participants for their time and efforts in our projects—**reciprocity**. Most often, our research is done within the context of a college or university setting where we need to provide evidence to institutional review boards or committees that our study design follows their guidelines for conducting ethical research. We have guiding standards for qualitative research ethics and different ethical considerations are especially important at different times during the research process. Thus, learning about and then engaging in thinking and writing about potential ethical issues specific to the study is an important component of the design process (Iphofen & Tolich, 2018; Poth, 2019, 2021). To reflect a necessary emphasis on **research ethics**, we devote the following section to introducing and providing guidance for qualitative research ethics.

PRACTICAL GUIDANCE FOR QUALITATIVE RESEARCH ETHICS

The approval processes of many ethics review boards (e.g., institutional, organizational, and community) are guided by policies requiring evidence of awareness of relevant ethical situations for the study and plans for addressing ethical issues related to three principles: respect for persons, concern for welfare, and justice. **Respect for persons** encompasses the treatment of persons and their data during the research process, providing evidence of measures for respecting the privacy of participants and ensuring the clear communication of the consent process. This consent includes the right of participants to withdraw from the study. **Concern for welfare** involves researchers ensuring adequate protection of participants, providing evidence the participants are not placed at risk. **Concern for justice** refers to the need to treat people fairly and equitably. This means we must carefully consider recruitment and justifications for sampling strategies, data collection methods, site selection, analysis strategies, and how and to whom we provide access to study findings. Completion of the review by institutional review boards or committees is required prior to accessing the study site and participants and, in some cases, for access to funding. Equally important is to examine standards for ethical conduct of research available from professional organizations in a researcher's disciplinary field, such as the American Historical Association, the American Sociological Association, the International Communication Association, the American Evaluation Association, the Canadian Evaluation Society, the Australasian Evaluation Society, and the American Educational Research Association (Lincoln, 2009).

It is not enough to simply seek and gain approval for your study from ethical review boards. During the process of planning and designing a qualitative study, researchers need to consider what ethical situations (meaning the various phases in a study) might surface during the study and to plan for how to handle the arising ethical issues. A common misconception is that these issues only surface during data collection. They arise, however, during several phases of the research process. They also are ever-expanding in scope as inquirers become more sensitive to the needs of participants, sites, stakeholders, and publishers of research. To help researchers in making decisions about how to respond to arising issues, they can engage in a careful and thorough assessment of different options related to the facts, circumstances, and ethical issues—ethical reasoning. It is also important that researchers take the time to learn from their experiences and apply their understandings to future studies. Creswell and Báez (2021), for example, provide important access to the insights they derived from the ethical situations they faced as qualitative researchers. Examine Figure 3.4 for this helpful anticipate-mitigate-respond-learn (AMRL) cycle for ethical qualitative research. This model, extended from worked presented in Poth (2021), makes explicit to researchers their responsibilities throughout the qualitative study. First, when study planning, researchers need to anticipate ethical situations. When conducting the study, researchers need to use procedures (e.g., consent) to mitigate ethical issues. As ethical issues arise, researchers need to respond appropriately (e.g., adapt their procedures). Finally, as the study proceeds and when the study concludes, researchers should take the time to learn from their experiences and apply their new understandings to their future studies.

Ethical Situations Across the Research Process

One way to examine ethical situations across the research process is to consider the catalogue of possibilities such as provided by Weis and Fine (2000). They ask us to

- Consider ethical considerations involving our roles as insiders/outsiders to the participants;

- Assess issues that we may be fearful of disclosing;
- Establish supportive, respectful relationships without stereotyping and using labels that participants do not embrace;
- Acknowledge whose voices will be represented in our final study; and
- Write ourselves into the study by reflecting on who we are and who are the people we study.

FIGURE 3.4 ■ Ethical Qualitative Research Involves an Anticipate, Mitigate, Respond, and Learn (AMRL) Cycle

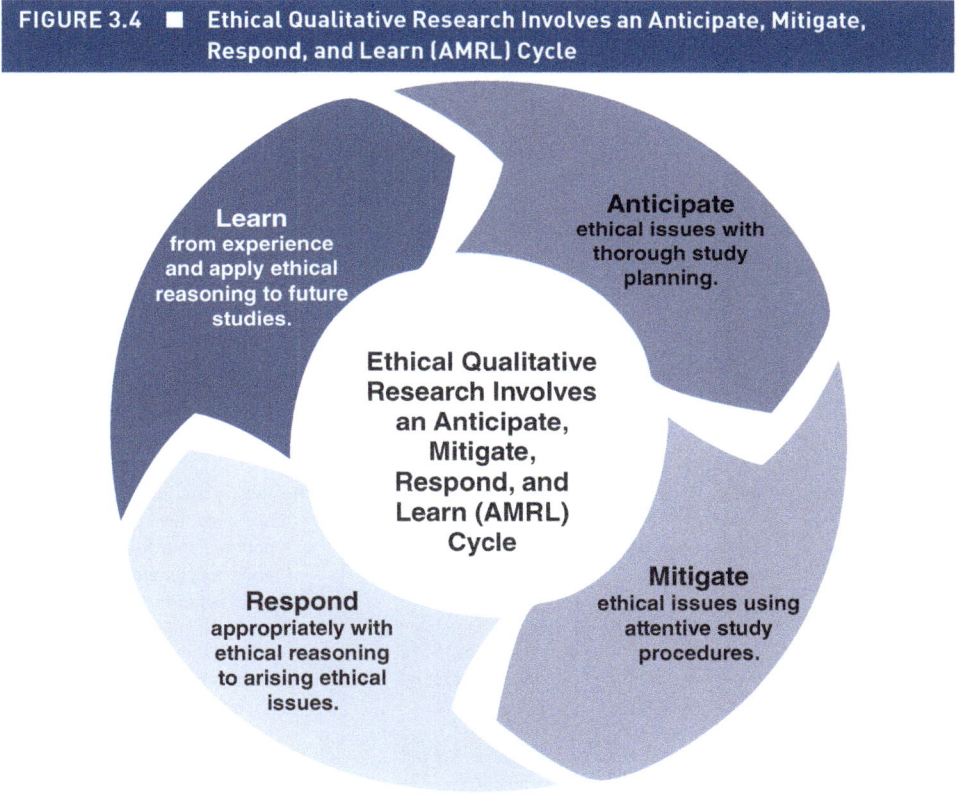

Source: Adapted from Poth (2021).

Our preferred approach in thinking about ethical issues in qualitative research is to examine them as they apply to different phases of the research process. Important recent books provide useful insight into how ethical situations array in phases, such as found in writings by Creswell and Guetterman (2019), Iphofen and Tolich (2018), Lincoln (2009), and Ravitch and Carl (2020). As shown in Table 3.1, ethical situations in qualitative research can be described as occurring prior to conducting the study, at the beginning of the study, during data collection, in conducting data analysis, in reporting the data, and in publishing a study. In this table, we also

TABLE 3.1 ■ Ethical Issues and Addressing Them in the Phases of the Research Process

Timing During Research Process Phases	Guiding Design Questions	Type of Ethical Issues to Anticipate and Address	How a Researcher Potentially Addresses the Situation
Prior to conducting the study	• What is the study focus?	• Formulate a study with benefits and minimal risks for those involved.	• Researcher identifies the risks and benefits for society and participants.
	• Where is the study taking place?	• Select a site without a vested interest in the outcome of the study.	• Researcher selects a site that will not raise power issues with participants.
	• What study approvals do I need?	• Seek necessary ethical reviews.	• Researcher submits for institutional and, if needed, organizational, and community review board approvals.
	• What guidelines do I need to follow?	• Examine professional association standards.	• Researcher consults appropriate professional ethical standards.
	• What research site permissions do I need?	• Gain local access permissions.	• Researcher identifies and goes through local approvals for the site and participants; finds a gatekeeper to help.
	• Who are my study participants?	• Assess capacity to consent for participants.	• Researcher identifies any vulnerabilities and plans for participant protections.
	• What instruments or protocols am I using, and do I need permissions?	• Create or select appropriate instruments or protocols and • Seek permission for use of unpublished instruments or procedures that other researchers might consider to be theirs.	• Researcher creates or selects protocols that treat people fairly and equitably and obtains permission for use of any material that may be considered proprietary and gives credit.
	• Who am I recognizing as a study author?	• Negotiate authorship for publication (if multiple authors).	• Researcher gives credit for work done on the project; decides on author order for planned publications.

Timing During Research Process Phases	Guiding Design Questions	Type of Ethical Issues to Anticipate and Address	How a Researcher Potentially Addresses the Situation
Beginning to conduct the study	• How am I treating people fairly and equitably and protecting vulnerable participants?	• Respect norms and charters of Indigenous societies. • Have sensitivity to the needs of vulnerable populations (e.g., children).	• Researcher finds out about cultural, religious, gender, and other differences that need to be respected. • Researcher obtains appropriate consent (e.g., parents as well as children).
	• How am I ensuring free and **informed consent** of participants?	• Disclose the purpose of the study. • Refrain from pressuring participants into signing consent forms.	• Researcher contacts participants and inform them of the general purpose of the study. • Researcher assures participants that their participation is voluntary and provide information about how to withdraw
Collecting data	• Who do I need to consult about potential disruptions to the research site?	• Respect the study site and minimize disruptions.	• Researcher builds trust and conveys the extent of anticipated disruption in gaining access.
	• What purposes and uses for their data am I communicating to participants?	• Avoid deceiving participants.	• Researcher discusses the purpose and use of the study data. • Researcher communicates any changes that occur.
	• How am I recruiting participants?	• Avoid bias in sampling by using recruitment strategies that remove as many participation barriers as possible.	• Researcher recruits using methods that ensure equitable participation. • Researcher describes criteria for selection and exclusion.
	• What measures am I taking to protect participants' well-being?	• Respect potential power imbalances and avoid exploitation of participants.	• Researcher avoids leading questions, sharing personal impressions, and disclosing sensitive information.

(Continued)

TABLE 3.1 ■ Ethical Issues and Addressing Them in the Phases of the Research Process (*Continued*)

Timing During Research Process Phases	Guiding Design Questions	Type of Ethical Issues to Anticipate and Address	How a Researcher Potentially Addresses the Situation
	• How am I planning for reciprocity with my site, community members, and individuals?	• Do not "use" participants by gathering data and leaving the site without giving back.	• Researcher provides rewards and covers expenses for participating and attends to opportunities for reciprocity that respect community norms.
	• What measures are protecting data privacy and confidentiality? • Who am I permitting to have data access?	• Store data and materials (e.g., raw data and protocols) using appropriate security measures.	• Researcher stores data and materials in secure locations for 5 years (APA, 2020). • Researcher limits access to the study data. • Researcher becomes familiar with local privacy laws.
Analyzing data	• What measures are avoiding bias in my interpretations?	• Avoid siding with participants and disclosing only positive results.	• Researcher reports multiple perspectives, and also reports contrary findings.
	• What measures are protecting the identities of my participants?	• Respect the privacy of participants.	• Researcher assigns fictitious names or aliases; develops composite profiles.
Reporting data	• What strategies are promoting validity in my inferences?	• Avoid falsifying authorship, evidence, data, findings, and conclusions.	• Researcher reports findings honestly. • Researcher uses memoing, audit trails, and descriptive accounts for making meaning of the data.
	• What measures are protecting my participants from harm?	• Avoid disclosing information that would harm participants.	• Researcher uses composite stories so that individuals cannot be identified.

Timing During Research Process Phases	Guiding Design Questions	Type of Ethical Issues to Anticipate and Address	How a Researcher Potentially Addresses the Situation
	• How am I providing access to study findings?	• Communicate in clear, straightforward, appropriate language.	• Researcher uses language appropriate for audiences of the research.
	• How am I giving credit where it is due?	• Do not plagiarize.	• Researcher uses APA (2020) guidelines for permissions needed to reprint or adapt the work of others.
Publishing study	• How am I offering access to study reports?	• Share reports with others and tailor the reporting to diverse audience(s).	• Researcher shares practical results, considers how participants and stakeholders can best access them (e.g., paper copies, website distribution, language translations).
	• What is my publication/ knowledge mobilization plan?	• Do not duplicate or divide the report of a research study in different publications.	• Researcher refrains from using the same material for more than one publication.
	• How am I documenting adherence to standards of ethical research?	• Complete proof of compliance with ethical issues and lack of conflict of interest.	• Researcher discloses funders for research and who will profit from the research.

Sources: Adapted from APA (2020); Creswell (2013, 2018); Lincoln (2009); Mertens and Ginsberg (2009); Poth (2021).

present some guiding questions and possible ways to mitigate ethical issues so that these can be actively written into a research design or plan. This table should not be considered exhaustive but rather a way of starting the conversation about different types of ethical issues that need addressing in qualitative research. These ethical concerns will be further developed throughout the chapters in this book.

Prior to conducting a study, it is necessary to make decisions about the focus of the study so that you can consider the benefits and risks to those involved. Who will be involved is needed because we need to be sensitive to vulnerable populations, imbalanced power relations, and placing participants at risk (Hatch, 2002). It is also important to begin thinking about where your study will take place because this has implications for what approvals you might need before you can begin. It is necessary to gather college or university approval from the institutional review board for the study, but it may also be required that you gather approval from community or organizational ethical review boards as well. Local permissions to gather data from individuals and sites also need to be obtained at an early stage in the research and interested parties and gatekeepers can assist in this endeavor. Sites should not be chosen that have a vested interest in the outcomes of the study. Also, at this early stage, researchers should consider any permissions they might need for data collection such as for instruments or protocols. Importantly, who is recognized as a study author matters. Authorship should be negotiated among researchers involved in the qualitative study, if more than one individual undertakes the research. The American Psychological Association (APA, 2020) has useful guidelines for negotiating authorship and how it might be accomplished.

> **TRY THIS NOW 3.2**
> **PLANNING FOR COMMON ETHICAL ISSUES IN YOUR QUALITATIVE RESEARCH**
>
> Providing evidence of planning for ethical situations is an essential part of qualitative research. What are some common ethical issues that you need to consider prior to conducting a study? Use the guiding questions in Table 3.1 to get you started.

Beginning the study involves initial contact with the site and with individuals. It is important to protect participants and treat them fairly. A key aspect is ensuring participants' free and **informed consent** to be involved in the research by first disclosing the purpose of the study to the participants and expectations of their participation. This is often stated on an informed consent form prepared in advance of the college or university institutional ethical review board submission for approval. This form should indicate that participating in the study is voluntary and that it would not place the participants at undue risk. Special provisions are needed (e.g., child and parent consent forms) for vulnerable populations (Mertens, 2021). Further, at this stage, the researcher needs to anticipate and respect cultural, religious, gender, or other differences in the participants and the sites. Qualitative writings have made us aware of this respect, especially for Indigenous populations (LaFrance & Crazy Bull, 2009; Lovern & Locust, 2013). For example, as American Indian tribes take over the delivery of services to their members, they have reclaimed their right to determine what research will be done and how it will be reported in a way sensitive to tribal cultures and charters.

We have also become more sensitive to potential issues that may arise in *collecting data* and accessing existing data. Researchers need to seek permission to conduct research on-site and convey to gatekeepers or individuals in authority how their research will provide the least disruption to the activities at the site. The participants should not be deceived about the nature of the research and, in the process of providing data (e.g., through interviews, documents, and so forth), should be informed of any changes to the inquiry. We need to minimize potential bias in our studies and employ equitable procedures. This will help researchers to remove as many potential participation barriers as possible with the aim of offering equal opportunities to participate. Technology continues to influence data collection in new and important ways. For example, discussions surrounding publicly accessible online data have implications for how consent is navigated by researchers.

Researchers need to attend to how data collection processes could cause harm to participants through power, sensitive topics, and privacy. Interviews can create a power imbalance through a hierarchical relationship between the researcher and the participant. This potential power imbalance needs to be acknowledged and actions taken to address it such as building trust and avoiding leading questions. Also, the simple act of collecting data may contribute to harming participants and the study site for the personal gain of the researcher. Strategies such as providing mental health supports when researching sensitive topics can contribute to the protection and well-being of participants. Who has access to the data and the measures taken to ensure data security and storage are important considerations for researchers. Be sure to become familiar with relevant professional guidelines and local privacy laws.

In *analyzing the data*, certain ethical issues also surface. Because qualitative inquirers often spend considerable time at research sites, they may lose track of the need to present multiple perspectives and a complex picture of the central phenomenon. They may side with the participants on issues, and only disclose positive results that create a biased, and in this case, an overly optimistic portrait of the issues. *Reporting* multiple perspectives needs to be kept in mind for the final report. Also, the research results may unwittingly present a harmful picture of the participants or the site, and qualitative researchers need to be mindful of protecting the participants' privacy through masking identities and, in some situations, developing composite profiles or cases.

The principles outlined in the recent APA (2020) ethical, legal, and professional standards offer helpful guidance across a wide variety of situations researchers may encounter; key among those are discussions about authorship and the proper disclosure of information. For example, honesty—and how authors should not falsify authorship, the evidence provided in a report, the actual data, the findings, and the conclusions of a study—is stressed. Reports should also not disclose information that will potentially harm participants in the present or in the future. The form of report writing should communicate in clear, appropriate language for the intended audiences of the report. Finally, plagiarism should be avoided by knowing about the types of permissions needed to cite the works by others in a study.

Another area of emerging interest in the APA (2017) standards on ethics resides in the *publication of a study*. It is important to share information from a research study with participants and stakeholders. This may include sharing practical information, posting information on websites, and publishing in languages that can be understood by a wide audience. To address the concern about multiple publications from the same research sources, researchers are well served by a publication or knowledge mobilization plan that makes clear what data is reported in what publication for what purpose and audience. It can help researchers to be thoughtful in their publications and avoid overlapping or piecemeal division of studies into publications. Finally, publishers often ask authors to sign letters of compliance with ethical practices, disclose sources of funding, and state that they do not have a conflict of interest in the results and publication of the studies.

THE DESIGN STRUCTURES OF A QUALITATIVE RESEARCH PLAN OR PROPOSAL

Researchers are tasked with the responsibility of clearly outlining their research in a plan or a proposal. The audiences for these plans and proposals vary from supervisory committee members to funding review panels. A review of final written products for qualitative research points to great diversity. No set format exists, yet there are some design elements for *engaging* your reader, and several writers suggest general topics to be included in a written plan or *proposal* for a qualitative study. In the following section, we describe six design elements that might make the study plan or proposal attractive to a reader.

Design Considerations Useful for Engaging Readers

In many cases, it is advantageous for research to be distinctive. In our experience, benefits from such types of research have ranged from securing funding to publishing opportunities. We think qualitative research should be interesting to read as well as rigorous in its approach. The following list provides some ideas for study elements to consider when thinking creatively about your study design and these are further expanded by Creswell and Báez (2021).

- *Study a unique or understudied sample.* Is there a sample or population that has not yet been studied? By studying an unusual group of people, researchers may gain new insights into well-established research areas and understudied populations.

- *Assume an unconventional perspective.* Are there angles or perspectives that may not be expected in your area of study? It might well be the reverse side (the shadow side) of what *is* expected or simply a perspective that is unconventional to study.

- *Observe an uncommon research site.* Is there an unusual group of people or an unusual location that could be accessed? It may be that access is now available in cases where it was not previously or that the research site has recently emerged in society.

- *Collect atypical forms of data.* Are there atypical data sources available for the research (e.g., collect sounds, have participants take pictures)? It may also be that the combination of data forms has not been used previously.

- *Present findings in an unusual way.* Are there ways of presenting findings that are influenced by the data collected? Diverse options exist such as through the creation of analogies (see Wolcott, 2010) or maps or other types of figures and tables. Visuals (or hyperlinks to digital representations of photos and videos) are becoming more common in digitally accessed reports.

- *Focus on a timely topic.* Is there a topic warranting research that is drawing a lot of attention? When many individuals are discussing topics, often these topics are also being covered by the news media (e.g., climate change, infectious diseases, aging brains). In some cases, funding priorities may also shift toward those topics.

Explore some of the design ideas as they appear in published qualitative studies in Example 3.1.

EXAMPLE 3.1 DESIGN IDEAS USEFUL FOR ENGAGING READERS

Notice how the ideas for engaging study elements (sampling, perspectives, research sites, data forms, and findings presentations) are presented for readers in the following journal articles:

1. Travers, J. L., Schroeder, K., Norful, A. A., & Aliyu, S. (2020). The influence of empowered work environments on the psychological experiences of nursing assistants during COVID-19: A qualitative study. *BMC Nursing, 19*, 98–110. https://doi.org/10.1186/s12912-020-00489-9

   See the introduction of nursing assistants as an essential yet *understudied population* in Travers et al. (2020), which makes the well-argued case that they are "undervalued, underutilized, and poorly treated" (p. 99).

2. Churchill, S. L., Plano Clark, V. L., Prochaska-Cue, M. K., Creswell, J. W., & Onta-Grzebik, L. (2007). How rural low-income families have fun: A grounded theory study. *Journal of Leisure Research, 39*(2), 271–294. https://doi.org/10.1080/00222216.2007.11950108

   See the literature review in Churchill et al. (2007) positioning the study's *unique perspective* on how low-income families have fun together as a gap in the literature:

   While previous approaches using an ecological perspective have provided a general framework to understand the influences and contexts of family leisure, there are a number of gaps left unaddressed in the literature. Little previous work has examined family fun from the perspectives of participants. This study is unique in that it focuses specifically on family fun and not directly on family leisure activities. (p. 275)

3. Navon, S., & Noy, C. (2022). Like, share, and remember: Facebook memorial Pages as social capital resources. *Journal of Computer-Mediated Communication, 28*(1), 1–12. https://doi.org/10.1093/jcmc/zmac021

   See the Navon and Noy (2022) introduction explicating the *uncommon aspect* of the digital ethnography studies of Facebook memorial Pages:

   Over the last two decades, online practices of death, mourning, and memorialization have grown into a vibrant field of interest and research. Studying the intersection of death and digital media sheds light on novel commemorative practices, affective performances, and oscillations between personal and public spheres. . . . The oscillations between personal and public spheres are integrated into Facebook's internal logic and infrastructure. . . . Interestingly, users commonly employ Pages in a memorial capacity and create Pages to memorialize and publicize ordinary people. In this article, we look at memorial Pages that are dedicated to ordinary people who died in non-ordinary circumstances (terror attacks, murder, suicide, etc.). (p. 1)

4. Malecki, J. S., Rhodes, P., Ussher, J. M., & Boydell, K. (2022). A feminist phenomenological approach to the analysis of body maps: Childhood trauma and anorexia nervosa. Health Care for Women International. https://doi.org/10.1080/07399332.2022.2096026

See the "background" section in Malecki et al. (2022) describing the contribution of the arts-based research technique called body mapping as an *atypical form of data* in the study of childhood trauma and anorexia nervosa:

> Body mapping offers researchers an innovative method to explore how child abuse influences the embodied processes in anorexia and contributes to anorexic subjectivities—the experience of living in and sensing the world from the embodied realities of being anorexic. In this article, the authors describe the methods of data collection and analysis of the body maps of four women abused during childhood who developed anorexia and four women who were abused during childhood but did not develop anorexia. We aim to equip an international audience with detailed knowledge about the methods and analysis of data and more specifically, stimulate dialogue about how to adapt the methodology to women's health issues across multidisciplinary settings. (p. 1)

5. Job, J., Poth, C., Pei, J., Wyper, J., O'Riordan, T., & Taylor, L. (2014). Combining visual methods with focus groups: An innovative approach for capturing the multifaceted and complex work experiences of Fetal Alcohol Spectrum Disorder prevention specialists. *International Journal of Alcohol and Drug Research, 3*(1), 71–80. https://doi.org/10.7895/ijadr.v3i1.129

See pages 73–77 in Job et al. (2014) describing and then discussing the use of a unique quilting process combined with focus groups to capture the experiences of prevention specialists working with women at risk of drug and/or alcohol-exposed pregnancies. The researchers *present findings in an unusual way*:

> In a time when research is increasingly expected to show its relevance to policy and social change, images have the ability to reach a wide audience, breaking through common resistance and engaging viewers in a new way of seeing FASD [Fetal Alcohol Spectrum Disorder] (Weber, 2008). Sharing the quilt with government officials involved in the FASD-CMC [Cross-Ministry Committee] may provoke critical questions about the value of FASD services and spark individual and collective action toward superior strategic planning and programming in this area (Deshpande et al., 2005). It is also plausible that emotional engagement created through visual research data may push policymakers to listen to advocates' concerns and suggestions more readily, providing a different framework for the health, justice, social, and educational issues surrounding FASD. (p. 77)

6. Critelli, F. M., Lewis, L. A., Yalim, A. C., & Ibraeva, J. (2021). Labor migration and its impact on families in Kyrgyzstan: A qualitative study. *Journal of International Migration and Integration, 22*, 907–928. https://doi.org/10.1007/s12134-020-00781-2

See the introduction in Critelli et al. (2021) for a description of a *current topic* involving crossing national borders to seek employment in the study exploring the impact of labor migration on families from Kyrgyzstan.

General Writing Structures

Comparing the differing formats for writing qualitative studies (e.g., Creswell & Guetterman, 2019; Marshall et al., 2021; Ravitch & Carl, 2020), we see common structures for guiding the process of writing a proposal. Next, we first describe each of the six common parts of a proposal followed by three parts we see as important. In our descriptions we highlight the topics where there might be variation due to the inherent nature of the different perspectives adopted in qualitative studies. For each section, we provide examples that list the arguments to be advanced in a qualitative proposal (adapted from Creswell, 2014; Maxwell, 2013). These structures and resources, in addition to the guidance in *Completing Your Qualitative Dissertation* (Bloomberg, 2022), are especially helpful for the student who has never written a thesis or dissertation project. Greater details for composing common parts of the proposal are addressed in subsequent chapters in this book.

1. *Introduce the problem to be studied.* The introduction generally includes three sections: statement of the problem, purpose of the study, and research questions. The sections within the study introduction may vary across studies adopting different perspectives; for example, whereas a separate section reviewing literature may be optional in a study adopting a constructivist/interpretivist perspective, the identification of specific transformative issues being explored is expected in studies adopting a transformative perspective. Researchers may find the following questions useful for guiding their introductory arguments: What do you propose to study? What do readers need to know about your topic? What do readers need to better understand your topic? We further discuss how to introduce and focus a qualitative study in Chapter 6.

2. *Describe your researcher positioning.* Embedded in the proposal should be details about what you bring to the study. As already discussed in Chapter 2, whether we are aware of it or not, we always bring certain beliefs and philosophical assumptions to our research. These, in turn, affect how we go about planning and designing our studies. Engaging in reflexive practices and working on making our assumptions explicit can help us and others become aware of our researcher positionality.

3. *Discuss the theoretical and interpretive frameworks for your study.* Various theoretical and interpretive frameworks can inform qualitative studies. In Chapter 2, we explored a few examples and offered guidance in how these can be written into proposals. These descriptions may appear throughout a proposal.

4. *Describe the procedures guiding the study.* The description of the study procedures generally includes eight sections: philosophical assumptions or worldview, qualitative research approach used, role of the researcher, data collection procedures, data analysis procedures, strategies for validating findings, proposed narrative structure of the study, and anticipated ethical issues. Variation in how the procedures are described may occur across studies adopting different perspectives; for example, a collaborative form in data collection is emphasized in studies adopting a transformative perspective and trustworthiness is emphasized in place of what we have been calling validation. Researchers may find the following questions useful for guiding their procedural arguments: What is the setting, and who are the people you will study? What methods do you plan to use to collect data? How will you analyze the data? How will you validate your findings? What ethical issues will your study present? In Chapters 7

and 8, we further discuss what information to include in your description of data procedures.

5. *Outline the anticipated study implications.* This section generally involves specifying the significance of the study. The descriptions of anticipated outcomes are expected to vary across studies adopting different perspectives; for example, whereas a study adopting a constructivist or interpretivist perspective may describe expected impacts, a study adopting a transformative perspective mentions or advocates for the anticipated changes that the research study will likely bring. Researchers may find the following questions useful for guiding their implications arguments: What significance does the study intend to have? Who are the audiences that are likely to be interested in the study outcomes?

Other important aspects of a proposal include the following:

6. *Report the preliminary study findings (if available).* The report of preliminary study findings may be available if the researcher completed a pilot study (or this section may be omitted completely). Researchers may find the following question useful for guiding their findings arguments: What do preliminary results (if available) indicate about the practicability and value of the proposed study?

7. *List the references cited in the study.* This section involves listing the references cited in the proposal. It is important that only references that have been cited within the text are included in this list and not those references that were simply consulted during the writing process. A helpful guide in creating reference lists and guiding in-text citations is APA (2020).

8. *Include essential documents as appendices.* The focus and quantity of the appendices will differ by study and audience for the proposal. Most common are the inclusion of entry letters, methods protocols (e.g., interview questions, observation forms), and proposed timelines. Less common are the inclusion of informational documents such as a proposed budget and a summary of the proposed content of each chapter in the final study.

Together these parts, in our experience, if adequately addressed and used as an organizing structure, create a well-written qualitative study proposal. It is important to note that these structures speak only to designing a plan or proposal for a qualitative study. In addition to these topics in the proposal, the complete study will include additional data findings, interpretations, a discussion of the overall results, limitations of the study, and future research needs.

CHAPTER CHECK-IN

1. What writing structures do published qualitative studies follow in practice? Select one of the articles in Appendices A through E. Begin with identifying where the problem to be studied is introduced. Then look for where (or if) the researcher describes their

positioning and evidence of the theoretical and interpretive frameworks for the study. Find the descriptions of the procedures for the study and where (and how) the findings are presented. Finally note where the study implications are discussed. Then see where each of these key writing structures appears in the article and identify the sequence of ideas using arrows. For example, one study may start with a discussion about the problem and then move on to a theoretical model, the purpose, and so forth.

2. What ethical issues do you recognize, and what options are available for addressing them? Choose one of the ethical issues that can arise during the process of qualitative research from Table 3.1. Identify why the issue matters in relation to one of the three ethical principles (respect for persons, concern for welfare, and justice). Consider a situation that would give rise to this ethical issue within a research study you would like to conduct and then describe as many options as possible for how you might address it in the design of your study.

3. What design considerations can you use to begin designing your qualitative study plan or proposal? Consider which (one or more) of the design ideas for engaging readers (see Example 3.1) fit your project and discuss how they relate to your study. Finally, develop a general outline for how you might organize and present the topics in your own study.

SUMMARY

In this chapter, we provided an overview of when to use qualitative research and what is required. A qualitative approach is appropriate for exploring a research problem when a complex, detailed understanding is needed; when the researcher wants to write in a literary, flexible style; and when the researcher seeks to understand the context or settings of participants. Qualitative research takes time and expertise as it involves ambitious data collection and analysis and extensive reporting of results. Although qualitative research does not have firm guidelines, consensus exists as to the criteria for a good study: rigorous data collection and analysis; the use of a qualitative approach (e.g., narrative, phenomenology, grounded theory, ethnography, case study); a single focus; a persuasive account; a reflection on the researcher's own history, culture, personal experiences, and politics; and ethical practices.

The design of a qualitative study emerges during inquiry, but it generally follows the pattern of scientific research. It starts with broad assumptions central to qualitative inquiry, an interpretive or theoretical lens, and a topic of inquiry. After stating a research problem or topic, the inquirer asks several open-ended research questions, gathers multiple forms of data to answer these questions, and makes sense of the data by grouping information into codes, themes or categories, and larger dimensions. The final narrative the researcher composes will have diverse formats—from a scientific type of study to narrative stories.

Ethical situations need to be anticipated and planned for in designing a qualitative study. Ethical issues arise in many phases of the research process. They develop prior to conducting the study when researchers seek approval for the inquiry. They arise at the beginning of the study when the researchers first contact the participants; gain consent to participate in the study; and acknowledge the customs, culture, and charters of the research site. Ethical issues can arise unexpectedly during data collection in respect to the site and the participants and in gathering data in ways that encourage reciprocity and mitigate power imbalances. They also come during the data analysis phase when researchers do not side with participants, shape findings in a particular direction, and fail to respect the privacy of individuals as their information is reported. In the reporting phase of research, inquirers need to be honest, and not plagiarize the work of others; refrain from presenting information that potentially harms participants; and communicate in a useful, clear way to stakeholders. In publishing research studies, inquirers need to openly share data with others, avoid duplicating their studies, and comply with procedures asked by publishers.

Finally, the structure of a plan or proposal for a qualitative study will vary, and considering ways to engage readers is useful. We describe common elements that researchers need to include in proposals.

CHAPTER KEY TERMS

Abstraction
Autobiography
Collective reflexivity
Concern for justice
Concern for welfare
Data management
Ethical reasoning

Ethical review
Informed consent
Methodological congruence
Reciprocity
Reflexivity
Research ethics
Respect for persons

FURTHER READINGS

The following resources are offered as foundational references for designing a qualitative study. The list should not be considered exhaustive, and readers are encouraged to seek out additional readings in the end-of-book reference list.

American Psychological Association. (2020). *Publication manual of the American Psychological Association* (7th ed.). Author.

A must-have resource for guiding effective communication with words and data, each new edition reflects the latest guidelines—for example, referencing electronic and online sources in the seventh edition.

Bloomberg, L. D. (2022). *Completing your qualitative dissertation* (5th ed.). Sage.

Linda D. Bloomberg provide a useful guide for navigating the challenges when proposing, writing, and defending doctoral research. In particular, we found the updated chapters on ethical considerations and data collection helpful.

Creswell, J. W., & Creswell, J. D. (2023). *Research design: Qualitative, quantitative, and mixed methods approaches* (6th ed.). Sage.

John W. Creswell and J. David Creswell present an excellent updated resource across three approaches to research. Using the research process as the organizing structure allows the reader to see how each approach is operationalized in a study.

Hatch, J. A. (2002). *Doing qualitative research in education settings*. State University of New York Press.

J. Amos Hatch adopts a step-by-step approach to study development emphasizing learning the craft of doing qualitative research. He uses data from real studies to elucidate analyses processes, which is useful for any researcher.

Iphofen R., & Tolich, M. (Eds.). (2018). *The SAGE handbook of qualitative research ethics*. Sage.

Handbooks provide a foundation, and editors Ron Iphofen and Martin Tolich deliver a useful starting point for research ethics. Of particular note are the chapters about specific approaches such as Chapter 7 about ethnography and Chapter 32 about grounded theory.

Maxwell, J. A. (2013). *Qualitative research design: An interactive approach* (3rd ed.). Sage.

Joe Maxwell describes a stepwise approach to planning qualitative research emphasizing how the research design components interact with one another. A noteworthy aspect of this book is the embedded commentary within two examples of qualitative dissertation proposals.

May, T., & Perry, B. (2017). *Reflexivity: The essential guide*. Sage.

As the title alludes, Tim May and Beth Perry provide an essential guide and introduce the why, what, and how of reflexivity. Of particular note for qualitative researchers is their excellent Chapter 7 on reflexive practice.

Poth, C. (2021). *Little quick fix: Research ethics*. Sage.

Cheryl Poth helps the reader to identify the ethical considerations of their research, protect the privacy of their subjects, develop an ethical research design, and respond to ethical issues as they arise.

Richards, L., & Morse, J. M. (2013). *README FIRST for a user's guide to qualitative methods* (3rd ed.). Sage.

Lyn Richards and Janice M. Morse provide easy-to-follow guidance for beginning a qualitative study. We find Chapter 7 on abstracting to be noteworthy in their clear explanations of this feature of a "good" qualitative study.

Tracy, S. J., & Hinrichs, M. M. (2017). Big tent criteria for qualitative quality. In *The international encyclopedia of communication research methods* (pp. 1–10). Wiley. https://doi.org/10.1002/9781118901731.iecrm0016

Sarah J. Tracy and Margaret M. Hinrichs present the "eight big-tent criteria" for qualitative research quality in a concise and accessible manner.

4 FIVE QUALITATIVE APPROACHES TO INQUIRY

> **QUESTIONS FOR DISCUSSION**
>
> - How does a researcher decide to use one of the five approaches (narrative research, phenomenological research, grounded theory research, ethnographic research, and case study research)?
> - What is narrative research?
> - What is phenomenological research?
> - What is grounded theory research?
> - What is ethnographic research?
> - What is case study research?
> - How do the five approaches differ?

We want to present a couple of scenarios to illustrate differences across the five qualitative **research approaches**. In the first, the qualitative researcher does not identify any specific approach to qualitative research they are using. Perhaps the methods discussion is short and simply limited to the collection of face-to-face interviews. The findings of the study are presented as a thematic workup of major categories of information collected during the interviews. Contrast this with a second scenario. The researcher adopts a specific approach to qualitative research, such as a **narrative research** approach. Now the methods section is detailed describing the meaning of such an approach, why it was used, and how it informed the procedures of the study. The findings in this study convey the specific story of an individual, and it is told chronologically, highlighting some of the tensions in the story. Details about the specific organization in which the individual's story takes place provide important contextual information. Which approach would you find to be the most scholarly? The most inviting? The most sophisticated? We think that you would opt for the second approach.

We need to identify our approach to qualitative inquiry in order to present it as a sophisticated study; to offer it as a specific type so that reviewers can properly assess it; and, for the beginning researcher, who can profit from having **writing structures** to follow, to offer ways of organizing ideas that can be grounded in the scholarly literature of qualitative research.

Of course, this beginning researcher could choose several qualitative approaches, such as narrative research and **phenomenological research**, but we would leave this more advanced methodological approach to more experienced researchers. We often say that the beginning researcher needs to first understand one approach thoroughly and then venture out to try another approach before combining different ways of conducting qualitative research.

This chapter will help you begin the mastery of one of the qualitative approaches to inquiry as well as to distinguish among the five approaches: **narrative research**, **phenomenological research**, **grounded theory research**, **ethnographic research**, and **case study research**. We take each approach, one by one, and provide a definition, discuss its origin, identify the key defining features of it, explore the various types of ways to use it, and describe the procedures involved in conducting a study within the approach. Then we consider dilemmas that you will likely encounter as you proceed and outline the emerging directions associated with the approach. We conclude the chapter with a comparison of the five approaches across foundational considerations, data procedures, and research reporting.

DECIDING AMONG THE FIVE APPROACHES

In this book, we use the term *research approach* to identify types of qualitative research. In earlier editions of our book, we referred to these types as *traditions*, recognizing their origin as types often found in discipline fields. Other qualitative sources may refer to them as *inquiry* approaches (Denzin & Lincoln, 2018b; Levitt et al., 2018). Regardless of the appropriate term, in this book we consider different styles of conducting qualitative research.

After the need for identifying an approach is established, the next pressing concern is deciding *which* among the five approaches is best suited to addressing your **research focus**. A research focus represents a more general area of study interest, such as a study objective or goal, and is distinguishable from a more specific **research problem**. A research problem refers to the issue or concern that leads to a need to conduct the study. We will build upon these concepts in Chapter 5, where we examine how to introduce the research problem and create suitable **research questions** to guide each of the five approaches. The research question also makes clear the **unit of analysis** for the study. The unit of analysis refers to the main subject or entity that the researcher intends to comment on, for example, an individual, a group of individuals, or individual experiences.

Gaining foundational knowledge about each of the five approaches is recommended, and the sections about each of the approaches can be read in any order. You may also read the chapters in the order that best fits your qualitative research learning needs.

Figure 4.1 guides researchers in assessing the fit of the five qualitative research approaches when considering their research focus or overall intent, research participants, and desired **research outcome** for each. The research intent indicates what the inquirer intends to accomplish with the research. The participants indicate the typical individuals or groups from which data will be collected to address the intent. The outcomes indicate what the researcher hopes to end up with at the conclusion of a study. On all three dimensions of Figure 4.1, we see differences among the five approaches. Sometimes the procedures of the five are similar; however, we

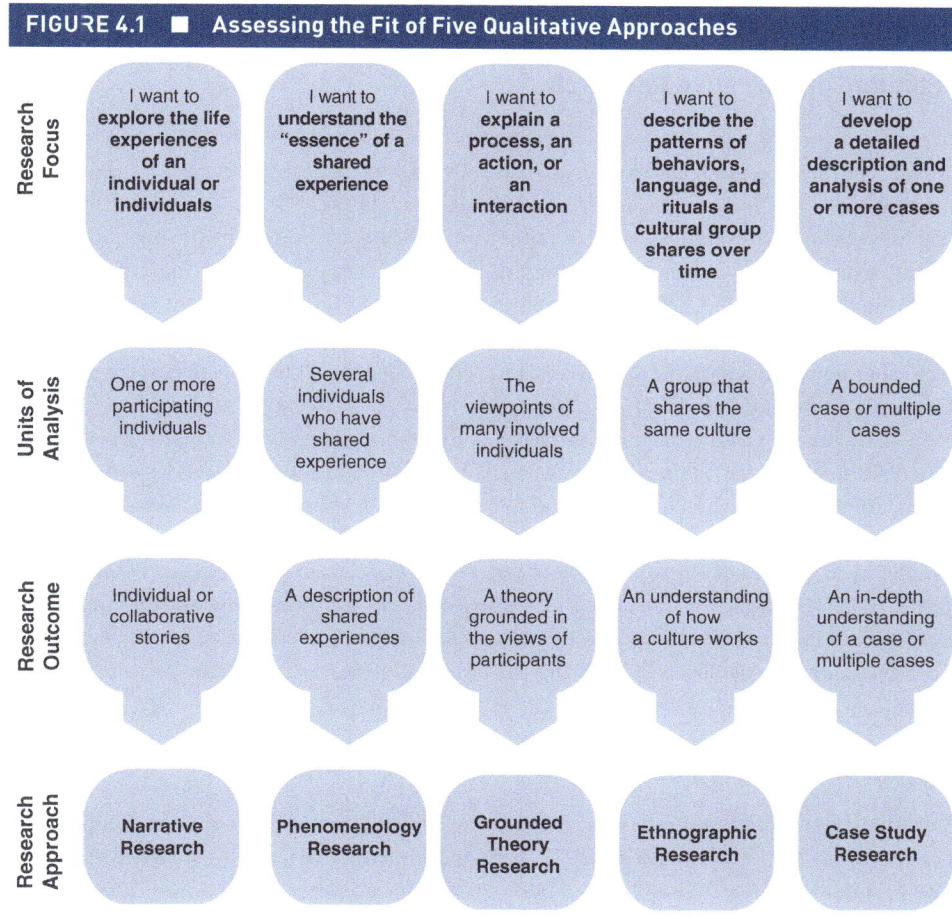

FIGURE 4.1 ■ Assessing the Fit of Five Qualitative Approaches

see the outcomes of the five approaches to be quite different. As you begin to decide on which approach best fits your problem, consider what outcome will result if you follow one approach or another.

TRY THIS NOW 4.1
CONSIDERING THE FOCUS OF YOUR QUALITATIVE RESEARCH

A research focus relates your study interests and, together with your desired unit of analysis and research outcome, can help you decide what qualitative approach to use. Consider the outcome of your qualitative study. At the end of your project, what type of outcome do you hope to have? We consider this approach "working backward" from the final outcome of your study. Use the statements in Figure 4.1 to get you started.

NARRATIVE RESEARCH

Definition of Narrative Research

Narrative research is a qualitative research approach for exploring the life of one or more individuals. Narrative research has many forms, uses a variety of analytic practices, and is rooted in different social and humanities disciplines (Daiute & Lightfoot, 2004). "Narrative" might be the phenomenon being studied, such as a narrative of illness, or it might be the method used in a study, such as the procedures of analyzing stories told (Chase, 2005; Clandinin & Connelly, 2000; Pinnegar & Daynes, 2007). As a method, it begins with the experiences as expressed in lived and told stories of individuals. Clandinin (2023) makes the case for the need for attending to the context in which the narrative is embedded, advising, "the focus of narrative inquiry is not only valorizing individuals' experience but is also an exploration of the social, cultural, familial, linguistic, and institutional narratives within which individuals' experiences were, and are, constituted, shaped, expressed and enacted" (p. 7). Writers have provided ways for analyzing and understanding the stories lived and told. Czarniawska (2004) defines narrative research as a specific type of qualitative design in which "narrative is understood as a spoken or written text giving an account of an event/action or series of events/actions, chronologically connected" (p. 17). The procedures for implementing this research consist of focusing on studying one or more individuals, gathering data through the collection of their stories, reporting individual experiences, and chronologically ordering the meaning of those experiences (or using key life events).

Origins of Narrative Research

Narrative inquiry offers a means of opening many "possibilities to think about a complex and interconnected world" (Caine et al., 2022, p. 3) and is distinctive with its own definitions and a well-established view as both a methodology and phenomenon (Clandinin, 2007, 2023). Narrative research originated from literature, history, anthropology, sociology, sociolinguistics, and education, yet different fields of study have adopted their own approaches (Chase, 2005; Kim, 2015). We find a postmodern, organizational orientation in Czarniawska (2004); a human developmental perspective in Daiute and Lightfoot (2004); a psychological approach in Lieblich et al. (1998); sociological approaches in Cortazzi (1993) and Riessman (1993, 2008); and quantitative (e.g., statistical stories in event history modeling) and qualitative approaches in Elliott (2005). Caine et al. (2022) point to the ontological and epistemological philosophical underpinnings of narrative inquiry in the pragmatic philosophy of the educational philosopher, John Dewey (1938). Interdisciplinary efforts at narrative research have also been encouraged by *The Narrative Study of Lives* annual series that began in 1993 (see, e.g., Josselson & Lieblich, 1993), the *Handbook of Narrative Inquiry* (Clandinin, 2007), and the journal *Narrative Inquiry*. Chase (2018) cites the publication of many books and articles and the establishment of academic and professional centers around the world as evidence that narrative inquiry is "still flourishing" (p. 546). In the discussion of narrative research, we rely on an accessible book called *Engaging in Narrative Inquiry* (Clandinin, 2023) that walks the reader through the justifications and practicalities of engaging in narrative research. We also bring into the sections that follow the data collection procedures and varied analytic strategies of Riessman (2008), two seminal works we often cite (Clandinin & Connelly, 2000; Czarniawska, 2004), and two texts we recommend to narrative researchers (Daiute, 2014; Kim, 2015).

Defining Features of Narrative Studies

Reading through a number of narrative articles published in journals and reviewing major books on narrative inquiry, a specific set of features emerged that define its boundaries. Not all narrative projects contain these elements, but many do, and the list is not exhaustive of possibilities. In Figure 4.2, we list the following common defining features of narrative studies:

- *Narrative researchers enable collaborative storytelling about the* **lived experiences** *of individuals.* These **stories** may emerge from a story told to the researcher, a story that is co-constructed between the researcher and the participant, and a story intended as a performance to convey some message or point (Riessman, 2008). Thus, a collaborative feature is typical in narrative research as the story emerges through the interaction or dialogue of the researcher and the participant(s) (Kim, 2015).

FIGURE 4.2 ■ Defining Features of Narrative Studies

List of Defining Features of Narrative Studies

Not all narrative projects contain these elements but many do and can help you distinguish narrative research from other qualitative approaches.

 Narrative researchers enable collaborative storytelling about the lived experiences of individuals.

 Narrative stories tell of individual experiences, and they may shed light on the identities of individuals and how they see themselves.

 Narrative stories occur and are described within specific places or situations.

 Narrative stories are gathered through many different forms of data including conversations, observations, and artifacts.

 Narrative stories are analyzed using varied strategies.

 Narrative stories heard by researchers and co-created with participants are often shaped into a chronology.

 Narrative stories often contain turning points as organizing structures.

- *Narrative stories tell of individual experiences, and they may shed light on the identities of individuals and how they see themselves.* The stories of individual experiences can vary greatly in their focus. Social media represents a massive contemporary epic narrative created by individuals with an eye to representing their lives using words and images to a vast network of actual and imagined audiences (Daiute, 2014).

- *Narrative stories occur and are described within specific places or situations.* Temporality becomes important for the researcher's telling of the story within a place. Such contextual details may include descriptions of the physical, emotional, and social situations (Clandinin, 2023).

- *Narrative stories are gathered through many different forms of data including conversations, observations, and* **artifacts**. The methods used can vary but common forms of data include interviews and observations as primary forms of data collection along with documents, pictures, and other sources of qualitative data and artifacts.

- *Narrative stories are analyzed using varied strategies.* An analysis can be made about what was said (thematically), the nature of the telling of the story (structural), who the story is directed toward (dialogic/performance), or using visual analysis of images or interpreting images alongside words (Riessman, 2008). Other options for analysis involve foci on values, plot, significance, or character mapping and time (Daiute, 2014).

- *Narrative stories heard by researchers and co-created with participants are often shaped into a* chronology. Stories may be conveyed chronologically although they may not be told that way by the participant(s). There is a temporal change that is conveyed when individuals talk about their experiences and their lives. They may talk about their past, their present, or their future (Clandinin & Connelly, 2000). Other options for telling stories involve using **life course stages** or key life events.

- *Narrative stories often contain turning points as organizing structures.* In addition to turning points (Denzin, 1989), researchers also highlight specific tensions or transitions or interruptions in the telling of stories. Such incidents can help organize the recounting of the story, including the lead-up and consequences. Daiute (2014) identifies four types of patterns (across narratives of one individual or two or more) for meaning-making related to similarities, differences, change, or coherence.

Types of and Variations Within Narrative Research

The many forms of narrative inquiry result from various influences including (but not limited to) the narrative studied (e.g., that of a life history, life story, biography, autobiography, or autoethnography), the lived experience explored (e.g., that of a **single individual** or multiple individuals as members of a group such as a community, organization, or institution), the interpretive theories or frameworks guiding the study (e.g., feminist, critical, or critical race theory among many others; see also Chapter 2), the strategies for data collecting, analyzing, interpreting, and **restorying**). This is not meant to be an exhaustive list but rather to provide a glimpse of the infinite possibilities narrative studies afford researchers interested in exploring the life of an individual or individuals. We note the promising use of narrative inquiry to bring to light the lived experiences of people who have experienced injustices, oppression, and structural racism to enact important social change in our communities and institutions. We recognize as have others (e.g., Chase, 2018; Kim, 2015) that although this interest is not new for narrative inquiry, further examples can be inspiring.

We differentiate narrative studies along two main influences. The first line considers the data analysis strategy used by the narrative researcher, whereas the second considers the types of narratives studied. We see the choice between the two types of approaches influenced by (among other factors) the positionality and disciplinary background of the researcher (see also Chapter 2), the nature of the life experiences explored, the story-generating process, and the audience for the narrative. For example, if the experiences span much of a life, then it might make sense for the researcher to consider guiding the collection as part of a **life history**, whereas the same story could also be analyzed using a thematic approach. The best guidance is finding a fit for the particular story function. Riessman (2008) outlines the variety of functions a narrative can serve from telling stories for individual and/or group identity formation to claiming a point aimed at mobilizing marginalized groups and initiating political action.

With a focus on the data analysis strategy, Polkinghorne (1995) discusses narrative in which the researcher extracts themes that hold across stories or taxonomies of types of stories, and a more storytelling mode in which the narrative researcher shapes the stories based on a plotline, or a literary approach to analysis. Polkinghorne (1995) goes on to emphasize the second form in his writings. Chase (2005) suggests analytic strategies based on parsing constraints on narratives—narratives that are composed interactively between researchers and participants and the interpretations developed by various narrators. Combining both of these approaches, we see an insightful analysis of strategies for analyzing narratives in Riessman (2008). She conveys three types of approaches used to analyze narrative stories: a thematic analysis in which the researcher identifies the themes "told" by a participant; a structural analysis in which the meaning shifts to the "telling" and the story can be cast during a conversation in comic terms, tragedy, satire, romance, or other forms; and a dialogic or performance analysis in which the focus turns to how the story is produced (i.e., interactively between the researcher and the participant) and performed (i.e., meant to convey some message or point). Chase (2018) acknowledges both the difficulties narrative researchers face in analysis and that narrative researchers often apply analytic strategies common to other qualitative approaches.

Narrative researchers can select from various types of narratives for guiding the collection of stories including biographical, autobiographical, and art-based narrative inquiry. A **biographical study** is a form of narrative study in which the researcher writes and records the experiences of another person's life. Common approaches involve the use of a life history and an **oral history**. A life history portrays an individual's entire life, while a personal experience story is a narrative study of an individual's personal experience found in single or multiple episodes, private situations, or communal folklore (Denzin, 1989). An oral history consists of gathering personal reflections of events and their causes and effects from one individual or several individuals (Plummer, 1983). An **autobiographical study** is a form of narrative study in which the researcher takes themselves as the subject of study and uses "the story of the researcher's self" (Kim, 2015, p. 121). A common approach, an **autoethnography**, is written and recorded by the individuals who are the subject of the study (Ellis, 2004; Muncey, 2010). Muncey (2010) defines *autoethnography* as the idea of multiple layers of consciousness, the vulnerable self, the coherent self, critiquing the self in social contexts, the subversion of dominant discourses, and the evocative potential. An autoethnography contains the personal story of the author as well as the larger cultural meaning for the individual's story. **Arts-based study** is a form of narrative inquiry in which creative literary forms of writing (e.g., poetry, nonfiction) and use of visuals (e.g., photos, photovoice, **digital storytelling**) is part of the research product or performance (Kim, 2015). Digital storytelling refers to a short (e.g., 3-to-5-minute) visual narrative integrating any number of images of photos, artwork, and video with audio recordings of voice and music (Willox et al., 2012). Explore the variations in narrative research in Example 4.1.

Procedures for Conducting Narrative Research

Using the approach taken by Clandinin and Connelly (2000) as a general procedural guide, the methods of conducting a narrative study do not follow a lockstep approach but instead represent an informal collection of topics. Clandinin (2023) recently reiterated her stance by saying,

> I highlight narrative inquiry as a fluid inquiry, not a set of procedures or linear steps to be followed but a relational inquiry methodology that is open to where stories of participants' experience take each researcher. (p. 19)

In Figure 4.3, we represent seven procedural topics diagramed as steps building on each other, but recognizing that in any given research project, the order may be altered to fit a particular study.

- *Determine if a narrative approach is the best fit to study the research problem.* Narrative research is best for capturing the detailed stories or life experiences of a single individual or the lives of a small number of individuals. The individuals studied may represent a variety of lives, such as a person of distinction (recognized or not), one who struggles, another with a life cut short, or yet another having an ordinary life. Of importance is that your narrative research seeks to explore how individuals make meaning of their life experiences.

- *Select one or more individuals and gather their stories through multiple types of information.* Researchers may interview or observe individuals and record field notes. Research participants may record their stories in a journal or diary. Researchers may also collect letters sent by the individuals; assemble stories about the individuals from family members; gather documents such as memos or official correspondence about the individuals; or obtain photographs, memory boxes (collection of items that trigger memories), and other personal, family, or social artifacts.

FIGURE 4.3 ■ Procedures for Conducting Narrative Research

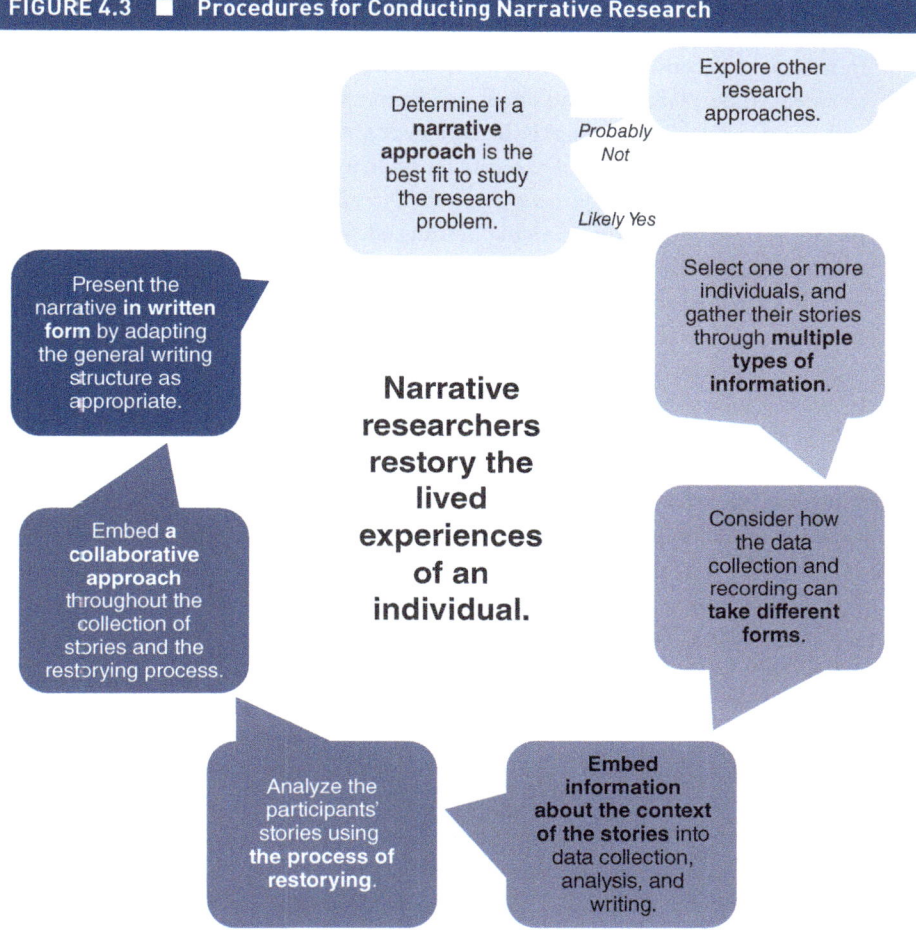

- *Consider how the data collection and recording can take different forms and embed a collaborative approach.* Riessman (2008) illustrates different ways that researchers can transcribe interviews to develop different types of stories. The transcription can highlight the researcher as a listener or a questioner, emphasize the interaction between the researcher and the participant, convey a conversation that moves through time, or include shifting meanings that may emerge through translated material.

- *Embed information about the context of the stories into data collection, analysis, and writing.* Narrative researchers situate individual stories within participants' personal experiences (their jobs, their homes), their culture (racial or ethnic), and their **historical contexts** (time and place). Being context-sensitive is considered essential to narrative inquiry (Czarniawska, 2004).

- *Analyze the participants' stories using the process of restorying.* The researcher may take an active role and "restory" the stories into a framework that makes sense. This framework may consist of gathering stories, analyzing them for key elements of the story (e.g., time, place, plot, and scene), and then rewriting the stories to place them within a chronological sequence (Ollerenshaw & Creswell, 2002). Cortazzi (1993) suggests that the chronology of narrative research, with an emphasis on sequence, sets narrative apart from other genres of research. One aspect of the chronology is that the stories have a beginning, a middle, and an end. Similar to basic elements found in good novels, these aspects involve a predicament, conflict, or struggle; a protagonist, or main character; and a sequence with implied causality (i.e., a plot) during which the predicament is resolved in some fashion (Carter, 1993). Further, the story might include other elements typically found in novels, such as time, place, and scene (Connelly & Clandinin, 1990). The plot, or story line, may also include Clandinin and Connelly's (2000) three-dimensional narrative inquiry space: the personal and social (the interaction); the past, present, and future (continuity); and the place (situation). This story line may include information about the setting or context of the participants' experiences. Beyond the chronology, researchers might detail themes that arise from the story to provide a more detailed discussion of the meaning of the story (Huber & Whelan, 1999). Thus, the qualitative data analysis may be a description of both the story and themes that emerge from it. A postmodern narrative writer, such as Czarniawska (2004), adds another element to the analysis: a deconstruction of the stories, an unmaking of them by such analytic strategies as exposing dichotomies, examining silences, and attending to disruptions and contradictions. Finally, the analysis process consists of the researcher looking for themes or categories; the researcher using a microlinguistic approach and probing for the meaning of words, phrases, and larger units of discourse, such as is often done in conversational analysis (see Gee, 1991); or the researcher examining the stories for how they are produced interactively between the researcher and the participant (or community) or performed by the participant to convey a specific agenda or message (Riessman, 2008).

- *Embed a collaborative approach throughout the telling and restorying processes.* Clandinin and Connelly (2000) describe active involvement of participants as central to their work; that is, "narrative inquiry is a way of understanding experience; it is collaboration between researcher and participants, over time, in a place or series of places, and in social interactions with milieus" (p. 17). As researchers hear stories, they negotiate relationships, smooth transitions, and provide ways to be useful to the participants. In narrative research, a key theme has been the turn toward the relationship between the researcher and the researched in which both parties will learn and change in the encounter (Pinnegar & Daynes, 2007). In this process, the parties negotiate the meaning of the stories, adding a validation check to the analysis (Creswell & Miller, 2000). Within the story may be **epiphanies**, turning points, or disruptions in which the story line changes direction dramatically. Also within the participant's story may also be an interwoven story of the researcher gaining insight into their own life (see Huber & Whelan, 1999). In the end, the narrative study tells the story of individuals unfolding in a chronology of their experiences, set within their personal, social, and historical context, and including the important themes in those lived experiences. Clandinin and Connelly (2000) say that "narrative inquiry is stories lived and told" (p. 20).

- *Present the narrative in written form by adapting the general narrative writing structures as appropriate.* The general writing structures for narrative inquiry are as follows: an introduction to familiarize the reader with the participant(s) and the intended purpose for the story; research procedures to provide a rationale for use of a narrative and details about data collection and analysis; telling of the story to theorize about participant lives, with narrative segments; and patterns of meaning articulated around events, processes, epiphanies, or themes; and a final interpretation of the meaning of the story. Attending to all the different aspects of a life experience can be difficult to synthesize into a final report.

Challenges and Opportunities in Narrative Research

Given these procedures and the characteristics of narrative research, narrative research is a challenging approach to use. Here, we focus on three key challenges narrative researchers can expect to encounter and practical ways to prepare. We conclude our discussion of narrative research with a look forward to two opportunities gaining prominence.

The collection of extensive information about the participant(s) and their lived experiences needs to occur in ways that protect the well-being of everyone involved. It takes effort on the part of the researcher to recognize the potential influence their positioning (e.g., their personal history and background; see also Chapters 1 and 2) brings to the narrative inquiry. It also takes a keen eye for the researcher to identify source material that gathers the particular stories and captures the individual's experiences. As Edel (1984) comments, it is important to uncover the "figure under the carpet" that explains the multilayered context of a life. We find engaging in reflective practice helpful to uncover our assumptions and minimize bias as narrative inquirers.

The collaboration of the researcher with the participant(s) is key to generating an understanding of the multifaceted contexts of the lived experience and shaping how they "restory" the account. Reflecting the embedded nature of narrative stories within the larger social, cultural, familial, linguistic, and institutional dimensions allows a more complex understanding to be attended to (Clandinin, 2023), yet is difficult to realize. It is not uncommon for researchers to find the process of finalizing reports challenging, "because it is at this point that we make our texts visible to public audiences, unknown audiences who may be far removed from the lived and told experiences of participants" (Clandinin, 2023, p. 31). We point to usefulness of the templates found in Chapter 7 of Daiute (2014) for organizing our findings as we engaged in writing.

The ethical issue of power relations is of principal concern in narrative inquiry (Clandinin & Connelly, 2000). Multiple ethical issues can arise in the collecting, analyzing, and telling of individual stories and building awareness of this responsibility is crucial (Czarniawska, 2004). We suggest narrative researchers are well served by considering the following questions raised by

Pinnegar and Daynes (2007): Who owns the story? Who can tell it? Who can change it? Whose version is convincing? What happens when narratives compete? As a community, what do stories do among us? We also suggest reviewing the discussions about research ethics in Chapter 3 and consider any unique implications for narrative research.

We are encouraged by the ways narrative studies are being used to advance social justice around the world. *Testimonios* have become powerful ways of promoting social justice across a variety of research settings, such as reporting women's voices being silenced during South Africa's Truth and Reconciliation Commission hearings (Gready, 2013) or the distrust of forced migrants in purportedly protective spaces for refugees in the United States, Germany, and Hong Kong (Witteborn, 2012). Oral histories may be told to disrupt the dominant discourse around teenage pregnancy (Muncey, 2010) or to highlight the isolation and limited access to maternal care in a rural community (Orkin & Newberry, 2014).

We anticipate further use of arts-based narrative inquiry for attaining more complex understandings. There are several ways that visuals, artifacts, and videos are being integrated and many more to be imagined—key among them are telling the story with arts-based methods, telling the story about the arts-based methods, and using arts-based methods to inform the storytelling (whether the art is found or made within the process). In addition, further bridges will need to be considered with both established and innovative methodologies; for example, the use of photovoice within narrative inquiry in research involving sensitive topics such as gender-based research with South African schoolgirls (see Simmonds et al., 2015) and the use of printmaking with narrative inquiry in research involving vulnerable populations, such as with trans young adults and refugee families from Syria with preschool children (see Lavoie & Caine, 2022).

EXAMPLE 4.1 NARRATIVE RESEARCH VARIATIONS

Notice how variations within narrative research are presented for readers in the following four journal articles.

1. Ruohotie-Lyhty, M. (2013). Struggling for a professional identity: Two newly qualified language teachers' identity narratives during the first years at work. *Teaching and Teacher Education, 30*, 120–129. https://doi.org/10.1016/j.tate.2012.11.002

    In this *biographical study*, see how Ruohotie-Lyhty (2013) records the experiences of another person's life as a researcher exploring the professional identity of two newly qualified language teachers in Finland. Through contrasting the teachers' experiences (a painful and an easy beginning), the stories offer insights into the role of reflection on life experiences as a useful means of supporting identity development.

2. Ellis, C. (1993). "There are survivors": Telling a story of sudden death. *The Sociological Quarterly, 34*(4), 711–730. https://doi.org/10.1111/j.1533-8525.1993.tb00114.x

    This *autoethnography* is written and recorded by Ellis (1993) as the individual who is the subject of the study. See how the researcher engages in a personal exploration of the family drama enacted in the aftermath of the author's brother's death in an airplane crash. She tells her story about childhood interactions with her brother, the crash, and the context for which he was traveling (to visit the author), their adulthood relationship, and the experience of going to the family home for the funeral followed by her return to her home. The author raises other issues as well, such as her personal and professional life and the larger cultural meaning of her story.

3. Fabricius, A. H. (2014). The transnational and the individual: A life-history narrative in a Danish university context. *Journal of Education for Teaching: International Research and Pedagogy, 40*(3), 284–299. https://doi.org/10.1080/02607476.2014.903027

    In this *life history*, see how Fabricius (2014) portrays the entire life of a Danish academic's position and perspectives to illustrate the complexity of internationalization.

4. Quayle, A. F., & Sonn, C. C. (2019). Amplifying the voices of Indigenous elders through community arts and narrative inquiry: Stories of oppression, psychosocial suffering, and survival. *American Journal of Community Psychology, 64*(1–2), 46–58. https://doi.org/10.1002/ajcp.12367

    In this *critical narrative inquiry*, community researchers Quayle and Sonn (2019) with four Noongar Elders co-create an archive of their stories explicating the history and ongoing legacy of racialized expression in their lives. Note in the article how the researchers explain their own positioning for this work and the work's purpose to serve as a resource for healing, reclamation, and examining a painful and unjust past.

PHENOMENOLOGICAL RESEARCH

Definition of Phenomenological Research

Whereas a narrative study reports the stories of experiences of a single individual or several individuals, a phenomenological study describes the common meaning for several individuals of their lived experiences of a concept or a **phenomenon**. Phenomenologists focus on describing what all participants have in common as they experience a phenomenon (e.g., grief is universally experienced). The basic purpose of phenomenology is to reduce individual experiences with a phenomenon to a description of the universal essence (a "grasp of the very nature of the thing"; van Manen, 1990, p. 177). To this end, qualitative researchers identify a phenomenon, an "object" of human experience (van Manen, 1990, p. 163). Recently, van Manen (2014) describes phenomenological research as beginning "with wonder at what gives itself and how something gives itself. It can only be pursued while surrounding to a state of wonder" (p. 27). Beck (2020) describes the aim of phenomenology as "gaining a deeper understanding of the meaning of experiences in everyday life" (p. 1). This human experience may be a phenomenon such as insomnia, being left out, anger, grief, or undergoing coronary artery bypass surgery (Moustakas, 1994). The inquirer then collects data from persons who have experienced the phenomenon and develops a composite description of the essence of the experience for all of the individuals. This description consists of "what" they experienced and "how" they experienced it (Moustakas, 1994).

Origins of Phenomenological Research

Phenomenology has a strong philosophical component to it. It draws heavily on the writings of the German mathematician Edmund Husserl (1859–1938; 1970) and those who expanded on his views, such as Heidegger, Sartre, and Merleau-Ponty (Spiegelberg, 1982). Phenomenology is popular in the social and health sciences, especially in sociology (Borgatta & Borgatta, 1992; Swingewood, 1991), psychology (Giorgi, 1985, 2009; Polkinghorne, 1989; Wertz, 2005), nursing and the health sciences (Nieswiadomy, 1993; Oiler, 1986), and education (Tesch, 1988; van Manen, 1990, 2014). Husserl's ideas are abstract, and Merleau-Ponty (1962) raised this question: "What is phenomenology?" In fact, Husserl was known to call any project currently under way "phenomenology" (Natanson, 1973). It was van Manen (2014, 2023) who adopted the phrase **phenomenology of practice** to describe the meaning-giving methods of phenomenology based on the primary literature of these scholars.

Writers following in the footsteps of Husserl also seem to point to different philosophical arguments for the use of phenomenology today (contrast, e.g., the philosophical basis stated in Moustakas, 1994; in Stewart and Mickunas, 1990; and in van Manen, 1990). Looking across all of these perspectives, however, we see that the philosophical assumptions rest on some common grounds: the study of the **lived experiences** of persons, the view that these experiences are conscious ones (van Manen, 2023), and the development of descriptions of the essences of these experiences, not explanations or analyses (Moustakas, 1994). At a broader level, Stewart and Mickunas (1990) emphasize four *philosophical perspectives* in phenomenology:

- *A return to the traditional tasks of philosophy*. By the end of the 19th century, philosophy had become limited to exploring a world by empirical means, which was called scientism. The return to the traditional tasks of philosophy that existed before philosophy became enamored with empirical science is a return to the Greek conception of philosophy as a search for wisdom.

- *A philosophy without presuppositions*. Phenomenology's approach is to suspend all judgments about what is real—the "natural attitude"—until they are founded on a more certain basis.

- *The* **intentionality of consciousness**. This idea is that consciousness is always directed toward an object. The reality of an object, then, is inextricably related to one's consciousness of it. Thus, reality, according to Husserl involves the dual Cartesian nature of both subjects and objects as they appear in consciousness.

- *The refusal of the subject–object dichotomy*. This theme flows naturally from the intentionality of consciousness. The reality of an object is only perceived within the meaning of the experience of an individual.

An individual writing a phenomenology should include some discussion about the philosophical presuppositions of phenomenology along with the methods in this form of inquiry. Moustakas (1994) devotes over 100 pages to the philosophical assumptions before he turns to the methods. We rely on two books for our primary information about phenomenology: van Manen (2023), based on a human science orientation, and Moustakas (1994), taken from a psychological perspective. We also return to the substantial work of van Manen (1990) in our descriptions of methods and traditions within phenomenology and we recommend Beck's work for phenomenological researchers (Beck, 2020).

Defining Features of Phenomenology

There are several features that are typically included in all phenomenological studies. In Figure 4.4, we list the following common defining features of a phenomenology:

- *An emphasis on a phenomenon to be explored.* The phenomenon is phrased in terms of a single concept or idea, such as the educational idea of "professional growth," the psychological concept of "grief," or the health idea of a "caring relationship."

- *The exploration of the phenomenon with a group of individuals who have all experienced the phenomenon.* Thus, the researcher identifies a heterogeneous group with a shared experience that may vary in size from 3 to 4 individuals to 10 to 15.

- *A philosophical discussion about the basic ideas involved in conducting a phenomenology.* This turns on the lived experiences of individuals and how they have both subjective experiences of the phenomenon and objective experiences of something in common with other people. Thus, there is a rejection of the subjective–objective perspective, and

FIGURE 4.4 ■ Defining Features of a Phenomenology

List of Defining Features of a Phenomenology

Not all phenomenological projects contain these elements but many do and can help you distinguish phenomenological research from other qualitative approaches.

 An emphasis on a phenomenon to be explored.

 The exploration of the phenomenon with a group of individuals who have all experienced the phenomenon.

 A philosophical discussion about the basic ideas involved in conducting a phenomenology.

 In some forms of phenomenology, the researcher brackets themself out of the study by discussing personal experiences with the phenomenon.

 A data collection procedure typically involves interviewing individuals who have experienced the phenomenon.

 A systematic data analysis that moves from narrow units of analysis, to broader units, and a final descriptive "essence" of the phenomenon.

A descriptive ending for phenomenology of the essence of participants' experience with the lived phenomenon.

- *In some forms of phenomenology, the researcher brackets themselves out of the study by discussing personal experiences with the phenomenon.* This does not take the researcher completely out of the study, but it does serve to identify personal experiences with the phenomenon and to partly set them aside so that the researcher can focus on the experiences of the participants in the study. This strategy is an ideal, but readers learn about the researcher's experiences and can judge for themselves whether the researcher focused solely on the participants' experiences in the description without bringing themselves into the picture. Giorgi (2009) sees this bracketing as a matter not of forgetting what has been experienced, but of not letting past knowledge be engaged while determining experiences. He then cites other aspects of life where this same demand holds. For example, a juror in a criminal trial may hear a judge say that a piece of evidence is not admissible, or a scientific researcher may hope that a pet hypothesis will be supported but then note that the results do not support it. Van Manen (2014, 2023) describes the processes of bracketing and reduction as **phenomenological reflection**.

- *Data collection typically involves interviewing individuals who have experienced the phenomenon.* This is not a universal trait, however, as some phenomenological studies involve varied sources of data, such as poems, observations, and documents.

- *A systematic data analysis that moves from narrow units of analysis, to broader units, and a final descriptive "essence" of the phenomenon.* Data analysis follows systematic procedures that move from the narrow units of analysis (e.g., significant statements), to broader units (e.g., meaning units), and on to detailed descriptions of the essence of the experience.

- *A descriptive ending for phenomenology of the essence of participants' experience with the lived phenomenon.* In this ending passage, the phenomenological researcher discusses the essence of the experience for individuals incorporating "what" they have experienced and "how" they have experienced it (Moustakas, 1994). The "essence" is the culminating aspect of a phenomenological study.

Types of and Variations Within Phenomenology

Two approaches to phenomenology are highlighted in this discussion. The first, **hermeneutical phenomenology** (van Manen, 1990, 2023), is also known as interpretive phenomenology (Beck, 2020; Suddick et al., 2020). Hermeneutics involves the theory and practice of interpretation, which in turn is essential to understanding. In hermeneutic phenomenology, it is said that "understanding is achieved through co-constructing the data with the research participants as understanding is achieved through a continual movement between the parts and the whole of the text of the participants' descriptions" (Beck, 2020, p. 1). The second approach, **transcendental phenomenology** (Moustakas, 1994), is also known as descriptive, empirical, or psychological phenomenology. Transcendental phenomenology focuses less on the interpretations of the researcher and more on a description of the experiences of participants. Explore the types of phenomenology in Example 4.2. Note that researchers do not clearly identify the type of phenomenology they are using.

As an educator, van Manen (1990) has written an instructive book on hermeneutical phenomenology in which he describes research as oriented toward lived experience (phenomenology) and interpreting the "texts" of life (hermeneutics; p. 4). Although van Manen does not approach phenomenology with a set of rules or methods, he discusses it as a dynamic interplay among six research activities. Researchers first turn to a phenomenon, an "abiding concern" (van Manen, 1990, p. 31), which seriously interests them (e.g., reading, running, driving, mothering). In the process, they reflect on essential themes, what constitutes the nature of this lived experience. They write a description of the phenomenon, maintaining a strong relation to the topic of inquiry and balancing the parts of the writing to the whole. In so doing, the researcher makes an interpretation of the meaning of the lived experiences (van Manen, 2023).

With less involvement of the researcher in the interpretive process, Moustakas's (1994) transcendental phenomenology instead focuses on the researchers' description of the experiences of participants. In addition, Moustakas focuses on one of Husserl's concepts, **epoché**, also referred to by others as *bracketing*, in which investigators set aside their experiences, as much as possible, to take a fresh perspective toward the phenomenon under examination. Hence, *transcendental* means "in which everything is perceived freshly, as if for the first time" (Moustakas, 1994, p. 34). Moustakas admits that this state is seldom perfectly achieved. However, we see researchers who embrace this idea when they begin a project by describing their own experiences with the phenomenon and bracketing out their views before proceeding with the experiences of others.

Besides bracketing, transcendental phenomenology draws on the *Duquesne Studies in Phenomenological Psychology* (e.g., Giorgi, 1985, 2009) and the data analysis procedures of Van Kaam (1966) and Colaizzi (1978). The procedures, illustrated by Moustakas (1994), consist of identifying a phenomenon to study, bracketing out one's experiences, and collecting data from several persons who have experienced the phenomenon. The researcher then analyzes the data by reducing the information to significant statements or quotes and combines the statements into themes. Following that, the researcher develops a **textural description** of the experiences of the persons (what participants experienced), a **structural description** of their experiences (how they experienced it in terms of the conditions, situations, or context), and a combination of the textural and structural descriptions to convey an overall essence of the experience.

Procedures for Conducting Phenomenological Research

We use the psychologist Moustakas's (1994) approach because it has systematic steps in the data analysis procedure and guidelines for assembling the textural and structural descriptions. The conduct of psychological phenomenology has been addressed in a number of writings, including Dukes (1984), Tesch (1990), Giorgi (1985, 1994, 2009), Polkinghorne (1989), and, most recently, Moustakas (1994). Pereira (2012) offers reflections on the rigor in phenomenological research from the perspective of a novice researcher. In Figure 4.5, we represent the major procedural steps in the process as tending to build one upon the other. However,

FIGURE 4.5 ■ **Procedures for Conducting Phenomenological Research**

a researcher may engage in the steps in a different order than we present and return to prior steps for revisions.

- *Determine if the research problem is best examined using a phenomenological approach.* The type of problem best suited for this form of research is one in which it is important to understand several individuals' common or shared experiences of a phenomenon of lived experience. It would be important to understand these common experiences in order to develop practices or policies, or to develop a deeper understanding about the features of the phenomenon.

- *Identify a phenomenon of interest to study and describe it.* Examples of a phenomenon include emotional states such as anger and social constructs such as professionalism.

A phenomenon can also involve gaining understandings of a clinical descriptor—for example, what it means to be underweight or a professional descriptor like what it means to be a wrestler. Moustakas (1994) provides numerous examples of phenomena that have been studied, and van Manen (1990) identifies such phenomena as the experience of learning, the beginning of fatherhood, riding a bicycle, and so on.

- *Distinguish and specify the broad philosophical assumptions of phenomenology.* For example, one could write about the combination of objective reality and individual experiences. These lived experiences are furthermore "conscious" and directed toward an object. To fully describe how participants view the phenomenon, researchers must bracket out, as much as possible, their own experiences.

- *Collect data using in-depth and multiple interviews from individuals who have experienced the phenomenon.* Polkinghorne (1989) recommends that researchers interview from 5 to 25 individuals who have all experienced the phenomenon. The participants are asked two broad, general questions (Moustakas, 1994): What have you experienced in terms of the phenomenon? What contexts or situations have typically influenced or affected your experiences of the phenomenon? Other open-ended questions may also be asked, but these two, especially, focus attention on gathering data that will lead to a textual and structural description of the experiences, and ultimately provide an understanding of the common experiences of the participants. Other forms of data may also be collected, such as observations, journals, poetry, music, and other forms of art.

- *Generate themes from the analysis of significant statements.* **Phenomenological data analysis** steps are generally similar for all psychological phenomenologists who discuss the methods (Moustakas, 1994; Polkinghorne, 1989). Building on the data from the first and second research questions, data analysts go through the data (e.g., interview transcriptions) and highlight "significant statements," sentences, or quotes that provide an understanding of how the participants experienced the phenomenon. Moustakas (1994) calls this step **horizontalization**. Next, the researcher develops **clusters of meaning** from these significant statements into themes.

- *Develop textual and structural descriptions of the phenomenon.* The significant statements and themes are then used to write a description of what the participants experienced (textual description). They are also used to write a description of the context or setting that influenced how the participants experienced the phenomenon, called structural description or imaginative variation. Moustakas (1994) adds a further step: Researchers also write about their own experiences and the context and situations that have influenced their experiences. We like to shorten Moustakas's procedures and reflect these personal statements at the beginning of the phenomenology, or include them in a methods discussion of the role of the researcher (Marshall et al., 2021).

- *Report the "essence" of the phenomenon by using a composite description.* From the structural and textual descriptions, the researcher then writes a composite description that presents the "essence" of the phenomenon, called the **essential, invariant structure**

(or essence). Primarily this passage focuses on the common experiences of the participants. For example, it means that all experiences have an underlying structure (grief is the same whether the loved one is a puppy, a parakeet, or a child).

- *Present the understanding of the essence of the experience in written form.* The practice of phenomenological inquiry is considered by van Manen (2014) to be inseparable from the practice of writing. He goes on to explain that one of the challenges with writing is that "one must bring into presence a phenomenon that cannot be represented in plain words" (p. 370). There are numerous "ways" of communicating phenomenological research, including by systematic exploration, meaning the phenomenon is placed in the context of the existential (e.g., temporality or spatiality), or by organizing the account reflective of an ever-deepening understanding of the phenomenon experienced. A general writing structure for phenomenology includes an introduction to familiarize the reader with the phenomenon and in some cases, a personal statement of experiences from the researcher (Moustakas, 1994); research procedures to provide a rationale for the use of phenomenology, and philosophical assumptions and details about data collection and analysis; a report of how the phenomenon was experienced with significant statements; and a conclusion with a composite description of the essence of the phenomenon.

Challenges and Opportunities in Phenomenological Research

A phenomenology provides a deep understanding of a phenomenon as experienced by several individuals. Knowing some common experiences can be valuable for groups such as therapists, teachers, health personnel, and policymakers. Here, we focus on three challenges faced by phenomenological researchers and offer some practical suggestions.

Phenomenology requires at least some understanding of the broader philosophical assumptions, and researchers should identify these assumptions in their studies. These philosophical ideas are abstract concepts and not easily seen in a written phenomenological study. Bracketing personal experiences may be difficult for the researcher to implement because interpretations of the data always incorporate the assumptions that the researcher brings to the topic (van Manen, 1990, 2014, 2023). Beck (2020) describes how researchers must attempt what is difficult, "to put aside their past experiences, biases, everyday understanding, and presuppositions about what they are studying in order to learn to see the phenomenon with fresh eyes" (p. 1). Thus, the researcher needs to decide how and in what way their personal understandings will be introduced into the study and how to document the changes the researcher experiences as well. Indeed, the practice of engaging in phenomenological research has the potential for lasting effects on the researcher, which merit further study as a phenomenon itself. Van Manen (1990) describes the potential impact on the researcher, saying, "phenomenology projects and their methods often have [a] transformative effect on the researcher himself or herself. Indeed, phenomenological research is often itself a form of deep learning, leading to a transformation of consciousness, heightened perceptiveness, increased thoughtfulness" (p. 163). We suggest researchers can benefit from reading *The Routledge Handbook of Phenomenology and Phenomenological Philosophy*

(De Santis et al., 2021), which offers an in-depth discussion of the philosophical discussions influencing the development of and current phenomenological research practices.

Phenomenology requires the careful selection of individuals who have all experienced the phenomenon in question and extensive time for developing a description of the lived phenomenon. Finding individuals who have all experienced the phenomenon and who are willing to participate may be difficult given particular research topics. The ethical issue of free and informed consent and participants' right to withdrawal is of principal concern in phenomenology. Phenomenology can involve a streamlined form of data collection by including only a single rather than multiple interviews with participants. To enhance feasibility, we suggest the Moustakas (1994) approach for analyzing the data, providing a structured approach for novice researchers. We also recognize that this approach may be too structured for some qualitative researchers.

A final challenge for phenomenological researchers is how (or for many *if*) interpretive phenomenological analysis fits with phenomenology. J. A. Smith et al. (2009, 2022) have led the development of interpretive phenomenological analysis as a qualitative research framework grounded in psychology and influenced by phenomenology and hermeneutics, as well as idiography. With a focus on the particular, a thorough and systematic approach to analysis examines "how a particular phenomenon has been understood from the perspective of particular people, in a particular context" (J. A. Smith et al., 2009, p. 51). Interpretive phenomenological analysis involves a double hermeneutic as it integrates not only the participant's sense of their lived experience but also the researcher's attempt to understand how the participant makes sense of their personal and social world (J. A. Smith et al., 2009). We note the usefulness of the structured approach to analyze the descriptions provided by the participants' interviews and the concept of a "gem" as a focal point. J. A. Smith (2017) defined a "gem" as "a singular utterance made by a participant with great resonance across the case and corpus" (p. 303).

EXAMPLE 4.2 PHENOMENOLOGICAL RESEARCH VARIATIONS

Notice how the types of phenomenological research are presented for readers in the following four journal articles:

1. Asgeirsdottir, G. H., Sigurbjornsson, E., Traustaddottir, R., Sigurdartottir, V., Gunnardottir, S., & Kelly, E. (2013). "To cherish each day as it comes": A qualitative study of spirituality among persons receiving palliative care. *Support Cancer Care, 21*, 1445–1451. https://doi.org/10.1007/s00520-012-1690-6

    In this *hermeneutic phenomenology*, see how Icelandic researchers examine the experience of spirituality and its influence on the lives of 10 persons receiving palliative care and their well-being. Both the religious and nonreligious aspects were emphasized and implications for the function of a theological approach in palliative care are discussed.
2. van der Hoorn, B. (2015). Playing projects: Identifying flow in the "lived experience." *International Journal of Project Management, 33*(5), 1008–1021. http://dx.doi.org/10.1016/j.ijproman.2015.01.009

> In this study of the *lived experience* of projects discourse, see how the researcher uses Csikszentmihalyi's flow theory to demonstrate findings supporting a Heideggerian paradigm and personal perspective of what a project is, using an arts-based elicitation activity.
>
> 3. Mefteh, K. Y. (2022). Circumstances precipitating rural older adults for co- residential family care arrangements in Central Ethiopia. *Gerontology and Geriatric Medicine, 8*, 1–11. https://doi.org/10.1177/23337214221113100
>
>   In this *transcendental phenomenology*, see how Mefteh (2022) explores the circumstances that precipitate rural older adults co-residential family care arrangements. The study involving 12 rural older adults offer policy implications for practices toward maintaining a positive living environment for rural older adults and tackling challenges in a co-residential family care setting.
>
> 4. Paparo, S. A. (2022). Singing with awareness: A phenomenology of singers' experience with the Feldenkrais Method. *Research Studies in Music Education, 44*(3), 541–553. https://doi.org/10.1177/1321103X211020642
>
>   In this *transcendental phenomenology*, see how Paparo (2022) examines the experiences of undergraduate vocal music education majors enrolled in an elective, 7-week Feldenkrais course with a specific focus on how singers describe their participation and how their experiences inform their understanding of how they sing. Note how Paparo (2022) describes the researcher's lens and role. The author also notes that total objectivity is not possible in presenting data analysis, engagement in the process of horizontalization, and member checking.

GROUNDED THEORY RESEARCH

Definition of Grounded Theory Research

While narrative research focuses on individual stories told by participants and phenomenology emphasizes the common experiences for a number of individuals, the intent of a *grounded theory study* is to move beyond description and to *generate or discover a theory*, a "unified theoretical explanation" (Corbin & Strauss, 2007, p. 107) for a process or an action. Participants in the study would all have experienced the process, and the development of the theory might help explain a practice or provide a framework for further research. A key idea is that this theory development does not come "off the shelf" but rather is generated or "grounded" in data from participants who have experienced the process (Strauss & Corbin, 1998). Thus, grounded theory is a qualitative research design in which the inquirer generates a general explanation (a theory) of a process, an action, or an interaction shaped by the views of a large number of participants. We agree with Morse, Bowers, Clarke et al. (2021) who highlight the unique value of grounded theory as allowing for

- Description, understanding, and analysis of both action and change.
- Generalization through theoretical development and abstraction.
- Broad application that is also *applied, useful and widely used*. (emphasis in original, p. 3)

Origins of Grounded Theory Research

This qualitative design was developed in sociology in 1967 by two researchers, Barney Glaser and Anselm Strauss, who felt that theories used in research were often inappropriate and ill-suited for participants under study. They elaborated on their ideas through several books (Corbin & Strauss, 2007, 2015; Glaser, 1978; Glaser & Strauss, 1967; Strauss, 1987; Strauss & Corbin, 1990, 1998). In contrast to the a priori, theoretical orientations in sociology, grounded theorists held that theories should be "grounded" in data from the field, especially in the actions, interactions, and social processes of people. Thus, grounded theory provided for the generation of a theory (complete with a diagram and hypotheses) of actions, interactions, or processes through interrelating categories of information based on data collected from individuals.

Despite the initial collaboration of Glaser and Strauss that produced such works as *Awareness of Dying* (Glaser & Strauss, 1965) and *Time for Dying* (Glaser & Strauss, 1968), the two authors ultimately disagreed about the meaning and procedures of grounded theory. Glaser has criticized Strauss's approach to grounded theory as too prescribed and structured (Glaser, 1992). Introducing another perspective into the conversation about procedures is Charmaz's (2006, 2014) advocacy for **constructivist grounded theory**. Through these different interpretations and publications such as *The SAGE Handbook of Grounded Theory* (Bryant & Charmaz, 2007b) and *The SAGE Handbook of Current Developments in Grounded Theory* (Bryant & Charmaz, 2019), grounded theory has gained popularity across diverse fields. For concise historical accounts, see Bryant and Charmaz (2007a), Kenny and Fourie (2014), and Morse, Bowers, Clarke et al. (2021).

Another recent grounded theory perspective is that of Clarke (Clarke, 2005; Clarke et al. 2015), who, along with Charmaz, seeks to reclaim grounded theory from its "positivist roots" (Clarke et al., 2017, p. 15). Clarke, however, goes further than Charmaz, suggesting that social "situations" should form our unit of analysis in grounded theory and that three sociological modes can be useful in analyzing these social situations—situational, social world/arenas, and positional cartographic maps for collecting and analyzing qualitative data. Clarke further expands grounded theory "after the postmodern turn" (Clarke, 2005, p. xxiv) and relies on postmodern perspectives (i.e., the political nature of research and interpretation, reflexivity on the part of researchers, a recognition of problems with representing information, questions of legitimacy and authority, and repositioning the researcher away from the "all knowing analyst" to the "acknowledged participant" [Clarke, 2005, pp. xxvii, xxviii]). Clarke frequently turns to the postmodern, poststructural writer Michel Foucault (1972) to base the grounded theory discourse. In our discussion of grounded theory, we rely on Corbin and Strauss (2015), who provide a structured approach to grounded theory, and Charmaz (2014), who offers a constructivist and interpretive perspective on grounded theory. We also refer to two practical texts we recommend to grounded theory researchers (Birks & Mills, 2023; Urquhart, 2022).

FIGURE 4.6 ■ Defining Features of Grounded Theory Studies

List of Defining Features of Grounded Theory Studies

Not all grounded theory projects contain these elements but many do and can help you distinguish grounded theory research from other qualitative approaches.

 Grounded theory research focuses on a process, action, or interaction that has distinct steps or phases that occur over time.

 In a grounded theory study, the researcher seeks, in the end, to develop a theory of this process, action, or interaction.

 Memoing involves the grounded theory researcher writing down ideas about the evolving theory.

 The data and analysis procedures are considered to be undertaken simultaneously and iteratively.

 The inductive procedures involved in data analysis are described in relation to the type of grounded theory approach.

 A detailed description of the theoretical model emerging from the data is conveyed. This can take many different forms including both written and visual representations.

Defining Features of Grounded Theory

There are several major characteristics of grounded theory that might be incorporated into a research study. In Figure 4.6, we list the following common defining features of grounded theory studies:

- *Grounded theory research focuses on a process, action, or interaction that has distinct steps or phases that occur over time.* Thus, a grounded theory study has "movement" or some action that the researcher is attempting to explain. A process might be "developing a general education program" or the process of "supporting faculty to become good researchers."

- *In a grounded theory study, the researcher seeks, in the end, to develop a theory of this process, action, or interaction.* There are many definitions of a theory available in the literature, but in general, a theory is an explanation of something or an understanding that the researcher develops. This explanation or understanding is a drawing together, in grounded theory, of theoretical categories that are arrayed to show how the theory works. For example, a theory of support for faculty may show how faculty are supported over time by specific resources, by specific actions taken by individuals, and with individual outcomes that enhance the research performance of a faculty member (Creswell & Brown, 1992).

- *Memoing involves the grounded theory researcher writing down ideas about the evolving theory.* The process of **memoing** becomes part of developing the theory as the researcher writes down ideas as data are collected and analyzed. In these memos, the ideas are recorded in an effort to formulate the process seen by the researcher and to sketch out the flow of this process.

- *The data and analysis procedures are considered to be undertaken simultaneously and iteratively.* The primary form of data collection is often interviewing, in which the grounded theory researcher is constantly comparing data gleaned from participants with ideas about the emerging theory. The process consists of going back and forth between the participants, gathering new interviews, and then returning to the evolving theory to fill in the gaps and to elaborate on how it works.

- *The inductive procedures involved in data analysis are described in relation to the type of grounded theory approach.* The procedures can be structured and follow the pattern of developing open categories, one **category** (called a "core" phenomenon) to be the focus of the theory, and then detailing additional categories (**axial coding**) to form a theoretical model. The intersection of the categories becomes the theory (called **selective coding**). This theory can be presented as a diagram, as **propositions** (or hypotheses), or as a discussion (Corbin & Strauss, 2015; Strauss & Corbin, 1998). Data analysis can also be less structured and based on developing a theory by piecing together implicit meanings about a category (Charmaz, 2014).

- *A detailed description of the theoretical model emerging from the data is conveyed.* This can take many different forms including both written and visual representations.

Types of and Variations Within Grounded Theory Studies

The two popular approaches to grounded theory are the systematic procedures of Anselm Strauss and Juliet Corbin (Corbin & Strauss, 2007, 2015; Strauss & Corbin, 1990, 1998) and the constructivist approach of Kathy Charmaz (2005, 2006, 2014). Important concepts of the approach associated with Strauss and Corbin involve the categories, codes, and the systematic procedures guided by the constant comparison of data from the field with emerging categories. In contrast, in the constructivist approach, Charmaz emphasizes theory development resulting from a co-construction process dependent upon researcher interactions with participants in their natural settings. Explore the variations in grounded theory research in Example 4.3.

In the more systematic, analytic procedures of Strauss and Corbin (Corbin & Strauss, 2007, 2015; Strauss & Corbin, 1990, 1998), the investigator seeks to systematically develop a theory that explains process, action, or interaction on a topic (e.g., the process of developing a curriculum, the therapeutic benefits of sharing psychological test results with clients). The researcher typically conducts 20 to 30 interviews based on several site visits to collect interview data to saturate the categories (or find information that continues to add to them until no more can be found). A category represents a unit of information that comprises events, happenings, and instances (Strauss & Corbin, 1990). The researcher also collects and analyzes observations and documents, but these data forms are seldom used. While the researcher collects data, they also begin analysis. Our image for data collection in a grounded theory study is a zigzag process: out to the field to gather information, into the office to analyze the data, back to the field to gather more information, into the office, and so forth. The participants interviewed are theoretically chosen (called **theoretical sampling**) to help the researcher best form the theory. How many times the researcher returns to the data sources depends on whether the categories of information become saturated—usually considered to be reached when no new ideas are emerging—and whether the theory is elaborated in all of its complexity. This process of taking information from data collection and comparing it to emerging categories is called the **constant comparative** method of data analysis.

The researcher begins with **open coding**, that is, coding the data for its major categories of information. Coding involves a data aggregating and meaning-making process described as "doing analysis and denoting concepts to stand for data" (Corbin & Strauss, 2015, p. 216). When researchers use the exact words of the interviewee in naming the codes, these are referred to as **in vivo codes**. From open coding, axial coding emerges, in which the researcher identifies one open coding category to focus on (called the "core" phenomenon) and then goes back to the data and creates categories around this core phenomenon. Strauss and Corbin (1990) prescribe the types of categories identified around the core phenomenon. They consist of **causal conditions** (what factors caused the core phenomenon), strategies (actions taken in response to the core phenomenon), contextual and **intervening conditions** (broad and specific situational factors that influence the strategies), and consequences (outcomes from using the strategies). These categories relate to and surround the core phenomenon in a visual model called the axial coding paradigm. The final step, then, is selective coding, in which the researcher takes the model and develops propositions (or hypotheses) that interrelate the categories in the model or assembles a story that describes the interrelationship of categories in the model. This theory, developed by the researcher, is articulated toward the end of a study, and can assume several forms (Urquhart, 2022), such as a narrative statement (Strauss & Corbin, 1990), a visual picture (S. L. Morrow & Smith, 1995), or a series of hypotheses or propositions (Creswell & Brown, 1992).

In their discussion of grounded theory, Corbin and Strauss (2015) take the model one step further to develop a **conditional or consequential matrix**. They advance the conditional matrix as an analysis strategy to help the researcher make connections between the macro and micro conditions influencing the phenomenon, and in turn identify the range of consequences that result from the interactions. This matrix is a set of expanding concentric circles with labels that build outward from the individual, group, and organization to the community, region, nation, and global world. In our experience, this matrix is seldom used in grounded theory research, and researchers typically end their studies with a theory developed in selective coding, a theory that might be viewed as a substantive, low-level theory rather than an abstract, grand theory (e.g., see Creswell & Brown, 1992. Although making connections between the substantive theory and its larger implications for the community, nation, and world in the conditional matrix is important (e.g., a model of work flow in a hospital, the shortage of gloves, and the national guidelines on AIDS may all be connected; see this example provided by Strauss & Corbin, 1998), grounded theorists seldom have the data, time, or resources to employ the conditional matrix. A further example explores the larger historical, social, political, cultural, and environmental conditions in which the Vietnam War combat experience took place and was survived by U.S. soldiers, and includes the use of a consequential matrix (see Corbin & Strauss, 2015).

A second variant of grounded theory is found in the constructivist writing of Charmaz (2005, 2006, 2014). Instead of embracing the study of a single process or core category as in the Strauss and Corbin (1998) approach, a social constructivist perspective emphasizes diverse local worlds, multiple realities, and the complexities of worlds, views, and actions (Charmaz, 2014). According to Charmaz (2006, 2014), constructivist grounded theory lies squarely within the interpretive approach to qualitative research with flexible guidelines; a focus on theory developed that depends on the researcher's view; and learning about the experience within embedded, hidden networks, situations, and relationships, as well as making visible hierarchies of power, communication, and opportunity. Charmaz places more emphasis on the views, values, beliefs, feelings, assumptions, and ideologies of individuals than on the methods of research, although she does describe the practices of gathering rich data, coding the data, memoing, and using theoretical sampling (Charmaz, 2006, 2014). She suggests that complex terms or jargon, diagrams, conceptual maps, and systematic approaches (such as Strauss & Corbin, 1990) detract from grounded theory and represent an attempt to gain power in their use. She advocates using active codes, such as gerund-based phrases like *recasting life*. Moreover, for Charmaz, a grounded theory procedure does not minimize the role of the researcher in the process. The researcher makes decisions about the categories throughout the process, brings questions to the data, and advances personal values, experiences, and priorities. Any conclusions developed by grounded theorists are, according to Charmaz (2005), suggestive, incomplete, and inconclusive.

Procedures for Conducting Grounded Theory Research

In this discussion, we include Charmaz's (2014) interpretive approach (e.g., reflexivity, being flexible in structure, as discussed in Chapter 2) and rely on Corbin and Strauss's (2015) helpful systematic approach for learning about and applying grounded theory research procedures.

In so doing, we adopt the advice offered by Charmaz (2014): "Grounded theory guidelines describe steps of the research process and provide a path through it. You can adopt and adapt them to solve varied problems and to conduct diverse studies" (p. 16). In Figure 4.7, we represent eight procedures as tending to build upon each other, and yet, the outcomes can result in revisions to the previous procedures in a cycle.

- *Determine if grounded theory is the best fit to study the research problem.* Grounded theory is a good design to use when a theory is not available to explain or understand a process. The literature may have models available, but they were developed and tested on samples and populations other than those of interest to the qualitative researcher. Also, theories may be present, but they are incomplete because they do not address potentially valuable variables or categories of interest to the researcher. On the practical side, a theory may be needed to explain how people are experiencing a phenomenon, and the grounded theory developed by the researcher will provide such a general framework.

102 Qualitative Inquiry and Research Design

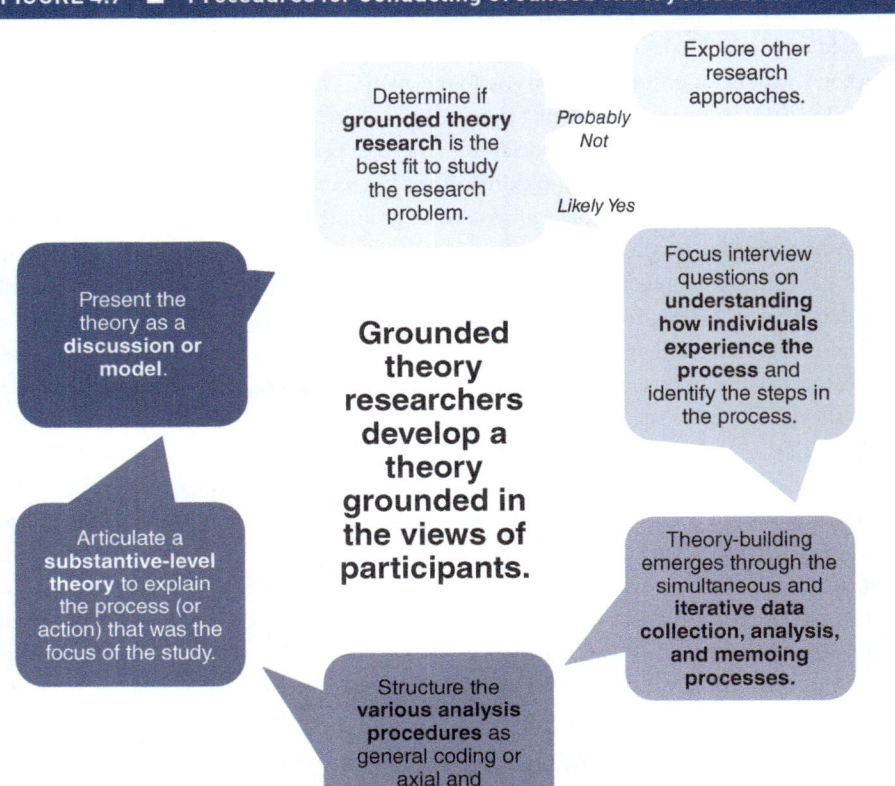

FIGURE 4.7 ■ Procedures for Conducting Grounded Theory Research

- *Focus the interview questions on understanding how individuals experience the process and identify the steps in the process.* Researchers use questions such as What was the process? How did it unfold? After exploring these initial questions, the researcher then returns to the participants and asks more detailed questions that help to shape the axial coding phase by identifying the core phenomenon, causal conditions, strategies, and consequences, such as What was central to the process? What influenced or caused this phenomenon to occur? What strategies were employed during the process? What effect occurred? These questions are typically asked in interviews, although other forms of data may also be collected, such as observational accounts, written documents, and visual items. The point is to gather enough information to fully develop (or **saturate**) the model. This may involve 20 to 60 interviews.

- *Theory-building emerges through the simultaneous and iterative data collection, analysis, and memoing processes.* In memoing, the researcher writes down ideas about the evolving theory throughout the data procedures in an effort to discover patterns (Birks & Mills, 2023; Lempert, 2007). The role of memoing as an essential habit for theory development is highlighted by Corbin and Strauss (2015): "Writing memos should begin with the first analytical session and continue throughout the research process" (p. 117) and "memos begin as rudimentary representations of thought and grow in complexity, density, clarity, and accuracy as the research progresses" (p. 117).

- *Structure the various analysis procedures as general coding and/or axial and selective coding.* In open coding, the researcher forms categories of information about the phenomenon being studied by segmenting information. Within each category, the investigator finds several **properties**, or subcategories, and looks for data to be **dimensionalized**, to show the extreme possibilities on a continuum of the property.

- *In axial coding, the investigator assembles the data in new ways after open coding.* In this structured approach, the investigator presents a **coding paradigm or logic diagram** (i.e., a visual model) in which they identify a **central phenomenon** (i.e., a core category about the phenomenon), explore causal conditions (i.e., categories of conditions that influence the phenomenon), specify strategies (i.e., the actions or interactions that result from the central phenomenon), identify the **conditional context** and intervening conditions (i.e., the narrow and broad conditions that influence the strategies), and delineate the **consequences or outcomes of the strategies** for this phenomenon. Researchers are advised when focusing on a particular theory component (i.e., condition) that the "explanation needs to remain at a conceptual level, using selected data fragments to provide supporting evidence" (Birks & Mills, 2023, p. 225).

- *In selective coding, the researcher may write a "story line" that connects the categories.* Alternatively, propositions or hypotheses may be specified that state predicted relationships. A model can serve as a helpful visual representation of the relationships among categories (Urquhart, 2022) and serve to increase grounded theory research impact (Birks & Mills, 2023).

- *Articulate a substantive-level theory for communication purposes.* A **substantive-level theory** is written by a researcher close to a specific problem or population of people. Alternatively, the study may end at this point with the generation of a theory as the goal of the research. The focus on presentation for communication purposes is made by Charmaz et al. (2018) in advancing the potential for grounded theory methods to change the world for the better. They argue that this change is only possible if findings are presented in such a way that substantive-level theory can make an impact.

- *Present the theory as a discussion or model.* Writing is intertwined into every aspect of conducting grounded theory research and how a grounded theory is presented depends on the audience and the process being explained (e.g., see Birks & Mills, 2023; Charmaz, 2014; Corbin & Strauss, 2015). A general writing structure for a grounded theory study includes an introduction to familiarize the reader with the process (or action) that the theory is intended to explain; research procedures to provide a rationale for grounded theory and details about data collection and analysis; a theory description involving the major categories from open coding; conditions around a core phenomenon from axial coding; and a proposition describing the interrelationships of categories in the model from selective coding. A model can be useful for providing a summative, concise visual representation of the theory and conclude with a discussion of the theory and (if appropriate) connections and contradictions with extant literature, significance of findings, and implications and limitations.

Challenges and Opportunities in Grounded Theory Research

A grounded theory study challenges researchers for numerous reasons. The investigator needs to set aside, as much as possible, theoretical ideas or notions so that the analytic, substantive theory can emerge. Despite the evolving, inductive nature of this form of qualitative inquiry, the researcher must recognize that this is a systematic approach to research with specific steps in data analysis, if approached from the Corbin and Strauss (2007, 2015) perspective.

Wide adoption of grounded theory has resulted in greater attention and the emergence of guidance for researchers for some of the more abstract procedural concepts—for example, memoing (Lempert, 2007) and saturation. The grounded theory researcher faces the difficulty of determining when categories are saturated or when the theory is sufficiently detailed. Corbin and Strauss (2015) note that saturation is "more than a matter of no new concepts. It also denotes the development of concepts in terms of their properties and includes showing their dimensional variation" (p. 134). Thus, the researcher needs to recognize that the primary study outcome is a theory, grounded in data, with specific components: a core phenomenon, causal conditions, strategies, conditions and context, and consequences. These are prescribed categories of information in the theory, so the Strauss and Corbin (1990, 1998) or Corbin and Strauss (2007, 2015) approach may not have the flexibility desired by some qualitative researchers. In this case, the Charmaz (2006, 2014) approach, which is less structured and more adaptable, may be used.

The use of grounded theory research and the benefits from conducting grounded theory research are well established (Morse, Bowers, Charmaz et al., 2021), including generating theory relevant to the context of the study and providing flexibility for addressing real-world issues (Corbin & Strauss, 2015).

Using different theoretical lenses and frameworks can contribute in important ways to social justice; for example, Hadley (2019) identifies critical grounded theory as highlighting "social process and phenomena pertaining to the problems of power inequality and discrimination in all its varied manifestations" (p. 565). We anticipate further broadening of the data collected and the theoretical lenses chosen by the grounded theory researcher because of the influence of these choices on the substantive area of enquiry studied.

We have seen increased interest in research designs intersecting grounded theory with mixed methods. Mixed methods–grounded theory designs are useful for testing the empirical verification of the substantive-level theory with quantitative data to determine if it can be generalized to a sample and population (for additional discussions, see Creamer, 2022; Creswell & Plano Clark, 2018).

EXAMPLE 4.3 GROUNDED THEORY RESEARCH VARIATIONS

Notice how variations within grounded theory research are presented for readers in the following four journal articles:

1. Thornton, R., Nicholson, P., & Harms, L. (2020). Creating evidence: Findings from a grounded theory of memory-making in neonatal bereavement care in Australia. *Journal of Pediatric Nursing, 53*, 29–35. https://doi.org/10.1016/j.pedn.2020.04.006

   Using the more structured analytic procedures of Corbin and Strauss (2015), see how this *grounded theory study* explored the significance of memory-making for 18 bereaved parents and its impact on parents' experience of loss following neonatal loss. The authors discuss the process of taking photographs, creating mementos, and allowing friends and family to be included in their time with the babies.

2. Harley, A. E., Buckworth, J., Katz, M. L., Willis, S. K., Odoms-Young, A., & Heaney, C. A. (2009). Developing long-term physical activity participation: A grounded theory study with African American women. *Health Education & Behavior, 36*(1), 97–112. https://doi.org/10.1177/1090198107306434

   This *grounded theory study* sought to develop a theory of the behavioral process of 15 African American women that explains the pathways linking key factors together in the integration of physical activity into their lifestyles. The authors use interviews with follow-up focus groups as their data collection methods. The authors presented the three-phase theoretical model as a figure, advanced categories within each of these phases, specified the context (i.e., African American social and cultural contexts) and the conditions influencing the physical activity integration. The authors then took one of the conditions, the planning practices for physical activity, and elaborated on these possibilities in a figure of the taxonomy of planning methods. This elaboration enabled the researchers to draw specific results for practice to advance important lessons for future efforts at physical activity program design for African American women.

3. Morehead-Gee, A., Üsküp, D. K., Omokaro, U., Shoptaw, S., Harawa, N. T., & Heilemann, M. V. (2022). Relating "to her human side": A grounded theory analysis of cosmetologists' and aestheticians' relationships with clients in Black American beauty salons to inform sexual health interventions. *Culture, Health & Sexuality, 25*(9), 1180–1197. https://doi.org/10.1080/13691058.2022.2141331

   In this *constructivist grounded theory study*, see how the researchers examined Black American women stylists' experiences discussing sex-related topics with Black American women clients. The authors describe how they used reflexivity to acknowledge the influence of our values, situatedness, and prior knowledge on data collection, analyses, and interpretation of interviews with 16 participants. The importance of three practices is discussed relating how stylists built relationships with their clients.

4. McBride, K., Franks, C., Wade, V., King, V., Rigney, J., Burton, N., Dowling, A., Mitchell, J. A., Van Kessel, G., Howard, N., Paquet, C., Hiller, S., Nicholls, S. J., & Brown, A. (2022). Getting to the heart of the matter: A research partnership with Aboriginal women in South and Central Australia. *Critical Public Health, 33*(3), 1–12. https://doi.org/10.1080/09581596.2022.2147417

   In this empirical/methodological contribution, see how the researchers explore bringing together Indigenous ways of working with *grounded theory* with Aboriginal

> communities in Australia. Of importance for this six-stage research approach is placing Indigenous voices and ways of doing at the center of research by working in intercultural partnership, bringing together Indigenous and Western knowledges.

ETHNOGRAPHIC RESEARCH

Definition of Ethnographic Research

Although a grounded theory researcher develops a theory from examining many individuals who share in the same process, action, or interaction, the study participants are not likely to be in the same place or interact in a way that they develop shared patterns of behavior, beliefs, and language. An ethnographer is interested in examining these shared patterns, and the unit of analysis is typically larger than the 20 or so individuals involved in a grounded theory study. An **ethnography** focuses on an entire **culture-sharing group**. Granted, sometimes this cultural group may be small (a few teachers, a few social workers), but typically it is large, involving many people who interact over time (teachers in an entire school, a community social work group). Thus, ethnography is a qualitative design in which the researcher describes and interprets the shared and learned patterns of values, behaviors, beliefs, and language of a culture-sharing group (M. Harris, 1968). As both a process and an outcome of research (Agar, 1996), ethnography is a way of studying a culture-sharing group as well as the final, written product of that research. As a process, ethnography involves extended observations of the group, most often through **participant observation**, in which the researcher is immersed in the day-to-day lives of the people and observes and interviews the group participants. Ethnographers study the meaning of the behavior, the language, and the interaction among members of the culture-sharing group.

Origins of Ethnographic Research

Ethnography had its beginning in comparative cultural anthropology conducted by early 20th-century anthropologists, such as Boas, Malinowski, Radcliffe-Brown, and Mead. Although these researchers initially took the natural sciences as a model for research, they differed from those using traditional scientific approaches through the firsthand collection of data concerning existing "primitive" cultures (Atkinson & Hammersley, 1994). In the 1920s and 1930s, sociologists such as Park, Dewey, and Mead adapted anthropological field methods to the study of cultural groups in the United States (Bogdan & Biklen, 1992). Scientific approaches to ethnography have expanded to include "schools" or subtypes of ethnography with different theoretical orientations and aims, such as structural functionalism, symbolic interactionism, cultural and cognitive anthropology, feminism, Marxism, ethnomethodology, critical theory, cultural studies, and postmodernism (Atkinson & Hammersley, 1994). This has led to a lack of orthodoxy in ethnography and has resulted in pluralistic approaches. Many excellent books are available on ethnography, including those by Van Maanen (1988,

FIGURE 4.8 ■ Defining Features of an Ethnography

List of Defining Features of an Ethnography

Not all ethnographic projects contain these elements but many do and can help you distinguish an ethnography from other qualitative approaches.

 Ethnographic research focuses on developing a complex, complete description of the culture of a group—the entire culture-sharing group or a subset of a group.

 Ethnographic researchers look for patterns among the group's various activities that develop over time.

 Ethnographic researchers use theory to focus their attention.

 Ethnographic researchers engage in extensive data collection and fieldwork.

 An ethnography includes verbatim quotes as well as the views of the participants (emic) and of the researcher (etic).

 An ethnography represents a cultural portrait of a culture-sharing group or a subset of a group.

2011) on the many forms of ethnography; LeCompte and Schensul (1999) on procedures of ethnography presented in a tool kit of short books; Przybylski (2020) on use of hybrid ethnography; Shrum and Scott (2017) on use of video ethnography; Atkinson (2015) on **ethnographic fieldwork**; and Madison (2019) on **critical ethnography**. Major ideas about ethnography developed in our discussion will draw on Fetterman's (2019) and Wolcott's (2008a) approaches, in addition to Wolcott's (2010) companion "primer" on ethnographic lessons and Hammersley and Atkinson (2019) on the practices of ethnography.

Defining Features of Ethnographies

From a review of published ethnographies, a brief list of defining characteristics of ethnographies can be assembled. In Figure 4.8, we list the following common defining features of ethnographic studies:

- *Ethnographic research focuses on developing a complex, complete description of the culture of a group—the entire culture-sharing group or a subset of a group.* The culture-sharing group must have been intact and interacting for long enough to develop social behaviors of an identifiable group for study. Key to ethnographic research is the focus on these discernible working patterns, not the study of a **culture** (Wolcott, 2008a).

- *Ethnographic researchers look for patterns among the group's various activities that develop over time.* Patterns are also described as rituals, customary social behaviors, or regularities of the group's mental activities, such as their ideas and beliefs expressed through language, or material activities, such as how they behave within the group as expressed through their actions observed by the researcher (Fetterman, 2019). Said in another way, the researcher looks for patterns of social organization (e.g., social networks) and ideational systems (e.g., worldview, ideas; Wolcott, 2008a).

- *Ethnographic researchers use theory to focus their attention.* Theory plays an important role in focusing the researcher's attention when conducting an ethnography. For example, ethnographers start with a theory—a broad explanation as to what they hope to find—drawn from cognitive science to understand ideas and beliefs, or from materialist theories, such as techno-environmentalism, Marxism, acculturation, or innovation, to observe how individuals in the culture-sharing group behave and talk (Fetterman, 2019).

- *Ethnographic researchers engage in extensive data collection and fieldwork.* Using the theory and looking for patterns of a culture-sharing group involves engaging in extensive fieldwork, collecting data primarily through interviews, observations, symbols, artifacts, and many diverse sources of data (Atkinson, 2015; Fetterman, 2019).

- *An ethnography includes verbatim quotes as well as the views of the participants (emic) and of the researcher (etic).* In an analysis of this data, the researcher relies on the participants' views as an insider **emic** perspective and reports them in verbatim quotes and then synthesizes the data filtering it through the researchers' **etic** scientific perspective to develop an overall **cultural interpretation**. This cultural interpretation is a description of the group and themes related to the theoretical concepts being explored in the study. Typically, in good ethnographies, not much is known about how the group functions (e.g., how a gang operates), and the reader develops a new, and novel, understanding of the group.

- *An ethnography often contains a cultural portrait of a culture-sharing group or a subset of a group.* An ethnography describes an understanding of how the culture-sharing group works—how it functions, the group's way of life. Wolcott (2010) provides two helpful questions that, in the end, must be answered in an ethnography: "What do people in this setting have to know and do to make this system work?" and "If culture, sometimes defined simply as shared knowledge, is mostly caught rather than taught, how do those being inducted into the group find their 'way in' so that an adequate level of sharing is achieved?" (p. 74).

Types of and Variations Within Ethnographies

There are many forms of ethnography, such as a confessional ethnography, life histories, auto-ethnography, feminist ethnography, ethnographic novels, as well as the visual ethnography found in photography, video, and electronic media (Denzin, 1989; Fetterman, 2019; LeCompte et al., 1992; Pink, 2013; Van Maanen, 1988). Two popular forms of ethnography will be emphasized here: the **realist ethnography** and the critical ethnography. Explore the variations of ethnographic studies in Example 4.4.

The realist ethnography is a traditional approach used by cultural anthropologists. Characterized by Van Maanen (1988, 2011), it reflects a particular stance taken by the researcher toward the individuals being studied. Realist ethnography is an objective account of the situation, typically written in the third-person point of view and reporting objectively on the information learned from participants at a site. In this ethnographic approach, the realist ethnographer narrates the study in a third-person dispassionate voice and reports on what is observed or heard from participants. The ethnographer remains in the background as an omniscient reporter of the "facts." The realist also reports objective data in a measured style uncontaminated by personal bias, political goals, and judgment. The researcher may provide mundane details of everyday life among the people studied. The ethnographer also uses standard categories for cultural description (e.g., family life, communication networks, work life, social networks, status systems). The ethnographer produces the participants' views through closely edited quotations and has the final word on how the culture is to be interpreted and presented.

For many researchers, ethnography employs a "critical" approach (Carspecken & Apple, 1992; Madison, 2019; J. Thomas, 1993) by including in the research an advocacy perspective. This approach is in response to current society, in which the systems of power, prestige, privilege, and authority serve to marginalize individuals who are from different classes, races, and genders. The critical ethnography is a type of ethnographic research in which the authors advocate for the emancipation of groups marginalized in society (J. Thomas, 1993). Critical researchers typically are politically minded individuals who seek, through their research, to speak out against inequality and domination (Carspecken & Apple, 1992). For example, critical ethnographers might study schools that provide privileges to certain types of students, or counseling practices that serve to overlook the needs of underrepresented groups. The major components of a critical ethnography include a value-laden orientation, empowering people by giving them more authority, challenging the status quo, and addressing concerns about power and control A critical ethnographer will study issues of power, empowerment, inequality, inequity, dominance, repression, hegemony, and victimization using a variety of approaches or theoretical frameworks to guide their study (e.g., participatory, critical race theory, autoethnography).

Procedures for Conducting an Ethnography

As with all qualitative inquiry, there is no single way to conduct ethnographic research. Although current writings provide more guidance to this approach than ever (e.g., see the excellent overview found in Wolcott, 2008a; and for a concise description, see Jachyra et al., 2015), the approach taken here includes elements of both realist ethnography and critical approaches. In Figure 4.9, we represent the seven procedural steps we would use to conduct an ethnography as tending to build upon each other, and yet are interactive with revisions made as the study progresses.

FIGURE 4.9 ■ **Procedures for Conducting Ethnographic Research**

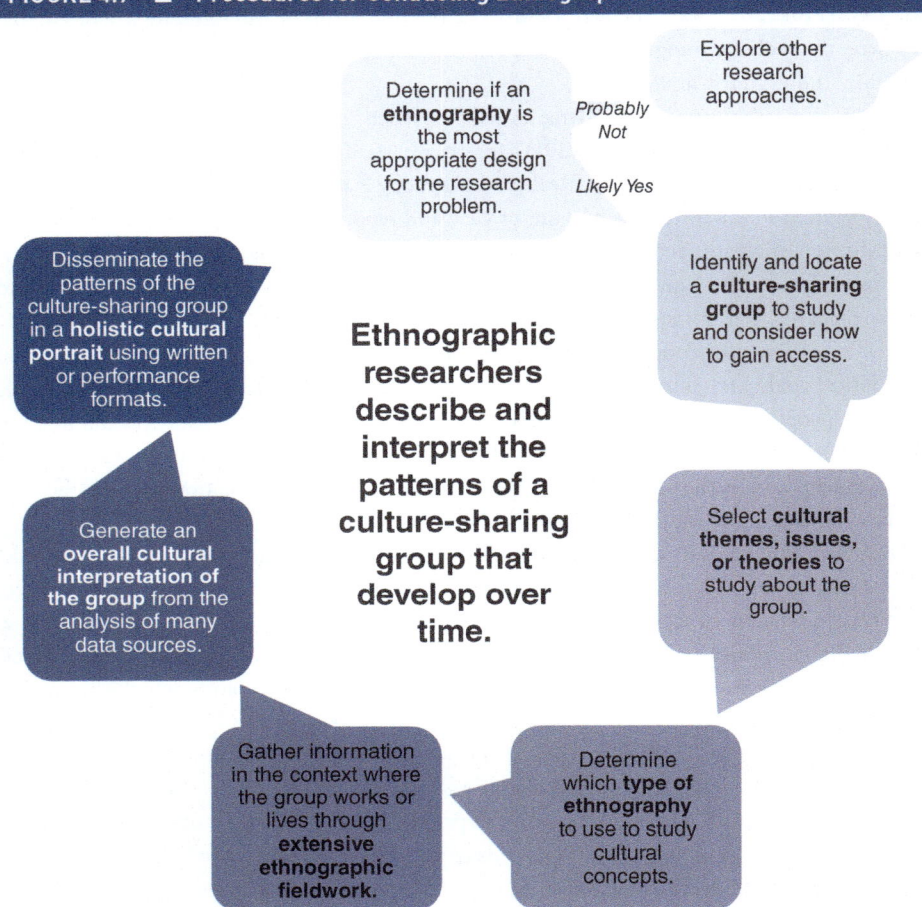

- *Determine if ethnography is the most appropriate design for studying the research problem.* Ethnography is appropriate if the needs are to describe how a cultural group works and to explore the beliefs, language, behaviors, and issues facing the group, such as how power, resistance, and dominance emerge over time. The literature may be deficient in knowing how the group works because the group is not in the mainstream, people may not be familiar with the group, or its ways are so different that readers may not identify with the group.

- *Identify and locate a culture-sharing group to study and consider how to gain access.* Typically, this group is one whose members have been together for an extended period of time so that their shared language, patterns of behavior, and attitudes have merged into discernable patterns. This may also be a group that has been marginalized by society. Because ethnographers spend time talking with and observing this group, access may require finding one or more individuals in the group who will allow the researcher into the culture-sharing group.

- *Select cultural themes, issues, or theories to study about the group.* These themes, issues, and theories provide an orienting framework for the study of the culture-sharing group. It also informs the **analysis of the culture-sharing group**. The themes may include such topics as enculturation, socialization, learning, cognition, domination, inequality, or child and adult development (LeCompte et al., 1992). As discussed by Hammersley and Atkinson (2019), Wolcott (1987, 1994, 2008a), and Fetterman (2019), the ethnographer begins the study by examining people in interaction in ordinary settings and discerns pervasive patterns such as life cycles, events, and cultural themes.

- *Determine which type of ethnography to use to study cultural concepts.* Perhaps how the group works needs to be described, or a critical ethnography can expose issues such as power, hegemony, and advocacy for certain groups. A critical ethnographer, for example, might address an inequity in society or some part of it; use the research to advocate and call for changes; and specify an issue to explore, such as inequality, dominance, oppression, or empowerment.

- *Gather information in the context where the group works or lives through extensive ethnographic fieldwork.* This fieldwork often involves **key informants (or participants**; Wolcott, 2008a). Gathering the types of information typically needed in an ethnography involves going to the research site, respecting the daily lives of individuals at the site, and collecting a wide variety of materials. The attention of the ethnographer can be focused on the **cultural behaviors**, interactions, and **language** of the group studied. It is important to realize that these patterns develop over time. The group needs to be together for a considerable time for these patterns to become set. Also, the ethnographer needs to spend considerable time gathering data from the group. LeCompte and Schensul (1999) organize types of ethnographic data into observations, tests and measures, surveys, interviews, content analysis, elicitation methods, audiovisual methods, spatial mapping, and network research. Participant observation (as a **complete participant**) is a common role researchers play as they fully engage with people they are observing. It is also possible to engage in **nonparticipant observation** such as watching an activity as part of the data collection or as a **complete observer** where the researcher is neither seen nor noticed by participants.

- *Generate an overall cultural interpretation of the group from the analysis of patterns across many data sources.* The researcher begins by compiling a detailed **description of the culture-sharing group**, focusing on a single event, on several activities, or on the group over a prolonged period of time. The ethnographer moves into a theme analysis of patterns or topics that signifies how the cultural group works and lives, and ends with an "overall picture of how a system works" (Fetterman, 2019, p. 13). Fetterman (2019) describes the function of thick description for the reader, stating, "ideally the ethnographer shares the participant's understanding of the situation with the reader. Thick description is a written record of cultural interpretation" (p. 134). This description includes verbatim quotes reflective of cultural concepts such as **social structure**, kinship, political structure, and the social relations or functions among members incorporating the views of the participants (emic) as well as the views of the researcher (etic).

- *Present the patterns of the culture-sharing group in a holistic cultural portrait using written or performance formats.* This is often accomplished by describing a working set of rules or generalizations as to how the culture-sharing group functions. This may also be referred to as a holistic **cultural portrait**. Writing ethnographies involves an interactive analysis and writing process often begun during fieldwork. A general writing structure for an ethnography includes an introduction to familiarize the reader with the culture-sharing group; research procedures to provide a rationale for the use of an ethnography; details about data collection and analysis; and an interpretation of the culture using a variety of methods. The final product is a holistic cultural portrait of the group from the participants and the interpretation by the researcher, which might also advocate for the needs of the group or suggest changes in society. Other products may be more performance based, such as theatrical plays or poems.

Challenges and Opportunities in Ethnographic Research

Ethnography is challenging to use for several reasons. Culture is a broad yet central concept in ethnography. The ethnographic researcher needs to understand cultural anthropology, the meaning of a social–cultural system, and the concepts typically explored by those studying cultures. Here we focus on challenges often encountered in ethnography and offer some practical suggestions for embedding responsive practices.

Ethnographers are tasked with documenting the complexities inherent to a culture-sharing group. Fetterman (2019) describes culture as "dynamic (not static), constantly evolving, and co-created, making description difficult and largely an illusion in reality" (p. 21). We agree that culture is an amorphous term and it is something researchers attribute to a group when looking for patterns of its social world. It is inferred from the words and actions of members of the group, and it is assigned to this group by the researcher. It consists of what people do (behaviors), what they say (language), the potential tension between what they do and ought to do, and what they make and use, such as artifacts (Spradley, 1980). Such themes are diverse, as illustrated in Winthrop's (1991) *Dictionary of Concepts in Cultural Anthropology*. Fetterman (2019) discusses how ethnographers describe a **holistic perspective** of the group's history, religion, politics, economy, and environment. In this work, researchers must keep an open mind about the groups or cultures they are studying and minimize the influences of their biases and assumptions (Fetterman, 2019). There is a possibility that the researcher becomes compromised in or unable to complete the study. This is but one issue in the complex array of fieldwork issues facing ethnographers who venture into an unfamiliar cultural group or system.

Ethnographic fieldwork requires close attention to the ethical issues of respect, reciprocity, deciding who owns the data, and others (Hammersley & Atkinson, 2019). Ethnographers bring a sensitivity to fieldwork issues such as attending to how they gain access, giving back or reciprocating with the participants, and engaging in ethical research, such as presenting themselves honestly and describing the purpose of the study. Sensitivity to the needs of individuals being studied is especially important, and the researcher must access and report their impact in conducting the study on the people and the places being explored. **Deception**, involving the researcher intentionally deceiving the informants to gain information, is a field issue that has become less of a problem since ethical standards were introduced in the 1960s requiring informed consent. For an ethnography-specific discussion of research ethics including informed consent, see Hammersley and Atkinson (2019).

Ethnographers must be agile in their thinking and invested with their time and energy. Fetterman (2019) describes how ethnographers must consider multiple perspectives and interpretations as they straddle the roles of storyteller and scientist saying, "the ethnographic study allows multiple interpretations of reality and alternative interpretations of data throughout the study" (p. 1). The time to collect data for an ethnography is extensive, involving prolonged time engaged in fieldwork, yet discussions abound about how funding often limits time for ethnographic fieldwork. The data collected naturally shapes the generation of a compelling ethnography. In much ethnography, the narratives are written in a literary, almost storytelling approach, an approach that may limit the audience for the work and may be challenging for authors accustomed to traditional approaches to scientific writing. We suggest Hammersley and Atkinson's (2019) discussion of writing ethnography and their reminder that images and other materials can accompany written text and "unless and until we 'write up,' any ethnography remains largely inert and invisible" (p. 198).

We anticipate further use of critical and realist lenses both separately and likely in combination by ethnographers. Among the key challenge for researchers is the lack of guiding examples. As described by Banfield (2020), "while specific applications of critical realism to ethnography are few, theoretical developments are promising and await more widespread development. This is especially the case for progressive and critical forms of ethnography that strive to be, in critical realist terms, an 'emancipatory science'" (p. 1034).

EXAMPLE 4.4 ETHNOGRAPHIC RESEARCH VARIATIONS

Notice how variations within ethnographic research are presented for readers in the following journal articles:

1. García-Rapp, F. (2019). Trivial and normative? Online fieldwork within YouTube's beauty community. *Journal of Contemporary Ethnography, 48*(5), 619–644. https://doi.org/10.1177/0891241618806974

In this *realist ethnography* of YouTube's beauty community, see how García-Rapp (2019) describes her multiyear dissertation fieldwork that sought to "understand online popularity framed by local norms and practices and shed light into the local significance of knowledge, expertise, and self-development" (p. 619). Note her self-reflections on the fieldwork process and visual representations of her findings.

2. Adler-Nissen, R., & Eggeling, K. A. (2022). Blended diplomacy: The entanglement and contestation of digital technologies in everyday diplomatic practice. *European Journal of International Relations, 28*(3), 640–666. https://doi.org/10.1177/13540661221107837

   In this *realist ethnography*, see how Adler-Nissen and Eggeling (2022) seek to understand the place of digital diplomatic work in the European Union multilateral setting in Brussels.

   This work, drawing on ethnographic observations of everyday diplomatic work and interviews with ambassadors, attachés, seconded diplomats, spokespersons, and interpreters, reveals how diplomatic actors demarcate their professional territory and protect their positions through boundary work. Note the researchers' use of vignettes that relay typical scenes of diplomatic work written in the form of the "impressionist tales" of Van Maanen (2011).

3. Hirani, S. A. A., & Wagner, J. (2022). Impact of COVID-19 on women who are refugees and mothering: A critical ethnographic study. *Global Qualitative Nursing Research, 9*, 1–12. https://doi.org/10.1177/23333936221121335

   In this *critical ethnography*, see how Hirani and Wagner (2022) explore the effects of COVID-19 on 27 women who are refugees and mothering young children aged 2 years and under in Saskatchewan, Canada. The areas in which refugee women are at high risk of experiencing add-on stressors due to isolation, difficulty in accessing health care, COVID-19–related restrictions in hospitals, limited follow-up care, limited social support, financial difficulties, and compromised nutrition are discussed.

4. Tan, E., & Faircloth, B. (2023). One world: Refugee youth incubating epistemologies toward rightful presence with/in community-driven STEM. *Journal of Research in Science Teaching.* https://doi.org/10.1002/tea.21846

   In this *critical participatory autoethnography*, see how Tan and Faircloth (2023) investigate recently resettled refugee youth engaged in learning and creating products integrating science, technology, engineering, and mathematics (STEM) in an after-school community. Note how the researchers describe their layering of critical and participatory approaches to their ethnography fieldwork with refugee youth, who innovated and created products that they needed but did not have access to at their residential community center.

CASE STUDY RESEARCH

Definition of Case Study Research

The entire culture-sharing group in ethnography may be considered a *case*, but the intent in ethnography is to determine how the culture works rather than to either develop an in-depth understanding of a single case or explore an issue or problem using the case as a specific illustration. Thus, case study research involves the study of a **case** (or cases) within a real-life, contemporary context or setting (Yin, 2017). This case may be a concrete entity, such as an individual, a small group, an organization, or a partnership. At a less concrete level, it may be a community, a relationship, a decision process, or a specific project (see Yin, 2017). G. Thomas (2021) describes case studies as "analyses of persons, events, decisions, periods, projects, policies, institutions or other phenomena which are studied holistically by one or more methods to illuminate and explicate some analytical theme" (p. 23). Stake (2005) states that case study research is not a methodology but a choice of what is to be studied (i.e., a case within a **bounded system,** bounded by time and place) whereas others present it as a strategy of inquiry, a methodology, or a comprehensive research strategy (Denzin & Lincoln, 2005; Merriam & Tisdell, 2015; Yin, 2017). Similar to Stake (2005), G. Thomas (2021) argues, "Your case study is defined not so much by the methods that you are using to do the study, but the edges you put around the case" (p. 19).

We choose to view case study research as a methodology: a type of design in qualitative research that may be an object of study as well as a product of the inquiry. Case study research is defined as a qualitative approach in which the investigator explores a real-life, contemporary bounded system (a case) or multiple bounded systems (cases) over time, through detailed, in-depth data collection involving **multiple sources of information** (e.g., observations, interviews, audiovisual materials, and documents and reports), and reports a **case description** and **case themes**. The unit of analysis in the case study might be multiple cases (a **multisite case study**) or a single case (a **within-site case study**).

Origins of Case Study Research

The case study approach is familiar to social scientists because of its popularity in psychology (Freud), medicine (case analysis of a problem), law (case law), and political science (case reports). Case study research has a long, distinguished history across many disciplines. Hamel, Dufour, and Fortin (1993) trace the origin of modern social science case studies through anthropology and sociology. They cite anthropologist Malinowski's study of the Trobriand Islands, French sociologist LePlay's study of families, and the case studies of the University of Chicago Department of Sociology from the 1920s and 1930s through the 1950s (e.g., W. I. Thomas and Znaniecki's 1958 study of Polish peasants in Europe and America) as antecedents of qualitative case study research. Today, the case study writer has a large array of texts and approaches from which to choose. Yin (2017), for example, espouses both quantitative and qualitative approaches to case study development and discusses explanatory, exploratory, and descriptive qualitative case studies. Merriam and Tisdell (2015) advocate a general approach to qualitative case studies in the field of education. Stake (1995) systematically establishes procedures for case study research and cites them extensively in his example of "Harper School." Stake's (2006) most recent book on multiple case study analysis presents a step-by-step approach and provides rich illustrations of multiple case studies in Ukraine, Slovakia, and Romania. In discussing the case study approach, we will rely on G. Thomas (2021) and Yin (2017) to form the distinctive features of this approach. We also return to the impactful work of Stake (1995, 2005).

FIGURE 4.10 ■ Defining Features of Case Studies

List of Defining Features of Case Studies

Not all case study projects contain these elements but many do and can help you distinguish case study research from other qualitative approaches.

 Case study research begins with the identification of an intention for the case study and a focus of analysis on the specific case or cases that will be described and analyzed.

 The key to the case identification is that it is bounded and relevant to the intent of conducting the case study.

 The intent of conducting the case study is important to focus the procedures for the particular type.

 A case study presents an in-depth understanding of the case, drawing on many forms of data.

 The selection of how to approach the data analysis in a case study will differ and often depend on type.

 The case description involves identifying and interpreting themes.

 Case studies often end with conclusions formed by the researcher about the overall meaning delivered from the case(s).

Defining Features of Case Studies

A review of many qualitative case studies reported in the literature yields several defining characteristics of most of them. In Figure 4.10, we list the following common defining features of case studies:

- *Case study research begins with the identification of an intention for the case study and a focus of analysis on the specific case or cases that will be described and analyzed.* Examples of a case for study are an individual, a community, a decision process, or an event. A single case can be selected or multiple cases identified so that they can be compared. Typically, case study researchers study current, real-life cases that are in progress so that they can gather accurate information not lost by time.

- *The key to the case identification is that it is bounded and relevant to the intent of conducting the case study.* A bounded case means it can be defined or described within certain parameters. Examples of parameters for bounding a case study are

- *The intent of conducting the case study is important to focus the procedures for the particular type.* A qualitative case study can be composed to illustrate a unique case, a case that has unusual interest in and of itself and needs to be described and detailed. This is called an *intrinsic case* (Stake, 1995). Alternatively, the intent of the case study may be to understand a specific issue, problem, or concern (e.g., teenage pregnancy) and a case or cases selected to best understand the problem. This is called an *instrumental case* (Stake, 1995).

- *A case study presents an in-depth understanding of the case drawing on many forms of data.* To accomplish this, the researcher collects and integrates many forms of qualitative data, ranging from interviews, to observations, to documents, to audiovisual materials. Relying on one source of data is typically not enough to develop this in-depth understanding.

- *The selection of how to approach the data analysis in a case study will differ and often depend on type.* Some case studies involve the analysis of multiple units within the case (e.g., the students, the school, the school district), while others report on the entire case (e.g., the school district). Also, in some studies, the researcher selects multiple cases to analyze and compare while, in other case studies, a single case is analyzed.

- *The case description involves identifying and interpreting themes.* These themes may also represent issues or specific situations to study in each case. A complete findings section of a case study would then involve both a description of the case and themes or issues that the researcher has uncovered in studying the case. Examples of how the case themes might be organized by the researcher include a chronology, an analysis across cases to extract similarities and differences among the cases, or a presentation as a theoretical model.

- *Case studies often end with conclusions formed by the researcher about the overall meaning delivered from the case(s).* These are called **assertions** by Stake (1995) or building "patterns" or "explanations" by Yin (2017). We think of these as general lessons learned from studying the case(s).

Types of and Variations Within Case Studies

Qualitative case studies differ by the focus of analysis for the bounded case, such as whether the case involves studying one individual, several individuals, a group, an entire program, or an activity. They may also be distinguished in terms of the intent of the case analysis, such as whether to gain insights of the particular case or the issue, to demonstrate differing perspectives within a group of cases, to evaluate the effectiveness of an intervention (Stake, 1995; G. Thomas, 2021; Yin, 2017). We focus here on three common types: the single instrumental case study, the collective or multiple case study, and the intrinsic case study. Explore the variations in case study research in Example 4.5.

In a single **instrumental case study**, the researcher focuses on an issue or concern and then selects one bounded case to illustrate this issue. Stake (1995) describes his use of an instrumental case study as having "a research question, a puzzlement, a need for general understanding, and feel that we may get insight into the question by studying a particular case" (p. 3). A single instrumental case study is used to gain insights about a specific case that in turn, illuminates the subject of interest of the case more generally.

In a **collective case study** (or multiple case study), the one issue or concern is again selected, but the inquirer selects multiple case studies to illustrate the issue. The researcher might select for study several programs from several research sites or multiple programs within a single site. Often the inquirer purposefully selects multiple cases to show different perspectives on the issue. Some researchers, like Lieberson (2000), argue for the use of a small group of comparison cases because of the potential to draw otherwise inaccessible conclusions. Yin (2017) suggests that the multiple case study design uses the logic of replication, in which the inquirer replicates the procedures for each case. As a general rule, qualitative researchers are reluctant to generalize from one case to another because the contexts of cases differ. To best generalize, however, the inquirer needs to select representative cases for inclusion in the qualitative study.

The final type of case study design is an **intrinsic case study** in which the focus is on the case itself (e.g., evaluating a program, or studying a student having difficulty; see Stake, 1995; G. Thomas, 2021) because the case presents an unusual or unique situation. This resembles the focus of narrative research, but the case study analytic procedures of a detailed description of the case, set within its context or surroundings, still hold true. Stake (2005) suggests that the case study is intrinsic "if the study is undertaken because, first and last, one wants better understanding of this particular case. It is not undertaken primarily because the case represents other cases or because it illustrates a particular trait or problem, but instead because, in all its particularity and ordinariness, the case itself is of interest" (p. 445). An intrinsic case study is also referred to as descriptive or holistic by Yin (2017).

Procedures for Conducting a Case Study

Several procedures are available for conducting case studies (see Merriam & Tisdell, 2015; Stake, 1995; G. Thomas, 2021; Yin, 2017). For a concise description from a novice perspective, see also Baxter and Jack (2008). In Figure 4.11, we represent five procedural topics we would use to conduct a case study as tending to build upon each other, and yet are also iterative.

- *Determine if a case study approach is appropriate for studying the research problem.* A case study is a good approach when the inquirer has clearly identifiable cases with boundaries and seeks to provide an in-depth understanding of the cases or a comparison of several cases.

- *Identify the intent of the study and select the case (or cases).* In conducting case study research, we recommend that investigators consider the intent of the study (i.e., to focus on a single case or collective cases, multisite cases or within-site cases) and the type of case study (i.e., intrinsic, instrumental). The case(s) selected may involve an

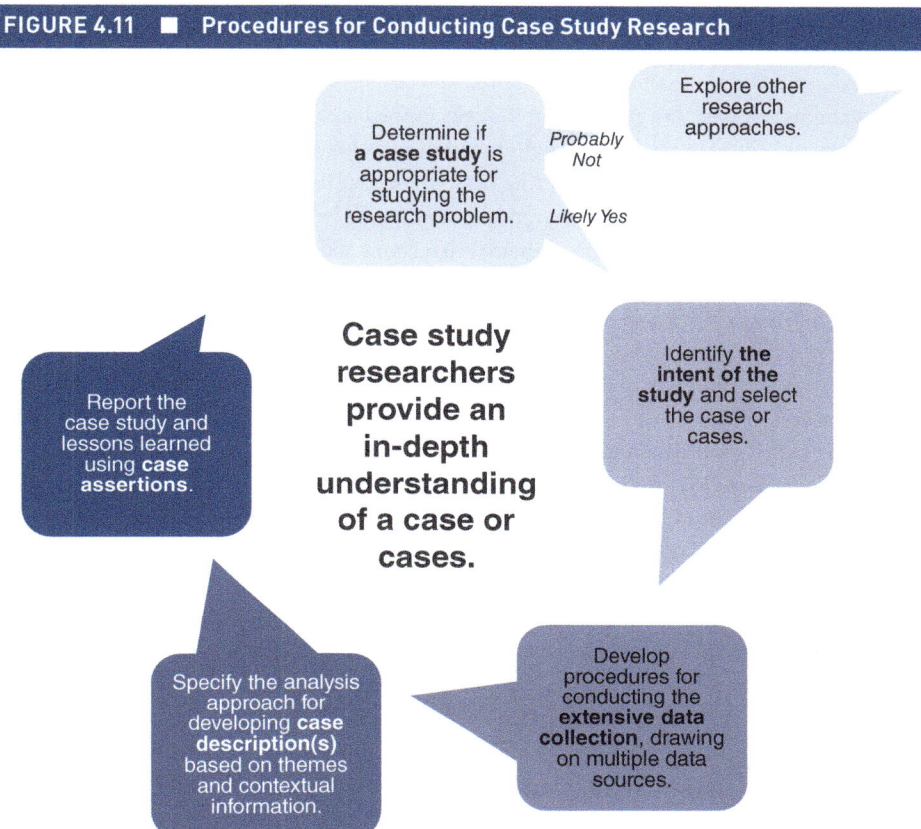

FIGURE 4.11 ■ Procedures for Conducting Case Study Research

individual, several individuals, a program, an event, or an activity (Stake, 1995; Yin, 2017) with an array of possibilities for **purposeful case sampling**. Often we have found selecting cases that show different perspectives on the problem, process, or event preferable (called purposeful maximal sampling; see Creswell & Creswell, 2023), but ordinary cases, accessible cases, or unusual cases are also desirable options.

- *Develop procedures for conducting the extensive data collection, drawing on multiple data sources.* Among the common sources of information are observations, interviews, documents, and audiovisual materials. For example, Yin (2017) recommends six types of information to collect: documents, archival records, interviews, direct observations, participant observation, and physical artifacts. A researcher will then identify **patterns** and look for correspondence across data sources.

- *Specify the analysis approach on which the case description integrates analysis themes and contextual information.* The type of analysis of these data can be a **holistic analysis** of the entire case or an **embedded analysis** of a specific aspect of the case (Yin, 2017). Through data collecting and analysis, a detailed description of the case (Stake, 1995) emerges in which the researcher details such aspects as the history of the case, the chronology of events, or a day-by-day rendering of the activities of the case. For example, the gunman case study (Asmussen & Creswell, 1995) involved tracing the campus response to a gunman for 2 weeks immediately following the near-tragedy on campus. Then the researcher might focus on a few key issues (or **analysis of themes**, or case themes), not for generalizing beyond the case but for understanding the complexity of the case. One analytic strategy would be to identify issues within each case and then look for common themes that transcend the cases (Yin, 2017). This analysis is rich in the **context of the case** or setting in which the case presents itself (Merriam, 1988). Another analytic strategy would be **direct interpretation**, where the researcher looks at a single instance and draws meaning from it without looking for multiple instances of it (Stake, 1995). When multiple cases are chosen, a typical format is to provide first a detailed description of each case and themes within each case, called a **within-case analysis**, followed by a thematic analysis across the cases, called a **cross-case analysis**, as well as assertions or an interpretation of the meaning of the case. Researchers can derive meaning from learning about the issue of the case (an instrumental case) or learning about an unusual situation (an intrinsic case). As Lincoln and Guba (1985) mention, this phase constitutes the lessons learned from the case, and Stake (1995) describes them as assertions. Stake (1995) focuses some of the assertions on lessons learned about the case, stating, "Having presented a body of relatively uninterpreted observations, I will summarize what I feel I understand about the case and how my generalizations about the case have changed conceptually or in level of confidence" (Stake, 1995, p. 123). In so doing, a case study researcher makes clear what the reader learns from the case that may be applicable to other cases—also known as **naturalistic generalizations**.

- *Report the case study and lessons learned using case assertions.* Writing case descriptions involves a reflective process, and the sooner you begin, our experiences tell us, the easier it is to finish. Certainly, the architecture for what works best for individual studies will emerge and be shaped differently by the study assertions. We adopt the advice forwarded by Stake (1995): "The report needs to be organized with readers in mind" (p. 122). A general writing structure for a case study includes an entry vignette to provide the reader with an inviting introduction to the feel of the context in which the case takes place, an introduction to familiarize the reader with the central features including rationale and research procedures, an extensive narrative description of the case or cases and its or their context, which may include historical and organizational information important for understanding the case. Then the issue description draws from additional data sources and integrates with the researcher's own interpretations of the issues and both confirming and disproving evidence are presented followed by the presentation of overall case assertions. Finally, a closing vignette provides the reader with a final experience. Stake (1995) portrays the purpose of the closing vignette as a way of cautioning the reader to the specific case context, saying, "I like to close on an experiential note, reminding the reader that the report is just one person's encounter with a complex case" (p. 123).

Challenges and Opportunities in Case Study Research

A case study challenges researchers in several ways. The case study researcher must develop a detailed case description and analysis of a bounded entity. Researchers need to recognize when they have collected "sufficient" information about a case. Despite its complexities, encouraging the use of case study research is an expressed goal of the editors of the *Encyclopedia of Case Study Research* (Mills et al., 2010). Here we focus on three challenges encountered by case study researchers and conclude our discussion with a look to the future.

One of the challenges inherent in qualitative case study development is that the researcher must identify and bound the case. The case selected may be broad in scope (e.g., the Boy Scout organization) or narrow in scope (e.g., a decision-making process at a specific college). Case selection requires establishing a rationale for its purposeful sampling and for gathering information about the case. Identifying the type of case study is helpful as is creating a data collection matrix to plan the information to be collected about the case. Deciding the "boundaries" of a case—how it might be constrained in terms of time, events, and processes—may be challenging. Some case studies may not have clean beginning and ending points, and the researcher will need to set boundaries that adequately surround the case. The case study researcher must decide which bounded system to study, recognizing that several might be possible candidates for this selection and realizing that either the case itself or an issue, which a case or cases are selected to illustrate, is worthy of study. The researcher must consider whether to study a single case or multiple cases.

Feasibility issues can limit the use of multiple or collective case studies. As the use of multiple case studies increases, it is important to consider three issues: resource limitations, case selection, and cross-case analysis. First, it is not surprising given resource limitations (i.e., both time and financial) that the study of more than one case dilutes the overall analysis; the more cases an individual studies, the less the depth in any single case can be. Second, when a researcher chooses multiple cases, the issue becomes, "How many cases?" There is no one answer to this question. However, researchers typically choose no more than four or five cases. What motivates the researcher to consider a large number of cases is the idea of *generalizability*, a term that holds little meaning for most qualitative researchers (Glesne & Peshkin, 1992; Lincoln & Guba, 2000). Finally, "What guides the cross-case analysis?" In the analysis of single case studies, we are guided by instrumental or intrinsic purposes; in multiple case studies, such explicit purpose identification up-front is not always made.

Having enough information to present an in-depth picture of the case limits the value of some case studies. One of the concerns that has historically plagued case study research is the rigor. Certainly, evidence of poor quality case study research exists, and it is with providing illustrative examples that we can continue to curtail such practices. Our students find G. Thomas's (2021) Chapter 4 discussion of rigor and quality in case study helpful to get started.

Case study research has experienced growing recognition during the past 30 years, evidenced by its more frequent application in published research and increased availability of reference works (e.g., G. Thomas, 2021; Yin, 2017). Engaging researchers is a focus of a number of publications aimed at guiding those new to the approach (e.g., Baxter & Jack, 2008; Flyvbjerg, 2006; Schwandt & Gates, 2018). We anticipate that we will see more diverse forms of data collected as a part of case study and further applications of various theoretical frameworks guiding our case study work. We, like others (e.g., Schwandt & Gates, 2018) have seen an increased interest in case study designs informed by insights from the field of complexity sciences. Studying complex systems as cases or cases as complex systems opens up new ways of thinking about boundaries and requires new ways of thinking about data to capture an in-depth understanding.

EXAMPLE 4.5 CASE STUDY RESEARCH VARIATIONS

Notice how variations within case study research are presented for readers in the following three journal articles:

1. Asmussen, K. J., & Creswell, J. W. (1995). Campus response to a student gunman. *Journal of Higher Education, 66*(5), 575–591. https://doi.org/10.1080/00221546.1995.11774799

    In this *instrumental case study*, see how Asmussen and Creswell (1995) explore the issue of campus violence, using the single case of one institution to illustrate the reaction of the campus to a potentially violent incident. The findings from multiple sources of information advanced five themes (denial, fear, safety, retriggering, and campus planning) and assertions in terms of two overriding responses of the campus community to the gunman incident (mentioned briefly in Chapter 1 and explored further in Chapter 11): organizational and social–psychological. This case study should not be seen as an intrinsic case study because campus gun violence has occurred, unfortunately, on several higher education campuses.

2. Anderson, R. A., Toles, M. P., Corazzini, K., McDaniel, R. R., & Colon-Emeric, C. (2014). Local interaction strategies and capacity for better care in nursing homes: A multiple case study. *BMC Health Services Research, 14*, 244–261. https://doi.org/10.1186/1472-6963-14-244

    In this *multiple case study*, see how R. A. Anderson et al. (2014) focus on the relationship patterns and management practices across four UK nursing homes involving 406 managers and staff over 6 months. The findings suggested that the capacity for delivering better resident care resulted from positive interaction strategies and pointed to the need for positive staff engagement with one another as a prerequisite for quality care.

3. Van Hout, M. C., & Bingham, T. (2013). "Silk Road," the virtual drug marketplace: A single case study of user experiences. *International Journal of Drug Policy, 23*(5), 385–391. https://doi.org/10.1016/j.drugpo.2013.01.005

    In this *intrinsic case study*, see how Van Hout and Bingham's study of the Silk Road as an online drug marketplace explored an individual user's "motives for online drug purchasing, experiences of accessing and using the website, drug information sourcing, decision making and purchasing, outcomes and settings for use and perspectives around security" (p. 385). The findings point to differences in relationships, participation, and feelings of safety compared with more traditional online and street sources of drug supply and shed light on the utility of Silk Road to maximize consumer decision making and harm reduction.

4. Frelin, A. (2015). Relational underpinnings and professionality—A case study of a teacher's practices involving students with experiences of school failure. *School Psychology International, 36*(6), 589–604. https://doi.org/10.1177/0143034315607412

   In this *instrumental case study*, see how Frelin's (2015) study of one teacher's practices negotiating relationships with students who have a history of school failure is bounded by the participant (Gunilla), by time (limited to data collection), and by place (situated at an institution offering the Swedish Introduction Programme). The study pointed to the importance of connecting to students with experiences of school failure and advanced practical implications for school psychologists to support teachers in negotiating student–teacher relationships.

TRY THIS NOW 4.2
LOCATING DEFINING FEATURES OF A QUALITATIVE APPROACH IN JOURNAL ARTICLES

Defining features help distinguish among qualitative approaches. Examine a journal article that identifies the use of each approach, such as the ones that appear in Appendices A–E and use the checklists in Figures 4.2, 4.4, 4.6, 4.8, and 4.10 to locate each defining feature. Where, in the article, did you find each defining feature? Which defining features were easy to find? Which ones were hard to find or even absent in a particular article? How might you use the defining features when designing your own studies?

COMPARING THE FIVE APPROACHES

All five approaches have in common the general process of research that begins with a research problem and proceeds to the questions, the data, the data analysis and interpretations, and the research report. Qualitative researchers have found it helpful at this point to see an overall sketch for each of the five approaches. From these sketches of the five approaches, we can identify fundamental differences among these types of qualitative research. Finally, we compare the five approaches relating the dimensions of foundational considerations (Table 4.1), data procedures (Table 4.2), and research reporting (Table 4.3).

In Table 4.1, we present four dimensions for distinguishing among the foundational considerations for the five approaches. At a most fundamental level, the five differ in what they are trying to accomplish—their research foci or the primary objectives of the studies. Exploring a life is different from generating a theory or describing the behavior of a cultural group. A couple of potential similarities among the designs should be noted. Narrative research, ethnography, and case study research may seem similar when the unit of analysis is a single individual. True, one may approach the study of a single individual from any of these three approaches; however, the types of data one would collect and analyze would differ considerably. In *narrative research*, the inquirer

TABLE 4.1 ■ Contrasting Foundational Considerations of Five Qualitative Approaches

Foundational Considerations	Narrative Research	Phenomenology	Grounded Theory	Ethnography	Case Study
Research focus of approach	Exploring the life of an individual	Understanding the essence of the experience	Developing a theory grounded in data from the field	Describing and interpreting a culture-sharing group	Developing an in-depth description and analysis of a case or multiple cases
Unit of analysis	Studying the lived experiences of one or more individuals	Studying several individuals who have shared the experience	Studying a process, an action, or an interaction involving many individuals	Studying a group that shares the same culture	Studying a bounded case such as an event, a program, an activity, or one or more individuals
Type of research problem best suited for approach	Restorying individual experiences	Describing the essence of a lived phenomenon	Grounding a theory in the views of participants	Describing and interpreting the shared patterns of culture of a group	Providing an in-depth understanding of a case or cases
Nature of disciplinary origins	Drawing from the humanities including anthropology, literature, history, psychology, and sociology	Drawing from philosophy, psychology, and education	Drawing from sociology	Drawing from anthropology and sociology	Drawing from psychology, law, political science, and medicine

TABLE 4.2 ■ Contrasting Data Procedures of Five Qualitative Approaches

Data Procedures	Narrative Research	Phenomenology	Grounded Theory	Ethnography	Case Study
Forms of data collection	Using primarily interviews and documents with a small number of individuals; artifacts may also be involved	Using primarily interviews with individuals who have shared the experience; documents, observations, and artifacts may also be considered	Using primarily interviews with individuals	Using primarily observations and interviews but perhaps collecting other sources during extended time in the ethnographic field site	Using multiple sources, such as interviews, observations, documents, and artifacts
Typical sample range	1 to 6 individuals (can be more)	5 to 25 individuals	20 to 60 individuals (can be fewer)	Varies greatly; often 10 to 30 individuals	1 to 6 cases
Strategies of data analysis	Analyzing data for stories, engaging in "restorying" and developing themes, often using a chronology	Analyzing data for significant statements, meaning units, textual and structural description, and description of the "essence"	Analyzing data through open coding, axial coding, and selective coding	Analyzing data through description of the culture-sharing group and themes about the group	Analyzing data through description of the case and themes of the case as well as cross-case themes

TABLE 4.3 ■ Contrasting Research Reporting of Five Qualitative Approaches

Research Reporting	Narrative Research	Phenomenology	Grounded Theory	Ethnography	Case Study
Introduction of written report	Focusing on participant(s) and nature of the story	Focusing on explaining the phenomenon	Focusing on the process (or action) that the theory is intended to explain	Focusing on the culture-sharing group being studied	Using entry vignette and then focusing on central features of the case
Description of research procedures	Stating the rationale, significance of individual experiences, and data procedures	Stating the rationale, philosophical assumptions, and data procedures	Stating the rationale and data procedures	Stating the rationale, type, and data procedures	Stating the rationale, type, and data procedures
Organization of research outcomes	Telling stories using a variety of ways involving restorying, theorizing, and narrative segments	Reporting how the phenomenon was experienced using significant statements and discussing meaning of themes	Developing theory involving open coding categories, axial coding, selective coding, theoretical propositions, and a model	Describing the culture and analyzing patterns of cultural themes with verbatim quotes	Providing first extensive description of the case followed by key issues (themes or issues) in the case
Concluding format	Interpreting patterns of meaning	Describing the "essence" of the experience	Advancing a theory and discussing lessons learned	Describing how a culture-sharing group works using a cultural portrait	Making case study assertions and advancing a closing vignette

focuses on the stories told by the individual and arranges these stories often in chronological order; in *ethnography*, the focus is on setting the individuals' stories within the context of their culture and culture-sharing group; in *case study research*, the single case is typically selected to illustrate an issue, and the researcher compiles a detailed description of the setting for the case. Our approach is to recommend—if the researcher wants to study a single individual—the narrative approach or a single case study because ethnography requires a much broader picture of the culture. Then, when comparing a narrative study and a single case to study a single individual, we feel that the narrative approach is seen as more appropriate because narrative studies *tend* to focus on a single individual, whereas case studies often involve more than one individual within a bounded case. The process of developing research question(s), which is covered in Chapter 6, can often be helpful in determining the suitability of the research problem for a specific approach. Moreover, although overlaps exist in discipline origin, some approaches have single-disciplinary traditions (e.g., grounded theory originating in sociology, ethnography founded in anthropology or sociology), and others have broad interdisciplinary backgrounds (e.g., narrative, case study).

The approaches employ similar data collection processes, including, in varying degrees, interviews, observations, documents, artifacts, and audiovisual and social media materials (see Table 4.2). The differences are apparent in terms of emphasis (e.g., more observations in ethnography, more interviews in grounded theory) and extent of data collection (e.g., only interviews in phenomenology, multiple forms in case study research to provide the in-depth case picture). At the data analysis stage, the differences are most pronounced. Not only is the distinction one of specificity of the analysis phase (e.g., grounded theory most specific, narrative research less defined) but the number of steps to be undertaken can vary (e.g., extensive steps in phenomenology, fewer steps in ethnography). We hesitate to offer exact sample sizes because samples can vary greatly and depend on various factors. Key considerations for researchers involve the time and financial resources available for the study as well as the study topic and the number of participants willing and available to be involved.

The research reporting of each approach, the written report, takes shape from all the processes before it (see Table 4.3). Stories about an individual's life comprise narrative research. A description of the essence of the experience of the phenomenon becomes a phenomenology. A theory, often portrayed in a visual model, emerges in grounded theory, and a holistic view of how a culture-sharing group works results in an ethnography. An in-depth study of a bounded system or a case (or several cases) becomes a case study. The general writing structures of the study report may be used in designing a journal-article-length study. However, because of the numerous steps in each, they also have applicability as chapters of a dissertation or a book-length work. We discuss the differences here because the reader, with an introductory knowledge of each approach, now can sketch the general "architecture" of a study within each approach. Certainly, this architecture will emerge and be shaped differently by the conclusion of the study, but it provides a framework for the design issues to follow. For each approach, the introduction describes the particular focus of the research and tends to familiarize the reader to the research problem and research question(s). The research procedures are subsequently outlined, often including a rationale for use of the approach and details related to the data procedures for the study.

Note the unique organizing framework related to each approach and specifically the variations in how the research outcomes can be presented. Providing in-depth descriptions is common across all the approaches, but how the descriptions are organized varies; whereas narrative research might use a chronology for telling stories, a phenomenology may use significant statements as the organizing structure for reporting how the phenomenon was experienced. Similarly, how a research report concludes also varies by the approach; whereas it is common practice to use a closing vignette in a case study, a cultural portrait is commonly used in an ethnography referring to overall interpretations, lessons learned, and questions raised representing the group. These structures should be considered as general templates at this time. In Chapter 5, we will examine five published journal articles, with each study illustrating one of the five approaches, and further explore the writing structure of each.

CHAPTER CHECK-IN

1. What research problems are appropriate for each of the approaches?
   - List three different research problems that are of interest to you. Begin with identifying the research foci and identify which approaches might be appropriate. Then consider the unit of analysis for your study and identify which approaches might be appropriate. Use Table 4.1 to help you. Can you see the subtle differences among the research approaches and the problems that best fit each approach?

2. What defining features can you apply within a qualitative study design for each of the five approaches?
   - Select one of the five approaches, and write a brief description of the approach, including a definition and the procedures associated with the approach. Include at least five references to the literature to ground your proposal. Can you include at least two new references not mentioned in this Chapter?

3. Can you transform the study focus, procedures, and writing structure for each of the five approaches?
   - Access a proposed qualitative study that you would like to conduct. Begin with presenting it as a narrative study, and then shape it into a phenomenology, a grounded theory, an ethnography, and finally a case study. Compare differences across each approach related to the focus of the study and the data collection and analysis procedures. Can you discuss how the written report would be differently structured across the approaches?

SUMMARY

In this chapter, we introduced each of the five approaches to qualitative research—narrative studies, phenomenology, grounded theory, ethnography, and case study. In each description, we provided a focus and definition, some history of the development of the approach, defining features, and the popular forms it has assumed, as well as detailed major procedures for conducting each approach. Finally, we discussed some of the major challenges in conducting each approach, and emerging directions. To highlight some of the differences among the approaches, we provided overview tables that contrast foundational considerations (research focus, unit of analysis, type of research problem, nature of disciplinary origins), data procedures (forms of data collection, sample size ranges, and data analysis strategies), and research reporting (research outcomes and structure of written report). In the next chapter, we will examine five studies that illustrate each approach and look more closely at the compositional structure of each type of approach.

CHAPTER KEY TERMS

Case study research
Ethnographic research
Grounded theory research
Narrative research
Phenomenological research
Research approaches

Research focus
Research outcome
Research problem
Research questions
Unit of analysis
Writing structures

TERMS SPECIFIC TO NARRATIVE RESEARCH

Artifacts
Arts-based study
Autobiographical study
Autoethnography
Biographical study
Digital storytelling
Epiphanies

Historical contexts
Life course stages
Life history
Lived experiences
Oral history
Restorying
Stories

TERMS SPECIFIC TO PHENOMENOLOGICAL RESEARCH

Clusters of meaning
Epoché (or bracketing)
Essential, invariant structure (or essence)
Hermeneutical (or interpretive) phenomenology
Horizontalization
Intentionality of consciousness
Lived experiences

Phenomenology of practice
Phenomenological reflection
Structural description
Transcendental (or descriptive, empirical, psychological) phenomenology
Textural description
Phenomenological data analysis
Phenomenon

TERMS SPECIFIC TO GROUNDED THEORY RESEARCH

Axial coding
Category
Causal conditions
Central phenomenon
Coding paradigm or logic diagram
Conditional or consequential matrix
Conditional context
Constant comparative
Constructivist grounded theory
Dimensionalized

Intervening conditions
In vivo codes
Memoing
Open coding
Properties
Propositions
Selective coding
Substantive-level theory
Theoretical sampling

TERMS SPECIFIC TO ETHNOGRAPHIC RESEARCH

Analysis of the culture-sharing group
Complete observer
Complete participant
Critical ethnography
Cultural behaviors
Cultural interpretation
Cultural portrait
Culture
Culture-sharing group
Deception
Description of the culture-sharing group

Emic
Etic
Ethnographic fieldwork
Ethnography
Holistic perspective
Key informants (or participants)
Nonparticipant observation
Language
Participant observation
Realist ethnography
Social structure

TERMS SPECIFIC TO CASE STUDY RESEARCH

Analysis of themes
Assertions
Bounded system
Case
Case description
Case themes
Collective case study
Context of the case
Cross-case analysis
Direct interpretation
Embedded analysis

Intrinsic case study
Instrumental case study
Holistic analysis
Multisite case study
Multiple sources of information
Naturalistic generalizations
Patterns
Purposeful case sampling
Within-case analysis
Within-site case study

FURTHER READINGS

Several readings extend this brief overview of each of the five approaches to inquiry. In Chapter 1, we presented the key books that were used to craft discussions about each approach. Here we expand this list for each of the qualitative approaches in the chapter. The list should not be considered exhaustive, and readers are encouraged to seek out additional readings in the end-of-book reference list.

Narrative Research

Clandinin, D. J., & Connelly, F. M. (2000). *Narrative inquiry: Experience and story in qualitative research*. Jossey-Bass.

Jean Clandinin and Michael Connelly weave helpful references throughout the text, describing their own journey of becoming narrative researchers. Of particular help to the beginning narrative researcher is the final chapter on persistent concerns and the comprehensive discussion of ethics within narrative inquiry.

Czarniawska, B. (2004). *Narratives in social science research*. Sage.

Barbara Czarniawska explores the various uses of narrative and its analysis in this important resource. Especially helpful is the use of her own research examples to illustrate concepts from conceptualization to telling of the stories.

Daiute, C. (2014). *Narrative inquiry: A dynamic approach*. Sage.

Colette Daiute provides essential scaffolding for undertaking what she calls dynamic narrative inquiry using examples, activities, and tips. Of particular note is how she builds on practices of daily life and makes connections to narrative research.

Phenomenological Research

De Santis, D., Hopkins, B. C., & Majolino, C. (Eds.). (2022). *The Routledge handbook of phenomenology and phenomenological philosophy*. Routledge.

This book is essential reading for researchers in philosophy studying phenomenology. We found Chapter 44 on Heidegger and Chapter 46 on Husserl particularly helpful.

Giorgi, A. (2009). *A descriptive phenomenological method in psychology: A modified Husserlian approach*. Duquesne University Press.

Amedeo Giorgi uses illustrative research examples to offer practical steps for applying the descriptive phenomenological method. This is essential reading for those working in the psychology field

Stewart, D., & Mickunas, A. (1990). *Exploring phenomenology: A guide to the field and its literature* (2nd ed.). Ohio University Press.

In this important work, David Stewart and Algis Mickunas provide an essential introduction to Husserl, Heidegger, and the various strands of phenomenology through the first half of the 20th century. Particularly helpful is the discussion about traditional challenges inherent to phenomenology.

van Manen, M. (1990). *Researching lived experience: Human science for an action sensitive pedagogy*. State University of New York Press.

Max van Manen describes the phenomenological tradition and presents methods and processes for engaging in phenomenological research. Among the key contributions is Chapter 5 focused on writing phenomenology.

Grounded Theory Research

Birks, M., & Mills, J. (2023). *Grounded theory: A practical guide* (3rd ed.). Sage.

Melanie Birks and Jane Mills's use of figures and pedagogical features throughout helps the reader to make sense of the text. In particular, the critical thinking questions guide the reader in self-assessment of the material and the "window into grounded theory" feature provides important insights.

Bryant, A., & Charmaz, K. (Eds.). (2007b). *The SAGE handbook of grounded theory*. Sage.

Handbooks are often a logical starting place for researchers new to an approach, and Alan Bryant and Kathy Charmaz provide useful guiding practices for conducting grounded theory. Specifically, we found the chapters on historical development by the editors and memo-writing by Lora Lempert to be noteworthy.

Clarke, A. E. (2005). *Situational analysis: Grounded theory after the postmodern turn*. Sage.

Adele Clarke represents her thinking using illustrative maps to enhance visibility of complexity. A unique aspect is her conceptualization of a situation as including the missing data (e.g., environmental factors) in addition to what has typically been considered as context.

Urquhart, C. (2022). *Grounded theory for qualitative research* (2nd ed.). Sage.

Cathy Urquhart's extensive examples are helpful for guiding researchers new to grounded theory. The chapter on theoretical sampling is especially unique.

Ethnographic Research

Atkinson, P. A. (2015). *For ethnography*. Sage.

At the heart of Paul Atkinson's book is the use of field research in ethnographic studies. He provides easy-to-follow guiding principles for engaging in ethnographic fieldwork.

Hammersley, M., & Atkinson, P. (2019). *Ethnography: Principles in practice* (4th. ed.). Routledge.

Martyn Hammersley and Paul Atkinson offer access to current discussions about practices in ethnography. We find the chapter on ethics especially helpful.

Madison, D. S. (2019). *Critical ethnography: Method, ethics, and performance* (3rd ed.). Sage.

D. Soyini Madison provides important insights about the role of theory in planning processes in a critical ethnography through the use of three case studies.

Wolcott, H. F. (2010). *Ethnography lessons: A primer*. Left Coast.

Harry Wolcott presents challenges and successes through his 5-decade ethnographic career sprinkled with personal interactions with notable anthropologists. Important contributions are the ethical dilemmas experienced by Wolcott and his students, and the lessons relevant for all qualitative researchers.

Case Study Research

Gomm, R., Hammersley, M., & Foster, P. (Eds.). (2000). *Case study method: Key issues, key texts*. Sage.

Robert Gomm, Martyn Hammersley, and Peter Foster have brought together authors to discuss practices and challenges in case study research. Specifically, we found the chapters on generalizability by Yvonna Lincoln and Egon Guba and case comparison by Stanley Lieberson to be noteworthy.

Mills, A. J., Durepos, G., & Wiebe, E. (Eds.). (2010). *Encyclopedia of case study research*. Sage.

In the entries, the authors trace the long history of case study research and offer examples and their perspectives of future directions.

Schwandt, T., & Gates, E. F. (2018). Case study methodology. In N. K. Denzin & Y. S. Lincoln (Eds.), *Handbook of qualitative research* (5th ed., pp. 341–358). Sage.

In this chapter, Thomas Schwandt and Emily F. Gates provide an updated view of case study research. Their discussion across the case study approaches of Stake and Yin is noteworthy.

Stake, R. E. (2006). *Multiple case study analysis*. Guilford.

This book offers a rare focus on multiple case studies, yet Robert Stake also includes a chapter on single cases. The book leads the reader through conducting an example of a multiple case study (and provides worksheets)—the multinational Step by Step Case Study Project.

5 FIVE DIFFERENT QUALITATIVE STUDIES

> **QUESTIONS FOR DISCUSSION**
>
> - What stories are collaboratively told in the sample narrative study?
> - What shared experience is explored in the sample phenomenological study?
> - What theory is developed in the sample grounded theory study?
> - What culture-sharing group is described in the sample ethnographic study?
> - What understandings of the case are presented in the sample case study?
> - How do the defining features of the five approaches differ across the samples?
> - How does a researcher choose among the five approaches for a particular study?

We have always felt that the best way to learn how to write a qualitative study is to view a number of published qualitative journal articles and to look closely at the way they were composed. If an individual plans on undertaking, for example, a grounded theory study, we would suggest that they collect about 20 grounded theory published journal articles, study each one carefully, select the most complete one that advances *all* the defining characteristics of grounded theory, and then model their own project after that one. This same process would hold true for an individual conducting any of the other approaches to qualitative inquiry, such as a narrative study, a phenomenology, an ethnography, or a case study. Short of this ideal, we want to get you started toward building this collection by suggesting an exemplar of each approach as discussed in this chapter.

Each of these five published studies represents one of the types of qualitative approaches being discussed in this book. They are found in Appendices A, B, C, D and E. The best way to proceed, we believe, is to first read the entire article in the appendix and then return to our summary of the article to compare your understanding with ours. Next, read our analysis of how the article illustrates a good model of the approach to research and incorporates the defining characteristics we introduced in Chapter 4. At the conclusion of this chapter, we reflect on why one might choose one approach over another when conducting a qualitative study.

The first study, by Chan (2010), as found in Appendix A, illustrates a narrative study of a single Chinese immigrant student, Ai Mei Zhang, as she attends a Canadian middle school and as she interacts with her family. The second article, a phenomenological study by Chance (2022), located in Appendix B, is a study about individuals who have experienced adversity as Black women in higher education leadership. The third article is a grounded theory study by Trip et al. (2019), as found in Appendix C. It presents a study of the caregiving relationship between aging people who have intellectual disabilities and their families. The study offers an explanation of navigating transitions across the life course. The fourth article is an ethnographic study by Mac an Ghaill and Haywood (2015), as presented in Appendix D, about the changing cultural condition of British-born, working-class Pakistani and Bangladeshi young Muslim men during the late 2000s. The local experiences of growing up in a rapidly changing Britain shaped the identity of young Muslim men as members of a broader social community. The final article, Goodrum et al. (2022), located in Appendix E is a qualitative case study of a school shooting where two students died. It examines the match between guidelines and activities in the threat assessment process and how that match influenced decision-making. In so doing the case study describes the way the school's organizational structure and culture shaped and hindered violence prevention practices. These exemplars were chosen for their usefulness as models of the defining features for each approach discussed in Chapter 4, as well as for their disciplinary, geographical, and participant diversity.

A NARRATIVE STUDY (CHAN, 2010; SEE APPENDIX A)

Chan, E. (2010). Living in the space between participant and researcher as a narrative inquirer: Examining ethnic identity of Chinese Canadian students as conflicting stories to live by. *The Journal of Educational Research, 103*(2), 113–122. https://doi.org/10.1080/00220670903323792

This is the story of a Chinese immigrant student, Ai Mei Zhang, a seventh- and eighth-grade student at Bay Street School in Toronto, Canada. Ai Mei was chosen for study by the researcher because she could inform how ethnic identity is shaped by expectations from school and her teacher, her peers at school, and her home. Ai Mei told stories about specific incidents in her life (e.g., a family dinner, new student orientation), and the author based her narrative article on these stories as well as observations in her classroom. The researcher also conducted interviews with Ai Mei and other students, took extensive field notes, and sought active participation in Ai Mei's school activities (e.g., Multicultural Night), and classroom conversations between Ai Mei and her classmates. The author's overriding interest was in exploring the conflicting stories that emerged during this data collection.

The author introduced the study citing changing school demographics and the need for greater understanding of the lived experiences of immigrant and minority students' daily transitions between home and school. The author identified Dewey's (1938) philosophy of the interconnectedness between experience and education as the theoretical foundation for the study of a three-dimensional narrative inquiry space (Clandinin & Connelly, 2000). In this study, the author followed procedures by Clandinin and colleagues (2006) for describing the interwoven lives of children and teachers.

From a thematic analysis of these data, the author presented several conflicting stories: tensions in friendship because Ai Mei hid her home language at school because it was seen as a hindrance to being accepted by English-speaking peers, pressure to use the school Chinese language and to use her maternal language at home with her family, multiple conflicting influences of parental versus peer expectations for behavior, and conflicts between family needs to help in the family business and teacher expectations to complete homework and prepare for tests and assignments. As a final element of the findings, the author reflected on her experiences in conducting the study, such as how the different events she participated in shaped her understanding, how opportunities arose to build trust, how her relationship with Ai Mei was negotiated, and how she developed a sense of advocacy for this young student. In the end, the study contributed to understanding the challenges of immigrant or minority students; the intersecting expectations of students, teachers, peers, and parents; and how the values of individuals in ethnic communities shaped these interactions. In a larger sense, this study informed the work of teachers and administrators working with diverse student populations, and served as an example of a "life-based literary narrative" (Chan, 2010, p. 121).

Examine Table 5.1 to see how this sample narrative study (Chan, 2010) presented well the defining features of a narrative study introduced in Chapter 4 (see also the text leading into Figure 4.2). Notice how each of the guiding design questions can help narrative researchers get started with a study idea.

TABLE 5.1 ■ Defining Features of Narrative Studies as Presented in Chan (2010) and Guiding Design Questions

Defining Features of Narrative Studies	As Presented in Chan (2010) Sample of a Narrative Study	Guiding Design Questions for a Narrative Researcher
Narrative researchers enable collaborative storytelling about the lived experiences of individuals.	The researcher made explicit the collaborative nature of how the stories about the lived experiences of a single individual were collected and the relationship that was built over time between the researcher and the participant in the study.	What individual (or individuals) will you study? How will you build a collaborative relationship with the individual(s)?
Narrative stories tell of individual experiences, and they may shed light on the identities of individuals and how they see themselves.	The research focused on the experiences of one individual, a Chinese immigrant student, Ai Mei Zhang and the cultural identity of this student and how parents, peers, and teachers shaped this identity.	What individual experiences will you focus on?
Narrative stories occur and are described within specific places or situations.	The researcher discussed the physical and social site of Bay Street School where most of the incidents reported in the narrative occurred.	What will be the contexts for your story?

(Continued)

Defining Features of Narrative Studies	As Presented in Chan (2010) Sample of a Narrative Study	Guiding Design Questions for a Narrative Researcher
Narrative stories are gathered through many different forms of data including conversations, observations, and artifacts.	The researcher gathered personal observations, interviews, school documents, samples of student work, and field notes that included attendance at events.	What data forms will inform your story?
Narrative stories are analyzed using varied strategies.	The researcher reported themes about "what happened" to the individual student, her parents, and at her school. The researcher also embedded excerpts of dialogue from her field notes.	How will you analyze the stories?
Narrative stories heard by researchers and co-created with participants are often shaped into a chronology.	The researcher did not use a chronology (after collecting data from the fall of 2001 to June 2003). From the themes, it was difficult to determine if one theme led to another.	How will you tell the overall story?
Narrative stories often contain turning points as organizing structures.	The overall narrative did not convey a specific turning point or epiphany. The researcher, however, highlighted specific tensions that arose in each of the themes (e.g., the tension between using Mandarin and Fujianese at home).	What writing structures, such as turning points, will you use to present your story?

Table 5.1 — Defining Features of Narrative Studies as Presented in Chan (2010) and Guiding Design Questions (*Continued*)

TRY THIS NOW 5.1
APPLYING THE DEFINING FEATURES OF NARRATIVE RESEARCH TO YOUR STUDY DESIGN

The defining features help guide researchers in designing their narrative inquiry. Use the guiding design questions from Table 5.1 to start thinking about the key aspects of the stories of the individual lived experiences you want to tell. Which of the questions were easier to answer for your study idea and which ones were harder?

A PHENOMENOLOGICAL STUDY (CHANCE, 2022; SEE APPENDIX B)

Chance, N. L. (2022). Resilient leadership: A phenomenological exploration into how Black women in higher education leadership navigate cultural adversity. *Journal of Humanistic Psychology, 62*(1), 44–78. https://doi.org/10.1177/00221678211003000

This study explored adversity and the lived experiences of U.S. Black women in higher education leadership. The researcher studied this topic because of the extensive personal and professional adversity that Black people, especially women, continue to face and overcome as a group. Thus, the purpose of this phenomenological study was "to explore and describe how Black women in higher education leadership navigate intersectionality, stereotype threat, and tokenism" (Chance, 2022, p. 52). The overall goal of exploring how Black women overcome adverse experiences within the context of higher education was to help develop and provide training and mentoring programs for Black women seeking leadership opportunities.

The author introduced the study by referring to the leadership ambitions of Black women and the significant challenges and adversity they experienced in higher education leadership. She turned to the literature to illustrate the many aspects of discrimination that Black women have had to navigate. She noted several studies exploring adversity experienced by Black women in higher education. However, their experiences had not been studied with a focus on intersectionality (such as the intersection of racism, sexism, and agism), stereotype threat, and isolation and tokenism. A phenomenological research design was the most appropriate design to allow Chance to explore and understand the lived experiences of Black women in higher education leadership positions.

Blending convenience, purposive, and snowball sampling techniques, the design involved recruiting participants who (a) were Black women; (b) served as president/chancellor, vice president/chancellor, or provost of a 4-year college or university in the United States; and (c) had obtained or were completing a terminal degree. A total of nine participants were involved in the study and completed a Lived Experiences Timeline activity, a demographic survey, and an interview using Zoom videoconferencing software. During the interviews, the researcher asked participants about their experiences, learnings, challenges, or obstacles they faced to achieve their positions, to overcome adversity, and to help future generations facing adversity.

The author used Moustakas's (1994) modified Stevick-Colaizzi-Keen phenomenological data analysis procedures. The interviews were transcribed, and participants were asked to review the transcripts and verify the content and accuracy. Following this member-checking, the researcher manually reviewed each transcript and used the qualitative data coding and analysis software Dedoose to further analyze the transcripts. Horizontalizing helped the author to move from general descriptions to specific examples and ultimately to the structural and textual descriptions of context and setting. Throughout the analysis, the investigator engaged in the reflexive process of epoché, using notetaking and reviewing bracketed information for each code. The intersectionality framework was used "as a lens to observe, understand, and describe the themes that emerged" (Chance, 2022, p. 56). Through the recurring patterns in the transcripts, the author identified themes expressing the meanings of participants about their lived experiences. Member checking was further used by asking participants to validate the identified themes. The analysis led to four primary themes and two subthemes that addressed how participants navigated the adversity that they faced. The findings section of this study reported each of the themes and subthemes and provided many quotes and perspectives.

The study ended with a discussion where the authors described the overall "essence" of the nine Black women's leadership experiences with adversity as promoting resilience and leadership development. The implications advanced knowledge that will enlighten the next generation of young aspiring Black women leaders experiencing adversity and it called for closing the racial-gender leadership gap for Black women. The limitations pointed to the need for further research of the lived experiences of Black, Indigenous, and People of Color in leadership within and outside of academia to expand the overall understanding of leadership development.

Examine Table 5.2 for how this sample phenomenology (Chance, 2022) illustrated the defining features of phenomenology introduced in Chapter 4 (see also the text leading into Figure 4.4). Notice how each of the guiding design questions can help phenomenological researchers get started with a study idea.

TABLE 5.2 ■ Defining Features of Phenomenology as Presented in Chance (2022) and Guiding Design Questions

Defining Features of Phenomenology	As Presented in Chance (2022) Sample of Phenomenology	Guiding Design Questions for Phenomenological Researchers
An emphasis on a phenomenon to be explored	The author examined the phenomenon of adversity and the lived experiences of Black women in higher education leadership.	What is the phenomenon you are exploring?
The exploration of the phenomenon with a group of individuals who have all experienced the phenomenon	The research sought to explore and understand how nine Black women in higher education leadership navigated the adverse challenges of intersectionality, stereotype threat, and tokenism.	Has the group of individuals in your study all experienced the phenomenon you are exploring?
A philosophical discussion about the basic ideas involved in conducting a phenomenology	The researcher only briefly mentioned that she ascribed to the hermeneutic school of thought and was personally vested and experienced with the phenomenon.	Have you studied and incorporated in your study some of the basic philosophical assumptions of phenomenology?
In some forms of phenomenology, the researcher brackets themselves out of the study by discussing personal experiences with the phenomenon.	The researcher described epoché through notetaking. This bracketing helped to reflect on the context of the codes and set aside personal beliefs and experiences.	What bracketing efforts will you take in your study?

Defining Features of Phenomenology	As Presented in Chance (2022) Sample of Phenomenology	Guiding Design Questions for Phenomenological Researchers
A data collection procedure typically involves interviewing individuals who have experienced the phenomenon.	The data collection consisted of nine interviews conducted over Zoom videoconferencing software and incorporating the Lived Experiences Timeline activity and a demographic survey.	What data forms will you use to capture individuals' experiences of the phenomenon?
A systematic data analysis moves from narrow units of analysis, to broader units, and a final descriptive "essence" of the phenomenon.	The authors followed Moustakas's (1994) procedures. These procedures included a table illustrating the theme clusters and meanings and working from the raw data to the "essence" of the study of the phenomenon.	How will you systematically analyze your data to develop the "essence" of the shared phenomenon?
A descriptive ending for phenomenology of the essence of participants' experience with the lived phenomenon	Following the presentation of four themes, the study ended by describing the "essence" of adversity promoting resilience and yielding leadership development.	Will you conclude your study with an "essence" description of the phenomenon including "what" the participants experienced and "how" they experienced it?

TRY THIS NOW 5.2
APPLYING THE DEFINING FEATURES OF PHENOMENOLOGY TO YOUR STUDY DESIGN

Applying the defining features helps guide researchers in designing their own phenomenological research. Use the guiding design questions from Table 5.2 to start thinking about the key aspects of a shared experience of a phenomenon you want to explore. Which of the questions were easier to answer for your study idea and which ones were harder?

A GROUNDED THEORY STUDY (TRIP ET AL., 2019; SEE APPENDIX C)

Trip, H., Whitehead, L., Crowe, M., Mirfin-Veitch, B., & Daffue, C. (2019). Aging with intellectual disabilities in families: Navigating ever-changing seas—A theoretical model. *Qualitative Health Research, 29*(11), 1595–1610. https://doi.org/10.1177/1049732319845344

This grounded theory study sought to develop a theory of the nature and dynamics of caregiving and receiving for older people with intellectual disability and their families.

It was premised on studies about aging and future planning that provided little evidence about the characteristics of the caregiving relationship. To this end, the researchers described using the constructivist grounded theory approach to explore the dynamic nature of the caregiving relationship between people with an intellectual disability and family members. This relationship involved a process of engagement in building a collective understanding of experiences requiring constant reflexivity on the part of the researchers (Charmaz, 2006, 2014). The authors interviewed 19 people with intellectual disabilities who met specific criteria: approximately 40 years of age, a mild to moderate level of intellectual disability, expressive language, ability to consent to participate, and living with or supported by someone they identified as "family' for at least 5 years. These participants then nominated 28 family members to participate in the research. Participants were recruited in various ways, including through primary health care settings, advertisements and public notices, and snowball sampling.

The methods in this study followed the Charmaz constructivist approach to grounded theory (Charmaz, 2014). The data collection and preliminary analysis procedures were undertaken simultaneously as the researchers refined their understandings of the caregiving relationship. The researchers used semi-structured open-ended questions to guide the sharing of experiences. Up to three face-to-face contacts were made with participants and their family members ranging from 30 to 150 minutes. Participants were invited to review the transcripts as a means of member checking. The data were analyzed through coding, categorizing, development of concepts, and theorizing. The authors described their extensive use of memoing to capture reflexivity and to distill the historical, current, and prospective context offered by participants. The researchers used tables to display how their codes evolved into categories and eventually to concepts.

The authors presented demographic information about the participants alongside a figure of the theoretical model advancing three concepts visually representing "navigating ever-changing seas." The researchers embedded quotes within their descriptions and discussed the "sea" as a metaphor representing a lack of a definitive beginning or ending in understanding aging and future planning. This metaphor also extended to include "navigation" (decision-making and purpose) as ongoing, and the ever-changing intrinsic and extrinsic factors of the participants. In their discussion of the theoretical model, the authors centered on how decision-making tended to shift, evolve, and devolve in the caregiver relationship and how it compared with existing theoretical models in the literature. In conclusion, this grounded theory study further elucidated the complexities of intergenerational caregiving by identifying the experiences of those in the caregiving relationship as negotiating and navigating decision-making. Using this model with individuals and their families can help unpack the nature of caregiving and decision-making, promote engagement with health and disability systems, enable future planning, and improve health care outcomes of all members in the system of care.

Examine Table 5.3 to see how this sample grounded theory (Trip et al., 2019) met the defining features of a grounded theory study discussed in Chapter 4 (see also the text leading into Figure 4.6). Notice how each of the guiding design questions can help grounded theory researchers get started with a study idea.

TABLE 5.3 ■ Defining Features of Grounded Theory Studies as Presented in Trip et al. (2019) and Guiding Design Questions

Defining Features of Grounded Theory	As Presented in Trip et al. (2019) Sample of Grounded Theory	Guiding Design Questions for Grounded Theory Researchers
Grounded theory research focuses on a process or an action that has distinct steps or phases that occur over time.	This study's central focus was to understand the caregiving relationship process of aging people with intellectual disabilities in families and advance a theoretical model consisting of three major concepts.	What action or process are you exploring in your study?
In a grounded theory study, the researcher seeks, in the end, to develop a theory of this process or action.	A theory emerged to help explain how people with intellectual disability and their caregivers navigate ever-changing transitions in the life course. The theoretical model used the metaphor of a "sea" to advance the theory.	What theoretical model will you present as an outcome of your study?
Memoing involves the grounded theory researcher writing down ideas about the evolving theory.	The researchers described their extensive use of memoing to capture reflexivity and to distill the historical, current, and prospective context offered by participants.	Will you engage in and report on your use of memoing in your study?
The data collection and analysis procedures are undertaken simultaneously and iteratively.	The researchers described the simultaneous data collection and analysis involving a series of face-to-face interviews with participants and their family members (see Figure 1 in Appendix C).	What types of data will you collect in your project? Will you be engaging in data collection and analysis simultaneously?
The inductive procedures involved in data analysis are described in relation to the type of grounded theory approach.	The researchers analyzed the data by developing codes, categories, concepts, and a theoretical model using the constructivist approach of Charmaz (2014).	Will you use systematic or constructivist steps in your data analysis? What will these steps be?
A detailed description of the theoretical model emerging from the data is conveyed.	The researchers provided a detailed description of the theoretical model including verbatim quotes and a visual representation (see Figure 2 in Appendix C).	How will you present your theoretical model in your study?

> **TRY THIS NOW 5.3**
> **APPLYING THE DEFINING FEATURES OF GROUNDED THEORY RESEARCH TO YOUR STUDY DESIGN**
>
> Applying the defining features helps guide researchers in designing their own grounded theory study. Use the guiding design questions from Table 5.3 to start thinking about the key aspects of developing a theory to explain a concept, action, or process that occurs over time. Which of the questions were easier to answer for your study idea and which ones were harder?

AN ETHNOGRAPHIC STUDY (MAC AN GHAILL & HAYWOOD, 2015; SEE APPENDIX D)

Mac an Ghaill, M., & Haywood, C. (2015). British-born Pakistani and Bangladeshi young men: Exploring unstable concepts of Muslim, Islamophobia and racialization. *Critical Sociology, 41*(1), 97–114. https://doi.org/10.1177/0896920513518947

This ethnographic study described the changing cultural conditions of a group of British born, working-class Pakistani and Bangladeshi young men over 3 years. The study involved young men born and raised in Birmingham, England, an area with the highest number of self-identified Muslims for a local authority in the United Kingdom. The authors focused on the group's culturally reductive representations of Islam, the Muslim community, and being a young Muslim man within the "urgent need to critically interrogate the assumed social separateness, cultural fixity and boundedness of religious, ethnic and national categories of difference that they [the group under study] claim are imputed to them" (Mac an Ghaill & Haywood, 2015, p. 98). The participants were young men who were not only friends but also part of a broader social community described as attending the same youth and community organizations and colleges, sharing the same employers, and participating together in leisure activities. The study explored the group of 25 young men's "geographically-specific local experiences of growing up in a rapidly changing Britain" (p. 99). The researchers described how their established reputation for social commitment to the area and previous work with families in the local community enabled access to the participants.

Ethnographic data collection methods provided insights into the young men's growing up, family, schooling, social life, and local community. The researchers collected in-depth group and life history interviews during extensive ethnographical fieldwork over a 3-year period. Further understandings were gleaned from observations, informal conversations, and interviews with parents and community representatives through snowball sampling. Braun and Clarke's (2006) thematic analysis guided the data analysis of each of the methods. From the integration of data sources, the authors described group members' generational-specific experiences in relation to the racialization of their ethnicities and changes in how they negotiated the meanings attached to being Muslim. The authors ended with a broad level of abstraction beyond the themes to suggest how the group made sense of the range of social and cultural exclusions they experienced during a time of rapid change within their city. In short, the authors identified a complex situation for a group of Bangladeshi and Pakistani young men and how they interacted and experienced ethnicity and demarcation of religious and cultural belonging. Unlike other critical approaches, the study did not end with a call for social transformation. Instead, it ended with a call for further efforts to validate the findings such as through member checking with group members. The authors cautioned readers to carefully consider ways to understand the young men's own participation and the influence of local contexts and broader social and economic processes in identity formation.

Examine Table 5.4 to see how Mac an Ghaill and Haywood's (2015) sample ethnography illustrated the defining features of an ethnographic study as mentioned in Chapter 4 (see also the text leading into Figure 4.8). Notice how each of the guiding design questions can help grounded theory researchers get started with a study idea.

TABLE 5.4 ■ Defining Features of Ethnography as Presented in Mac an Ghaill and Haywood (2015) and Guiding Design Questions

Defining Features of Ethnography	As Presented in Mac an Ghaill & Haywood (2015) Sample of Ethnography	Guiding Design Questions for Ethnographic Researchers
Ethnographic research focuses on developing a complex, complete description of the culture of a group—the entire culture-sharing group or a subset of a group.	This ethnographic research examined the culture-sharing group of British-born, working-class Pakistani and Bangladeshi young men. This group had been in contact for some time as a community.	What is the culture-sharing group you are studying?
Ethnographic researchers look for patterns among the group's various activities.	The researchers described the group of 25 British-born, working-class Pakistani and Bangladeshi young men and their ideas of their generational-specific experiences (e.g., racialization of religion, the central role that religion plays in the process of racialization, and Islamophobia as a contemporary form of racialization of Muslims).	Has the group been in contact over a period of time to develop shared patterns? What patterns (e.g., of behavior, language, rituals, actions) will you be looking for as you study this culture-sharing group?
Ethnographic researchers use theory to focus their attention.	Consistent with critical ethnography, the researchers used a combination of materialist and postcolonial theoretical frameworks and young men's accounts to explain the groups' changing cultural condition.	How will you use theory in your study?

(Continued)

TABLE 5.4 ■ Defining Features of Ethnography as Presented in Mac an Ghaill and Haywood (2015) and Guiding Design Questions (*Continued*)

Defining Features of Ethnography	As Presented in Mac an Ghaill & Haywood (2015) Sample of Ethnography	Guiding Design Questions for Ethnographic Researchers
Ethnographic researchers engage in extensive data collection and fieldwork.	The authors engaged in participant observation of the group for 3 years. They also conducted in-depth group and life history interviews, had informal conversations, and interviewed parents and community representatives.	What types of data will you collect about the culture-sharing group?
An ethnography includes verbatim quotes as well as the views of the participants (emic) and of the researcher (etic).	The researchers formed a cultural interpretation from the participant (emic) data and the researcher's field notes (etic data). Their interpretation took the form of themes (i.e., racialization of their ethnicities and changes in terms of how they negotiated the meanings attached to being Muslim).	How will you present the information collected from the cultural group?
An ethnography often contains a cultural portrait of a culture-sharing group or a subset of a group.	The researchers' cultural portrait suggested how the group made sense of the range of social and cultural exclusions they experienced during a time of rapid change within their city. The portrait also presented a complex view of Bangladeshi and Pakistani young men, their interaction and their ethnicity, religion, and cultural belonging.	What description will you advance to give readers an understanding of how the culture-sharing group works?

TRY THIS NOW 5.4
APPLYING THE DEFINING FEATURES OF ETHNOGRAPHY TO YOUR STUDY DESIGN

Applying the defining features helps guide researchers in designing their own ethnography. Use the guiding design questions from Table 5.4 to start thinking about the key aspects of the culture-sharing group you want to describe. Which of the questions were easier to answer for your study idea and which ones were harder?

A CASE STUDY (GOODRUM ET AL., 2022; SEE APPENDIX E)

Goodrum, S., Slepicka, J., Woodward, W., & Kingston, B. (2022). Learning from error in violence prevention: A school shooting as an organizational accident. *Sociology of Education, 95*(4), 257–275. https://doi.org/10.1177/00380407221120431

This qualitative case study of a school shooting—in which two students died—examined how the school's organizational structure and culture impeded the prevention of violence. The authors presented the case to provide "a rich and meaningful investigation of the structural factors that influenced the situation and decision-making" (Goodrum et al., 2022, p. 261). The authors introduced the study by citing descriptive statistics indicating the increased frequency of and higher number of casualties from school shootings. The authors point to studies from the fields of sociology and organizational psychology suggesting that these school failures of foresight to prevent shootings arise from loosely coupled organizational structures and from a U.S. gun culture. By highlighting the unique circumstances of the current case as "one of only two known cases where a threat assessment was conducted with a student prior to their deadly attack" (p. 260), the focus of the study on the case itself represented an "intrinsic" case study despite the lack of the authors' explicit identification as such.

The case study procedures were guided by Stake (1995, 2005) and Yin (2017) among others, and drew primarily on existing depositions from an investigative arbitration of the circumstances leading to the school attack. The various sources of data included deposition testimony from 12 school officials and more than 4,000 pages of school and law enforcement records. Each deposition testimony lasted between 2 and 8 hours and offered participants' perceptions and experiences in their own words detailing narrative accounts of the circumstances, interactions, and communications prior to the attack. The data analysis of the deposition testimonies was guided by Strauss's (1987) guidelines for line-by-line coding; the qualitative software program NVivo aided the analysis. The records provided supplementary contextual information. The case centered on examining educators' decision-making processes to understand the organization's management of and response to a troubled student. As a result of this understanding, the authors aimed to develop effective intervention strategies.

Following a description of background information on the school, the student, and his family, the results from the data analysis illustrated themes about "the ways the tightly and loosely coupled components of the school and district influenced the implementation of federal threat assessment guidelines, encouraged a culture of autonomous decision-making, and created structural secrets about the extent and seriousness of the student's troubles" (Goodrum et al., 2022, p. 262). The case assertion claimed that the "organizational structure and culture of schools may impede the prevention of violence in America's schools, specifically threat assessment and management for students of concern" (p. 257). The case study concluded with discussions of recommendations for building organizational structures and cultures that support violence prevention in schools.

Examine Table 5.5 for more on how this sample case study (Goodrum et al., 2022) illustrated the defining features of a case study introduced in Chapter 4 (see also the text leading into Figure 4.10). Notice how each of the guiding design questions can help case study researchers get started with a study idea.

TABLE 5.5 ■ Defining Features of Case Study Research as Presented in Goodrum et al. (2022) and Guiding Design Questions

Defining Features of Case Study Research	As Presented in Goodrum et al. (2022) Sample of a Case Study	Guiding Design Questions for Case Study Researchers
Case study research begins with the identification of an intention for the case study and a focus of analysis on the specific case or cases that will be described and analyzed.	The case in this study consisted of one high school that experienced school violence when two students died at the hands of an armed student.	What will be the case(s) you are studying?
The key to the case identification is that it is bounded and relevant to the intent of conducting the case study.	The case described in this study was a bounded system, delimited by the unique circumstance of a high school shooting where a threat assessment had been conducted with a student prior to his deadly attack.	How will your case be bounded by time and place?
The intent of conducting the case study is important to focus the procedures for the particular type.	The intent was to report an intrinsic case study. Thus, the focus was on the case itself as "one of only two known cases where a threat assessment was conducted with a student prior to their deadly attack" (p. 260).	Will your case study be an instrumental or intrinsic case?
A case study presents an in-depth understanding of the case drawing on many forms of data.	The extensive sources of data included deposition testimony from school and district officials, materials from the sheriff's investigation, documents from the school district, and exhibits produced during deposition testimony.	What data forms will you use to describe and analyze the case?
The selection of how to approach the data analysis in a case study will differ and often depend on type.	The analysis began with a detailed case background discussion of the school.	How will you analyze your data to describe the case?
The case description involves identifying and interpreting themes.	The researchers reported on themes about tightly and loosely coupled structure, and structural secrets about a student of concern.	What themes will you develop about your case?
Case studies often end with conclusions formed by the researcher about the overall meaning delivered from the case(s).	The study concluded with the presentation of an assertion about the impeding roles of organizational structure and culture of schools to prevent violence in America's schools, specifically threat assessment and management of students of concern. The authors discussed recommendations for building organizational structures and cultures that support violence prevention in schools.	What generalizations and recommendations will you make about your case?

TRY THIS NOW 5.5
APPLYING THE DEFINING FEATURES OF CASE STUDY RESEARCH TO YOUR STUDY DESIGN

Applying the defining features helps guide researchers in designing their own case study research. Use the guiding design questions from Table 5.5 to start thinking about the key aspects of the case you want to understand. Which of the questions were easier to answer for your study idea and which ones were harder?

DIFFERENCES AMONG THE APPROACHES

A useful perspective to begin the process of differentiating among the five approaches is to assess the defining features of each approach beginning with the focus of the research or the study purpose. As shown in Table 5.6, the focus of a narrative is on the life of an individual, and the focus of a phenomenology is on a concept or phenomenon and the essence of the phenomenon of lived experiences of persons. In grounded theory, the aim is to develop a theory, whereas in ethnography, it is to describe a culture-sharing group. In a case study, a specific case is examined, often with the intent of examining an issue with the case illustrating the complexity of the issue. Turning to the five studies, the defining features of foundational considerations for the approaches to qualitative research become more evident.

The story of Ai Mei Zhang, the Chinese immigrant student in a Canadian middle school, is a case in point—one decides to write a narrative when a single individual needs to be studied as the research focus, and that individual can illustrate with experiences the issue of being an immigrant student and the conflicting concerns that she faced (Chan, 2010). Furthermore, the researcher needs to make a case for the need to study this particular individual—someone who illustrates a problem, someone who has had a distinguished career, someone in the national spotlight, or someone who lives an ordinary life (Clandinin, 2023). The process of data collection and analysis involves gathering material about the person, such as from conversations or observations to stories of individual experiences.

The phenomenological study, on the other hand, focuses not on the life of an individual but rather on understanding the lived experiences of individuals around a phenomenon, such as how individuals represent the adversity faced by Black women in higher education leadership (Chance, 2022). Furthermore, the researcher selects individuals who have experienced the phenomenon, and asks participants to provide data, often through interviews (van Manen, 2014, 2023). The researcher takes these data and, through several steps of reducing the data, ultimately develops a description of the experiences about the phenomenon that all individuals have in common—the essence of the lived experience.

Whereas the phenomenological project focuses on the meaning of people's experience regarding a phenomenon, researchers in grounded theory have a different objective—to

TABLE 5.6 ■ Contrasting the Defining Features of Foundational Considerations for the Five Studies

Defining Features of Foundational Considerations	Five Qualitative Studies				
	Narrative Research (Chan, 2010)	Phenomenology (Chance, 2022)	Grounded Theory (Trip et al., 2019)	Ethnography (Mac an Ghaill & Haywood, 2015)	Case Study (Goodrum et al., 2022)
Research focus of approach	Exploring the life of a Chinese immigrant student in a Canadian middle school	Understanding the essence of the experience of adversity by a group of U.S. Black women in higher education leadership	Developing a theory grounded in data about the caregiving relationships of aging people with intellectual disabilities in families	Describing and interpreting a culture-sharing group of British-born, working-class Pakistani and Bangladeshi young men	Developing an in-depth description and analysis of an intrinsic case of the unique circumstances of a school shooting
Unit of analysis	One individual: Ai Mei Zhang	Several individuals who have shared the experience of adversity: nine Black women in higher education leadership roles	A process, an action, or an interaction involving many individuals: 19 people with intellectual disability who also nominated 28 family members to participate	A group that shares the same culture: 25 British-born, working-class Pakistani and Bangladeshi young men	A bounded case such as an event, a program, an activity, or one or more individuals: A school where shooting killed two students
Type of research problem best suited for approach	Telling the story of individual experiences	Describing the essence of a lived phenomenon	Grounding a theory in the views of participants	Describing and interpreting the shared patterns of the cultural group that develop over time	Providing an in-depth description and generalizing from a case or cases

generate a substantive theory, such as the theory about the caregiving relationship of aging people with intellectual disabilities in families that explains navigating transitions across the life course (Trip et al., 2019). Thus, grounded theorists undertake research to develop theory about a process or action. The data collection method primarily involves interviewing, and the collecting and analyzing processes are undertaken simultaneously and iteratively. Researchers may use constructivist procedures for analyzing and developing this theory, by way of generating codes, themes, and concepts in a theoretical model, as illustrated by Trip et al. (2019) and suggested by Charmaz (2014). The theory is then presented in a discussion or theoretical model, generating an overall tone of a grounded theory study as one of rigor and scientific credibility.

An ethnographic design is chosen when one wants to study the behaviors of a culture-sharing group, such as the British-born, working-class Pakistani and Bangladeshi young Muslim men (Mac an Ghaill & Haywood, 2015). In an ethnography, the researcher studies an intact culture-sharing group that has been interacting long enough to have shared or regular patterns of language and behavior (Fetterman, 2019). A detailed description of the culture-sharing group is essential at the beginning, and then the author may turn to identify patterns of the group around some cultural concept such as acculturation, politics, or economy and the like. The ethnography ends with summary statements about how the group functions and works in everyday life. In this way, a reader understands a group that may be previously unfamiliar.

Finally, a case study is chosen to study a case with clear boundaries, such as the organizational structure of a school where two students died in a school shooting and the culture that shaped and hindered violence prevention practices (Goodrum et al., 2022). In this type of intrinsic case study, the researchers illustrated a unique case, a case that has unusual interest in and of itself and needs to be described and detailed. It is important, too, for the researcher to have contextual material available to describe the setting for the case and draw upon multiple sources of information about the case to provide an in-depth picture of it. Central to writing a case study, the researcher describes the case in detail, and mentions several issues or focuses on a single issue that emerged when examining the case (Stake, 1995).

Selecting Your Approach

Based now on a more thorough understanding of the five approaches, how do you choose one approach over the other? We recommend that you start with distinguishing among the foci of the research approach and the units of analysis (see Table 5.6). In addition, other factors need also to be considered:

- *The audience question*: What approach is frequently used by gatekeepers in your field (e.g., committee members, advisors, editorial boards of journals)?
- *The background question*: What training do you have in the inquiry approach (e.g., courses completed, books read)? Or what resources are accessible to guide you in your work (e.g., committee members, books, workshops)?
- *The scholarly literature question*: What is needed most as contributing to the scholarly literature in your field (e.g., a study of an individual, an exploration of the meaning of a concept, a theory, a portrait of a culture-sharing group, an in-depth case study)?

- *The personal preference question*: Do you prefer a more structured approach to research or a storytelling approach (e.g., narrative research, ethnography)? Do you prefer a more well-defined approach to research or a more flexible approach (e.g., grounded theory, case study, phenomenology)?

CHAPTER CHECK-IN

1. What defining features of the five approaches were easy to apply to your study design and which ones were more difficult?
   - Reflect on your "Try This Now" activities in this chapter and add any additional information for your study.
2. Do you understand the key differences among the five approaches?
   - Read qualitative journal articles that adopt different approaches across diverse fields. See Examples 4.1–4.5 for ideas or find your own through an online search.

SUMMARY

This chapter examined five different qualitative journal articles to illustrate good models for writing a narrative study, a phenomenology, a grounded theory study, an ethnography, and a case study. These articles reflected many of the defining features of each approach (see also Chapter 4) and should enable readers to see differences in composing and writing structures of qualitative studies. Choose a narrative study to examine the life experiences of an individual when the individual is willing to share stories. Choose a phenomenology to examine a phenomenon and the meaning it holds for individuals. Choose a grounded theory study to generate or develop a theory grounded in the views of participants. Choose an ethnography to describe and interpret how a culture-sharing group (or individual) works. Choose a case study to examine a case, bounded in time or place, and look for contextual material to provide an in-depth picture of the case. These are important distinctions among the five approaches to qualitative inquiry. By studying an example of each approach in detail, we can learn more about how to proceed and how to narrow our choice of which approach to use. In the next chapter, we will see how to incorporate each of the five approaches into a scholarly introduction in a qualitative project.

FURTHER READINGS

Several readings extend this brief overview and comparison of articles for each of the five approaches. Here we continue to expand the list of books about each approach (see also Key Book Readings in Chapter 1 and Further Readings in Chapter 4). The list should not be considered exhaustive, and readers are encouraged to seek out additional readings in the end-of-book reference list.

Clandinin, D. J., Huber, J., Huber, M., Murphy, M. S., Murray Orr, A., Pearce, M., & Steeves, P. (2006). *Composing diverse identities: Narrative inquiries into the interwoven lives of children and teachers*. Routledge.

Through this book, the authors illustrate the usefulness of narrative research for capturing the complex interactions among children, families, teachers, and administrators within the school environment. This should be required reading for anyone engaging in narrative research with children.

Colaizzi, P. F. (1978). Psychological research as the phenomenologist views it. In R. Valle & M. King (Eds.), *Existential phenomenological alternatives for psychology* (pp. 48–71). Oxford University Press.

This key resource introduces existential phenomenology as a philosophical and methodological approach within the field of psychology. Within this chapter, Paul Colaizzi advances procedures for conducting phenomenological analysis that remain relevant to this day.

Denzin, N. K., & Lincoln, Y. S. (2013). *Strategies of qualitative inquiry*. Sage.

Norman Denzin and Yvonna Lincoln take a new approach in this accessible version of a handbook on qualitative research. In particular, we find the case study chapter by Flyvberg to be helpful in delineating case study research from the other approaches.

Goffman, A. (2014). *On the run: Fugitive life in an American city*. University of Chicago Press.

Alice Goffman contributes an ethnographic study of a group of young Black men in a poor community in West Philadelphia over 6 years. She also introduces several ethical issues that are worthy of further exploration for those engaging in ethnographic research.

Gorski, P. C., & Pothini, S. G. (2018). *Future directions for case studies: Case studies on diversity and social justice in education*. Routledge.

Paul C. Gorski and Seema G. Pothini guide readers through examining case studies across a variety of topics including school culture, bullying, and parent and community engagement. They describe the usefulness of case studies to practice seeing the full complexity of educational settings.

Spradley, J. P. (1979). *The ethnographic interview*. Holt, Rinehart & Winston.

This book by James Spradley has enduring influence for how to conduct open-ended interviews. In addition to suggestions about how to phrase research questions, he offers the reader useful guidance for comparing data during analyses.

6 INTRODUCING AND FOCUSING THE STUDY

> **QUESTIONS FOR DISCUSSION**
>
> - How are research problems, purpose statements, and research questions connected?
> - How can the problem statement be best written to reflect one of the approaches to qualitative research?
> - How can the purpose statement be best written to convey the orientation of an approach to research?
> - How can a central question be written so that it encodes and foreshadows an approach to qualitative research?
> - How can subquestions be presented so that they subdivide the central question into several parts?

The beginning of a study, as was mentioned earlier, is the most important part of a research project. If the purpose of the study is unclear, if the research questions are vague, and if the research problem or issue is not clearly identified, then a reader has difficulty following the remainder of the study. Consider a qualitative research journal article that you have recently read. Did it read quickly? If so, that is usually an indication that the study is well tied together: The problem leads to certain research questions, and the data collection naturally follows, and then the data analysis and interpretation relate closely to the questions, which, in turn, helps the reader to understand the research problem. The author uses transitions to bridge from one part to another. Often the logic is back and forth between these components in an integrated, consistent manner so that all parts interrelate (Morse & Richards, 2013) and are interactive (Maxwell, 2013). This integration of all parts of a good qualitative introduction begins with the identification of a clear problem that needs to be studied. It then advances the primary intent of the study, called the purpose or study aim. Of all parts of a research project, the **purpose statement** is most important. It sets the stage for the reader and conveys what the author hopes to accomplish in the study. It is so important, we believe, that we have scripted a purpose statement that you might use in your qualitative project. All you need to do is insert several components into this script to have a clear, short, and concise qualitative purpose statement that will be easy for readers to follow. Then, the qualitative research questions extend and often narrow the purpose statement into questions that will be answered during the course of the study. In this chapter, we will discuss how to compose a good problem statement for a qualitative study, how to compose a clear purpose statement, and how to further specify the research through qualitative research questions. Moreover, we will suggest how these sections of an introduction can be adjusted to fit all five of the approaches to qualitative inquiry addressed in this book.

INTERRELATING THE STUDY PROBLEM, PURPOSE, AND QUESTIONS WITHIN RESEARCH

A qualitative study begins with identifying a clear problem in need of investigation, advancing the primary purpose of the study, and specifying the questions guiding the study design. The problem, purpose, and questions provide the foundation on which to base subsequent decisions related to the research methods. To help this process, we provide a guiding framework in Figure 6.1. First, the researcher identifies a problem and creates a research problem statement; this statement then narrows to the study purpose. Second, the researcher creates a research

FIGURE 6.1 ■ Interrelating a Study's Research Problem, Purpose, and Questions

Research Problem Statement
Identify a particular issue in need of investigation.

Research Purpose Statement
Advance the major objective for beginning the study.

Research Questions
Specify the guiding query for narrowing the study.

purpose statement (hereafter, we will call this the purpose statement, recognizing that some researchers call it a study aim or study objective). From the purpose statement we then advance a primary study goal that is ultimately operationalized by specific research questions. These central research questions and subquestions subsequently guide the study design and methods. We consider this a narrowing process that is similar across the five approaches; yet some distinguishing features will be discussed within the sections that follow. In Figure 6.1, we recognize that study problems, purposes, and questions are grounded in and influenced by previous research, our experiences, and our viewpoints of what needs to be studied. Also implicit in Figure 6.1 is the importance of informing the selection of data collection methods and data analysis strategies where the outcome addresses the specified research questions, contributes to the primary study purpose, and investigates the identified research problem.

THE RESEARCH PROBLEM STATEMENT

How does one begin a qualitative study? Have you realized that all good research begins with an issue or problem that needs to be studied? Qualitative studies start with an introduction advancing the research problem or issue in a study. The term *problem* may be a misnomer, and individuals unfamiliar with writing research may struggle with this writing passage. Rather than calling this passage the problem, it might be clearer if we call it "the need for the study" or "creating a rationale for the need for the study." The intent of a research problem in qualitative research is to provide a rationale or need for studying a particular issue or problem. A discussion of this research problem begins a qualitative study. But the actual research problem is framed within several other components in an opening paragraph in a good qualitative study. Here, we want to analyze what these opening paragraphs might look like and to illustrate how they might be tailored to fit one of the five approaches. Ideas for structuring a good qualitative study introduction came from examining opening passages in good research articles and generating a model or template for authors to use (see Creswell & Creswell, 2023, for further discussions).

First, examine the model used to structure the introduction for a multiple case study of teen smoking in high schools represented in Figure 6.2. This article uses a "deficiencies model of an introduction" (Creswell & Creswell, 2023, p. 110) and is referred to by this name because it centers on deficiencies in the current literature and how studies add to a body of literature. We know now that qualitative studies not only add to the literature but they can also give voice to underrepresented groups; probe a deep understanding of a central phenomenon; and lead to specific outcomes such as stories, the essence of a phenomenon, the generation of theory, the cultural life of a group, and an in-depth analysis of a case. In Figure 6.2, you will see the five elements of a good introduction: the topic, the research problem, the evidence from the literature about the problem, the deficiencies in the evidence, and the importance of the problem for select audiences. Added as a final sixth element in this statement would be the purpose statement, a topic to be covered later in this chapter.

FIGURE 6.2 ■ Sample Research Problem Section (Introduction) to a Study

1. Advance topic
- Exploring the conceptions and misconceptions of teen smoking in high schools

2. Discuss research problem
- Tobacco use is a leading cause of cancer in American society (McGinnis & Foefe, 1993). Although smoking among adults has declined in recent years, it has actually increased for adolescents. The Centers for Disease Control and Prevention reported that smoking among high school students had risen from 27.5 percent in 1991 to 34.8 percent in 1995 (USDHHS, 1996). Unless this trend is dramatically reversed, an estimated 5 million of our nation's children will ultimately die a premature death (CDC, 1996).

3. Summarize scholarly literature
- Previous research on adolescent tobacco use has focused on four primacy topics. Several studies have examined the question of the initiation of smoking by young people, noting that tobacco use initiation begins as early as junior high school (e.g., Heishman et al., 1997). Other studies have focused on the prevention of smoking and tobacco use in schools. This research has led to numerous school-based prevention programs and interventions (e.g., Sussman et al., 1995). Fewer studies have examined "quit attempts" or cessation of smoking behaviors among adolescents, a distinct contrast to the extensive investigations into adult cessation (Heishman et al., 1997). Of interest as well to researchers studying adolescent tobacco use has been the social context and social influence of smoking (Fearnow et al., 1998). For example, adolescent smoking may occur in work-related situations, at home where one or more parents or caretakers smoke, at teen social events, or at areas designated as "safe" smoking places near high schools (McVea et al., in press).

4. Point to deficiencies in evidence
- Minimal research attention has been directed toward the social context of high schools as a site for examining adolescent tobacco use. During high school, students form peer groups, which may contribute to adolescent smoking. Often peers become a strong social influence for behavior in general, and belonging to an athletic team, a music group, or the "grunge" crowds can impact thinking about smoking (McVea et al., in press). Schools are also places where teachers and administrators need to be role models for abstaining from tobacco use and enforcing policies about tobacco use (O'Hara et al., 1999). Existing studies of adolescent tobacco use are primarily quantitative with a focus on outcomes and transtheoretical models (Pallonen, 1998). Qualitative investigations, however, provide detailed views of students in their own words, complex analyses of multiple perspectives, and specific school contexts of different high schools that shape student experiences with tobacco (Creswell, in press). Moreover, qualitative inquiry offers the opportunity to involve high school students as co-researchers, a data collection procedure that can enhance the validity of students' views uncontaminated by adult perspectives.

5. Argue importance of study for audiences
- By examining these multiple school contexts, using qualitative approaches and involving students as co-researchers, we can better understand the conceptions and misconceptions adolescents hold about tobacco use in high schools. With this understanding, researchers can better isolate variables and develop models about smoking behavior. Administrators and teachers can plan interventions to prevent or change attitudes toward smoking, and school officials can assist with smoking cessation or intervention programs.

Source: Adapted from McVea, Harter, McEntarffer, and Creswell (1999).

The five components of a good introduction are as follows:

1. *Advance the topic or general subject matter of the research study in a few beginning sentences or a paragraph to create reader interest.* A good first sentence—called a narrative hook in literature composition—would create reader interest through stating timely topics, advancing a key controversy, using numbers, or citing a leading study. We suggest staying away from quotes for the first sentence because they often require the reader to focus in on the key idea of the quote and need appropriate lead-in and lead-out features. Proceed beyond the first sentence to advance a general discussion about "what is the topic being addressed in the study" (see Creswell & Creswell, 2023, for further discussion about deciding on a topic).

2. *Discuss the research problem or issue that leads to a need for the study.* Readers simply need to be told about the issue or concern that you plan on addressing in your qualitative project. Another way to frame the research problem is to view it as an argument addressing "why my study topic matters." In this way, you can present to the reader the study's importance (Ravitch & Riggan, 2012). Qualitative research methods books (e.g., Marshall et al., 2021; Ravitch & Carl, 2020) advance several sources for locating research problems. Research problems are found in personal experience with an issue, a job-related problem, an advisor's research agenda, or the scholarly literature (Creswell & Creswell, 2023; Creswell & Guetterman, 2019). We like to think about the research problem as coming from real-life issues or from a gap in the literature, or both. Real-life problems might be that students struggle with their ethnic identity given the demands of friends, family, and schools, such as in Chan's (2010) study (see Appendix A). Caregivers of aging people with intellectual disabilities struggle with navigating transitions across the life course (Trip et al., 2019; see Appendix C). The need for a study also comes from certain deficiencies or gaps in the existing scholarly literature. Authors mention these gaps in future research sections or in introductions of their published studies. Studies can inspire dialogue and further understandings of issues that can inform practice improvements. Besides dialogue and understanding, a qualitative study may lead to new insights, fill a void in existing literature, establish a new line of thinking, lift up the voices of individuals who have been marginalized in our society, or assess an issue with an understudied group or population.

3. *Summarize the scholarly literature.* Briefly discuss any recent evidence that has addressed this research problem. "Has anyone studied my research problem or a closely related topic?" Although opinions differ about the extent of literature review needed before a study begins, qualitative research authors (e.g., Creswell & Creswell, 2023; Marshall et al., 2021; Ravitch & Carl, 2020) refer to the need to review the literature so that one can provide the rationale for the problem and position one's study within the ongoing literature about the topic. We have found it helpful to visually depict where our study can be positioned in the larger literature. For example, one might develop a visual or figure—a research map (see Creswell & Báez, 2021, for further discussion)—depicting existing literature and show in this figure the topics addressed in the

literature and how one's proposed research fits into or extends the existing literature. We also see this section as not providing detail about any one study, such as what one finds in a complete literature review, but as a statement about the general literature—the groups of literature, if you will—that have addressed the problem. If no groups of literature have addressed the problem, then discuss the extant literature closest to the topic. In the best scenario, a good qualitative study has not already been done, and no or few studies directly address the topic being proposed in your study.

4. *Point to deficiencies in evidence using the current literature or discussions.* Indicate in what ways gaps exist in understanding the problem. Mention several reasons, such as inadequate methods of data collection, a need for further research, or inadequate research. It is here, in the deficiencies section of an introduction, that information can be inserted that relates to one of the five qualitative approaches. In a problem statement for a narrative study, for example, writers can mention how individual stories need to be told to gain personal experiences about the research problem. In a phenomenological study, the researcher makes the case that a need exists to know more about a particular phenomenon and the common experiences of individuals with the phenomenon. For a grounded theory study, authors state that we need a theory that explains a process because existing theories are inadequate, are nonexistent for the population under study, or need to be modified for an existing population. In an ethnographic study, the problem statement advances why it is important to describe and interpret the cultural behavior of a certain group of people or how a group is marginalized and kept silent by others. For a case study, the researcher might discuss how the study of a case or cases can help inform the issue or concern. In all of these illustrations, the researcher presents the research problem as relating to the particular approach to qualitative research taken in the study and addresses "What gaps remain about my problem? And how can my chosen qualitative approach contribute to filling those gaps?"

5. *Argue the importance of the study for audiences.* Present how audiences or stakeholders will profit from your study addressing the problem. Consider different types of audiences and point out, for each one, the ways they will benefit from the study. These audiences could be other researchers, policymakers, practitioners in the field, or students. It also is here, in the audience section of an introduction, that information can be inserted about one of the five qualitative approaches. When describing the audience for a narrative study, for example, writers can mention how others such as teachers and clinicians will benefit from restorying the lived experiences of individuals addressing the research problem. In a phenomenological study, the researcher identifies who and how audiences benefit from knowing more about a particular phenomenon and the common experiences of individuals with the phenomenon. For a grounded theory study, authors describe the audience for an explanatory theory about an action, process, or interaction. In an ethnographic study, the benefits for the study audience involve interpreting the patterns of a certain group of people. For a case study, the researcher might discuss how the in-depth descriptions will benefit others' understanding of a unique context or be instrumental for understanding similar cases. In all of these illustrations, the

researcher presents the audience and study contributions as relating to the particular approach to qualitative research taken in the study addressing, "How can my study profit the intended audiences?"

The introduction then proceeds on to the purpose statement because, at this point, a reader has a clear understanding of the problem leading to a need for the study and is encouraged to read on to see what the overall intent of the study might be (purpose) as well as the types of questions (research questions) that will be answered in the study.

> **TRY THIS NOW 6.1**
> **IDENTIFYING THE FIVE ELEMENTS OF A RESEARCH PROBLEM SECTION (INTRODUCTION) IN THE APPENDIX STUDIES**
>
> Identifying the five elements of a Research Problem Section (Introduction) in a published qualitative study helps guide researchers in creating their own study introductions. Choose one of the Appendix studies to identify the five elements illustrated in Figure 6.2. Can you find evidence of each of the five elements in the Appendix studies?

THE PURPOSE STATEMENT

This interrelationship between design and approach continues with the purpose statement, a statement that provides the major objective, intent, or "road map" for the study. As the most important statement in an entire qualitative study, the purpose statement needs to be carefully constructed and written in clear and concise language. Unfortunately, all too many writers leave this statement implicit, causing readers extra work in interpreting and following a study. This need not be the case, so we have created the following "script" for a purpose statement containing several sentences and blanks that an individual fills in (see also Creswell & Báez, 2021; Creswell & Creswell, 2023; and Example 6.1):

> The purpose of this _____ (narrative, phenomenological, grounded theory, ethnographic, case) study is (was? will be?) to _____ (understand? describe? develop? discover?) the _____ (central phenomenon of the study) for _____ (the participants) at _____ (the site). At this stage in the research, the _____ (central phenomenon) will be generally defined as _____ (a general definition of the central phenomenon).

As this script shows, several terms can be used to encode a passage for a specific approach to qualitative research. The following occurs in the purpose statement:

- The writer identifies the specific qualitative approach used in the study by mentioning the type (e.g., narrative study). The name of the approach comes first in the passage, foreshadowing the inquiry approach for data collection, analysis, and report writing.

- The writer encodes the passage with words that indicate the action of the researcher and the focus of the approach to research. For example, certain words encode the statement as qualitative research, such as *understand experiences* (useful in narrative studies), *describe* (useful in case studies, ethnography, and phenomenology), *ascribe meaning* (associated with phenomenology), *develop* or *generate* (useful in grounded theory), and *discover* (useful in all approaches). See Table 6.1 for specific words that a researcher would include in a purpose statement to encode it for a qualitative approach. These words indicate not only researchers' actions but also the foci and outcomes of the studies.
- The writer identifies the central phenomenon. The central phenomenon is the one central concept being explored or examined in the research study. Qualitative researchers focus on only one concept at the beginning of a study. For example, a school shooting as an organizational accident (Appendix E: Goodrum et al., 2022) or the behaviors of a culture-sharing group, such as the British-born, working-class Pakistani and Bangladeshi young Muslim men (Appendix D: Mac an Ghaill & Haywood, 2015). Comparing groups or looking for linkages can be included in the study as one gains experiences in fieldwork and proceeds on with analysis after initial exploration of the central phenomenon.
- The writer foreshadows the participants and the site for the study, whether the participants are one individual (i.e., narrative or case study), several individuals (i.e., grounded theory or phenomenology), a group (i.e., ethnography), or a site (i.e., program, event, activity, or place in a case study).

We also suggest including a *general definition* for the central phenomenon. This definition is a tentative, preliminary definition that the researcher intends to use at the outset of the

TABLE 6.1 ■ Words to Use in Encoding the Purpose Statement Across Five Qualitative Research Approaches

Narrative	Phenomenology	Grounded Theory	Ethnography	Case Study
- Narrative study - Stories - Epiphanies - Lived experiences - Chronology	- Phenomenology - Describe - Experiences - Meaning - Essence	- Grounded theory - Generate - Develop - Propositions - Process - Substantive theory	- Ethnography - Culture-sharing group - Cultural behavior and language - Cultural portrait - Cultural themes	- Case study - Bounded - Single or collective case - Event, process, program, individual

study (Clandinin, 2023). The definition may be difficult to determine with any specificity in advance. But, for example, in a narrative study, a writer might define the types of stories to be collected such as life stages, childhood memories, the transition from adolescence to adulthood, attendance at an Alcoholics Anonymous meeting, or even the family situation enacted in the aftermath of the death of a sibling (Ellis, 1993; see also Examples 4.1 and 6.1). In a phenomenology, the central phenomenon to be explored is clearly specified (van Manen, 2023). For example, the phenomenon might be specified as the meaning of grief, anger, or even chess playing (Aanstoos, 1985) or surviving a stroke (Suddick et al., 2020; see also Example 4.2). In grounded theory, the central phenomenon might be identified as a concept central to the process being examined (Corbin & Strauss, 2015)—for example, the effect of past relationships on post-bereavement remarried couples (Brimhall & Engblom-Deglmann, 2011) or even the significance of memory-making in neonatal bereavement (Thornton et al., 2020; see also Example 4.3). In an ethnography, the writer might identify the key cultural concepts (often drawn from cultural concepts in anthropology) being examined, such as roles, behaviors, acculturation, communication, myths, stories, or other concepts that the researcher plans to take into the field at the beginning of the study (Wolcott, 2008a). For example, refugee and mother roles in a study on the impact of COVID-19 (Hirani & Wagner, 2022; see also Example 4.4). Finally, in a case study such as an "intrinsic" case study (Stake, 1995), the writer might define the boundaries of the case, specifying how the case is uniquely bounded in time and place such as in the study of the Silk Road as an online drug marketplace (Van Hout & Bingham, 2013; see also Example 4.5). If an "instrumental" case study is being examined, then the researcher might specify and define generally the issue being examined in the case such as the campus response to a student gunman (Asmussen & Creswell, 1995; see also Example 4.5).

Several examples of purpose statements follow (Examples 6.1–6.5) that illustrate the ***encoding*** and foreshadowing of the five approaches to research.

EXAMPLE 6.1 NARRATIVE RESEARCH PURPOSE STATEMENTS

Notice how the lived experience is emphasized in each of the following examples.

a. A single individual and the life history of the individual in Fabricius (2014, p. 284):
   The article addresses the narrated life history of an academic employed in Denmark who teaches in both Danish and English and shows how he represents the interplay of local and transnational in his history in order to make sense of his present position and opinions.

b. The family and friends of an airplane crash victim and the reactions of these individuals by Ellis (1993, p. 712):
   The story I tell here describes the aftermath of the crash as my family and friends in Lurary, the town where I was born and where Rex lived, react to and cope with this unanticipated tragedy.

EXAMPLE 6.2 PHENOMENOLOGICAL RESEARCH PURPOSE STATEMENTS

See in the following examples how the phenomenon is clearly described.

a. The role of a group of individuals as older rural adults by Mefteh (2022, p. 3):
   The general objective of this study is to explore and describe rural older adults lived experiences on the circumstances that precipitate them for seeking family care in a co-residential family care arrangement.
b. The meaning individuals attributed to a health care experience in Brown et al. (2006, p. 120):
   The purpose of our phenomenological study was to explore what meaning people with liver failure ascribe to the experience of waiting for a transplant at a major midwestern transplant center.

EXAMPLE 6.3 GROUNDED THEORY RESEARCH PURPOSE STATEMENTS

In the following examples, the researchers advance a theory by studying a process around the

a. Leadership identity of an individual by Komives et al. (2005, p. 594):
   The purpose of this study was to understand the processes a person experiences in creating a leadership identity.
b. Resilience development by a group of women in an isolated setting in Leipert and Reutter (2005, p. 50):
   The purpose of this study was to explore how women maintain their health in geographical, social, political, economic, and historical contexts.

EXAMPLE 6.4 ETHNOGRAPHIC RESEARCH PURPOSE STATEMENTS

A portrait of a culture-sharing group was sought in each of the following examples.

a. The "ballpark" culture of the employees described by Trujillo (1992, p. 351):
   This article examines how the work and the talk of stadium employees reinforce certain meanings of baseball in society, and it reveals how the work and the talk create and maintain ballpark culture.
b. The core values of the straight edge (sXe) movement as stated by Haenfler (2004, p. 410):
   This article fills a gap in the literature by giving an empirical account of the sXe movement centered on a description of the group's core values.

EXAMPLE 6.5 CASE STUDY RESEARCH PURPOSE STATEMENTS

The focus on understanding the bounded system is evident in each of the following examples.

a. A multiple case study of the integration of technology by Staples et al. (2005, p. 287):
   The purpose of this study was to describe the ways in which three urban elementary schools, in partnership with a local, publicly funded multipurpose university, used a similar array of material and human resources to improve their integration of technology.
b. An intrinsic case study of the campus reaction to a gunman event in Asmussen and Creswell (1995, p. 576):
   The study presented in this article is a qualitative case analysis that describes and interprets a campus response to a gun incident.

TRY THIS NOW 6.2
EXAMINING ENCODING WORDS IN THE PURPOSE STATEMENTS OF THE APPENDIX STUDIES

Examining the encoding words in purpose statements in a published qualitative study helps guide researchers in focusing their own studies. Choose one of the Appendix studies to locate the purpose statement and note what (if any) encoding words are used. What (if any) information is provided about the qualitative approach, the central phenomenon, participants, and the site.

For example, in Chance (2022; Appendix B): The purpose of this phenomenological study was to "*explore and describe how Black women in higher education leadership navigate* intersectionality, stereotype threat, and tokenism" (italics added, p. 62).

THE RESEARCH QUESTIONS

The intent of qualitative research questions is to narrow the purpose to several questions that will be addressed in the study. We distinguish between the purpose statement and research questions so that we can clearly see how they are conceptualized and composed; other authors may combine them or more typically state only a purpose statement in a journal article and leave out the research questions. However, in many types of qualitative studies, such as dissertations and theses, the research questions are distinct and stated separately from the purpose statement. Once again, we find that these questions provide an opportunity to encode and foreshadow an approach to inquiry.

The Central Question

Some writers offer suggestions for writing qualitative research questions (e.g., Creswell & Báez, 2021; Creswell & Creswell, 2023; Creswell & Guetterman, 2019; Marshall et al., 2021). Qualitative research questions are open-ended, evolving, and nondirectional. They restate the purpose of the study in more specific terms and typically start with a word such as *what* or *how* rather than *why* in order to explore a central phenomenon. This is because *why* suggests possible cause-and-effect directional language, not open-ended language that is more apparent with the use of *what* or *how*. Questions are few in number (five to seven) and posed in various forms, from the "grand tour" (Spradley, 1979, 1980) that asks, "Tell me about yourself," to more specific questions.

We recommend that a researcher reduce their entire study to a single, overarching **central question** and several **subquestions**. Drafting this central question often takes considerable work because of its breadth and the tendency of some to form specific questions based on traditional training. To reach the overarching central question, we ask qualitative researchers to state the broadest question they could possibly pose to address their research problem. We find writing good research questions to be difficult and time-consuming because it often takes several drafts. Students can benefit from creating dozens of research questions about a research topic, categorizing them, and then eliminating questions that can be easily answered (e.g., "googled" or "yes," "no"). Here are some suggestions for getting started with writing, revising, and refining central questions:

- Start with several questions and then answer some of the questions as you begin to read the literature.
- Read literature and discuss your research questions with others to help you revise and refine your questions using your chosen research approach.
- Check to ensure your research questions are worded in ways that are
  - Interesting to a reader in your discipline (e.g., engaging, evocative)
  - Contributing something new (e.g., unique insights, perspectives)
  - Relevant to the conversation (e.g., extending previous work, related topic)
  - Clear in their wording (e.g., avoiding the use of jargon, concise)

The central question can be encoded with the language of each of the five approaches to inquiry. Morse (1994) spoke directly to this issue as she reviewed the types of research questions. Although she did not refer to narratives or case studies, she mentioned that one finds descriptive cultural questions in ethnographies, process questions in grounded theory studies, and meaning questions in phenomenological studies.

For example, we searched through the five studies presented in Chapter 5 to see if we could find or imagine their central research questions. We recognized immediately that the authors of these journal articles typically provided purpose statements rather than research questions—often the case in journal articles. Still, it is helpful to consider what their central questions, if asked, might have been for the Chapter 5 articles. In Examples 6.6–6.10, we present our version (or the authors' version) of the research questions guiding the studies included in the appendices. Additional examples, based on studies in Chapter 5, are also provided to illustrate research questions for each approach.

EXAMPLE 6.6 NARRATIVE STUDY RESEARCH QUESTIONS

Notice how the focus on the lived experience is emphasized in each of the following narrative research question examples.

a. How gathering stories from Ai Mei, the Chinese immigrant student, might have been written by Chan (2010; see Appendix A):
   What are the conflicting stories of ethnic identity that Ai Mei experienced in her school, with her peers, and with her family?
b. How eliciting life narratives, the comparison of code-switching patterns of two African American women, might have been written by Nelson (1990):
   What are the patterns and significance of code-switching and other contextualization cues that African American women experienced as participants in American culture during the latter part of the 20th century?

EXAMPLE 6.7 PHENOMENOLOGY RESEARCH QUESTIONS

See how the focus on describing the phenomenon is articulated in the following examples of phenomenological research questions.

a. Capturing the experience of how Black women in higher education leadership navigate cultural adversity was stated by Chance (2022, p. 62; see Appendix B):
   How [do] Black women in higher education leadership navigate intersectionality, stereotype threat, and tokenism?
b. Describing the meaning a woman attributed to the lived experience of a long-term disability was stated by Padilla (2003, p. 415):
   What is the lived experience of disability for a woman who sustained a head injury many years ago?

EXAMPLE 6.8 GROUNDED THEORY STUDY RESEARCH QUESTIONS

In the following grounded theory research question examples, the focus on advancing a theory is clearly represented.

a. Explaining the process of caregiving relationships of families with aging individuals with intellectual disabilities might have been expressed by Trip and colleagues (2019; see Appendix C) as follows:

What caregiving relationship process theory explains the transitions across the life course of 19 people with intellectual disability and their 28 family members?

b. Generating an understanding of what the process of remarrying involves between post-bereavement couples might have been represented by Brimhall and Engblom-Deglmann (2011) as follows:

What relational process theory describes the effects of past relationships on post-bereavement remarried couples?

EXAMPLE 6.9 ETHNOGRAPHY RESEARCH QUESTIONS

Note how the portrait of a culture-sharing group was sought in each of the following research question examples for ethnography.

a. Representing the changing cultural condition inhabited by a group of British-born, working-class Pakistani and Bangladeshi young men over 3 years might have been expressed by Mac an Ghaill and Haywood (2015; see Appendix D) as follows:

What are the core beliefs related to ethnicity, religion, and cultural belonging of the group of British-born, working-class Pakistani and Bangladeshi young men, and how do the young men construct and understand their geographically specific experiences of family, schooling, social life as well as both growing up and interacting within their local community in a rapidly changing Britain?

b. Describing the core values of the members of the sXe movement might have been advanced by Haenfler (2004) as follows:

What are the core values of the sXe movement, and how do the members construct and understand their subjective experiences of being a part of the subculture?

EXAMPLE 6.10 CASE STUDY RESEARCH QUESTIONS

The focus on understanding the bounded system is evident in each of the following examples of case study research questions.

a. Tracing the lessons learned from a school shooting as an organizational accident might have been proposed by Goodrum et al. (2022; see Appendix E) as follows:
    What is it about the organizational structures and culture of schools that failed to prevent violence even after a student of concern had been identified?
b. Describing and interpreting the campus response to a gun incident was taken on by Asmussen and Creswell (1995, p. 576) using five central guiding questions in the introduction:
    What happened? Who was involved in response to the incident? What themes of response emerged during the eight-month period that followed this incident? What theoretical constructs helped us understand the campus response, and what constructs were unique to this case?

Example 6.10 illustrates describing individuals' experiences and then in developing themes representing responses of individuals on the campuses. As these examples show, authors may or may not pose a central question, although they are implicit, if not explicit, in all studies. When writing journal articles, central questions may be used less than purpose statements to guide the research. However, for individuals' graduate research, such as theses or dissertations, the trend is toward writing both purpose statements and central questions.

Subquestions

An author typically presents a small number of subquestions that subdivide the central question into its parts. For example, a central question such as "What does it mean to be a college professor?" would be analyzed in subquestions on topics like "What does it mean to be a college professor in the classroom? As a researcher? As a thesis supervisor? As a colleague in a department?" In this example, the subquestions focus on the roles or responsibilities this particular college professor undertakes as an instructor, researcher, supervisor of students, and colleague within a department. The subquestions will vary if the college professor has different roles assigned—for example, as administrator or practicum supervisor. Subquestions can be used to create specific questions asked during the data collection, such as in interviews or in the observations.

Here are some suggestions for writing these subquestions:

- State a small number of subquestions to further refine the central question. We generally recommend five to seven subquestions. New questions may arise during data collection, and, as with all qualitative research, questions may change or evolve during the research process.

- Think about how the central question might be divided into smaller questions. Ask yourself, "If the central question were divided into some areas that I would like to explore, what would the areas or parts be?" A good illustration comes from ethnography. Wolcott (2008a) said that the grand tour or central question such as "What is going on here?" can only be addressed when fleshed out with detail: "In terms of what?" (p. 74).

- Create open-ended subquestions that begin with *how* or *what*. These words should reflect a similar manner as the central question.

You can write the subquestions focused on further analyzing the central phenomenon that relates to the type of qualitative research being used. In a narrative study, these questions may further probe the meaning of stories. In a phenomenology, they will help to establish the components of the essence of the study. In a grounded theory, they will help to detail the emerging theory, and in an ethnography, they will detail the aspects of the culture-sharing group you plan to study, such as members' rituals, their communication, their economic way of life, and so forth. In a case study, the subquestions will address the elements of the case or the issue that you seek to understand. Examples 6.11–6.15 present subquestions (asked or possibly asked) in the Appendix studies.

EXAMPLE 6.11 NARRATIVE STUDY RESEARCH SUBQUESTIONS

Subquestions for gathering stories from Ai Mei, the Chinese immigrant student, that might have been written by Chan (2010; see Appendix A) include the following:

What and how did school experiences contribute to Ai Mei's ethnic identity?

How might peer experiences have contributed to Ai Mei's ethnic identity?

What family experiences does Ai Mei describe as influential to her ethnic identity?

EXAMPLE 6.12 PHENOMENOLOGY RESEARCH SUBQUESTIONS

Subquestions for exploring adversity and the lived experiences of Black women in higher education leadership by Chance (2022, p. 62; see Appendix B) were stated as the following:

What influence does a Black women's identity have on her ability to lead in higher education administration?

What influence does stereotype threat have on Black women's leadership in higher education administration?

What influence does tokenism have on Black women's leadership style and ability in higher education administration?

EXAMPLE 6.13 GROUNDED THEORY STUDY RESEARCH SUBQUESTIONS

Subquestions for guiding the development of a theory of the caregiving relationship process of aging people with intellectual disabilities in families navigating life course transitions might have been written by Trip and colleagues (2019; see Appendix C) as the following:

How do the people with intellectual disability perceive their aging process and future?

What are the greatest challenges for families involved in caregiving for aging people with intellectual disability?

What has motivated the future planning for caregivers of aging people with intellectual disability?

EXAMPLE 6.14 ETHNOGRAPHIC RESEARCH SUBQUESTIONS

Subquestions for documenting the changing cultural conditions inhabited by a group of British-born, working-class Pakistani and Bangladeshi young men might have been expressed by Mac an Ghaill and Haywood (2015; see Appendix D) as the following:

What core beliefs do group members describe related to ethnic identity?

What experiences do group members attribute as influencing their cultural identity?

What social experiences do group members describe as contributing to core beliefs?

EXAMPLE 6.15 CASE STUDY RESEARCH SUBQUESTIONS

Subquestions for tracing the organizational structure and culture of a school where two students died in a shooting might have been expressed by Goodrum (2022; see Appendix E) as follows:

What decisions represent key threats in the assessment process for students of concern?

What aspects of school organizational structure and culture hinder violence prevention practices?

What is the match between the guidelines and activities in the threat assessment process for the student of concern?

In Chapter 7, we will examine the phases of data collection common to all approaches and then discuss how data collection differs among the five approaches.

INTRODUCING AND FOCUSING YOUR STUDY

Based now on a more thorough understanding of how to introduce and focus a qualitative study, we recommend that you start drafting an interrelated problem statement, purpose statement, and research question(s) for your chosen approach. The following questions can help guide you in this work:

- *What is my study about?* Once you have a topic in mind, you can narrow the research focus and specify a research problem (see also Chapter 4). For example, the topic of classroom disruptions could become focused on the disruptions caused by at-risk students and specifically on exploring the environmental contributors to classroom disruptions by at-risk students.

- *Why is my study needed?* Once you have an idea for a specific research problem to pursue, you can examine the scholarly literature to find out what is known about your problem and the ways your problem has been studied to identify gaps for your study to address. For example, the disruptions caused by at-risk students have been studied from the perspective of teachers but not the lived experience from the student perspective.

- *What is my study's contribution?* Once you have determined your study purpose, you can create your statement identifying a qualitative research approach and draft your research questions. For example, a narrative study would allow you to capture the lived experiences of individual at-risk students or a small group of students. This is also a good opportunity to think about how your intended audience and society might benefit from your study's outcomes.

CHAPTER CHECK-IN

1. Can you identify evidence of an introduction with interrelated parts being used by the author(s) as illustrated in Figure 6.2? Select one of the qualitative journal articles listed in Examples 4.1–4.6. Identify the interrelated parts as mentioned in the example. What parts are present? Are missing?

2. Can you identify the research problem investigated in the selected study (from Examples 4.1–4.6)? State the research problem in a single sentence. Finally, review the article for evidence of research questions. Assess to what extent the author(s) state a central research question and subquestions.

3. What purpose statements are appropriate for each of the approaches? Use the script provided in this chapter to rewrite the purpose statement for each of the Appendix studies A–E and compare it with what was stated in the journal article (see Try This Now 6.2). Note the similarities and differences between the two statements.

4. Apply the suggestions presented in this chapter for composing research questions. Specifically, write the first draft of your central question, starting with *how* or *what*. Consider whether you have addressed four key elements of a central question: the central phenomenon, the participants, the site, and the approach to inquiry.

SUMMARY

In this chapter, we addressed how to introduce and focus a qualitative study by the problem statement, the purpose statement, and the research questions. We began with describing the need for the parts to be interrelated and a guiding framework for implementation. After discussing the general features of designing each part in a qualitative study, we related each to the five approaches advanced in this book. The problem statement should advance the topic, discuss the research problem, summarize the literature about the problem, point to the deficiencies in this literature, and argue the importance for the audience who will profit from the study insights. It is in the deficiencies section that an author can insert specific information related to their approach. For example, authors can advance the need for stories to be told, the need to find the "essence" of the experience, the need to develop a theory, the need to portray the life of a culture-sharing group, and the need to use a case to explore a specific issue. A script may be used to construct the purpose statement. This script should include the type of qualitative approach being used and incorporate words that signal the use of one of the five approaches. The research questions divide into one central question and about five to seven subquestions that subdivide the central questions into several parts of inquiry. The central question can be encoded to accomplish the intent of one of the approaches, such as the development of stories in narrative projects or the generation of a theory in grounded theory. Subquestions also can be used in the data collection process as the key questions asked during an interview or to guide an observation.

CHAPTER KEY TERMS

Central question
Encoding

Purpose statement
Subquestions

FURTHER READINGS

Several readings extend this brief overview and comparison of articles for each of the five approaches. Here we continue to expand the list of books about each approach (see also the Key Book Readings in Chapter 1 and Further Readings in Chapter 4). The list should not be considered exhaustive, and readers are encouraged to seek out additional readings in the end-of-book reference list.

Creswell, J. W., & Báez, J. (2021). *30 essential skills for the qualitative researcher* (2nd ed.). Sage.

John W. Creswell and his new coauthor Johanna Báez's updated book offers an innovative way for guiding the qualitative researcher through its organization by skills. In so doing, researchers can easily access specific skills information. This resource may be particularly helpful for those new to qualitative research.

Marshall, C., Rossman, G. B., & Blanco, G. L. (2021). *Designing qualitative research* (7th ed.). Sage.

In the most recent edition, Catherine Marshall and Gretchen Rossman are joined by Gerardo L. Blanco and enhance their practical resource by expanding the scope of contemporary issues, methods, and considerations in qualitative research. The interwoven vignettes providing access to potential questions, which are helpful for defending the proposal, afford a unique perspective.

Ravitch, S. M., & Carl, N. M. (2020). *Qualitative research: Bridging the conceptual, theoretical, and methodological* (2nd ed.). Sage.

Sharon Ravitch and Nicole Mittenfelner Carl offer an accessible resource on the processes involved in qualitative research. Chapter 11 provides important guidance for thinking about qualitative research ethics and the relational quality of research.

7 DATA COLLECTION

QUESTIONS FOR DISCUSSION

- What are the steps in the overall data collection process of qualitative research?
- What are key ethical considerations when collecting data?
- How does a researcher find people or places to study?
- What are typical access and rapport issues?
- What decisions influence the selection of a purposeful sampling strategy?
- What are typical forms of data collection across the five qualitative approaches?
- How is information recorded and organized?
- What are common fieldwork issues when collecting data?
- How is information securely stored?
- What do I need to consider when planning data collection across the five approaches?

A typical reaction to thinking about qualitative data collection is to focus attention on the actual types of data and the procedures for gathering them. Data collection, however, involves much more. It means anticipating and responding to arising ethical issues, gaining permissions to study sites and individuals, selecting **purposeful sampling** strategies, developing means for collecting and recording information, mitigating fieldwork issues as they arise, and storing the data securely. Also, in the actual forms of data collection, researchers often opt for only conducting interviews and observations. As will be seen in this chapter, the array of qualitative sources of data are ever expanding, and we encourage researchers to use newer, innovative methods in addition to interviews and observations. In addition, new forms of data and the steps in the process of collecting qualitative data need to be sensitive to the outcomes expected for each of the five different approaches to qualitative research. Engaging in reflexivity can help researchers recognize the influence of their "positioning" on data collection decisions (see also Chapter 2). Attention to reciprocity for participants can help researchers plan for giving back to participants for their time and efforts during data collection (Poth, 2021).

We find it useful to visualize the phases of data collection common to all approaches. A "circle" of interrelated activities best displays this process, a process of engaging in activities that include but go beyond collecting data. We begin this chapter by presenting this circle of activities, briefly introducing each activity. These activities are locating a site or an individual, gaining access and building rapport, sampling purposefully, collecting data, recording and organizing information, exploring fieldwork issues, and storing data. Then we explore how these activities differ in the five approaches to inquiry, and we end with a few summary comments about comparing the data collection activities across the five approaches.

THE DATA COLLECTION CIRCLE

We visualize data collection as a series of interrelated activities aimed at gathering good information to answer emerging research questions. As shown in Figure 7.1, a qualitative researcher engages in a series of activities in the process of collecting data. Data collection is iterative and much less stepwise than it appears in Figure 7.1. How researchers plan for and ultimately collect data for their study varies. Although we start with locating a site or an individual to study,

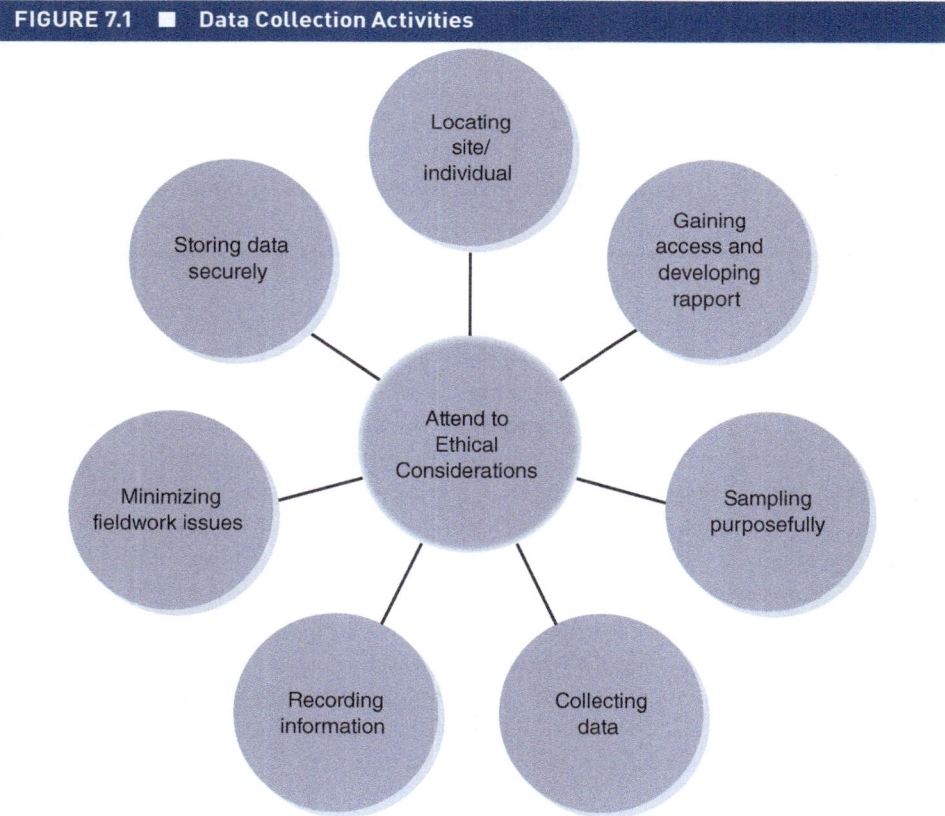

FIGURE 7.1 ■ Data Collection Activities

an investigator may begin at another entry point in the circle. Most important, we want the researcher to consider the multiple activities often involved in collecting data—activities that extend beyond the typical reference point of conducting interviews or making observations. By placing ethics at the intersection of the data collection circle, we emphasize the need to attend to ethical considerations across the phases.

An important step in the process is to find people or places to study and to gain access to and establish rapport with participants so that they will provide good data. A closely interrelated step in the process involves determining a strategy for the **purposeful sampling** of individuals or sites. This is not a probability sample that will enable a researcher to determine statistical inferences to a population; rather, it is a purposeful sample that will intentionally sample a group of people that can best inform the researcher about the research problem under examination. Thus, the researcher needs to determine which type of purposeful sampling will be best to use.

Once the inquirer selects the sites or people, decisions need to be made about the most appropriate data collection approaches. Increasingly, a qualitative researcher has more choices regarding forms of data and modes of collection and recording—for example, the various types of interviews generate different interactions and subsequently influence the information recorded. Typically, the qualitative researcher will collect data from more than one source. To guide data collection, the researcher develops protocols for recording the information and needs to pilot the forms for recording the data, such as interview or observational protocols. Also, the researcher needs to anticipate and respond to arising fieldwork issues of data collection, such as experiencing recruitment challenges or needing to prematurely conclude fieldwork. Finally, a qualitative researcher must decide how they will store data securely so that it can be easily retrieved and protected from damage or breaches.

We now turn to each of these seven data collection activities and ethical considerations, and we address each for general procedures and within each approach to inquiry. As shown in Table 7.1, these activities are both different and similar across the five approaches to inquiry.

Ethical Considerations for Data Collection

Regardless of the approach to qualitative inquiry, a qualitative researcher faces many ethical issues that arise during fieldwork data collection and in analysis and dissemination of qualitative reports. In Chapter 3, we discussed some of these issues, but ethical issues loom large in the data collection phase of qualitative research (see Table 3.1 for a summary of ethical issues in qualitative research). Planning and conducting an ethical study means that the researcher considers and addresses all anticipated and emergent ethical issues in the study. Typically, these ethical issues relate to three principles guiding ethical research: respect for persons (i.e., privacy and consent), concern for welfare (i.e., minimize harm and augment reciprocity), and justice (i.e., enhance inclusivity and equitable treatment). A researcher protects the anonymity of the participants, for example, by assigning numbers or aliases to individuals. To gain free and informed consent from participants, a qualitative researcher conveys the voluntary expectations of participating in the study, explains the purpose of the study and that participants can withdraw from the study, and does not engage in **deception** about the study nature, procedures, or expected outcomes.

TABLE 7.1 ■ Data Collection Activities by Five Qualitative Approaches

Data Collection Activity	Narrative	Phenomenology	Grounded Theory	Ethnography	Case Study
What is traditionally studied (sites or individual[s])?	Single individual, accessible, and distinctive in their stories of experience	Multiple individuals who have experienced the phenomenon	Multiple individuals who have responded to an action or participated in a process about a central phenomenon	Members of a culture-sharing group or individuals representative of the group	A bounded system, such as a process, an activity, an event, a program, or multiple individuals
What are typical access and rapport procedures (access and rapport)?	Gaining permission from individuals, obtaining access to information in archives	Finding people who have experienced the phenomenon	Locating a homogeneous sample	Gaining access through the gatekeeper, gaining the confidence of informants	Gaining access through the gatekeeper, gaining the confidence of participants
How does one select a site or individuals to study (purposeful sampling strategies)?	Several strategies, depending on the person (e.g., convenient, politically important, typical, a critical case)	Finding individuals who have experienced the phenomenon, a "criterion" sample	Finding a homogeneous sample, a "theory-based" sample, a "theoretical" sample	Finding a cultural group to which one is a "stranger," a "representative" sample	Finding a "case" or "cases," an "atypical" case, or a "maximum variation" or "extreme" case
What type of information is typically collected (forms of data)?	Documents and archival material, open-ended interviews, subject journaling, participant observation, casual chatting; typically a single individual	Interviews with a range of people (e.g., 5 to 25)	Primarily interviews with 20 to 30 people to achieve detail in the theory	Participant observations, interviews, artifacts, and documents of a single culture-sharing group	Extensive forms, such as documents and records, interviews, observation, and physical artifacts for 1 to 4 cases

Data Collection Activity	Narrative	Phenomenology	Grounded Theory	Ethnography	Case Study
How is information recorded (recording information)?	Notes, interview protocol	Interviews, often multiple interviews with the same individuals	Interview protocol, field notes, memoing	Field notes, interview and observational protocols	Field notes, interview and observational protocols
What are common data collection issues (fieldwork issues)?	Access to materials, authenticity of account and materials	Bracketing one's experiences, logistics of interviewing	Interviewing issues (e.g., logistics, openness)	Field issues (e.g., reflexivity, reactivity, reciprocity, divulging private information, deception)	Interviewing and observing issues
How is information typically stored (storing data)?	File folders, digital files	Transcriptions, digital files	Transcriptions, digital files	Field notes, transcriptions, digital files	Field notes, transcriptions, digital files

What if the study is on a sensitive topic and the participants decline to be involved if they are aware of the topic? The researcher needs to allow the participant to decline involvement. Another issue likely to develop is when participants share information off the record. Although in most instances this information is deleted from analysis by the researcher, the issue becomes problematic when the information, if reported, harms individuals. Finally, we point to the increased focus on how we elicit and record information in appropriate ways for participants. In doing so, it is the responsibility of the researcher to become familiar with the research context and participants and to respect different knowledge systems and ways of interacting. Many excellent resources exist with help for situating research in diverse contexts and/or with marginalized and vulnerable populations (e.g., Chilisa, 2020; Clandinin et al., 2006; Stanfield, 2011).

Institutional Review Boards

Prior to beginning data collection, a key activity involves the researcher seeking and obtaining the permission of institutional review boards (Creswell & Creswell, 2023; Hatch, 2002; Iphofen & Tolich, 2018; Mertens, 2018). The purpose of this activity is to provide evidence to the review boards that the study design follows guidelines for conducting ethical research. Most qualitative studies are exempt from a lengthy review (e.g., the expedited or full review), but studies involving individuals who are minors (i.e., 18 years or under) or studies of vulnerable populations (e.g., those who have experienced trauma, or those with addictions, disabilities, or illnesses) require a thorough review—a process involving detailed, lengthy applications and an extended time for review. The review process involves submitting a proposal that details project procedures for selection, access, and permissions for sites and individuals; the selection, sampling, and collection strategies for data; and the management of recording, storage, and use of information. Table 7.2 summarizes the ethical issues by the data collection activities where each of these procedures will be further described. See also Mertens (2018) for an in-depth discussion of the ethics of qualitative data collection.

The Site or Individual

We are often asked how a researcher locates a site or an individual to study, and our answer typically refers to the approach we have decided to use. In a narrative study, one needs to find one or more individuals to study—individuals who are accessible, willing to provide information, and distinctive for their accomplishments and ordinariness or who shed light on a specific phenomenon or issue being explored. Plummer (1983) recommends two sources of individuals to study. The pragmatic approach is where individuals are met on a chance encounter, emerge from a wider study, or are volunteers. Alternatively, one might identify a "marginal person" who lives in conflicting cultures, a "great person" who impacts the age in which they live, or an "ordinary person" who provides an example of a large population. An alternative perspective is available from Gergen (1994), who suggests that narratives "come into existence" (p. 280) not as a product of an individual, but as a facet of relationships, as a part of culture, and as reflected in social roles such as gender and age. Thus, to ask which individuals will participate is not to focus on the right question. Instead, narrative researchers need to focus on the stories to emerge, recognizing that all people have stories to tell. Yet Daiute (2014) suggests that sensemaking of

TABLE 7.2 ■ Ethical Situations to Anticipate and Address by Data Collection Activity

Data Collection Activity	Examples of Types of Ethical Situations to Anticipate and Address	Examples of How a Researcher Potentially Addresses the Situation
The site or individual selection	Situations where site selection might raise power issues with researchers (e.g., research within own work context)	Researcher presents a rationale and procedures for site or individual selection and engages in procedures to minimize power issues. Could also consider alternatives with lessened power concerns.
Access and rapport	Situations where sites might require local site approvals for access	Researcher seeks local approval and contacts a gatekeeper for help.
	Situations where participants need to be informed of study procedures and their rights	Researcher seeks consent from appropriate individuals for participation.
	Situations requiring respect for the participants and sites	Researcher identifies cultural, religious, gender, and other differences and how they will be respected and honored.
Sampling strategy	Situations requiring participant knowledge about their selection for the sample, their inclusion/exclusion in the sample, and the equal distribution of risks and benefits to participants	Researcher states rationale for participant selection, identifies inclusion/exclusion criteria, and recruits in ways that equally distribute risks/benefits for participants.
Forms of data	Situations where data collection might disrupt the site and be inappropriate for the participants	Researcher describes potentially disruptive situations and how they will be addressed.
	Situations requiring eliciting information from participants, providing rewards for their participation, and reciprocating back to participants	Researcher identifies procedures for eliciting information, giving rewards, and reciprocating back to participants.
Recording procedures	Situations when recording might be intrusive and inappropriate for the participants	Researcher identifies handling intrusive situations and maintaining confidentiality of the data.
Field issues	Situations related to entry and access, appropriateness of data forms, and procedures for information collection	Researcher discusses entry/access, use of the data forms, and procedures for data collection.
Data storage	Situations about the secure storage of data and the intended use of the data	Researcher details secure data storage approaches and intended use of the data.

the narratives begins with sampling relevant time and space dimensions. Also instructive in considering the individual in narrative research is to consider whether first-order or second-order narratives are the focus of inquiry (Elliott, 2005). In first-order narratives, individuals tell stories about themselves and their own experiences, while in second-order narratives, researchers construct a narrative about other people's experiences (e.g., biography) or present a collective story that represents the lives of many.

In a phenomenological study, the participants may be located at a single site, although they need not be. Most important, they must be individuals who have all experienced the phenomenon being explored and can articulate their lived experiences (van Manen, 2023). The more diverse the characteristics of the individuals, the more difficult it will be for the researcher to find common experiences, themes, and the overall essence of the experience for all participants. In a grounded theory study, the individuals may not be located at a single site; in fact, if they are dispersed, they can provide important contextual information useful in developing categories in the axial coding phase of research. They need to be individuals who have participated in the process or action the researcher is studying in the grounded theory study. For example, Creswell and Brown (1992) interviewed 32 department chairpersons located across the United States who had mentored faculty in their departments. In an ethnographic study, a single site, in which an intact culture-sharing group has developed shared values, beliefs, and assumptions, is often important (Fetterman, 2019). The researcher needs to identify a group (or an individual or individuals representative of a group) to study, preferably one to which the inquirer is a "stranger" (Agar, 1986) and can gain access. For a case study, the researcher needs to select a site or sites to study, such as programs, events, processes, activities, individuals, or several individuals. Although Stake (1995) refers to an individual as an appropriate "case," we turn to the narrative biographical approach or the life history approach in studying a single individual. However, the study of multiple individuals, each defined as a case and considered a collective case study, is acceptable practice.

Self-Study Considerations

A question that students often ask is whether they can study their own organization, place of work, or themselves. Such a study may raise issues of power and risk to the researcher, the participants, and the site. To study one's own workplace, for example, raises questions about whether good data can be collected when the act of data collection may introduce a power imbalance between the researcher and the individuals being studied. Although studying one's own "backyard" is often convenient and eliminates many obstacles to collecting data, researchers can jeopardize their jobs if they report unfavorable data or if participants disclose private information that might negatively influence the organization or workplace. A hallmark of all good qualitative research is the report of multiple perspectives that range over the entire spectrum of perspectives (see the section in Chapter 3 on the characteristics of qualitative research). We are not alone in sounding this cautionary note about studying one's own organization or workplace. Glesne and Peshkin (1992) question research that examines "your own *backyard*—within your own institution or agency, or among friends or colleagues" (p. 21), and they suggest that such information is "dangerous knowledge" that is political and risky for an "inside" investigator.

When it becomes important to study one's own organization or workplace, we typically recommend that multiple strategies of validation (see Chapter 10) be used to ensure that the account is accurate and insightful.

Studying yourself can be a different matter. As mentioned in Chapter 4, autoethnography provides an approach or method for studying yourself. Several helpful books are available on autoethnography that discuss how personal stories are blended with larger cultural issues (see Ellis, 2004; Muncey, 2010). Ellis's (1993) story of the experiences of her brother's sudden death illustrates the power of personal emotion and the use of cultural perspectives around one's own experiences. We recommend that individuals wanting to study themselves and their own experiences turn to autoethnography or biographical memoir for scholarly procedures in how to conduct their studies.

Access and Rapport

Qualitative research involves the study of a research site(s) and gaining permission to study the site in a way that will enable the easy collection of data. Gaining access to sites and individuals also involves several steps. All qualitative approaches to inquiry, if collecting data from participants, require permissions from a human subjects review board. This means obtaining approval from university or college institutional review boards as well as individuals at the research site—and in some cases from an organizational body such as a school board or hospital-based research review committee. Evidence of having gained approval(s) should be stated in a research report or proposal (if applicable). While the approval processes are dependent upon the individual study and participant circumstances and as a result the necessary evidence can vary greatly, we offer four examples from journal articles to examine in Example 7.1.

EXAMPLE 7.1 EVIDENCE OF ETHICAL REVIEWS AND APPROVALS

See how the evidence of a review and approval is presented for readers in the following four journal articles.

a. Referencing a university-based institutional review board in Harley et al. (2009, p. 99):
   The study was approved by the Institutional Review Board of The Ohio State University.
b. Referencing the ethical application filing number and a governmental institutional review board followed by a rationale for and description of the consent procedures used with the vulnerable study population in Trip et al. (2019, pp. 1599–1600; see Appendix C):
   Ethical approval (URA/11/02/004) was received from the Upper South A Regional Ethics Committee, Ministry of Health, New Zealand . . . As with the general population, people with intellectual disability must be "assumed to have capacity to consent, unless it is proven otherwise" (Dye, Hendy, Hare, & Burton, 2004, p. 145). Consent by proxy was used by one person with intellectual disability who was able to assent to participate but was unable to provide informed consent (Veenstra et al., 2010): This means that

their legal guardian could consent to their participation having ascertained their understanding about the project even if the logistics of research process per se are unclear to them. All the remaining participants consented for themselves.

c. Referencing community-based initiators, review procedures, and an institutional review board affiliated with a university in Healey (2014, p. e134):

> The researcher was born and raised in Nunavut, lives and works in the community as a health researcher, and initiated the study at the request of fellow community members. The research project was designed and implemented in partnership with community wellness or research centres in each of the three communities. The project was supported in principle by Nunavut Tunngavik Incorporated and the Chief Medical Officer of Health for Nunavut. The research protocol was reviewed by community members and community wellness committees in the three communities, and their feedback was provided to the Nunavut Research Institute, which had granted a research license. Ethical approval was granted by the University of Toronto Community-Based HIV/AIDS Research Ethics Board.

d. Referencing that no ethical review approval was needed in Goodrum et al. (2022, p. 271; see Appendix E):

> Institutional review board approval was not required because the authors did not recruit or interview subjects. In addition, all parties in the case agreed to the public release of the project data to share lessons learned on violence prevention.

Letter of information

As part of the review process application, researchers include examples of materials that will be used in their study including a letter of information and a consent form for participants. The importance of such materials is noted by Poth (2021):

> Free and informed consent requires careful planning of research procedures, keeping in mind your participants and their capacity for decision-making and providing free and informed consent. By providing their informed consent, participants affirm that they understand the purpose of the research and what their participation in the research involves, and that their decision to participate is made voluntarily and free from coercion. (p. 41)

A letter of information can also be used as a recruitment tool and needs to be carefully constructed and written in clear and concise language. Unfortunately, all too many researchers do not provide sufficient information. This need not be the case, so we have created the following "script" for a letter of information containing several sentences and blanks that a researcher can fill in (see also Poth, 2021).

> You are invited to participate in _____(State study title) by _____ (Name researcher and contact information) because you _____(Specify criteria for inclusion). From this research about _____(Describe study topic/phenomenon), we wish to learn _____(Outline the study purpose and benefits).

This _____(Identify the type of qualitative approach—narrative, phenomenological, grounded theory, ethnographic, case) study will involve _____(Describe the data collection methods—interviews, observations, artifacts). The study will take place _____(Describe the study location—online, on campus, at an office) on _____(Provide approximate dates) and should take approximately _____ (Explain duration—minutes, hours, months).

The results of this research will be used to _____(Describe use of data—for publication, conferences, public talks) and will be accessible to _____(Describe who will have access—research team members, investigators). We anticipate the risks of participation to be low; however, should you experience _____(Describe possible risks) please _____ (Describe what to do if problems occur—list of resources or contacts if applicable).

We will take all measures to ensure the confidentiality of your responses, including _____(Describe secure data storage—where, how, what form, and for how long). For your participation, you will receive _____(Describe any research incentives—compensations or reimbursements of expenses). Your participation in this research is strictly voluntary: You may withdraw from this project, without penalty by _____(Detail how to withdraw and contact details). If you should have any questions or concerns about the project at any time you are urged to contact _____(Describe who to contact for questions and provide details). The plan for this study has been reviewed by _____(Describe any ethical reviews completed).

If you wish to participate in this study, please _____(Describe how to access or who to contact—name and contact details). If you wish to receive a summary of the study findings, please ____(Describe how to access or who to contact or what contact information to provide).

As this script shows, several terms can be used to encode a passage for a specific approach to qualitative research by identifying the approach when introducing the study, the central phenomenon in the study description, the focus of the study in the purpose statement, and the study outcome in the benefits details.

Documenting Consent

A key procedure for ensuring free and informed consent to participate involves participants affirming their willingness to participate and documenting their consent to participate. It is helpful to examine a sample consent form that participants need to review and sign in a qualitative study. Examine the example of a consent form in Figure 7.2.

This consent form often requires that specific elements be included, such as the following:

- The right of participants to voluntarily withdraw from the study at any time (and have no obligation to participate) and how participants can withdraw if they so choose
- The right of participants to contact someone if they have questions or need clarifications

- The central purpose of the study and the procedures to be used in data collection
- The protection of the confidentiality of the respondents
- The known risks associated with participation in the study
- The expected benefits for study participants

FIGURE 7.2 ■ Sample Human Subjects Consent-to-Participate Form

"Experiences in Learning Qualitative Research: A Qualitative Case Study"

Dear Participant,

The following information is provided for you to decide if you wish to participate in the present study. You should be aware that you are free to decide not to participate or to withdraw at any time without affecting your relationship with this department, the instructor, or the University of XX. To withdraw contact the research assistant (listed below) at any time as the instructor will not have access to data or know who is participating until the course is completed.

The purpose of this case study is to understand the process of learning qualitative research in a doctoral-level college course. At this stage in the research, the process will be generally defined as the perceptions of the course and making sense out of qualitative research at different phases in the course.

Data will be collected at three points—at the beginning of the course, at the midpoint, and at the end of the course. Data collection will involve documents (journal entries made by students and the instructor, student evaluations of the class and the research procedure), audiovisual material (a video of the class), interviews (transcripts of interviews between students), and classroom observation field notes (made by students and the instructor). Individuals involved in the data collection will be the instructor and the students in the class.

Do not hesitate to ask any questions about the study either before participating or during the time that you are participating. We would be happy to share our findings with you after the research is completed and we will send a summary to the entire class. However, your name will not be associated with the research findings in any way, and only the researchers will know your identity as a participant.

There are no known risks and/or discomforts associated with this study. The expected benefits associated with your participation are the information about the experiences in learning qualitative research, the opportunity to participate in a qualitative research study, and coauthorship for those students who participate in the detailed analysis of the data. If submitted for publication, a byline will indicate the participation of all students in the class.

The plan for this study has been reviewed for its adherence to ethical guidelines and approved by Research Ethics Board at the University of XX. Please sign your consent with full knowledge of the nature and purpose of the procedures. A copy of this consent form will be given to you to keep.

Date

Signature of Participant

John W. Creswell, PhD, University of XX, Principal Investigator, XX@XX

Sara Johnson, MEd, University of XX, Research Assistant, XX@XX

- The instructions for participants to access the findings
- The signature of the participant as well as the researcher

While it has been typical practice for participants to document written consent by signing a paper-based form, there may be situations where alternatives might be offered and so it is important to become familiar with other common approaches described by Poth (2021):

- Typing their name to a digital consent form may be a reasonable alternative to providing a digital signature.

- Stating their name verbally may be preferable if the research involves participants for whom writing is a challenge, who are not accustomed to signing their names, or who wish, by not documenting their consent in writing, to remain anonymous in the data records.

- Providing an overt action may be sufficient if the data is being collected anonymously such as clicking 'yes' to begin an online interview.

- Offering a waiver and having a second eyewitness if the research has no other record of participants' identities and where their identity is the main risk for potential harm.

- Protecting vulnerable participants such as minors (i.e., 18 years or under) might involve a designate providing consent verbally or in writing on their behalf.

Gaining access also means finding individuals who can provide access to the research site and facilitate the collection of data. The permissions and building of rapport will differ depending on the type of qualitative approach being used and the participants sought. For a narrative study, inquirers gain information from individuals by obtaining their permission to participate in the study. Study participants should be apprised of the motivation of the researcher for their selection, granted anonymity (if they desire it), and told by the researcher about the purpose of the study. This disclosure helps build rapport. As in the Chan (2010; see Appendix A) narrative study of a single individual, access to family and community members, biographical documents, and archives required permission from the individual(s).

In a phenomenological study in which the sample includes individuals who have experienced the phenomenon, it is also important to obtain participants' consent to be studied. This is the case in the Chance (2022; see Appendix B) study of the lived experiences of adversity as Black women in higher education leadership. In such a study of a sensitive topic, it was important to have in place measures to protect the identities of participating individuals.

In a grounded theory study, the participants need to provide permission to be studied, while the researcher should have established rapport with the participants so that they will disclose detailed perspectives about responding to an action or a process. The grounded theorist starts with a homogeneous sample and individuals who have commonly experienced the action or process. In the grounded theory study of the caregiving relationship process of aging people with intellectual disabilities in families, Trip and colleagues (2019; see Appendix C) initially approached residential and vocational intellectual disability service providers to seek their guidance to ascertain if people accessing their services met the inclusion criteria. In an ethnography, access typically begins with a **gatekeeper**, an individual who is a member of or has insider status with a cultural group. This gatekeeper is the initial contact for the researcher and leads the researcher to other participants (Atkinson, 2015). An example of such a gatekeeper are the two young men who provided the initial access point to the group studied in the ethnography described by Mac an Ghaill and Haywood (2015; see Appendix D).

A gatekeeper can be especially important when seeking access to vulnerable groups because of the trust, culture, and language concerns identified by Creswell and Guetterman (2019). Approaching this gatekeeper and the cultural system of a community slowly is necessary. See Chilisa (2020) and Tuhiwai Smith (2023) to learn about how Indigenous ways of knowing and being can inform your work with Indigenous communities and help you gain awareness about the harm of colonial practices and the promise of current decolonizing practices. For both ethnographies and case studies, gatekeepers require information about the studies that often includes answers from the researchers to the following questions, as Bogdan and Biklen (1992) suggest:

- Why was the site chosen for study?
- What will be done at the site during the research study? How much time will be spent at the site by the researcher(s)?
- Will the researcher's presence be disruptive?
- How will the results be reported?
- What will the gatekeeper, the participants, and the site gain from the study (reciprocity)?

In case study, it is often the researchers who are seeking access to a specific bounded system. Similar to other qualitative approaches, rapport must be built, and participants must consent to be studied if the researchers are going to collect data. In situations where researchers rely on existing data, such as the one described in Goodrum et al., (2022; see Appendix E) inquirers must negotiate data access but not site access or permissions from participants. See Poth (2019) for guidance about what methodological details (including ethical procedures followed in the original study) to report when using existing (also referred to as reusing) qualitative data.

Purposeful Sampling Strategies

Three considerations go into the purposeful sampling approach in qualitative research, and these considerations vary depending on the specific approach. They include whom to select as participants (or sites) for the study, the specific type of sampling strategy, and the size of the sample to be studied. Such decisions are essential to enhance equity and promote diversity in recruitment and sampling (Poth, 2021).

Participants in the Sample

In a narrative study, the researcher reflects more on whom to sample—the individual may be convenient to study because they are available; a politically important individual who attracts attention or is marginalized; or a typical, ordinary person. All of the individuals need to have stories to tell about their lived experiences. Inquirers may select several options, depending on whether the person is marginal, great, or ordinary (Plummer, 1983). The schoolgirls, who consented to participate and provided insightful information about gender-based violence, poverty, and HIV/AIDS (Simmonds et al., 2015), were convenient to study but also provided a critical illustration of the types of challenges surrounding broader issues of gender within an African society. Ai Mei Zhang was a Chinese immigrant student in Canada who could inform an understanding of the ethnic identity through student, teacher, and parent narratives (Chan, 2010; see Appendix A).

We have found, however, a much narrower range of sampling strategies for phenomenological studies. It is essential that all participants have experience of the phenomenon being studied. Criterion sampling works well when all individuals studied represent people who have experienced the phenomenon. Participants in the Chance (2022; see Appendix B) phenomenology were recruited by blending convenience, purposive, and snowball sampling techniques. All participants met the following three criteria for participation: (a) Black women; (b) president/chancellor, vice president/vice chancellor, or provost of a 4-year college or university in the United States; (c) individuals who had obtained or had been completing a terminal degree. Chance (2022) describes her sampling population as unique, small, and limited. However, they all experienced leadership, the phenomenon under study.

In a grounded theory study, the researcher chooses participants who can contribute to the development of the theory. Corbin and Strauss (2015) refer to theoretical sampling, which is a process of sampling individuals who can contribute to building the opening and axial coding of the theory. This begins with selecting and studying a homogeneous sample of individuals (e.g., all women who have experienced childhood abuse) and then, after initially developing the theory, selecting and studying a heterogeneous sample (e.g., types of support groups other than women who have experienced childhood abuse). The rationale for studying this heterogeneous sample is to confirm or disconfirm the conditions, both contextual and intervening, under which the model holds. The Trip et al. (2019; see Appendix C) grounded theory study used nonprobability sampling and recruited using "advertisements placed in a religious publication, a carers newsletter, and public notices in local newspapers and on websites" (p. 1597). The 19 people with intellectual disabilities met specific criteria of being approximately 40 years of age, having a mild to moderate level of intellectual disability, having expressive language, having the ability to consent to participate, and having lived with or been supported by someone they identified as "family" for at least 5 years. These participants then nominated 28 family members to contribute their perspectives to develop a theory of the caregiving relationship process of aging people with intellectual disabilities in families that explains navigating transitions across the life course.

In ethnography, once the investigator selects a site with a cultural group, the next decision is who and what will be studied. Thus, within-culture sampling proceeds and several authors offer suggestions for this procedure. Fetterman (2019) recommends proceeding with the big net approach, where at first the researcher mingles with everyone. Ethnographers rely on their judgment to select members of the subculture or unit based on their research questions. They take advantage of opportunities (i.e., opportunistic sampling; Miles et al., 2019) or establish criteria for studying select individuals (criterion sampling). The criteria for selecting who and what to study, according to Hammersley and Atkinson (2019), are based on gaining some perspective on chronological time in the social life of the group, people representative of the culture-sharing group in terms of demographics, and the contexts that lead to different forms of behavior. In their ethnography of British-born, Pakistani and Bangladeshi young men, Mac an Ghaill and Haywood (2015; see Appendix D) attribute their access as "greatly enabled by our being known for our social commitment to the local area, working with families in the local community" (p. 100) and snowball sampling from the initial two young men as effective for identifying participants.

In a case study, we prefer to select unusual cases in collective case studies and employ maximum variation as a sampling strategy to represent diverse cases and to fully describe multiple perspectives about the cases. Extreme and deviant cases may comprise a collective case study, such as the study of the unusual user experience of the Silk Road, the virtual drug marketplace (Van Hout & Bingham, 2013; see also Example 4.5) and the unusual case studied by Goodrum et al. (2022; see Appendix E) as one of only two known cases where a school threat assessment was conducted with a student prior to a deadly school attack.

Types of Sampling Strategies

The concept of purposeful sampling is used in qualitative research. This means that the inquirer selects individuals and sites for study because they can purposefully inform an understanding of the research problem and central phenomenon in the study. Decisions need to be made about who or what should be sampled, what form the sampling will take, and how many people or sites need to be sampled. Further, the researchers need to decide if the sampling will be consistent with the information within one of the five approaches to inquiry.

We will begin with some general remarks about sampling and then turn to sampling within each of the five approaches. The decision about who or what should be sampled can benefit from the conceptualization of Marshall et al. (2021), who provide an example of sampling four aspects: people, actions, events, and/or processes. They also note that sampling can change during a study and that researchers need to be flexible; but despite this, researchers need to plan ahead as much as possible for their sampling strategy. We like to think in terms of levels of sampling in qualitative research. Researchers can sample at the site level, at the event or process level, and at the participant level. In a good plan for a qualitative study, one or more of these levels might be present, and each one needs to be identified.

On the question of what form the sampling will take, we need to note that there are several qualitative sampling strategies available (see Table 7.3 for a list of possibilities). These strategies have names and definitions, and they can be described in research reports. Also, researchers might use one or more of the strategies in a single study. Looking down the list, **maximum variation sampling** is listed first because it is a popular approach in qualitative studies.

TABLE 7.3 ■ Types of Sampling Strategies in Qualitative Inquiry

Type of Sampling	Purpose
Maximum variation	Documents diverse variations of individuals or sites based on specific characteristics
Homogeneous	Focuses, reduces, simplifies, and facilitates group interviewing
Critical case	Permits logical generalization and maximum application of information to other cases
Theory based	Elaborates on and examines a construct of a theory or the entire theory
Confirming and disconfirming cases	Elaborates on initial analysis, seeks exceptions, and looks for variation
Snowball or chain	Identifies cases of interest from people who know people who know what cases are information-rich
Extreme or deviant case	Learns from highly unusual manifestations of the phenomenon of interest
Typical case	Highlights what is normal or average
Intensity	Seeks information-rich cases that manifest the phenomenon intensely but not extremely
Politically important	Attracts desired attention or avoids attracting undesired attention
Random purposeful	Adds credibility to sample when potential purposeful sample is too large
Stratified purposeful	Illustrates subgroups and facilitates comparisons
Criterion	Seeks cases that meet some criterion; useful for quality assurance
Opportunistic	Follows new leads; taking advantage of the unexpected
Combination or mixed	Meets multiple interests and needs through triangulation, flexibility
Convenience	Saves time, money, and effort, but at the expense of information and credibility

Source: Miles and Huberman (1994, p. 28). Reprinted with permission from Sage.

This approach consists of determining in advance some criteria that differentiate the sites or participants and then selecting sites or participants that are quite different from the criteria. This approach is often selected because when a researcher maximizes differences at the beginning of the study, it increases the likelihood that the findings will reflect differences or different perspectives—an ideal in qualitative research. Other sampling strategies frequently used are critical cases, which provide specific information about a problem, and convenience cases, which represent sites or individuals from which the researcher can easily access and collect data.

Sample Size

The size question is an important decision in sampling. One general guideline for **sample size** in qualitative research is to study a few sites or individuals and collect extensive detail about each site or individual studied. The intent in qualitative research is not to generalize the information (except in some forms of case study research) but to elucidate the particular, the specific (Pinnegar & Daynes, 2007). Beyond these general suggestions, each of the five approaches to research raises specific sample size considerations. See also Guest et al. (2013) for their discussion of sampling considerations across data forms.

In narrative research, we have found many examples with one or two individuals, unless a larger pool of participants is used to develop a collective story (Huber & Whelan, 1999). In phenomenology, we have seen the number of participants range from 1 (Padilla, 2003) up to 325 (Polkinghorne, 1989). Dukes (1984) recommends studying 3 to 10 participants, and in one phenomenology, Edwards (2006) studied 33 individuals. In grounded theory, we recommend including 20 to 30 individuals to develop a well-saturated theory, but this number may be much larger (Charmaz, 2014). In ethnography, we like well-defined studies of single culture-sharing groups, with numerous artifacts, interviews, and observations collected until the workings of the cultural group are clear. For case study research, we would recommend four or five cases in a single study (Yin, 2017). This number should provide ample opportunity to identify themes of the cases as well as conduct cross-case theme analysis. Wolcott (2008a) maintains that any case over one dilutes the level of detail that a researcher can provide.

Forms of Data

New forms of qualitative data continually emerge in the literature (see Creswell & Creswell, 2023; Creswell & Guetterman, 2018; Fielding et al., 2017; Merriam & Tisdell, 2015; Paulus & Lester, 2021; Warren & Xavia Karner, 2014), but all forms might be grouped into basic types. They may be interviews ranging from synchronous (where online exchanges may occur at the same time) to asynchronous (where we may post or send a message not knowing when a response will be received online or in-person). Also interviews may range from one-to-one to group interactions. Observations are also popular in qualitative research (ranging from nonparticipant to participant). Researchers also collect documents and artifacts (ranging from personal to public), and audiovisual and social media materials (ranging from photographs to social media posts). Over the years, a compendium with an evolving list of data types has emerged, as shown in Figure 7.3.

We organize the list into the four basic types, although some forms may not be easily placed into one category or the other. Once considered new forms of data such as journaling in narrative story writing, interviewing via e-mail messages, and observing through examining videos and photographs are now joined by journaling in text messaging, observing using social media posts, and interviewing using avatars. Particularly noteworthy have been the emergence of procedures for qualitative research using online, visual, social media, and arts-based research methods (Morris & Paris, 2022; Pauwels & Mannay, 2019; Quan-Haase & Sloan, 2022). Common formats of computer-mediated data collection for qualitative

FIGURE 7.3 ■ A Compendium of Data Forms in Qualitative Research

Interviews

- Conduct one-on-one synchronous interviews online or in person
- Conduct synchronous focus group interviews online or in person
- Conduct asynchronous interviews through e-mail, chat rooms, listservs

Observations

- Conduct an observation as a participant
- Conduct an observation as an observer
- Conduct an observation shifting positions from participant to observer (and vice versa)

Documents

- Keep a research journal during the study
- Have a participant keep a written journal, diary, or blog during the research study
- Examine autobiographies and biographies
- Collect personal letters from participants
- Have participants take photographs, record audio messages or videos
- Analyze organizational documents (e.g., reports, strategic plans, charts, medical records)
- Analyze public documents (e.g., official memos, minutes, records, archival information)
- Conduct chart audits and reviews of medical records

Audiovisual and Social Media Materials

- Examine physical trace evidence (e.g., footprints in the snow)
- Video or film a social situation or an individual or group
- Have a participant keep a video journal or blog during the research study
- Examine photographs or videos
- Examine websites, social media posts
- Collect e-mails or electronic text messages
- Collect sounds (e.g., musical sounds, a child's laughter, car horns honking)
- Examine possessions, artifacts, or ritual objects

research include virtual focus groups and asynchronous interviews via e-mail or text-based chat rooms, weblogs and life journals (such as open-ended diaries online), and social media posts and interactions (Halfpenny & Procter, 2015; Paulus & Lester, 2021; Warren & Xavier Karner, 2014). Some ethnographic researchers have conducted advanced qualitative studies online, collecting data through e-mail, chat room interactions, instant messaging, videoconferencing, and the images and sounds of the websites (Garcia et al., 2009). Paulus and Lester (2021) describe the widespread benefits of adopting new digital technologies in our data collection for cost and time efficiency in terms of reduced costs for travel and data transcription and increased ease of collaboration and communications. Asynchronous data collection can provide temporal flexibility that allows more time for participants to consider and respond to requests for information. Virtual focus groups (when compared to face-to face) can create a nonthreatening and comfortable environment, providing greater ease for participants discussing sensitive issues (Nicholas et al., 2010). Importantly, online data collection can increase the pool of potential study participants by reaching individuals who are geographically dispersed, socially isolated, and hard-to-reach (due to practical constraints, disability, or language or communication barriers). Reaching these groups leads to more equitable qualitative research procedures and outcomes (Salmons, 2022).

There are, however, increased ethical concerns with online data collection, such as participants' privacy protection, new power differentials, ownership of the data, authenticity, and trust in the data collected (Marshall et al., 2021; Nicholas et al., 2010; Salmons, 2022). This is particularly noteworthy when working with children, such as the ethnographic study conducted by Jachyra et al. (2015) with adolescent boys using social media. See Figure 7.4 for an innovative visual representation by Salmons of the interconnectedness of online research ethics among the researcher, human participants, data quality, and online research site.

Moreover, online qualitative research brings new requirements to both participants and researchers. For instance, participants are required to have some technical skills, access to the Internet, and necessary reading and writing proficiency. Online qualitative researchers have to adapt to new data quality and ethical responsibilities (Tiidenberg, 2018) and ways of interacting (Salmons, 2022), for example, conducting screen-based observations, building rapport virtually, and using written chat functions. We encourage individuals designing qualitative projects to explore and include new and creative data collection methods that will encourage readers and editors to examine their studies. While the choice of creative qualitative data collection methods depends upon the individual study and participant circumstances, we offer four examples from journal articles in Example 7.2.

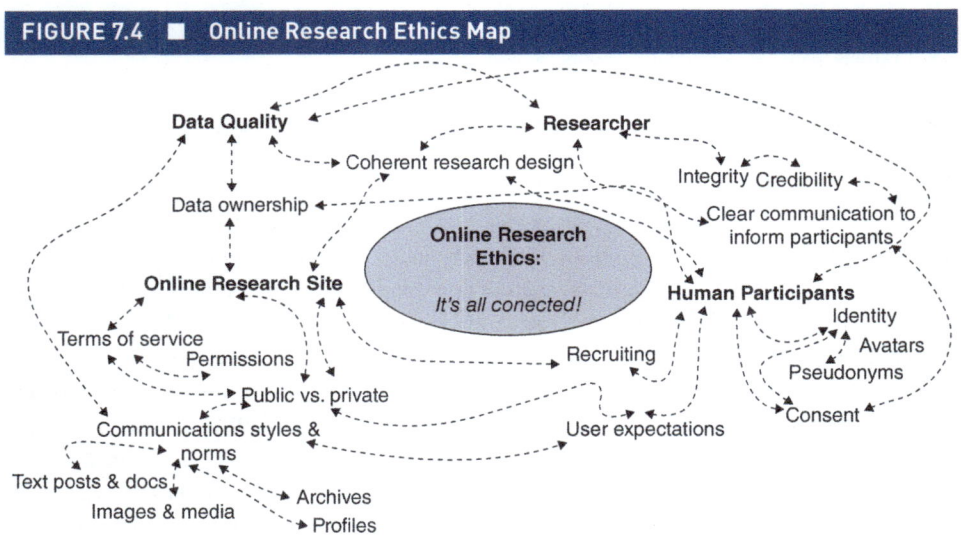

FIGURE 7.4 ■ Online Research Ethics Map

Source: Salmons (2022, p. 79). Used with permission from Sage.

EXAMPLE 7.2 CREATIVE QUALITATIVE DATA COLLECTION METHODS AND RATIONALES FOR THEIR USE

See how the rationale for the use of creative qualitative data collection methods is presented for readers in the following four journal articles.

1. Employing an arts-based inquiry method (musical improvisation on a xylophone and/or glockenspiel) was well suited to the research focus of capturing a "lived experience" perspective in van der Hoorn (2015, p. 1008):

    To capture a "lived experience" perspective, this study leverages an arts-based inquiry research method. The selected method echoes Whitty's (2010) artefacts and emotions study that required project managers to characterize the concept of a project in the form of a line drawing and provide a subsequent explanation of their representation. This study draws on musical improvisation as a device to access the "lived experience" rather than drawing. The improvisation is followed by a semi-structured discussion between researcher and participant regarding the meaning behind the improvised sounds played. In the analysis priority and weight are given to the discussion rather than the actual improvisation. The musical instrument is simply a methodological device for creating a musical improvisation that enables a discourse to take place that discloses a personal perspective of managing a project. It facilitates an exploration of the perceived "lived experience" of managing a project.

2. Using "photo elicitation" interviews was well suited to the research focus of understanding everyday commuting practices by Guell and Ogilvie (2015, pp. 203–204):

    We chose participant-produced photography for several reasons. In its use as photo-elicitation, it would allow us to meet the busy participants for a follow-up interview that could be more participant driven and unstructured. Changes in the participants' lives could thus be captured, and participants would have the opportunity to place emphasis on special aspects of their experience and raise issues that were not anticipated by the researcher. Most importantly, we chose it in its function as photovoice, using the photos as data in their own right. Both the photos and the follow-up interviews provide a more nuanced and richer data set and allow for an ethnographic analysis beyond content analysis of singular interview transcripts.

3. Drawing on multiple forms of data (interviews, participant observation, and documents) was unusual yet helpful to the study focus of explaining the process of software development in Adolph et al. (2012, pp. 1272–1273):

    Participant observation was a major data collection method rather than a supplement to our interviews because it allowed the primary researcher to observe what people did rather than having them comment on what they believed they did. In total, over the year, the primary researcher conducted 20 interviews and spent some 42 days observing participants at work. . . . Document analysis helped us understand the context of the organization (e.g., the organizational charts), and the event history derived from project plans and status reports.

4. Drawing on multiple forms of data (participant observation over 14 years including attending 250 shows, maintaining the lifestyle of the cultural group, regularly associating with group members, collecting interviews, and documenting a variety of sources) uniquely positioned the researcher to generate a detailed description of the core values of the straight edge (sXe) movement in Haenfler (2004, pp. 413–414):

> The data I present result from more than fourteen years of observing the sXe movement in a variety of settings and roles and interviewing members of the scene. . . . To supplement my participant observation, I conducted unstructured, in-depth interviews . . . with [individuals with] differing levels of involvement in the scene. . . . In addition to participant observation, casual conversation, and interviews, I examined a variety of other sources including newspaper stories, music lyrics, World Wide Web pages, and sXe 'zines, coding relevant snippets of information into my field notes.

The particular approach to research often directs a qualitative researcher's attention toward preferred approaches to data collection, although these preferred approaches cannot be seen as rigid guidelines. Researchers need to consider visual ethnography (Marion & Crowder, 2013; Pink, 2013) or the possibilities of narrative research to include living stories, metaphorical visual narratives, and digital archives (see Clandinin, 2007). Czarniawska (2004) mentions three ways to collect data for stories: recording spontaneous incidents of storytelling, eliciting stories through interviews, and asking for stories through such mediums as the Internet. Clandinin and Connelly (2000) suggest collecting field texts through a wide array of sources—autobiographies, journals, researcher field notes, letters, conversations, interviews, stories of families, documents, photographs, and personal-family-social artifacts. The conflicting stories of Ai Mei's ethnic identity were generated through personal observations, interviews, field notes, and attendance at events (Chan, 2010; see Appendix A).

For a phenomenological study, the process of collecting information involves primarily in-depth interviews (e.g., the discussion about the long interview in McCracken, 1988) with as many as 10 individuals. The important point is to describe the meaning of the phenomenon for a small number of individuals who have experienced it. Often multiple interviews are conducted with each of the research participants. The unprecedented study circumstances of the COVID-19 pandemic for higher education leaders was a probable barrier to multiple interviews for Chance (2022; see Appendix B). To personalize the semi-structured interview protocol questions ahead of her interviews, Chance asked participants to complete the Lived Experiences Timeline activity and demographic survey. Besides interviewing and self-reflection, Polkinghorne (1989) advocates gathering information from depictions of the experience outside the context of the research projects, such as descriptions drawn from novelists, poets, painters, and choreographers. We recommend Lauterbach (1993), the study of wished-for babies from mothers, as an especially rich example of phenomenological research using diverse forms of data collection.

Interviews play a central role in the data collection in a grounded theory study. This was the case for Trip et al. (2019; see Appendix C) with the interview protocols informed by the Family Quality of Life questionnaire. In another study, each interview with 33 academic chairpersons lasted approximately an hour (Creswell & Brown, 1992). Other data forms besides interviewing, such as participant observation, researcher reflection or journaling (memoing), participant journaling, and focus groups, may be used to help develop the theory (Birks & Mills, 2023; Corbin & Strauss, 2015).

In an ethnographic study, the investigator collects descriptions of behavior through observations, interviews, documents, and artifacts (Atkinson, 2015; Fetterman, 2019; Spradley, 1980), although observing and interviewing appear to be the most popular forms of ethnographic data collection. In the study by Mac an Ghaill and Haywood (2015; see Appendix D), group and life history interviews provided the framework through which to explore a range of critical incidents experienced by the British-born Pakistani and Bangladeshi young men. Ethnography has the distinction among the five approaches, we believe, of advocating the use of quantitative surveys and tests and measures as part of data collection. For example, examine the wide array of forms of data in ethnography as advanced by LeCompte and Schensul (1999). They reviewed ethnographic data collection techniques of observation, tests and repeated measures, sample surveys, interviews, content analysis of secondary or visual data, elicitation methods, audiovisual information, spatial mapping, and network research.

Like ethnography, case study data collection involves a wide array of procedures as the researcher builds an in-depth picture of the case. We are reminded of the multiple forms of data collection recommended by Yin (2017) in his book about case studies. He referred to six forms: documents, archival records, interviews, direct observation, participant observation, and physical artifacts. This was the case for Goodrum et al. (2022; see Appendix E) whose study drew upon deposition testimony, investigation reports, and exhibits. To represent the extensive data collection involved in a campus gun incident case study, Asmussen and Creswell (1995) used a matrix of information of the four types of data (interviews, observations, documents, and audiovisual materials) in the columns and the specific forms of information (e.g., students at large, central administration) in the rows. The use of a matrix, which is especially applicable in an information-rich case study, might serve the inquirer equally well in all approaches of inquiry to convey the depth and multiple forms of data collection.

Of the four forms of data collection in Figure 7.3, documents, audiovisual material, and social media are typically used to supplement interviews and observations. Yet it is important to recognize the important historical and contextual information generated by a review of existing individual and organizational documents and artifacts (Prior, 2003). To mitigate many of the challenges of reviewing documents, audiovisual, and social media materials, we recommend negotiating access to materials ahead of time, defining clear inclusion or exclusion criteria based on the purpose for the data, and allocating adequate time for review and synthesis.

Interviewing and observing deserve special attention because they are frequently used in all five of the approaches to research. Entire books are available on these two topics (e.g., on interviewing: Brinkman, 2018; Brinkmann & Kvale, 2015; Rubin & Rubin, 2012; on observing: Angrosino, 2007; Bernard, 2017); thus, we highlight basic procedures that we recommend to prospective interviewers and observers.

Interviewing

An interview is a social interaction based on a conversation (Rubin & Rubin, 2012; Warren & Xavia Karner, 2014). According to Brinkmann and Kvale (2015), an interview is where "knowledge is constructed in the interaction between the interviewer and the interviewee" (p. 4). The qualitative research interview is further described as "attempts to understand the world from the subjects' point of view, to unfold the meaning of their experience, to uncover their lived world" (p. 3). Who is interviewed and what questions are asked depends on the purpose of the study and research questions guiding the study. It is not surprising given the complex skills necessary for conducting a good interview, that interviewing is often referred to as a "craft" that is developed through practice (Brinkmann & Kvale, 2015; Rubin & Rubin, 2012). One might view interviewing as consisting of a series of steps. As shown in Figure 7.5, authors have specified the steps necessary to conduct qualitative interviews.

The Brinkmann and Kvale (2015) seven stages of an interview inquiry report a logical sequence starting with thematizing the inquiry; designing the study; interviewing; transcribing the interview; analyzing the data; verifying the validity, reliability, and generalizability of the findings; and finally, reporting the study. The seven steps described by Rubin and Rubin (2012), called the responsive interviewing model, are similar in scope to Brinkmann and Kvale (2015), but they view the sequence as not fixed, allowing the researcher to change the questions asked, the sites chosen, and the situations to study. Both approaches to the stages of interviewing sweep across the many phases of research from deciding on a topic to the actual writing of the study. In the approach presented here, we focus on the data collection process in some detail, recognizing that this process is embedded within a larger sequence of research. The steps are as follow:

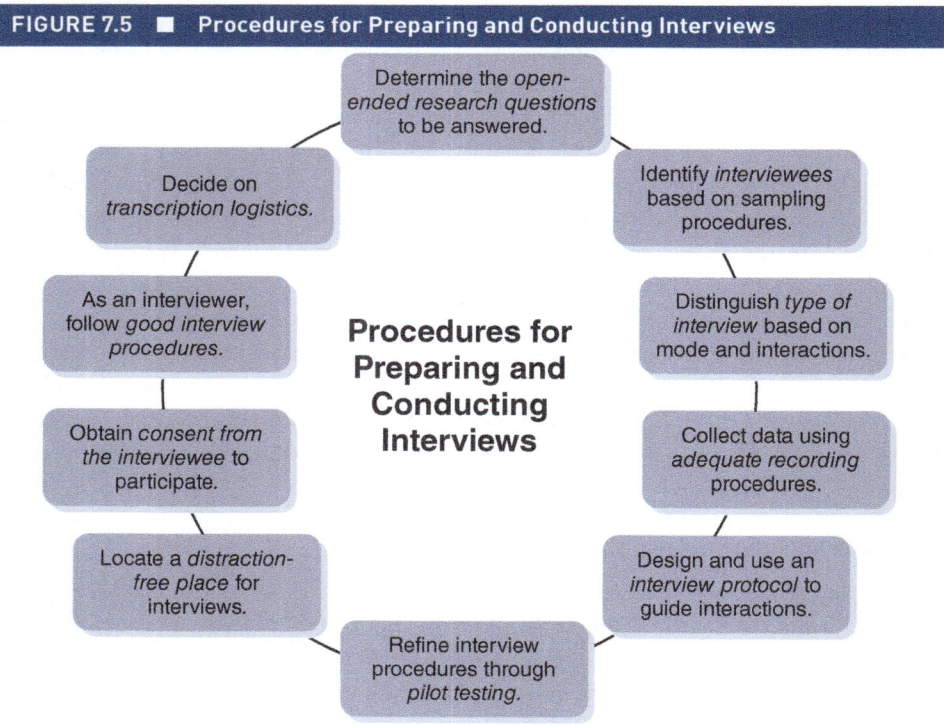

FIGURE 7.5 ■ Procedures for Preparing and Conducting Interviews

- *Determine the research questions that will be answered by interviews.* These questions are open-ended, general, and focused on understanding your central phenomenon in the study.

- *Identify interviewees who can best answer these questions based on one of the purposeful sampling procedures mentioned in the preceding discussion* (see Table 7.3).

- *Distinguish the type of interview by determining what mode is practical and what interactions will net the most useful information to answer research questions.* We recommend assessing the types available and deciding the best fit for the context.

- *Collect data using adequate recording procedures when conducting one-on-one or focus group interviews.* We recommend microphone equipment that is sensitive to the acoustics of the room from its location, such as the use of lapel microphones or headsets. We also recommend using more than one recording device placed at different locations in a group environment.

- *Design and use an interview protocol, or interview guide* (Brinkmann & Kvale, 2015). Use approximately five to seven open-ended questions and ample space between the questions to write responses to the interviewee's comments (see the sample protocol in Figure 7.6).

- *Refine the interview questions and the procedures through pilot testing.* In an ethnography of boat pilots aboard cargo vessels, Sampson (2004) used pilot testing to refine and develop research instruments, assess the degrees of observer bias, frame questions, collect background information, and adapt research procedures. In case study research, Yin (2017) recommends a pilot test to refine data collection plans and develop relevant lines of questions. These pilot cases are selected based on convenience, access, and geographic proximity.

- *Locate a distraction-free place for conducting the interview.* Find, if possible, a physical setting where a private conversation can be held that lends itself to audiotaping.

- *Obtain consent from the interviewee to participate in the study by completing a consent form approved by the human relations review board.* At the beginning of the interview, review the purpose of the study, the amount of time that will be needed to complete the interview, their right to withdraw from the study, and plans for using the results from the interview (offer a copy of the report or an abstract of it to the interviewee).

- *As an interviewer, follow good interview procedures.* Stay within the study boundaries you have reviewed, use the protocol to guide your questions, complete the interview within the time specified, be respectful and courteous, and offer few questions and advice. This last point is an important reminder of how a good interviewer is a good listener rather than a frequent speaker during an interview.

- *Decide on transcription logistics ahead of time.* For example, what will be transcribed if needed? If software will be used, then how will it be checked? Decisions here need to be made about verbal cues and extraneous words and utterances (e.g., "hmms"). Analysis will be limited if you don't include certain things.

One step in the procedure we will highlight: designing an interview protocol. Earlier (in Chapter 6) we spoke about how the research subquestions could be used as the key questions during an interview. An **interview protocol**, contains these key questions, and they are bounded on the front end by questions inviting the interviewee to open up and talk and located at the end by questions about "Whom should I talk to in order to learn more?" or comments thanking the participants for their time for the interview. Figure 7.6 illustrates a sample interview protocol or guide.

How the interactions take place depends on the choice of interview approach. A basic consideration is the degree to which the researcher structures the interview. In a structured interview the researcher predetermines the questions and provides response options. This approach is typically used in quantitative research. In semi-structured interviewing, the research uses some structured questions as well as open-ended questions without response options. In unstructured interviews, the researcher asks open-ended questions without specifying in advance the response options. For qualitative research, we favor using unstructured interviews, providing open-ended questions, and learning participant views about the central phenomenon being explored.

The type of interview options vary considerably. Variations for one-on-one interviews include both the interviewee and interviewer being physically located in the same room, talking face-to-face using technology (e.g., Zoom or avatars in a virtual environment), or talking over the phone. An alternative to talking is to interact in writing using text messaging or an online chat function. Focus groups are advantageous when the interaction among interviewees will likely yield the best information, when interviewees are similar and cooperative with each other,

---

FIGURE 7.6 ■ Sample Interview Protocol or Guide

Interview Protocol Project: University Reaction to a Campus Shooting Incident

Time of interview:

Date:

Place:

Interviewer:

Interviewee:

Position of interviewee:

(Briefly describe the project)

Questions:

1. What has been your role in the incident?
2. What has happened since the event that you have been involved in?
3. What has been the impact on the university community of this incident?
4. What larger ramifications, if any, exist from the incident?
5. To whom should we talk to find out more about campus reaction to the incident?

Thank the individual for participating in this interview. Describe the measures to ensure participant of confidentiality of responses and potential future interviews.

when time to collect information is limited, and when individuals interviewed one-on-one may be hesitant to provide information (Krueger & Casey, 2014; Morgan, 1997, 2019). Krueger and Casey (2014) discuss the use of focus groups on the Internet, including the use of chat room and bulletin board groups. They discuss how to manage the Internet groups as well as how to develop questions for the groups. Problems that require planning for online focus groups include scheduling across international time zones, documenting informed consent, and ensuring participants avoid talking "over" one another. Regardless of interview mode, care must be taken to create an environment as comfortable as possible and, in group settings, to encourage all participants to talk and to monitor individuals who may dominate the conversation.

Observing

Observation is one of the key tools for collecting data in qualitative research. It is the act of noting a phenomenon in a field setting through the five senses of the observer, often with a note-taking instrument, and recording it for scientific purposes (Angrosino, 2007). The observations are based on the research purpose and questions. During observations, researchers watch the physical setting, participants, activities, interactions, conversations, and their own behavior. Researchers also use their senses, including sight, sound, touch, smell, and taste. Writing down everything is impossible. Thus, we recommend starting the observation broadly and then concentrating on addressing the research questions. To one degree or another, the observer is usually involved in that which they are observing.

The extent to which the observer is engaged in terms of participating and observing is usually distinguished into four observation *types*:

- *Complete participant.* The researcher is fully engaged with the people he or she is observing. This engagement may help the researcher establish greater rapport with the people being observed (Angrosino, 2007).

- *Participant as observer.* The researcher is participating in the activity at the site. The participant role is more salient than the researcher role. This involvement may help the researcher gain insider views and subjective data. However, it may be distracting for the researcher to record data when they are integrated into the activity (Bogdewic, 1999).

- *Nonparticipant observer.* The researcher is an outsider of the group under study, watching and taking field notes from a distance. As an observer, the researcher records data without direct involvement with the activity or people (Bernard, 2017).

- *Complete observer.* The researcher is neither seen nor noticed by the people under study.

As a good qualitative observer, changing roles during an observation may occur, such as starting as a nonparticipant and then moving into the participant role, or vice versa. Participant observation, for example, offers possibilities for the researcher on a continuum from being a complete outsider to being a complete insider (Fetterman, 2019). The approach of changing one's role from that of an outsider to that of an insider through the course of the ethnography is well documented in ethnographic fieldwork (Bernard, 2017). Wolcott's (1994) study of the Principal Selection Committee illustrates an outsider perspective, as he observed and recorded events in the process of selecting a principal for a school without becoming an active participant in the committee's conversations and activities.

Observing in a setting involves special researcher skills such as impression management to not disclose reactions. The researcher may also experience marginalization in a strange setting or deception by the people being interviewed (Atkinson, 2015). Like interviewing, we also see observing as a series of procedural steps that involve preparing for and conducting observations as summarized in Figure 7.7.

- *Select a site to be observed and gain access.* Obtain the required permissions needed to gain access to the site.

- *At the site, identify who or what to observe, when, and for how long.* A gatekeeper helps in this process.

- *Select an observational role as an observer.* This role can range from that of a complete participant (going native) to that of a complete observer. We especially like the procedure of being an outsider initially, followed by becoming an insider over time.

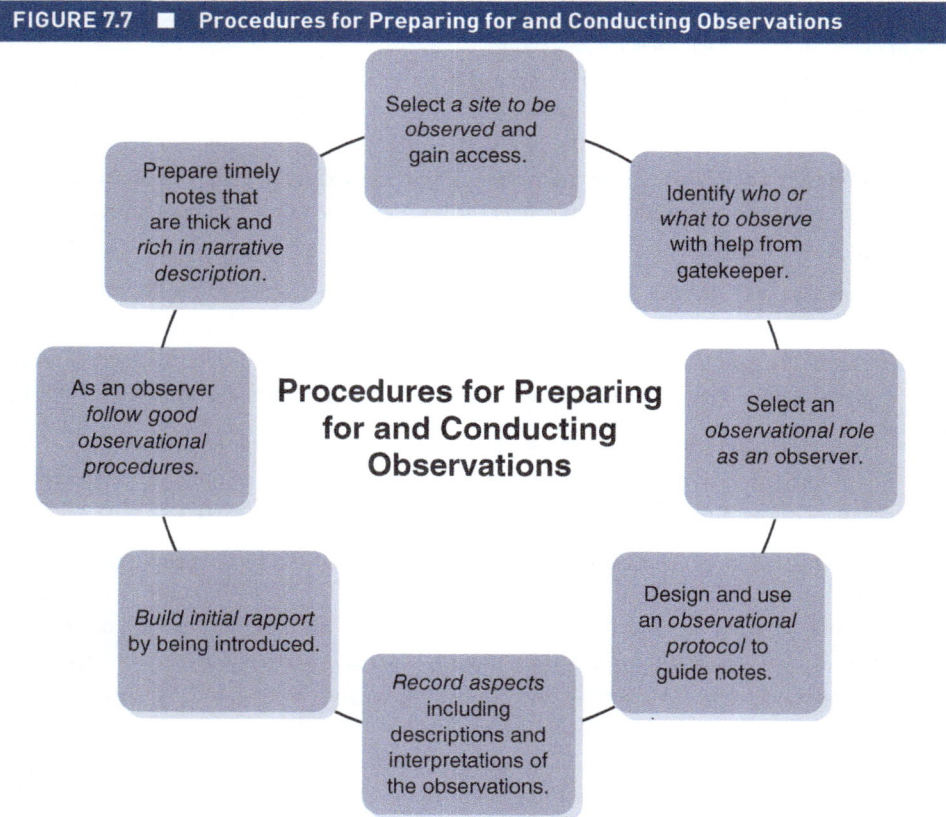

FIGURE 7.7 ■ Procedures for Preparing for and Conducting Observations

- *Design and use an **observational protocol** as a method for recording field notes.* Include in this protocol both descriptive and reflective notes (i.e., notes about your experiences, hunches, and learnings). Make sure the protocol is headed by the date, place, and time of observation (Angrosino, 2007). See Figure 7.8 for a sample observational protocol.

- *Record aspects such as portraits of the participants, the physical setting, particular events and activities, and personal reactions* (Bogdan & Biklen, 1992). Describe what happened including personal reflections, insights, ideas, confusions, hunches, initial interpretations, and breakthroughs.

- *Build initial rapport by being introduced by someone if an outsider, having a passive and friendly attitude, and starting with limited objectives in the first few sessions of observation.* The early observational sessions may be times in which to take minimal notes and simply observe.

- *As an observer, follow good observational procedures.* After observing, slowly withdraw from the site, thanking the participants and informing them of the use of the data and their access to the study.

- *Prepare timely notes that are thick and rich in narrative description after the observation.* Give a full description of the people and events under observation (Emerson et al., 2011).

Recording Information Procedures

In discussing interviewing and observing procedures, we mention the use of a protocol, a pre-designed form used to guide information collection during an interview or observation. The interview protocol helps a researcher organize thoughts on interviewee responses to particular questions, items such as headings, information about starting the interview, concluding ideas, information on ending the interview, and thanking the respondent. Figure 7.6 provided the interview protocol used in the gunman case study (Asmussen & Creswell, 1995).

Besides the five open-ended questions in the study, this form contains several features we recommend. The instructions for using the interview protocol are as follows:

- Use a header to record essential information about the project and as a reminder to go over the purpose of the study with the interviewee. This heading might also include information about confidentiality and address aspects included in the consent form.

- Place space between the questions in the protocol form. Recognize that an individual may not always respond directly to the questions being asked. For example, a researcher may ask Question 2, but the interviewee's response may be to Question 4. Be prepared to write notes on all of the questions as the interviewee speaks.

- Memorize the questions and their order to minimize losing eye contact with the participant. Provide appropriate verbal transitions from one question to the next.

- Write out the closing comments that thank the individual for the interview and request follow-up information, if needed, from them.

FIGURE 7.8 ■ Sample Observational Protocol

Length of Activity: 90 Minutes	
Descriptive Notes	*Reflective Notes*
General: What are the experiences of graduate students as they learn qualitative research in the classroom?	
See classroom layout and comments about physical setting at the bottom of this page.	*Overhead with details: I wonder if the back of the room was able to read it.*
Approximately 5:17 p.m., Dr. Creswell enters the filled room, introduces Dr. Wolcott. Class members seem relieved.	*Overhead projector not plugged in at the beginning of the class: I wonder if this was a distraction (when it took extra time to plug it in).*
Dr. Creswell gives brief background of guest, concentrating on his international experiences; features a comment about the educational ethnography "The Man in the Principal's Office."	*Lateness of the arrival of Drs. Creswell and Wolcott: Students seemed a bit anxious. Maybe it had to do with the change in starting time to 5 p.m. (some may have had 6:30 classes or appointments to get to).*
Descriptive Notes	*Reflective Notes*
Dr. Wolcott begins by telling the class he now writes out educational ethnography and highlights this primary occupation by mentioning two books: *Transferring Qualitative Data* and *The Art of Fieldwork*.	*Drs. Creswell and Wolcott seem to have a good rapport between them, judging from many short exchanges that they had.*
While Dr. Wolcott begins his presentation by apologizing for his weary voice (due to talking all day, apparently), Dr. Creswell leaves the classroom to retrieve the guest's overhead transparencies.	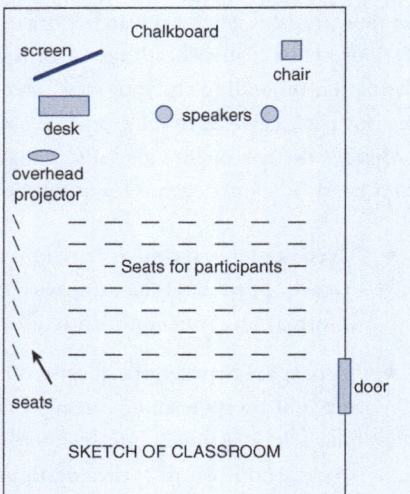
Seemed to be three parts to this activity: (1) the speaker's challenge to the class of detecting pure ethnographical methodologies, (2) the speaker's presentation of the "tree" that portrays various strategies and substrategies for qualitative research in education, and (3) the relaxed "elder statesman" fielding class questions, primarily about students' potential research projects and prior studies Dr. Wolcott had written.	
The first question was "How do you look at qualitative research?" followed by "How does ethnography fit in?"	

During an observation, use an observational protocol to record information. As shown in Figure 7.8, this protocol contains notes taken by a student on a class visit by the late professor Harry Wolcott. We provide only one page of the protocol, but this is sufficient for one to see what it includes. It has a header giving information about the duration of the observational session and then includes a "descriptive notes" section for recording a description of activities. The section with a box around it in the "descriptive notes" column indicates the observer's attempt to summarize, in chronological fashion, the flow of activities in the classroom. This can be useful information for developing a chronology of the ways the activities unfolded during the class session. There is also a "reflective notes" section for notes about the process, reflections on activities, and summary conclusions about activities for later theme development. A line down the center of the page divides descriptive notes from reflective notes. A visual sketch of the setting and a label for it provide additional useful information.

Recording information is essential and can take various forms, such as observational field notes, interview write-ups, and documents as well as mapping responses onto a protocol, photographing, shooting video, and recording sound. An informal process may occur in recording information comprising initial "jottings" (Emerson et al., 2011). These on-the-spot notes, daily logs, or summaries build upon the jottings, and can be useful during data analysis. See Marshall et al. (2021) and Sanjek (1990) for examples of field notes. These forms of recording information are popular in narrative research, ethnographies, and case studies. Once information is recorded, consider "member checking," taking themes or stories back to participants to check for accuracy (see also Chapter 10).

Fieldwork Issues

Researchers engaged in studies within all five approaches face fieldwork issues when gathering data that need to be anticipated. Resources for guiding fieldwork and arising issues have expanded considerably in scope and number as interpretive frameworks (see Chapter 2) have been widely discussed. Beginning researchers are often overwhelmed by the amount of time needed to collect qualitative data and the richness of the data encountered. As a practical recommendation, we suggest that beginners start with limited data collection and engage in a pilot project to gain some initial experiences (Sampson, 2004). This limited data collection might consist of one or two interviews or observations so that researchers can estimate the time needed to collect data and revise their protocols accordingly.

One way to think about and anticipate the types of issues that may arise during data collection is to view the issues as they relate to several aspects of data collection, including entry and organizational access, procedures for participant observations, dynamics between interviewer and interviewee, and availability of documents and audiovisual or social media materials.

Entry and Organizational Access

Gaining access to organizations, sites, and individuals to study has its own challenges. Recruiting individuals to participate in the study, building trust and credibility at the field site, and engaging people from a site are all important access challenges. Factors related to considering the appropriateness of a site need to be considered as well (see Weis & Fine, 2000).

For example, researchers may choose a site that is one in which they have a vested interest (e.g., employed at the site, a study of superiors or subordinates at the site), thus limiting the researcher's ability to develop diverse perspectives on coding data or developing themes. A researcher's own particular "stance" within the group may limit acknowledging all dimensions of the experiences. The researcher may hear or see something uncomfortable when collecting data. In addition, participants may be fearful that their issues will be exposed to people outside their community. Also related to access is the changing nature of situations and appropriate timing for specific contexts. For example, in K–12 education settings avoid trying to access sites at the beginning or the end of the year, which are times of school transitions.

Procedures for Participant Observations

The types of challenges experienced during observations will closely relate to the role of the inquirer in observation, such as whether the researcher assumes a participant, nonparticipant, or middle-ground position. There are challenges as well with the mechanics of observing, such as remembering to take field notes, recording quotes accurately for inclusion in field notes, determining the best timing for moving from a nonparticipant to a participant (if this role change is desired), keeping from being overwhelmed with information, and learning how to funnel the observations from the broad picture to a narrower one in time. Differences in researcher experiences as participant observers is highlighted by the commentaries of Labree (2002) and Ezeh (2003). Labaree (2002), who was a participant in an academic senate on a campus, noted the advantages of this role and discussed dilemmas associated with entering the field, disclosing oneself to the participants, sharing relationships with other individuals, and attempting to disengage from the site. Ezeh (2003), a Nigerian researcher who studied the Orring, a little-known minority ethnic group in Nigeria, found that being of the same nationality did not reduce challenges at the research site. Although he found that during his initial contact the group was supportive, the more he became integrated into the host community, the more he experienced human relations problems, such as being accused of spying, pressured to be more generous in his material gifts, and suspected of trysts with women.

Dynamics Between Interviewer and Interviewee

Challenges in qualitative interviewing often focus on the mechanics of conducting the interview. Roulston et al. (2003) chronicled the challenges in interviewing encountered by postgraduate students during a 15-day intensive course. These challenges related to unexpected participant behaviors and students' ability in creating good instructions, negotiating questions, dealing with sensitive issues, and developing transcriptions. Suoninen and Jokinen (2005), from the field of social work, asked whether the phrasing of interview questions led to subtle persuasive questions, responses, or explanations.

Undoubtedly, conducting interviews is taxing, especially for inexperienced researchers engaged in studies that require extensive interviewing, such as phenomenology, grounded theory, and case study research. Equipment issues loom large as a problem in interviewing, and both recording and transcribing equipment need to be organized in advance of the interview.

The process of building rapport and asking questions during an interview (e.g., saying little, handling emotional outbursts, using icebreakers) includes problems that an interviewer must address. Many inexperienced researchers express surprise at the difficulty of conducting interviews and the lengthy process involved in reviewing transcripts and (if applicable) transcribing interview recordings. In addition, in phenomenological interviews, asking appropriate questions and relying on participants to discuss the meaning of their experiences require patience and skill on the part of the researcher.

Recent discussions about qualitative interviewing highlight the importance of reflecting about the relationship that exists between the interviewer and the interviewee (Brinkmann & Kvale, 2015; Nunkoosing, 2005; Weis & Fine, 2000). For example, the research interview often raises the power asymmetry (unequal power dynamic) between interviewer and interviewee. A research interview should not be regarded as a completely open and free dialogue between egalitarian partners, because the interview is directed by the interviewer. The interview is dialogue that is conducted one-way, provides information for the researcher, is based on the researcher's agenda, and leads to the researcher's interpretations. It can also contain "counter control" elements by the interviewee, who may withhold information. To correct for this asymmetry, Brinkmann and Kvale (2015) suggest more collaborative interviewing, where the researcher and the participant approach equality in questioning, interpreting, and reporting.

On the problems of power and resistance, Nunkoosing (2005) distinguishes truth from authenticity, the impossibility of consent, and projection of the interviewers' own self (their status, race, culture, and gender). Weis and Fine (2000) raise additional questions for consideration: Are your interviewees able to articulate the forces that interrupt, suppress, or oppress them? Do they erase their history, approaches, and cultural identity? Do they choose not to expose their history or go on record about the difficult aspects of their lives? These questions and the points raised about the nature of the interviewer–interviewee relationship cannot be easily answered for all interview situations. They do, however, sensitize us to important challenges in qualitative interviewing that need to be anticipated.

A final issue is whether the researcher shares personal experiences with participants in an interview setting such as in a case study, a phenomenology, or an ethnography. This sharing minimizes the "bracketing" that is essential to construct the meaning of participants in a phenomenology and reduces information shared by participants in case studies and ethnographies.

Availability of Documents and Audiovisual and Social Media Materials

In document research, many issues involve locating materials, often at sites far away, accessing public materials, and obtaining permissions to use the materials (Marshall et al., 2021). For biographers, the primary form of data collection might be archival materials from documents that may be online. New and emerging online qualitative research methods and data forms continue to raise important ethical considerations (Paulus & Lester, 2021; Salmons, 2022).

When researchers ask participants in a study to keep journals or to create audiovisual materials and documents during the process of research, additional fieldwork issues emerge. Journaling is a popular data collection process in case studies and narrative research. What instructions should be given to individuals prior to writing in their journals? Are all participants equally comfortable with journaling? Is it appropriate, for example, with small children who express themselves well verbally but have limited writing skills? The researcher also may have difficulty reading the handwriting of participants who journal. Video recordings raise issues for the qualitative researcher such as deciding on the best location for the camera and determining whether to provide close-up shots or distant shots.

Data Storage and Security

We are surprised at how little attention is given in books and articles to managing data storage of qualitative data. Richards (2021) states that the usefulness of data storage systems is dependent on whether qualitative researchers can find and retrieve the records: "Mountains of transcripts of interviews will distance any researcher from an understanding of the topic if there is no way of finding the data needed" (p. 93). Technology advances continue to dramatically shift data management and storage practices, with Evers (2018) noting, "storing information in and working 'from the cloud' is becoming standard procedure" (p. 67). The approach to storage will reflect the type of information collected, which varies by approach to inquiry and mode of collection. In writing a narrative life history, the researcher needs to organize researcher field notes, artifacts, and interview recordings. Creating backup copies of digital files requires the researcher to ensure the files are in the appropriate form (i.e., de-identified), in the proper location (e.g., external storage devices such as flash drives or cloud-based storage), and secure (i.e., password protected and encrypted), as described in the research ethics review board application. With large databases being created and used by some qualitative researchers, data storage and security assumes major importance.

Some common data storage and handling procedures for qualitative research include the following:

- Create backup systems for all digital files.
- Use more than one audio recording device for interviews.
- Develop a data collection matrix as a summary of information gathered, including file names for a study and storage location.
- Protect the anonymity of participants by masking their names and using pseudonyms in the data files for analysis.
- Develop a source list of participant names and pseudonyms.
- Store the source list separately from the data files for analysis.

TRY THIS NOW 7.1
COMPARING DATA COLLECTION ACTIVITY DESCRIPTIONS IN THE APPENDIX STUDIES

Comparing the similarities and differences in data collection rationales and plans across published qualitative studies helps guide researchers in presenting their own studies. Choose two of the Appendix studies to compare. What evidence of the seven data collection activities and ethics summarized in Figure 7.1 can you find? Then compare the descriptions for each of the data collection activities across the articles. Note which elements are similar and which are different.

COMPARING THE FIVE APPROACHES IN DATA COLLECTION

Returning to Table 7.1, we see there are both differences and similarities among the activities of data collection for the five approaches to inquiry. Among the differences, certain approaches seem more directed toward specific types of data collection than others. For case and narrative studies, the researcher uses multiple forms of data to build the in-depth case or the storied experiences. For grounded theory studies and phenomenological projects, inquirers rely primarily on interviews as data. Ethnographers highlight the importance of participant observation and interviews, but as noted earlier, they may use many different sources of information. Unquestionably, some mixing of forms occurs, but in general these patterns of collection by approach hold true.

Second, the unit of analysis for data collection varies among the five approaches. Narrative researchers, phenomenologists, and grounded theorists study individuals; case study researchers examine groups of individuals participating in an event or activity or an organization; and ethnographers study entire cultural systems or subcultures of systems.

Third, we found the amount of discussion about field issues to vary among the five approaches. Ethnographers have written extensively about field issues (e.g., Atkinson, 2015; Hammersley & Atkinson, 1995). This may reflect historical concerns about imbalanced power relationships, imposing objective, external standards on participants, and failures to be sensitive to marginalized groups. Narrative researchers are less specific about field issues, although concerns have been voiced about how to conduct the interviews (Elliott, 2005). Across all approaches, ethical issues are widely discussed.

Fourth, the approaches vary in their level of intrusiveness in data collection. Conducting interviews seem less intrusive in phenomenological projects and grounded theory studies than in the high level of access needed in personal narratives, the prolonged stays in ethnographic fieldwork, and the immersion into programs or events in case studies.

These differences do not lessen some important similarities that need to be observed. All qualitative studies sponsored by public institutions need to be approved by a human subjects review board, at least in the United States and in many countries around the globe. Also, the use of interviews and observations is central to many of the approaches. Furthermore, observational and interview protocols can be similar regardless of approach (although specific questions on each protocol will reflect the language of the approach). Finally, the issue of data storage of information is closely related to the form of data collection and the basic objective of researchers, regardless of approach, and requires some management system for organized retrieval of information and secure storage. In Chapter 8, we build upon the data collection circle with a data analysis spiral (see Figure 8.1) that provides essential guidance for qualitative researchers, before we detail specific analysis procedures for each of the five approaches.

CHAPTER CHECK-IN

1. Can you identify evidence of connections between the study purpose and data being collected by the author(s)? Read qualitative journal articles that adopt different approaches across diverse fields, such as those listed in Examples 4.1–4.5.
   a. Begin by identifying the forms of data collected in the study. What rationales are presented for their use?
   b. Then review the study introduction and note the research purpose (and research questions if present) and qualitative approach adopted.
   c. Next, assess to what extent the forms of data collection are appropriate for the approach and purpose for conducting the study. In brief, can the data collected address the articulated purpose? Why or why not?
2. Can you begin to sketch the data collection circle for a qualitative study? Examine Figure 7.1 for the eight activities and Table 7.2 for information about ethical situations researchers may encounter. Develop a data collection description for all seven activities for your project. Follow these steps:
   a. State the site and/or individuals that are the focus of your study and rationale for their choice in a couple of sentences.
   b. Discuss the processes by which you will gain access and develop a rapport with individuals and/or gatekeepers (if applicable).
   c. Present the strategy for purposeful sampling and a rationale that reflects your approach to the research.
   d. Describe the forms of data you will collect and provide a rationale for the appropriateness of their use, referring to the approach you chose.
   e. Outline the procedures you will develop for recording information.
   f. Consider the ethical situations and issues that may emerge as you begin fieldwork. Present a plan for resolving each of them.

g. Apply the suggestions presented in this chapter for storing data securely and draft the procedures you will follow.
h. Look across the descriptions of the activities within the data collection circle for any ethical issues that need to be addressed.

SUMMARY

In this chapter, we addressed several components of the data collection process. The process involves locating a site or person to study; gaining access to and building rapport at the site or with the individual(s); sampling purposefully using one or more of the many approaches to sampling in qualitative research; collecting information through many forms, such as interviews, observations, documents, audiovisual and social media materials, and newer forms emerging in the literature; establishing approaches for recording information such as the use of interview or observational protocols; anticipating and addressing fieldwork issues; and developing a system for storing and securely handling the databases. The five approaches to inquiry differ in the diversity of information collected, the unit of study being examined, the extent of field issues discussed in the literature, and the intrusiveness of the data collection effort. An essential aspect for researchers, regardless of approach, is the collection and management of data in an ethical manner. This typically involves gaining institutional approvals—and in some cases, organizational and community approvals—from review boards prior to beginning the research and then following the consent, recording, and storage protocols that are described in the application.

CHAPTER KEY TERMS

Gatekeeper
Maximum variation sampling
Observational protocol

Purposeful sampling
Sample size

FURTHER READINGS

Several readings extend this introduction to data collection, beginning with general resources and then by specific data forms. The list should not be considered exhaustive, and readers are encouraged to seek out additional readings in the end-of-book reference list.

Chilisa, B. (2020). *Indigenous research methodologies* (2nd ed.). Sage.

Bagele Chilisa describes diverse Indigenous research methodologies and provides illustrative case studies from around the globe. She also provides practical guidance for researchers within Indigenous contexts.

Creswell, J. W., & Guetterman, T. G. (2018). *Educational research: Planning, conducting, and evaluating quantitative and qualitative research* (5th ed.). Pearson.

John W. Creswell and Timothy G. Guetterman introduce the steps for conducting qualitative research alongside those for conducting quantitative research. This approach can be especially helpful for the researcher who has some existing research expertise or experience and finds the discussions about sampling and data collection to be essential reading.

Flick, U. (Ed.). (2018). *The SAGE handbook of qualitative data collection*. Sage.

As the handbook editor, Uwe Flick has compiled an excellent resource. Noteworthy chapters include Chapter 3 on "Ethics in Qualitative Research Data Collection" by Donna Mertens and Chapter 30 on "Ethics in Digital Research" by Katrin Tiidenberg.

Salmons, J. E. (2022). *Doing qualitative research online*. Sage.

Janet Salmons offers practical guidance for getting started in online qualitative data collection. Of particular note is the chapter on online interviews.

FOR GUIDANCE RELATED TO INTERVIEWING

Brinkmann, S., & Kvale, S. (2015). *InterViews: Learning the craft of qualitative research interviewing* (3rd ed.). Sage.

Svend Brinkmann and Steinar Kvale describe seven stages of an interview investigation to structure their comprehensive guidance for conducting interviews.

Krueger, R. A., & Casey, M. A. (2014). *Focus groups: A practical guide for applied research* (5th ed.). Sage.

A good overview for planning and conducting focus groups, this new edition expands guidance on developing questions. Particularly useful is the discussion on moderating skills in different contexts (e.g., young participants, cross-cultural settings).

Rubin, H. J., & Rubin, I. S. (2012). *Qualitative interviewing: The art of hearing data* (3rd ed.). Sage.

Herbert Rubin and Irene Rubin describe their seven-step responsive interviewing approach. The writing is accessible and provides access to the lessons learned from their extensive interview experiences.

For Discussions About Making Observations and Taking Field Notes

Angrosino, M. V. (2007). *Doing ethnographic and observational research*. Sage.

Michael Angrosino provides a comprehensive guide to the process of conducting ethnographic research. Of particular note is his discussion of ethical considerations and descriptions of a variety of data collection techniques for participant observer field researchers.

Bernard, H. R. (2017). *Research methods in anthropology: Qualitative and quantitative approaches* (6th ed.). Rowman & Littlefield.

In this comprehensive resource, Russ Bernard outlines procedures for sampling, collecting, and analyzing data. We find his guidance for observational procedures to be particularly helpful.

Emerson, R. M., Fretz, R. I., & Shaw, L. L. (2011). *Writing ethnographic fieldnotes* (2nd ed.). University of Chicago Press.

Robert Emerson, Rachel Fretz, and Linda Shaw outline practical guidance for creating and interpreting field notes. Through embedding illustrative examples, they make accessible a difficult process to describe.

For Information About Issues and Use of Documents, Audiovisual, and Social Media Materials

Bauer, W. M., & Gaskell, G. D. (Eds.). (2007). *Qualitative research with text, image and sound: A practical handbook for social research*. Sage.

Noteworthy within this handbook are chapters related to the use of video, film, and photographs (Chapter 6), analysis guidance of conversations (Chapter 11), images (Chapters 13 and 14), and music (Chapter 15).

Merriam, S. B., & Tisdell, E. J. (2015). *Qualitative research: A guide to design and implementation* (4th ed.). Jossey-Bass.

This is a useful resource for designing, conducting, and reporting qualitative research. Of particular note is their description of documents including popular culture documents (e.g., cartoons, movies), visual data (e.g., video, web-based media), physical materials (e.g., personal, favorite objects), and artifacts (e.g., tools, electronics).

Warren, C. A., & Xavia Karner, T. (2014). *Discovering qualitative methods: Ethnography, interviews, documents, and images* (3rd ed.). Oxford University Press.

Carol Warren and Tracey Xavia Karner describe the decisions and processes involved in sampling, collecting, and analyzing a variety of types of documents and images.

8 DATA ANALYSIS AND REPRESENTATION

> **QUESTIONS FOR DISCUSSION**
>
> - What are three common data analysis strategies?
> - What steps are involved in qualitative data analysis?
> - How do you use computer qualitative data analysis software (QDAS)?
> - How do you conduct qualitative data analysis within each of the five approaches?

Analyzing text and multiple other forms of data presents a challenging task for qualitative researchers. Deciding how to **represent the data** in tables, matrices, and narrative form adds to the challenge. Often, qualitative researchers equate data analysis with approaches for analyzing text and image data. The process of analysis is much more. It involves organizing the data, conducting a preliminary read-through of the database, **coding** and organizing **themes**, representing the data, and forming an interpretation of them. These steps are interconnected and form a spiral of activities all related to the analysis and representation of the data. It also includes engaging in reflexivity, attending to ethical issues, and deciding whether (or not) to use computers and **qualitative data analysis software (QDAS)**. Computers and specialized software programs can assist in qualitative data analysis to facilitate making some tasks easier and more efficient, but they do not analyze the data for researchers. Patton (2015) notes the role of software in the process of analysis, saying that while "many swear by it because it can offer leaps in productivity for those adept at it, using software is not a requisite for qualitative analysis. Whether you do or do not use software, the real analytical work takes place in your head" (pp. 530–531). Paulus and Lester (2020) remind researchers "that qualitative research is a time intensive process remains true even when using a QDAS package" (p. 422).

In this chapter, we begin with a summary of three general approaches to analysis so that we can see how leading authors follow similar processes as well as different ones. Next, we present a visual model—a data analysis spiral—that we find useful to conceptualize a larger picture of all activities involved in the data analysis process in qualitative research. Alongside this discussion we weave a review of key ethical issues in need of attention during data analysis and how reflexivity can help researchers recognize the influence of their "positioning" on data analysis decisions. We introduce the use of computers and QDAS and describe a sample of five software programs—ATLAS.ti, Dedoose, HyperRESEARCH, MAXQDA, and NVivo—that researchers may decide to use (or not). Finally, we use this spiral as a conceptualization to further examine specific data procedures, representations, and templates for coding data within each of the five approaches to inquiry. We conclude this chapter by comparing the data analysis activities across the five approaches.

THREE ANALYSIS STRATEGIES

Data analysis in qualitative research consists of preparing and organizing the data (i.e., text data as in transcripts, image data as in photographs, or recordings as audio files) for analysis; then reducing the data into themes through a process of coding and condensing the codes; and finally representing the data in figures, tables, or a discussion. Across many books on qualitative research, this is the general process that researchers use. Undoubtedly, there will be some variations in this approach. An important point to note is that beyond these steps, the five approaches to inquiry have additional analysis steps. Before examining the specific analysis steps in the five approaches, it is helpful to have in mind the general analysis procedures that are fundamental to all forms of qualitative research.

Table 8.1 presents typical general analysis procedures as illustrated through the writings of three qualitative researchers. We have chosen these three authors because they represent different perspectives. Madison (2005, 2012, 2019) presents an interpretive framework taken from critical ethnography; Huberman and Miles (1994) adopt a systematic approach to analysis that has a long history of use in qualitative inquiry; and Wolcott (1994) uses a more traditional approach to research from ethnography and case study analysis. These three influential sources advocate many similar processes, as well as a few different approaches to the analytic phase of qualitative research.

All of these authors comment on the central steps of coding the data (reducing the data into meaningful segments and assigning names for the segments), combining the codes into broader categories or themes, and displaying and making comparisons in the data graphs, tables, and charts. These are the core elements of qualitative data analysis.

Beyond these elements, the authors present different phases in the data analysis process. Huberman and Miles (1994), for example, provide more detailed steps in the process, such as writing marginal notes, drafting summaries of field notes, and noting relationships among the categories. The practical application of many of these strategies were recently described, and in some cases, expanded upon by Bazeley (2013, 2021)—for example, how participants can be involved, the use of visuals, and the role of software. Madison (2012, 2019) introduces the need to create a point of view—a stance that signals the interpretive framework (e.g., critical, feminist) taken in the study. This point of view is central to the analysis in critical, theoretically oriented qualitative studies. Wolcott (1994), on the other hand, discusses the importance of forming a description from the data, as well as relating

TABLE 8.1 ■ General Data Analysis Strategies Advanced by Select Authors

Analytic Strategy	Madison (2005, 2012, 2019)	Huberman and Miles (1994)	Wolcott (1994)
Taking notes while reading		Write margin notes in field notes.	Highlight certain information in description.
Sketching reflective thinking		Write reflective passages in notes.	
Summarizing field notes		Draft a summary sheet on field notes.	
Working with words		Make metaphors.	
Identifying codes	Use abstract coding or concrete coding.	Write codes and memos.	
Reducing codes to themes	Identify salient themes or patterns.	Note patterns and themes.	Identify patterned regularities.
Counting frequency of codes		Count frequency of codes.	
Relating categories		Note relations among variables, and build a logical chain of evidence.	
Relating categories to analytic framework in literature			Contextualize with the framework from literature.
Creating a point of view	Create a point of view for scenes, audience, and readers.		
Displaying and reporting the data	Create a graph or picture of the framework.	Make contrasts and comparisons.	Display findings in tables, charts, diagrams, and figures; compare cases; compare with a standard case.

the description to the literature and cultural themes in cultural anthropology. A review of recent editions of introductory qualitative research texts revealed the majority address the use of computers and QDAS programs (e.g., Creswell & Guetterman, 2019; Flick, 2023; Paulus & Lester, 2021).

THE DATA ANALYSIS SPIRAL

Data analysis is not off-the-shelf; rather, it is custom-built, revised, and "choreographed" (Huberman & Miles, 1994). The processes of data collection, data analysis, and report writing are not distinct steps in the process—they are interrelated and often go on simultaneously in a research project. Bazeley (2021) attributes success in data analysis to early preparation, cautioning "from the time of [your research project's] conception you will take steps that will either facilitate or hinder your interpretation and explanation of the phenomena you observe" (p. 3). One of the challenges is making the data analysis process explicit because qualitative researchers often "learn by doing" (Dey, 1993, p. 6). This leads critics to claim that qualitative research is largely intuitive, soft, and relativistic or that qualitative data analysts fall back on the three I's—"insight, intuition, and impression" (Dey, 1995, p. 78). Undeniably, qualitative researchers preserve the unusual and serendipitous, and writers craft studies differently, using analytic procedures that often evolve while they are in the field. Despite this uniqueness, we believe that the analysis process conforms to a general contour.

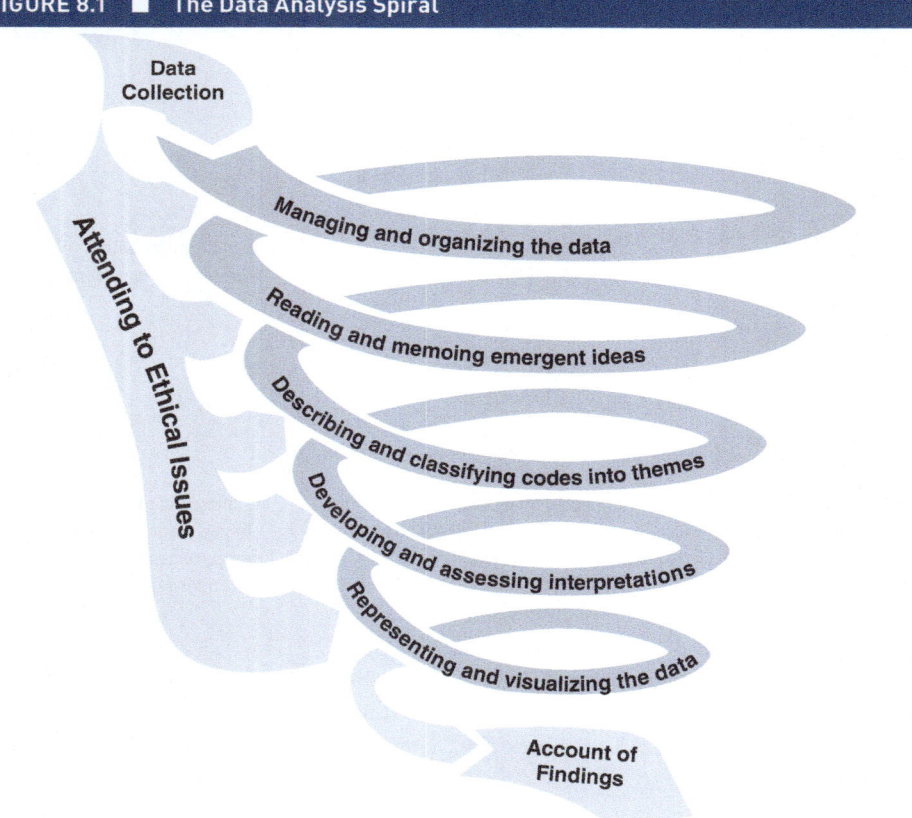

FIGURE 8.1 ■ The Data Analysis Spiral

We choose to represent data analysis using a spiral image, a data analysis spiral. As shown in Figure 8.1, to analyze qualitative data, the researcher engages in the process of moving in analytic circles rather than using a fixed linear approach. One enters with data of text or audiovisual materials (e.g., images, sound recordings) and exits with an account or a narrative. In between, the researcher touches on several facets of analysis and circles around and around including a sensitivity to ethical considerations. Within each spiral, the researcher uses analytic strategies for the goal of generating specific analytic outcomes—all of which will be further described in the following sections and a summary in Table 8.2. We begin with ethical issues during data analysis.

Data Analysis Spiral Activities	Analytic Strategies	Analytic Outcomes
Managing and organizing the data	Preparing files and units	Giving a name to a file system, and organizing database files and units of text, images, and recordings
	Ensuring ongoing secure storage of files	Creating long-term file storage plan
	Selecting mode of analysis	Using computers and QDAS, analyzing by hand, or using a hybrid approach
Reading and memoing emergent ideas	Taking notes while reading	Writing memos leading to code development, reflections over time, and/or summaries across files or questions or project
	Sketching reflective thinking	
	Summarizing ideas and field notes	
Describing and classifying codes into themes	Working with words	Naming of initial codes
	Identifying codes	Listing code categories and descriptions
	Applying codes	Assigning the codes to units of text, images, and recordings
	Reducing codes to themes	Finalizing list of codes
Developing and assessing interpretations	Relating categories/themes/families	Contextualizing understandings and diagrams
	Relating categories/themes/families to analytic framework in literature	Developing theories and propositions
Representing and visualizing the data	Creating a point of view	Developing matrices, trees, and models
	Displaying and reporting the data	Presenting an account of the findings

TABLE 8.2 ■ The Data Analysis Spiral Activities, Strategies, and Outcomes

Ethical Considerations in Data Analysis

Among the key challenges researchers encounter during the data analysis and representation process are ethical situations related to participant protection from harm, researcher bias, disclosure of comprehensive findings, and participant engagement (see Table 8.3). This review, positioned in advance of our discussion of specific analysis strategies, reminds us to carefully consider ethical issues throughout data analysis across all approaches to inquiry (see our initial discussion in Chapter 3 and Table 3.1 for a summary of ethical situations and issues in qualitative research).

For the protection of participants from harm, it is essential that researchers mask participant names as soon as possible to avoid inclusion of identifiable information in the analysis files. Researchers may also create composite profiles to avoid situations where participants might be identifiable in the reporting documents. To minimize bias and ensure reliable assignment of codes, the researcher can engage in reflexive practice and check their coding reliability with others. During the disclosure of findings, it is researchers who are responsible for embedding the use of and describing the procedures for member-checking strategies to enhance confidence in the data interpretations (for further discussion see Chapter 10). Engaging participants in the

TABLE 8.3 ■ Ethical Situations to Anticipate and Address by Data Analysis Activity

Data Analysis Activity	Types of Ethics Situations to Anticipate and Address	How a Researcher Potentially Addresses the Situation
Managing and organizing the data	Situations where information in the data might identify participants	Researcher masks personal identifiers (i.e., names, places, attributes) to protect participants' anonymity.
Reading and memoing emergent ideas	Situations requiring the researcher to minimize any biases they may consciously or unconsciously bring to their close reading of data	Researcher engages in reflexivity to recognize the influence of their "positioning" on data analysis decisions.
Describing and classifying codes into themes	Situations where codes are unreliably assigned	Researcher checks reliability of coding with others and uses a codebook.
Developing and assessing interpretations	Situations where interpretations extend beyond the data or only represent partial (i.e., one perspective) findings	Researcher uses and explains use of validation strategies such as member checking and an audit trail.
		Researcher presents multiple perspectives reflective of a complex picture.
Representing and visualizing the data	Situations where descriptions of findings might be identifiable to a particular source	Researcher avoids disclosing information that would harm or identify participants.

data analysis may foster collaboration in data interpretation and representation, to the ultimate benefit of participants and society.

Managing and Organizing the Data

Data management, the first loop in the spiral, begins the process. At an early stage in the analysis process, researchers typically organize their data into digital files and create a file naming system. The consistent application of a file naming system ensures materials can be easily located in large databases of text (or images or recordings) for analysis either by hand or by computer (Bazeley, 2021). A searchable spreadsheet or database by data form, participant, and date of collection (among other contextual features) is critical for locating files efficiently. This helps researchers to prepare for managing their qualitative data analysis and thus avoiding, to the extent they can, the situation described by Miles et al. (2019) that, "Qualitative studies, especially those done by the lone researcher or the novice graduate student, can be notorious for their vulnerability to poor study management" (p. 39). Patton (1980) offers the following caution:

> The data generated by qualitative methods are voluminous. I have found no way of preparing students for the sheer massive volumes of information with which they will find themselves confronted when data collection has ended. Sitting down to make sense out of pages of interviews and whole files of field notes can be overwhelming. (p. 297)

In our experience, computer use and QDAS can be especially helpful in managing a large number of as well as various types of digital files (i.e., images, text, recordings) for data analysis. Similar to Bazeley (2021), we also suggest becoming familiar with the tools offered by the computer software you intend to use *even before* data collection begins.

Besides organizing files, researchers prepare data records and make plans for long-term secure file storage. Data file preparation requires the researcher to make decisions about appropriate text units of the data (e.g., a word, a sentence, an entire story) and digital representations of the audiovisual materials. Audiovisual materials such as images or artifacts (e.g., letter, clay sculpture, and clothing) and recordings of conversations (naturally occurring, focus groups, and interviews) can be represented as digital files (Grbich, 2013; Richards, 2021). It is important for researchers to carefully consider these early organizational decisions because of the potential impact on future analysis—for example, if the researcher intends to compare files, then how the individual files are initially set up and (if applicable) uploaded to a software program matter. Initial file organization may hinder making comparisons over chronological time, across multiple participants, or across forms of data (e.g., interviews, focus groups, documents).

Reading and Memoing Emergent Ideas

Following the organization of the data, researchers continue analysis by getting a sense of the whole database. Richards (2021) notes the importance of identifying early ideas and explanations from the data: "This means that the quality of the analysis is dependent not only on the quality of the data records but also on working up from them to ideas and explanation" (p. 101). To do this, Agar (1980) suggests that researchers "read the transcripts in their entirety several times. Immerse yourself in the details, trying to get a sense of the interview as a whole before breaking it into parts" (p. 103). Similarly, Bazeley (2021) describes her read, reflect, play, and explore strategies as an "initial foray into new data sources, in expectation of more concentrated work to come" (p. 128). Writing notes or memos in the margins of field notes or transcripts or under images helps in this initial process of exploring a database.

We have found QDAS helpful for organizing our memos, capturing both emerging holistic understandings as well as more nuanced details. Scanning the text with a holistic intention allows the researcher to build a sense of the data as a whole without getting caught up in the details of coding. Scanning (or rapid reading) also offers the benefits of approaching texts in a new light, "as if they had been written by a stranger" (Emerson et al., 2011, p. 145). In contrast, by reading line-by-line and thinking about the meaning of each sentence and idea, the researcher engages in an active reading strategy. This can help researchers carefully consider each idea they encounter as they review the data files.

Memos are short phrases, ideas, or key concepts that occur to the reader as they examine various data files. Mihas (2021) eloquently describes memo writing as "a practice that documents our understanding—our incremental awareness as well as "aha" moments—along the qualitative research life cycle" (p. 223). Its distinctive role is reflected in the helpful definition of memos as "not just descriptive summaries of data but attempts to synthesize in them into higher level analytic meanings" (Miles et al., 2019, p. 88). Grbich (2013) suggests guiding the examination of the content and context of the material using the following questions: What is it? Why, when, how, and by whom was it produced? What meanings does the material convey? Guidance for the analysis of audiovisual data is available from general resources (e.g., Estrada & Koolen, 2018; Rose, 2016) as well as for specific forms of audiovisual data, for example, for images, see Banks (2014); for film and video, see Mikos (2014) and Knoblauch et al. (2014); for sounds, see Maeder (2014); and for virtual data, see Marotzki et al. (2014). Researchers can write their memos into their data files either on the digital representation itself or in an accompanying text file. In this way, we have found QDAS helpful for managing various memos that can be linked to individual data segments, code descriptions, and files. The subsequent searching and sorting of memos that are linked within QDAS often takes less effort than was required when hand sorting.

Memoing procedures were used in the gunman case study (Asmussen & Creswell, 1995); first, the authors scanned all the databases to identify major organizing ideas. Then, looking over their field notes from observations, interview transcriptions, physical trace evidence, and audio and visual images, the authors disregarded predetermined questions so they could "see" what interviewees said. They then reflected on the larger thoughts presented in the data and formed initial categories. These categories were few (about 10), and they looked for multiple forms of evidence to support each. Moreover, they found evidence that portrayed multiple perspectives about each category (Stake, 1995).

Common to both of our analysis experiences, we have found memoing to be a worthy investment of our time as a means of creating a digital **audit trail** that can be retrieved and examined (Richards, 2021; Silver & Lewins, 2014). Using an audit trail as a validation strategy for documenting thinking processes that clarify understandings over time will be discussed in Chapter 10. Here are some recommendations that guide our memoing practice (see also Corbin & Strauss, 2015; Mihas, 2021a; Miles et al., 2019; Ravitch & Carl, 2020).

- *Prioritize memoing throughout the analysis process.* Begin memoing during the initial read of your data and continue all the way to the writing of the conclusions. For example, we recommend memoing during each and every analytic session and often return to the memos written during the early analysis as a way of tracking the evolution of codes and theme development. Miles et al. (2019) describes the urgency of memoing as "when an idea strikes, *stop* whatever else you are doing and write the memo. . . . Include your musings of all sorts, even the fuzzy and foggy ones" (p. 90; emphasis in original).

- *Individualize a system for memo organization.* Memos can quickly become unwieldy unless they are developed with an organizational system in mind. At the same time researchers often tout the usefulness of memoing, there is a lack of consensus about guiding procedures for it. We approach memoing so that the process meets our individualized needs. For example, we use a system based on the unit of text associated with the memo and create captions reflective of content to assist in sorting. Three levels can be used in analysis:
  - Segment memos capture ideas from reading phrases in the data. This type of memo is helpful for identifying initial codes and is similar to a precoding memo described by Ravitch and Carl (2020) or a key quotation memo described by Mihas (2021a).
  - Document memos capture researcher reflections on concepts developed from reviewing an individual file or as a way of documenting evolving ideas from the review across multiple files. This type of memo is helpful for summarizing the initial understanding of a particular transcript (Mihas, 2021a) and identifying code categories for themes and/or comparisons across questions or data forms.
  - Project memos capture the integration of ideas across one concept or as a way of documenting how multiple concepts might fit together across the project. This type of memo is like a summary memo described by Corbin and Strauss (2015) as useful for helping to move the research along because all the major ideas of the research are accessible.

- *Embed sorting strategies for memo retrieval.* Memos need to be easily retrievable and sortable across time, content, data form, or participant. To that end, dating and creating identifiable captions become very important when writing memos. Corbin and Strauss (2015) forward the use of conceptual headings as a feature for enhanced memo retrieval.

To conclude this section, we emphasize the role memoing plays in systematic analysis because it helps track the development of ideas through the process. This, in turn, lends credibility to the qualitative data analysis process and outcomes because "the qualitative researcher should expect to uncover some information through informed hunches, intuition, and serendipitous occurrences that, in turn, will lead to a richer and more powerful explanation of the setting, context, and participants in any given study" (Janesick, 2016, p. 147). In Chapter 9, as we discuss contributions to writing up qualitative studies, we will return to memoing as a helpful practice. Similar to Mihas (2021b), we find that the practice of writing memos helps in developing "our writing voice for a particular study. Every project comes with its own lexicon and unwieldy thoughts—contradictions and mysteries—that we work through in writing" (p. 223).

Describing and Classifying Codes Into Themes

The next step consists of moving from reading and memoing in the spiral to describing, classifying, and interpreting the data. In this loop, forming *codes* or *categories* (these two terms will be used interchangeably) represents the heart of qualitative data analysis. Here, researchers build detailed descriptions, apply codes, develop themes or dimensions, and provide an interpretation of their views or perspectives reflected in relevant literature. *Detailed description* means that authors describe what they see. This detail is provided in situ—that is, within the context of the setting of the person, place, or event. Description becomes a good place to start in a qualitative study (after reading and managing data), and it plays a central role in ethnographic and case studies.

The process of coding is central to qualitative research and involves making sense of the text collected from interviews, observations, and documents. Coding involves aggregating the text or visual data into small categories of information, seeking evidence for the code from different databases being used in a study, and then assigning a label to the code. We think about "winnowing" the data here; not all information is used in a qualitative study, and some may be discarded (Wolcott, 1994). Researchers develop a short list of tentative codes (e.g., 25 to 30 or so) that match text segments, regardless of the length of the database.

Beginning researchers tend to develop elaborate lists of codes when they review their databases. We recommend proceeding differently with a short list—only expanding the list of initial codes as necessary. This approach is called "lean coding," because it begins with five or six categories with shorthand labels or codes and then it expands as review and re-review of the database continues. Typically, regardless of the size of the database, we recommend a final code list of no more than 25 to 30 categories of information, and we find ourselves working to reduce and combine them into the five or six themes that we will use in the end to write a narrative. Those researchers who end up with 100 or 200 categories—and it is easy to find this many in a complex database—struggle to reduce the analysis to the five or six themes typically advanced in most publications. For audiovisual materials, identify codes and classify codes into themes by relating the material to other aspects of the phenomenon of interest. Grbich (2013) suggests a guide for the coding process of audiovisual materials using the following questions: What codes would be expected to fit? What new codes are emergent? What themes relate to other data sources?

In our experience, QDAS offer helpful features for researchers to identify a text segment or image segment, assign a code label, search through the database and retrieve the text segments that have the same code label. This enables researchers to "see" if the coded segments within the original document which is important for verifying interpretation. In this process it is essential to remember it is the researcher, not the computer software application, that does the coding and classifying codes into themes.

Figure 8.2 illustrates the coding process used to describe one of three themes (i.e., fostering relationships) from a study conducted by Job et al. (2013). The study involved analyzing 11 focus groups and 3 interviews with teachers, administrators, caregivers, and allied professionals for the purpose of supporting the educational success of students with fetal alcohol spectrum disorders. This illustration shows the development of the theme beginning with the naming of three initial codes (i.e., attitudes, behavior, and strategies), the expansion from three to a total of six codes, followed by the reduction to two final code categories (i.e., respectful interactions and candid communication). The description of the theme is organized in the published paper by the two final code categories (sometimes called subthemes) and the methodology includes a general description of the coding process without examples. This is an unusual practice for articles, yet some dissertations include such examples in an appendix (for an example of a case study, see Poth, 2008).

Finalizing a list of codes and creating descriptions provides the foundation for a **codebook**. Table 8.4 illustrates the codebook used to guide the development of the theme, fostering relationships, from the final two codes (i.e., respectful interactions and candid communication) from the study conducted by Job et al. (2013). This illustration provides a description of the boundaries for each of the two code categories (i.e., respectful interactions with one another, candid communication among stakeholders) using a definition, criteria guiding use, and example of a segment of text from the study.

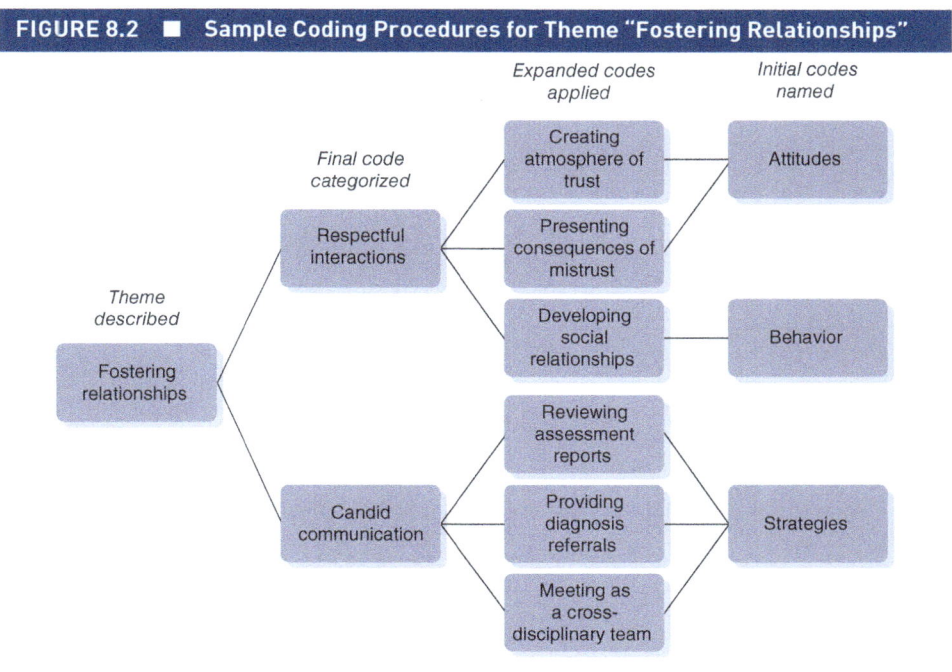

FIGURE 8.2 ■ Sample Coding Procedures for Theme "Fostering Relationships"

Source: Adapted Job et al. (2013).

TABLE 8.4 ■ Sample Codebook Entry for Theme "Fostering Relationships"

Theme	Code Name (shortened name)	Code Definition	When to Use Code	When Not to Use Code	Example Text Segment From Analysis
Fostering relationships	Respectful interactions with one another (Respectful interactions)	Any evidence recognizing individual contributions as "mattering" or efforts that are valued	Use when interaction led to or hindered student success or trust/mistrust	When text refers to outcomes instead use "actions or training" code	"This is their turf and I don't [want to] go in there and impose my will on [them]."
	Candid communications among stakeholders (Candid communication)	Any evidence referring to communication relevant for informing student success	Descriptions of timing, quality, and frequency of information sharing—reports, referrals, team meetings	When text refers to supports instead use "awareness or availability" code	". . . we have to have [an] openness and . . . willingness to listen without being judgmental. And I think when that comes, everything else will . . . come too. But for right now, there are still too many people that are willing to judge. . ."

Source: Adapted from Job et al. (2013).

A codebook should contain the following information (adapted from Bazeley, 2013, 2021; Bernard & Ryan, 2016:

- Name for the code and, if necessary, a shortened label suitable to apply in a margin
- Description of the code defining boundaries through the use of inclusion and exclusion criteria
- Example(s) of the code using data from the study for illustration purposes

The codebook articulates the distinctive boundaries for each code and plays an important role in assessing interrater reliability among multiple coders (discussed in Chapter 10). The methodology of the published paper includes a general description of the interrater coding assessment procedures and outcomes without the guiding codebook. This is not unusual, as published papers do not typically include code lists, yet our experience as supervisors, members of supervisory committees, and examiners tells us that qualitative researchers often use a codebook and provide an example of it in an appendix.

Several issues are important to address in this coding process. The first is whether qualitative researchers should count codes. Huberman and Miles (1994), for example, suggest that investigators make preliminary counts of data codes and determine how frequently codes appear in the database. Counting frequencies of codes, co-occurrences of the double coding, words and phrases and their locations are particularly easy to do using QDAS search and retrieval features. This issue remains contentious as some (but not all) qualitative researchers feel comfortable counting and reporting the number of times the codes appear in their databases. It does provide an indicator of frequency of occurrence, something typically associated with quantitative research or systematic approaches to qualitative research. In our own work, we may look at the number of passages associated with each code as a pattern indicator, but we do not report counts in articles. This is because we, along with others (e.g., Bazeley, 2021; Hays & Singh, 2012; Sandelowski, 2001), consider counting as conveying a quantitative orientation of magnitude and frequency contrary to qualitative research. In addition, a count conveys that all codes should be given equal emphasis, and it disregards that the passages coded may represent contradictory views. Miles et al. (2019) provide the following helpful guidance:

> It's important in qualitative research to know (a) that we are sometimes counting and (b) when it is a good idea to work self-consciously with frequencies and when it's not. There are three good reasons to resort to numbers: to see rapidly what you have in a large batch of data; to verify a hunch or hypothesis; and to keep yourself analytically honest, protecting against bias. (p. 279)

Another issue is the use of preexisting or a priori codes that guide our coding process. Again, we have a mixed reaction to the use of this procedure and a variety of terms such as "deductive coding" (e.g., Saldaña, 2021) and "prefigured" categories (Crabtree & Miller, 2022). Using prefigured codes or categories (often from a theoretical model or the literature) is popular in the health sciences (Crabtree & Miller, 2022), but use of these codes does serve to limit the analysis to the prefigured codes rather than opening up the codes to reflect the views of participants in a traditional qualitative way. If a prefigured coding scheme is used in analysis, we typically encourage the researchers to be open to additional codes emerging during the analysis. Patton (2015) referred to codes brought to the data by the researcher as "sensitising concepts" (p. 545). He noted the value of looking at how these were manifested in the data and are given meaning in the context of the data.

Another issue is the question as to the origin of the code names or labels. Code labels emerge from several sources. They might be in vivo codes, which are code names that are the exact words used by participants. They might also be code names drawn from the social or health sciences (e.g., coping strategies), names the researcher composes that seem to best describe the information, or from metaphors we associate with the codes (Bazeley, 2021). In the process of data analysis, we encourage qualitative researchers to look for code segments that can be used to describe information and develop themes. These codes can represent the following:

- Expected information that researchers hope to find
- Surprising information that researchers did not expect to find
- Conceptually interesting or unusual information for the researcher, the participants, or the audiences that is conceptually interesting or unusual to researchers (and potentially participants and audiences)

A final issue is the types of information a qualitative researcher codes. The researcher might look for stories (as in narrative research); individual experiences and the context of those experiences (in phenomenology); processes, actions, or interactions (in grounded theory); cultural themes and how the culture-sharing group works that can be described or categorized (in ethnography); or a detailed description of the case or cases (in case study research). Another way of thinking about the types of information would be to use a deconstructive stance, a stance focused on issues of desire and power (Czarniawska, 2004). Czarniawska identifies the data analysis strategies used in deconstruction, adapted from Martin (1990, p. 355), that help focus attention on types of information to analyze from qualitative data in all approaches:

- Dismantling a dichotomy, exposing it as a false distinction (e.g., public/private, nature/culture)
- Examining silences—what is not said (e.g., noting who or what is excluded by the use of pronouns such as *we*)
- Attending to disruptions and contradictions; places where a text fails to make sense or does not continue
- Focusing on the element that is most alien or peculiar in the text—to find the limits of what is conceivable or permissible
- Interpreting metaphors as a rich source of multiple meanings
- Analyzing double entendres that may point to an unconscious subtext, often sexual in content
- Separating group-specific and more general sources of bias by "reconstructing" the text with substitution of its main elements

Moving beyond coding, classifying pertains to taking the text or qualitative information apart and looking for categories, themes, or dimensions of information. As a popular form of analysis, classification involves identifying five to seven general themes. Themes in qualitative research (also called categories) are broad units of information that consist of several codes aggregated to form a common idea. These themes, in turn, we view as a family of themes with children, or subthemes, and even grandchildren represented by segments of data. It is difficult, especially in a large database, to reduce the information down into five or seven "families," but our process involves winnowing the data (i.e., reducing them to a small, manageable set of themes to write into a final narrative). Among the key challenges for beginning qualitative researchers is the leap from codes to themes. We forward the following strategies for exploring and developing themes (inspired by ideas from Bazeley, 2013, 2021):

- *Use memoing to capture emerging thematic ideas.* As you work with the data, write memos and include details about relevant codes. For example, an early project memo identified relationships as important in the study of educational success and it was not until later that how and what relationships needed to be fostered became clear from the coding process (Job et al., 2013).

- *Highlight noteworthy quotes as you code.* In addition to its identification, include a description of why this quote was noteworthy. For example, include an initial code called noteworthy quotes simply for the purpose of keeping track of the quotes deemed as noteworthy. These "noteworthy quotes" can also inform the development of themes. Researchers can assign interesting quotes into this code label and easily retrieve them to use in a qualitative report.

- *Create diagrams representing relationships among codes or emerging concepts.* Visual representations are helpful for seeing overlap among codes and many QDAS offer such features. For example, use a network diagram of codes in ATLAS.ti to visualize the relationships among codes and the concurrence tool to review possible overlaps among codes.

- *Draft summary statements reflective of recurring or striking aspects of the data.* Noting recurrences or outliers in the data may help to see patterns between conditions and consequences.

- *Recognize the role of thematic analysis.* Prior to transitioning to focus on the process of interpreting, it is important to recognize that some present thematic analysis as an alternative to coding. In our work, we emphasize the integral role of coding in the development of themes. This view is eloquently described by Bazeley (2021): "The consensus among those who seek to interpret, analyse, and theorise qualitative data, however, is that the development of themes usually builds on a labelling or coding process" (p. 242).

Developing and Assessing Interpretations

Researchers engage in interpreting the data when they conduct qualitative research. Interpretation involves making sense of the data, the "lessons learned," as described by Lincoln and Guba (1985). Patton (2015) describes this interpretative process as requiring both creative and critical faculties in making carefully considered judgments about what is meaningful in the patterns, themes, and categories generated by analysis. Richards (2021) describes the challenges for researchers in achieving a "balance [between] being close to your data with finding distance? How to see the 'big picture' but also test its basis?" (p. 209).

Interpretation in qualitative research involves abstracting out beyond the codes and themes to the larger meaning of the data. It is a process that begins with the development of the codes, the formation of themes from the codes, and then the organization of themes into larger units of abstraction to make sense of the data. Several forms exist, such as interpretation based on hunches, insights, and intuition (for further details about strategies for relating codes and connecting concepts, see the following: Bazeley, 2021; Ravitch & Carl, 2020; Richards, 2021). Interpretation also might be within a social science construct or idea or a combination of personal views as contrasted with a social science construct or idea. Thus, the researcher would link their interpretation to the larger research literature developed by others. For postmodern and interpretive researchers, these interpretations are seen as tentative, inconclusive, and questioning. In our experience, computer software offers helpful features such as concept mapping that enables the researcher to visualize relationships among codes and themes useful for interpreting. These interactive modeling features allow for exploring relationships and building theory through a visual representation that we often included in the final reporting.

As part of the iterative interpretative process, Marshall et al. (2021) encourages "scrupulous qualitative researchers to be on guard" (p. 228) for alternative understandings using such strategies as challenging ones' own interpretations through comparisons with existing data, relevant literature, or initial hypotheses. Specific to audiovisual materials, develop and assess interpretations of the materials using strategies to locate patterns and develop stories, summaries, or statements. Grbich (2013) suggests guiding the interpretation using the following questions: What surprising information did you not expect to find? What information is conceptually interesting or unusual to participants and audiences? What are the dominant interpretations and what are the alternate notions?

The researcher might obtain peer feedback on early data interpretations or on their audit trail (discussed further in Chapter 10) and procedures. This can be helpful for assessing "how do I know what I know or think I know?" because it requires the researcher to clearly articulate the patterns they see in the data themes or categories. A researcher might use diagramming as a way of representing the relationships among concepts visually at this point, and in some cases, these representations are used in the final report.

Representing and Visualizing the Data

In the final phase of the spiral, researchers represent the data, a packaging of what was found in text, tabular, or figure form. In our experience, computer software as well as specific QDAS packages offer helpful data visualizing features. Among the many options for data representations is a comparison table or a matrix—for example, a 2-x-2 table that compares men and women in terms of one of the themes or categories in the study or a 6-x-6 effects matrix that displays assistance location and types (see Miles & Huberman, 1994; Miles et al., 2019). The cells contain text, not numbers, and depending on the content, researchers use matrices to compare and cross-reference categories to establish a picture of data patterns or ranges (Marshall et al., 2021). A hierarchical tree diagram represents another form of presentation (Angrosino, 2007; Creswell & Guetterman, 2019). This shows different levels of abstraction, with the boxes in the top of the tree representing the most abstract information and those at the bottom representing the least abstract themes. Figure 8.3 illustrates the levels of abstraction from the gunman case

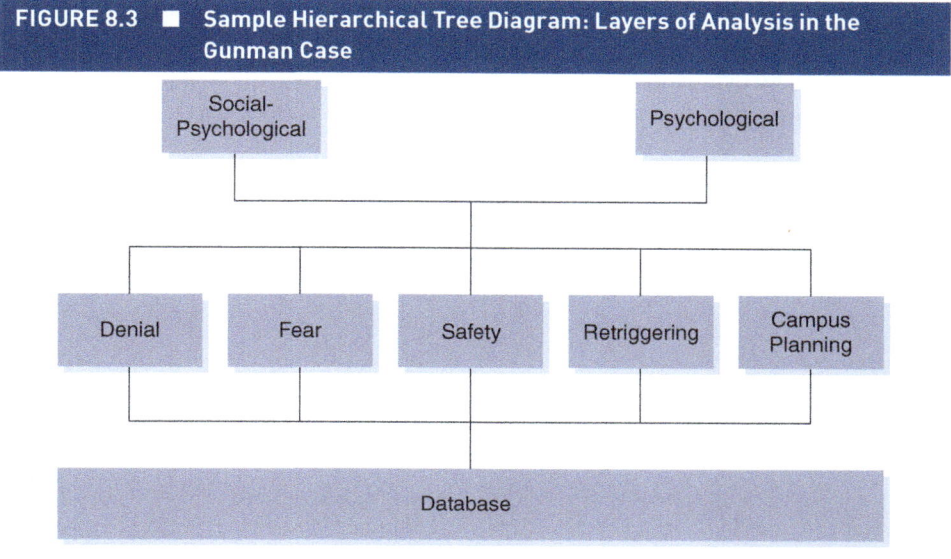

FIGURE 8.3 ■ Sample Hierarchical Tree Diagram: Layers of Analysis in the Gunman Case

Source: Asmussen and Creswell (1995).

(Asmussen & Creswell, 1995). This illustration shows inductive analysis that begins with the raw data consisting of multiple sources of information and then broadens to several specific themes (e.g., safety, denial) and on to the most general themes represented by the two perspectives of social-psychological and psychological factors.

Given the variety of displays available to researchers, it can be difficult to decide which one works best. We forward the following guidance for creating and using matrix displays (adapted from Miles et al., 2019):

- *Search data and select level and type of data to be displayed.* Begin by revisiting the research question and available data. Decide what forms and types of data will appear, such as direct quotes, paraphrases, or researcher explanations or any combination of these forms.. Use search functions within software (or hand search data) to locate potential material.

- *Sketch and seek feedback on initial formatting ideas.* Select labels for row and column headings as part of the initial sketching process. Be sure to balance the amount and type of information. Ask colleagues to review your initial sketches and provide feedback about suggestions for alternative ways of displaying data.

- *Assess completeness and readability and modify as needed.* Look for areas of missing or ambiguous data, and if warranted, show this explicitly in the display. Reduce the number of rows or columns if possible—ideally no more than five or six is considered manageable—create groups within rows or columns or multiple displays as appropriate. Do not feel restricted by the formats you see, rather "*Think display*. Adapt and invent formats that will serve you best" (emphasis in original, Miles et al., 2019, p. 107).

- *Note patterns and possible comparisons and clusters in the display.* Examine the display using various strategies and summarize initial interpretations. The process of writing is essential for refining and clarifying ideas. Displays always need accompanying text as they "never speak for themselves" (Miles et al., 2019, p. 117).

- *Revisit accompanying text and verify conclusions.* Check that the text goes beyond a descriptive summary of the data presented and instead offers explanations and conclusions. Then verify the conclusions against raw data or data summaries because "if a conclusion does not ring true at the 'ground level' when you try it out there, it needs revision" (Miles et al., 2019, p. 117).

Hypotheses or propositions that specify the relationship among categories of information also represent qualitative data. In grounded theory, for example, investigators advance propositions that interrelate the causes of a phenomenon with its context and strategies. Finally, authors present metaphors to analyze the data, literary devices in which something borrowed from one domain applies to another (Hammersley & Atkinson, 1995). Qualitative writers may compose entire studies shaped by analyses of metaphors. For additional ideas for innovative styles of data display and guidance, see Bazeley (2021), Grbich (2013), and Richards (2021).

At this point, the researcher might obtain feedback on the initial summaries and data displays by taking information back to informants, a procedure to be discussed in Chapter 10 as a key validation step in research.

HOW TO USE COMPUTER QUALITATIVE DATA ANALYSIS SOFTWARE (QDAS)

How the researcher intends to use computers and software programs in their data analysis and the "complexity" of the study itself are key use considerations. The range of software and features for supporting qualitative data analysis has increased since they first became available in the 1980s. It is important to note that the process used for qualitative data analysis is the same for hand coding or using a computer and it is the researcher, not the computer software, that completes the process. Marshall et al. (2021) explain the role of software as a qualitative analysis tool: "We caution that software is only a tool to help with some of the mechanical and management aspects of analysis; so the hard analytic thinking must be done by the researcher's own internal hard drive!" (p. 249). For beginner users of computer software for qualitative analysis the choice can be overwhelming.

Researchers can choose to use computers and familiar word-processing and spreadsheet software to organize files, take notes, and code their data. As the QDAS packages continue to evolve in response to researcher feedback, the audience who are willing to learn and integrate the specialized coding, retrieval, and visualizing features is broadening. Kuckartz and Rädiker (2023) note, "For over three decades, the field of computer-assisted analysis of qualitative data has been considered one of the most innovative fields of social science methodology development" (p. 160). Using QDAS packages may not be of interest to all qualitative researchers nor necessary for all studies. While there are several advantages to using QDAS packages that are worthwhile to explore, it is essential for researchers to be aware of their limitations and need for resource investments.

Advantages and Disadvantages

In our view, QDAS is useful for helping researchers in organizing, retrieving, coding, sorting, visualizing, and sharing. We suggest Niedbalski and Ślęzak's (2022) advice for beginner users of computer software for qualitative data analysis as an excellent introduction. In our experience, most QDAS packages offer features to ease and create efficiencies in relation to the following tasks:

- Creating an organized storage system for managing various file formats
- Locating files using search and retrieval functions
- Engaging researchers in coding by facilitating reading line by line
- Sorting data segments for purposes of generating categories and themes
- Producing visual representations for helping with interpreting and reporting
- Enabling collaborative analysis by facilitating sharing among team members

We feel that while QDAS is most helpful with a large number of text files in a database, it can also have value for small databases. Software is essential in research with diverse file formats (i.e., images, recordings) and helpful for teams of multiple researchers. We have found QDAS to be essential to facilitate communication and file access when working with a geographically dispersed research team. Without QDAS, researchers might complete work independently without a common purpose or use codes that are difficult to integrate.

The disadvantages of QDAS go beyond its cost, because of the time involved in learning how to set up and run a software package. This is sometimes a daunting task that is above and beyond the learning required for understanding the procedures of qualitative research. A researcher's comfort with and capacity for technology integration may also impact the time investment. Differences in features and terminology across various QDAS may require learning different terminology and procedures. In our experience, we could get up and running with the basic functions (i.e., file import or memoing) quickly across programs but found gaining proficiency in the specific search, retrieval, and diagramming features to require additional time investment. We find features allowing changes in coding and themes to be desirable, yet we acknowledge some researchers will find some QDAS packages easier to navigate than others. Some researchers note concerns with positioning computers between the researcher and the actual data by producing an uncomfortable distance or hindering the creative process of analysis (e.g., Friese, 2022; Gibbs, 2014, 2018; Jackson & Bazeley, 2019). Finally, while resources to guide the use of QDAS continue to grow, sometimes guidance remains limited or can quickly become outdated. It is important to note the availability of online resources through software websites and books that are both general to the use of QDAS and specific to QDAS packages (e.g., Friese, 2019; Jackson & Bazeley, 2019; Salmona et al., 2019; Silver & Lewins, 2014).

Other resources provide access to researchers' descriptions of QDAS use and experiences (e.g., Cypress, 2019; Estrada & Koolen, 2018; LeBlanc, 2017; Oswald, 2017). For comparisons across QDAS programs, see Gibbs (2018).

> ## TRY THIS NOW 8.1
> ### ALIGNING YOUR QUALITATIVE DATA ANALYSIS NEEDS WITH COMPUTER AND SOFTWARE CAPACITIES
>
> Exploring your study needs and your own capacity can be helpful for deciding whether to use QDAS programs or more familiar computer applications such as word-processing and spreadsheet programs. Address the following questions: What file formats and data quantity do I anticipate my study to involve? What tasks would benefit from my use of QDAS? How many researchers do I anticipate my study to involve? What capacity for integrating computer software do I bring as a researcher and what resources am I able to invest? Include describing your data analysis needs (i.e., complexity and people involved) and the necessary investments (i.e., time, finances, etc.) that inform decisions about whether and how to use QDAS.

A Sampling of Computer Software for Qualitative Data Analysis

The various options of QDAS and unique features continue to expand considerably, making the selection of a program challenging for novice qualitative researchers. Indeed, a key challenge for researchers is learning about the unique features across QDAS packages. In our work, we have found it sometimes difficult to predict what features will be most important. We join Gilbert et al. (2014), who ask, "what analytical tasks will I be engaged in, and what are the different ways I can leverage technology to do them well" (p. 221)? Among the challenges for researchers is accounting for the use of QDAS in research descriptions (Flick, 2023). Paulus et al. (2017) provide essential guidance for researchers about the details to include in research reports:

- Identify the QDAS package by name and version because software features change frequently.

- Use the active rather than passive voice when describing use of QDAS to avoid the misconception of the software conducting the analysis.

- Provide a rationale for choice of QDAS to make explicit why it was selected and how particular features were used.

Each QDAS package may not have the features or capability that researchers need, so researchers can shop comparatively to find a program that meets their needs. See Davidson and di Gregorio (2011) and Paulus and Lester (2020, 2021) for detailed historical descriptions of the evolution of QDAS and specific software features. Below we provide descriptions across a sample of five QDAS packages we have used to help you become familiar with the key uses, considerations, and available guiding resources. We have intentionally left out the version numbers and have presented a general discussion of the programs because the developers are continually upgrading the programs. Our selection of QDAS to highlight in this chapter reflects those that are currently most popular. Other QDAS packages available include Quirkos (http://www.quirkos.com), Transana (http://www.transana.org), F4Analyse (http://www.audiotranskription.de/en/f4analyse), and QDA Miner (http://provalisresearch.com). The new REFI-QDA exchange standard offers users of some QDAS the option of moving coded data files between programs. This can be especially helpful when analysis needs emerge during the process when, for example, a researcher does not anticipate the need for multimedia features (see Evers et al., 2020). We anticipate the flexibility of the exchange standards will eventually bring new users to QDAS.

ATLAS.ti (http://www.atlasti.com)

This program enables you to organize your text, graphic, audio, and visual data files, along with your coding, memos, and findings, into a project. Further, you can code, annotate, and compare segments of information. You can drag and drop codes within an interactive margin screen. You can rapidly search, retrieve, and browse all data segments and notes relevant to an idea and, importantly, build unique visual networks that allow you to connect visually selected passages, memos, and codes in a concept map. Data can be exported to programs such as SPSS, HTML, XML, and CSV. This program also allows for a group of researchers to work on the same project and make comparisons of how each researcher coded the data. Friese (2019, 2022) offers a useful resource specific to the features offered by ATLAS.ti, and a demonstration software package is available to test out this program, which is described by and available from Scientific Software Development in Germany.

Dedoose (http://www.dedoose.com)

This cloud-based program, is accessible for you to use through a website, allowing collaborative analyses. An internet connection is required to use this program with storage, organizing, coding, and retrieving features. Dedoose was developed by SocioCultural Research Consultants to meet the needs of research teams working in real time. The practical strategies offered by Salmona et al. (2019) are complemented by case study descriptions of researchers' use of Dedoose.

HyperRESEARCH (http://www.researchware.com)

This program is an easy-to-use qualitative software package enabling you to code and retrieve, build theories, and conduct analyses of the data. Now with advanced multimedia and language capabilities, HyperRESEARCH allows the researcher to work with text, graphics, and audio and video sources—making it a valuable research analysis tool. HyperRESEARCH is a solid code-and-retrieve data analysis program, with additional theory-building features provided by the Hypothesis Tester. This program also allows the researcher to draw visual diagrams, and it now has a module that can be added, called HyperTRANSCRIBE that will allow researchers to create a transcript of video and audio data. This program, developed by Researchware, is available in the United States.

MAXQDA (http://www.maxqda.com)

MAXQDA is a computer software program that helps you systematically evaluate and interpret qualitative texts. It is also a powerful tool for developing theories and testing theoretical conclusions. The main menu has four windows: the data, the code or category system, the text being analyzed, and the results of basic and complex searches. It uses a hierarchical code system, and the researcher can attach a weight score to a text segment to indicate the relevance of the segment. Memos can be easily written and stored as different types of memos (e.g., theory memos or methodological memos). It has a visual mapping feature for producing different types of conceptual maps representing theoretical associations, empirical relations, and data dependencies. Data can be exported to statistical programs, such as SPSS or Excel, and the software can import Excel or SPSS program files as well. Multiple coders on a particular project can easily collaborate using the program. Images and video segments can also be stored and coded in this program. The mobile companion, MAXApp, allows researchers to use smartphones for data gathering, coding, and memoing, which can be directly imported into your ongoing project for further analysis. MAXQDA is distributed by VERBI Software in Germany. The Corbin and Strauss (2015) book focused on grounded theory contains an extensive illustration of the use of MAXQDA. A demonstration program is available to learn more about the unique features of this program.

NVivo (http://www.qsrinternational.com)

NVivo is the latest version of software from QSR International. NVivo combines the features of the popular software program N6 (or NUD*IST 6) and NVivo 2.0. NVivo helps manage, shape, and analyze qualitative data. It provides security by storing the database and files together in a single file, enables a you to use multiple languages, has a merge function for team research, and enables the researcher to easily manipulate the data and conduct searches. Further, it can display graphically the codes or categories. It can integrate social media data including profile data from Facebook, X—the platform formerly known as Twitter, and LinkedIn. A good overview of the evolution of the software from N6 to NVivo is available from Bazeley (2002) and a resource specific to using NVivo from Jackson and Bazeley (2019). NVivo is distributed by QSR International in Australia. A demonstration copy is available to see and try out the features of this software program.

Steps in Using a QDAS Program

QDAS programs provide a convenient way to store diverse forms of data across each of the five qualitative approaches. These files consist of information from one discrete unit of information, such as a transcript from one interview, one set of observational notes or recordings, or photos of an artifact. After organizing the data files, the researcher embarks on a general reading and memoing of information to develop a sense of the data and to begin the process of making sense of them. When using QDAS programs the researcher goes through the text or images one line or image at a time and asks, "What is the person saying (or doing) in this passage?" Then the researcher assigns a code label using the words of the participant, employing social or human science terms, or composes a term that seems to relate to the situation. After reviewing many pages or images or other types of files, the researcher can use the search function of the program to locate all the text or image segments that fit a code label. In this way, the researcher can easily see how participants are discussing the code or theme in a similar or different way.

The search process can then be extended to include retrieving and reviewing common passages that relate to two or more code labels. For example, the code label "sources of stress" might be combined with "workplace stresses" to yield text segments in which participants are discussing "sources of stress." Alternatively, "sources of stress" might be combined with "home stresses" to generate text segments in which participants describe "sources of stress." The co-occurrence features highlight the frequency of the double coding. After reviewing the frequency of these code combinations, the researcher can use the search function of the program to look for specific words to see how frequently they occur in the texts. In this way, the researcher can create new codes or possible themes based on the frequency of the use of specific words describing the focus for each of the approaches—for example, patterns among story elements for narrative research, significant statements for phenomenology, properties representing multiple perspectives for grounded theory, group thought and behavior for ethnography, and instances for case study.

If the researcher makes both of these requests about workplace and home stresses, data then exists for making comparisons among the source locations described by participants and their views about the "sources of stress." QDAS thus enables a researcher to interrogate the database about the interrelationship within or among differing codes and themes. The researcher can easily retrieve the relevant data segments associated with these codes and themes and use the concept-mapping feature of many QDAS programs during the development of themes, models, and abstractions relevant for each approach.

To support the researcher in conceptualizing different levels of abstraction, QDAS provides a means for organizing codes hierarchically so that smaller units, such as codes, can be placed under larger units, such as themes. For example, the familial hierarchy of children and their parents represented by codes illustrates two levels of abstraction under the theme of coping mechanisms. In this way, the computer program helps the researcher to build levels of analysis and see the relationship between the raw data and the broader themes. Abstraction thus contributes to the development of the story for narrative research, the description of the essence in phenomenology, the theory in grounded theory, cultural interpretation in ethnography, and the case assertions in case study.

Then, all approaches, with the exception of grounded theory, have a phase dedicated to description in which the inquirer seeks to begin building toward a theory of the action or process. This description represents the researcher's interpretations of codes and themes drawn from the data. Many QDAS programs contain the features of concept maps, data charts and cluster analysis so that the user can generate a visual diagram of the codes and themes and their interrelationships. In this way, the researcher can continually move around and reorganize these codes and themes under new categories of information as the project progresses. Also, keeping track of the different versions of the diagrams creates an audit trail comprising a log of the analytic process that can be revisited as needed (see Chapter 10 for further discussion).

Another source of an audit trail involves documenting and managing researchers' memos to capture emerging ideas and insights throughout the data analysis. QDAS programs provide the capability to write and store memos associated with different units of data—for example, segments of text or images, codes, files, and the overall project. In this way, the researcher can begin to create the codebook or qualitative report during data analysis or simply record insights as they emerge.

ANALYSIS WITHIN APPROACHES TO INQUIRY

Think about the process of qualitative data analysis as having two layers. The first layer is to cover the processes we have described in the general spiral analysis. The second layer is to build on this general analysis by using specific analytic procedures advanced for each of the five approaches to inquiry. These procedures will take data analysis beyond a "generic" approach to analysis into a more advanced set of procedures. Our organizing framework for this discussion is found in Table 8.5. With the discussion of each of the five approaches, we address specific analysis and representing characteristics including a template for coding within each approach. It is important to note that while these codes were initially developed in earlier editions of this book as a hierarchical picture, they could be drawn as circles or in a less linear fashion as well. At the end of this discussion, we return to significant differences and similarities among the five approaches.

Narrative Research Analysis and Representation

We think that Riessman (2008) says it best when she comments that narrative analysis "refers to a family of methods for interpreting texts that have in common a storied form" (p. 11). The data collected in a narrative study need to be analyzed for the story of lived experiences the participant tells, a chronology of unfolding events, and turning points or epiphanies. Within this broad sketch of analysis, several options exist for the narrative researcher.

A narrative researcher can take a literary orientation to their analysis. For example, using a story in science education told by four fourth graders in one elementary school included several approaches to narrative analysis (Ollerenshaw & Creswell, 2002). One approach is a process advanced by Yussen and Ozcan (1997) that involves analyzing text data for five elements of plot structure (i.e., characters, setting, problem, actions, and resolution). A narrative researcher could use an approach that incorporates different elements that go into the story. The three-dimensional space approach of Clandinin and Connelly (2000) includes analyzing the data for three elements: interaction (personal and social), continuity (past, present, and future), and situation (physical places or the storyteller's places). In the Ollerenshaw and Creswell (2002) narrative, we saw common elements of narrative analysis: by collecting stories of personal experiences in the form of field texts such as conducting interviews or having conversations, retelling the stories based on narrative elements (e.g., three-dimensional space approach and the five

TABLE 8.5 ■ Data Analysis and Representation by Five Qualitative Approaches

Data Analysis and Representation	Narrative	Phenomenology	Grounded Theory Study	Ethnography	Case Study
Managing and organizing the data	• Create and organize data files.	• Create and organize data files.	• Create and organize data files.	• Create and organize data files.	• Create and organize data files.
Reading and memoing emergent ideas	• Read through text, make margin notes, and form initial codes.	• Read through text, make margin notes, and form initial codes.	• Read through text, make margin notes, and form initial codes.	• Read through text, make margin notes, and form initial codes.	• Read through text, make margin notes, and form initial codes.
Describing and classifying codes into themes	• Describe the patterns across the objective set of experiences. • Identify and describe the stories into a chronology.	• Describe personal experiences through epoché. • Describe the essence of the phenomenon.	• Describe open coding categories. • Select one open coding category to build toward central phenomenon in process.	• Describe the social setting, actors, and events; draw a picture of the setting.	• Describe the case and its context.
Developing and assessing interpretations	• Locate epiphanies within stories. • Identify contextual materials.	• Develop significant statements. • Group statements into meaning units.	• Engage in axial coding—causal condition, context, intervening conditions, strategies, and consequences. • Develop the theory.	• Analyze data for themes and patterned regularities.	• Use categorical aggregation to establish themes or patterns.
Representing and visualizing the data	• Re-story and interpret the larger meaning of the story.	• Develop a textural description—"what happened." • Develop a structural description—"how the phenomenon was experienced." • Develop the "essence," using a composite description.	• Engage in selective coding and interrelate the categories to develop a "story" or propositions or matrix.	• Interpret and make sense of the findings—how the culture "works."	• Use direct interpretation. • Develop naturalistic generalizations of what was "learned."

elements of plot), rewriting the stories into a chronological sequence, and incorporating the setting or place of the participants' experiences.

A chronological approach can also be taken in the analysis of the narratives. Denzin (1989) suggests that a researcher begin biographical analysis by identifying an objective set of experiences in the subject's life. Having the individual journal a sketch of their life may be a good beginning point for analysis. In this sketch, the researcher looks for life-course stages or experiences (e.g., childhood, marriage, employment) to develop a chronology of the individual's life. Stories and epiphanies will emerge from the individual's journal or from interviews. The researcher looks in the database (typically interviews or documents) for concrete, contextual biographical materials. During the interview, the researcher prompts the participant to expand on various sections of the stories and asks the interviewee to theorize about their life. These theories may relate to career models, processes in the life course, models of the social world, relational models of biography, and natural history models of the life course. Then, the researcher organizes larger patterns and meaning from the narrative segments and categories. Daiute (2014) identifies four types of patterns for meaning-making related to similarities, differences, change, or coherence. Finally, the individual's biography is reconstructed, and the researcher identifies factors that have shaped the life. This leads to the writing of an analytic abstraction of the case that highlights (a) the processes in the individual's life, (b) the different theories that relate to these life experiences, and (c) the unique and general features of the life. Embedded within narrative analysis and representation processes is a collaborative approach whereby participants are actively involved (Clandinin, 2023; Clandinin & Connelly, 2000).

In narrative research in QDAS (see Figure 8.4), we create codes that relate to the story, such as the chronology, the plot or the three-dimensional space model, and the themes that might arise from the story. The analysis might proceed using the plot structure approach or

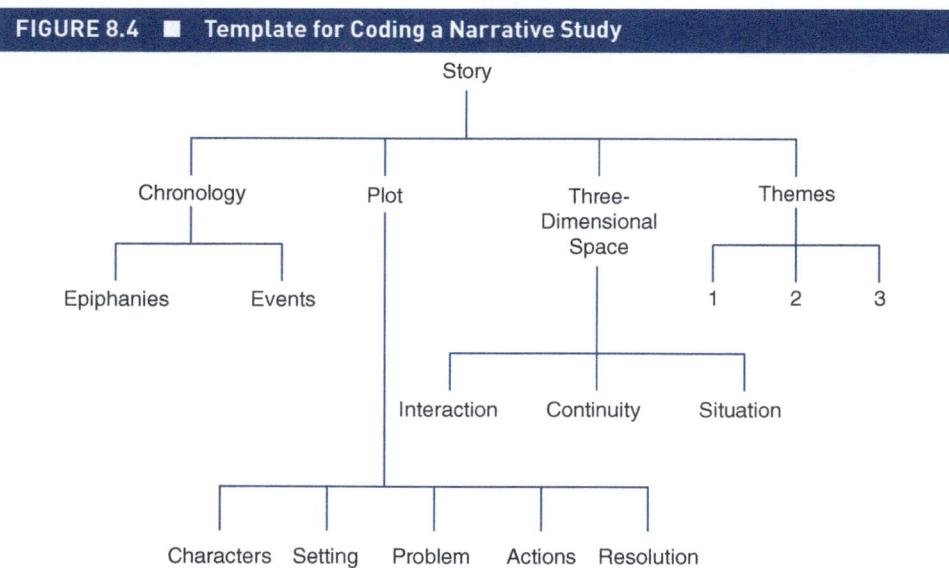

FIGURE 8.4 ■ Template for Coding a Narrative Study

the three-dimensional model, but we placed both in the figure to provide the most options for analysis. The researcher will not know what approach to use until he or she actually starts the data analysis process. The researcher might develop a code, or "story," and begin writing out the story based on the elements analyzed.

Another approach to narrative analysis turns on how the narrative report is composed. Riessman (2008) suggests a typology of four analytic strategies that reflect this diversity in composing the stories. Riessman calls it thematic analysis when the researcher analyzes "what" is spoken or written during data collection. She comments that this approach is the most popular form of narrative studies, and we see it in the Chan (2010) narrative project reported in Appendix A. A second form in Riessman's (2008) typology is called the structural form, and it emphasizes "how" a story is told. This brings in linguistic analysis in which the individual telling the story uses form and language to achieve a particular effect. Discourse analysis, based on Gee's (1991) method, would examine the storytellers' narrative for such elements as the sequence of utterances, the pitch of the voice, and the intonation. A third form for Riessman (2008) is the dialogic or performance analysis, in which the talk is interactively produced by the researcher and the participant or actively performed by the participant through such activities as poetry or a play. The fourth form is an emerging area of using visual analysis of images or interpreting images alongside words. It could also be a story told about the production of an image or how different audiences view an image.

In the narrative study of Ai Mei Zhang, the Chinese immigrant student presented by Chan (2010) in Appendix A, the analytic approach begins with a thematic analysis similar to Riessman's (2008) approach. After briefly mentioning a description of Ai Mei's school, Chan then discusses several themes, all of which have to do with conflict (e.g., home language conflicts with school language). That Chan saw conflict introduces the idea that she analyzed the data for this phenomenon and rendered the theme development from a postmodern type of interpretive lens. Chan then goes on to analyze the data beyond the themes to explore her role as a narrative researcher learning about Ai Mei's experiences. Thus, while overall the analysis is based on a thematic approach, the introduction of conflict and the researcher's experiences adds a thoughtful conceptual analysis to the study.

Phenomenological Analysis and Representation

The suggestions for narrative analysis present a general template for qualitative researchers. In contrast, in phenomenology, there have been specific, structured methods of analysis advanced, especially by Moustakas (1994). Moustakas reviews several approaches in his book, but we see his modification of the Stevick-Colaizzi-Keen method as providing the most practical, useful approach. Our approach, a simplified version of this method discussed by Moustakas (1994), is as follows:

- *Describe personal experiences with the phenomenon under study.* The researcher begins with a full description of their own experience of the phenomenon. This is an attempt to set aside the researcher's personal experiences (which cannot be done entirely) so that the focus can be directed to the participants in the study.

- *Develop a list of significant statements in the data.* The researcher then finds statements (in the interviews or other data sources) about how individuals are experiencing the topic; lists these significant statements (horizontalization of the data) and treats each statement as having equal worth; and works to develop a list of nonrepetitive, nonoverlapping statements.

- *Group the significant statements into broader units of information.* These larger units, also called meaning units or themes, provide the foundation for interpretation.

- *Create a description of "what" the participants in the study experienced with the phenomenon.* This is called a textural description of the experience—what happened—and includes verbatim examples.

- *Draft a description of "how" the experience happened.* This is called structural description, and the inquirer reflects on the setting and context in which the phenomenon was experienced. For example, in a phenomenological study of the smoking behavior of high school students (McVea et al., 1999), the authors provided a structural description about where the phenomenon of smoking occurs, such as in the parking lot, outside the school, by student lockers, in remote locations at the school, and so forth.

- *Write a composite description of the phenomenon.* A composite description incorporates both the textural and structural descriptions. This passage is the "essence" of the experience and represents the culminating aspect of a phenomenological study. It is typically a long paragraph that tells the reader "what" the participants experienced with the phenomenon and "how" they experienced it (i.e., the context).

Moustakas (1994) is a psychologist, which may explain why, in his writings, the essence typically is of a phenomenon in psychology, such as grief or loss. Giorgi (2009), also a psychologist, provides an analytic approach similar to that of Stevick, Colaizzi, and Keen. Giorgi discusses how researchers read for a sense of the whole, determine meaning units, transform the participants' expressions into psychologically sensitive interpretations, and then write a description of the essence. Most helpful in Giorgi's discussion is the example he provides of describing jealousy as analyzed by himself and another researcher.

In a phenomenological study of individuals who have experienced adversity, as in the case of Black women in higher education leadership by Chance (2022; see Appendix B; reviewed in Chapter 5), the author used Moustakas's (1994) modified Stevick-Colaizzi-Keen phenomenological data analysis procedures. The approach follows the general guideline of horizontalizing the transcripts by reviewing each transcript to identify possible codes, applying the codes, and moving from naïve descriptions to specific examples to presenting an exhaustive description of the participants lived experiences of the phenomenon. Chance describes using the QDAS program Dedoose, engaging in the reflexive process of epoché through notetaking, and advancing an intersectionality framework as a lens to "observe, understand, and describe the themes that emerged" (Chance, 2022, p. 56).

In the template for coding a phenomenological study (see Figure 8.5), we used the categories mentioned earlier in data analysis. We placed codes for epoché or bracketing (if this is used), significant statements, meaning units, and textural and structural descriptions (which both might be written as memos). The code at the top, "essence of the phenomenon," is written as a memo about the "essence" that will become the essence description in the final written report.

A less structured approach is found in van Manen (1990, 2014, 2023) for use when two conditions for the possibility of doing phenomenological analysis are met with an appropriate question and data. First, the phenomenological question guiding the study is critical because "if the question lacks heuristic clarity, point, and power, then analysis will fail for the lack of reflective focus" (van Manen, 2014, p. 297). Second, the experiential quality of the data is necessary because "if the material lacks experiential detail, concreteness, vividness, and lived-thoroughness, then the analysis will fail for lack of substance" (van Manen, 2014, p. 297). He begins discussing data analysis by calling it "phenomenological reflection" (van Manen, 1990, p. 77). The basic idea of this reflection is to grasp the essential meaning of something. The wide array of data sources of expressions or forms that we would reflect on might be transcribed taped conversations, interview materials, daily accounts or stories, suppertime talk, formally written responses, diaries, other people's writings, film, drama, poetry, novels, and so forth. Recently, van Manen (2023) described intentional analysis as "descriptive and focuses on the whole rather than on the parts" (p. 136).

Van Manen (1990) places emphasis on gaining an understanding of themes by asking, "What is this example an example of?" (p. 86). These themes should have certain qualities such as focus, a simplification of ideas, and a description of the structure of the lived experience (van Manen, 1990, 2014, 2023). The process involves attending to the entire text (holistic reading approach), looking for statements or phrases (selective reading or highlighting approach), and examining every sentence (the detailed reading or line-by-line approach). Attending to four guides for reflection was also important: the space felt by individuals (e.g., the modern bank), physical or bodily presence (e.g., what does a person in love look like?), time (e.g., the dimensions of past, present, and future), and the relationships with others (e.g., expressed through a handshake). In the end, analyzing the data for themes, using different approaches to examine the information, and considering the guides for reflection should yield an explicit structure of the meaning of the lived experience.

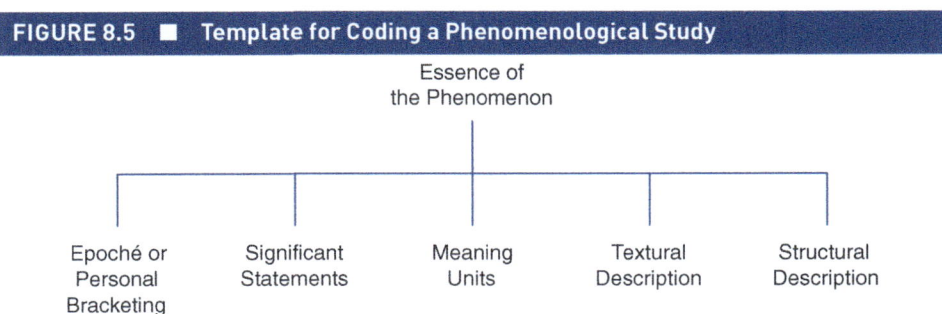

FIGURE 8.5 ■ Template for Coding a Phenomenological Study

We suggest Suddick et al.'s (2020) experiential reflection of phenomenology as an example to emulate in which the researchers described how individuals in the acute stroke unit lived meaningfully. To visually represent the processes undertaken, the researchers used visual maps (see Figure 8.6) to offer opportunities to enter the hermeneutic circle and thus be able to "work with part and whole and embrace a more dynamic, textured, holistic understanding of the lived experience" (Suddick, et al., 2020, p. 7). The study involved four stroke survivors' experiential accounts and how the acute stroke unit emerged as a lived space in two meaningful and interconnected forms: holding space and transitional space. In the final reflection, Suddick et al. (2020) describe their contribution as having attempted "to convey the somewhat abstract and less articulated process that occurs in hermeneutic phenomenological research. It illustrates the texts alterity and integral interplay between part and whole, as meaning unfolds and is apprehended" (p. 12).

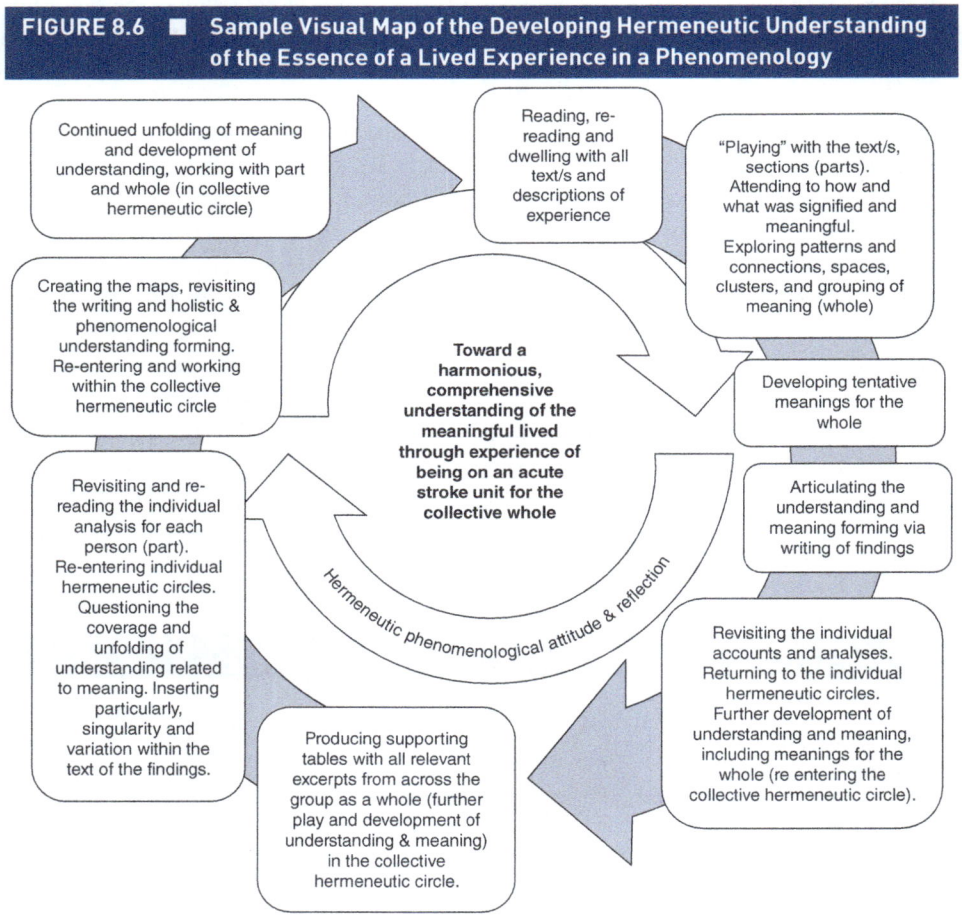

FIGURE 8.6 ■ Sample Visual Map of the Developing Hermeneutic Understanding of the Essence of a Lived Experience in a Phenomenology

Source: Suddick et al. (2020), Fig. 1. Used with permission from Sage

Grounded Theory Analysis and Representation

Similar to phenomenology, grounded theory uses detailed procedures for analysis. It consists of three phases of coding—open, axial, and selective—as advanced by Strauss and Corbin (1990, 1998) and Corbin and Strauss (2007, 2015). Grounded theory provides a procedure for developing categories of information (open coding), interconnecting the categories (axial coding), building a "story" that connects the categories (selective coding), and ending with a discursive set of theoretical propositions (Strauss & Corbin, 1990). In the template for coding a grounded theory study (see Figure 8.7), we included the three major coding phases: open coding, axial coding, and selective coding. We also included a code for the conditional matrix if that feature is used by the grounded theorist. The researcher can state a name for the diagram, "Theory Description or Visual Model," thus linking the codes.

In the open coding phase, the researcher examines the text (e.g., transcripts, field notes, documents) for salient categories of information supported by the text. Using the constant comparative approach, the researcher attempts to "saturate" the categories—to look for instances that represent the category and to continue looking (and interviewing) until the new information obtained does not provide further insight into the category. These categories comprise subcategories, called properties, that represent multiple perspectives about the categories. Properties, in turn, are **dimensionalized** and presented on a continuum. Overall, this is the process of reducing the database to a small set of themes or categories that characterize the process or action being explored in the grounded theory study.

Once an initial set of categories has been developed, the researcher identifies a single category from the open coding list as the central phenomenon of interest. The open coding category selected for this purpose is typically one that is extensively discussed by the participants or one of special conceptual interest because it seems central to the process being studied in the grounded theory project. The inquirer selects this one open coding category

FIGURE 8.7 ■ Template for Coding a Grounded Theory Study

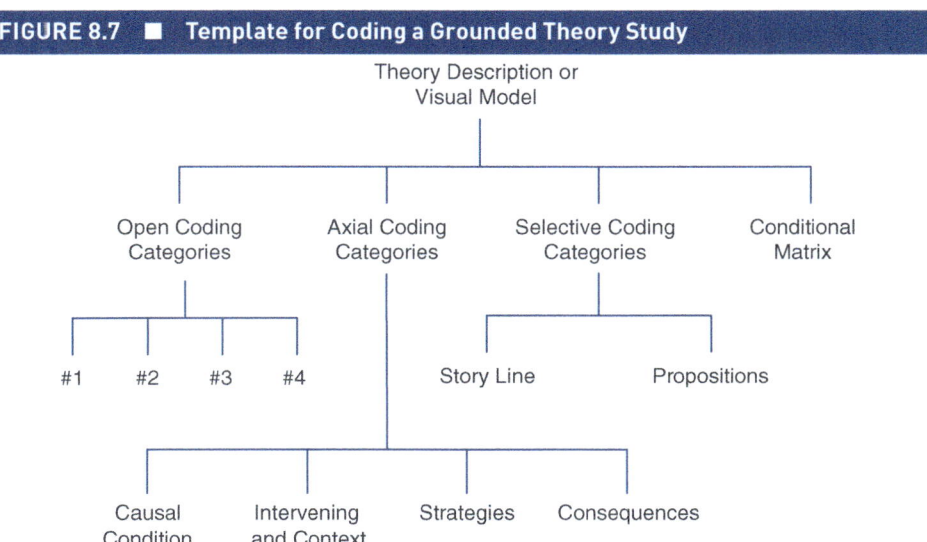

(a central phenomenon), positions it as the central feature of the theory, and then returns to the database (or collects additional data) to understand the categories that relate to this central phenomenon. Specifically, the researcher engages in the coding process called axial coding in which the database is reviewed (or new data are collected) to provide insight into specific coding categories that relate to or explain the central phenomenon. These are causal conditions that influence the central phenomenon, the strategies for addressing the phenomenon, the context and intervening conditions that shape the strategies, and the consequences of undertaking the strategies. Information from this coding phase is then organized into a figure (i.e., a coding paradigm) that presents a theoretical model of the process under study. In this way, a theory is built or generated. From this theory, the inquirer generates propositions (or hypotheses) or statements that interrelate the categories in the coding paradigm. This is called selective coding. Finally, at the broadest level of analysis, the researcher can create a conditional matrix. This matrix is an analytical aid—a diagram—that helps the researcher visualize the wide range of conditions and consequences (e.g., society, world) related to the central phenomenon (Corbin & Strauss, 2015; Strauss & Corbin, 1990). Seldom have we found the conditional matrix used in studies.

A key to understanding the difference that Charmaz brings to grounded theory data analysis is to hear her say, "Avoid imposing a forced framework" (Charmaz, 2006, p. 66). Her approach emphasized an emerging process of forming the theory. Her analytic steps began with an initial phase of coding each word, line, or segment of data. At this early stage, she was interested in having the initial codes treated analytically to understand a process and larger theoretical categories. This initial phase was followed by focused coding, using the initial codes to sift through large amounts of data, analyzing for syntheses and larger explanations. She did not support the Strauss and Corbin (1998) formal procedures of axial coding that organized the data into conditions, actions/interactions, consequences, and so forth. However, Charmaz (2006, 2014) did examine the categories and began to develop links among them. She also believed in using theoretical coding, first developed by Glaser (1978). This step involved specifying possible relationships between categories based on a priori theoretical coding families (e.g., causes, context, ordering). However, Charmaz (2006, 2014) goes on to say that these theoretical codes needed to earn their way into the grounded theory that emerges. The theory that emerged for Charmaz emphasizes understanding rather than explanation. It assumes emergent, multiple realities; the link of facts and values; provisional information; and a narrative about social life as a process. It might be presented as a figure or as a narrative that pulls together experiences and shows the range of meanings.

The specific form for presenting the theory in grounded theory may differ among studies. In a study of department chairs, theory is presented as hypotheses (Creswell & Brown, 1992). In Trip et al.'s study (2019) of the caregiving relationship process with aging people having intellectual disabilities, the authors explain navigating transitions across the life course (see Appendix C). Trip et al. (2019) present a discussion of a theoretical model as displayed in a figure. Their study also describes the use of constant comparative analysis, initial and focused coding requiring the fracturing of data exploring the "inter-relationships between the data, enabling it be reassembled as theory emerges" (p. 1599). The visual representation of these procedures appears in Figure 8.8 and is effective in conveying the iterative nature of the analysis

Chapter 8 • Data Analysis and Representation   247

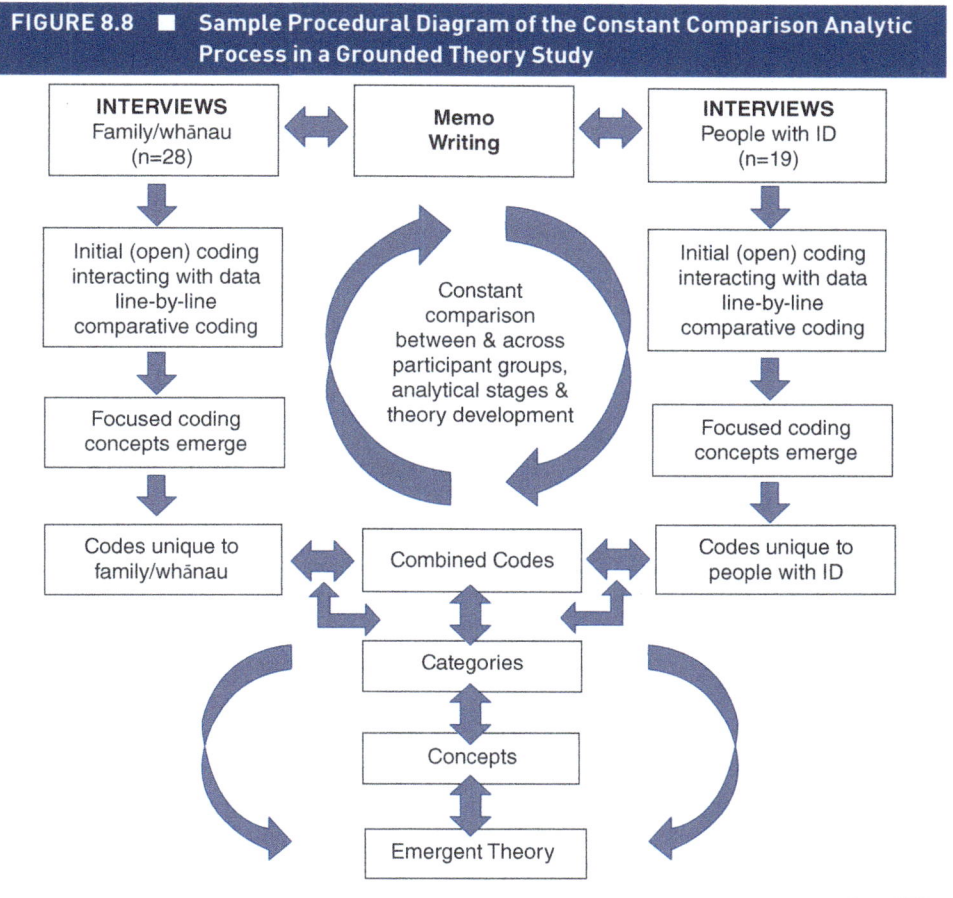

FIGURE 8.8 ■ Sample Procedural Diagram of the Constant Comparison Analytic Process in a Grounded Theory Study

Source: Trip et al. (2019), Fig. 1. Used with permission from Sage.

and the key role of memoing in grounded theory research. Trip et al. (2019) describe the use of Excel software in the initial coding and printing the coded data from across the participants. Trip describes working in partnership with coauthors who were her supervisors and specialist advisors with clinical and research expertise in the field.

Ethnographic Analysis and Representation

For ethnographic research, we recommend the three aspects of data analysis advanced by Wolcott (1994): description, analysis, and interpretation of the culture-sharing group. Wolcott (1990b) believes that a good starting point for writing an ethnography is to describe the culture-sharing group and setting:

> Description is the foundation upon which qualitative research is built. . . . Here you become the storyteller, inviting the reader to see through your eyes what you have seen.

. . . Start by presenting a straightforward description of the setting and events. No footnotes, no intrusive analysis—just the facts, carefully presented and interestingly related at an appropriate level of detail. (p. 28)

From an interpretive perspective, the researcher may present only one set of facts; other facts and interpretations await the reading of the ethnography by the participants and others. But this description may present information gleaned from the analysis of data presented in chronological order. The writer describes through progressively focusing the description or chronicling a "day in the life" of the group or individual. Finally, other techniques involve focusing on a critical or key event, developing a "story" complete with a plot and characters, writing it as a "mystery," examining groups in interaction, following an analytical framework, or showing different perspectives through the views of participants.

Analysis for Wolcott (1994) is a sorting procedure—"the quantitative side of qualitative research" (p. 26). This involves highlighting specific material introduced in the descriptive phase or displaying findings through tables, charts, diagrams, and figures. The researcher also analyzes through using systematic procedures such as those advanced by Spradley (1979, 1980), who called for building taxonomies, generating comparison tables, and developing semantic tables. Perhaps the most popular analysis procedure, also mentioned by Wolcott (1994), is the search for patterned regularities in the data. Other forms of analysis consist of comparing the cultural group to others, evaluating the group in terms of standards, and drawing connections between the culture-sharing group and larger theoretical frameworks. Other analysis steps include critiquing the research process and proposing a redesign for the study. See Figure 8.9 for a screen capture image of the spreadsheet created by García-Rapp (2019) as part of her file organization and her visual map of the integrative model of phenomenon for the video analysis of a multiyear ethnographic examination of YouTube's beauty community. As part of an experiential reflection on her ethnographic fieldwork on YouTube, she explains how the content within cells of the spreadsheet are hyperlinked to files documenting comments or pictures of YouTube videos (see Example 4.4 for an introduction to García-Rapp's study). García-Rapp describes how color printing her coding helped her to further analyze her data manually. She then diagramed and used visual maps to create the integrative model that was also described in text.

Making an ethnographic interpretation of the culture-sharing group is a data transformation step as well. Here the researcher goes beyond the database and probes "what is to be made of them" (Wolcott, 1994, p. 36). The researcher speculates outrageous, comparative interpretations that raise doubts or questions for the reader. The researcher draws inferences from the data or turns to theory to provide structure for their interpretations. The researcher also personalizes the interpretation: "This is what I make of it" or "This is how the research experience affected me" (p. 44). Finally, the investigator forges an interpretation through expressions such as poetry, fiction, or performance.

In the template for coding an ethnography (see Figure 8.10), we included a code that might be a memo or reference to text about the theoretical lens used in the ethnography, codes on the description of the culture and an analysis of themes, a code on field issues, and a code on interpretation. The name at the top, "Cultural Portrait of Culture-Sharing Group—'How It Works,'"

Chapter 8 • Data Analysis and Representation   249

FIGURE 8.9 ■ Sample File Organization and Visual Model Mapping in an Ethnography

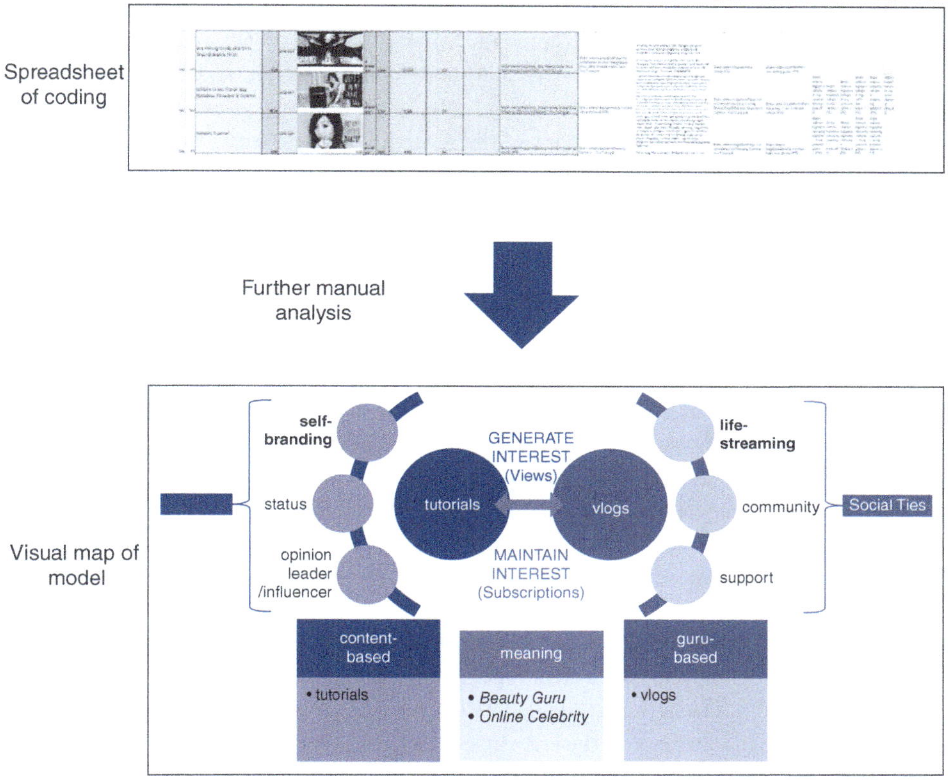

Spreadsheet of coding

Further manual analysis

Visual map of model

Source: García-Rapp (2019), Figs. 1 and 2. Used with permission from Sage.

FIGURE 8.10 ■ Template for Coding an Ethnography

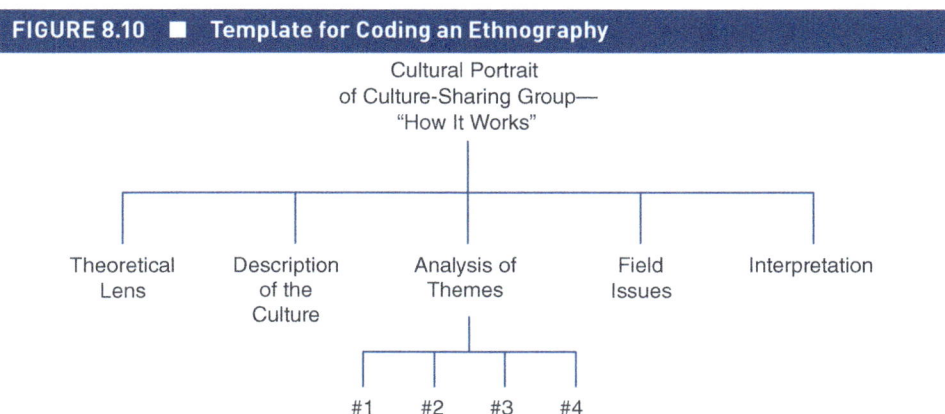

Cultural Portrait of Culture-Sharing Group—"How It Works"

- Theoretical Lens
- Description of the Culture
- Analysis of Themes
  - #1
  - #2
  - #3
  - #4
- Field Issues
- Interpretation

can be a statement in which the ethnographer writes a memo summarizing the major cultural rules that pertain to the group.

Multiple forms of analysis represent Fetterman's (2019) approach to ethnography. He did not have a lockstep procedure but recommended triangulating the data by testing one source of data against another, looking for patterns of thought and behavior, and focusing in on key events that the ethnography can use to analyze an entire culture (e.g., ritual observance of the Sabbath). Ethnographers also draw maps of the setting, develop charts, design matrices, and sometimes employ statistical analysis to examine frequency and magnitude. They might also crystallize their thoughts to provide "a mundane conclusion, a novel insight, or an earth-shattering epiphany" (Fetterman, 2019, p. 117).

The ethnography presented in Appendix D by Mac an Ghaill and Haywood (2015) was guided by Braun and Clarke's (2006) thematic analysis. The authors describe the group of Bangladeshi and Pakistani young men's generational-specific experiences in relation to the racialization of their ethnicities and changes in terms of how they negotiated the meanings attached to being Muslim. The final section offered a broad level of abstraction beyond the themes to suggest how the group made sense of the range of social and cultural exclusions they experienced during a time of rapid change within their city. The authors situate their conclusions within their own experiences of listening to the group's narratives over 3 years and resisting representing their identities "using popular and academic explanations" (Mac an Ghaill & Haywood, p. 111). Instead, they chose to emphasize the need for careful consideration and facilitation of ways for understanding the young men's own participation and the influence of local contexts and broader social and economic processes in identity formation. Another example of an ethnography applied a critical perspective to the analytic procedures of ethnography (Haenfler, 2004). Haenfler provides a detailed description of the straight edge core values of resistance to other cultures and then discusses five themes related to these core values (e.g., positive, clean living). Then, the conclusion to the article includes broad interpretations of the group's core values, such as the individualized and collective meanings for participation in the subculture. However, Haenfler began the methods discussion with a self-disclosing, positioning statement about his background and participation in the straight edge (sXe) movement. This positioning was also presented as a chronology of his experiences following the group from 1989 to 2001.

Case Study Analysis and Representation

For a case study, as in ethnography, analysis consists of making a detailed description of the case and its setting. If the case presents a chronology of events, we then recommend analyzing the multiple sources of data to determine evidence for each step or phase in the evolution of the case. Moreover, the setting is particularly important. For example, in Goodrum et al.'s (2022) case study of a school shooting where two students died, the researchers analyzed existing documents to examine the match between guidelines and activities in the threat assessment process and how that match influenced decision making (see Appendix E). The analysis involved line-by-line coding with the QDAS NVivo. The case centered on examining educators' decision-making processes to understand the organization's management of and response to a troubled student. The authors described their resulting understandings of how the school's organizational structure and culture shaped and hindered violence prevention practices with the aim of developing effective intervention strategies. In another study, the gunman on campus case (Asmussen & Creswell, 1995), the authors sought to establish how the incident fit into the setting—in this situation, a tranquil, peaceful Midwestern community.

Stake (1995) advocates four forms of data analysis and interpretation in case study research. In categorical aggregation, the researcher seeks a collection of instances from the data, hoping that issue-relevant meanings will emerge. In the template for coding a case study (see Figure 8.11), we chose a multiple case study to illustrate the pre-code specification. For each case, codes exist for the context and description of the case. Also, we advanced codes for themes within each case, and for themes that are similar and different in cross-case analysis. Finally, we included codes for assertions and generalizations across all cases. In direct interpretation, on the other hand, the case study researcher looks at a single instance and draws meaning from it without looking for multiple instances. It is a process of pulling the data apart and putting them back together in more meaningful ways. Also, the researcher establishes patterns and looks for a correspondence between two or more categories. This correspondence might take the form of a table, possibly a 2-x-2 table, showing the relationship between two categories. Yin (2017) advances a cross-case synthesis as an analytic technique when the researcher studies two or more cases. He suggests that a word table can be created to display the data from individual cases according to some uniform framework. The implication of this is that the researcher can then look for similarities and differences among the cases. Finally, the researcher develops naturalistic generalizations from analyzing the data, makes generalizations that people can learn from the case for themselves, applies learnings to a population of cases, or transfers them to a similar context.

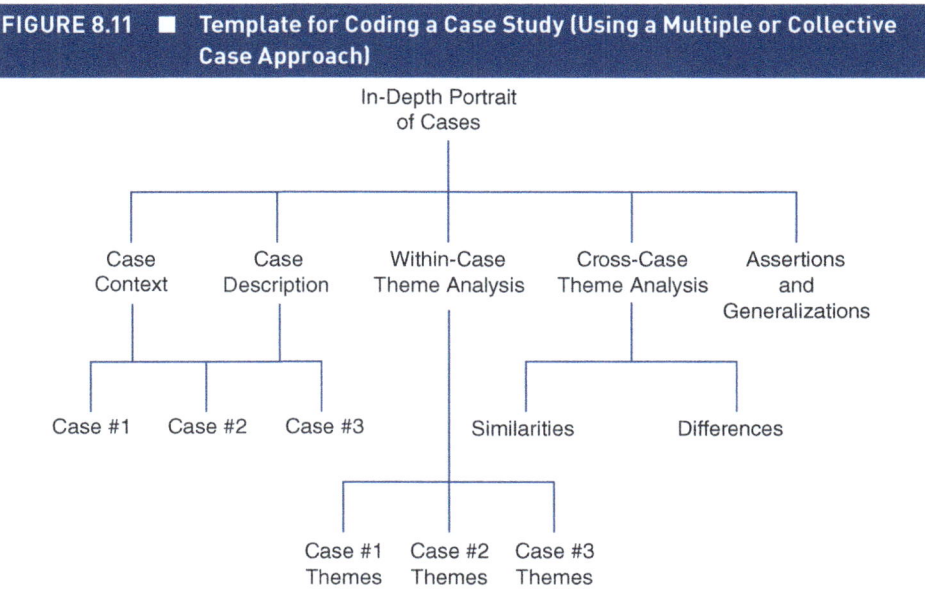

FIGURE 8.11 ■ Template for Coding a Case Study (Using a Multiple or Collective Case Approach)

To these analysis steps we would add description of the case—a detailed view of aspects about the case, the "facts." In Frelin's (2015) case study, the author illustrates relational practices chronologically, describing how relationships were negotiated and the qualities of trust and humaneness (see Example 4.5 for our introduction to Frelin's study). The final section discusses the complex and temporal nature of teachers' work in the literature about the population of students with experiences of school failure and considers the transferability of the findings related to teachers to the roles of school psychologists within similar contexts. To provide another account, in the gunman case study, we have access to greater details about the analytic processes (Asmussen & Creswell, 1995). The case description centers on the events for the 2 weeks following the gunman incident and highlights the major players, the sites, and the activities. The data were then aggregated into about 20 categories (categorical aggregation) and collapsed into five themes. The final section of the study presents generalizations about the case in terms of the themes and how they compared and contrasted with published literature on campus violence.

TRY THIS NOW 8.2
COMPARING DATA ANALYSIS DESCRIPTIONS IN THE APPENDIX STUDIES

Comparing the similarities and differences in data analysis descriptions across published qualitative studies helps guide researchers in presenting their own studies. Choose two of the Appendix studies to compare. What evidence of the data spiral activities summarized in Table 8.2 can you find? Then compare the descriptions for each of the data analysis activities across the articles. Note which elements are similar and which are different.

COMPARING THE FIVE APPROACHES IN DATA ANALYSIS

Returning to Table 8.5, data analysis and representation in the five qualitative approaches have several common and distinctive features. Across all five approaches, the researcher typically begins by creating and organizing files of information. Then, all approaches have a phase dedicated to description.

However, several important differences exist in the five approaches. Grounded theory and phenomenology have the most detailed, explicated procedure for data analysis, depending on the author chosen for guidance on analysis. Ethnography and case studies have analysis procedures that are common, and narrative research represents the least structured procedure. Also, the terms used in the phase of classifying show distinct language among these approaches (see glossary for terms used in each approach); what is called open coding in grounded theory is similar to the first stage of identifying significant statements in phenomenology and to categorical aggregation in case study research. The researcher needs to become familiar with the definition of these terms of analysis and employ them correctly in the chosen approach to inquiry. Finally, the presentation of the data, in turn, reflects the data analysis steps, and it varies from a narration in narrative to tabled statements, meanings, and description in phenomenology to a visual model or theory in grounded theory.

CHAPTER CHECK-IN

1. What general coding strategies can you use to practice coding text to develop an analysis within one of the five approaches?
    a. To conduct this practice, obtain a short text file, which may be a transcript of an interview, field notes typed from an observation, or a digital file of a document, such as a newspaper article.
    b. Next, read and assign memos by bracketing large text segments and asking yourself the following questions:
        i. What is the content being discussed in the text?
        ii. What would you expect to find in the database?
        iii. What surprising information did you not expect to find?
        iv. What information is conceptually interesting or unusual to participants?
    c. Develop and assign code labels to the text segments using information in this chapter and guided by such questions as the following:
        i. What codes would be expected to fit?
        ii. What new codes are emergent?
        iii. What codes relate to other data sources?
    d. Finally, revisit the segments assigned to each of the code labels and consider which ones might be useful in forming themes in your study.
2. What general coding strategies can you use to practice coding images to develop an analysis within one of the five approaches?
    a. To conduct this practice, obtain pictures from one of your projects or select pictures from magazine articles and prepare a digital file.
    b. Next, examine one of the images and assign memos by asking yourself the following questions:
        i. What is in the picture?
        ii. Why, when, how, and by whom was it produced?
        iii. What meanings does the image convey?
    c. Develop and assign code labels to the image using information in this chapter and guided by such questions as the following:
        i. What codes would be expected to fit?
        ii. What new codes are emergent?
        iii. What codes relate to other data sources?
    d. Finally, revisit the image segments assigned to each of the code labels and consider which ones might be useful in forming themes in your study.

3. What considerations should guide your use of QDAS programs?
   a. Using a qualitative study you want to pursue, consider how QDAS could be helpful.
   b. Go to the website of a QDAS program, and find the demonstration program and resources to help you get started.
   c. Try out the QDAS program. If possible, input a small database to try out the program features related to memoing, coding, sorting, retrieving, and diagramming.
   d. Now, you might experiment with demonstrations from different QDAS programs. Consider which one has the features that work best for you. Why?

SUMMARY

This chapter presented data analysis and representation. We began by reviewing the procedures advanced by three authors and noted the common features of coding, developing themes, and providing a visual representation of the data. We also noted some of the differences among their approaches. We then advanced a spiral of data analysis that captured the general process and we began our discussion by attending to ethical considerations specific to data analysis. This spiral contained aspects of managing and organizing data; reading and memoing emergent ideas; describing and classifying codes into themes; developing and assessing interpretations; and representing and visualizing data. We next described how computers and qualitative data analysis software could be used and the features specific to five programs. We introduced and discussed how each of the five approaches to inquiry had unique data analysis steps beyond the "generic" steps of the spiral. Finally, we ended with comparing the data analysis activities across the five approaches.

CHAPTER KEY TERMS

Audit trail
Codebook
Coding
Dimensionalized

Qualitative data analysis software (QDAS)
Represent the data
Themes

FURTHER READINGS

Several readings extend this brief introductory overview of data analysis, beginning with general resources and then moving to more specific ones for using QDAS. The list should not be considered exhaustive, and readers are encouraged to seek out additional readings in the end-of-book reference list.

For Information About Procedures and Issues in Qualitative Data Analysis

Bazeley, P. (2021). *Qualitative data analysis: Practical strategies* (2nd ed.). Sage.

Pat Bazeley provides a comprehensive description of analysis including illustrative examples of her practical strategies. This book should be essential reading because of its usefulness for a researcher at any level of expertise.

Creswell, J. W., & Báez, J. C. (2021). *30 essential skills for the qualitative researcher* (2nd ed.). Sage.

John Creswell and Johanna Báez developed a book intended to be an introductory textbook for students learning qualitative research for the first time. Specific chapters detail the process of coding, theme development, and intercoder agreement strategies. The authors constructed this practical, applied book based on their experiences in conducting qualitative research.

Flick, U. (Ed.). (2014). *The SAGE handbook of qualitative analysis*. Sage.

Handbooks offer diverse perspectives on a common theme as a starting place. The chapter authors provide guidance about the basics of qualitative research, general analytic strategies, and data analysis strategies for specific data forms.

Grbich, C. (2013). *Qualitative data analysis: An introduction* (2nd ed.). Sage.

Carol Grbich uses the background a researcher needs, the processes involved in research, and the displays used for presenting findings on which to organize this easy-to-read book. Noteworthy are her practical explanations related to coding (Chapter 21) and theorizing from data (Chapter 23).

Miles, M. B., Huberman, A. M., & Saldaña, J. (2019). *Qualitative data analysis: A sourcebook of new methods* (4th ed.). Sage.

In this newest edition, Johnny Saldaña continues to update Matthew B. Miles and A. Michael Huberman's seminal resource. This text is a must-read for researchers.

Vanover, C., Mihas, P., & Saldaña, J. (Eds.). (2021). *Analysing and interpreting qualitative research: After the interview*. Sage.

Edited books provide access to multiple perspectives. The chapter authors cover many topics from coding to memo writing and interpretive strategies across diverse types of data. Particularly noteworthy is Chapter 14 on memo writing strategies by Paul Mihas.

Wolcott, H. F. (1994). *Transforming qualitative data: Description, analysis, and interpretation*. Sage.

In this classic work, Harry Wolcott describes the process of data analysis and representation using nine studies. He makes the case for the need for a good written description as a study outcome.

For Information About Procedures and Issues About the Use of Qualitative Data Analysis Software

Evers, J. C. (2018). Current issues in qualitative data analysis software (QDAS): A user and developer perspective. *The Qualitative Report*, *23*(13), 61–73. https://doi.org/10.46743/2160-3715/2018.3205

Jeanine Evers describes a range of issues from differences in features and terminology across various QDAS to security and possible future directions involving artificial intelligence and migrating between software packages.

Friese, S. (2019). *Qualitative data analysis with ATLAS.ti* (3rd ed.). Sage.

Susanne Friese provides a step-by-step guide for using ATLAS.ti, based on a method for QDAS involving noticing things, collecting things, and thinking about things.

Jackson, K., & Bazeley, P. (2019). *Qualitative data analysis with NVivo* (3rd ed.). Sage.

Kristi Jackson and Pat Bazeley provide a comprehensive guide using examples to illustrate the use of NVivo features for getting started, coding, interpreting, and diagramming.

Kuckartz, U., & Rädiker, S. (2023). *Qualitative content analysis: Methods, practice and software* (2nd ed.). Sage.

In this updated edition, Udo Kuckartz, creator of MAXQDA, and Stefan Rädiker provide an essential grounding in three types of qualitative content analysis—structuring, evaluative, and type-building. In addition, Chapter 8 focuses on using software during the analysis process.

Niedbalski, J., & Ślęzak, I. (2022). Encounters with CAQDAS: Advice for beginner users of computer software for qualitative research. *The Qualitative Report*, *27*(4), 1114–1132. https://doi.org/10.46743/2160-3715/2022.4770

Jakub Niedbalski and Izabela Ślęzak provide those contemplating using QDAS an essential user perspective balancing both the advantages and disadvantages.

Paulus, T. M., & Lester, J. N. (2021). *Doing qualitative research in a digital world*. Sage.

Trena Paulus and Jessica Lester provide an essential introduction to the history and current status of qualitative data analysis software in Chapter 3. Newcomers may find the overview of various QDAS packages and the description of what QDAS packages do *not* do especially helpful (see pages 81 and 78, respectively).

9 WRITING A QUALITATIVE STUDY

> **QUESTIONS FOR DISCUSSION**
>
> - What ethical issues require attention when writing a qualitative study?
> - What are several broad writing strategies associated with crafting a qualitative study?
> - What are the overall writing structures used within each of the five approaches of inquiry?
> - What are the embedded writing structures within each of the five approaches of inquiry?
> - How do the writing structures differ across the five approaches?

Writing and composing the narrative report brings the entire study together. We like the description by Denzin and Lincoln (2018a) of the qualitative research writer as creating "narratives, braided compositions woven into and through field experiences" (p. 21). Borrowing a term from Strauss and Corbin (1990), we are fascinated by the *architecture* of a study, how it is composed and organized by writers. We also like Strauss and Corbin's (1990) suggestion that writers use a "spatial metaphor" (p. 231) to visualize their full reports or studies. To consider a study spatially, they ask the following questions: Is coming away with an idea like walking slowly around a statue, studying it from a variety of interrelated views? Like walking downhill step-by-step? Like walking through the rooms of a house? We are intrigued by what Pelias (2011) refers to as *realization* (the writer's process) and *record* (the completed text)—specifically how we might make this progression less obscure. Engaging in the process of writing a qualitative study can be considered ambiguous because "we may not realize what we have or know where we are going" (Charmaz, 2014, p. 290). In short, we may not be able to trace the path our writing process has taken until we complete the written report.

In this chapter, we assess the general architecture of a qualitative study, and then we invite the reader to enter specific rooms of the study to see how they are composed. Readers may be interested in reviewing Levitt et al.'s (2017) recommendations for designing and reviewing qualitative research specific for the field of psychology. We begin with revisiting the key ethical considerations for writing a qualitative study. Then we present four writing strategies for addressing issues in the rendering of a study regardless of approach: reflexivity and representation, audience, encoding, and quotes. Then we take each of the five approaches to inquiry and assess two writing structures: **overall writing structures** (i.e., overall organization of the report or study) and **embedded writing structures** (i.e., specific narrative devices and techniques that the writer uses in the report). We return once again to the five examples of studies in Chapter 5 to illustrate overall and embedded structures. Finally, we compare the writing structures within and across the five approaches. In this chapter, we will not address the use of grammar and syntax and will refer readers to books that provide a detailed treatment of these subjects (e.g., Creswell & Guetterman, 2019; Strunk & White, 2000; Sword, 2012; Weaver-Hightower, 2019).

ETHICAL CONSIDERATIONS FOR WRITING

Before considering the architecture underpinning writing qualitative studies, we carefully consider relevant ethical issues (see initial discussion in Chapter 3). We must protect our participants, ensure report access, plan for knowledge mobilization, and comply with ethical publishing practices (see Table 9.1).

TABLE 9.1 ■ Ethical Questions, Issues, and Situations in Writing a Qualitative Study

Guiding Question in Writing a Study	Ethical Issues Often Arising During the Writing Process	How a Researcher Might Address the Situation When Writing a Study
How do I protect participants from harm in study reports?	Avoid disclosing information that would harm participants.	Researcher uses composite stories so that individuals cannot be identified.
How am I ensuring accessible reports?	Communicate in clear, straightforward, appropriate language.	Researcher uses language appropriate for audiences of the research.
Am I offering access to study reports?	Share reports with others and tailor the reporting to diverse audiences.	Researcher shares practical results and considers how participants and stakeholders can best access them (e.g., paper copies, website distribution, language translations).
What is my publication/knowledge distribution plan?	Do not duplicate or divide reports of a research study into fragments for different publications.	Researcher refrains from using the same material for more than one publication.
How am I giving credit where it's due?	Do not plagiarize.	Researcher uses APA (2020) guidelines for permissions needed to reprint or adapt the work of others.
How am I documenting adherence to standards of ethical research?	Complete proof of compliance with ethical issues and lack of conflict of interest.	Researcher discloses funders for research and who profits from the research.

For protecting our participants, we must avoid disclosing identifying information, ensure report access, tailor reports to diverse audiences, and use language appropriate for target audiences. To comply with ethical publishing practices, researchers must seek permissions as needed, ensure that the same material is not used for more than one publication, and disclose funders and beneficiaries of the research.

Creswell & Báez (2021, pp. 57–58) present an adapted version of the "Ethical Compliance Checklist" (American Psychological Association [APA], 2020, p. 26) to inform writing. These are questions that should be considered by all qualitative researchers about their study manuscripts and research proposals:

- Have I obtained permission for use of unpublished instruments, procedures, or data that other researchers might consider theirs (proprietary)?
- Have I properly cited other published work presented in portions of the manuscript?
- Am I prepared to answer questions about institutional review of my study or studies?
- Am I prepared to answer editorial questions about the informed consent and debriefing procedures used in the study?
- Have all authors reviewed the manuscript and agreed on the responsibility for its content?
- Have I adequately protected the confidentiality of research participants, clients-patients, organizations, third parties, or others who provided information presented in this manuscript?
- Have all authors agreed to the order of the authorship?
- Have I shared participant data in accordance with the agreement written in my informed consent?
- Have I obtained permission for including any copyrighted material?

SEVERAL WRITING STRATEGIES

Unquestionably, narrative forms are extensive in qualitative research. In reviewing the forms, Glesne (2016) notes that narratives tell stories that blur the lines between fiction, journalism, and scholarly studies. Qualitative forms often engage the reader through a chronological approach as events unfold slowly over time, whether the subject is a study of a culture-sharing group, the narrative story of the life of an individual, or the evolution of a program or an organization. Another form is to expand and narrow the story focus, evoking the metaphor of a camera lens zooming out, in, and then out again. Some reports rely heavily on description of events, whereas others advance a small number of "themes" or perspectives. A narrative might capture a "typical day in the life" of an individual or a group. Some reports are heavily oriented toward theory, whereas others, such as Stake's (1995) "Harper School," employ little literature and theory. In addition, since the publication of Clifford and Marcus's (1986) edited volume *Writing Culture* in ethnography, qualitative writing has been shaped by a need for researchers to be self-disclosing about their role in the writing, the impact of their writing on participants, and the potential effect of their study on audiences.

Reflexivity and Representations in Writing

Qualitative researchers today are much more self-disclosing about their qualitative writings than they were a few years ago. Ronald Pelias (2011) describes reflexive writers as "ethically and politically self-aware, make themselves part of their own inquiry" (p. 662). No longer is it acceptable to be the omniscient, distanced qualitative writer. Postmodern thinkers "deconstruct" the narrative of an omniscient narrator, challenging text as contested terrain that cannot be understood without references to ideas being concealed by the author and contexts within the author's life (Agger, 1991). This theme is espoused by Denzin (2001) in his "interpretive" approach to biographical writing. As a response, qualitative researchers today acknowledge that the writing of a qualitative text cannot be separated from the author, how it is received by readers, and how it impacts the participants and sites under study.

How we write is a reflection of our own interpretation based on the cultural, social, gender, class, and personal politics that we bring to research. All writing is "positioned" and within a stance. All researchers shape the writing that emerges, and qualitative researchers need to accept this interpretation and be open about it in their writings. According to Richardson (1994), the best writing acknowledges its own "undecidability" forthrightly, that all writing has "subtexts" that "situate" or "position" the material within a particular historical and local specific time and place. In this perspective, no writing has "privileged status" (p. 518) or is superior over other writings. Indeed, writings are co-constructions, representations of interactive processes between researchers and the researched (Gilgun, 2005).

An increased concern about the impact of the writing on the participants has led to important questions. How will they see the write-up? Will they be marginalized because of it? Will they be offended? Will they hide their true feelings and perspectives? Have the participants reviewed the material and interpreted, challenged, or disputed the interpretation (Weis & Fine, 2000)? Perhaps researchers' writing objectively, in a scientific way, silences both the participants and researchers. Czarniawska (2004) and Gilgun (2005) make the point that this silence is contradictory to qualitative research that seeks to hear all voices and perspectives.

Also, the writing has an impact on the reader, who also makes an interpretation of the account and may form an entirely different interpretation from that of the author or the participants. Should the researcher be concerned that certain people will see the final report? Can the researcher give any kind of definitive account when it is the reader who makes the ultimate interpretation of the events? Is there a risk of potential misinterpretations? Indeed, the writing may be a performance, and the standard writing of qualitative research into text has expanded to include split-page writings, theater, poetry, photography, music, collage, drawing, sculpture, quilting, stained glass, and dance (Gilgun, 2005). Language may "kill" whatever it touches, and qualitative researchers understand that it is impossible to truly "say" something (van Manen, 2006).

Weis and Fine (2000) discussed a "set of self-reflective points of critical consciousness around the questions of how to represent responsibility" in qualitative writings (p. 33). They present questions that should be considered by all qualitative researchers about their writings:

- Should I write about what people say or recognize that sometimes they cannot remember or choose not to remember?

- What are my political reflexivities that need to come into my report?

- Has my writing connected the voices and stories of individuals back to the set of historic, structural, and economic relations in which they are situated?

- How far should I go in theorizing the words of participants?

- Have I considered how my words could be used for progressive, conservative, and repressive social policies?

- Have I backed into the passive voice and decoupled my responsibility from my interpretation?

- To what extent has my analysis (and writing) offered an alternative to common sense or the dominant discourse?

Qualitative researchers need to "position" themselves in their writings. This is the concept of reflexivity in which the writer engages in self-understanding about the biases, values, and experiences that he or she brings to a qualitative research study. One characteristic of good qualitative research is that the inquirer makes his or her "position" explicit in a report (Hammersley & Atkinson, 2019). We think about reflexivity as having two parts. The researcher first talks about their experiences with the phenomenon being explored. This involves relaying past experiences through work, schooling, family dynamics, and so forth. The second part is to discuss how these past experiences shape the researcher's interpretation of the phenomenon. Researchers often overlook or leave out this second part because it is challenging (van Manen, 2014, 2023).

We suggest writing reflexive comments about what is being experienced as the study progresses—these might be observations during data collection, hunches about what the findings might indicate, and reactions from participants during the study. These comments can be easily captured and retrieved using memo functions in qualitative software programs. Reviewing and then discussing biases, values, and experiences that impact emerging understandings represent the heart of reflexive thinking. It is important for the researcher to detail experiences with the phenomenon and be self-conscious about how these experiences may potentially shape the findings, the conclusions, and the interpretations drawn in a study. Thus, the act of writing a qualitative text cannot be considered separate from the author, the study participants, or the readers. The placement of reflexive comments in a study also needs some consideration.

The reflexive comments may be positioned in one or more positions in a qualitative study. Among the most popular placements are in the opening (or closing) passage of the study, in a methods discussion in which the writer talks about his or her role in the study, and in personal comments threaded throughout the study. It is not unusual to begin with a personal statement in a phenomenology where the authors disclose their backgrounds (see Brown et al., 2006). Similarly, a case study may open with a personal vignette (see Stake, 1995) or end with an epilogue (see Asmussen & Creswell, 1995). As part of a methods description, a phenomenological researcher may disclose the experiences they bring to the research and attempt to bracket those experiences. In the phenomenology describing the adversity faced by Black women in higher education leadership, Chance (2022; see Appendix B) acknowledged being "personally vested and experienced with the phenomenon" (p. 52). Finally, the researcher may talk about "position" in the introduction, the methods, and the findings or themes as is often the case in an ethnographic study (e.g., see Mac an Ghaill & Haywood, 2015; see Appendix D).

Audience for Our Writings

A basic axiom holds that all writers write for an audience. As Clandinin and Connelly (2000) say, "A sense of an audience peering over the writer's shoulder needs to pervade the writing and the written text" (p. 149). Thus, writers consciously think about their audience or multiple audiences for their studies (Richardson, 1990, 1994). Tierney (1995), for example, identified four potential audiences: colleagues, those involved in the interviews and observations, policymakers, and the general public. More recently, Silverman (2022) differentiated the expectations of academic and practitioner colleagues in that the former sought theoretical, factual, or methodological insights from research, whereas the latter drew practical suggestions for better procedures or reform of existing practices. Identifying target audiences helps inform choices during the writing process. In short, how the report is structured depends on the readers to be engaged with the writing. For example, because Fischer and Wertz (1979) disseminated information about their phenomenological study at public forums, they produced several expressions of their findings, all responding to different audiences. One form was a general structure, four paragraphs in length, an approach that they admitted lost its richness and concreteness. Another form consisted of case synopses, each reporting the experiences of one individual and each two and a half pages in length. MacKenzie et al. (2015) discussed the challenges they experienced while trying to communicate their participatory research results with their Indigenous participants. Ravitch and Carl (2020) discussed 14 questions related to the purpose and audience of a study. Their questions about intended audiences should be considered by all qualitative researchers.

- For what audience(s) is this study being written? What informs these choices?
- What am I hoping to achieve with this report to my audience?
- What writing structures would my audience expect?

- Are there other audiences who could benefit from my learning and knowledge?
- How might I structure my writing to fit other audiences' needs?

Encoding Our Writings

A closely related topic is recognizing the importance of language in shaping our qualitative texts. The words we use encode our report, revealing how we perceive the needs of audiences. Earlier, in Chapter 6, we presented encoding the problem, purpose, and research questions; now, we consider encoding the entire narrative report.

Using Goodrum et al.'s (2022; see Appendix E) case study examining how the school's organizational structure and culture impeded the prevention of violence, we can consider how a writer can shape a work differently for a trade audience, an academic audience, or a moral or political audience. For a trade audience, such as law enforcement, the authors could encode their work with literary devices such as the following:

> Poignant titles focused on the crime, statistics, specialized law enforcement jargon, marginalization of methodology, law-world metaphors and images, and book blurbs and prefatory material about the "law enforcement" interest in the material.

For the moral or political audience, the authors could encode through devices such as the following:

> Media-grabbing headline words in the title, for example, campus gun crime; the moral or activist "credentials" of the author, such as the author's role in particular social movements; references to moral and activist authorities; empowerment metaphors, and book blurbs and prefatory material encoded how this work related to real people's lives.

For an academic audience (e.g., journals, conference papers, academic books), the authors could mark it by the following:

> Prominent display of academic credentials of author, references, footnotes, methodology sections, use of familiar academic metaphors and images (such as "crime prevention theory" and "leadership roles" and book blurbs and prefatory material about the science or scholarship involved encode the study for an academic audience.

Although we emphasize academic writing here, researchers encode qualitative studies for audiences other than academics. For example, in the social and human sciences, policymakers may be a primary audience, and this necessitates writing with minimal methods, more parsimony, and a focus on practice and results.

The Goodrum et al. (2022; see Appendix E) example initiated thoughts about how one might encode a qualitative narrative. Such encoding might include the following:

- An overall structure that does not conform to the standard quantitative introduction, methods, results, and discussion format. Instead, the methods might be called procedures, and the results might be called findings. In fact, the researcher might phrase the headings for themes in the words of participants in the study as they discuss "denial," "retriggering," and so forth, as was done in the gunman case (Asmussen & Creswell, 1995).

- A writing style that is personal, familiar, perhaps "up-close," highly readable, friendly, and applied for a broad audience. Our qualitative writings should strive for a "persuasive" effect (Czarniawska, 2004, p. 124). Readers should find the material interesting and memorable, the "grab" in writing (Gilgun, 2005).

- A level of detail that makes the work come alive—**verisimilitude** comes to mind (Richardson, 1994, p. 521). This word indicates the presentation of a good literary study in which the writing becomes "real" and "alive"—writing that transports the reader directly into the world of the study, whether this world is the subcultural setting of youths' multilayered resistance (Haenfler, 2004) or an immigrant student in a school classroom (Chan, 2010; see Appendix A). Still, we must recognize that the writing is only a representation of what we see or understand.

Quotes in Our Writings

In addition to encoding text with the language of qualitative research, authors bring in the voice of participants in the study. A good rule of thumb is that quotes should be as illustrative as possible and be contextualized, interpreted, and incorporated within the text of the manuscript (Brinkmann & Kvale, 2015). Writers use ample quotes, and we find Richardson's (1990) discussion about three types of quotes most useful: short quotes, embedded quotes, and long quotes. The short quotes consist of short, eye-catching quotations. These are easy to read, take up little space, and stand out from the narrator's text and are indented to signify different perspectives. For example, in the grounded theory study about the caregiving relationship process of aging people with intellectual disabilities in families navigating transitions across the life course (Trip et al., 2019; see Appendix C) used short quotes from various caregivers within a paragraph describing the various perspectives of reciprocating relationships:

> Reciprocating relationships denotes connections within the caregiving system of support evidenced by the roles, relationships, sense of duty, and expectations. Challenging the common expectations about who provides and who receives care, one sister reflected about her brother that "amazingly, it got to a place where he has become a caregiver for Mum." Conversely, he felt he had to co-ordinate the services involved with his mother as it was like a "train station—people coming and going." Another stated that while it could be trying at times, her flatmate, who has intellectual disability and mental health needs, is "a really good friend and you've always got company." (p. 1601)

The second approach consists of embedded quotes, briefly quoted phrases within the analyst's narrative. These quotes, according to Richardson (1990), prepare a reader for a shift in emphasis or display a point and allow the writer (and reader) to move on. Chan (2010; see Appendix A) used short, embedded quotes extensively in her narrative study because they consumed little space and provided specific concrete evidence, in the participants' words, to support a theme such as Home Language Conflicting With School Language:

One day, as we were walking back to her homeroom classroom after art class, she has told me about an incident when she felt embarrassed when she attempted to order drinks at a shopping mall and the vendor could not understand her because "[her] English accent was so bad!" (pp. 116–117)

A third type of quote is the longer quotation used to convey more complex understandings. Longer quotes are difficult to use because of space limitations in publications and because they often contain many ideas. The reader needs to be guided both "into" the quote and "out of" the quote to focus attention on the writer's controlling idea. Chance (2022; see Appendix B) used longer quotes to describe the impact of experiences of discrimination in her leadership role:

And then throughout my experience, sometimes your voice was marginalized. When men said something versus when a woman said something, but I didn't experience it that much until I got to [University]. . . . Though there was gender discrimination at [University] to the point where even HR and the Title IX coordinator mentioned that I should file a complaint, I did not file a complaint. Because, when you file a complaint in higher education, whether you're right or wrong, it follows you through your career and can impact future employment. The fact that you filed a complaint is a problem. (p. 61)

> **TRY THIS NOW 9.1**
> **IDENTIFYING USE OF WRITING STRATEGIES IN THE APPENDIX STUDIES**
>
> Comparing the use of writing strategies across published qualitative studies can provide helpful guidance. Choose two of the Appendix studies to compare. What evidence of the four writing strategies (i.e., reflexivity and representations, audience, encoding, and quotes) can you find? How might different approaches impact your use of various writing strategies?

OVERALL AND EMBEDDED WRITING STRATEGIES

In addition to these writing approaches, the qualitative researcher needs to address how to compose the overall narrative structure of the report and use embedded structures within the report to provide a narrative within the approach of choice. We offer Table 9.2 as a guide for the following discussion in which we list many overall and embedded structural approaches as they apply to the five approaches of inquiry.

Narrative Writing Structures

As we read about the writing of studies in narrative research, we find authors unwilling to prescribe a tightly structured writing strategy (Clandinin, 2013, 2023; Clandinin & Connelly, 2000; Czarniawska, 2004; Riessman, 2008). Instead, we find the authors suggesting maximum flexibility in structure (see Daiute, 2014; Ely, 2007) but emphasizing core elements that might

TABLE 9.2 ■ Overall and Embedded Writing Structures Within the Five Approaches

Approach	Overall Writing Structures	Embedded Writing Structures
Narrative	• Flexible and evolving processes (Clandinin, 2013, 2023; Clandinin & Connelly, 2000) • Three-dimensional space inquiry model (Clandinin & Connelly, 2000) • Story chronologies (Clandinin & Connelly, 2000) or temporal or episodic ordering of information (Kim, 2015; Riessman, 2008) • Reporting what participants said (themes), how they said it (order of their story), or how they interacted with others (dialogue and performance; Riessman, 2008)	• Epiphanies (Denzin, 2001) and significance (Daiute, 2014) • Key events or plots (Czarniawska, 2004; Daiute, 2014; L. M. Smith, 1994) • Metaphors and transitions (Clandinin & Connelly, 2000; Lomask, 1986) • Progressive–regressive methods (Czarniawska, 2004; Denzin, 2001; Ellis, 1993; Huber & Whelan, 1999) • Threads across multiple narrative accounts (Clandinin, 2013, 2023; Clandinin & Connelly, 2000) • Themes or categories (Chan, 2010; Riessman, 2008) • Dialogues or conversations (Chan, 2010; Riessman, 2008)
Phenomenology	• Structure of a "research manuscript" (Moustakas, 1994) • The "research report" format (Polkinghorne, 1989) • The "lived experiences descriptions" (van Manen, 2023) starting with examples (vignette-like or anecdotal stories and sketches) to make the unknowable knowable	• Figures or tables reporting essences (Chance, 2022; Grigsby & Megel, 1995) • Philosophical discussions (Harper, 1981) • Creative closings (Moustakas, 1994) • Engage with other authors; use time, space, and other dimensions in description of essence (van Manen, 2014)
Grounded theory	• Grounded theory study components (May, 1986) • Results of open, axial, and selective coding (Strauss & Corbin, 1990, 1998) • Focus is on theory and arguments that support it (Charmaz, 2014)	• Extent of analysis (Chenitz & Swanson, 1986; Creswell & Brown, 1992; Kus, 1986) • Propositions (Conrad, 1978; Strauss & Corbin, 1990) • Visual diagrams (S. L. Morrow & Smith, 1995; Trip et al., 2019) • Emotions, rhythm, rhetorical questions, tone, pacing, stories, evocative writing (Charmaz, 2014)

Approach	Overall Writing Structures	Embedded Writing Structures
Ethnography	• Types of tales (Van Maanen, 2011) • Description, analysis, and interpretation (Wolcott, 1994) • "Thematic narrative" (Emerson et al., 2011)	• Tropes or metaphors (Fetterman, 2019; Hammersley & Atkinson, 2019; Rhoads, 1995) • "Thick" description (Denzin, 2001; Fetterman, 2010) • Verbatim quotations (Fetterman, 2019; Haenfler, 2004; Mac an Ghaill & Haywood, 2015) • Dialogue (Nelson, 1990) or scenes (Emerson et al., 2011) • Literary devices, such as voices of different speakers, metaphors, irony, and similes (Fetterman, 2019)
Case study	• Format with vignettes (Stake, 1995) • Substantive case report format (Lincoln & Guba, 1985) • Types of cases (Yin, 2017) • Alternative structures based on linear and nonlinear approaches (Yin, 2017)	• Chronological and funnel approaches (Asmussen & Creswell, 1995; Frelin, 2015; Staples et al., 2005) • Description (Goodrum et al., 2022; Merriam, 1988; Merriam & Tisdell, 2015)

go into the narrative study. In so doing, Clandinin (2023) describes the writer as well positioned for matching the narrative structures to the particular study context:

> As narrative inquirers, we need to hold open and to make visible the ways that participants, and we, struggle for that coherence, sometimes successfully, sometimes not. In the composing, co-composing and negotiation of interim and final research texts, we must make visible the multiplicity as well as the narrative coherence and lack of narrative coherence of our lives, the lives of participants, and the lives we co-compose in the midst of our narrative inquiries. (p. 30)

Overall Structures

Narrative researchers encourage individuals to write narrative studies that experiment with form (Clandinin, 2023; Clandinin & Connelly, 2000). Researchers can come to their narrative form by first looking to their own preferences in reading (e.g., memoirs, novels), reading other narrative dissertations and books, and viewing the narrative study as back-and-forth writing, as a process (Clandinin & Connelly, 2000). Within these general guidelines, Clandinin and Connelly (2000) review two doctoral dissertations that employ narrative research. The two have different narrative structures: One provides narratives of a chronology of the lives of three women; the other adopts a more classical approach to a dissertation including an introduction, a literature review, and a methodology. For this second example, the remaining chapters then go into a discussion that tells the stories of the author's experiences with the participants. Reading through these two examples, we are struck by how they both reflect the three-dimensional inquiry space that Clandinin and Connelly (2000) discuss. This space, as mentioned earlier, is a text that looks backward and forward, looks inward and outward, and situates the experiences within place. For example, the dissertation of He, cited by Clandinin and Connelly (2000), is a study about the lives of two participants and the author in their past life in China and in their present situation in Canada. The story does the following:

> [It] looks backward to the past for her and her two participants and forward to the puzzle of who they are and who they are becoming in their new land. She looks inward to her personal reasons for doing this study and outward to the social significance of the work. She paints landscapes of China and Canada and the in-between places where she imagines herself to reside. (Clandinin & Connelly, 2000, p. 156)

Later in Clandinin and Connelly (2000), there is a story about Clandinin's advice for students about the narrative form of their studies. This form again relates to the three-dimensional space model:

> When they came to Jean for conversations about their emerging texts, she found herself responding not so much with comments about preestablished and accepted forms but with [a] response that raised questions situated within the three-dimensional narrative inquiry space. (Clandinin & Connelly, 2000, p. 165)

Notice in this passage how Clandinin "raised questions" rather than told the student how to proceed, and how she returned to the larger **rhetorical** structure of the three-dimensional inquiry space model as a framework for thinking about the writing of a narrative study. This framework also suggested a chronology to the narrative report, and this ordering within the chronology might further be organized by time or by specific episodes (Riessman, 2008).

In narrative research, as in all forms of qualitative inquiry, there is a close relationship between the data collection procedures, the analysis, and the form and structure of the report writing. For example, the larger writing structure in a thematic analysis would be the presentation of several themes (Riessman, 2008). In a more structured approach—analyzing how the individual tells a story—the elements presented in the report might follow six elements, what Riessman (2008) calls a "fully formed narrative" (p. 84). These would be the elements of the following:

- A summary and/or the point of the story
- Orientation (the time, place, characters, and situations)
- Complicating action (the event sequence, or plot usually with a crisis or turning point)
- Evaluation (where the narrator comments on meaning or emotions)
- Resolution (the outcome of the plot)
- Coda (ending the story and bringing it back to the present)

In a narrative study focused on the interrogation between speakers (such as the interviewer and the interviewee), the larger writing structure would focus on direct speech and dialogue. Further, the dialogue might contain features of a performance, such as direct speeches, asides to the audience, repetition, expressive sounds, and switches in verb tense. The entire report may be a poem, a play, or another dramatic rendering. In previous chapters, we have described narrative studies that illustrate these narrative elements (see Example 4.1 and featured narrative study example Chan, 2010; see Appendix A), and we encourage reviewing them for similarities and differences in presentation.

Embedded Structures

Assuming that the larger writing structure proceeds with experimentation and flexibility, the writing structure at the more micro level relates to several elements of writing strategies that authors might use in composing a narrative study. These are drawn from Clandinin (2013, 2023), Clandinin and Connelly (2000), Czarniawska (2004), and Riessman (2008).

The writing of a narrative needs to not silence some of the voices, and it ultimately gives more space to certain voices than others (Czarniawska, 2004). In addition, there can be a spatial element to the writing, such as in the **progressive–regressive method** (Denzin, 2001) whereby the biographer begins with a key event in the participant's life and then works forward and backward from that event, such as in Denzin's (2001) study of alcoholics. Alternatively, there can be a "zooming in" and "zooming out," such as describing a large context to a concrete field of study (e.g., a site) and then telescoping out again (Czarniawska, 2004). Huber and Whelan's (1999) retelling of the narrative of a teacher's identity shaping refers to personal background influences as she talks about more current professional experiences. Similarly, Ellis's (1993) personal narrative of a family drama enacted in the aftermath of her brother's death in airplane crash is told by alternating between descriptions of childhood experiences and those surrounding the crash.

The writing may emphasize the "key event" or the epiphany, defined as interactional moments and experiences that mark people's lives (Denzin, 2001). Denzin distinguishes four types: the major event that touches the fabric of the individual's life; the cumulative or representative events or experiences that continue for some time; the minor epiphany, which represents a moment in an individual's life; and episodes or relived epiphanies, which involve reliving the experience. Czarniawska (2004) introduces the key element of the plot or the emplotment, a means of introducing structure that allows for making sense of the events reported.

Themes can be reported in narrative writing. L. M. Smith (1994) recommends finding a theme to guide the development of the life to be written. This theme emerges from preliminary knowledge or a review of the entire life, although researchers often experience difficulty in distinguishing the major theme from lesser or minor themes. Clandinin and Connelly (2000) refer to writing research texts at the reductionistic boundary, an approach consisting of a "reduction downward" (p. 143) to themes in which the researcher looks for common threads or elements across participants. Clandinin (2013, 2023) describes these threads as important for composing multiple narrative accounts. See also Kim (2015) for guidelines for writing a life history.

Specific narrative writing strategies also include the use of dialogue, such as that between the researcher and the participants (Riessman, 2008). Sometimes in this approach the specific language of the narrator is interrogated and is not taken at face value. The dialogue unfolds in the study, and often it is presented in different languages, including the language of the narrator and an English translation. An example is provided by Chan's (2010; see Appendix A) story of one Chinese immigrant student and the affiliation this student had with other students, her teacher, and her family where dialogue between the researcher and the student provided evidence for each theme. Each dialogue segment was titled to shape the meaning of the conversation, such as "Susan doesn't speak Fujianese" (Chan, 2010, p. 117).

Other narrative rhetorical devices include the use of transitions. Lomask (1986) refers to these as built into the narratives in natural chronological linkages. Writers insert them through words or phrases, questions (which Lomask calls being lazy), and time-and-place shifts moving the action forward or backward. In addition to transitions, narrative researchers employ **foreshadowing**, the frequent use of narrative hints of things to come or of events or themes to be developed later. Narrative researchers also use metaphors, and Clandinin and Connelly (2000) suggest the metaphor of a soup to describe a narrative text (i.e., the combination of description of people, places, and things; arguments for understandings; and richly textured narratives of people situated in place, time, scene, and plot) all combined within containers (i.e., dissertations, journal articles).

Phenomenological Writing Structures

Those who write about phenomenology (e.g., Moustakas, 1994; van Manen, 2014, 2023) provide more extensive attention to overall writing structures than to embedded ones. However, as in all forms of qualitative research, one can learn much from a careful study of research reports in journal articles (see Example 4.2 and featured phenomenological study example Chance, 2022; Appendix B), monographs, or books.

Overall Structures

The highly structured approach to analysis by Moustakas (1994) presents a detailed form for composing a phenomenological study. The analysis steps—identifying significant statements, creating meaning units, clustering themes, advancing textural and structural descriptions, and ending with a composite description of textural and structural descriptions with an exhaustive description of the essential invariant structure (or essence) of the experience—provide a clearly articulated procedure for organizing a report (Moustakas, 1994). In our experience, individuals are quite surprised to find highly structured approaches to phenomenological studies on sensitive topics (e.g., "being left out," "insomnia," "being criminally victimized," "life's meaning," "voluntarily changing one's career during midlife," "longing," "adults being abused as children" (Moustakas, 1994, p. 153). But the data analysis procedure, we think, guides a researcher in that direction and presents an overall structure for analysis and ultimately the organization of the report.

Consider the overall organization of a report as suggested by Moustakas (1994). He recommends specific chapters in "creating a research manuscript":

Chapter 1: *Introduction and statement of topic and outline.* Topics include an autobiographical statement about experiences of the author leading to the topic, incidents that lead to a puzzlement or curiosity about the topic, the social implications and relevance of the topic, new knowledge and contribution to the profession to emerge from studying the topic, knowledge to be gained by the researcher, the research question, and the terms of the study.

Chapter 2: *Review of the relevant literature.* Topics include a review of databases searched, an introduction to the literature, a procedure for selecting studies, the conduct of these studies and themes that emerged in them, and a summary of core findings and statements as to how the present research differs from prior research (in question, model, methodology, and data collected).

Chapter 3: *Conceptual framework of the model.* Topics include the theory to be used as well as the concepts and processes related to the research design (Chapters 3 and 4 might be combined).

Chapter 4: *Methodology.* Topics include the methods and procedures in preparing to conduct the study; in collecting data; and in organizing, analyzing, and synthesizing the data.

Chapter 5: *Presentation of data.* Topics include verbatim examples of data collection, data analysis, a synthesis of data, horizontalization, meaning units, clustered themes, textural and structural descriptions, and a synthesis of meanings and essences of the experience.

Chapter 6: *Summary, implications, and outcomes.* Sections include a summary of the study, statements about how the findings differ from those in the literature review, recommendations for future studies, the identification of limitations, a discussion about implications, and the inclusion of a creative closure that speaks to the essence of the study and its inspiration for the researcher.

A second model, not as specific, is found in Polkinghorne (1989) where he discusses the "research report." In this model, the researcher describes the procedures to collect data and the steps to move from the raw data to a more general description of the experience. Also, the investigator includes a review of previous research, the theory pertaining to the topic, and implications for psychological theory and application. We especially like Polkinghorne's (1989) comment about the impact of such a report:

> Produce a research report that gives an accurate, clear, and articulate description of an experience. The reader of the report should come away with the feeling that "I understand better what it is like for someone to experience that." (p. 46)

A third model of the overall writing structure of a phenomenological study comes from van Manen (1990, 2014). He begins his discussion of "working the text" (van Manen, 1990, p. 167) with the thought that studies that present and organize transcripts for the final report fall short of being a good phenomenological study. Instead, he recommends several options for writing the study. The study might be organized thematically, examining essential aspects of the phenomenon under study. It might also be presented analytically by reworking the text data into larger ideas (e.g., contrasting ideas), or focused narrowly on the description of a particular life situation or lived experience description (van Manen, 2023). It might begin with the essence description and then present varying examples using vignette-like anecdotal stories or sketches) of how the essence is manifested. Other approaches include engaging one's writing in a dialogue with other phenomenological authors and weaving the description against time, space, the lived body, and relationships to others. In the end, van Manen suggests that authors may invest new ways of reporting their data or combine approaches. We find van Manen's (2023) concept of wonder inspiriting as writers reflect a holistic account of the essence of an experience. He notes,

> Phenomenological writing not only finds its starting point in wonder, it must also induce wonder. For a phenomenological text to "lead" the way to human understanding, it must lead the reader to wonder. Our text must induce a questioning wonder. But what is wonder? Can we make someone wonder? (p. 9)

Embedded Structures

Turning to embedded rhetorical structures, a writer presents the "essence" of the experience for participants in a study through sketching a short paragraph about it in the narrative or by enclosing this paragraph in a figure. This latter approach is used effectively in a study of the caring experiences of nurses who teach (Grigsby & Megel, 1995). Another structural device is to educate the reader through a discussion about phenomenology and its philosophical assumptions. Harper (1981) uses this approach and describes several of Husserl's major tenets as well as the advantages of studying the meaning of "leisure" in a phenomenology.

Finally, we like Moustakas's (1994) suggestion: "Write a brief creative close that speaks to the essence of the study and its inspiration to you in terms of the value of the knowledge and future directions of your professional-personal life" (p. 184). Despite the phenomenologist's inclination to bracket himself or herself out of the narrative, Moustakas introduces the reflexivity that psychological phenomenologists can bring to a study, such as casting an initial problem statement within an autobiographical context. In previous chapters, we have described phenomenology that follows general outlines (Chance, 2022; see Appendix B), and we encourage you to review them for similarities and differences in how the studies are presented. Specifically, Chance's phenomenology of individuals who have experienced adversity as Black women in higher education leadership represented many of these overall and embedded writing structures. The overall article has a structured organization, opening with an introduction to the leadership ambitions of Black women and the significant challenges and adversity experienced in higher education leadership. Chance draws upon an extensive literature review of the many aspects of discrimination that Black women have had to navigate followed by a methodological description and findings organized by four themes with embedded quotes throughout, It followed Colaizzi's (1978) phenomenological methods by reporting significant statements and a table of meaning themes (see Table 3 in Chance, 2022, p. 58). Informed by Moustakas (1994), Chance (2022) ended with an in-depth, exhaustive description of the essence: Adversity promotes resilience and yields leadership development:

> These findings suggest that for Black women, leadership development results from resilience, and the cost of resilience is lived adversity. As they have been exposed to greater adversity historically and culturally, Black women have naturally developed greater resilience. Research has suggested that Black women are socialized to be independent,

emphasizing self-determination and education (Thomas & King, 2007). This sort of socialization promotes resilience over the oppression of the negative stereotypes and images. Therefore, these women are being taught at an early age to have tough skin and endure. Regardless of the adverse experiences these Black women have faced, they consistently found ways to rise above and over-come. Jade shared that she thinks "part of [her] ability to move up in the ranks" has been due to her resilience. (p. 68)

The final discussion was significant for its implications advancing knowledge aimed at enlightening the next generation of young aspiring Black women leaders experiencing adversity and calling for closing the racial-gender leadership gap for Black women.

Grounded Theory Writing Structures

From reviewing grounded theory studies in journal articles, qualitative researchers can view a general form (and variations) for composing the narrative. The problem with journal articles is that the authors present abbreviated versions of the studies to fit within the parameters of the journals. Thus, a reader emerges from a review of a particular study without a full sense of the entire project.

Overall Structures

It is of paramount importance that authors present the theory in any grounded theory narrative. To do this requires the writer to engage in an iterative process: "It means going back and forth between the sections to rethink, revise, and sometimes recast and rewrite" (Charmaz, 2014, p. 285). As May (1986) comments, "In strict terms, the findings are the theory itself, i.e., a set of concepts and propositions which link them" (p. 148). May (1986) continues to describe the research procedures in grounded theory:

- The research questions are broad. They will change several times during data collection and analysis.

- The literature review "neither provides key concepts nor suggests hypotheses" (p. 149). Instead, the literature review in grounded theory shows gaps or bias in existing knowledge, thus providing a rationale for this type of qualitative study.

- The methodology evolves during the course of the study, so writing it early in a study poses difficulties. However, the researcher begins somewhere, and she or he describes preliminary ideas about the sample, the setting, and the data collection procedures.

- The findings section presents the theoretical scheme. The writer includes references from the literature to show outside support for the theoretical model. Also, segments of actual data in the form of vignettes and quotes provide useful explanatory material. This material helps the reader form a judgment about how well the theory is grounded in the data.

- The final discussion section discusses the relationship of the theory to other existing knowledge and the implications of the theory for future research and practice.

Strauss and Corbin (1990) also provide broad writing parameters for their grounded theory studies. They suggest the following:

- Develop a clear analytic story. This is to be provided in the selective coding phase of the study.

- Write on a conceptual level, with description kept secondary to concepts and the analytic story. This means that one finds little description of the phenomenon being studied and more analytic theory at an abstract level.

- Specify the relationship among categories. This is the theorizing part of grounded theory found in axial coding when the researcher tells the story and advances propositions.

- Specify the variations and the relevant conditions, consequences, and so forth for the relationships among categories. In a good theory, one finds variation and different conditions under which the theory holds. This means that the multiple perspectives or variations in each component of axial coding are developed fully. For example, the consequences in the theory are multiple and detailed.

More specifically, in a structured approach to grounded theory as advanced by Strauss and Corbin (1990, 1998), specific aspects of the final written report contain a section on open coding that identifies the various open codes that the researcher discovered in the data, and the axial coding, which includes a diagram of the theory and a discussion about each component in the diagram (i.e., causal conditions, the central phenomenon, the intervening conditions, the context, the strategies, and the consequences). Also, the report contains a section on the theory in which the researcher advances theoretical propositions tying together the elements of the categories in the diagram, or discusses the theory interrelating the categories. In previous chapters, we have described grounded theory studies that follow this general outline (see Example 4.3 and featured grounded theory study example Trip et al., 2019; Appendix C), and we encourage a review of them for similarities and differences in how the studies are presented.

For Charmaz (2006, 2014), a less-structured approach flows into her suggestions for writing the draft of the grounded theory study. She emphasizes the importance of allowing the ideas to emerge as the theory develops, revising early drafts, asking yourself questions about the theory (e.g., have you raised major categories to concepts in the theory?), constructing an argument about the importance of the theory, and closely examining the categories in the theory. Thus, Charmaz does not have a template for writing a grounded theory study but focuses our attention on the importance of the argument in the theory and the nature of the theory. An example is provided by Trip et al.'s (2019; see Appendix C) grounded theory study seeking to develop a theory of the nature and dynamics of caregiving and receiving for older people with intellectual disability and their family. The study began with a description of the background on which the study was premised and referencing studies about aging and future planning that provided little evidence about the characteristics of the caregiving relationship. Following a detailed description of the grounded theory study design, data procedures, and ethical considerations, the authors presented their findings organized by three theoretical concepts. Trip et al. (2019) explain and discuss the theoretical model of "navigating ever-changing seas," using text along with a visual representation as an evocative metaphor:

> A new meta-level of understanding commonalties thus emerged and allowed for the shared evolution of caregiving experiences. As a result, these three concepts represent dynamic, cyclical, and evolving trans-generational relationships, and illustrate the realities of individuals and their family who found themselves Navigating Ever-Changing Seas (Figure 2). The "sea" as a metaphor represents no definitive beginning or ending in understanding aging and future planning and in which "navigation" (decision-making and purpose) is ongoing, and the intrinsic and extrinsic factors that underpin participant perspectives are ever-changing. At the heart of this theoretical model is that decision-making in the frame of health and disability tends to shift, evolve, and devolve as an ongoing function of the dynamic and fluid intersections between relationships (personal, familial, and formal service systems) and the perceptions and beliefs held by the very occupants of those systems with regard to caregiving and receiving across the lifespan. (p. 1603)

Embedded Structures

In grounded theory studies, the researcher varies the narrative report based on the extent of data analysis. Chenitz and Swanson (1986), for example, present six grounded theory studies that vary in the types of analysis reported in the narrative. In a preface to these examples, they mention that the analysis (and narrative) might address one or more of the following: description; the generation of categories through open coding; linking categories around a core category in axial coding, thus developing a substantive, low-level theory; and/or a substantive theory linked to a formal theory.

We have seen grounded theory studies that include one or more of these analyses. For example, in a study of gays and their "coming out" process, Kus (1986) uses only open coding in the analysis and identifies four stages in the process of coming out: identification, in which a gay person undergoes a radical identity transformation; cognitive changes, in which the individual changes negative views about gays into positive ideas; acceptance, a stage in which the individual accepts being gay as a positive life force; and action, the process of the individual's engaging in behavior that results from accepting being gay, such as self-disclosure, expanding the circle of friends to include gays, becoming politically involved in gay causes, and volunteering for gay groups. Set in contrast to this focus on the process, Creswell and Brown (1992) follow the coding steps in Strauss and Corbin (1990). First, they examined the faculty development practices of chairpersons who enhance the research productivity of their faculties. They begin with open coding, move to axial coding complete with a logic diagram, and state a series of explicit propositions in directional (as opposed to the null) form. Sometimes, authors present these propositions in "discursive" form, or describing the theory in narrative form. Strauss and Corbin (1990) present such a model in their theory of "protective governing" (p. 134) in the health care setting. Another example is seen in Conrad's (1978) formal propositions about academic change in the academy.

Another embedded structure is the presentation of the "logic diagram," the "mini-framework," or the "integrative" diagram, where the researcher presents the actual theory in the form of a visual model. The researcher identifies elements of this structure in the axial coding phase, and then tells the "story" in axial coding as a narrative version of it. How is this visual model presented? A good example of this diagram is found in the S. L. Morrow and Smith (1995) study of women who have survived childhood sexual abuse. Their diagram shows a theoretical model that contains the axial coding categories of causal conditions, the central phenomenon, the context, intervening conditions, strategies, and consequences. It is presented with directional arrows indicating the flow of causality from left to right, from causal conditions to consequences. Arrows also show that the context and intervening conditions directly impact the strategies. Presented near the end of the study, this visual form represents the culminating theory for the study. Trip et al. (2019; see Appendix C) advance a visual of the theory representing "navigating ever-changing seas." The visual depicted the concepts of Riding the Waves, Shifting Sands—Changing Tides, and Uncovering Horizons as interpretive co-constructions of the participants' narrative experiences. In so doing, the researchers gave voice to the individual perspectives within and between systems and thus allowed an overlaying of all contributions.

Charmaz (2006, 2014) provides an array of embedded writing strategies useful in grounded theory reports including a centering of the analytical frameworks. Examples of grounded theory studies illustrate imparting mood or emotions into a theoretical discussion, straightforward language, and ways that writing can be accessible to readers such as the use of rhythm and time (e.g., "Days slip by" [Charmaz, 2006, p. 173]). Charmaz also invites the use of unexpected definitions and assertions by the grounded theory author. Rhetorical questions are also useful, and the writing includes pacing and a tone that leads a reader into the topic. Stories can be told in grounded theory studies, and overall the writing brings evocative language to persuade the reader of the theory.

Ethnographic Writing Structures

Ethnographers write extensively about narrative construction, from how the nature of the text shapes the subject matter to the "literary" conventions and devices used by authors (Atkinson & Hammersley, 1994). The general shapes of ethnographies and embedded structures are well detailed in the literature.

Overall Structures

The overall writing structure of ethnographies varies. For example, Van Maanen (1988, 2011) provides the alternative forms of ethnography. Some ethnographies are written as realist tales, reports that provide direct, matter-of-fact portraits of studied cultures without much information about how the ethnographers produced the portraits. In this type of tale, a writer uses an impersonal point of view, conveying a "scientific" and "objective" perspective. A confessional tale takes the opposite approach, and the researcher focuses more on their fieldwork experiences than on the culture. The final type, the impressionistic tale, is a personalized account of "the fieldwork case in dramatic form" (Van Maanen, 1988, p. 7). It has elements of both realist and confessional writing and, in our opinion, presents a compelling and persuasive story.

In both confessional and impressionistic tales, the first-person point of view is used, conveying a personal style of writing. Van Maanen states that other, less frequently written tales also exist—critical tales focusing on large social, political, symbolic, or economic issues; formalist tales that build, test, generalize, and exhibit theory; literary tales in which the ethnographers write like journalists, borrowing fiction-writing techniques from novelists; and jointly told tales in which the production of the studies is jointly authored by the fieldworkers and the participants, opening up shared and discursive narratives.

On a slightly different note, but yet related to the larger rhetorical structure, Wolcott (1994) provides three components of good qualitative inquiry representing the centerpiece of good ethnographic writing as well as steps in data analysis. First, an ethnographer writes a "description" of the culture that answers this question: "What is going on here?" (Wolcott, 1994, p. 12). Wolcott offers useful techniques for writing this description: chronological order, the researcher or narrator order, a progressive focusing, a critical or key event, plots and characters, groups in interaction, an analytical framework, and a story told through several perspectives. Second, after describing the culture using one of these approaches, the researcher "analyzes" the data. Analysis includes highlighting findings, displaying findings, reporting fieldwork procedures, identifying patterned regularities in the data, comparing the case with a known case, evaluating the information, contextualizing the information within a broader analytic framework, critiquing the research process, and proposing a redesign of the study. Of all these analytic techniques, the identification of "patterns" or themes is central to ethnographic writing. Third, interpretation is involved in the rhetorical structure. This means that the researcher can extend the analysis, make inferences from the information, do as directed or as suggested by gatekeepers, turn to theory, refocus the interpretation itself, connect with personal experience, analyze or interpret the interpretive process, or explore alternative formats. Of these interpretive strategies, we like the approach of interpreting the findings both within the context of the researcher's experiences and within the larger body of scholarly research on the topic.

A more detailed, structured outline for ethnography was found in Emerson et al. (2011). They discuss developing an ethnographic study as a "thematic narrative," a story "analytically thematized, but often in relatively loose ways . . . constructed out of a series of thematically organized units of fieldnote excerpts and analytic commentary" (p. 202). This thematic narrative builds inductively from a main idea or thesis that incorporates several specific analytic themes and is elaborated throughout the study. It is structured as follows:

- First is an introduction that engages the reader's attention and focuses the study, and then the researcher proceeds to link his or her interpretation to wider issues of scholarly interest in the discipline.

- After this, the researcher introduces the setting and the methods for learning about it. In this section, too, the ethnographer relates details about entry into and participation in the setting as well as advantages and constraints of the ethnographer's research role.

- The researcher presents analytic claims next. Emerson and colleagues (2011) indicate the utility of "excerpt commentary" units, whereby an author incorporates an analytic point, provides orientation information about the point, presents the excerpt or direct quote, and then advances analytic commentary about the quote as it relates to the analytic point.

- In the conclusion, the researcher reflects and elaborates on the thesis advanced at the beginning. This interpretation may extend or modify the thesis in light of the materials examined; relate the thesis to general theory or a current issue; or offer a metacommentary on the thesis, methods, or assumptions of the study.

In previous chapters, we have described ethnographies that follow this general outline (Example 4.4 and featured ethnographic study example Mac an Ghaill & Haywood, 2015; see Appendix D), and we encourage a review of them for similarities and differences in how the studies are presented.

Embedded Structures

Ethnographers use embedded rhetorical devices such as figures of speech or "tropes" (Fetterman, 2010, 2019; Hammersley & Atkinson, 2019). Metaphors, for example, provide visual and spatial images or dramaturgical or theatrical characterizations of social actions. Another trope is the synecdoche, in which ethnographers present examples, illustrations, cases, and/or vignettes that form a part but stand for the whole. See Rhoads (1995) for an example of an effective opening vignette in an ethnography of fraternity life on campus. Ethnographers present storytelling tropes examining cause and sequence that follow grand narratives to smaller parables. A final trope is irony, in which researchers bring to light contrasts of competing frames of reference and rationality.

More specific rhetorical devices depict scenes in ethnography (Emerson et al., 2011). Writers can incorporate details or "write lushly" (E. Goffman, 1989, p. 131) or "thickly" a description that creates verisimilitude and produces for readers the feeling that they experience, or perhaps could experience, the events described (Denzin, 2001; Fetterman, 2019). The ethnographic study of the core values of the straight edge (sXe) movement illustrated many of these writing conventions (Haenfler, 2004). He told a persuasive story, with colorful elements (e.g., T-shirt slogans), "thick" description, and extensive quotes. Denzin (2001) talks about the importance of using "thick description" in writing qualitative research. By this, he means that the narrative "presents detail, context, emotion, and the webs of social relationships . . . [and] evokes emotionality and self-feelings. . . . The voices, feelings, actions, and meanings of interacting individuals are heard" (Denzin, 2001, p. 100). As an example, Denzin (2001) first refers to an illustration of thick description from Sudnow (1978) and then provides his own version as if it were a thin description:

> "Sitting at the piano and moving into the production of a chord, the chord as a whole was prepared for as the hand moved toward the keyboard, and the terrain was seen as a field relative to the task. . . . There was chord A and chord B, separated from one another. . . . A's production entailed a tightly compressed hand, and B's . . . an open and extended spread. . . . The beginner gets from A to B disjointly." (Sudnow, 1978, pp. 9–10)

> "I had trouble learning the piano keyboard." (Denzin, 2001, p. 102)

Also, ethnographers present dialogue, and the dialogue becomes especially vivid when written in the dialect and natural language of the culture (see, e.g., the articles on Black English vernacular or "code switching" in Nelson, 1990). Writers also rely on characterization in which human beings are shown talking, acting, and relating to others. Longer scenes take the form of sketches, a "slice of life" (Emerson et al., 2011, p. 75), or larger episodes and tales. The ethnographic study describing the changing cultural conditions of a group of British-born, working-class Pakistani and Bangladeshi young men over 3 years (Mac an Ghaill & Haywood, 1995; see Appendix D) offers such a scene. They use the following segment to effectively illustrate their (M.M. represents the first author's initials) discussion with the young men (Wasim and Imran) about their use of the term Muslim as a collective self-referent:

Wasim: When you asked us were we proper Muslims, we all laughed and said, no. So, things around prayers, fasting and going to the mosque, no, not real Muslims for most of us, for younger people.
Imran: Groups can label themselves, like we label ourselves Muslim. But it's not the same as when white people use the label.
M.M: What do you mean?
Imran: It's hard to explain, we're both using the same word. But they use Muslim and they don't even know us, or they mean something bad. For us it's a definite good thing or just a normal thing.
M.M: And do you know what it means?
Imran: A good question. I think if I'm been honest, then no. I think a lot of the time, we don't know what Muslim means. Like we're saying here, it can mean lots of things. (pp. 103–104)

Ethnographic writers tell "a good story" (Richardson, 1990). Thus, one of the forms of "evocative" experimental qualitative writing for Richardson (1990) is the fictional representation form in which writers draw on the literary devices such as flashback, flash-forward, alternative points of view, deep characterization, tone shifts, synecdoche, dialogue, interior monologue, and sometimes the omniscient narrator. Similarly, Wolcott (2008a) emphasizes the use of techniques for telling the story as a travelogue, life history, or organized around specific themes.

Case Study Writing Structures

Turning to case studies, we are reminded of contrasting writing structures. Merriam (1988) stated, "there is no standard format for reporting case study research" (p. 193). G. Thomas (2021) suggested that "there are essential elements to any [case study] project that must be incorporated in the write-up" (p. 262). Unquestionably, some case studies generate theory, some are simply descriptions of cases, and others are more analytical in nature and display cross-case or inter-site comparisons. The overall intent of the case study undoubtedly shapes the larger structure of the written narrative. Still, we find it useful to conceptualize a general form, and we turn to key texts on case studies for their guidance.

Overall Structures

One can open and close the case study narrative with vignettes to draw the reader into the case. This approach is suggested by Stake (1995), who provides an outline of topics that might be included in a qualitative case study. We feel that this is a helpful way to stage the topics in a good case study:

- The writer opens with a vignette. This is so the reader can develop a vicarious experience to get a feel for the time and place of the study.

- Next, the researcher identifies the issue, the purpose, and the method of the study so that the reader learns about how the study came to be, the background of the writer, and the issues surrounding the case.

- This is followed by an extensive description of the case and its context—a body of relatively uncontested data. This is a description the reader might make if he or she had been there.

- Issues are presented next, a few key issues, so that the reader can understand the complexity of the case. This complexity builds through references to other research or the writer's understanding of other cases.

- Next, several of the issues are probed further. At this point, too, the writer brings in both confirming and disconfirming evidence.

- Assertions are presented. These are a summary of what the writer understands about the case and whether the initial naturalistic generalizations, conclusions arrived at through personal experience or offered as vicarious experiences for the reader, have been changed conceptually or challenged.

- Finally, the writer ends with a closing vignette, an experiential note. It is to remind the reader that this report is one person's encounter with a complex case.

We like this general outline because it provides a description of the case; presents themes, assertions, or interpretations of the researcher; and begins and ends with realistic scenarios. In previous chapters, we have referred to case studies that follow this general outline (see Example 4.5 and featured case study example Goodrum et al., 2022; see Appendix E), and we encourage a review of similarities and differences in how authors present cases. While the Goodrum et al. (2022) case description does not begin with a vignette, its initial paragraph succinctly describes both the larger, societal issue for the case and the focus of the current case:

> School administrators, law enforcement officials, and federal agencies have increasingly taken active measures to prevent targeted acts of school violence in the United States. . . . Despite these prevention efforts, there were 57 active shooter incidents in U.S. schools from 2000 to 2018 (Blair and Schweit 2014; Federal Bureau of Investigation 2016, 2018, 2019). In 2020–2021, more school shootings with casualties occurred in the United States than in any other academic year since data

collection began (Irwin et al. 2022); as of July 2022, 27 school shootings have resulted in injury or death in the United States this academic year ("School Shootings This Year" 2022). The investigations that follow these tragic events consistently identify "failures of foresight" to recognize and interrupt the attacker's path toward violence within schools and across communities. (pp. 257–258)

Following descriptions of the procedures undertaken and the emergent themes, the case report concludes with discussions of recommendations for building organizational structures and cultures that support violence prevention in schools.

A similar model is found in Lincoln and Guba's (1985) substantive case report. They describe a need for the explication of the problem, a thorough description of the context or setting, a description of the transactions or processes observed in that context, saliences at the site (elements studied in-depth), and outcomes of the inquiry ("lessons learned").

At a more general level yet, we find Yin's (2017) 2-x-2 matrix representing 4 types of case studies helpful. Case studies can be either single-case or multiple-case designs and either holistic (single unit of analysis) or embedded (multiple units of analysis). Yin comments further that a single case is best when a need exists to study a critical case, an extreme or unique case, or a revelatory case. Whether the case is single or multiple, the researcher decides to study the entire case, a holistic design, or multiple subunits within the case (the embedded design). Although the holistic design may be more abstract, it captures the entire case better than the embedded design does. However, the embedded design starts with an examination of subunits and allows for the detailed perspective should the questions begin to shift and change during fieldwork.

Yin (2017) also presents several possible structures for composing a case study report. In a "linear-analytic approach," the researcher discusses the problem, the methods, the findings, and the conclusions. An alternative, a "comparative structure," repeats the same case study several times and presents alternative descriptions or explanations of the same case. A "chronological structure" presents the case study in a sequence, such as sections or chapters that address the early, middle, and late phases of a case history. In a "theory-building structure," the case study advances various hypotheses or propositions. In a departure from the norm, researchers may use a "suspense structure," in which the study begins with an answer or outcome to the problem and then builds an explanation for this outcome in the remaining parts of the research. Finally, the "unsequenced structure" is "one in which the sequence of sections of chapters assumes no particular importance" (Yin, 2017, p. 231). The unsequenced structure provides the author great flexibility in organizing their case description.

Embedded Structures

What specific narrative devices, embedded structures, do case study writers use to "mark" their studies? One might approach the description of the context and setting for the case in a chronology from a broader picture to a narrower one. The gunman case (Asmussen & Creswell, 1995) begins with a description of the actual campus incident in terms of the city in which the situation developed, followed by the campus, and, narrower yet, the actual classroom on campus. This represents a funneling approach that narrowed the setting from a calm city environment to a potentially volatile campus classroom, and finally, to a chronology of events focused on the campus shooting.

Another example is provided by the multiple case study of technology integration across three schools (Staples et al., 2005). Each case description begins with the technology context that existed prior to the study, details the changes that occurred during the study, and concludes with future projections. The chronological approach seemed to work best when events unfolded and followed a process; case studies often are bounded by time and cover events over time (Yin, 2017).

The case study examining how the school's organizational structure and culture impeded the prevention of violence (Goodrum et al., 2022; see Appendix E) also represented a single case study (Yin, 2017). This case of a single school shooting where two students died involved unique circumstances as "one of only two known cases where a threat assessment was conducted with a student prior to their deadly attack" (p. 260). In multiple case studies (e.g., Chirgwin, 2015; Staples et al., 2005), researchers first present each case and then provide an analysis across all cases (Yin, 2017). Another narrative format is to pose a series of questions and answers based on the case study database (Yin, 2017).

Finally, researchers need to be cognizant of the amount of description in their case studies versus the amount of analysis and interpretation or assertions (Merriam & Tisdell, 2015; G. Thomas, 2021). In comparing description and analysis, Merriam (1988) suggests that the proper balance might be 60% to 40% or 70% to 30% in favor of description. An examination of the gunman case by Asmussen and Creswell (1995) revealed a balance of elements in equal thirds (33% to 33% to 33%)—first, a concrete description of the setting and the actual events (and those that occurred within 2 weeks after the incident); second, the five themes; and third, the interpretation and the lessons learned, reported in the discussion section. Writers must make these decisions while keeping in mind their audience (G. Thomas, 2021; Yin, 2017), and it is conceivable that a case study might contain mainly descriptive material, especially if the bounded system, the case, is quite large and complex.

COMPARING WRITING STRUCTURES ACROSS THE FIVE APPROACHES

Looking back over Table 9.1, we see many diverse structures for writing the qualitative report. What major differences exist in the structures depending on one's choice of approach?

First, we are struck by the diversity of discussions about narrative structures. We found little crossover or sharing of structures among the five approaches, although, in practice, this undoubtedly occurs. The narrative tropes and the literary devices, discussed by ethnographers and narrative researchers, have applicability regardless of approach. Second, the writing structures are highly related to data analysis procedures. A phenomenological study and a grounded theory study follow closely their data analysis steps. In short, we are reminded once again that it is difficult to separate the activities of data collection, analysis, and report writing in a qualitative study. Third, the emphasis given to writing the narrative, especially the embedded narrative structures, varies among the approaches. Ethnographers lead the group in their extensive discussions about narrative and text construction. Phenomenologists and grounded theory writers spend less time discussing this topic. Fourth, the overall narrative structure is clearly specified in some approaches (e.g., a grounded theory study, a phenomenological study, and perhaps a case study), whereas it is flexible and evolving in others (e.g., a narrative, an ethnography). Perhaps this conclusion reflects the more structured approach versus the less structured approach, overall, among the five approaches of inquiry.

CHAPTER CHECK-IN

1. Do you see the overall writing structures within a particular approach to qualitative research and can you adapt it to guide your own work? Select one of the qualitative articles presented in Appendices B through F that fits your particular approach.
   a. Begin with diagramming its overall structure by identifying the flow within its components. How does the article start? With a personal vignette, a statement of the problem, a literature review? What comes next? How does the article end?
   b. Then look within each component and identify the embedded strategies used—for example, metaphors, quotes, and diagrams.
2. Can you identify the characteristics of thick description to apply our understandings to a practical experience in writing qualitative research? To do this, turn to novels in which the author provides exquisite detail about an event, a thing, or a person. For example, turn to page 14 in Paul Harding's (2009) award-winning book, *Tinkers*, and read the passage about how George repaired a broken clock at a tag sale.
   a. Write about how Harding incorporates a physical description, includes a description of the steps (or movement), uses strong action verbs, draws on references or quotes, and relies on the five senses to convey detail (sight, hearing, taste, smell, touch).
   b. Use this type of detail in your qualitative descriptions or themes.

SUMMARY

In this chapter, we discussed writing the qualitative report. We began by revisiting ethical considerations and then by discussing several writing strategies. These strategies include writing reflexively and with representation, identifying intended audiences, determining the appropriate encoding (or the importance of language), and deciding how best to use quotes. Then we turned to each of the five approaches of inquiry and presented overall writing structures for organizing the entire study as well as specific embedded structures, writing devices, and techniques that the researcher incorporates into the study. We concluded with observations about the differences in writing structures among the five approaches.

CHAPTER KEY TERMS

embedded writing structures
foreshadowing
overall writing structures
progressive–regressive method
rhetorical
verisimilitude

FURTHER READINGS

In addition to many of the resources already suggested in earlier chapters, which include strategies and guidance for writing and communicating qualitative research, we highlight a few here focused on information about procedures and issues when writing. The list should not be considered exhaustive, and readers are encouraged to seek out additional readings in the end-of-book reference list.

Denzin, N. K. (2001). *Interpretive interactionism* (2nd ed.). Sage.

In this second edition, Norman Denzin expands his guidance about how "to do" interpretive interactionism—that is to make the lived experiences successfully accessible to a reader.

Gilgun, J. F. (2005). "Grab" and good science: Writing up the results of qualitative research. *Qualitative Health Research*, 15, 256–262. https://doi.org/10.1177/1049732304268796

Jane Gilgun presents compelling historical and contemporary arguments for the use of first-person voice, and other guidance for writing qualitative research.

Richardson, L. (1990). *Writing strategies: Reaching diverse audiences*. Sage.

Laurel Richardson offers an important resource for guiding qualitative writing and how it needs to be adjusted based on the target audience.

Strunk, W., & White, E. B. (2000). *The elements of style* (4th ed.). Pearson.

William Strunk and E. B. White convey the principles of English style in an accessible manner with illustrative examples accompanying detailed descriptions. This is essential reading.

Sword, H. (2012). *Stylish academic writing*. Harvard University Press.

Helen Sword describes the elements of stylishness for scholars writing for larger audiences. Of particular note are her chapters on "tempting titles" and "hooks and sinkers."

Van Maanen, J. (2011). *Tales of the field: On writing ethnography* (2nd ed.). University of Chicago Press.

John Van Maanen unpacks the styles associated with written representations of culture. In so doing, he offers valuable advice to an ethnographer through illustrative examples and practices.

Weaver-Hightower, M. B. (2019). *How to write qualitative research*. Routledge.

Marcus B. Weaver-Hightower provides practical guidance about how to write qualitative research including important processes such as revising for clarity and creating and writing about visuals.

Weis, L., & Fine, M. (2000). *Speed bumps: A student-friendly guide to qualitative research*. Teachers College Press.

Lois Weis and Michelle Fine provide an excellent resource focused on reflexivity. Specifically, they clearly explain the potential impact of qualitative writing on readers, audiences, and the participants studied.

Wolcott, H. F. (2008b). *Writing up qualitative research* (3rd ed.). Sage.

Harry Wolcott leads the reader through a time-tested process of interpreting and communicating qualitative research. Noteworthy are his guidance with respect to perseverance in writing and tightening the message.

10 STANDARDS OF VALIDATION AND EVALUATION

> **QUESTIONS FOR DISCUSSION**
>
> - What are some perspectives on validation within qualitative research?
> - What are some procedures useful in establishing validation in qualitative research?
> - How is reliability realized in qualitative research?
> - What are some stances on evaluating the quality of qualitative research?
> - How do quality criteria differ by types of approaches to qualitative inquiry?

Qualitative researchers strive for "understanding," that deep structure of knowledge that comes from visiting personally with participants, spending extensive time in the field, and probing to obtain detailed meanings. During or after a study, qualitative researchers ask, "Did we get it right?" (Stake, 1995, p. 107) or "Did we publish a 'wrong' or inaccurate account?" (J. Thomas, 1993, p. 39). Is it possible to even have a right answer? To answer these questions, researchers need to look to themselves, to the participants, and to the readers. There are multi- or polyvocal discourses at work here that provide insight into the validation and evaluation of a qualitative research account.

In this chapter, we address two interrelated questions: Is the account valid, and by whose standards? and How do we evaluate the quality of qualitative research? Answers to these questions take us into the many perspectives on validation to emerge within the qualitative community and the multiple standards for evaluation discussed by authors with procedural, interpretive, and postmodern perspectives. Then, we examine the **quality criteria** for each of the five approaches to inquiry and compare standards of evaluation across the approaches. To represent the diversity of qualitative perspectives, we weave our own stances in with those of others from the literature.

VALIDATION AND RELIABILITY IN QUALITATIVE RESEARCH

Validation of qualitative research occurs throughout the research process, yet it is often only in the written study description that a reader becomes aware of the procedures researchers take to ensure the accuracy of their findings and generate evidence of **credibility**. It is important that we define our qualitative approach to **validity** and **reliability**. We define qualitative validity as the researcher checking for the accuracy of the findings by employing certain procedures (Creswell & Creswell, 2023). Qualitative reliability indicates that the researcher's approach is consistent across different researchers and among different projects (Gibbs, 2018). In the sections to follow, we introduce some of the diverse perspectives that exist regarding the importance of validation in qualitative research and the terms and procedures used by researchers to describe and establish a valid account. We then discuss reliability related to the procedures qualitative researchers use to promote and assess coding consistency across multiple researchers and data sets.

Perspectives on Validation Within Qualitative Research

We begin by recognizing the diverse perspectives within the qualitative community for description of and procedures for establishing the accuracy of a research account. Our view of validation as an evolving construct means that a broad understanding of both traditional and contemporary perspectives is essential for informing the work and reading of qualitative research. In Table 10.1, we present a sample of the perspectives, arranged chronologically, available on validation in the qualitative literature. These perspectives represent positioning validation in qualitative research in a range of ways including (but not limited to) terms of quantitative equivalents, postmodern and interpretive lenses, metaphors used for visualization, and present validity use. Evidence of evolving thinking about validation in qualitative research is apparent within and across authors, and we conclude this section by advancing a rationale for our own stance.

Writers have searched for and found qualitative equivalents that parallel traditional quantitative approaches to validation. LeCompte and Goetz (1982) took this approach when they compared the issues of validation and reliability to their counterparts in experimental design and survey research. They contended that qualitative research had garnered much criticism in the scientific ranks for its failure to "adhere to canons of reliability and validation" (LeCompte & Goetz, 1982, p. 31) in the traditional sense. They applied threats to internal validation in experimental research to ethnographic research (e.g., history and maturation, observer effects, selection and regression, mortality, spurious conclusions). They further identified threats to external validation as "effects that obstruct or reduce a study's comparability or translatability" (LeCompte & Goetz, 1982, p. 51).

Some writers argue that authors who use positivist terminology facilitate the acceptance of qualitative research in a traditionally focused quantitative world. Ely and colleagues asserted that using quantitative terms tended to be a defensive measure that muddied the waters and that "the language of positivistic research is not congruent with or adequate to qualitative work" (1991, p. 95). Lincoln and Guba (1985) offered alternative terms that, they contended, adhere more to naturalistic research. To establish the "**trustworthiness**" of a qualitative study, Lincoln and Guba (1985) advanced the use of unique terms, such as *credibility, authenticity, transferability, dependability*, and *confirmability* as "the naturalist's equivalents" for the qualitative equivalent of quantitative *internal validation, external validation, reliability*, and *objectivity* (p. 300).

TABLE 10.1 ■ Perspectives and Terms Used for Validation in Qualitative Research

Authors	Perspectives	Terms
LeCompte & Goetz (1982)	Use of parallel, qualitative equivalents to their quantitative counterparts in experimental and survey research	Internal validity, external validity, reliability, and objectivity
Lincoln & Guba (1985)	Use of alternative terms equivalent to quantitative counterparts that apply more to naturalistic axioms	Credibility, transferability, dependability, and confirmability
Eisner (1991)	Use of alternative terms that provide reasonable standards for judging the credibility of qualitative research	Structural corroboration, consensual validation, and referential adequacy
Lather (1991)	Use of four types for reconceptualizing validity	Triangulation, construct validation, face validation, and catalytic validation
Lather (1993)	Use of four frames of validity	Ironic validity, paralogic validity, rhizomatic validity, and situated or embedded voluptuous validity
Wolcott (1990a, 1994)	Use of terms other than *validity* because it neither guides nor informs qualitative research	Understanding is a better word than validity
Angen (2000)	Use of two types of validation within the context of interpretive inquiry	Ethical validation and substantive validation
Whittemore et al. (2001)	Use of synthesized perspectives of validity to organize key validation criteria into primary and secondary	Primary criteria: credibility, authenticity, criticality, and integrity Secondary criteria: explicitness, vividness, creativity, thoroughness, congruence, and sensitivity
Richardson & St. Pierre (2005, 2018)	Use of a metaphorical, reconceptualized form of validity as a crystal	Crystals as growing, changing, altering, reflecting externalities, and refracting within themselves
Lincoln et al. (2011)	Use of authenticity, transgression, and ethical relationships	Fairness representing views, raised awareness, and action; hidden assumptions and repressions, the crystal that can be turned many ways; relationships with research participants
Creswell & Poth (this book)	Use of validation strategies for assessing the accuracy of the findings as best described by the researcher and the participants	Process involves a combination of qualitative research strategies—for example, extensive field time, thick description, closeness of researcher to participants and member checking

To operationalize these new terms, they proposed techniques such as prolonged engagement in the field and the **triangulation** of data sources, methods, and investigators to establish credibility. They described "thick description" as necessary to ensure the transferability of findings between the researcher and those being studied. Rather than a focus on the reliability of an approach, researchers sought dependability that the results would be subject to change and instability. The naturalistic researcher looked for confirmability rather than objectivity in establishing the value of the data. Both dependability and confirmability were established through an auditing of the research process. We find the Lincoln and Guba criteria still popular today in qualitative reports.

Rather than using the term *validation*, Eisner (1991) constructed standards such as structural corroboration, consensual validation, and referential adequacy as evidence for asserting the credibility of qualitative research. In structural corroboration, the researcher used multiple types of data to support or contradict the interpretation. Eisner described his purpose to "seek a confluence of evidence that breeds credibility, that allows us to feel confident about our observations, interpretations, and conclusions" (1991, p. 110). He further illustrated this purpose with an analogy drawn from detective work: The researcher compiles bits and pieces of evidence to formulate a "compelling whole." At this stage, the researcher looked for recurring behaviors or actions and considered disconfirming evidence and contrary interpretations. Moreover, Eisner recommended that to demonstrate credibility, the weight of evidence should become persuasive. In consensual validation, the researcher sought the opinion of others, which Eisner described as "an agreement among competent others that the description, interpretation, evaluation, and thematics of an educational situation are right" (1991, p. 112). Referential adequacy suggested the importance of criticism, and Eisner described the goal of criticism as illuminating the subject matter and bringing about more complex and sensitive human perception and understanding.

Qualitative researchers also have reconceptualized validation with a postmodern perspective. Lather (1991) initially identified four types of validation (i.e., triangulation, construct validation, face validation, and catalytic validation) as a "reconceptualization of validation." Lather commented that "paradigmatic uncertainty in the human sciences is leading to the reconceptualizing of validation" and called for "new techniques and concepts for obtaining and defining trustworthy data which avoids the pitfalls of orthodox notions of validation" (1991, p. 66). For Lather, the character of a social science report changed from a closed narrative with a tight argument structure to a more open narrative with holes and questions and an admission of situatedness and partiality. In *Getting Smart*, Lather (1991) described triangulation as drawing upon multiple data sources, methods, and theoretical schemes. Construct validation recognized the constructs that existed rather than imposing theories or constructs on informants or the context. Face validation was best explained by Kidder (1982) as "a 'click of recognition' and a 'yes, of course,' instead of 'yes, but' experience" (p. 56). Catalytic validation energized participants to consider knowing reality to transform it.

In a later article, Lather's (1993) terms became more unique and closely related to feminist research in "four frames of validation." The first, *ironic* validation, was where the researcher presented truth as a problem. The second, *paralogic* validation, was concerned with undecidables, limits, paradoxes, and complexities. This validation moved away from theorizing things and toward providing direct exposure to other voices in an almost unmediated way. The third, *rhizomatic* validation, pertained to questioning proliferations, crossings, and overlaps without underlying structures or deeply rooted connections. The researcher should also question taxonomies, constructs, and interconnected networks in which the reader jumped from one assemblage to another and consequently moved from judgment to understanding. The fourth type was situated, embodied, or *voluptuous* validation, which meant that the researcher sets out to understand more than one can know and to write toward what one does not understand.

Other writers, such as Wolcott (1990a), had little use for validation, suggesting that "validation neither guides nor informs" his work (p. 136). He did not dismiss validation but rather placed it in a broader perspective. Wolcott's (1990a) goal was to identify "critical elements" and write "plausible interpretations from them" (p. 146). He ultimately tried to understand rather than convince, and he voiced the view that validation distracted from his work of understanding what was really going on. Wolcott (1990a, 1994) claimed that the term *validation* did not capture the essence of what he sought, adding that perhaps someone would coin a term more appropriate for the naturalistic paradigm. But for now, he said, the term *understanding* seemed to encapsulate the idea as well as any other (Wolcott, 1994).

Validation has also been cast within an interpretive approach to qualitative research marked by a focus on the importance of the researcher; a lack of truth in validation; a form of validation based on negotiation and dialogue with participants; and interpretations that are temporal, located, and always open to reinterpretation (Angen, 2000). Angen suggested that within interpretative research, validation was "a judgment of the trustworthiness or goodness of a piece of research" (2000, p. 387). She espoused an ongoing, open dialogue on the topic of what made interpretive research worthy of our trust. Considerations of validation were not definitive as the final word on the topic, nor should every study be required to address them. Further, she advanced two types of validation: ethical validation and substantive validation. Ethical validation meant that all research agendas must question their underlying moral assumptions, their political and ethical implications, and the equitable treatment of diverse voices. It also required research to provide some practical answers to questions. Angen (2000) also proposed that our interpretive qualitative research should have a "generative promise" (p. 389) and raise new possibilities, open up new questions, stimulate new dialogue, and provide nondogmatic answers to the questions posed. In so doing, interpretive qualitative research must have transformative value leading to action and change. Substantive validation meant understanding one's own topic, understandings derived from other sources, and the documentation of this process in the written study. Self-reflection contributed to the validation of the work. The interpretive qualitative researcher, as a sociohistorical interpreter, interacted with the subject matter to co-create the interpretations derived. Understandings derived from previous research gave substance to the inquiry. Interpretive research also was a chain of interpretations that must be documented for others to judge the trustworthiness of the meanings arrived at in the end. Written accounts must resonate with their intended audiences, and must be compelling, powerful, and convincing.

A synthesis of validation perspectives comes from Whittemore et al. (2001), who analyzed 13 writings about validation and extracted key validation criteria from these studies. They organized these criteria into primary and secondary criteria. They found four primary criteria: credibility (Are the results an accurate interpretation of the participants' meaning?); authenticity (Are different voices heard?); criticality (Is there a critical appraisal of all aspects of the research?); and integrity (Are the investigators self-critical?). Secondary criteria related to explicitness, vividness, creativity, thoroughness, congruence, and sensitivity. In summary, with these criteria, it seemed like the validation standard had moved toward the interpretive lens of qualitative research, with an emphasis on researcher reflexivity and on researcher challenges that included raising questions about the ideas developed during a research study.

A postmodern perspective drew on the metaphorical image of a crystal. Richardson (in Richardson & St. Pierre, 2005) described this image:

> I propose that the central imaginary for "validation" for postmodern texts is not the triangle—a rigid, fixed, two-dimensional object. Rather the central imaginary is the crystal, which combines symmetry and substance with an infinite variety of shapes, substances, transmutations, multidimensionalities, and angles of approach. Crystals grow, change, and are altered, but they are not amorphous. Crystals are prisms that reflect externalities and refract within themselves, creating different colors, patterns, and arrays casting off in different directions. What we see depends on our angle of response—not triangulation but rather crystallization. (p. 963)

A final perspective was drawn from Lincoln et al. (2011). They captured the many perspectives developed through the years. They suggested that the question of validity criteria is not whether we should have such criteria or whose criteria the scientific community might adopt, but rather how criteria needed to be developed within the projected transformations being suggested by social scientists. To this end, they reviewed establishing authenticity but framed it within the perspectives of a balance of views, raising the level of awareness among participants and other stakeholders, and advancing action on the part of research participants and their training. Lincoln et al. (2011) also saw a role for validity in understanding hidden assumptions and ethical relationships with research participants through such standards as positioning themselves, having discourses, encouraging voices, and being self-reflective.

Given the many perspectives of validation within the qualitative research community, we acknowledge the ongoing debate regarding the many types of and terms for validation in qualitative research (e.g., Beck, 2020). We suggest the need for authors to choose the types and terms with which they are comfortable and reference the terms and strategies writers use.

To summarize our own stance, we consider "validation" in qualitative research to be an attempt to assess the "accuracy" of the findings, as best described by the researcher, the participants, and the readers (or reviewers). This view also suggests that any report of research is a representation by the author. We also view validation as a distinct strength of qualitative research by the researcher spending extensive time in the field setting, detailing thick description in their work, and remaining close to participants in the study. We use the term *validation* to emphasize a process (see Angen, 2000; Hayashi et al., 2019), rather than *verification* (which has quantitative overtones) or historical words such as *trustworthiness* and *authenticity* (recognizing that many qualitative writers do return to these words, suggesting the "staying power" of Lincoln and Guba's, 1985, standards; see Whittemore et al., 2001). Our adoption of a "process view" to validation is based on the longstanding premise that the question of whether the account is valid cannot and should not be based on a single strategy. Instead, validation strategies generating evidence should be embedded throughout the qualitative research process and be sufficiently flexible to the multiple contexts in which the qualitative research takes place. As an illustration, we suggest Hayashi et al.'s (2019) reflections highlighting contextual influences on validation strategies throughout their research process.

The subject of validation arises in several of the approaches to qualitative research (e.g., Corbin & Strauss, 2015; Riessman, 2008; Stake, 1995), but we do not think that distinct validation approaches exist for the five approaches to qualitative research. At best, there might be less emphasis on validation in narrative research and more emphasis on it in grounded theory, case study, and ethnography, especially when the authors of these approaches want to employ systematic procedures. We recommend using multiple validation strategies regardless of the type of qualitative approach.

Our framework for thinking about validation in qualitative research is to suggest that researchers employ accepted strategies to document the accuracy of their studies. These we call **validation strategies**.

TRY THIS NOW 10.1
CONVEYING YOUR PERSPECTIVE ON VALIDATION IN QUALITATIVE RESEARCH

Perspectives on validation are shaped by many influences including the researcher's lived experience and their reading of literature. What and who are key influences on your perspective of validation as a qualitative researcher? What works might you reference in your qualitative reporting?

Validation Strategies

It is not enough for researchers to be able to define and describe the essential role of validation in qualitative research. They need to be able to translate their understandings of validation into practice as strategies. We describe nine strategies frequently used by qualitative researchers during the process of validation adapted from the work of Creswell and Miller (2000) and provide some general guidance about how we go about implementing these strategies (see Figure 10.1).

The strategies are not presented in any specific order of importance but are organized in three groups by the lens the strategy represents: researcher's lens, participant's lens, and reader's or reviewer's lens (Creswell & Báez, 2021).

292 Qualitative Inquiry and Research Design

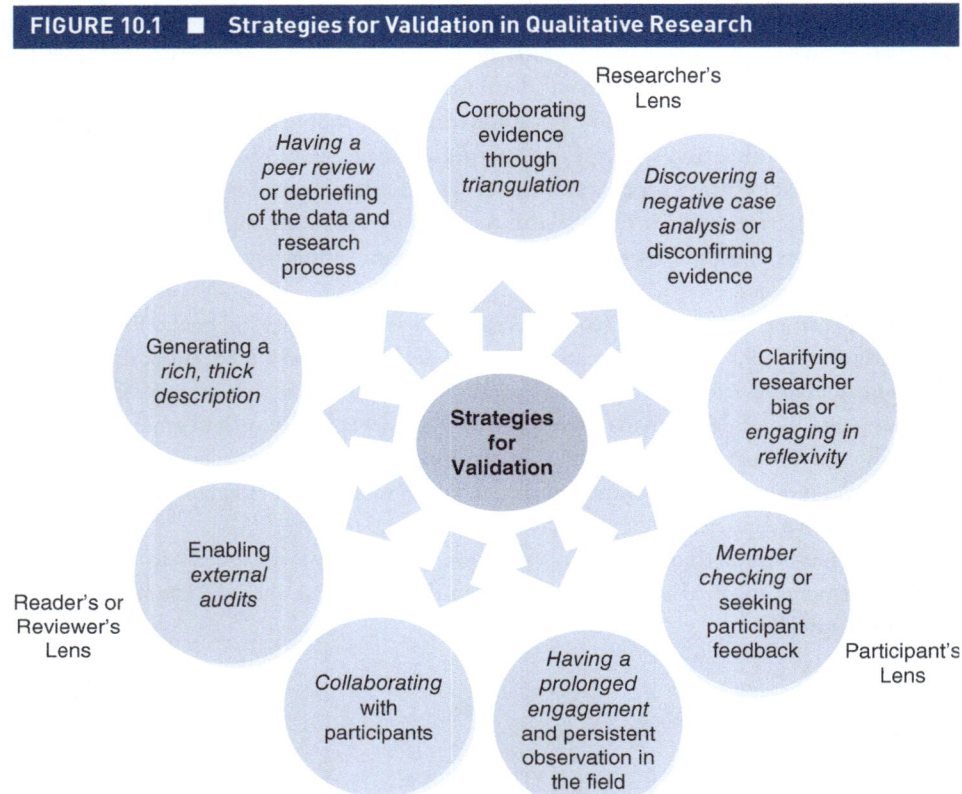

FIGURE 10.1 ■ Strategies for Validation in Qualitative Research

Researcher's Lens

Among the many roles a researcher undertakes is checking the accuracy of a qualitative account and any of the following validation strategies can assist the researcher in this effort:

- *Corroborating evidence through triangulation of multiple data sources.* The researcher makes use of multiple and different sources, methods, investigators, and theories to provide corroborating evidence (Bazeley, 2021; Ely et al., 1991; Erlandson et al., 1993; Gibbs, 2018; Glesne, 2016; Lincoln & Guba, 1985; Miles & Huberman, 1994; Patton, 1980, 1990, 2015; Yin, 2017). Typically, this process involves corroborating evidence from different sources or researchers to shed light on a theme or perspective. When qualitative researchers locate evidence to document a code or theme in different sources of data, they are triangulating information and providing validity to their findings. For this validation strategy, we begin considering how various data sources can be used in tandem when planning the study. Then, as data is collected, we further explore evidence of corroboration and use these insights in our interpretation and writing. See Goodrum et al. (2022; Appendix E) for a description of their data triangulation efforts involving multiple components and official documents.

- *Discovering a negative case analysis or disconfirming evidence.* The researcher refines working hypotheses as the inquiry advances in light of negative or rival evidence (Ely et al., 1991; Lincoln & Guba, 1985; Miles & Huberman, 1994; Patton, 1980, 1990, 2015; Yin, 2017). Not all evidence will fit the pattern of a code or a theme. It is necessary then to report this negative evidence, and in doing so, the researcher provides a realistic assessment of the phenomenon under study. In real life, not all evidence is either positive or negative; it is some of both. For this validation strategy, we both admit that we tend to be attentive to such evidence and make a point of following what we call "points of intrigue" throughout the study. We find these points are often our key points of discussion in our writing.

- *Clarifying researcher bias or engaging in reflexivity.* The researcher discloses their understandings about the biases, values, and experiences that they bring to a qualitative research study from the outset of the study so that the reader understands the position from which the researcher undertakes the inquiry (Hammersley & Atkinson, 1995, 2019; Merriam & Tisdell, 2015). In this clarification, according to Weiner-Levey and Popper-Giveon (2013), the researcher illuminates what they call the "dark matter" that is often omitted in qualitative research by commenting on past experiences, biases, prejudices, and orientations that have likely shaped the interpretation and approach to the study. For this validation strategy, we embed opportunities throughout a study for writing and discussing connections that emerge with our past experiences and perspectives. See Trip et al. (2019; Appendix C) for their description of how memoing helped them engage in reflexivity.

Participant's Lens

Participants can play an important role in the following validation strategies:

- *Member checking or seeking participant feedback.* The researcher solicits participants' views of the credibility of the findings and interpretations (Bazeley, 2021; Ely et al., 1991; Erlandson et al., 1993; Glesne, 2016; Lincoln & Guba, 1985; Merriam & Tisdell, 2015; Miles & Huberman, 1994). This technique is considered by Lincoln and Guba (1985) to be "the most critical technique for establishing credibility" (p. 314). This approach, *writ large* in most qualitative studies, involves taking data, analyses, interpretations, and conclusions back to the participants so that they can judge the accuracy and credibility of the account. According to Stake (1995), participants should "play a major role directing as well as acting in case study" research (p. 115). They should be asked to examine rough drafts of the researcher's work and to provide alternative language, "critical observations or interpretations" (Stake, 1995, p. 115). In so doing, participants play a critical role because they are asked "how well the ongoing data analysis represents their experience" (Hays & Singh, 2012, p. 206). For this validation strategy, we often convene a focus group made up of participants in the study either in person or virtually and ask them to reflect on the accuracy of the account. We do not take back to participants the transcripts or the raw data, but the preliminary analyses consisting of description or themes. We are interested in their views of these written analyses as well as what was missing. Another option is to use e-mail to share a summary of the preliminary findings with focus group participants and seek written feedback. See Richards (2021) for practical guidance about how to interpret participant feedback. Also see Chance (2022; Appendix B) for her description of member checking with participants.

- *Having a prolonged engagement and persistent observation in the field.* The researcher makes field-based decisions about what is salient to study, relevant to the purpose of the study, and of interest for focus. Researchers build rapport with participants and gatekeepers, learn the culture and context, and check for misinformation that stems from distortions introduced by themselves or informants (Ely et al., 1991; Erlandson et al., 1993; Glesne, 2016; Lincoln & Guba, 1985; Merriam & Tisdell, 2015). Fetterman (2019) contended that "participant observation requires close, long-term contact with the people under study" (p. 50). For this validation strategy, we spend as much time in the field as feasible during the study. We begin data collection by familiarizing ourselves with the site and participants. Throughout the study we also reflect upon our observations and documents as our understandings evolve and emerge. See Mac an Ghaill and Haywood (2015; Appendix D) for their description of their 3-year ethnographic work and how access to the community was "greatly enabled by our being known for our social commitment to the local area, working with families in the local community" (p. 111).

- *Collaborating with participants.* The researcher embeds opportunities for participants to be involved throughout the research process in varying ways and degrees. Among the various ways is involvement in key research decisions such as developing data collection protocols and contributing to data analysis and interpretation. The degree to which participants are involved can vary along a continuum from minimal to extensive. Participant involvement is based on the idea (and ever-growing body of research) that the study is more likely to be supported and findings used when participants are involved (Patton, 2011, 2015). For this validation strategy, we are often guided by community-based participatory research practices that involve participants as co-researchers in the study (see, e.g., Hacker, 2013, Wallerstein et al., 2018, for further discussions).

Reader's or Reviewer's Lens

Including others beyond the researcher and those involved in the research contribute in the following validation strategies:

- *Enabling external audits.* The researcher facilitates auditing by securing the services of an external consultant, the auditor, to examine both the process and the product of the account to assess their accuracy (Erlandson et al., 1993; Lincoln & Guba, 1985; Merriam & Tisdell, 2015; Miles & Huberman, 1994). This auditor should have no connection to the study. In assessing the study, the auditor examines whether or not the findings, interpretations, and conclusions are supported by the data. Lincoln and Guba (1985) compared this, metaphorically, with a fiscal audit, and the procedure provided a sense of interrater reliability to a study. This process can be assisted by the creation of documentation, sometimes referred to as an audit trail and described by Silver and Lewins (2014) as "comprising a log of all the processes followed, describing the small analytic leaps contributing to the analysis as a whole" (p. 140). For this validation strategy, we engage in two processes: First, we create a tracking document at the beginning of a study on which we detail our key decisions including rationale and potential consequences. Second, when resources permit, we use an auditor to review our process and findings.

- *Generating a rich, thick description.* The researcher allows readers to make decisions regarding transferability because the writer describes in detail the participants or setting under study (Erlandson et al., 1993; Lincoln & Guba, 1985; Merriam & Tisdell, 2015). With such a detailed description, the researcher enables readers to transfer information to other settings and to determine whether the findings can be transferred "because of shared characteristics" (Erlandson et al., 1993, p. 32). Thick description means that the researcher provides details when describing a case or when writing about a theme. According to Stake (2010), "a description is rich if it provided abundant, interconnected details" (p. 49). Detail can emerge through physical description, movement description, and activity description. It can also involve describing from the general ideas to the narrow, interconnecting the details, and using strong action verbs and quotes. For this validation strategy, we devote time to revisiting our raw data soon after its collection to add further description that might be helpful during the analysis—for example, contextual descriptions like atmosphere. See Chan (2010; Appendix A) for her description of how she was able to generate such a detailed narrative story about an individual's lived experiences from her varied interactions over 2 years that took place at home, at school, with those around her, and the use of extensive field notes.

- *Having a peer review or debriefing of the data and research process.* The researcher seeks an external check by "someone who is familiar with the research or the phenomenon explored" (Creswell & Miller, 2000, p. 129), in much the same spirit as interrater reliability in quantitative research (Ely et al., 1991; Erlandson et al., 1993; Glesne, 2016; Lincoln & Guba, 1985; Merriam & Tisdell, 2015). Lincoln and Guba (1985) defined the role of the peer debriefer as a "devil's advocate," an individual who kept the researcher honest; asked hard questions about methods, meanings, and interpretations; and provided the researcher with the opportunity for catharsis by sympathetically listening to the researcher's feelings. For this validation strategy, we involve colleagues and students as reviewers (and for our students we play this role) in what Lincoln and Guba (1985) called peer debriefing sessions during which both the reviewers and the researcher keep written accounts of the sessions.

Examining these nine validity strategies as a whole (just discussed and outlined in Figure 10.1), we advise that researchers engage in at least *two of them* in any given qualitative study. Unquestionably, procedures such as triangulating among different data sources (assuming that the investigator collects more than one), writing with detailed and thick description, and taking the entire written narrative back to participants in member checking all are reasonably easy procedures to conduct. They also are the most popular and cost-effective procedures. Other procedures, such as peer audits and external audits, are more time-consuming in their application and may also involve substantial costs to the researcher. We also point out that differences among the validity lenses (i.e., researchers, participants, readers, and reviewers) can be attributed to the philosophical orientation of the researcher and may therefore impact their use of specific validation strategies (see Creswell & Báez, 2021, for further discussion).

> **TRY THIS NOW 10.2**
> **COMPARING VALIDATION STRATEGY DESCRIPTIONS IN THE APPENDIX STUDIES**
>
> Comparing the descriptions of validation strategies and evidence across published qualitative studies helps guide researchers in presenting their own studies. Choose two of the Appendix studies to compare. What evidence of the nine data validation strategies summarized in Figure 10.1 can you find in each of the studies? Underline examples of the strategy in use and consider its effectiveness. Could the strategy be used as effectively in other approaches? How might different approaches impact your use of various validation strategies?

Reliability Perspectives and Procedures

Reliability can be addressed in qualitative research in several ways (Bazeley, 2021). Richards (2021) described the need for conveying to readers transparent details about the data-handling processes. This information assured the reliable examination of data records and consistent application of codes and categories. Reliability can be enhanced if the researcher kept detailed field notes and checked the accuracy and completeness of transcriptions of recordings. This completeness included mentioning the trivial, but often crucial, pauses and overlaps. Further coding checks can be done by researchers using a codebook (possibly held by individuals not previously involved in the study). Bazeley (2021) emphasized the need for training a research team and documenting coding and the reliability of coding through computer QDAS programs.

Our focus on reliability here will be on **intercoder agreement** based on the use of multiple coders to analyze transcript data. In qualitative research, *reliability* often refers to the stability of responses by multiple coders of data sets. It is important to develop codes and assess the reliability among coders as part of the analysis process (Kuckartz, & Rädiker, 2023; Richards &

Morse, 2013; Saldaña, 2021). Saldaña (2021) described intercoder agreement as providing a "crowd-sourcing reality check" for each other in the data analysis process (p. 53).

We find this practice especially used in qualitative health science research and within the form of qualitative research in which inquirers want an external check on the highly interpretive coding process. What seems to be largely missing in the literature (with the exception of Armstrong et al., 1997; Bernard, 2017; Campbell et al., 2013; Miles & Huberman, 1994; and Miles et al., 2014, 2019) is a discussion about the procedures of actually conducting intercoder agreement checks. One of the key issues is determining what exactly the coders agree on, whether they seek agreement on code names, the coded passages, or the same passages coded the same way. We also need to decide on whether researchers seek agreement based on codes, themes, or both codes and themes (see Armstrong et al., 1997). Finally, we need to carefully interpret our findings—as Richards (2021) wisely advised, we cannot expect to find complete consistency in coding over time or between coders. Undoubtedly, there is flexibility in the process, and researchers need to fashion an approach consistent with the resources and time to engage in coding.

Drawing upon our experiences working with multiple coders, we propose the following procedures for assessing intercoder agreement in coding of qualitative research (see Figure 10.2):

- *Establish a common platform for coding and develop a preliminary code list.* The researchers decide which software program or paper-based methods they will use; a common platform is essential to be able to easily share the results of their initial read and preliminary coding efforts. In our recent work, we have often used computer-assisted qualitative data analysis software packages (MAXQDA, ATLAS.ti, or NVivo, depending on familiarity across researchers) and have implemented training sessions at the beginning of the study. Each researcher then reads several transcripts

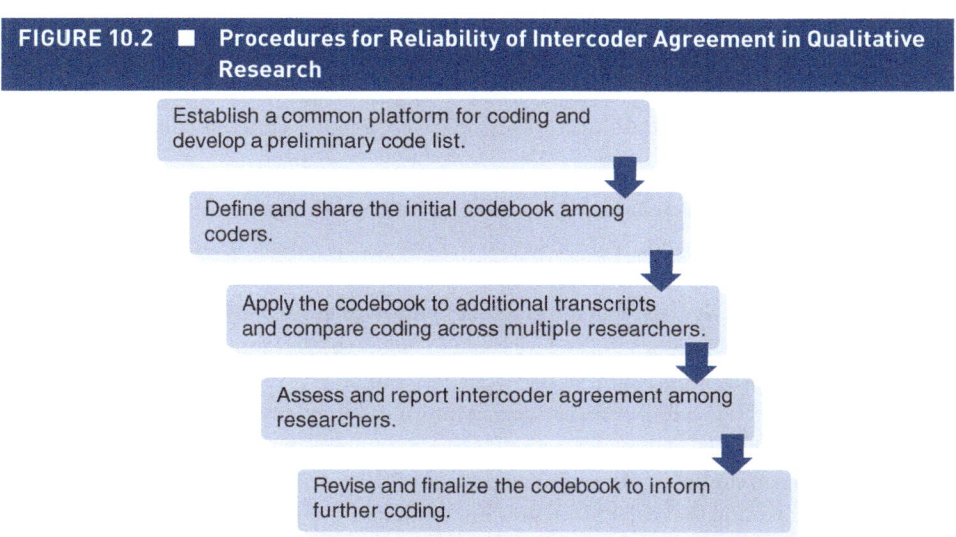

FIGURE 10.2 ■ Procedures for Reliability of Intercoder Agreement in Qualitative Research

independently and develops a list of preliminary codes. As discussed in Chapter 8, computer software programs have features that facilitate the creation of these lists.

- *Develop and share the initial codebook among coders.* The researchers develop a shared understanding of codes to create a codebook that is stable and represents the coding analysis of four independent coders. To do this, after coding, say, three transcripts (i.e., A, B, and C), we then meet and examine the codes, their names, and the text segments that each researcher codes. We begin developing an initial codebook of the major codes. This codebook contains a definition of each code and the text segments that we assigned to each code. In this initial codebook, we had main codes and subcodes. In this initial codebook, we focus on the main codes we were finding in the data rather than forming an exhaustive list. Additional codes are added as the analyses proceed.

- *Apply the codebook to additional transcripts and compare coding across multiple researchers.* The researchers independently apply the shared codebook to additional transcripts and then compare their coding to assess consistency. To do this, the researchers had to agree upon a type of data segment to compare, whether it be a phrase, sentence, or paragraph, and then each researcher independently codes three additional transcripts (i.e., D, E, and F). With no clear guidance in the literature as to what the appropriate data segment should be for coding, consensus can be difficult to reach (Hruschka et al., 2004). To streamline the process in their exploratory study, Campbell and colleagues (2013) suggested having the lead researcher determine the type of data segments to be coded. We feel it is more important to have agreement on the type of data segments we were assigning to codes than to have the same, exact passages coded. The decision about the type of data segment is crucial because it becomes the basis on which intercoder agreement is defined, when we are ready to actually compare our coding. Thus, intercoder agreement means that we agree that when we assign a code word to a passage, we all assign this same code word to the passage. It does not mean that we all code the same passages—an ideal that we believe would be hard to achieve because some people code short passages and others longer passages. Nor does it mean that we all bracket the exact same lines for our code word, another ideal difficult to achieve.

- *Assess and report intercoder agreement among researchers.* The researchers define individual instances of intercoder agreement before assessing overall intercoder agreement. In our work, we tend to take a realistic stance, look at the passages that are coded across researchers, and ask ourselves whether we all assign the same code word to the passage based on our tentative definitions in the codebook. The decision would be either a yes or a no, and we could calculate the percentage of agreement among all researchers on this passage that we all code. We seek to establish a high level of agreement on coding of these passages informed by an 80%-to-90% range that seems a minimal benchmark by many (Miles & Huberman, 1994; Saldaña, 2021). This range is similar to the recommendation by Miles et al. (2014, 2019). We suggest keeping in mind that there is no agreed-upon standard to indicate a high level of intercoder agreement and that the size and range of the coding scheme means it can be difficult (or even impossible) for researchers to reach the 80%-to-90% range of agreement. Many QDAS packages include features to facilitate the calculation among multiple coders. Other researchers might actually calculate a kappa reliability statistic on the agreement, but we feel that a percentage is sufficient to report in our published studies (see also Creswell & Báez, 2021, for practical guidance about three different approaches to intercoder agreement).

- *Revise and finalize the codebook to inform further coding.* The researchers review and refine the codebook to further differentiate code definitions. In our work, after the process continues through several more transcripts, we then revise the codebook and conduct anew an assessment of passages that all researchers code to determine if we apply the same or different codes. With each phase in the intercoder agreement process, we hope to achieve a higher percentage of agreed-upon codes and themes for data segments. Then we can collapse codes into broader themes and can conduct the same process with themes, to see if the passages all coded as themes by the researchers were consistent in the use of the same theme.

TRY THIS NOW 10.3
ASSESSING INTERCODER AGREEMENT IN YOUR CODING PRACTICE

Intercoder agreement represents a key practice for assessing reliability across coders. To conduct this practice, obtain a short text file such as a transcript of an interview or observational field notes. Next, have two or more coders go through a transcript and record their codes. Then look at the passages all coders have identified and see whether their codes are similar or match. Look back at the procedures we propose for intercoder agreement in Figure 10.2 and see which procedures were easy to implement and which ones were more challenging.

EVALUATION CRITERIA FOR QUALITATIVE RESEARCH

In reviewing validation in the qualitative research literature, we are struck by how validation is sometimes used in discussing the quality of a study (e.g., Angen, 2000). Although validation is certainly an aspect of evaluating the quality of a study, other criteria are also useful. In reviewing evaluation criteria, we find that here, too, the standards vary within the qualitative community (see Creswell & Guetterman, 2019, who contrast three approaches to qualitative evaluation). To discuss evaluation, we reprise the features of a "good" qualitative study introduced in Chapter 3, and review three standards (i.e., general standards, interpretive and postmodern standards, and publication standards), and then turn to specific criteria within each of our five approaches to qualitative research.

In Figure 10.3, we present the criteria of a "good" qualitative study presented earlier in our Chapter 3 discussion about the characteristics of qualitative research. Also in Figure 10.3, we reference key content covered in different chapters of this book for each of the "good" features. In this way, readers can review detailed content for each feature.

Other writers provide additional thoughts about helpful evaluation criteria. A methodological perspective comes from Howe and Eisenhardt (1990), who suggested that only broad, abstract standards are possible for qualitative (and quantitative) research. Moreover, to determine, for example, whether a study is a good ethnography cannot be answered apart from whether the study contributes to our understanding of important questions. Silverman (2022) advanced four criteria that good research must satisfy. The following five standards are adapted from Howe and Eisenhardt (1990) and are put in question form for researchers to apply to their work:

FIGURE 10.3 ■ Reprising the Features of a "Good" Qualitative Study

Does the qualitative study do the following?

☐ 1. Meet the assumptions and distinguishing features of the qualitative approach to research?
- The author provides evidence of the defining characteristics described in Table 1.1.

☐ 2. Provide evidence of an ethical study?
- The author provides evidence of having anticipated and addressed the ethical issues described in Tables 3.1, 7.2, 8.3, and 9.1.

☐ 3. Use procedures of a recognizable approach to inquiry?
- The author may refer to the procedures described in Figures 4.3 (narrative), 4.5 (phenomenology), 4.7 (grounded theory), 4.9 (ethnography), and 4.11 (case study).

☐ 4. Explore a single focus or concept?
- The author describes the study focus using research purpose statements such as those in Examples 6.1–6.5.

☐ 5. Employ rigorous data collection procedures?
- The author provides evidence of data collection activities described in Figure 7.1 and Table 7.1.

☐ 6. Detail rigorous data analysis methods?
- The author provides evidence of data spiral activities described in Figure 8.1 and Table 8.5.

☐ 7. Present evidence of multiple levels of abstraction?
- The author provides evidence of the validation strategies in Figure 10.1 and Table 10.2.

☐ 8. Convey the reader experience of "being there" persuasively?
- The author provides evidence of writing structures described in Table 9.2.

☐ 9. Present the researcher's situated role?
- The author provides evidence of their guiding philosophical assumptions and interpretive frameworks described in Tables 2.1, 2.2, and 2.3.

- Does the research question drive the data collection and analysis? (That is, rather than the reverse?) Silverman (2022) states similar criteria about good research using "methods which are demonstrably appropriate to the research problem" (p. 425).

- To what extent are the data collection and analysis techniques competently applied? (That is, in a technical sense?) Silverman (2022) states similar criteria about good research developing "empirically sound, reliable, and valid findings" (p. 425).

- Are the researcher's assumptions made explicit? (That is, such as the researcher's own subjectivity?)

- Does the study have overall warrant? (That is, is it robust, does it use respected theoretical explanations, and does it discuss disconfirmed theoretical explanations?) Silverman (2022) states similar criteria about good research thinking "theoretically through and with data" (p. 425).

- Does the study have value both in informing and improving practice in an ethical manner? (That is, does it contribute to the "so what?" question and is the study conducted ethically? Are participants protected from harm by taking all measures to protect the confidentiality, privacy, and truth telling of participants?) Silverman (2022) states similar criteria about good research contributing "where possible, to practice and policy" (p. 425).

A postmodern, interpretive framework forms a second perspective. Lincoln (1995) thought about the quality issue in terms of emerging criteria. She tracked her own thinking (and that of her late colleague, Guba). Her thinking extended from early approaches of developing parallel methodological criteria (Lincoln & Guba, 1985) to establishing the criteria of "fairness" (a balance of stakeholder views), to sharing knowledge and fostering social action (Guba & Lincoln, 1989), and on to her current stance. Her new emerging approach to quality was based on three new commitments: emergent relations with respondents, a set of stances, and a vision of research that enables and promotes justice. Based on these commitments, Lincoln (1995) then proceeded to identify several standards of quality:

- The standard is set in the inquiry community, such as by guidelines for publication. These guidelines admit that within diverse approaches to research, inquiry communities have developed their own traditions of rigor, communication, and ways of working toward consensus. These guidelines, she also maintains, serve to exclude legitimate research knowledge and social science researchers.

- The standard of positionality guides interpretive or qualitative research. Drawing on those concerned about standpoint epistemology, this means that the text should display honesty or authenticity about its own stance and about the position of the author.

- Another standard is under the rubric of community. This standard acknowledges that all research takes place in, is addressed to, and serves the purposes of the community in which it is carried out. Such communities might be feminist thought, Black scholarship, Native American studies, or ecological studies.

- Interpretive or qualitative research must give voice to participants so that their voice is not silenced, disengaged, or marginalized. Moreover, this standard requires that alternative or multiple voices be heard in a text.

- Critical subjectivity as a standard means that the researcher needs to have heightened self-awareness in the research process and create personal and social transformation. This "high-quality awareness" enables the researcher to understand his or her psychological and emotional states before, during, and after the research experience.

- High-quality interpretive or qualitative research involves reciprocity between the researcher and those being researched. This standard requires that intense sharing, trust, and mutuality exist.

- The researcher should respect the sacredness of relationships in the research-to-action continuum. This standard means that the researcher respects the collaborative and egalitarian aspects of research and "make[s] spaces for the lifeways of others" (Lincoln, 1995, p. 284).

- Sharing of the privileges acknowledges that in good qualitative research, researchers share their rewards with persons whose lives they portray. This sharing may be in the form of royalties from books or the sharing of rights to publication.

A final perspective uses interpretive standards for conducting qualitative research. Drawing from their own experience reviewing papers or monographs submitted for social science publication, Richardson (in Richardson & St. Pierre, 2018) suggests the following criteria:

- *Substantive contribution*. Does this piece contribute to our understanding of social life? Does the writer demonstrate a deeply grounded (if embedded) social scientific perspective? Does this piece seem "true"—a credible account of a cultural, social, individual, or communal sense of the "real"?

- *Aesthetic merit*. Does this piece succeed aesthetically? Does the use of creative analytical practices open up the text and invite interpretive responses? Is the text artistically shaped, satisfying, complex, and not boring?

- *Reflexivity*. How has the author's subjectivity been both a producer and a product of this text? Is there adequate self-awareness and self-exposure for the reader to make judgments about the point of view? Does the author hold himself or herself accountable to the standards of knowing and telling of the people he or she has studied?

- *Impact*. Does this piece affect me emotionally or intellectually? Does it generate new questions or move me to write? Does it move me to try new research practices or move me to action? (p. 823)

As applied research methodologists, we prefer the methodological standards of evaluation, but we can also support the postmodern and interpretive perspectives. We also agree with Flick (2014), who stated, "the problem of how to assess qualitative research has not yet been solved" (p. 480). Still, we return to our criteria for a "good" qualitative study as mentioned in Figure 10.3. Our features highlight the choice of a methodological approach (i.e., one of the five approaches mentioned in this book) and strong methods for data collection and analysis in a qualitative study. Next we discuss specific evaluative criteria for each of the five approaches.

EVALUATION CRITERIA SPECIFIC TO EACH OF THE FIVE APPROACHES

In the section that follows, we provide practical guidance of evaluation criteria specific to each of the five approaches of qualitative inquiry. What standards of evaluation, beyond those already mentioned, would signal a high-quality narrative study, a phenomenology, a grounded theory study, an ethnography, and a case study?

Narrative Research

In discussing what makes for a good narrative study, both Riessman (2008) and Clandinin (2013, 2023) pointed to seeking coherence of participants' narratives yet acknowledged that it may not always be possible. To that end, Riessman (2008) proposed questions for assessing coherence (p. 189):

- Do episodes of a life story hang together?
- Are sections of a theoretical argument linked and consistent?
- Are there major gaps and inconsistencies?
- Is the interpreter's analytic account persuasive?

In 2013, Clandinin proposed a way for "judging and responding to narrative inquiries" (p. 211) by describing what she and Vera Caine defined as touchstones:

> While one meaning directs our attention to a touchstone as a quality of example that is used to test the excellence or genuineness of others, we were also drawn to a touchstone as a hard black stone, such as jasper or basalt, that was used to test the quality of gold or silver by comparing the streak left on the stone by one of these metals with that of a standard alloy. We wondered, if we metaphorically touched or scratched a narrative inquiry, what kinds of streaks or marks would be left. (Clandinin & Caine, 2013, p. 191)

Clandinin (2023, p. 146) listed the following 12 touchstones and considered them as evolving (see also Clandinin & Caine, 2013, for in-depth touchstone descriptions):

1. Relational responsibilities
2. In the midst
3. Negotiation of relationships

4. Narrative beginnings
5. Negotiating entry to the field
6. Moving from field to field texts
7. Moving from field texts to interim and final research texts
8. Representing narratives of experience in ways that show temporality, sociality, and place
9. Relational response communities
10. Justifications—personal, practical, social
11. Attentive to multiple audiences
12. Commitment to understanding lives in motion

When writing an interpretive biography, Denzin (1989) was primarily interested in the problem of "how to locate and interpret the subject in biographical materials" (p. 26). Denzin (1989) advanced several guidelines for writing:

> The lived experiences of interacting individuals are the proper subject matter of sociology. The meanings of these experiences are best given by the persons who experience them; thus, a preoccupation with method, validation, reliability, generalizability, and theoretical relevance of the biographical method must be set aside in favor of a concern for meaning and interpretation.
>
> Students of the biographical method must learn how to use the strategies and techniques of literary interpretation and criticism (i.e., bring their method in line with the concern about reading and writing of social texts, where texts are seen as "narrative fictions." (p. 26)

Thus, within a humanistic, interpretive stance, Denzin (2001) identified "criteria of interpretation" as a standard for judging the quality of a biography. These criteria were based on respecting the researcher's perspective as well as thick description. Denzin (2001) advocated for the ability of the researcher to illuminate the phenomenon in a thickly contextualized manner (i.e., thick description of developed context) so as to reveal the historical, processual, and interactional features of the experience. Also, the researcher's interpretation engulfed what was learned about the phenomenon and incorporated prior understandings while always remaining incomplete and unfinished.

This focus on interpretation and thick description was in contrast to criteria established within the more traditional approach to biographical writing. For example, Plummer (1983) asserted three sets of questions for a good life history study:

- Is the individual representative? Edel (1984) asked a similar question: How has the biographer distinguished between reliable and unreliable witnesses?
- What are the sources of bias (about the participant, the researcher, and the participant–researcher interaction)? Or, as Edel (1984) questions, how has the researcher avoided making himself or herself simply the voice of the subject?

- Is the account valid when subjects are asked to read it, when it is compared to official records, and when it is compared to accounts from other participants?

In Figure 10.4, we advance five criteria for guiding what we would look for in a narrative study.

FIGURE 10.4 ■ Guiding Evaluative Criteria for a Narrative Study

Does the narrative study do the following?

☐ 1. Focus on an individual?

- The author may focus on one or more individuals.

☐ 2. Collect stories about a significant issue?

- The author may focus on the stories told by the individual or individuals.

☐ 3. Develop a chronology?

- The author may use a chronology to connect different phases or aspects of a story.

☐ 4. Tell a story?

- The author may, through the story, report what was said (themes), how it was said (unfolding story), or how speakers interact or perform the narrative.

☐ 5. Embed reflexivity?

- The author may use reflexive thinking and writing to bring himself or herself into the study.

Phenomenological Research

What criteria should be used to judge the quality of a phenomenological study? From the many readings about phenomenology, one can infer criteria from the discussions about steps (Giorgi, 1985) or the "core facets" of transcendental phenomenology (Moustakas, 1994, p. 58). We have found direct discussions of the criteria to be missing, but perhaps Polkinghorne's (1989) discussion of whether the findings are "valid" (p. 57) and van Manen's (2014) outline of validation and evaluative criteria come the closest in our readings.

For Polkinghorne, validation referred to the notion that an idea was well grounded and well supported. He asked, "Does the general structural description provide an accurate portrait of the common features and structural connections that are manifest in the examples collected?" (Polkinghorne, 1989, p. 57). He then proceeded to identify five questions that researchers might ask themselves:

- Did the interviewer influence the contents of the participants' descriptions in such a way that the descriptions do not truly reflect the participants' actual experience?

- Is the transcription accurate, and does it convey the meaning of the oral presentation in the interview?

- In the analysis of the transcriptions, were there conclusions other than those offered by the researcher that could have been derived? Has the researcher identified these alternatives?

- Is it possible to go from the general structural description to the transcriptions and to account for the specific contents and connections in the original examples of the experience?

- Is the structural description situation specific, or does it hold in general for the experience in other situations? (Polkinghorne, 1989)

Van Manen (2014) pointed to questions as a way to "test [a phenomenology's] level of validity" (p. 350).

- Is the study based on a valid phenomenological question? In other words, does the study ask, "What is this human experience like?" "How is this or that phenomenon or event experienced?" A phenomenological question should not be confused with empirical studies of a particular population, person(s), or group of people at a particular time and location. Also, phenomenology cannot deal with causal questions or theoretical explanations. However, a particular individual or group may be studied for the understanding of a phenomenological theme—such as a gender phenomenon, a sociopolitical event, or the experience of a human disaster.

- Is the analysis performed on experientially descriptive accounts, transcripts? (Does the analysis avoid empirical material that mostly consists of perceptions, opinions, beliefs, views, and so on?)

- Is the study properly rooted in primary and scholarly phenomenological literature—rather than mostly relying on questionable secondary and tertiary sources?

- Does the study avoid trying to legitimate itself with validation criteria derived from sources that are concerned with other (non-phenomenological) methodologies (van Manen, 2014, pp. 350–351)?

Van Manen (2014) also provided criteria for evaluative appraisal of phenomenological studies.

- *Heuristic questioning*: Does the text induce a sense of contemplative wonder and questioning attentiveness—*ti estin* (the wonder [of] what this is) and *hoti estin* (the wonder that something exists at all)?

- *Descriptive richness*: Does the text contain rich and recognizable experiential material?

- *Interpretive depth*: Does the text offer reflective insights that go beyond the taken-for-granted understandings of everyday life?

- *Distinctive rigor*: Does the text remain constantly guided by a self-critical question of distinct meaning of the phenomenon or event?

- *Strong and addressive meaning*: Does the text "speak" to and address our sense of embodied meaning?

- *Experiential awakening*: Does the text awaken prereflective or primal experience through vocative and presentative language?

- *Inceptual epiphany*: Does the study offer us the possibility of deeper and original insight, and perhaps, an intuitive or inspired grasp of the ethics and ethos of life commitments and practices? (pp. 355–356)

In Figure 10.5, we advance our five standards for assessing the quality of a phenomenology.

FIGURE 10.5 ■ Standards for Assessing the Quality of a Phenomenology

Does the phenomenology do the following?

☐ 1. Articulate a clear "phenomenon" to study in a concise way?
- The author may use a phenomenological question to guide the study.

☐ 2. Convey an understanding of the philosophical tenets of phenomenology?
- The author may ground the study in primary and scholarly phenomenological literature.

☐ 3. Use procedures of data analysis in phenomenology?
- The author may refer to procedures recommended by Moustakas (1994) or van Manen (1990, 2023).

☐ 4. Communicate the overall essence of the experience of the participants?
- The author may describe the context in which the experience occurred.

☐ 5. Embed reflexivity throughout the study?
- The author may explain the process and outcomes of reflexive thinking.

Grounded Theory Research

Strauss and Corbin (1990) identified criteria by which one judges the quality of a grounded theory study. They described seven criteria related to the general research process and six criteria related to the empirical grounding of a study. Corbin and Strauss (2015) advanced the term *checkpoint* in place of criteria, saying they "dislike using the word *criteria* because that makes the evaluative process seem so dogmatic, an 'all [or] nothing' approach to evaluation" (p. 350, emphasis in original).

Corbin and Strauss (2015) described 16 checkpoints for guiding researchers and reviewers in evaluating the "methodoloical consistency" of a grounded theory study:

1. What was the target sample population? How was the original sample selected?

2. How did sampling proceed? What kinds of data were collected? Were there multiple sources of data and multiple comparative groups?

3. Did data collection alternate with analysis?

4. Were ethical considerations taken into account in both data collection and analysis?

5. Were the concepts driving the data collection arrived at through analysis (based on theoretical sampling), or were concepts derived from the literature and established before the data were collected not true theoretical sampling)?
6. Was theoretical sampling used, and was there a description of how it proceeded?
7. Did the research demonstrate sensitivity to the participants and to the data?
8. Is there evidence or examples of memos?
9. At what point did data collection end or a discussion of saturation end?
10. Is there a description of how coding proceeded along with examples of theoretical sampling, concepts, categories, and statements of relations? What were some of the events, incidents, or actions (indicators) that pointed to some of these major categories?
11. Is there a core category, and is there a description of how that core category was arrived at?
12. Were there changes in design as the research went along based on findings?
13. Did the researcher(s) encounter any problems while doing the research? Is there any mention of a negative case, and how was that data handled?
14. Are methodological decisions made clear so that readers can judge their appropriateness for gathering data (theoretical sampling) and doing analysis?
15. Was there feedback on the findings from other professionals and from participants? And were changes made in the theory based on this feedback?
16. Did the researcher keep a research journal or notebook? (Corbin & Strauss, 2015, pp. 350–351)

Corbin and Strauss (2015) also advanced 17 checkpoints for researchers and reviewers to evaluate the "quality and applicability" of a grounded theory study:

1. What is the core category, and how do the major categories relate to it? Is there a diagram depicting these relationship?
2. Is the core category sufficiently broad so that it can be used to study other populations and similar situations beyond this setting?
3. Are each of the categories developed in terms of their properties and dimensions so that they show depth, breadth, and variation?
4. Is there descriptive data given under each category that brings that theory to life so that it provides understanding and can be used in a variety of situations?
5. Has context been identified and integrated into the theory? Conditions and consequences should be listed merely as background information in a separate section but woven into the actual analysis with explanations of how they impact and flow from action–interaction in the data.

6. Has process been incorporated into the theory in the form of changes in action–interaction in relationship to changes in conditions? Is action–interaction matched to different situations, demonstrating how the theory might vary under different conditions and therefore be applied to different situations?

7. How is saturation explained, and when and how was it determined that categories were saturated?

8. Do the findings resonate or fit with the experience of both the professionals for whom the research ended and the participants who took part in the study? Can participants see themselves in the story even if not every detail applies to them?

9. Are there gaps, or missing links, in the theory, leaving the reader confused and with a sense that something is missing?

10. Is there an account of extremes or negative cases?

11. Is variation built into the theory?

12. Are the findings presented in a creative and innovative manner? Does the research say something new or put old ideas together in new ways?

13. Do findings give insight into situation and provide knowledge that can be applied to develop policy, change practice, and add to the knowledge base of a profession?

14. Do the theoretical findings seem significant, and to what extent? It is entirely possible to complete a theory-generating study, or any research investigation, yet not produce findings that are significant.

15. Do the findings have the potential to become part of the discussion and ideas exchanged among relevant social and professional groups?

16. Are the limitations of the study clearly spelled out?

17. Are there suggestions for practice, policy, teaching, and application of the research? (Corbin & Strauss, 2015, pp. 351–352)

Charmaz (2014) reflected on the quality of the theory developed in a grounded theory study She suggested that grounded theorists look at their theory and ask themselves the following evaluative questions:

- Are the definitions of major categories complete?
- Have I raised major categories to concepts in my theory?
- How have I increased the scope and depth of the analysis in this draft?
- Have I established strong theoretical links between categories and between categories and their properties, in addition to the data?
- How have I increased understanding of the studied phenomenon?

- How does my grounded theory study make a fresh contribution?

- With which theoretical, substantive, or practical problems is this analysis most closely aligned? Which audiences might be most interested in it? Where shall I go with it?

- What implications does this analysis hold for theoretical reach, depth, and breadth? For methods? For substantive knowledge? For actions or interventions? (Charmaz, 2014, pp. 337–338)

See also Charmaz (2014, pp. 337–338) for guiding questions for assessing criteria for grounded theory studies organized by four categories: credibility, originality, resonance, and usefulness.

In Figure 10.6, we describe features of the general process and a relationship among the concepts we look for when evaluating a grounded theory study.

FIGURE 10.6 ■ Features for Evaluating a Grounded Theory Study

Does the grounded theory study do the following?

☐ 1. Focus on the study of a process, an action, or an interaction as the key element in the theory?

- The author may focus on the steps that unfold when studying a central phenomenon as a process, action, or interaction among individuals.

☐ 2. Integrate a coding process that works from the data to a larger theoretical model?

- The author may describe the data collection as alternating with data analysis to build a theoretical model.

☐ 3. Present the theoretical model in a figure or diagram?

- The author may use innovative means for presenting the theory in a creative and innovative manner.

☐ 4. Advance a story line or proposition connected with the categories in the theoretical model that presents further questions to be answered?

- The author may refer to the overall picture emerging in the current study as a springboard for future directions of research.

☐ 5. Use memoing through the process of research?

- The author may describe the different types of memos or ways of recording emerging ideas throughout the process of conducting the study.

☐ 6. Embed evidence of reflexivity for self-disclosure by the researcher about their study "positioning"?

- The author may describe how a research journal documented their reflexive thinking during the study.

Ethnographic Research

Few ethnographic writers identify criteria for quality ethnographies. Instead, the preference, it seems, for ethnographers is to describe the "basics" of ethnographical studies as prolonged fieldwork that generate thick and contextual descriptions reflective of triangulating multiple data sources (Fetterman, 2010, 2019; Wolcott, 2008a, 2010). An exception is Spindler and Spindler (1987).

The ethnographers Spindler and Spindler (1987) emphasized that the most important requirement for an ethnographic approach was to explain behavior from the "native's point of view" (p. 20) and to be systematic in recording this information using note taking, tape recorders, and cameras. This required that the ethnographer be present in the situation and engage in constant interaction between observation and interviews. These points were reinforced in Spindler and Spindler's (1987) nine criteria for a "good ethnography":

Criterion I. Observations are contextualized.

Criterion II. Hypotheses emerge *in situ* as the study goes on.

Criterion III. Observation is prolonged and repetitive.

Criterion IV. Through interviews, observations, and other eliciting procedures, the native view of reality is obtained.

Criterion V. Ethnographers elicit knowledge from informant-participants in a systematic fashion.

Criterion VI. Instruments, codes, schedules, questionnaires, agenda for interviews, and so forth are generated *in situ* as a result of inquiry.

Criterion VII. A transcultural, comparative perspective is frequently an unstated assumption.

Criterion VIII. The ethnographer makes explicit what is implicit and tacit to informants.

Criterion IX. The ethnographic interviewer must not predetermine responses by the kinds of questions asked. (p. 18)

This list, grounded in fieldwork, leads to a strong ethnography. Moreover, as Lofland (1974) contended, the study was located in wide conceptual frameworks; presented the novel but not necessarily new; provided evidence for the framework(s); was endowed with concrete, eventful interactional events, incidents, occurrences, episodes, anecdotes, scenes, and happenings without being "hyper-eventful"; and showed an interplay between the concrete and analytical and the empirical and theoretical.

In Figure 10.7, we advance seven evaluative criteria for an ethnography.

> **FIGURE 10.7 ■ Criteria for Evaluating an Ethnography**
>
> **Does the ethnography do the following?**
>
> ☐ 1. Convey evidence of clear identification of a culture-sharing group?
>
> - The author may describe the group in some detail—how the group was selected, how access to the group was facilitated including any involvement of gatekeepers, how the group interacts, how the group communicates, and so forth.
>
> ☐ 2. Specify a cultural theme that will be examined in light of this culture-sharing group?
>
> - The author may identify a cultural theme and the rationale for choosing it.
>
> ☐ 3. Describe the cultural group in detail?
>
> - The author may use creative analytical practices to convey these descriptions.
>
> ☐ 4. Communicate themes derived from an understanding of the cultural group?
>
> - The author may organize a thematic narrative or tale.
>
> ☐ 5. Identify issues that arose during fieldwork that reflect on the relationship between the researcher and the participants, the interpretive nature of reporting, and sensitivity and reciprocity in the co-creating of the account?
>
> - The author may describe a working set of rules or generalizations as to how the culture-sharing group functions.
>
> ☐ 6. Explain how the culture-sharing group works overall?
>
> - The author may describe a working set of rules or generalizations as to how the culture-sharing group functions.
>
> ☐ 7. Integrate self-disclosure and reflexivity by the researcher about their position in the research?
>
> - The author may describe their background experiences with the group and describe their reflections about interactions with the group.

Case Study Research

Yin (2017) reflected on the quality of the description presented in a case study. He described several characteristics for an exemplary case study.

- *Significant*: Has the researcher focused the case(s) as "unusual and of general public interest" or underlying issues as "nationally important—either in theoretical terms or in policy or practical terms" (p. 242)?

- *Complete*: Has the researcher clearly defined the case(s) boundaries, collected extensive evidence, and conducted the study absent "of certain artefactual conditions" (p. 244)—for example, if a time or resource constraint unwittingly ended the study?

- *Consider alternative perspectives*: Has the researcher considered rival propositions and sought to collect evidence from differing perspectives in the case(s)?

- *Display sufficient evidence*: Has the researcher reported the case(s) in such a way that a reader can "reach an independent judgment regarding the merits" (p. 246)?
- *Composed in an engaging manner*: Has the researcher presented the case(s) in a way that communicates "the results widely"—either in writing or performance (p. 247)?

G. Thomas (2021) asked case study researchers to consider the following three questions:

1. *How well has the case been chosen?* Thomas's discussions of quality are aptly focused on appropriate sampling and procedural decisions.
2. *How well has the context for the study been explained and justified?* Thomas pointed to the need for detailed contextual descriptions to be able to assess decisions justifying how analysis has been undertaken.
3. *How well have arguments been made?* Thomas explained the role of rival explanations to provide "space to think about alternative storylines for the same plot" (p. 81).

Stake (1995) described evaluative criteria for a case study using a rather extensive "critique checklist." In so doing, Stake (1995) shared criteria for assessing a good case study report:

- Is the report easy to read?
- Does it fit together, each sentence contributing to the whole?
- Does the report have a conceptual structure (i.e., themes or issues)?
- Are its issues developed in a serious and scholarly way?
- Is the case adequately defined?
- Is there a sense of story to the presentation?
- Is the reader provided some vicarious experience?
- Have quotations been used effectively?
- Are headings, figures, artifacts, appendixes, and indexes used effectively?
- Was it edited well—and then again with a last-minute polish?
- Has the writer made sound assertions, neither over- nor misinterpreting?
- Has adequate attention been paid to various contexts?
- Were sufficient raw data presented?
- Were data sources well-chosen and in sufficient number?
- Do observations and interpretations appear to have been triangulated?
- Is the role and point of view of the researcher nicely apparent?
- Is the nature of the intended audience apparent?

- Is empathy shown for all sides?
- Are personal intentions examined?
- Does it appear that individuals were put at risk? (p. 131)

In Figure 10.8, we describe our criteria for evaluating a case study.

FIGURE 10.8 ■ Evaluative Criteria for a Case Study

Does the case study do the following?

☐ **1.** Identify the case studied?
- The author may identify the boundaries and time parameters of a single case or multiple cases.

☐ **2.** Present a rationale for the case(s) selection?
- The author may identify rationales for selecting the case, such as the intent to understand a research issue or describe intrinsic merit.

☐ **3.** Describe the case(s) in detail?
- The author may begin with a rich description of the case(s) and its setting or context(s).

☐ **4.** Articulate the themes identified for the case(s)?
- The author may focus on a few key thematic issues for an individual case(s) or across cases.

☐ **5.** Report assertions or generalizations from the case analysis?
- The author may interpret how the case(s) provides insight into the issue, or the findings can be generalized to other cases. Sometimes this may take the form of a summary statement or a vignette.

☐ **6.** Embed researcher self-disclosure about their position in the study?
- The author may use reflexive practices and writing throughout the study.

COMPARING EVALUATION STANDARDS ACROSS THE FIVE APPROACHES

The standards discussed for each approach differ slightly depending on the procedures of the approaches. Certainly, less is mentioned about narrative research and its standards of quality, and more is available about the other approaches. From within the major books used for each approach, we have attempted to extract the evaluation standards recommended for their approach to research. To these, we have added our own standards that we use in our qualitative classes when we evaluate a project or study presented within each of the five approaches. We can compare these standards across the five approaches relating five dimensions summarized in Table 10.2.

TABLE 10.2 ■ Comparing the Evaluation Standards Across the Five Qualitative Approaches

Criterion	Narrative Research	Phenomenology	Grounded Theory	Ethnography	Case Study
What is the focus of the study?	Focuses on a single individual (or two or three individuals)	Articulates a "phenomenon" to study in a concise way	Studies a process, an action, or an interaction as the key element in the theory	Identifies a culture-sharing group	Identifies the study case (or multiple cases)
How does the study proceed?	Collects stories about a significant issue related to the individual's life	Conveys an understanding of the philosophical tenets of phenomenology Uses recommended procedures of data analysis in phenomenology	Integrates a coding process that works from the data to a larger theoretical model Uses memoing throughout the process of research	Specifies a cultural theme that will be examined in light of this culture-sharing group Identifies issues that arose in the field	Rationalizes case(s) selection in terms of understandings that will be generated Identifies themes for the case (or across cases)
How is the study presented?	Develops a chronology that connects different phases or aspects of a story	Presents a discussion of "what" is the essence of the phenomenon and "how" individuals have experienced the phenomenon	Presents the theoretical model in a figure or diagram	Communicates themes derived from an understanding of the cultural group	Reports assertions or generalizations from the case analysis
What is the study outcome?	Tells a story that reports what was said (themes), how it was said (unfolding story), and how speakers interact or perform	Communicates the overall essence of the experience of the phenomenon	Advances a story line or proposition that connects categories in the theoretical model and presents further questions	Describes the cultural group in detail Explains how the culture-sharing group works overall	Details a description of the case(s)
What does a researcher bring to the study?	Uses reflexive thinking and writing	Embeds reflexivity throughout the study	Self-discloses his or her stance	Integrates reflexivity about her or his position	Uses reflexivity about his or her position

At the most fundamental level, the five differ in the focus of the study. A couple of potential similarities should be noted. Phenomenology, grounded theory, and ethnography typically focus the study on a singular phenomenon, process (or action or interaction), and culture-sharing group, respectively. One may also focus narrative research or a case study on a single individual or case but it also possible to focus on two or three individuals or multiple cases. The study procedures offer distinguishing features for each approach in which some research features the collection of stories (i.e., narrative), specification of cultural themes (i.e., ethnography), and selection of cases (i.e., case study). Others such as phenomenology are distinguishable by initial conveyance of an understanding of the philosophical tenets or integration of analysis into data collection activities and use of memoing (i.e., grounded theory). When examining a study, the approach can be identifiable by its presentation and outcomes of a story chronology for narrative research, theoretical diagramming for grounded theory research, explanation of how a culture-sharing group works for ethnography, and the assertions for a case study. Common across all the qualitative approaches is the use of reflexive and self-disclosing practices for embedding what the researcher brings to the study.

CHAPTER CHECK-IN

1. Can you identify the characteristics of "thick description" to develop a deeper understanding of how cases, settings, and themes are presented in a qualitative study?
    a. Look for a detailed description in a short story or a novel. If you do not find one, you might use the short story about the "Cat 'n' Mouse" as found in Steven Millhauser's book (2008), *Dangerous Laughter*.
    b. Next, identify passages in which Millhauser (2008) creates detail by physical passages, movement, or activity description.
    c. Finally, identify how the author interconnects the details.
2. Can you apply the specific evaluation criteria for each of the five approaches presented in Figures 10.4–10.8 to assess the quality of a published account? Select one of the approaches, find a journal article that uses the approach, and then see if you can find the key evaluation criteria for that approach in the article.

SUMMARY

In this chapter, we discussed validation, reliability, and standards of evaluation in qualitative research. Validation approaches vary considerably, such as strategies that emphasize using qualitative terms comparable to quantitative terms, the use of distinct terms, perspectives from postmodern and interpretive lenses, syntheses of different perspectives, descriptions based on metaphorical images, or some combination of these perspectives on validity. Reliability is used in qualitative research in several ways, one of the most popular being the use of intercoder agreements when multiple coders analyze and then compare their code segments to establish the reliability of the data analysis process. A detailed procedure for establishing intercoder agreement is described in this chapter. Also, diverse standards exist for evaluating the quality of qualitative research, and these criteria are based on methods perspectives, general research perspectives, postmodern perspectives, and interpretive perspectives. Within each of the five approaches to inquiry, specific standards also exist; these were reviewed in this chapter. Finally, we advanced standards that we use to assess the quality of studies presented in each approach and we compare the evaluating standards across the five approaches.

CHAPTER KEY TERMS

Credibility
Intercoder agreement
Quality criteria
Reliability

Triangulation
Trustworthiness
Validation strategies
Validity

FURTHER READINGS

In addition to many of the resources already suggested in earlier chapters that include perspectives and guidance for evaluation, validation, and reliability in qualitative research, we highlight a few key resources here. The list should not be considered exhaustive and readers are encouraged to seek out additional readings in the end-of-book reference list.

Resources Focused on Validation Perspectives

Angen, M. J. (2000). Evaluating interpretive inquiry: Reviewing the validity debate and opening the dialogue. *Qualitative Health Research, 10*(3), 378–395. https://doi.org/10.1177/104973230001000308

Maureen Jane Angen traces the origins of validity and suggests its application within interpretive approaches. In so doing, she relates validity to terms of trustworthiness and validation strategies.

Lincoln, Y. S., & Guba, E. G. (1985). *Naturalistic inquiry.* Sage.

In this classical text, Yvonna Lincoln and Egon Guba describe the alternative terms for validation in qualitative research that remain in use today. This is a must-read for many researchers.

Richards, L. (2021). *Handling qualitative data: A practical guide* (4th ed.). Sage.

In this updated edition, Lyn Richards guides researchers in generating reliable coding and valid interpretations of qualitative data. The text is organized by setting up, handling, and making sense of data.

Whittemore, R., Chase, S. K., & Mandle, C. L. (2001). Validity in qualitative research. *Qualitative Health Research, 11*(4), 522–537. https://doi.org/10.1177/104973201129119299

In their exploration of validity issues in 13 writings of qualitative research, Robin Whittemore and colleagues extract key validation criteria and organize them into four primary and six secondary criteria. The article also provides a comprehensive description of historical development of validity issues in qualitative research.

Resources Focused on Reliability Perspectives

Armstrong, D., Gosling, A., Weinman, J., & Marteau, T. (1997). The place of inter-rater reliability in qualitative research: An empirical study. *Sociology, 31*(3), 597–606. https://doi.org/10.1177/0038038597031003015

The authors use the assessment of interrater reliability among six researchers as a springboard for discussing procedures of conducting intercoder agreement checks. Noteworthy is their focus on key issues related to what coding agreements specify.

Bernard, H. R. (2017). *Research methods in anthropology: Qualitative and quantitative approaches* (6th ed.). Rowman & Littlefield.

H. Russel Bernard's text is unique for its focus on qualitative and quantitative data about human thought and behavior. See his discussion on codebooks and intercoder agreement.

Campbell, J. L., Quincy, C., Osserman, J., & Pederson, O. K. (2013). Coding in-depth semistructured interviews: Problems of unitization and intercoder reliability and agreement. *Sociological Methods & Research, 42*(3), 294–320. https://doi.org/10.1177/0049124113500475

The authors provide practical procedures for reliability of coding in an exploratory study. Of particular interest was the discussion related to the possible impact of coder knowledge of the text being coded.

Miles, M. B., Huberman, A. M., & Saldaña, J. (2019). *Qualitative data analysis: A sourcebook of new methods* (4th ed.). Sage.

This book is a must-read for qualitative researchers. We especially like Chapter 11 "Drawing and Verifying Conclusions," and their discussion of reliability.

Resources Focused on Qualitative Evaluation Criteria

Howe, K., & Eisenhardt, M. (1990). Standards for qualitative (and quantitative) research: A prolegomenon. *Educational Researcher, 19*(4), 2–9. https://doi.org/10.3102/0013189X019004002

Kenneth Howe and Margaret Eisenhardt contribute important discussions of quality standards of research; methodological competence; making researcher assumptions explicit; and a study's warrant, practical, and theoretical implications. An essential read for understanding historical developments.

Lincoln, Y. S. (1995). Emerging criteria for quality in qualitative and interpretive research. *Qualitative Inquiry, 1*, 275–289. https://doi.org/10.1177/107780049500100301

In this work, Yvonna Lincoln relates the researcher's relationship with research participants as a measure of quality—for example, meeting ethical standards such as reciprocity would serve as necessary criteria.

Richardson, L., & St. Pierre, E. A. (2018). Writing: A method of inquiry. In N. K. Denzin & Y. S. Lincoln (Eds.), *The SAGE handbook of qualitative research* (5th ed., pp. 818–838). Sage.

Laurel Richardson and Elizabeth Adams St. Pierre offer two individual yet complementary perspectives on evaluative criteria. A hidden gem is the discussion of creative analytical writing practices.

Silverman, D. (2022). *Doing qualitative research: A practical handbook* (6th ed.). Sage.

David Silverman provides practical guidance for planning and conducting high-quality qualitative research. Of particular note is his discussion on reliability and illustrative examples embedded throughout.

11 "TURNING THE STORY" AND CONCLUSION

> **QUESTIONS FOR DISCUSSION**
>
> - How does turning the story across the five approaches differ?
> - What are seven key "takeaways" from this book?

How might the story be different if it were turned into a case study, a narrative project, a phenomenology, a grounded theory study, or an ethnography? Would the final report of some approaches appear more similar than others and if so, in what ways? In this final chapter, we demonstrate how the "story becomes turned" across the five approaches to qualitative inquiry discussed in this book. By "turning" we mean that the same problem is addressed by constructing a study using each of the five approaches.

Our illustrative example represents how we would think about and structure a qualitative study across the five approaches. In our experience, this chapter helps researchers choose among the five approaches by seeing the differences in the end results of a study. Throughout this book, we have developed understandings to help researchers be cognizant of their own positioning, the procedures of qualitative research, and the differences across five approaches of qualitative inquiry: a case study, a narrative project, a phenomenology, a grounded theory, and an ethnography. With increased interest in qualitative research, it is important that studies being conducted go forward with rigor and attention to the defining features (see Chapters 4, 5, and 6), theoretical frames and researcher worldviews (see Chapter 2), data procedures (see Chapters 7 and 8), writing structures (see Chapter 9), and quality standards (see Chapter 10) developed within approaches of inquiry.

We recognize the approaches to qualitative inquiry as many and inclusive of those beyond the scope of this book focused on five. The research procedures for some approaches are well documented within books and articles whereas for others only minimal guidance exists. A few writers classify the approaches, and some authors mention their favorites. Unquestionably, qualitative research cannot be characterized as of one type, attested to by the multivocal discourse surrounding qualitative research today. Adding to this discourse are diverse perspectives about philosophical, theoretical, and ideological stances.

In this chapter, prior to offering some final guidance to conclude this book, we again sharpen the distinctions among the approaches of inquiry, but we depart from our side-by-side approach used in prior chapters. We focus the lens in a new direction and "turn the story" of a case study—a campus response to a student gunman (Asmussen & Creswell, 1995)—into a narrative study, a phenomenology, a grounded theory, and an ethnography.

TURNING THE STORY ACROSS THE FIVE APPROACHES

Turning the story through different approaches of inquiry raises the issue of whether one should match a particular problem to an approach to inquiry. Much emphasis is placed on this relationship in social and human science research. We agree this needs to be done. But for the purposes of this book, our way around this issue is to pose a *general* problem—"How did the campus react?" in the illustrative case study—and then construct scenarios that address this specific problem. For instance, the specific problem of studying a single individual's reaction to the gun incident is different from the specific problem of how several students as a culture-sharing group reacted, but both scenarios are reactions to the general issue of a campus response to the incident. The general problem that we address is that we know little about how campuses respond to violence and even less about how different constituent groups on campus respond to a potentially violent incident. Knowing this information would help us devise better plans for reacting to this type of problem as well as add to the literature on violence in educational settings. This was the central problem in the gunman case study that is presented next in its complete, original form (Asmussen & Creswell, 1995), and then we briefly review the major dimensions of this case study before we begin "turning the story" across the remaining four approaches to inquiry discussed in this book.

The Original Story: "Campus Response to a Student Gunman"

To be able to turn the story across the five approaches to inquiry we must have an original story as a starting place. We note that the original story could be any of the approaches. For this chapter, we use the case study by Asmussen and Creswell (1995) but we could have begun with any of the approaches. To familiarize you with the original story, the complete, original form of Asmussen & Creswell (1995) precedes the discussion of how a case study can be turned into a narrative study, a phenomenology, a grounded theory study, and an ethnography. Figure 11.1 appears after the original story and its turnings with a summary of the story turning across the five approaches.

CAMPUS RESPONSE TO A STUDENT GUNMAN

Kelly J. Asmussen

John W. Creswell

With increasingly frequent incidents of campus violence, a small, growing scholarly literature about the subject is emerging. For instance, authors have reported on racial [12], courtship and sexually coercive [3, 7, 8], and hazing violence [24]. For the American College Personnel Association, Roark [24] and Roark and Roark [25] reviewed the forms of physical, sexual, and psychological violence on college campuses and suggested guidelines for prevention strategies. Roark [23] has also suggested criteria that high-school students might use to assess the level of violence on college campuses they seek to attend. At the national level, President Bush, in November 1989, signed into law the "Student Right-to-Know and Campus Security Act" (P.L. 101-542), which requires colleges and universities to make available to students, employees, and applicants an annual report on security policies and campus crime statistics [13].

One form of escalating campus violence that has received little attention is student gun violence. Recent campus reports indicate that violent crimes from thefts and burglaries to assaults and homicides are on the rise at colleges and universities [13]. College campuses have been shocked by killings such as those at The University of Iowa [16], The University of Florida [13], Concordia University in Montreal, and the University of Montreal-Ecole Polytechnique [22]. Incidents such as these raise critical concerns, such as psychological trauma, campus safety, and disruption of campus life. Aside from an occasional newspaper report, the postsecondary literature is silent on campus reactions to these tragedies; to understand them one must turn to studies about gun violence in the public school literature. This literature addresses strategies for school intervention [21, 23], provides case studies of incidents in individual schools [6, 14, 15], and discusses the problem of students who carry weapons to school [1] and the psychological trauma that results from homicides [32].

A need exists to study campus reactions to violence in order to build conceptual models for future study as well as to identify campus strategies and protocols for reaction. We need to understand better the psychological dimensions and organizational issues of constituents involved in and affected by these incidents. An in-depth qualitative case study exploring the context of an incident can illuminate such conceptual and pragmatic understandings. The study presented in this article is a qualitative case analysis [31] that describes and interprets a campus response to a gun incident. We asked the following exploratory research questions: What happened? Who was involved in response to the incident? What themes of response emerged during the eight-month period that followed this incident? What theoretical constructs helped us understand the campus response, and what constructs were unique to this case?

The Incident and Response

The incident occurred on the campus of a large public university in a Midwestern city. A decade ago, this city had been designated an "all-American city," but more recently, its normally tranquil environment has been disturbed by an increasing number of assaults and homicides. Some of these violent incidents have involved students at the university.

The incident that provoked this study occurred on a Monday in October. A forty-three-year-old graduate student, enrolled in a senior-level actuarial science class, arrived a few minutes before class, armed with a vintage Korean War military semiautomatic rifle loaded with a thirty-round clip of thirty caliber ammunition. He carried another thirty-round clip in his pocket. Twenty of the thirty-four students in the class had already gathered for class, and most of them were quietly reading the student newspaper. The instructor was en route to class.

The gunman pointed the rifle at the students, swept it across the room, and pulled the trigger. The gun jammed. Trying to unlock the rifle, he hit the butt of it on the instructor's desk and quickly tried firing it again. Again it did not fire. By this time, most students realized what was happening and dropped to the floor, overturned their desks, and tried to hide behind them. After about twenty seconds, one of the students shoved a desk into the gunman, and students ran past him out into the hall and out of the building. The gunman hastily departed the room and went out of the building to his parked car, which he had left running. He was captured by police within the hour in a nearby small town, where he lived. Although he remains incarcerated at this time, awaiting trial, the motivations for his actions are unknown.

Campus police and campus administrators were the first to react to the incident. Campus police arrived within three minutes after they had received a telephone call for help. They spent several anxious minutes outside the building interviewing students to obtain an accurate description of the gunman. Campus administrators responded by calling a news conference for 4:00 P.M. the same day, approximately four hours after the incident. The police chief as well as the vice-chancellor of Student Affairs and two students described the incident at the news conference. That same afternoon, the Student Affairs office contacted Student Health and Employee Assistance Program (EAP) counselors and instructed them to be available for any students or staff requesting assistance. The Student Affairs office also arranged for a new location, where this class could meet for the rest of the semester. The Office of Judicial Affairs suspended the gunman from the university. The next day, the incident was discussed by campus administrators at a regularly scheduled campuswide cabinet meeting. Throughout the week, Student Affairs received several calls from students and from a faculty member about "disturbed" students or unsettling student relations. A counselor of the Employee Assistance Program consulted a psychologist with a specialty in dealing with trauma and responding to educational crises. Only one student immediately set up an appointment with the student health counselors. The campus and local newspapers continued to carry stories about the incident.

When the actuarial science class met for regularly scheduled classes two and four days later, the students and the instructor were visited by two county attorneys, the police chief, and two student mental health counselors who conducted "debriefing" sessions. These sessions focused on keeping students fully informed about the judicial process and having the students and the instructor, one by one, talk about their experiences and explore their feelings about the incident. By one week after the incident, the students in the class had returned to their standard class format. During this time, a few students, women who were concerned about violence in general, saw Student Health Center counselors. These counselors also fielded questions from several dozen parents who inquired about the counseling services and the level of safety on campus. Some parents also called the campus administration to ask about safety procedures.

In the weeks following the incident, the faculty and staff campus newsletter carried articles about post-trauma fears and psychological trauma. The campus administration wrote a letter that provided facts about the incident to the board of the university. The administration also mailed campus staff and students information about crime prevention. At least one college dean sent out a memo to staff about "aberrant student behavior," and one academic department chair requested and held an educational group session with counselors and staff on identifying and dealing with "aberrant behavior" of students.

Three distinctly different staff groups sought counseling services at the Employee Assistance Program, a program for faculty and staff, during the next several weeks. The first group had had some direct involvement with the assailant, either by seeing him the day of the gun incident or because they had known him personally. This group was concerned about securing professional help, either for the students or for those in the group who were personally experiencing effects of the trauma. The second group consisted of the "silent connection," individuals who were indirectly involved and yet emotionally traumatized. This group recognized that their fears were a result of the gunman incident, and they wanted to deal with these fears before they escalated. The third group consisted of staff who had previously experienced a trauma, and this incident had retriggered their fears. Several employees were seen by the EAP throughout the next month, but no new groups or delayed stress cases were reported. The EAP counselors stated that each group's reactions were normal responses. Within a month, although public discussion of the incident had subsided, the EAP and Student Health counselors began expressing the need for a coordinated campus plan to deal with the current as well as any future violent incidents.

The Research Study

We began our study two days after the incident. Our first step was to draft a research protocol for approval by the university administration and the Institutional Review Board. We made explicit that we would not become involved in the investigation of the gunman or in the therapy to students or staff who had sought assistance from counselors. We also limited our study to the reactions of groups on campus rather than expand it to include off-campus groups (for example, television and newspaper coverage). This bounding of the study was consistent with an exploratory qualitative case study design [31], which was chosen because models and variables were not available for assessing a campus reaction to a gun incident in higher education. In the constructionist tradition, this study incorporated the paradigm assumptions of an emerging design, a context-dependent inquiry, and an inductive data analysis [10]. We also bounded the study by time (eight months) and by a single case (the campus community). Consistent with case study design [17, 31], we identified campus administrators and student newspaper reporters as multiple sources of information for initial interviews. Later we expanded interviews to include a wide array of campus informants, using a semi-structured interview protocol that consisted of five questions: What has been your role in the incident? What has happened since the event that you have been involved in? What has been the impact of this incident on the university community? What larger ramifications, if any, exist from the incident? To whom should we talk to find out more about the campus reaction to the incident? We also gathered observational data, documents, and visual materials (see table 11.1 for types of information and sources).

The narrative structure was a "realist" tale [28], describing details, incorporating edited quotes from informants, and stating our interpretations of events, especially an interpretation within the framework of organizational and psychological issues. We verified the description and interpretation by taking a preliminary draft of the case to select informants for feedback and later incorporating their comments into the final study [17, 18]. We gathered this feedback in a group interview where we asked: Is our description of the incident and the reaction accurate? Are the themes and constructs we have identified consistent with your experiences? Are there some themes and constructs we have missed? Is a campus plan needed? If so, what form should it take?

TABLE 11.1 ■ Data Collection Matrix: Type of Information by Source

Information/Information Source	Interviews	Observations	Documents	Audio-Visual Materials
Students involved	Yes		Yes	
Students at large	Yes			
Central administration	Yes		Yes	
Campus police	Yes	Yes		

(Continued)

TABLE 11.1 ■ Data Collection Matrix: Type of Information by Source *(Continued)*				
Information/Information Source	Interviews	Observations	Documents	Audio-Visual Materials
Faculty	Yes	Yes	Yes	
Staff	Yes			
Physical plant		Yes	Yes	
News reporters/papers/television	Yes		Yes	Yes
Student health counselors	Yes			
Employee Assistance Program counselors	Yes			
Trauma expert	Yes		Yes	Yes
Campus businesses			Yes	
Board members			Yes	

Themes

Denial

Several weeks later we returned to the classroom where the incident occurred. Instead of finding the desks overturned, we found them to be neatly in order; the room was ready for a lecture or discussion class. The hallway outside the room was narrow, and we visualized how students, on that Monday in October, had quickly left the building, unaware that the gunman, too, was exiting through this same passageway. Many of the students in the hallway during the incident had seemed unaware of what was going on until they saw or heard that there was a gunman in the building. Ironically though, the students had seemed to ignore or deny their dangerous situation. After exiting the building, instead of seeking a hiding place that would be safe, they had huddled together just outside the building. None of the students had barricaded themselves in classrooms or offices or had exited at a safe distance from the scene in anticipation that the gunman might return. "People wanted to stand their ground and stick around," claimed a campus police officer. Failing to respond to the potential danger, the class members had huddled together outside the building, talking nervously. A few had been openly emotional and crying. When asked about their mood, one of the students had said, "Most of us were kidding about it." Their conversations had led one to believe that they were dismissing the incident as though it were trivial and as though no one had actually been in danger. An investigating campus police officer was not surprised by the students' behavior:

> It is not unusual to see people standing around after one of these types of incidents. The American people want to see excitement and have a morbid curiosity. That is why you see spectators hanging around bad accidents. They do not seem to understand the potential danger they are in and do not want to leave until they are injured.

This description corroborates the response reported by mental health counselors: an initial surrealistic first reaction. In the debriefing by counselors, one female student had commented, "I thought the gunman would shoot out a little flag that would say 'bang.'" For her, the event had been like a dream. In this atmosphere no one from the targeted class had called the campus mental health center in the first twenty-four hours following the incident, although they knew that services were available. Instead, students described how they had visited with friends or had gone to bars; the severity of the situation had dawned on them later. One student commented that he had felt fearful and angry only after he had seen the television newscast with pictures of the classroom the evening of the incident.

Though some parents had expressed concern by phoning counselors, the students' denial may have been reinforced by parent comments. One student reported that his parents had made comments like, "I am not surprised you were involved in this. You are always getting yourself into things like this!" or "You did not get hurt. What is the big deal? Just let it drop!" One student expressed how much more traumatized he had been as a result of his mother's dismissal of the event. He had wanted to have someone whom he trusted willing to sit down and listen to him.

Fear

Our visit to the classroom suggested a second theme: the response of fear. Still posted on the door several weeks after the incident, we saw the sign announcing that the class was being moved to another undisclosed building and that students were to check with a secretary in an adjoining room about the new location. It was in this undisclosed classroom, two days after the incident, that two student mental health counselors, the campus police chief, and two county attorneys had met with students in the class to discuss fears, reactions, and thoughts. Reactions of fear had begun to surface in this first "debriefing" session and continued to emerge in a second session.

The immediate fear for most students centered around the thought that the alleged assailant would be able to make bail. Students felt that the assailant might have harbored resentment toward certain students and that he would seek retribution if he made bail. "I think I am going to be afraid when I go back to class. They can change the rooms, but there is nothing stopping him from finding out where we are!" said one student. At the first debriefing session the campus police chief was able to dispel some of this fear by announcing that during the initial hearing the judge had denied bail. This announcement helped to reassure some students about their safety. The campus police chief thought it necessary to keep the students informed of the gunman's status, because several students had called his office to say that they feared for their safety if the gunman were released.

During the second debriefing session, another fear surfaced: the possibility that a different assailant could attack the class. One student reacted so severely to this potential threat that, according to one counselor, since the October incident, "he had caught himself walking into class and sitting at a desk with a clear shot to the door. He was beginning to see each classroom as a 'battlefield.'" In this second session students had sounded angry, they expressed feeling violated, and finally [they] began to admit that they felt unsafe. Yet only one female student immediately accessed the available mental health services, even though an announcement had been made that any student could obtain free counseling.

The fear students expressed during the "debriefing" sessions mirrored a more general concern on campus about increasingly frequent violent acts in the metropolitan area. Prior to this gun incident, three young women and a man had been kidnapped and had later been found dead in a nearby city. A university football player who experienced a psychotic episode had severely beaten a woman. He had later suffered a relapse and was shot by police in a scuffle. Just three weeks prior to the October gun incident, a female university student had been abducted and brutally murdered, and several other homicides had occurred in the city. As a student news reporter commented, "This whole semester has been a violent one."

Safety

The violence in the city that involved university students and the subsequent gun incident that occurred in a campus classroom shocked the typically tranquil campus. A counselor aptly summed up the feelings of many: "When the students walked out of that classroom, their world had become very chaotic; it had become very random, something had happened that robbed them of their sense of safety." Concern for safety became a central reaction for many informants.

When the chief student affairs officer described the administration's reaction to the incident, he listed the safety of students in the classroom as his primary goal, followed by the needs of the news media for details about the case, helping all students with psychological stress, and providing public information on safety. As he talked about the safety issue and the presence of guns on campus, he mentioned that a policy was under consideration for the storage of guns used by students for hunting. Within four hours after the incident, a press conference was called during which the press was briefed not only on the details of the incident, but also on the need to ensure the safety of the campus. Soon thereafter the university administration initiated an informational campaign on campus safety. A letter, describing the incident, was sent to the university board members. (One board member asked, "How could such an incident happen at this university?") The Student Affairs Office sent a letter to all students in which it advised them of the various dimensions of the campus security office and of the types of services it provided. The Counseling and Psychological Services of the Student Health Center promoted their services in a colorful brochure, which was mailed to students in the following week. It emphasized that services were "confidential, accessible, and professional." The Student Judiciary Office advised academic departments on various methods of dealing with students who exhibited abnormal behavior in class. The weekly faculty newsletter stressed that staff needed to respond quickly to any post-trauma fears associated with this incident. The campus newspaper quoted a professor as saying, "I'm totally shocked that in this environment, something like this would happen." Responding to the concerns about disruptive students or employees, the campus police department sent plainclothes officers to sit outside offices whenever faculty and staff indicated concerns.

An emergency phone system, Code Blue, was installed on campus only ten days after the incident. These thirty-six ten-foot-tall emergency phones, with bright blue flashing lights, had previously been approved, and specific spots had already been identified from an earlier study. "The phones will be quite an attention getter," the director of the Telecommunications Center commented. "We hope they will also be a big detractor [to crime]." Soon afterwards, in response to calls from concerned students, trees and shrubbery in poorly lit areas of campus were trimmed.

Students and parents also responded to these safety concerns. At least twenty-five parents called the Student Health Center, the university police, and the Student Affairs Office during the first week after the incident to inquire what kind of services were available for their students. Many parents had been traumatized by the news of the event and immediately demanded answers from the university. They wanted assurances that this type of incident would not happen again and that their child[ren were] safe on the campus. Undoubtedly, many parents also called their children during the weeks immediately following the incident. The students on campus responded to these safety concerns by forming groups of volunteers who would escort anyone on campus, male or female, during the evening hours.

Local businesses profited by exploiting the commercial aspects of the safety needs created by this incident. Various advertisements for self-defense classes and protection devices inundated the newspapers for several weeks. Campus and local clubs [that] offered self-defense classes filled quickly, and new classes were formed in response to numerous additional requests. The campus bookstore's supply of pocket mace and whistles was quickly depleted. The campus police received several inquiries by students who wanted to purchase handguns to carry for protection. None [was] approved, but one wonders whether some guns were not purchased by students anyway. The purchase of cellular telephones from local vendors increased sharply. Most of these purchases were made by females; however, some males also sought out these items for their safety and protection. Not unexpectedly, the price of some products was raised as much as 40 percent to capitalize on the newly created demand. Student conversations centered around the purchase of these safety products: how much they cost, how to use them correctly, how accessible they would be if students should need to use them, and whether they were really necessary.

Retriggering

In our original protocol, which we designed to seek approval from the campus administration and the Institutional Review Board, we had outlined a study that would last only three months—a reasonable time, we thought, for this incident to run its course. But during early interviews with counselors, we were referred to a psychologist who specialized in dealing with "trauma" in educational settings. It was this psychologist who mentioned the theme of "retriggering." Now, eight months later, we begin to understand how, through "retriggering," that October incident could have a long-term effect on this campus.

This psychologist explained retriggering as a process by which new incidents of violence would cause individuals to relive the feelings of fear, denial, and threats to personal safety that they had experienced in connection with the original event. The counseling staffs and violence expert also stated that one should expect to see such feelings retriggered at a later point in time, for example, on the anniversary date of the attack or whenever newspapers or television broadcasts mentioned the incident again. They added that a drawn-out judicial process, during which a case was "kept alive" through legal maneuvering, could cause a long period of retriggering and thereby greatly thwart the healing process. The fairness of the judgment of the court as seen by each victim, we were told, would also influence the amount of healing and resolution of feelings that could occur.

As of this writing, it is difficult to detect specific evidence of retriggering from the October incident, but we discovered the potential consequences of this process firsthand by observing the effects of a nearly identical violent gun incident that had happened some eighteen years earlier. A graduate student carrying a rifle had entered a campus building with the intention of shooting the department chairman. The student was seeking revenge, because several years earlier he had flunked a course taught by this professor. This attempted attack followed several years of legal maneuvers to arrest, prosecute, and incarcerate this student, who, on more than one occasion, had tried to carry out his plan but each time had been thwarted by quick-thinking staff members who would not reveal the professor's whereabouts. Fortunately, no shots were ever fired, and the student was finally apprehended and arrested.

The professor who was the target of these threats on his life was seriously traumatized not only during the period of these repeated incidents, but his trauma continued even after the attacker's arrest. The complex processes of the criminal justice system, which, he believed, did not work as it should have, resulted in his feeling further victimized. To this day, the feelings aroused by the original trauma are retriggered each time a gun incident is reported in the news. He was not offered professional help from the university at any time; the counseling services he did receive were secured through his own initiative. Eighteen years later his entire department is still affected in that unwritten rules for dealing with disgruntled students and for protecting this particular professor's schedule have been established.

Campus Planning

The question of campus preparedness surfaced during discussions with the psychologist about the process of "debriefing" individuals who had been involved in the October incident [19]. Considering how many diverse groups and individuals had been affected by this incident, a final theme that emerged from our data was the need for a campuswide plan. A counselor remarked, "We would have been inundated had there been twenty-five to thirty deaths. We need a mobilized plan of communication. It would be a wonderful addition to the campus considering the nature of today's violent world." It became apparent during our interviews that better communication could have occurred among the constituents who responded to this incident. Of course, one campus police officer noted, "We can't have an officer in every building all day long!" But the theme of being prepared across the whole campus was mentioned by several individuals.

The lack of a formal plan to deal with such gun incidents was surprising, given the existence of formal written plans on campus that addressed various other emergencies: bomb threats, chemical spills, fires, earthquakes, explosions, electrical storms, radiation accidents, tornadoes, hazardous material spills, snowstorms, and numerous medical emergencies. Moreover, we found that specific campus units had their own protocols that had actually been used during the October gun incident. For example, the police had a procedure and used that procedure for dealing with the gunman and the students at the scene; the EAP counselors debriefed staff and faculty; the Student Health counselors used a "debriefing" process when they visited the students twice in the classroom following the incident. The question that concerned us was, what would a campuswide plan consist of, and how would it be developed and evaluated?

As shown in table 11.2, using evidence gathered in our case, we assembled the basic questions to be addressed in a plan and cross-referenced these questions to the literature about post-trauma stress, campus violence, and the disaster literature (for a similar list drawn from the public school literature, see Poland and Pitcher [21]). Basic elements of a campus plan to enhance communication across units should include determining what the rationale for the plan is; who should be involved in its development; how it should be coordinated; how it should be staffed; and what specific procedures should be followed. These procedures might include responding to an immediate crisis, making the campus safe, dealing with external groups, and providing for the psychological welfare of victims.

TABLE 11.2 ■ Evidence From the Case, Questions for a Campus Plan, and References

Evidence From the Case	Question for the Plan	Useful References
Need expressed by counselors	Why should a plan be developed?	Walker (1990); Bird et al. (1991)
Multiple constitutes reacting to incident	Who should be involved in developing the plan?	Roark & Roark (1987); Walker (1990)
Leadership found in units with their own protocols	Should the leadership for coordinating be identified within one office?	Roark & Roark (1987)
Several unit protocols being used in incident	Should campus units be allowed their own protocols?	Roark & Roark (1987)
Questions raised by students reacting to case	What types of violence should be covered in the plan?	Roark (1987); Jones (1990)
Groups/individuals surfaced during our interviews	How are those likely to be affected by the incident to be identified?	Walker (1990); Bromet (1990)
Comments from campus police, central administration	What provisions are made for the immediate safety of those in the incident?	
Campus environment changed after incident	How should the physical environment be made safer?	Roark & Roark (1987)
Comments from central administration	How will the external publics (e.g., press, businesses) be apprised of the incident?	Poland & Pitcher (1990)
Issue raised by counselors and trauma specialist	What are the likely sequelae of psychological events for victims?	Bromet (1990); Mitchell (1983)
Issue raised by trauma specialist	What long-term impact will the incident have on victims?	Zelikoff (1987)
Procedure used by Student Health Center counselors	How will the victims be debriefed?	Mitchell (1983); Walker (1990)

Discussion

The themes of denial, fear, safety, retriggering, and developing a campuswide plan might further be grouped into two categories, an organizational and a psychological or social-psychological response of the campus community to the gunman incident. Organizationally, the campus units responding to the crisis exhibited both a loose coupling [30] and an interdependent communication. Issues such as leadership, communication, and authority emerged during the case analysis. Also, an environmental response developed, because the campus was transformed into a safer place for students and staff. The need for centralized planning, while allowing for autonomous operation of units in response to a crisis, called for organizational change that would require cooperation and coordination among units.

Sherrill [27] provides models of response to campus violence that reinforce as well as depart from the evidence in our case. As mentioned by Sherrill, the disciplinary action taken against a perpetrator, the group counseling of victims, and the use of safety education for the campus community were all factors apparent in our case. However, Sherrill raises issues about responses that were not discussed by our informants, such as developing procedures for individuals who are first to arrive on the scene, dealing with non-students who might be perpetrators or victims, keeping records and documents about incidents, varying responses based on the size and nature of the institution, and relating incidents to substance abuse such as drugs and alcohol.

Also, some of the issues that we had expected after reading the literature about organizational response did not emerge. Aside from occasional newspaper reports (focused mainly on the gunman), there was little campus administrative response to the incident, which was contrary to what we had expected from Roark and Roark [25], for example. No mention was made of establishing a campus unit to manage future incidents—for example, a campus violence resource center—reporting of violent incidents [25], or conducting annual safety audits [20]. Aside from the campus police mentioning that the State Health Department would have been prepared to send a team of trained trauma experts to help emergency personnel cope with the tragedy, no discussion was reported about formal linkages with community agencies that might assist in the event of a tragedy [3]. We also did not hear directly about establishing a "command center" [14] or a crisis coordinator [21], two actions recommended by specialists on crisis situations.

On a psychological and social-psychological level, the campus response was to react to the psychological needs of the students who had been directly involved in the incident as well as to students and staff who had been indirectly affected by the incident. Not only did signs of psychological issues, such as denial, fear, and retriggering, emerge, as expected [15], gender and cultural group issues were also mentioned, though they were not discussed enough to be considered basic themes in our analysis. Contrary to assertions in the literature that violent behavior is often accepted in our culture, we found informants in our study to voice concern and fear about escalating violence on campus and in the community.

Faculty on campus were conspicuously silent on the incident, including the faculty senate, though we had expected this governing body to take up the issue of aberrant student or faculty behavior in their classrooms [25]. Some informants speculated that the faculty might have been passive about this issue because they were unconcerned, but another explanation might be that they were passive because they were unsure of what to do or whom to ask for assistance. From the students we failed to hear that they responded to their post-traumatic stress with "coping" strategies, such as relaxation, physical activity, and the establishment of normal routines [29]. Although the issues of gender and race surfaced in early conversations with informants, we did not find a direct discussion of these issues. As Bromet [5] comments, the sociocultural needs of populations with different mores must be considered when individuals assess reactions to trauma. In regard to the issue of gender, we did hear that women were the first students to seek out counseling at the Student Health Center. Perhaps our "near-miss" case was unique. We do not know what the reaction of the campus might have been had a death (or multiple deaths) occurred, although, according to the trauma psychologist, "the trauma of no deaths is as great as if deaths had occurred." Moreover, as with any exploratory case analysis, this case has limited generalizability [17], although thematic generalizability is certainly a possibility. The fact that our information was self-reported and that we were unable to interview all students who had been directly affected by the incident so as to not intervene in student therapy or the investigation also poses a problem.

Despite these limitations, our research provides a detailed account of a campus reaction to a violent incident with the potential for making a contribution to the literature. Events emerged during the process of reaction that could be "critical incidents" in future studies, such as the victim response, media reporting, the debriefing process, campus changes, and the evolution of a campus plan. With the scarcity of literature on campus violence related to gun incidents, this study breaks new ground by identifying themes and conceptual frameworks that could be examined in future cases. On a practical level, it can benefit campus administrators who are looking for a plan to respond to campus violence, and it focuses attention on questions that need to be addressed in such a plan. The large number of different groups of people who were affected by this particular gunman incident shows the complexity of responding to a campus crisis and should alert college personnel to the need for preparedness.

Epilogue

As we conducted this study, we asked ourselves whether we would have had access to informants if someone had been killed. This "near-miss" incident provided a unique research opportunity, which could, however, only approximate an event in which a fatality had actually occurred. Our involvement in this study was serendipitous, for one of us had been employed by a correctional facility and therefore had direct experience with gunmen such as the individual in our case; the other was a University of Iowa graduate and thus familiar with the setting and circumstances surrounding another violent incident there in 1992. These experiences obviously affected our assessment of this case by drawing our attention to the campus response in the first plan and to psychological reactions like fear and denial. At the time of this writing, campus discussions have been held about adapting the in-place campus emergency preparedness plan to a critical incident management team concept. Counselors have met to discuss coordinating the activities of different units in the event of another incident, and the police are working with faculty members and department staff to help identify potentially violence-prone students. We have the impression that, as a result of this case study, campus personnel see the interrelatedness and the large number of units that may be involved in a single incident. The anniversary date passed without incident or acknowledgment in the campus newspaper. As for the gunman, he is still incarcerated awaiting trial, and we wonder, as do some of the students he threatened, if he will seek retribution against us for writing up this case if he is released. The campus response to the October incident continues.

References

1. Asmussen, K. J. "Weapon Possession in Public High Schools." *School Safety* (Fall 1992), 28–30.
2. Bird, G. W., S. M. Stith, and J. Schladale. "Psychological Resources, Coping Strategies, and Negotiation Styles as Discriminators of Violence in Dating Relationships." *Family Relations*, 40 (1991), 45–50.
3. Bogal-Allbritten, R., and W. Allbritten. "Courtship Violence on Campus: A Nationwide Survey of Student Affairs Professionals." *NASPA Journal*, 28 (1991), 312–18.
4. Boothe, J. W., T. M. Flick, S. P. Kirk, L. H. Bradley, and K. E. Keough. "The Violence at Your Door." *Executive Educator* (February 1993), 16–22.
5. Bromet, E. J. "Methodological Issues in the Assessment of Traumatic Events." *Journal of Applied Psychology*, 20 (1990), 1719–24.

6. Bushweller, K. "Guards with Guns." *American School Board Journal* (January 1993), 34–36.
7. Copenhaver, S., and E. Grauerholz. "Sexual Victimization among Sorority Women." *Sex Roles: A Journal of Research*, 24 (1991), 31–41.
8. Follingstad, D., S. Wright, S. Lloyd, and J. Sebastian. "Sex Differences in Motivations and Effects in Dating Violence." *Family Relations*, 40 (1991), 51–57.
9. Gordon, M. T., and S. Riger. *The Female Fear*. Urbana: University of Illinois Press, 1991.
10. Guba, E., and Y. Lincoln. "Do Inquiry Paradigms Imply Inquiry Methodologies?" In *Qualitative Approaches to Evaluation in Education*, edited by D. M. Fetterman. New York: Praeger, 1988.
11. Johnson, K. "The Tip of the Iceberg." *School Safety* (Fall 1992), 24–26.
12. Jones, D. J. "The College Campus as a Microcosm of U.S. Society: The Issue of Racially Motivated Violence." *Urban League Review*, 13 (1990), 129–39.
13. Legislative Update. "Campuses Must Tell Crime Rates." *School Safety* (Winter 1991), 31.
14. Long, N. J. "Managing a Shooting Incident." *Journal of Emotional and Behavioral Problems*, 1 (1992), 23–26.
15. Lowe, J. A. "What We Learned: Some Generalizations in Dealing with a Traumatic Event at Cokeville." Paper presented at the Annual Meeting of the National School Boards Association, San Francisco, 4–7 April 1987.
16. Mann, J. *Los Angeles Times Magazine*, 2 June 1992, pp. 26–27, 32, 46–47.
17. Merriam, S. B. Case Study Research in Education: A Qualitative Approach. San Francisco: Jossey-Bass, 1988.
18. Miles, M. B., and A. M. Huberman. *Qualitative Data Analysis: A Sourcebook of New Methods*. Beverly Hills, Calif.: Sage, 1984.
19. Mitchell, J. "When Disaster Strikes." *Journal of Emergency Medical Services* (January 1983), 36–39.
20. NSSC Report on School Safety. "Preparing Schools for Terroristic Attacks." *School Safety* (Winter 1991), 18–19.
21. Poland, S., and G. Pitcher. *Crisis Intervention in the Schools*. New York: Guilford, 1992.
22. Quimet, M. "The Polytechnique Incident and Imitative Violence against Women." *SSR*, 76 (1992), 45–47.
23. Roark, M. L. "Helping High School Students Assess Campus Safety." *The School Counselor*, 39 (1992), 251–56.
24. ____. "Preventing Violence on College Campuses." *Journal of Counseling and Development*, 65 (1987), 367–70.
25. Roark, M. L., and E. W. Roark. "Administrative Responses to Campus Violence." Paper presented at the annual meeting of the American College Personnel Association/National Association of Student Personnel Administrators, Chicago, 15–18 March 1987.
26. "School Crisis: Under Control," 1991 [video]. National School Safety Center, a partnership of Pepperdine University and the United States Departments of Justice and Education.
27. Sherill, J. M., and D. G. Seigel (eds.). *Responding to Violence on Campus*. New Directions for Student Services, No. 47. San Francisco: Jossey-Bass, 1989.
28. Van Maanen, J. *Tales of the Field*. Chicago: University of Chicago Press, 1988.
29. Walker, G. "Crisis-Care in Critical Incident Debriefing." *Death Studies*, 14 (1990), 121–33.
30. Weick, K. E. "Educational Organizations as Loosely Coupled Systems." *Administrative Science Quarterly*, 21 (1976), 1–19.
31. Yin, R. K. *Case Study Research, Design and Methods*. Newbury Park, Calif.: Sage, 1989.
32. Zelikoff, W. I., and I. A. Hyman. "Psychological Trauma in the Schools: A Retrospective Study." Paper presented at the annual meeting of the National Association of School Psychologists, New Orleans, La., 4–8 March 1987.

FIGURE 11.1 ■ Turning the Story Across the Five Approaches With Case Study as the Original Study

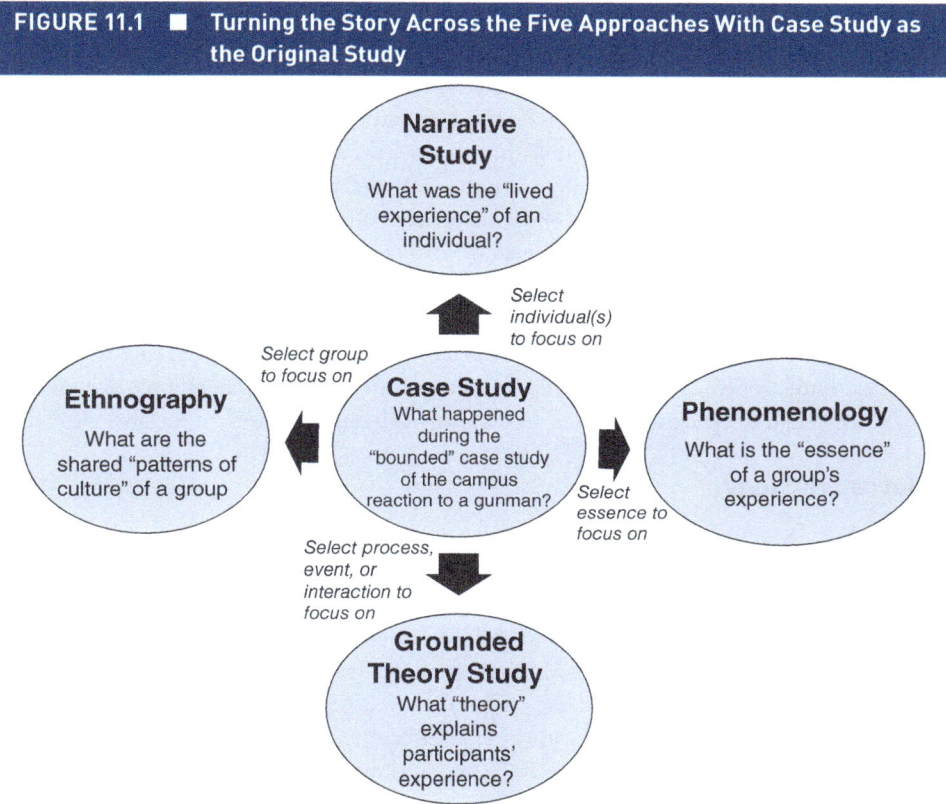

A Case Study

This qualitative case study (Asmussen & Creswell, 1995), as our original study (see also Figure 11.1), presented a campus reaction to a gunman incident in which a student attempted to fire a gun at his classmates. In so doing, the report addressed questions relating to the case bounded by those on campus at the time of the gunman incident, the 2 weeks following the incident when the researchers began data collection, and the 8-month period following the incident for completing the report. The authors based the composition of this case study on the "substantive case report" format of Lincoln and Guba (1985) and Stake (1995). These formats called for an explication of the problem; a thorough description of the context or setting and the processes observed; a discussion of important themes; and, finally, "lessons to be learned" (Lincoln & Guba, 1985, p. 362). After introducing the case study with the problem of violence on college campuses, the authors turned to a detailed description of the setting and a chronology of events immediately following the incident and events during the following 2 weeks. Then they presented the important themes related to denial, fear, safety, retriggering, and campus planning. In a process of layering of themes, the authors combined the more specific themes into two overarching themes: an organizational theme and a psychological or social–psychological theme. Asmussen and Creswell

(1995) gathered data through interviews with participants, observations, documents, and audiovisual materials. From the case emerges a proposed plan for campuses, and the case ends with an implied lesson for the specific Midwestern campus and a specific set of questions this campus or other campuses might use to design a plan for handling future campus terrorist incidents.

Turning to specific research questions in this case, the authors asked the following questions: What happened? Who was involved in response to the incident? What themes of response emerged during an 8-month period? What theoretical constructs helped us understand the campus response, and what constructs developed that were unique to this case? Asmussen and Creswell (1995) entered the field 2 days after the incident and did not use any a priori theoretical lens to guide our questions or the results. The narrative first described the incident, analyzed it through levels of abstraction, and provided some interpretation by relating the context to larger theoretical frameworks. The authors validated the case analysis by using multiple data sources for the themes and by checking the final account with select participants, or member checking.

A Narrative Study

How might we have approached this same general problem ("how did the campus react" to the incident) as an interpretive biographical study with a narrative approach? Rather than identifying responses from multiple campus constituents, we would have focused on one individual (see Figure 11.1), such as the instructor of the class involved in the incident. We would have tentatively titled the project, "Campus Confrontation: An Interpretive Biography of an African American Professor." This instructor, like the gunman, was African American, and his response to such an incident might be situated within racial and cultural contexts. Hence, as an interpretive biographer, we might have asked the following research question: What are the life experiences of the African American instructor of the class, and how do these experiences form and shape his reaction to the incident? This biographical approach would have relied on studying a single individual and situating this individual within his lived experiences. We would have examined *life events* or "epiphanies" culled from stories he told. Our approach would have been to "restory the stories" into an account of his experiences of the gunman that followed a chronology of events. We might have relied on the Clandinin and Connelly (2000) and Clandinin (2023) three-dimensional space model to organize the story into the personal, social, and interactional components. Alternatively, the story might have had a plot to tie it together, such as the theoretical perspective as described by Daiute (2014). This plot might have spoken to cultural aspects highlighted by the instructor and how the particular aspects played out both within the African American culture and other cultures. These perspectives may have shaped how the instructor viewed and experienced the student gunman incident. We also might have composed this report by discussing our own situated beliefs followed by those of the instructor and the changes he brought about as a result of his experiences. For instance, did he continue teaching? Did he share his experiences with others? Our narrative story about this instructor would be expected to contain a detailed description of the context to reveal the historical and interactional features of the experience (Chase, 2018; Denzin, 2001). We also would have acknowledged that any interpretation of the instructor's reaction would be incomplete, unfinished, and a rendering from our own perspectives and lived experiences as White researchers.

A Phenomenology

Rather than study a single individual as in a biography, we would have studied several individual students and examined a psychological concept in the tradition of psychological phenomenology (Moustakas, 1994). Our working title might have been, "The Meaning of Fear for Students Caught in a Near Tragedy on Campus." Our assumption would have been that students expressed this concept of fear during the incident, immediately after it, and several weeks later. To develop our understanding of the essence of their shared experience (see Figure 11.1), we might have posed the following questions: What fear did the students experience, and how did they experience it? What meanings did they ascribe to this experience? As a phenomenologist, we assume that human experience makes sense to those who live it and that human experience can be consciously expressed (Dukes, 1984). Thus, we would bring to the study a phenomenon to explore (fear) and a philosophical orientation to use (we want to study the meaning of the students' experiences). We would have engaged in extensive interviews with up to 10 students, and we would have analyzed the interviews using the steps described by Moustakas (1994). We would have begun with a description of our own fears and experiences (epoché) to position ourselves, recognizing that we could not completely remove ourselves from the situation. Then, after reading through all the students' statements, we would have located significant statements or quotes about their meanings of fear. These significant statements would then be clustered into broader themes. Our final step would have been to write a long paragraph providing a narrative description of what they experienced (*textural description*) and how they experienced it (*structural description*) and combine these two descriptions into a longer description that conveys the *essence* of their experiences. This would be the endpoint for the discussion. Our phenomenology procedures would be expected to reflect prolonged engagement to permit an in-depth understanding of the phenomenon under study (Beck, 2020).

A Grounded Theory Study

If a theory needed to be developed (or modified) to explain the campus reaction to this incident, we would have used a grounded theory approach (see Figure 11.1). For example, we might have developed a theory around a process—the "surreal" experiences of several students immediately following the incident, experiences resulting in actions and reactions by students. The draft title of our study might have been, "A Grounded Theory Explanation of the Surreal Experiences for Students in a Campus Gunman Incident." We might have introduced the study with a specific quote about the surreal experiences:

> In the debriefing by counselors, one female student commented, "I thought the gunman would shoot out a little flag that would say 'bang.'" For her, the event was like a dream.

Our research questions might have been as follows: What theory explains the phenomenon of the "surreal" experiences of the students immediately following the incident? What were these experiences? What caused them? What strategies did the students use to cope with them? What were the consequences of their strategies? What specific interaction issues and larger conditions influenced their strategies? Consistent with a structured approach to grounded theory (Corbin

& Strauss, 2015), we would not bring into the data collection and analysis a specific theoretical orientation other than to see how the students interact and respond to the incident. Instead, our intent would be to develop or generate a theory. In the results section of this study, we would have first identified the open coding categories that we found. Then, we would have described how we narrowed the study to a central category (e.g., the dream element of the process) and made that category the major feature of a theory of the process. This theory would have been presented as a *visual model*, and in the model we would have included *causal conditions* that influenced the central category, intervening and context factors surrounding it, and specific strategies and consequences (axial coding) as a result of it occurring. We would have advanced *theoretical propositions* or hypotheses that explained the dream element of the surreal experiences of the students (selective coding). We would have validated our account by judging the thoroughness of the research process and whether the findings are empirically grounded, two factors mentioned by Corbin and Strauss (1990, 2015). Our grounded theory procedures would be expected to include memoing as part of the process of theory development (Birks & Mills, 2023).

An Ethnography

In grounded theory, our focus was on generating a theory grounded in the data. In ethnography, we would turn the focus away from theory development to a description and understanding of the workings of the campus community as a *culture-sharing group* (see Figure 11.1). To keep the study manageable, we might have begun by looking at how the incident, although unpredictable, triggered quite predictable responses among members of the campus community. These community members might have responded according to their roles, and thus we could have looked at some recognized campus microcultures. Students constituted one such microculture, and they, in turn, comprised several further microcultures or subcultures. Because the students in this class were together for 16 weeks during the semester, they had enough time to develop some shared patterns of behavior and could have been seen as a culture-sharing group. Alternatively, we might have studied the entire campus community, comprising a constellation of groups each reacting differently.

Assuming that the entire campus comprised the culture-sharing group, the title of the study might have been, "Getting Back to Normal: An Ethnography of a Campus Response to a Gunman Incident." Notice how this title immediately invites a contrary perspective into the study. We would have asked the following questions: How did this incident produce predictable role performance within affected groups? Using the entire campus as a cultural system or culture-sharing group, in what roles did the individuals and groups participate? One possibility would be that they wanted to get the campus back to normal after the incident by engaging in predictable patterns of behavior. Although no one anticipated the exact moment or nature of the incident itself, its occurrence set in motion rather predictable role performances throughout the campus community. Administrators did not close the campus and start warning, "The sky is falling." Campus police did not offer counseling sessions, although the Counseling Center did. However, the Counseling Center served the student population, not others (who were marginalized), such as the police or groundskeepers, who also felt unsafe on the campus. In short, predictable performances by campus constituencies followed in the wake of this incident.

Indeed, campus administrators routinely held a news conference following the incident. Also, predictably, police carried out their investigation, and students ultimately and reluctantly contacted their parents. The campus slowly returned to normal—an attempt to return to day-to-day business, to a steady state, or to homeostasis, as the systems thinkers say. In these predictable role behaviors, one saw culture at work.

As we entered the field, we would seek to build rapport with the community participants, to not further marginalize them or disturb the environment more than necessary through our presence. It was a sensitive time on campus with people who had nerves on edge. We would have explored the cultural themes of the "organization of diversity" and "maintenance" activities of individuals and groups within the culture-sharing campus. Wallace (1970) defines the "organization of diversity" as "the actual diversity of habits, of motives, of personalities, of customs that do, in fact, coexist within the boundaries of any culturally organized society" (p. 23). Our data collection would have consisted of observations over time of predictable activities, behaviors, and roles in which people engaged that helped the campus return to normal. This data collection would depend heavily on interviews and observations of the classroom where the incident occurred and newspaper accounts. Our ultimate narrative of the culture-sharing campus would be consistent with Wolcott's (1994) three parts: a detailed description of the campus, an analysis of the cultural themes of "organizational diversity" and maintenance (possibly with taxonomies or comparisons; Spradley, 1979, 1980), and interpretation. Our interpretation would be couched not in terms of a dispassionate, objective report of the facts, but rather within our own experiences of not feeling safe in a soup kitchen for the homeless (Miller et al., 1998) and our own personal life experiences of having grown up in "safe" small Midwestern towns. For an ending to the study, we might have used the "canoe into the sunset" approach (H. F. Wolcott, personal communication, November 15, 1996) or the more methodologically oriented ending of checking our account with participants. Here is the canoe into the sunset approach:

> The newsworthiness of the event will be long past before the ethnographic study is ready, but the event itself is of rather little consequence if the ethnographer's focus is on campus culture. Still, without such an event, the ethnographer working in his or her own society (and perhaps on his or her own campus as well) might have a difficult time "seeing" people performing in predictable everyday ways simply because that is the way in which we expect them to act. The ethnographer working "at home" has to find ways in which to make the familiar seem strange. An upsetting event can make ordinary role behavior easier to discern as people respond in predictable ways to unpredictable circumstances. Those predictable patterns are the stuff of culture.

Here is the more methodological ending:

> Some of our "facts" or hypotheses may need (and be amenable to) checking or testing if we have carried our analysis in that direction. If we have tried to be more interpretive, then perhaps we can "try out" the account on some of the people described, and the cautions and exceptions they express can be included in our final account to suggest that things are even more complex than the way we have presented them.

We would expect that our description of ethnographic fieldwork would include details about our work with people as "ethnographers do not work in a vacuum" (Fetterman, 2019, p. 141).

CONCLUSION: SEVEN KEY TAKEAWAYS

We now reflect on how we have addressed our "compelling" question raised at the outset of this book at the qualitative research workshop at Vail, Colorado: How does the approach to inquiry shape the design of a study? When designing a qualitative study, we recommend that the author design the study within one of the approaches of qualitative inquiry.

We find distinctions as well as overlap among the five approaches, but designing a study attuned to procedures found within one of the approaches suggested in this book will enhance the sophistication of the project and convey a level of methodological expertise for readers of qualitative research. This means that components of the design process (e.g., interpretive framework, research purpose and questions, data collection, data analysis, report writing, validation evidence) will reflect the procedures of the selected approach and will be composed with the encoding and features of that approach. This is not to rigidly suggest that one cannot mix approaches and employ, for example, a grounded theory analysis procedure within a case study design. "Purity" is not our aim. But in this book, we suggest that the reader sort out the approaches first before combining them and see each one as a rigorous procedure in its own right. We offer seven key takeaways from this book in the sections that follow.

Study Focus

One of the most pronounced ways to differentiate among the five approaches is to examine the focus of the study. As discussed in Chapter 4, a theory differs from the exploration of a phenomenon or concept, from an in-depth case, and from the creation of an individual or group portrait. Please examine again Table 4.1, which establishes differences among the five approaches, especially in terms of foci.

However, this is not as clear-cut as it appears. A single case study of an individual can be approached either as a narrative study or as a case study. A cultural system may be explored as an ethnography, whereas a smaller "bounded" system, such as an event, a program, or an activity, may be studied as a case study. Both are systems, and the problem arises when one undertakes a micro-ethnography, which might be approached either as a case study or as an ethnography. However, when one seeks to study cultural behavior, language, or artifacts, then the study of a system might be undertaken as an ethnography. When researchers can clearly articulate their study focus, it can greatly help them choose among the many approaches to qualitative inquiry.

Interpretive Orientation

An interpretive orientation flows throughout qualitative research. As discussed in Chapter 2, we cannot step aside and be "objective" about what we see and write. Our words flow from our own personal experiences, culture, history, and backgrounds. When we engage in fieldwork to collect data, we need to approach the task with care for the participants and sites and to be reflexive about our role, our "positioning" and how it shapes what we see, hear, and write.

Ultimately, our writing represents an interpretation of events, people, and activities. While we might share our interpretations and they may ultimately be influenced by others, it begins with our interpretation. We must recognize that participants, readers, and other individuals reading our accounts will have their own interpretations. Within this perspective, our writing can only be seen as a discourse, one with tentative conclusions, and one that will be constantly changing and evolving. Qualitative research truly has an interpretation element that flows throughout the process of research. When researchers engage in reflexive practice, they can greatly benefit from opportunities to reflect upon and make explicit the experiential and theoretical influences on their designs.

Language Use

The approach to inquiry shapes the language of the research design procedures in a study, especially the terms used in the introduction to a study, the data collection, and the analysis phases of design. The embedded "Chapter Key Terms" in Chapter 4 can be particularly helpful for introducing some of the unique terms across the five approaches. We also incorporated these terms into Chapter 6, as we discussed the wording of purpose statements and research questions for different approaches to qualitative research.

Our language theme continued in Chapter 9 as we talked about encoding the text within an approach to research. The glossary presents a useful list and definitions of terms within each tradition that researchers might incorporate into the language of their studies. When researchers are familiar with the language associated with different approaches, it can be easier to convey meanings to others.

Participant Samples

The approach to research includes identifying the participants who are studied, and as discussed in Chapter 7, describing sampling and recruitment strategies as well as data collection procedures that are appropriate for the participants and their communities. A study may consist of one or two individuals (i.e., narrative study), groups of people (i.e., phenomenology, grounded theory), or an entire culture (i.e., ethnography). A case study might fit into all three of these categories as one explores a single individual, an event, or a large social setting.

In Chapter 7, we also highlighted how the approaches vary in the extent of data collection, from the use of mainly single sources of information (i.e., narrative interviews, grounded theory interviews, phenomenological interviews) to those that involve multiple sources of information (i.e., ethnographies consisting of observations, interviews, and documents; case studies incorporating interviews, observations, documents, archival material, and audiovisual and social media). Although these forms of data collection are not fixed, we see a general pattern that differentiates the approaches.

Analysis Strategies

The distinctions among the approaches are most pronounced in the data analysis phase, as discussed in Chapter 8. Data analysis ranges from unstructured to structured approaches. Among the less structured approaches, we include ethnographies (with the exception of Spradley, 1979, 1980) and narratives (e.g., as suggested by Clandinin, 2023; Clandinin & Connelly, 2000) and interpretive forms advanced by Denzin (1989). The more structured approaches consist of grounded theory with a systematic procedure and phenomenology (see Colaizzi's 1978 approach and those of Dukes, 1984, and Moustakas, 1994) and case studies (Stake, 1995; G. Thomas, 2021, Yin, 2017). These procedures provide direction for the overall structure of the data analysis in the qualitative report.

The approach also shapes the amount of relative weight given to description in the analysis of the data. In ethnographies, case studies, and biographies, researchers employ substantial description; in phenomenologies, investigators use less description; and in grounded theory, researchers seem not to use it at all, choosing to move directly into analysis of the data. We also point to the potential of computers and qualitative data analysis software for facilitating the ease and efficiency of data analysis and representations.

Report Writing

The approach to inquiry shapes the final written product as well as the embedded rhetorical structures used in the narrative. This explains why qualitative studies look so different and are composed so differently across the five approaches to inquiry, as discussed in Chapter 9. We see the writing structures (both overall and embedded) are highly related to data analysis procedures.

We are reminded again about the interrelatedness among different components of the research process. Take, for example, the presence of the researcher. Although reflexivity flows into all qualitative projects, the presence of the researcher is lessened in the more "objective" accounts provided in grounded theory. Alternatively, the researcher is center stage in ethnographies and possibly in case studies where "interpretation" plays a major role.

Research Quality

The criteria for assessing the quality of a study differ among the approaches, as discussed in Chapter 10. Although some overlap exists in the procedures for validation, the criteria for assessing the study quality of qualitative research relate to the defining features for each approach to inquiry. The features of a "good" qualitative study initially introduced in Chapter 3 can be seen in the quality criteria specific to qualitative research.

CHAPTER CHECK-IN

1. Can you "take" your proposed (or completed) qualitative study and turn the story into one of the other approaches of qualitative inquiry?

2. Can you construct a table that states the key seven takeaway points (study focus, interpretive orientation, language use, participant samples, analysis strategies, report writing, and research quality) in the first column and identifies ways each of the five approaches differ in a second column?

SUMMARY

In this final chapter, we demonstrate how an original study of a case study of a campus gunman by Asmussen and Creswell (1995) is turned first into a narrative study focused on the lived experience of an individual. Then the story is turned into a phenomenology focused on studying several individual students generating an understanding of the essence of the phenomenon experienced by the group. Next, the story becomes a grounded theory study focused on developing a theory explaining the surreal experiences of several students. Finally, the story becomes an ethnography focused on describing and understanding the workings of the campus community as a culture-sharing group. To conclude, we refer to specific book chapters in the description of our final guidance in the form of seven takeaways for qualitative researchers to attend to in their study design: study focus, interpretive orientation, language use, participant samples, analysis strategies, report writing, and research quality.

APPENDICES

Appendix A. A Narrative Research Study—"Living in the Space Between Participant and Researcher as a Narrative Inquirer: Examining Ethnic Identity of Chinese Canadian Students as Conflicting Stories to Live By"

Appendix B. A Phenomenological Study—"Resilient Leadership: A Phenomenological Exploration Into How Black Women In Higher Education Leadership Navigate Cultural Adversity"

Appendix C. A Grounded Theory Study—"Aging With Intellectual Disabilities in Families: Navigating Ever-Changing Seas—A Theoretical Model"

Appendix D. An Ethnography—"British-Born Pakistani and Bangladeshi Young Men: Exploring Unstable Concepts of Muslim, Islamophobia and Racialization."

Appendix E. A Case Study—"Learning From Error in Violence Prevention: A School Shooting as an Organizational Accident"

APPENDIX A

A Narrative Research Study—"Living in the Space Between Participant and Researcher as a Narrative Inquirer: Examining Ethnic Identity of Chinese Canadian Students as Conflicting Stories to Live By"

Elaine Chan

ABSTRACT

Schooling experiences of 1st-generation Canadians interact with cultural experiences in their immigrant households to shape a sense of ethnic identity both as Canadians and as members of an ethnic community. This long-term, school-based narrative inquiry is an examination of ways in which expectations for academic performance and behavior by teachers and peers at school and immigrant parents at home contributed to shaping the ethnic identity of an immigrant Chinese student as conflicting stories to live by. A narrative approach revealed challenges of supporting immigrant students in North American schools, and contributed to understanding of the nuances of multicultural education.

KEYWORDS

narrative inquiry, ethnic identity, curriculum, multicultural education, student experiences

Author's Note: Address correspondence to Elaine Chan, Department of Teaching, Learning, and Teacher Education, College of Education and Human Sciences, University of Nebraska–Lincoln, 24 Henzlik Hall, Lincoln, NE 68588-0355. (E-mail: echan2@unl.edu)

Source: The material in this appendix originally appeared in *The Journal of Educational Research, 103*(2), 133–122 (2010). Reprinted with permission of Taylor & Francis Ltd, http://www.tandfonline.com.

For children, school has enormous implications for their sense of identity as members of society, of their families, and of their ethnic communities. Each individual brings to their school context experiences shaped by their participation in schools, whether in Canada or in their home country, whether positive or negative, enriching or demoralizing. For a child of immigrant parents, tensions between home and school, the interaction of parent and teacher experiences of schooling, and their own experiences of schooling may be felt especially strongly, to the point of being experienced as conflicting stories to live by (Connelly & Clandinin, 1999). These students have their own ideas of how they should be in their school context, shaped by interaction with peers, exposure to popular culture and media, and prior experiences of schooling, schools, and teachers. At the same time, they are evaluated by teachers and supported by parents whose experiences of schooling may be vastly different, by nature of social and political influences as well as personal circumstances of the societies of which their own childhood schools were a part.

In the present study, I examined the experiences of one Chinese immigrant student, Ai Mei Zhang. I explore her participation in her Canadian middle school curriculum as the interaction of student, teacher, and parent narratives, a story of interwoven lives (Clandinin et al., 2006). I examined ways in which her sense of ethnic identity may be shaped by expectations for her academic performance and her behavior in her school and her home. I focus in particular on ways in which participation in her urban, multicultural school setting may contribute to shaping her sense of affiliation to family members and members of her ethnic and school communities, and contribute to her maternal-language development and maintenance. I also examined ways in which she experienced well-intended school practices and curriculum activities designed to support her academic performance in ways not anticipated by policymakers and educators. I explored these influences as conflicting stories to live by (Connelly & Clandinin, 1999).

I examined experientially the intersection of school and home influences from the perspective of one middle school student as a long-term, school-based narrative inquirer. I explored features of narrative inquiry, such as the critical role of researcher–participant relationships, and the role of temporal and spatial factors (Clandinin & Connelly, 2000) of the research context in contributing to a nuanced understanding of multicultural education in this diverse school context. The present study is holistic, in that I examined the impact of multiple influences in a connected way as they intersected in the life of one student rather than as examples of ways in which an issue or theme may be experienced by different members of the same ethnic group.

Given the increasing diversity of the North American population (Statistics Canada, 2008; U.S. Census Bureau, 2002) that is in turn reflected in North American schools (Chan & Ross, 2002; He, Phillion, Chan, & Xu, 2007), addressing the curricular needs of students of minority background and supporting the professional development of teachers who work with them is essential. The present study contributes to existing research in the area of multicultural education and, in particular, curriculum development for diverse student populations, and student experiences of multicultural education.

To date, research addressing the interaction of culture and curriculum is often presented as an argument for the inclusion of culture in the school curriculum or as documentation for ways in which the inclusion of culture in the curriculum was successful (Ada, 1988; Cummins et al., 2005). There is an abundance of research highlighting the importance of culturally relevant and responsive pedagogy (Gay, 2000; Ladson-Billings, 1995, 2001; Villegas, 1991) and a culturally sensitive curriculum that builds on the experiences and knowledge of immigrant and minority students (Ada; Cummins, 2001; Igoa, 1995; Nieto & Bode, 2008).

Acknowledging the cultural knowledge of minority students in the classroom has been found to have important implications for their well-being outside of school. For example, Banks (1995) highlighted the inclusion of culture in the curriculum as a means of helping students to develop positive racial attitudes. Rodriguez (1982), Wong-Fillmore (1991), and Kouritzin (1999) presented compelling accounts of ways in which the failure to support the maintenance and development of maternal-language proficiency for students of minority background had dire consequences for their sense of ethnic identity and their sense of belonging in their families and ethnic communities. McCaleb (1994), Cummins (2001), and Wong-Fillmore elaborated on some of the dangers, such as increased dropout rates among immigrant and minority youth as well as increased likelihood of gang involvement, or failing to recognize the cultural communities from which students come.

Existing research has been invaluable in highlighting the importance of acknowledging the cultural knowledge that immigrant and minority students bring to a school context, and the work of educators as they develop curricula and teach an increasingly diverse student population (Banks, 1995; Cummins, 2001; Moodley, 1995). Research has also accentuated the need to develop ways of learning about the ethnic, linguistic, and religious backgrounds of students to inform curriculum development and policymaking for students of diverse backgrounds. Cochran-Smith (1995), Ladson-Billings (1995, 2001), and Conle (2000) explored the practice of drawing on the cultural knowledge of preservice teachers as a resource for preparing them to teach in culturally diverse classrooms. It is interesting to note that although there is research that has acknowledged the potential difficulties of moving from home to school for students of a minority background, and the difficulties of moving from school back home when minority students have assimilated to the school and societal expectations that differ from those of their home cultures, the day-to-day transition as minority and immigrant students move from home to school and back home again seems to have been overlooked. In the present study, I examine the nuances that one student lives as she makes this transition on a daily basis.

This work addresses the need for experiential research, focusing specifically on exploring the intersection of home and school influences from the perspective of the students themselves. Presently, there is a surprising lack of research examining ways in which students, in general (Cook-Sather, 2002), and immigrant and minority students, in particular, personally experience their school curriculum and school contexts (He et al., 2007). Bullough's (2007) examination of a Muslim student's response to curriculum and peer interactions in his U.S. school is among the few pieces examining school-curriculum activities from the perspective of a student of ethnic-minority background. Feuerverger's (2001) ethnographic work exploring tensions that Israeli and Palestinian youth experience in their Israeli-Palestinian school is among few studies documenting and exploring student perspectives of their schooling experiences. Sarroub (2005) and Zine's (2001) accounts of Muslim students in American and Canadian schools, respectively, illustrate the complexities of negotiating a sense of identity among peers in a school context when values in the home differ significantly.

Within the relatively limited body of existing research addressing student experiences of schooling and curriculum presented, I present examples of student experiences thematically to address specific issues, topics, or arguments rather than ways that acknowledge multiple facets and tensions interacting at once to shape the experiences of an individual student. Smith-Hefner (1993), in her ethnographic study of female high school Khmer students, presented examples of Puerto Rican female students whose limited academic success was shaped by cultural and sociohistorical influences in their ethnic communities. Rolon-Dow (2004) examined tensions Puerto Rican students and their teachers experience when values supported in their home and in their ethnic communities seem to conflict with those encouraged in school. Lee's (1994, 1996) ethnographic study focused on ways in which Asian high school students' sense of identity and academic achievement was influenced by self-identified labels and membership in specific peer groups. There does not exist a large body of research examining the experiences of one student in the context of their North American school in a way that presents the stories to illustrate ways in which the interaction of multiple influences and issues of relevance may impact on an immigrant or minority student.

This narrative inquiry is intended to provide a glimpse of the intersection of complex influences shaping the life of an immigrant student. I drew on existing narrative and ethnographic accounts of immigrant and minority students attending North American schools to inform this work. Valdes's (1996) work documenting the experiences of a small number of Latino and Mexican American families in their school and community and Li's (2002) ethnographic study with Chinese families as they supported their children's literacy development provide a glimpse of ways in which transitions between home and school may be challenging, and even overwhelming, due to differences in expectations about the school curriculum and the work of teachers. Carger's (1996) long-term narrative account of a Mexican American family's experiences provides an organizational structure for the present study, in that it is an in-depth account of one family's experiences of supporting their child in school, taking into consideration the intersection of multiple influences shaping the child's education. Ross & Chan's (2008) narrative account of an immigrant student, Raj, and his family's academic, financial, and familial difficulties highlighted the many challenges the family encountered in the process of supporting their children's adaptation to their Canadian school and community. This examination of Ai Mei's experiences contributes to the growing but still limited body of research addressing Chinese students in North American schools (Chan, 2004; Kao, 1995; Kim & Chun, 1994; Lee, 1994, 1996, 2001; Li, 2002, 2005).

Theoretical Framework

Given the focus on experience in contributing to Ai Mei's sense of ethnic identity, I used Dewey's (1938) philosophy of the interconnectedness between experience and education as the theoretical foundation for this study. I examined, in particular, ways in which the many influences in her home, school, and neighborhood life with family members, peers, teachers, administrators, and school curriculum events intersected to contribute to her overall experience or learning of a sense of ethnic identity as an immigrant student in a Canadian school context. Ai Mei's stories are set into the framework of a three-dimensional narrative inquiry space (Clandinin & Connelly, 2000), with Bay Street School as the spatial dimension, the years 2001–2003 as the temporal dimension, and my interactions with Ai Mei, her classmates, her teachers, her parents, and other members of the Bay Street School community as the sociopersonal dimension. The stories are a means of exploring the interaction of influences contributing to Ai Mei's sense of identity; they highlight the extent to which this intersection of narratives may be interpreted as conflicting stories to live by (Connelly & Clandinin, 1999).

METHOD

I first met Ai Mei when I began observations in her seventh-grade class as a classroom-based participant observer for a research project exploring the ethnic identity of first-generation Canadian students. The focus on examining the intersection of culture and curriculum as experienced by Chinese Canadian students over the course of their 2 years in middle school was deliberate from the beginning. As I learned about the details of the students' experiences, the complex interaction of factors contributing to Ai Mei's sense of ethnic identity became apparent and merited further analysis.

Ai Mei's homeroom teacher, William, told me about how she had arrived at Bay Street School from an urban area of Fuchien province in China as a 7-year-old. Although she did not initially speak English at all, she was relatively proficient by the time I met her 4 1/2 years after her arrival. Her English was distinct from that of her native-English-speaking peers by the unusual turns of phrases and unconventional uses of some words, but the animated way in which she spoke about her experiences caught my attention from the beginning. I later appreciated this quality even more as I began to work more closely with her as a research participant. Her dark eyes, partially hidden behind wisps of hair, seemed to flicker and dance as she elaborated on details of interactions with peers and family members, especially when she recounted amusing or troublesome events pertaining to difficulties she had experienced in communicating with others. She also seemed to enjoy telling me about incidents that had occurred at home, at school, or in the community. As I learned about Ai Mei's stories of immigration and settlement, the conflicting influences and expectations of her family members, peers and teachers at school, and members of her ethnic community became more apparent, thus further contributing to my decision to focus on her stories in this study.

As a narrative inquirer, I learned about Ai Mei's stories of experience (Connelly & Clandinin, 1988) using a variety of narrative approaches, including long-term, school-based participant observations, document collection set into the context of ongoing conversational interviews with key participants, and the writing of extensive field notes following each school visit, interview, and interaction with participants (Clandinin & Connelly, 1994, 2000; Clandinin et al., 2006) to explore the interwoven quality of Ai Mei, her teacher, her classmates, and her family members' lives. I observed and interacted with her in the context of regular classroom lessons as I assisted her and her classmates with assignments, accompanied them on field trips, attended their band concerts and performances, and took part in school activities such as Multicultural Night, Curriculum and Hot Dog Night, school assemblies, and festivals. School visits began during the fall of 2001 as Ai Mei and her classmates began seventh grade and continued until June 2003 when they graduated from eighth grade at Bay Street School.

I conducted interviews as well as ongoing informal conversations with Ai Mei over the course of the 2 years I spent in her homeroom classroom. I also collected documents such as school notices, announcements of community and school events, notices from bulletin boards and classroom walls in the school, agendas and minutes from School Council meetings, and samples of student work. Descriptive field notes, interview transcripts, researcher journals, and theoretical memos written following school visits were computerized and filed into an existing research project archival system. I examined field notes pertaining to Ai Mei's experiences numerous times to identify recurring themes. Her stories were set into the context of field notes written about her classroom teacher, her peers, and her school community since I began research at the school in 2000.

RESULTS

Ai Mei's Stories of Home and School: Conflicting Stories to Live By

I subsequently present some of Ai Mei's stories of experience to explore challenges and complexities, harmonies and tensions (Clandinin & Connelly, 2002) she lived as she attempted to balance affiliation to her peers while at the same time accommodating for expectations placed on her by her teachers and parents. I explore ways in which parent, teacher, and peer expectations may contribute to shaping her sense of identity, and examine the contribution of narrative methodology in revealing nuances of the intersection of multiple influences in her life.

Bay Street School Context

Ai Mei's stories were set in the context of Bay Street School, a school known to consist of a diverse student community from the time of its establishment (Cochrane, 1950; Connelly, He, Phillion, Chan, & Xu, 2004), located in an urban Toronto neighborhood where the ethnic composition of residents is known to reflect Canadian immigration and settlement patterns (Connelly, Phillion, & He, 2003). Accordingly, the student population at the school reflects this diversity. An Every Student Survey administered to students during the 2001–2002 school year (Chan & Ross, 2002) confirmed the ethnic and linguistic diversity of the students. More specifically, 39 countries and 31 languages were represented in the school. This was the context in which Ai Mei's stories played out.

Home Language Conflicting with School Language

I subsequently present the story, "I was trying to hide my identity," as a starting point for examining Ai Mei's experiences of her academic program at Bay Street School.

"I was trying to hide my identity"

Ai Mei: When I first came to Bay Street School, I stayed with the IL (International Language)[1] teacher, Mrs. Lim . . . I stayed with her for the whole week, and she taught me things in English.
Elaine: What did she teach you?
Ai Mei: You know, easy things, like the alphabet, and how to say "Hello." Then I went to Ms. Jenkins' class. I sat with a strange boy.
Elaine: A strange boy?
Ai Mei: Well, he wasn't that strange. My desk was facing his desk, and he did this to me (Ai Mei demonstrates what the boy did), he stuck his tongue out at me. I didn't know what it meant. He had messy orange hair.
Elaine: Did you make any friends?
Ai Mei: No, not for a long time. Some people tried to talk to me but I didn't understand them. Then Chao tried to talk with me in Fujianese and I pretended I didn't understand her. She tried a few times, then gave up. Then one day, my sister said something to me in Fujianese and Chao heard. She looked at me—she was really surprised because she tried to talk with me and I pretended I couldn't understand her. She didn't like me at all.
Elaine: Why did you do that? Why did you pretend you couldn't understand her?
Ai Mei: I don't know. I was trying to hide my identity.
Ai Mei: (calling over to Chao): Chao, remember how I didn't talk with you, how I pretended I didn't understand you?
Chao: Yeah, I remember. (Chao scowls at Ai Mei.) I didn't like you for a long time.
Ai Mei: Yeah, a long time.

(Fieldnotes, April, 2003)

When Ai Mei arrived at Bay Street School, new students coming into the school spent a week or two with the respective International Language (IL) teacher prior to placement into a classroom. The new student orientation provided teachers the opportunity to assess the English and maternal- language proficiency of new students, identify potential learning difficulties, and learn about their previous schooling experiences. The orientation also provided students an opportunity to learn about school routines in their home language while being gradually introduced into their age-appropriate classroom.

Ai Mei's response to the new student orientation, however, was surprising for a number of reasons. From her teachers' perspective, Chao would have seemed like an ideal friend for Ai Mei—both girls were from the same rural province of southern China, grew up speaking Fujianese at home and Mandarin in school, and Chao could help Ai Mei to adapt to Bay Street School because she had arrived two years earlier. However, Ai Mei did not seem to welcome the opportunity to speak with Chao in Fujianese. Her teachers were also likely puzzled that she would try to "hide [her] identity," because, from their perspective, they worked hard to create programs that would acknowledge students' home cultures in a positive way.

In this context, it is possible that Ai Mei, similar to many students featured in research on immigrant and minority students (Cummins, 2001; Kouritzin, 1999), perceived her affiliation to her family's home language as a hindrance to acceptance by English-speaking peers. She seemed to appreciate learning English from her IL teacher and perhaps felt that her inability to speak in English was an obstacle to forming friendships with English-speaking peers. One day, as we were walking back to her homeroom classroom after art class, she has told me about an incident when she felt embarrassed when she attempted to order drinks at a shopping mall and the vendor could not understand her because "[her] English accent was so bad!" Ai Mei may have been attempting to distance herself from those she perceived as non-English-speaking when she said she "tried to hide [her] identity." Wong-Fillmore (1991) elaborated on how a language minority child might abandon the home language when she or he realizes the low status of this language in relation to the English that is used by peers in school. At the same time, in choosing not to respond to her Fujianese-speaking classmate who attempted to befriend her, Ai Mei was giving up the opportunity to make a friend at a time when she did not have the English proficiency to build friendships easily with English-speaking peers.

School Language Conflicting with Home Language

In addition to pressure to achieve a higher level of English proficiency, Ai Mei seemed to be under pressure from her IL Mandarin teacher, Mrs. Lim, to maintain and to develop her Mandarin proficiency. She was in a high level of language within her grade-level Mandarin program,[2] and she was doing well in the class, judging from the grades I saw when she showed me her Mandarin language textbook and workbooks. Her teacher has said that she did well in her assignments and tests, and that she was a strong student in Mandarin. She stated that it was important for Ai Mei to work hard to maintain the advantage she had over her Canadian-born Chinese peers. Mrs. Lim believed that Ai Mei has an easier time learning the characters that many Canadian-born Chinese students have difficulty with, due to her early years of schooling in China before arriving in Canada. She also felt that Ai Mei had an advantage over her Chinese-born peers, in that her schooling prior to leaving China was regular and uninterrupted in a way some of her Chinese-born peers had not experienced.

Maintenance of her Mandarin language proficiency is an achievement her parents support. At the same time, they would like her to maintain fluency in her family's home dialect of Fujianese. For Ai Mei and her parents, maternal language maintenance has important implications for communication within the family. Ai Mei told me about the following mealtime conversation involving her mother and her younger sister, Susan.

"Susan doesn't speak Fujianese"

> **Ai Mei**: We were eating supper and my mother said to my sister, "(phrase in Fujianese)." My sister asked me, "What did she say?" so I told her, "She wants to know if you want more vegetables."

Elaine: Your sister doesn't understand Fujianese?
Ai Mei: She does but not everything.
Elaine: What did your mother say? Is she worried that your sister doesn't understand her?
Ai Mei: She looked at her like this—(Ai Mei showed me how her mother gave her sister a dirty look).

(Fieldnotes, April, 2003)

From the fieldnote, it seems that Ai Mei's parents were beginning to feel the effects of maternal language loss within the family. Fujianese is not easy to develop and maintain because its use in Canada is not widely supported outside the home, with the exception of exposure to the dialect through other recent immigrants from Fuchien Province. Susan's inability to understand basic vocabulary in her home language likely worried her and Ai Mei's parents, but given the limited resources to support it and limited time to encourage her themselves, they might wonder what can be done. Ai Mei spoke about how her parents reminded her often to speak with her sister in Fujianese. Meanwhile, the sisters had long grown into the habit of speaking to one another in English; communication in their home language of Fujianese would have been stifled at that point due to the lack of ease both felt in using it as well as Susan's limited vocabulary. It might be the case that their parents, as they began to realize the extent of their daughter's maternal language loss, might already be too late to stop it. This pressure to develop and to maintain language proficiency interacted with other factors contributing to Ai Mei's sense of identity and affiliation in her school and in her home and ethnic communities.

Parent Values Conflicting with Peer Values

In addition to pressure to succeed academically, Ai Mei was also under pressure to behave according to the expectations of her peers, teachers, and parents. Through interaction with Ai Mei at Bay Street School over the course of two full academic years, it became apparent that being included within her peer group was very important to her. Like her peers, Ai Mei was becoming more firmly entrenched into popular movies, music, and fashion trends as she moved into adolescence. These influences were coupled with increasing pressure from peers to scoff at school success and downplay the importance of academic work. During the fall of 2001, there were a number of days when I arrived at Ai Mei's classroom to find her friends trying to console her after a popular and outspoken male classmate, Felix, had made unflattering comments about her appearance. Her homeroom teacher also told me about incidents when she had left school in tears after being excluded from an after school activity that had been planned by classmates. Another day, I overheard Felix mimicking one of the stories from Ai Mei's Mandarin IL text; although he spoke in English, the tone and storyline were along the lines of what might be found in the text. Ai Mei laughed at Felix's attempts and seemed to appreciate that he knew a little about what she did in IL class but I also wondered whether she was embarrassed or annoyed with him.

In addition to concerns about being excluded by her peers and feeling the pull of multiple influences in school to behave in certain ways, Ai Mei also seemed to live the tensions of parental expectations and standards for her behavior and comportment that, at times, conflicted with those of her peers, and ways in which she saw herself. I wrote the following fieldnote after a conversation with Ai Mei in which she complained about her mother's comments about her in relation to her mother's friend during a family outing.

"Dim Sum with her mother's friend"

Ai Mei told me today about going out to dim sum with her mother's friend and her family. She said she was very annoyed at being compared to her mother's friend's daughter who is close in age to Ai Mei but who seems like a perfect daughter in her mother's eyes. Ai Mei told me, "My mother said, 'Look at Ming Ming, so pretty and tall. And so quiet! She helps her mother do the cooking and the cleaning at home.' She said to Ming Ming's mother, 'Look at Ai Mei, 13 years old and so short. And she doesn't help me at home, and she doesn't cook!' She kept comparing us, saying how nice Ming Ming is and how terrible I am." Ai Mei rolled her eyes.

(Fieldnotes, April, 2003)

The interaction between Ai Mei and her mother highlighted the potential for tensions to develop when expressing differences in perspective about the value of certain kinds of behaviors over others. It sounded as if Ai Mei resented that her mother did not think she was quiet or helpful or tall enough when compared with her friend's daughter. Although a generational gap might account for some of the tension about what constituted appropriate behavior and goals for Ai Mei with respect to what she did to contribute to the family, some of this tension might also have been shaped by the very different contexts in which Ai Mei and her mother have spent their childhood. Ai Mei has spent a good portion of her childhood living in different homes in an urban, commercial district of Toronto. Her perception of appropriate behavior and practices has likely been shaped by influences different from what her mother experienced in rural Fuchien province of China where she spent her own childhood.

Teacher Expectations Conflicting with Parent Expectations

Moreover, although Ai Mei's parents and her teachers had in common the goal of academic success for her, tensions surfaced about the time commitment needed to fulfill these school and family responsibilities. Ai Mei seemed to be caught between pressures to help in the family business and teacher expectations for completed homework and thorough preparation for tests and assignments.

Ai Mei's family acquired a dumpling restaurant during the fall of her eighth-grade year, and since then, the whole family had devoted much time and energy toward building a successful business. I knew that Ai Mei's family owned a dumpling restaurant because she had told me about what she did to help.

Ai Mei: There's a door that no one can close but me.
Elaine: What's wrong with it?
Ai Mei: It's stuck, so I have to kick it shut. (She demonstrates as she says this, kicking to one side as she leans over.) Then, we go home, me, my mom, and my dad.

Elaine: How about your sister?

Ai Mei: She goes home a little earlier, with my grandmother and grandfather.

(Fieldnotes, October, 2002)

Each day after school, Ai Mei and her sister, Susan, after spending some time with their friends in the classroom or in the school yard, headed to the dumpling restaurant to spend the evening there helping their parents. Ai Mei's sister, Susan, has told me about how she helped their father by standing outside the restaurant where the family sells vegetables and fruits to watch for people who attempted to take food without paying for it. When I asked her whether this often happened, she nodded gravely.

The importance of Ai Mei and Susan's participation in the family business could be denied, but Ai Mei's teachers had questioned the time commitment involved. Late in the fall after the family acquired the dumpling restaurant, Ai Mei's teacher, William, noticed that she had begun to come to school looking very tired, and without her homework done. One day while he was meeting with her to discuss the report card that would soon be sent home to her parents, he told her that she could have done better had she submitted all of her homework and done a better job on recent tests. Ai Mei surprised him by bursting into tears. Little by little, William learned that Ai Mei had little opportunity to do her homework or to study because she was helping out at the restaurant during evenings and weekends. By the time the family had closed up the restaurant, traveled home, and eaten supper, it was past 11:00 pm or 12:00 am, beyond what William thought was appropriate for a 12-year-old. With a sense of professional responsibility to report potentially negligent situations to officials and the support of school board policies guiding his actions, William spoke with his principal about the situation. Both decided it was a borderline case, and with the principal's knowledge, William contacted the Children's Aid Society (CAS) about Ai Mei's family. I wrote the following field note the day William told me about his call to the CAS.

"I called the CAS"

I was helping William straighten up the textbooks, sort student assignments into piles, and organize pens, pencils, and chalk into appropriate places in the classroom. We have gotten into the habit of talking about events of the day as we tidy up the classroom after the students have left for French class toward the end of the day. Today, William said to me, "I called the CAS about Ai Mei. She doesn't do her homework or have time to study because she's up late working in the family restaurant. She's exhausted." (Fieldnotes, December, 2002)

The dumpling restaurant was tied to Ai Mei's family's dreams of financial success and family reunification. Ai Mei had spoken about how her parents had sponsored her maternal grandparents to come to Toronto from Fuchien province, and were in the process of trying to bring her paternal grandparents over to join the family as well. The importance of helping her family with their business could not be denied from her parents' perspective and, from what Ai Mei has said about the ways in which she helped the family, it could be assumed that she also recognized the importance of her role as well.

At the same time, it was beginning to become apparent that assisting her parents in the family business might have diverted her attention away from fulfilling her parents' desire for her to do well in school, in that time spent in the restaurant helping her family was time that she could have otherwise devoted to her school work. Ai Mei was caught between her parents' dreams of financial and business success, her sense of responsibility, as the oldest daughter in the family, to help them achieve this success, her parents' desire for her to perform well academically to secure her own future economic success, and her teacher's professional responsibility to report potentially negligent situations to officials. She lived the tensions of deciding how best to use her time to assist her parents in the family business as well as to perform well academically.

This situation also needed to be examined in terms of her teacher's professional tensions and ways in which these tensions might have contributed to Ai Mei's sense of identity. Her teacher, William, was aware that the cultural and social narratives guiding his professional practices might have differed from those guiding the practices of the parents of his students, and had expressed a commitment to acknowledging the diversity of his students. The potential for conflict between teacher, student, and parent perspectives pertaining to Ai Mei's use of time in the evenings and on weekends became apparent when William contacted child-protection officials to report that Ai Mei's time in the family's restaurant in the evenings was contributing to her late arrival at school in the mornings, without her assigned homework completed. He did so with the belief in the importance of protecting Ai Mei's time to ensure that she had adequate time and necessary conditions in her home to complete her school work.

William's call to the CAS, however well intentioned, had the potential to cause difficulties in Ai Mei's family as well as a rift in his own relationship with Ai Mei. In fact, he later told me about how Ai Mei, on realizing that he had reported her parents to the CAS, neither came around after school to spend time in his classroom nor did she tell him about what was happening in her life as she was accustomed to doing up until that time. He felt he had lost her trust and believed that his call to the CAS had been the cause. This example highlights some of the tension William felt as he attempted to balance his professional obligation to report potentially negligent situations to child protection officials and his ideal of the role of teacher as an advocate who supported students in ways they would appreciate.

Learning About Ai Mei's Experiences as a Narrative Inquirer

These stories highlight some of the complexities of the interaction of multiple influences in contributing to Ai Mei's sense of identity. Underlying these accounts of Ai Mei's experiences with her peers, teachers, and parents in the context of school and community-based events are accounts of my interactions with Ai Mei as a narrative inquirer. The narrative inquiry approach used in this study facilitated the identification of the many nuances of living as an immigrant student in a North American school context, and provided a framework in which to ponder these complexities. To begin, the stories of experience documenting Ai Mei's experiences as an immigrant student at Bay Street School were gathered over a long period of time as I spent 2 full school years in her homeroom classroom with her, her teachers, and her peers as a participant observer. During this time, I became a member of the classroom, joining the class for activities such as field trips, special school events, band concerts, and school assemblies.

More importantly, however, I was a part of their class during the uneventful days of lessons and regular school activities. It was during these times that I was able to build a relationship with Ai Mei and her peers and teachers. They grew to see me as an additional teacher in the classroom who was able to help them with assignments, act as an adult supervisor during in-school activities or field trips, and as a listening ear when they had disagreements with friends or with teachers.

I learned about the details of Ai Mei's life as she told me about her classmates, her parents, her family's dumpling restaurant, her sister, and family outings. I heard about her perceptions of how she fit into her peer group, her ethnic community, and her family as she told me about specific interactions, such as the family dinner when her sister did not understand what her mother had said in Fujianese, her mother's criticisms of her in comparison with her mother's friend's daughter, or her impressions of the new student orientation that was in place to ease her transition into the school as a new student from China.

As the students came to realize my interest in learning about their school lives, they began to update me on events I had missed between visits, and to fill me in on what they referred to as "gossip" at school. At one point partway through my second year with Ai Mei's homeroom class, I conducted interviews with the students. As I planned the questions and discussed them with William, I remember wondering whether this shift to a more formal kind of interaction with the students would change the relationship we had established. My concern about negatively impacting the relationship turned out to be unfounded. In fact, I was pleased to realize one day when Ai Mei approached me to tell me about a family dinner (see "Susan doesn't speak Fujianese") that the process had opened up further opportunities to learn about the students' lives. Realizing that I was interested in hearing about their interactions at home and in the community with members of their ethnic groups, the students began to tell me more about them. Our existing relationship had provided a foundation such that I could talk with the students about their experiences with family and members of their ethnic communities, and the interviews provided an opportunity for the students to learn, in a more explicit way, about my interest in hearing about out-of-school aspects of their lives. Our relationship was such that they knew they could trust that I would treat their stories and their perceptions of these stories with interest and respect.

I also saw Ai Mei in the neighborhood with her friends during the after school hours as they moved from house to house visiting one another in the housing project while their parents worked in nearby restaurants and shops, and on weekends as she shopped with her sister and her parents in the stores that lined the commercial area near the school. These brief interactions provided further glimpses of influences interacting in her life to contribute to shaping a sense of identity in ways that would not be possible through formal interviews or a more structured schedule of research observations. In addition, these interactions provided an opportunity for Ai Mei's friends and family to become familiar with my presence and participation in the school.

Tensions of acting as a researcher with a focus on learning about the experiences of my participants became more apparent as my role as researcher became less clear. As I got to know Ai Mei and her family, I felt the tensions she experienced as she balanced the multiple influences in her life and wanted to advocate for her. I felt a sense of responsibility to Ai Mei, to support her learning and to attempt to ease some of the tensions she experienced as she balanced affiliation to her home and school cultures. I understood a little of the betrayal she felt when her parents were reported to child protection officials, and the fear her parents might have felt. When she told me about how her parents would not be able to attend her eighth-grade graduation because they needed to work, I wanted to be sure to attend and to take photos of her with her sister so that she would have a record of the event. The nature of the researcher-participant relationship in contributing to understanding about the nuances of experiences lived by my student participant heightened my understanding of what the events might mean for her.

The role of narrative inquiry, and, more specifically, the role of long-term participation in the day to day school life of an immigrant student that was critical to this narrative inquiry, contributed to the researcher-participant relationship I was able to develop with Ai Mei, her peers, and her teachers. Careful attention to the details of life in classrooms (Jackson, 1990) and within the school, and respect for the ongoing negotiation so critical to building a research relationship from initial negotiation of entry into the school-research site to negotiation of exit towards the completion of school-based narrative inquiries—features foundational to Clandinin & Connelly's (2000) approach—further contributed to the development of a research relationship based on trust and familiarity with Ai Mei. This trust, in turn, engaged me in careful consideration of the potential implications of telling and retelling Ai Mei's stories, and what they might mean for her, as well as other immigrant and minority students who may struggle with similar challenges of balancing tensions of affiliation to home and school cultures in a North American school context. It was also through this commitment to examining these tensions narratively from multiple perspectives of others in Ai Mei's school, as well as in relation to temporal, spatial, and sociopersonal dimensions at play in her school, that enabled me to see some of the nuances and complexities of the conflicting influences in Ai Mei's life. In the process of examining Ai Mei's experiences narratively, I also became a participant, in that my experiences and interpretations of Ai Mei's stories were continually being examined and reflected on as I shared my interpretations with Ai Mei in an ongoing process to better understand the stories she told.

This relationship, in turn, was critical to my learning about the complexities of Ai Mei's experiences. In this way, this long-term, school-based narrative inquiry approach contributes not only to knowledge about the experiences of my participants as I focus on examining nuances of the research phenomenon at hand but it also raises awareness about the intricacies, and the impact, of the work of researchers in the lives of our participants.

DISCUSSION

Conflicting Student, Teacher, and Parent Stories to Live By: Implications for Practice, Research, and Theory

This examination of the intersection of home, school, and ethnic community influences in Ai Mei's life provided a glimpse of the challenges immigrant or minority students might encounter as they negotiate a sense of ethnic identity. More specifically, examining Ai Mei's stories reveals ways in which immigrant and minority students may be pulled in many directions, with some of these influences experienced as conflicting stories to live by as teacher, peer, and parent expectations intersect on a school landscape. The stories highlight the potential for conflict when immigrant students have values shaped by interaction with family and members of their ethnic community as well as values shaped by interaction with peers, teachers, and other members of their North American school communities.

As Ai Mei grows up, she needs to determine which aspects of her home and school communities she incorporates into her own set of values. The age-old tension between children and their parents as children move toward adulthood and make decisions pertaining to their education and the kind of life they see themselves leading is exacerbated by differences in perspective that are influenced by differences in culture between their new host society that the children are navigating and the landscape that their immigrant parents experienced as children in their home countries. This tension is further complicated by struggles that their parents have endured in the immigration process as they settle into new countries. Ai Mei's stories revealed the extent to which ideas for innovative curricula and the good intentions of teachers, administrators, researchers, and policymakers may unfold in unexpected ways. Learning about Ai Mei's conflicting stories to live by highlighted the importance of examining ways in which curriculum and school events may contribute to shaping the ethnic identity of immigrant and minority students in ways much more complex than anticipated by their teachers, their parents, and even the students themselves.

This knowledge, in turn, informs the work of teachers and administrators as they attempt to meet the needs of their increasingly diverse student populations. Teachers need to learn to meet the academic and social needs of their immigrant and minority students in a school context with sometimes little knowledge about the cultures and education systems from which they are coming. In this way, knowledge gained from this study has implications for teachers working in diverse school contexts, professional development for in-service and pre-service educators, and decision making pertaining to the development of curriculum policies for multicultural school contexts. Examining Ai Mei's experiences of the intersection of home and school influences informs the development and implementation of programs designed to facilitate the adaptation of immigrant students in North American schools. Ai Mei's stories of experience may be referred to as an example of a life-based literary narrative (Phillion & He, 2004), and contribute to the body of student lore introduced by Schubert and Ayers (1992) and recognized by Jackson (1992) in Pinar, Reynolds, Slattery, and Taubman's book, Understanding Curriculum (1995). Attention to the narratives of students and their families is a reminder not to lose sight of the diversity in student populations and highlights the need for attention to issues of social justice and equity in education. Not only does this research address the dearth of research focused specifically on students' experiences from their perspective, but it also contributes to understanding of the experiences of immigrant and minority students to provide insights into the experiences of a group about which educators and policymakers involved in developing and implementing school curriculum are desperately in need of better understanding.

CONCLUSION

Teachers and administrators with whom I shared this piece appreciated the acknowledgment of the challenges they encounter in their work with their students. William, as a beginning teacher, recognized the need for further attention to prepare teachers for diverse classrooms and felt that stories such as those presented in this article contributed to raising awareness of difficulties teachers may encounter; he recognized the potential of the stories as a forum to generate discussion among teachers and administrators. His administrators spoke of the challenges inherent to meeting the needs of their student population, and referred to the tensions of needing to abide by existing policies even as they lived the difficulties of implementing some of the policies with their students and teachers.

Exploring the multitude of influences shaping student participation in school curriculum using a narrative inquiry approach to examining student experiences is also a means of acknowledging the complexity of schooling and teacher preparation (Cochran Smith, 2006), and the need for guidance about how best to develop curriculum and pedagogy for students of minority background, and the challenges associated with working with diverse student populations. Given the increasingly diverse North American context, is it essential that educators and policymakers are well informed about the students for whom educational practices and policies are developed.

NOTES

1. Students at Bay Street School chose from IL classes in Cantonese or Mandarin Chinese, Vietnamese, Arabic, Swahili/Black History, or Spanish that were integrated into their regular school day.

2. The Mandarin texts used in the IL program were based on a multi-grade format in which each grade level was in turn divided into six levels of difficulty ranging from beginner to advanced to accommodate for differences in language proficiency among students in the same grade level.

REFERENCES

Ada, A. F. (1988). The Pajaro Valley experience: Working with Spanish-speaking parents to develop children's reading and writing skills in the home through the use of children's literature. In T. Skutnabb-Kangas & J. Cummins (Eds.), *Minority education: From shame to struggle* (pp. 223–237). Clevedon, UK: Multilingual Matters.

Banks, J. A. (1995). Multicultural education: Its effects on students' racial and gender role attitudes. In J. A. Banks & C. A. McGee Banks (Eds.), *Handbook of research on multicultural education* (pp. 617–627). Toronto, Canada: Prentice Hall International.

Bullough, R. V., Jr. (2007). Ali: Becoming a student—A life history. In D. Thiessen & A. Cook-Sather (Eds.), *International handbook of student experience in elementary and secondary school* (pp. 493–516). Dordecht, The Netherlands: Springer.

Carger, C. (1996). *Of borders and dreams: Mexican-American experience of urban education*. New York: Teachers College Press.

Chan, E. (2004). *Narratives of ethnic identity: Experiences of first generation Chinese Canadian students*. Unpublished doctoral dissertation, University of Toronto, Ontario, Canada.

Chan, E., & Ross, V. (2002). *ESL Survey Report. Sponsored by the ESL Work-group in collaboration with the OISE/UT Narrative and Diversity Research Team*. Toronto, Canada: Centre for Teacher Development, Ontario Institute for Studies in Education, University of Toronto, Ontario, Canada.

Clandinin, D. J., & Connelly, F. M. (1994). Personal experience methods. In N. K. Denzin & Y. S. Lincoln (Eds.), *Handbook of qualitative research in the social sciences* (pp. 413–427). Thousand Oaks, CA: Sage.

Clandinin, D. J., & Connelly, F. M. (2000). *Narrative inquiry: Experience and story in qualitative research*. San Francisco: Jossey-Bass.

Clandinin, D. J., & Connelly, F. M. (2002, October). Intersecting narratives: Cultural harmonies and tensions in inner-city urban Canadian schools. Proposal submitted to the Social Sciences and Humanities Research Council of Canada.

Clandinin, D. J., Huber, J., Huber, M., Murphy, M. S., Murray Orr, A., Pearce, M., et al. (2006). *Composing diverse identities: Narrative inquiries into the interwoven lives of children and teachers*. New York: Routledge.

Cochrane, M. (Ed.). (1950). *Centennial story: Board of education for the city of Toronto: 1850–1950*. Toronto, Canada: Thomas Nelson.

Cochran-Smith, M. (1995). Uncertain allies: Understanding the boundaries of race and teaching. *Harvard Educational Review, 65*, 541–570.

Cochran-Smith, M. (2006). Thirty editorials later: Signing off as editor. *Journal of Teacher Education, 57*(2), 95–101.

Conle, C. (2000). The asset of cultural pluralism: an account of cross-cultural learning in pre-service teacher education. *Teaching and Teacher Education, 16*, 365–387.

Connelly, F. M., & Clandinin, D. J. (1988). *Teachers as curriculum planners: Narratives of experience*. New York: Teachers College Press.

Connelly, F. M., & Clandinin, D. J. (1999). Stories to live by: Teacher identities on a changing professional knowledge landscape. In F. M. Connelly & D. J. Clandinin (Eds.), *Shaping a professional identity: Stories of educational practice* (pp. 114–132). London, Canada: Althouse Press.

Connelly, F. M., He, M. F., Phillion, J., Chan, E., & Xu, S. (2004). Bay Street Community School: Where you belong. *Orbit, 34*(3), 39–42.

Connelly, F. M., Phillion, J., & He, M. F. (2003). An exploration of narrative inquiry into multiculturalism in education: Reflecting on two decades of research in an inner-city Canadian community school. *Curriculum Inquiry, 33*, 363–384.

Cook-Sather, A. (2002) Authorizing students' perspectives: toward trust, dialogue, and change in education. *Educational Researcher, 31* (4), 3–14.

Cummins, J. (2001). *Negotiating identities: Education for empowerment in a diverse society* (2nd ed.). Ontario, CA: CABE (California Association for Bilingual Education).

Cummins, J., Bismilla, V., Chow, P., Cohen, S., Giampapa, F., Leoni, L., et al. (2005). Affirming identity in multilingual classrooms. *Educational Leadership*, 63(1), 38–43.

Dewey, J. (1938). *Experience and education*. New York: Simon & Schuster.

Feuerverger, G. (2001). *Oasis of dreams: Teaching and learning peace in a Jewish-Palestinian village in Israel*. New York: Routledge.

Gay, G. (2000). *Culturally responsive teaching: Theory, research, & practice*. New York: Teachers College Press.

He, M. F., Phillion, J., Chan, E., & Xu, S. (2007). Chapter 15—Immigrant students' experience of curriculum. In F. M. Connelly, M. F. He, & J. Phillion (Eds.), *Handbook of curriculum and instruction* (pp. 219–239). Thousand Oaks, CA: Sage.

Igoa, C. (1995). *The inner world of the immigrant child*. New York: St. Martin's Press.

Jackson, P. (1990). *Life in classrooms*. New York: Teachers College Press. Jackson, P. (1992). Conceptions of curriculum specialists. In P. Jackson (Ed.), *Handbook of research on curriculum* (pp. 3–40). New York: Peter Lang.

Kao, G. (1995). Asian Americans as model minorities? A look at their academic performance. *American Journal of Education, 103*, 121–159.

Kim, U., & Chun, M. J. B. (1994). The educational 'success' of Asian Americans: An indigenous perspective. *Journal of Applied Developmental Psychology*, 15, 329–339.

Kouritzin, S. G. (1999). *Face(t)s of first language loss*. Mahwah, NJ: Erlbaum.

Ladson-Billings, G. (1995). Multicultural teacher education: Research, practice, and policy. In J. A. Banks & C. A. McGee Banks (Eds.), *Handbook of research on multicultural education* (pp. 747–759). Toronto, Canada: Prentice Hall International.

Ladson-Billings, G. (2001). *Crossing over to Canaan: The journey of new teachers in diverse classrooms*. San Francisco: Jossey-Bass.

Lee, S. J. (1994). Behind the model-minority stereotype: Voices of high and low-achieving Asian American students. *Anthropology & Education Quarterly*, 25, 413–429.

Lee, S. J. (1996). *Unravelling the "model minority" stereotype: Listening to Asian American youth*. New York: Teachers College Press.

Lee, S. J. (2001). More than "model minority" or "delinquents": A look at Hmong American high school students. *Harvard Educational Review, 71*, 505–528.

Li, G. (2002). "East is East, West is West"? Home literacy, culture, and schooling. In J. L. Kincheloe & J. A. Jipson (Eds.), *Rethinking childhood book series* (Vol. 28). New York: Peter Lang.

Li, G. (2005). *Culturally contested pedagogy: Battles of literacy and schooling between mainstream teachers and Asian immigrant parents*. Albany, NY: SUNY Press.

McCaleb, S. P. (1994). *Building communities of learners: A collaboration among teachers, students, families and community*. New York: St. Martin's Press.

Moodley, K. A. (1995). Multicultural education in Canada: Historical development and current status. In J. A. Banks & C. A. McGee Banks (Eds.), *Handbook of research on multicultural education* (pp. 801–820). Toronto, Canada: Prentice Hall International.

Nieto, S., & Bode, P. (2008). *Affirming diversity: The sociopolitical context of multicultural education* (5th ed.). New York: Longman.

Phillion, J., & He, M. F. (2004). Using life based literary narratives in multicultural teacher education. *Multicultural Perspectives*, 6(2), 3–9.

Pinar, W. F., Reynolds, W. M., Slattery, P., & Taubman, P. M. (1995). *Understanding curriculum: An introduction to the study of historical and contemporary curriculum discourses*. New York: Peter Lang.

Rodriguez, R. (1982). *Hunger of memory: The education of Richard Rodriguez*. Boston: David R. Godine.

Rolon-Dow, R. (2004). Seduced by images: Identity and schooling in the lives of Puerto Rican girls. *Anthropology & Education Quarterly, 35*, 8–29.

Ross, V., & Chan, E. (2008). Multicultural education: Raj's story using a curricular conceptual lens of the particular. *Teaching and Teacher Education, 24*, 1705–1716.

Sarroub, L. K. (2005). *All-American Yemeni girls: Being Muslim in a public school*. Philadelphia: University of Pennsylvania Press.

Schubert, W., & Ayers, W. (Eds.) *Teacher lore: Learning from our own experience*. New York: Longman.

Smith-Hefner, N. (1993). Education, gender, and generational conflict among Khmer refugees. *Anthropology & Education Quarterly, 24*, 135–158.

Statistics Canada. (2008). *Canada's ethnocultural mosaic, 2006 census*. Retrieved July 1, 2008, from http://www12.statcan.ca/english/census06/analysis/ethnicorigin/pdf/97-562-XIE2006001.pdf

U.S. Census Bureau. (2002). *United States Census 2000*. Washington, D.C: U.S. Government Printing Office.

Valdes, G. (1996). *Con respeto: Bridging the distances between culturally diverse families and schools. An ethnographic portrait*. New York: Teachers College Press.

Villegas, A. M. (1991). *Culturally responsive pedagogy for the 1990's and beyond*. Princeton, NJ: Educational Testing Service.

Wong-Fillmore, L. (1991). When learning a second language means losing the first. *Early Childhood Research Quarterly, 6*, 323–346.

Zine, J. (2001). Muslim youth in Canadian schools: Education and the politics of religious identity. *Anthropology & Education Quarterly, 32*, 399–423.

AUTHOR NOTE

Elaine Chan is an assistant professor of Diversity and Curriculum Studies in the Department of Teaching, Learning, and Teacher Education at the College of Education and Human Sciences, the University of Nebraska–Lincoln. Her research and teaching interests are in the areas of: narrative inquiry, culture and curriculum; multicultural education; ethnic identity of first-generation North Americans; student experiences of schooling; and educational equity policies. She has taught and conducted long-term classroom-based research in Canadian, Japanese, and American schools. She is currently co-authoring a book on engaging ELL students in arts education with Margaret Macintyre Latta.

APPENDIX B

Resilient Leadership: A Phenomenological Exploration Into How Black Women in Higher Education Leadership Navigate Cultural Adversity

Nuchelle L. Chance[1]

[1]Fort Hays State University, Hays, KS, USA

Source: The material in this appendix originally appeared in the *journal of Humanistic Psychology,* 62(1), 44–78. https://doi.org/10.1177/00221678211003000. Copyright 2022, Sage Publications, Inc.

Corresponding author(s):

Nuchelle L. Chance, Department of Psychology, Fort Hays State University, 600 Park Street, 208 Martin Allen Hall, Hays, KS 67601-4099, USA. Email: nlchance0331@gmail.com

ABSTRACT

This article explores adversity and the lived experiences of Black women in higher education leadership. Using phenomenology, this study specifically explores how Black women in higher education leadership navigate the adverse challenges of intersectionality, stereotype threat, and tokenism. Black women in leadership undergo adversity including limited role models, the concrete ceiling, and the intersectionality of racism, sexism, and ageism, as well as tokenism. The current findings validate that Black women in higher education leadership experience adversity. Some of the more salient codes that emerged were discrimination such as racism, sexism, ageism, and the intersection of these challenges with identity, cultural diversity and belonging, resilience, and leadership callings. Referred to as "superwomen," Black women are resilient and strong. The results of this study reveal that Black women use adversity as fuel, thus helping them develop the necessary skills to prepare them for leadership. Their strength through adversity is driven by the resilience that has manifested as motivation factors such as family and relationships, mentorship and sponsorship, as well as the support of cultural identity and diversity. The current findings support the notion that adversity shapes Black women into leaders with an emphasis on higher education leadership.

KEYWORDS

resilience, adversity, leadership development, Black women, higher education, tokenism, stereotype threat, intersectionality, phenomenology, qualitative research

INTRODUCTION

Black women are continually emerging as leaders across all industries, organizations, nonprofits, government agencies, and academia ("The state of women-owned businesses," 2018). Leadership ambitions of this group are high, such that Black women are nearly three times more likely to aspire to senior leadership with prestigious titles than their counterparts (Hewlett & Green, 2015). With these goals, however, come intrinsic and extrinsic challenges.

As a collective, Black people have and continue to face substantial adversity both personally and professionally. Nevertheless, overcoming adversity is routine of the Black community. Black women; however, are doubly affected when adversity and challenges are rooted in race and gender differences. Identity markers such as being a "woman" and being "Black" do not exist independently of each other, thus creating a complex intersection of potential adverse experiences. Black women experience more adversity and are given less opportunity such that they perceive that failure is not an option (Rosette & Livingston, 2012). With that said, Black women who have reached leadership success have done so by beating the odds.

Although there has been a significant amount of research on leadership through times of crisis and adversity (Banutu-Gomez, 2004; Beaudan, 2002; Boin & Hart, 2003; Burnett, 1998; Goleman, 2000; Pillai & Meindl, 1991; Valle, 1999) and on women in higher education leadership (Dean et al., 2009; Longman & Madsen, 2014; Madsen, 2008; Wolverton et al., 2009); research specifically investigating minorities in higher education leadership is limited (Bower & Wolverton, 2009; Gutiérrez y Muhs et al., 2012; Valverde, 2003). Furthermore, research on the adverse experiences of Black women serving in college and university leadership is minimal (Davis & Maldonado, 2015; Jean-Marie, 2006).

Black women in higher education leadership face significant challenges and adversity; therefore, there is a need to examine what that adversity looks like and how it has influenced professional Black women and their leadership development. The purpose of this phenomenological study was to explore and describe how Black women in higher education leadership navigate intersectionality, stereotype threat, and tokenism. The following questions guided this study:

1. What influence does a Black women's identity have on her ability to lead in higher education administration?
2. What influence does stereotype threat have on Black women's leadership in higher education administration?
3. What influence does tokenism have on Black women's leadership style and ability in higher education administration?

While White men continue to dominate higher education leadership, the current research sheds light on Black women's methods of advancement and retention in higher education leadership by exploring the adverse lived experiences unique to Black women. Ultimately, this research attempts to provide direction and guidance to all women while emphasizing the challenges of specific underrepresented groups attempting to advance in the pipeline of higher education administrative leadership.

REVIEW OF THE LITERATURE

There has been a great deal of emphasis placed on the need to increase the number of women in higher education administration positions in American colleges and universities based on the equality of civil rights (American Council on Education [ACE], 2017). There are recent trends in examining leadership research to help leaders in higher education and those striving for leadership to thrive in the multifaceted global environment and effectively prepare for the challenge of leading complex institutions. Thus, focusing on Black women who serve in leadership roles at colleges and universities will help expand the knowledge base on higher education leadership, Black women in leadership, resilience, and overcoming adversity, therefore opening up the door for more access by this population.

Black women have had to overcome significant adversity to achieve professional success (Assari, 2017). Some of the challenges the Black women in higher education leadership have faced include underrepresentation (ACE, 2017; Bower & Wolverton, 2009; Davis & Maldonado, 2015; T. B. Jones et al., 2012) due to White male/male dominance (Chun & Evans, 2016; T. B. Jones et al., 2012) limited vertical mobility and the concrete ceiling (Baxter-Nuamah, 2015; Davis, 2012) perpetuated by racism, sexism, ageism (and the intersection of these), stereotype threat, isolation, and tokenism (Bower & Wolverton, 2009; Bright, 2010; Kanter, 1977; Sobers, 2014; Woods-Giscombé, 2010).

Underrepresentation and White Male Dominance

Findings from the American College President Study reported that women are still underrepresented, accounting for only 30% of all president positions in 2016, which is slightly up from 26% in 2012 (ACE, 2017). The emerging changes in this field are allowing women to make strides; however, of this 30%, only 9% represent Black women compared with the 83% who are White women. The positions of chancellor or president have traditionally been held by older, White men (Kirschman, 2009). However, even when controlling for race, males still dominate this senior higher education leadership population. Of the 8% of Black college presidents, only 34% were women compared with 66% who were men (ACE, 2017). Furthermore, Black women in these leadership positions serve almost exclusively at community colleges and historically Black colleges and universities (HBCUs; ACE, 2017). Thus, the barriers and obstacles that Black women in higher education administration face are not only personal, but also systemic.

Despite a few gains by women and minorities, leadership in U.S. higher education has consistently been dominated by White males (Chun & Evans, 2016). Western society is gradually moving toward equality between genders (Inglehart et al., 2003), yet there is a disproportional number of male versus female senior leaders of colleges and universities. That gap widens severely when specifically evaluating Black women compared to White men in higher education leadership (ACE, 2017).

Limited Vertical Mobility and the Concrete Ceiling

In academia, the glass ceiling has been restructured as the "concrete ceiling" for many Black women (Baxter-Nuamah, 2015; Davis, 2012). The concrete ceiling is a unique adverse obstacle that Black and other minority women face limiting their ascension into positions of leadership in business and academia. This concept is a metaphor for limiting upward career mobility and hindering Black women's ability to coexist in an organization, depicting that Black women are underrepresented and face adversity in seeking or being in senior levels of leadership in higher education. Although similar, this differs from the concept of the glass ceiling that all women have faced for years. With the glass ceiling, women can at least see what they were being blocked from as well as have the ability to see, shatter, and breakthrough glass. Concrete however; blocks vision and is nearly impenetrable.

There are several factors that perpetuate the challenges associated with the concrete ceiling; one being the lack of positive Black women role models (Galloway, 2016). This opens the door to increased exposure with no guidance to adverse experiences that include discrimination, which is reliant on stereotyping (S. Jackson & Harris, 2007), racism, sexism (Galloway, 2016), and their intersectionality. Vertical mobility for Black women in higher education has been limited due to these dueling forms of discrimination. Discrimination works not only to keep women of color out of positions of leadership but also works against their authentic inclusion when they make it into those positions. The literature further suggests that discrimination increases for Black women, the higher they climb in higher education leadership. (Baxter-Nuamah, 2015). The levels of mental and emotional labor that is required for a Black woman in a position of leadership while maintaining her authentic racial and sexual identity has been identified as exhausting (Erskine et al., 2020). Alas, once the hurdle of the concrete ceiling has been overcome for these female leaders a new series of challenges present. Higher education's power structure, gender-pay gap, and the limited access to power and privilege can result in feelings of tokenism and isolation, leading to diminished resilience thus presenting unique challenges for Black women in senior higher education leadership (Becks-Moody, 2004).

The Many Faces of Discrimination

Discrimination refers to the harmful and sometimes dangerous actions of some based on negative prejudice that is expressed in escalating levels of violence to others, ranging from spoken abuse to genocide, according to the seminal research of Allport (1954). Discrimination is fueled by stereotype threat and fear and is expressed as racism, sexism, ageism, classism, or ableism. Professional discrimination speaks to people's unfair and unethical treatment based on race, sex, age, religion, health, socioeconomic status, and class. It looks like harassment, preferential hiring practices, wrongful terminations, intentional demotions, or unjustly denied promotions, to name a few. One of the real dangers of racial discrimination that people of color experience is racial trauma or race-based stress. Experiences of discrimination compounded with fear of a real or perceived threat can lead to symptoms that mirror those of posttraumatic stress disorder (Comas-Díaz et al., 2019). Black women have to manage their identities of people of color and as women when navigating society and leadership.

Intersectionality. For Black women navigating identity, "race does not exist outside of gender . . . and gender does not exist outside of race" (Parker & Lynn, 2002, p. 12) as such, they face the dual discrimination of the of racism and sexism. The overlap or interaction of the various categories of identity discrimination is referred to as intersectionality (Crenshaw, 1989). Studies have found that the intersection of racism and sexism in the workplace can result in biases that alter the perceptions of Black women's competencies thus limiting their ascension into leadership (Hughes & Dodge, 1997; Moorosi et al, 2018; Patterson, 2006; Scott, 2011; Smith, 2016). This intersectionality has led to more examination and critique for Black women in administrative leadership, making it more difficult for them to succeed (Hughes & Dodge, 1997, Patterson, 2006).

Stereotype Threat. Stereotype threat is a construct that refers to the risk of self-confirming negative beliefs or stereotypes about one's racial, ethnic, gender, or cultural group in the eyes of others or one's self and has hindered professional advancement for Black women in and out of academic leadership. A growing body of evidence supports the notion that stereotype threat leads to the reduced performance of individuals that identify as part of the negatively stereotyped group. Other negative outcomes of stereotype threat include anxiety and increased use of self-defeating strategies (Stone, 2002), disengagement and disidentification (J. Steele et al., 2002), lowered academic performance (Croizet & Claire, 1998; Inzlicht & Ben-Zeev, 2000; C. M. Steele, 1997), and narrowed career options (Gupta & Bhawe, 2007; Murphy et al., 2007). C. M. Steele and Aronson (1995) speculated that decreased task performance caused by stereotype threat could specifically be due to factors such as narrowed attention, distraction, anxiety, self-consciousness, and reduced effort or over-effort. Alas, stereotype threat can adversely affect Black women's experiences in higher education senior leadership and the workforce in general. As it pertains to stereotype threat, Black women who hold senior leadership positions in various organizations, including higher education, battle with the inner turmoil of self-doubt, negative beliefs, low self-esteem. They further struggle with external forces of a hostile environment of racism and sexism daily (Alexander-Lee, 2014).

Black women have unique experiences that other groups of women cannot relate to regarding the impact of stereotype threat and negative stereotypes. In a study exploring the experiences of Black women as part of the African American Women's Voices Project, which collected data from 333 Black women from all over the United States between the ages of 18 and 88 years, C. Jones and Shorter-Gooden (2003) reported that 80% of Black women had been affected by a negative stereotype. For Black women in higher education leadership, the stigma of stereotypes has contributed to their underrepresentation and challenges in their climb to higher education senior leadership. Stereotype threat can further present a dissonance between what these women are perceived as opposed to how they feel they have to be as leaders instead of who they truly are and want to be as leaders (Beckwith et al., 2016; Brown, 2016). If stereotypes define these women's leadership capabilities, it can be mentally and physically damaging to these leaders (Hill et al., 2016), potentially leading to isolation and tokenism.

Isolation and Tokenism: The Battle Between Invisibility and Hypervisibility. As a woman of color working in an industry predominantly run by White men, tokenism's conflicting thoughts can further complicate an already difficult adjustment. Black women in academic leadership describe the challenges of discrimination and how it leads to marginalization and feelings of isolation and tokenism (Bower & Wolverton, 2009; Cho et al., 2013; Kaba, 2008; Miller & Groccia, 2011). Kanter (1977) described tokenism as the feelings and experiences of being one or few of a group in which they are the extreme minority, such as Black women in higher education. These feelings and experiences can include isolation, loneliness, limited support, and solo status associated with the organizational practices of meeting minimal legal and administrative compliance and public scrutiny in minority use and placement (Bright, 2010; Sobers, 2014).

As a social concept, tokenism stems from discrimination, marginalization, and oppression, as it refers to the practice of including a limited number of minorities to give the appearance of equality instead of true equality and diversity (Bower & Wolverton, 2009; Bright, 2010; Kanter, 1977; Sobers, 2014; Woods-Giscombé, 2010). Tokenism emerges from organizational calls for diversity and inclusion without genuine feelings of belongingness and equal access to resources. Tokenism in the workplace and, specifically, higher education can present in many ways. It can potentially look like hiring a minority person because of their race or ethnicity or an organization marketing their 1% minority population on their website to appear more diverse. In higher education leadership, Black women appointed to serve as a college/university president are continuously challenged and denied by their governing board at every impasse (Davis & Maldonado, 2015).

In the world of White academia, Black women, regardless of preparation, qualifications, or competency in administration, are invisible and isolated (Becks-Moody, 2004). Although the duality of invisibility and hypervisibility plague women in social settings, it significantly affects Black women in leadership positions (Dickens et al., 2019). Black women in higher education leadership are accounted for and visible when it comes to statistical reporting; however, they are discounted or deemed invisible when it comes to intelligence or academic ability (Baxter-Nuamah, 2015). The sociocultural phenomenon of Black women being invisible or going unnoticed or unheard is not rare. Sesko and Biernat (2010) found that Black women are more likely to be unheard, unnoticed, and least likely to be recognized in social situations. According to Benjamin (1997, as cited in Davis, 2012), the number of Black women in academia has increased; yet, they remain largely invisible, thus presenting as further adversity to overcome to have their voices heard.

Black women in higher education leadership are constantly challenged to prove that their success is justly due and achieved and not an effect of affirmative action, opportunity hiring, or tokenism (Baxter-Nuamah, 2015). Edwards (1997) notes that Black women are "more visible and equally isolated" because of their race and gender differences. Increased cognitive conflict can occur due to the token Black woman finding herself in situations where she is cognizant of her position as the only Black woman; however, she must "behave as though these differences do not exist" (p. 33).

Tokenism has significant effects and consequences. Lord and Saenz (1985) suggested that the token minority status in a group can cause deficits in cognitive functioning and memory, even in cases where a performance-relevant stereotype does not target that individual. It is further suggested that this is likely due to the outgrowth of the self-consciousness tokenism causes. Tokenism also leads to feelings of loneliness, isolation, and alienation; receiving heavy blame when there are adverse outcomes (Miller & Groccia, 2011); and exhaustion (Becks-Moody, 2004; Walker, 2016). These outcomes are all validated by early reporting's from Kanter (1977), finding poor social relationships, dismal self-imagery, frustrations from conflicting demands, inhibition of self-expression, feelings of inadequacy, and self-hatred.

There are significant and critical challenges for Black women associated with tokenism in higher education specifically. For instance, Holmes (2003) explored the experiences of mid-through senior-level Black women student affairs professionals employed by predominantly White institutions [PWIs] and found that these women experience feelings of alienation and isolation. The study participants further indicated that they felt their race dictated their actions in and outside of the university. Research intensive institutions (R1s and R2s) of higher education and PWIs such as the University of Pennsylvania and the University of Kentucky have been notorious for creating environments where people of color, specifically women, have extreme difficulty feeling accepted and becoming successful (Kelly et al., 2019). Tokenism affects the hiring practices of institutions (Trusteeship, 2002). Tokenism further leads to Black female higher education leaders struggling to feel accepted and treated somewhat as equals and not just an object of compliance in the reality of the White, male-dominated world of higher education (J. F. L. Jackson & O'Callaghan, 2009).

People of color in higher education administration and leadership positions are almost always the liaisons on all issues dealing with diversity (Becks-Moody, 2004). Kanter (1977) suggested that this is because the member(s) of the token group will become the representative of the group in general, thus being viewed and treated as symbols rather than individuals. The number of Black women in higher education senior leadership is essentially due to these challenges, which hinders these women's advancement and limits role models.

Black women have faced these challenges over the years yet, continued to strive for leadership success in all industries. With a focus on higher education administration and leadership, these adversities have been collectively examined to understand their influence on Black women in higher education and how they shape their leadership development. By exploring how these women overcome adverse experiences and applying that knowledge to the world of higher education leadership, we attempt to build the profile of a Black woman in higher education leadership. Understanding the processes and strategies these women have implemented will help develop and provide training and mentoring programs for Black women seeking leadership and advancement in higher education administration.

METHODOLOGY

The purpose of the current study was to understand better how Black women in higher education leadership navigate the adverse challenges of intersectionality, stereotype threat, and tokenism. The investigator employed a qualitative methodology using a phenomenological research design as most appropriate to understand the lived experiences of Black women in higher education leadership.

The investigator explored the impact of adversity on the leadership development of Black women in higher education leadership with a phenomenological inquiry. This approach allowed the investigator to explore and understand the participants' lived experiences while maintaining reflexivity. Objectivity was achieved by bridling personal subjectivity and personal bias throughout the data collection and analysis processes (Vagle, 2018). The investigator ascribed to the hermeneutic school of thought, and although personally vested and experienced with the phenomenon, maintaining objectivity allowed the investigator the ability to interpret the data as appropriate (Moustakas, 1994).

Participants

Participants in the study were recruited by blending convenience, purposive, and snowball sampling techniques. The criteria for participation were (a) Black women, (b) President/Chancellor, vice president/chancellor, or provost of a 4-year college or university in the United States, which have/had been (c) obtained or completing a terminal degree. The investigator conducted an exhaustive internet search to identify potential participants. Convenience sampling like, the name suggests, is the request for participation based on participant availability; however, the participants had to meet the criteria as outlined, which is purposive by definition. Purposive sampling is also found to increase representativeness in field research (Vogt & Johnson, 2011). With such a unique and small population to sample, the pool of participants was already limited, thus allowing snowball sampling to access more participants that met the criteria for participation (Naderifar et al., 2017). By networking with peers and colleagues in various colleges and universities, as well as professional organizations, social media, and affinity groups associated with higher education, the investigator was able to generate a list of potential participants and ask for a direct reference or recommendation to connect them with the potential participant. The investigator successfully recruited nine participants for the study outlined in Table 1.

TABLE 1 ■ Participant Demographic Summary Data					
Pseudonyms	Age, years	Degrees	Marital status	Children	Highest position in higher education leadership
Diamond	+65	Ph.D.	Married	Yes	President
Amethyst	46-50	J.D. and Ed.D.	Married	yes	President
Ruby	60-65	J.D.	Married	yes	President
Morganite	46-50	Ph.D.	Married	yes	President
Emerald	60-65	Ph.D.	Married	yes	President
Wonderstone	60-65	Ph.D.	Divorced	yes	President
Jade	40-45	MBA and MsEd; (Ph.D. in progress)	Single	no	Vice President
Opal	56-60	M.A. (Ed.D. in progress)	Divorced	yes	Assistant Vice President/ Asst. Provost
Fluorite	30-35	Ph.D.	Divorced	yes	Vice President and Dean

Procedures and Data Collection

After successfully recruiting each participant, the researcher then emailed preinterview documents that included the (a) Lived Experiences Timeline Activity (Figure 1), (b) a link to the demographic survey, and (c) a calendar request to schedule the interview. The results of the demographic survey are summarized in Table 1. The investigator required that the Lived Experiences Timeline activity and demographic survey be returned at least 2 to 3 days before the interview for adequate review time to personalize the semistructured interview protocol questions (see Table 2). Once all the preliminary documents were collected, semistructured interviews were scheduled and conducted via Zoom videoconference software.

The use of Zoom video conferencing software allowed the investigator to observe and recognize social cues such as body language and voice inflection during the interview (Opedenakker, 2006). This was beneficial as social distancing guidelines due to the COVID-19 pandemic has recommended avoiding unnecessary contact with people outside your immediate home. Along with using the interview questions and the timeline activity responses, the investigator took notes during the interviews as the participants shared their lived experiences. The notes helped guide the interview flow and assisted the investigator in understanding and preserving emerging themes during data analysis (Oltmann, 2016). The interviews were recorded digitally to allow for adequate and precise transcription. The study included the interview questions listed in Table 2.

FIGURE 1 ■ **Lived experiences timeline activity**

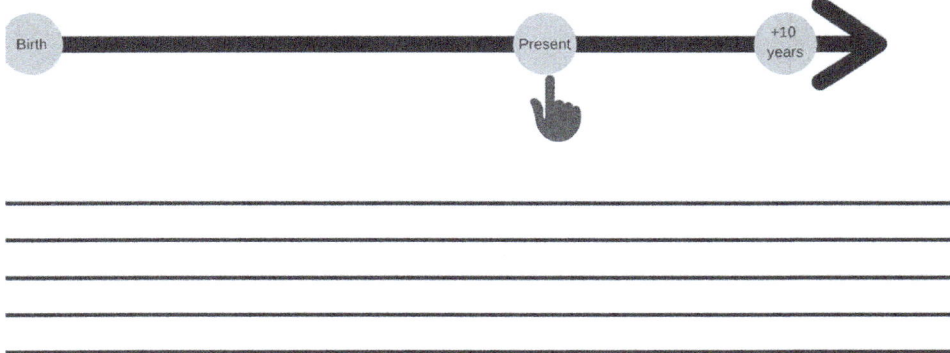

TABLE 2 ■ Interview Protocol	
Research questions	**Interview questions**
1. What influence does a Black women's identity have on her ability to lead in higher education administration? 2. What influence does stereotype threat have on Black women's leadership in higher education administration? 3. What influence does tokenism have on Black women's leadership style and ability in higher education administration?	1. Can you describe [specific experience]? 2. Referring to [specific experience], how do you recall handling it? 3. How did you process this experience? 4. What did you think about this experience afterwards? 5. Did you have any meaningful discussions about [specific experience] with anyone? How did that go? What did you get out of it? 6. What was the outcome of that experience? 7. Did you learn anything from [specific experience]? 8. Why do you think those were the outcomes? 9. How do you describe your experiences as they relate to your role in higher education senior leadership? 10. What were some of the challenges or obstacles you faced specifically to get to your [position]? 11. How did you recognize and respond to those obstacles in your career path to your [position]? 12. Do you think your position in HE leadership was driven by your experiences and ability to overcome adversities? 13. How can your experiences and the lessons you learned help influence a path for the next generation struggling thru adversity reach leadership?

Data Analysis

The audio recordings of the interviews were uploaded to Rev, an online professional transcription service. Once transcription was completed, the investigator utilized member checking by asking the participants to review the transcripts to verify the data's content and accuracy. The participants were able to confirm truthfulness, which increases validity. Member checking has been described as "the most crucial technique for establishing credibility" (Lincoln & Guba, 1985, p. 314).

The researcher utilized Moustakas's (1994) modified Stevick-Colaizzi-Keen phenomenological data analysis method to organize, analyze, and describe the findings. The investigator manually reviewed each transcript to identify possible codes and themes then used the qualitative data coding and analysis software, Dedoose, to further analyze the transcripts. Horizonalizing the transcripts' data allowed the investigator to move from naïve descriptions to specific examples, thus revealing the essential structures of the experience. The investigator first developed textural descriptions of what the participants experienced, followed by structural descriptions concerning the context and setting that affect how they experienced the phenomenon. These general descriptions revealed the composite essential structure of the lived experience of the participants.

The investigator further engaged in the reflexive process of epoché through note taking, which involved reviewing bracketed information and reflection on the context for each code (Creswell, 2013). This bracketing practice of setting aside personal beliefs, experiences, biases, and preconceived notions about the phenomenon helped the investigator to capture the ideas essential to the research (Moustakas, 1994). Vagle (2014) expanded on the practicality of this process and further described it as bridling. Dahlberg (2006, as cited in Vagle, 2014) suggested,

> bridling involves the essence of bracketing in that pre-understandings are restrained so they do not limit the openness [and] is an active project in which one continually tends to the understanding of the phenomenon as a whole throughout the study. (p. 67)

This data analysis method further included interpretive pre-reflection by the investigator and the participants' reflective descriptions to reach a "universal description of the experience" (Moustakas, 1994, p. 122). The intersectionality framework was used as a lens to observe, understand, and describe the themes that emerged. Multidimensional, phenomenological themes that expressed the participants' meanings of their lived experience by identifying recurring content and patterns in the transcripts and drawing connections among the transcripts' pages are discussed in the findings below. Additionally, the investigator further used member checking by asking the participants to validate the identified themes, strengthening the validity of the findings.

FINDINGS

This study suggests that leadership development for Black women in higher education administration is a result of overcoming adversity fueled by resilience. On coding and analyzing the data, four primary themes and two subthemes emerged that addressed how Black women in higher education leadership navigate the adversity of intersectionality, stereotype threat, and tokenism: (1) Intersectionality: Navigating the -isms; (2) Identity, Cultural Diversity, and Belonging; (3) Doing what we have to do: The many faces of resilience . . .; (3a) "I am strong, I am invincible, I am woman": Motivations of the strong Black woman (SBW)/Superwoman; (3b) Networking, Mentoring, and Professional Support; and (4) Leadership: "I am the master of my fate, I am the captain of my soul." Table 3 illustrates the themes and invariant meanings derived from the research question, connection to the theoretical framework, and frequency of mentions.

Theme 1: Intersectionality: Navigating the -isms

As previously discussed, intersectionality refers to the overlap or interaction of the various categories of discrimination (Crenshaw, 1989), such as the intersection of racism and sexism in Black women. This study's participants have shared several experiences where they have had to navigate discrimination on various fronts, whether on sex, race, age, education level, social class, and so on.

Ruby discussed dealing with ageism, sexism, and racism in several of her lived experiences. When reflecting on her legal career before entering higher education, Ruby dealt with sexism in

TABLE 3 ■ Invariant Meanings and Themes

Theme 1: Intersectionality: Navigating the -isms
1. Discrimination [37]
   a. Ageism
   b. Classism
   c. Education
   d. Racism
   e. Sexism

Theme 2: Identity, cultural diversity, and belonging [44]
   f. Imposter syndrome
   g. Tokenism
2. Microaggressions [16]

Theme 3: Doing what we have to do: The many faces of resilience . . .
3. Motivations [108]
   a. Being the best
   b. Seeking cultural diversity
   c. Faith/spirituality/religion
   d. Family: Partners and children
   e. Relationships/friendships
4. #Unbothered

Subtheme 3a: "I am strong, I am invincible, I am woman": Motivations of the strong Black woman (SBW)/superwoman
   a. SBW schema [17]
   b. Work ethic/work 2x as hard [3]

Subtheme 3b: Networking, mentoring, and professional support
   c. Mentorship and sponsorship [28]

Theme 4: Leadership: " . . . my head is bloody, but unbowed."

situations such as [women] being unable to "wear pants to the courthouse." When referencing challenges due to her race, Ruby shared the following:

> Even after I graduated and I went to work for [a government agency], I wore a wig for the first 9 months because I was afraid that my natural hair would not be something that would be taken seriously. It would be too radical . . . plus I had lost my hair from chemotherapy. I remember that when I started growing my hair back and I had to make that decision to come out of my wig. I remember having this conversation with a woman in the bathroom and she said, "Oh, I see you cut your hair off." And I said, "Yes." And she said, "And I see that you are . . . " I said, "Wearing it naturally like yours?" She just washed her hands and went out the bathroom. I just thought to myself, "Well, you've made a stand. If you can't continue in this line of work, then you'll just have to figure out something else to do." It was important to me to be my authentic self. When my hair grew back, I didn't go back to the wig and when people made those comments to

me about my hair, I would just say, "It's natural, just like yours." We had Jewish people working there with kinky hair and curly hair. We had Italian people there. So, I did that. My thing was if I can do the job and do it well, you shouldn't have any questions about my hair or what I wear. Those are accoutrements. That didn't have anything to do with the quality of my work or my performance.

Once in higher education, Ruby further experienced not only racism and sexism but also ageism:

More so because I was so young. I'm an associate dean and I'm so young. My Dean, he was 30 years my senior when he started doing the work that I was doing. Here I was in my thirties and I'm doing this work, but I think the imposter syndrome works differently for White women than it does for Black women. For Black women in the Academy, we really don't have time to be imposters because we're not seen as being equals anyway. It's not an imposter because whereas White women and White men might say, "That female could be replaced, placing me as a primary character because they're White and I'm White." There's no way anybody was going to look at and see me as a replacement for them because there were too many different characteristics. Not only am I Black, I'm a female, and I'm six foot one, and I've got this natural hair. The imposter syndrome wasn't really the mechanism for me. For me it was more the age piece. You've got all these old White men. My Dean, thank God was a woman.

Amethyst shared the unique experience of being both supported and yet marginalized by a White, male superior at a point in time in her career:

And absolutely he viewed himself as obviously incredibly intellectually superior, and he was a chauvinist, and you know I had some bizarre negative experiences with him. And so, while I say he was very supportive, and he professionally gave me lots of promotions and subsidized my doctoral work, on the flip side could also be incredibly . . . I had two children while working there. He didn't speak with me for probably eight months. Like he literally stopped speaking to me. He reassigns some of my work and he just, once we were at lunch with the person who will be taking over something while I was with family, and he moved the centerpiece in front of my face. And directed her and talked to the other person.

She further recalled a conversation with the same boss which she was reminded of after getting off a plane:

. . . the pilot, myself, and two other people and [the boss] is talking about another employee's wife and who thinks she's such a, you know, whatever. And I said, "I bet you talk about me behind my back too," like I just kind of joke. And he goes, "No, actually I agreed with that until you got knocked up." I mean, he was a chauvinist pig. He really was. And so, we don't think about. I mean, again, we just always that . . . kind of compartmentalize that went away and keep doing work. And I think Black women probably do a lot more of that then probably said.

Jade came to a great epiphany during the interview when considering her actions and the impact of institutional oppression on her thoughts and behaviors:

> I don't think I was as self-aware as I am now, so I think again, similar to some of my upbringing, I feel as though . . . in generalities, right? I think as women of color we're . . . at least, I was raised very much on respectability, you dress a certain way, you act a certain way, you speak a certain way and you'll be fine, and I realized that people were treated differently, but I don't think, until I got to [HBCU], I realized how systemic and institutional racism is . . . I don't know that I'm able to pinpoint and say, "Yep. It was definitely my race that was an issue" or whatever the case may be, because I don't think . . . I was so programmed to think about, "Well, what did I do? Did I speak a certain way? Did I say something that I shouldn't have? Did I do something I shouldn't have?" Without realizing how institutional oppression is, if that makes sense?

However, sexism and ageism are some of the most prominent expressions of discrimination she experienced, according to Jade. She discussed a particular experience that led to her being temporarily unemployed a few years after undergraduate education:

> So, I had recently quit a job, being 20 something years old, when I felt as though I was being discriminated against. I had my boss tell me that I was, quote, and I'm not paraphrasing. Quote, "You are too young to be making the money you make. How old are you anyway?" Yeah. Again, this was when I was still in the corporate world. Shortly after that I was like, "Yeah, I'm out. I quit." So, I was temping at various places while I tried to figure out what I wanted to do, so yeah. It was still relatively early in my career. I mean, I was only 6 years out of undergrad, but at that point, the job that I quit was a manager level position.

When evaluating her experiences in higher education, Jade shared that she has

> . . . worked at both PWIs and HBCUs. HBCUs are some of the sexist places you will ever experience. Very patriarchal, very male-dominated. I don't want to say old school, but like this very. . . . Oh goodness, I should know the word for this. Everyone was Mr. so-and-so and Ms. So-and-so, no one was [first name] or [first name]. It was very formal and very old school in certain ways, so in that space, I wouldn't say race played a role, but gender? Absolutely. Age? Absolutely. I was one of the youngest people on the cabinet and I definitely felt that. I felt kind of this undertone of, "Oh child, sit down. I could be your grandmother. You're just going to do what I said because that's what we always do." Whereas at PWIs you get all of that. You have the race component, you have the gender, because it's still very male-dominated, but not . . . I haven't had anyone explicitly dismiss me, but absolutely I've been dismissed many a times.

Fluorite echoed some of these sentiments as she discussed her transition from [University] to [University]:

> I was really looking for an environment where I could thrive as a Black woman and kind of be celebrated in that, and interestingly enough it was really difficult in that

environment. Because as an amazing of a place that [University] is, it is a place that kind of can tear you down. I didn't experience any racial or gender microaggressions, but my age was a factor for people because when I started there, I was 33, and so everybody who worked with me and reported to me was all significantly older than me. And so that was very difficult for people to work with . . . I was constantly microaggressed about that.

Professionally, Diamond experienced significant discrimination:

And then throughout my experience, sometimes your voice was marginalized. When men said something versus when a woman said something, but I didn't experience it that much until I got to [University]. . . . Though there was gender discrimination at [University] to the point where even HR and the Title IX coordinator mentioned that I should file a complaint, I did not file a complaint. Because, when you file a complaint in higher education, whether you're right or wrong, it follows you through your career and can impact future employment. The fact that you filed a complaint is a problem.

Navigating professional environments can be challenging when your physical self is not congruent to the expectations set on you; however, Opal is conscious that "it's the intersection of race and gender that is a challenge. Showing up as a Black woman who believes in presenting her true and authentic self is challenging." Although adversity can be subjective as it differs from person-to-person, there are overlapping similarities in these Black women leaders' experiences in higher education. Some of the overarching similarities lie in the discrimination experienced, intersectionality, and identity, cultural diversity, and belonging for this group of participants.

Theme 2: Identity, Cultural Diversity, and Belonging

Second-guessing yourself, imposter syndrome, and tokenism are just a few of the challenges associated with these participants' identities and belonging in academic and professional environments. Ruby summed up the notion of what it feels like to second-guess your talents and skills even when others see them:

At [University], [mentor] was an incredible mentor. He's the person who actually told me one day you're going to be a president. And I was like, "No, I'm not going to be president." He said, "In order for you to do that, you need to go to [Ivy League College]." And I was like, "[mentor], I'm not going to [Ivy League College]. I really appreciate it." Now you talk about imposter syndrome. I was like, "I really appreciate the fact that you think I'm that smart, but I'm really not that smart. I took a major that I loved, and I augmented that with speech, which I loved, and that's why I got good grades. So, don't be trying to send me to [Ivy League College]." He was like, "Well, [a colleague's] going to [Ivy League College]." I'm like, "She's brilliant." And he's like, "[another colleague's] gone to [Ivy League College]." I was like, "She's brilliant." And he was like, "And you're going to [Ivy League College]." I was like, "I am not brilliant." He put me in the IEM program, the management development program at [Ivy League College]. I'll never forget, I got accepted into that program and I went in his office like a kid on Christmas morning. I was like, "I got in, I got in, I got in." He just laughed at me like,

"You silly girl, of course you got in. Do you know how good you are?" I was like, "No." And I really, for a long time, I thought that he had pulled some strings and he swore, he didn't do anything except for support, my application. He was one of the ones who first opened that idea.

Jade echoed this sentiment as she discussed working in her role as a vice president:

Do they realize who they hired? I'm just some little girl from [an urban neighborhood] that . . . I shouldn't even be in this space, and wanting to help, because I know other people feel that way as well and wanting to never have other . . . It's 2020, why do we still feel that we shouldn't be here?

Amethyst, who "grew up around almost entirely White people . . . in a mixed-race family in West Virginia, which is a 3% minority state," talks about the challenge of reaching success based on identity and appearance as perceived by a subordinate:

There was definitely a sense of "I made you." Once he said to me, "you have everything it takes to be successful, you're smart, you're good looking, you're tall. You're dark but not Black." What does that mean? Like, you know, are we talking about like skin tone or are we talking about, like, I don't "act Black." And I mean—I'm dark but not Black. Yeah. Like I had everything it takes to be successful.

Wonderstone shared that although she "always know[s] that [she's] coming in and being a token . . . a twofer right, you get a female, and you get a person of color," expressed how she has pondered at times "Do I belong, can I fit? What do I need to do? And you do have to learn how to check the boxes." She was ever reminded of her uniqueness as she states, "I could look around myself and see, there weren't many people that looked like me in the academy that were administrative positions."

Morganite discusses the challenges of the sense of not belonging and wrestling with imposter syndrome as she stated, "I was something of a unicorn for them," and being told by peers, "Oh, I like you, you're Black. I like you, but I don't like most Black people." She goes on to say:

I wasn't particularly accepted anywhere so I learned how to deal with it, but certainly to my White colleagues - I mean, I was something of a unicorn for them. Most of them had never met or engaged with an equal Black woman . . .

For Black women in society in general, and specifically women in higher education senior leadership, this is a reoccurring theme. Wonderstone, cognizant of her position, goes on to say, "I was never a quiet token, so you're not going to just mistreat me" when dealing with adversity in her positions. On the concept of tokenism, Diamond states, "it's a very isolat[ing] experience," whether in classes back in school or in the board room.

The participants are highly aware of their positions and how their race, gender, and age impact that. The ability to successfully lead in the face of discrimination sets these women apart from those who shy away from leadership due to being marginalized by their demographics. Regardless of the industry, Black women are expected to navigate the compounding discriminations they face daily flawlessly.

Theme 3: Doing What We Have to Do: The Many Faces of Resilience

Resilience looks different for all people. In the face of trauma, adversity, and the stresses of life, developing and maintaining resilience has helped these women get through difficult experiences and promote personal and professional growth. Resilience does not imply that a person will not experience adversity, trauma, or distress—on the contrary, this author finds that resilience refers to those protective factors and positive adaptations a person makes in light of those situations. The women in this study have identified several resilience techniques and resources they have used in the face of adversity.

These women have been motivated to be the best from their early academics up through their career development. For instance, Ruby recalled part of her motivations in undergrad that pushed and built her for success:

> You had to get up and out that day and go to class. You had to study, you had to do your work. You had to be serious because you were setting the pace for the next group. And that was something that was drummed into you, not only by [our] Dean and his staff but, also by all the other students that were there. We knew that we had a unique opportunity with our presence.

Wonderstone was significantly motivated by her grandparents as a child during the civil rights movement of the 1960s. Her grandparents instilled in her the "importance of education . . . [and] service," and her grandmother would say, "people can take your house, your car, everything from you, but they can never take away your education." Emerald echoed the group's sentiments when reflecting on work ethic in that "you do it well or you don't do it at all."

Some participants recalled being motivated and inspired by their families (i.e., parents, siblings, children, and spouses), whereas others reflected on external and outside motivators. Ruby spoke of being able to see and hear Shirley Chisholm, the first Black woman elected to Congress, and to successfully run a full campaign for President of the United States, in person. She described it as a "galvanizing . . . life changing" experience that finalized her career goals of being "in service to others." Amethyst, while navigating her identity issues, spoke of being motivated by people such as her mother-in-law. She was inspired to become a member of several public service organizations, as well as to strive for leadership in her respective career field as she "sought out Black women that [she] thought could teach [her] how to be a Black woman." Several of the participants spoke of the supportive nature that their friends had provided them throughout their life and 1/3 of the participants referenced the supportive sisterhood of joining a Black Greek Letter Organization. Wonderstone summarized it best when she said, "you have different people in your life that you go to, depending on what it is that you're dealing with. Whether it's . . . in your personal life, you know you have a support system of others that are around you that you know will challenge you, listen to you . . . " Last, but not least, the participants unapologetically revealed their faith and spirituality as personal motivations through adversity. Having the mentality to remain steadfast, or #unbothered as the youth call it, in the face of adversity has served these Black female leaders well as they reached and continue to reach professional success.

Subtheme 3a: "I am Strong, I am Invincible, I am Woman": Motivations of the SBW/ Superwoman. According to the literature, the SBW schema "is a race-gender schema that prescribes culturally specific feminine expectations from [Black] women, including unyielding strength, assumption of multiple roles, and caring for other" (Liao et al., 2020, p. 84). However, to the women who live it, it is just the norm, as indicated by this study's results. Each participant mentioned their strength and resilience in overcoming adversity at least once.

Diamond shared the notion that " . . . Black women can't slow down" as she reflected on the resolve of her mother, that even after separation from her husband, she "kept working and tirelessly juggled multiple tasks." Diamond further stated that as Black women, " . . . that's what we do, and we learned to do it. We learned to be superwomen." Being a superwoman comes with its own unique set of drawbacks, however. In reflecting on professional experiences, Jade described it as " . . . there's always this ever-moving bar of justification and explanation of why you're in this space, why you should be allowed to make decisions." Setting clear boundaries of what will and will not be tolerated and accepted is critical. In reflecting on collective experiences of adversity, Amethyst wondered if Black women are "giving people license to treat [them poorly] because [their] resilience meter tends to be a little higher," however, "that's a coping mechanism, not nature." However, having a strong work ethic does not translate into being unbreakable for anyone, and having to always be the "SBW" as a source of resilience has its drawbacks and benefits.

Resilience is often seen or defined as overcoming hardships or something easily obtainable; however, that does not paint the whole picture. This particular definition of resilience does not consider systems of power, privilege, and oppression that impact marginalized people's lives every day. Black women in leadership have had to specifically take on the stereotypical role of the SBW or Black superwoman, uphold a ridiculous work ethic, and live by the mantra of having to work twice as hard to get half as far (or half the acknowledgment) than their White counterparts. Strength is undoubtedly a factor of resilience for Black women in higher education leadership.

Subtheme 3b: Networking, Mentoring, and Professional Support. These women's resilience has further been supported by networking relationships, advocates, mentors, sponsors, and professional support systems. Having the right support system has helped the participants in this group reflect on their setbacks and learn from them, allowing them to do better in the future. Having the right mentors helped the participants see failures as learning experiences. Each participant spoke of a mentor, a teacher, spiritual leader, or administrator while they were in college, a colleague, or a supervisor.

Opal spoke of her mentors and how they "provide[d] advice in the roles [she held] . . . helped [her] job search, not only to think about what [she'd] need to look for in a position but the social aspect of the city too." Fluorite had this to say of her mentors:

> They each play different roles depending on what is happening in my life. Is it personal, is it professional? Do I need to be boosted up, or do I need to be brought back to reality? I see them as like my own personal board of trustees. They tell me the good and the bad. They are there to support me and to push and challenge me.

Ruby describes the benefits of mentorship as follows:

> . . . more times than not, there are other people that can see greater things in you than you see for yourself. You need to listen to those people. Especially if they mean you well, you need to take their advice when they try to offer you opportunities and not shy away from them just because you can't see it for yourself.

In summarizing the participants' thoughts, having the right support system, whether it is mentors, sponsors, or advocates, is a valuable asset and resource to help advance professionals' success in all fields and industries, with higher education being no exception. It is necessary to state that although professional sponsorship is similar to mentorship, sponsorship goes to the next level of advocacy. Whereas a mentor is someone you value with career experience and the ability to help shape and drive career goals, a sponsor is a senior-level executive that helps their protégés network. For Black women in leadership, it has been stated that other Black women in leadership make great mentors (Grant, 2012); however, White male allies in senior leadership positions are the most influential sponsors.

This group of Black women leaders has further found that networking and having sufficient mentors, sponsors, and professional support systems have contributed to their resilience and leadership success. These support systems have helped the participants in this group reflect on their setbacks and learn from them, allowing them to do better in the future, thus helping them view their failures as transformational learning experiences. Mentors and sponsors have provided them the necessary resources, knowledge, skills, and motivations to climb the leadership ladder.

Theme 4: Leadership: ". . . My Head Is Bloody, but Unbowed."

Leadership for these women is not about a title but about fulfilling a calling. Ruby stated, "you can lead wherever you are . . . it doesn't have to be huge, you don't have to have a title in order to be a leader." For Black women in leadership,

> there are a series of compromises we make as people of color, series of compromises we make as women . . . to enable us to get to a certain level . . . and then once we're there . . . we can begin.

according to Amethyst. Similarly, Wonderstone advises that one

> decide[s] where you're going to be happy . . . you don't ever want to be in a place where you're miserable . . . [decide] if you want to advance, what does that look like where you still can be authentically you.

Jade understands that leadership comes with responsibility beyond the traditional workload as well. She states,

> it's the representation, it's the impact . . . for students to feel or to see someone [that looks like them] . . . You can't aspire to what you don't know. You can't aspire to what you don't see.

While Diamond suggests that one must "Lead with courage and integrity," Morganite identifies as " . . . a leader who thinks you have to connect with, engage, and see the humanity of the people you lead." Opal further recommends as a leader remaining

> . . . cognizant of the choices one makes and be ready for the challenges . . . while you may not know what is ahead, mentally, you can prepare yourself for the best and worst . . .

Regardless, developing leadership through adversity requires resilience. Fluorite summarizes this notion as she stated, "I thoroughly believe that setbacks are setups for comebacks. Everything that happens can teach us something, and at times we have to be made uncomfortable in order to grow and step out on faith." Taking ownership and mastering life's challenges has helped to forge leaders out of this group of women.

"My head is bloody, but unbowed" is the final line of the second stanza from the poem "Invictus" written by William Earnest Henley (1919, p. 1019). The Latin word "Invictus" translates to mean undefeated or unconquerable. There is no group more befitting this title than the women in this study. This poem's theme is resilience, the will to survive in the face of severe adversity, of which these Black female leaders in higher education have successfully done. This poem visualizes with metaphors overcoming hardships and personal adversities. Essentially, this poem imagines the practices of how a transformational leader resiliently overcomes adversity to achieve successful leadership.

Essence: Adversity Promotes Resilience and Yields Leadership Development

These findings suggest that for Black women, leadership development results from resilience, and the cost of resilience is lived adversity. As they have been exposed to greater adversity historically and culturally, Black women have naturally developed greater resilience. Research has suggested that Black women are socialized to be independent, emphasizing self-determination and education (Thomas & King, 2007). This sort of socialization promotes resilience over the oppression of the negative stereotypes and images. Therefore, these women are being taught at an early age to have tough skin and endure. Regardless of the adverse experiences these Black women have faced, they consistently found ways to rise above and overcome. Jade shared that she thinks "part of [her] ability to move up in the ranks" has been due to her resilience. Morganite affirms that her resilience prepared her for her role in higher education senior leadership by stating, "[it] is a job that will chew you up and you have to be able every day . . . you have to wake up and bounce back and have a renewed perspective, so I think that has helped." Emerald's words of advice when dealing with adversity further promote overcoming:

> You got to stay the course. You have to learn to be resilient. There's going to be some hurt and harm along the way, but you cannot give up. If that's your dream, you cannot give up on your dream. You just have to be resilient and keep on going.

Instead of folding under the pressures of adverse crucible experiences, this group's resilience supports the development of their leadership potential.

Leadership Development. Learning and adaptation support a positive correlation between the lived adverse experiences and leadership development in Black women (Pulley & Wakefield, 2001). The participants in this study are no strangers to adversity nor resilience. By not giving up after experiencing adverse situations and events, these women sharpened their swords of resilience and pressed onward and upward, reaching academic, administrative leadership. When considering her lived experiences with adversity and overcoming with resilience and the impact that adverse experience had on her leadership development, Wonderstone stated that she always ponders "how character and strength is developed. [Her] resounding answer is when you have walked through the valleys of life . . . you grow and hopefully learn how to be resilient in the face of adversity."

Although this group of Black women leaders is in higher education, many of them suspect the leadership skills and tools they developed along the way apply to any leadership position. Perhaps, Black women who experience adversity and overcome with renewed resilience will indeed make the best leaders (Gaudiano, 2019).

DISCUSSION

This study explored how Black women in higher education leadership navigate the adverse challenges of intersectionality, stereotype threat, and tokenism. The results revealed that Black women in higher education leadership experienced and overcame adversity, thus revealing an association of their ability to develop the necessary leadership skills to advance their careers. The participants described their adversities as fuel to overcome, thus developing the necessary skills to prepare them for leadership. Their strength through adversity is driven by resilience. Resilience has manifested itself in many ways for this study's participants, varying from motivation factors such as family and relationships, mentors, community support, and the support of cultural identity and diversity.

The data collected from nine participants provided various perspectives and narratives about their lived experiences, focusing on discrimination and intersectionality, prejudice and stereotype threat, and tokenism and the impact those had on their leadership development. All of the rich, textural data obtained from the participants and the literature provide a wealth of information for young Black women seeking guidance in overcoming adversity and leadership development.

Implications

This study aims to disseminate knowledge to enlighten the next generation of young Black women struggling through adversity and aspiring leaders to find Black women role models who have successfully broken through the barriers of race and gender (S. Jackson & Harris, 2007). Exploring Black women's experiences in leadership and higher education expands the approach to analyze leadership development programs for women of color. Black women are still underrepresented at the top ranks of leadership in the academy and across the board, both domestic and abroad; therefore, educating and motivating other Black women with leadership potential to strive for leadership remains a high priority.

Closing the racial-gender leadership gap for Black women is imperative. The majority of leadership development and empowerment programs geared toward women have shortcomings regarding Black women; however, this disparity may not be by design. Conventional programs that emphasize specific skills such as speaking up, being assertive, negotiating, being confident, self-promoting, setting career goals, and developing a personal brand or image yield unfavorable responses for women of color. Black women are consistently challenged with the stereotype threat of being perceived as an "angry Black woman," dressing appropriately to meet European beauty standards, not appearing intimidating or scary, and not appearing to congregate and socialize unprofessionally. As such, the duality of needing to be an assertive and confident female leader is continually struggling against the need to tone it down as a Black woman.

The results of the explored experiences of Black women in higher education leadership can further provide decision making individuals and bodies such as boards of trustee members, regents, and other key decision makers with information essential in evaluating Black women in higher education poised to assume leadership at 4-year colleges and universities (Gasman et al., 2015; Rein, 2017). Overall, the current findings intend to inform the readers about the participants' experiences and provide themes or patterns that can be used to better understand Black women's experiences who have assumed these roles.

Limitations and Future Research

Limitations of the current study must be addressed to protect the reliability and trustworthiness of the research. All research has limitations (Creswell, 2013; Moustakas, 1994), and this study is not an exception. The following exclusion criteria have delimited the current study: participants were Black women working toward or had completed terminal degrees, and participants are or previously had served as president/chancellor, vice president/chancellor, or provosts at 4-year universities in the United States. As there are not many Black women in this role from which to choose, there were challenges recruiting participants for the study. Furthermore, by the study only exploring the experiences of a small group (approximately 8-10) limited by race and sex in a specific and notable career, the findings are not generalizable. Nor can we expect the data to reflect all Black women's experiences in higher education senior leadership at 4-year colleges and universities.

Although limitations exist, these findings speak to the investigator's best effort to understand the lived experiences of the Black women in higher education leadership who participated in this study. These findings open the door to future research opportunities such as those related to the scarcity of Black women in higher education leadership in 4-year colleges and universities that are not HBCUs. It is evident how few Black women have reached higher education leadership. Further research is suggested to explore the experiences and perceptions of the Black women that have and do hold these positions with particular emphasis on PWIs and top-tier research schools. More advanced research will help understand the challenges these women face and their recommendations to increase Black women's representation in these positions where they may not have initially felt they had a place.

Another future suggestion for research involves exploring the lived experiences of Black, Indigenous, People of Color [BIPOC] in leadership outside of academia. BIPOC women have been making significant advances in leadership in industries such as politics, government and military, automotive, retail, finance, technology, and emergency management, to name a few. Investigating how their lived experiences influenced their leadership development will expand the overall understanding of leadership development and women's studies.

CONCLUSION

Black women in higher education leadership have overcome stereotypes and multilayered intersectional discrimination and pushed past organizational oppressions such as limited role models, the concrete ceiling, and tokenism with the use of resilience. Fortunately, these challenges have merely been speed bumps on the road to success for this group. They have been diligent in their drive to climb the ranks of leadership in the ivory tower. Factors such as resilience, social support, and leadership development all contribute to that climb.

There have been several strategies indicated by the participants for Black women to increase their likelihood of successfully achieving higher education senior leadership. They will need to be educationally prepared and credentialed, know themselves, have a mentor/sponsor, develop coping mechanisms to handle adversity, and most importantly, reach back and help others (Baxter-Nuamah, 2015). This interview process allowed the participants to be vulnerable and transparent when reflecting on and sharing their lived adverse experiences and their impact on their resilience and leadership development. This study has made evident that adversities shared, whether minor or significant, were not enough to break these women's spirit, drive, and resilience.

ACKNOWLEDGMENTS

First, I am beyond appreciative for the amazing participants in my study. You women, who are leaders and decision makers at your colleges and universities took time out of your extremely hectic and busy schedules to complete this research, and I am forever humbled and grateful. To say that I was inspired and motivated after the conversations with all these amazing Black women who are pioneering level leadership in their various institutions of higher education is an understatement. You all are #BlackGirlMagic #BlackExcellence and #MelaninMagic personified.

DECLARATION OF CONFLICTING INTERESTS

The author declared no potential conflicts of interest with respect to the research, authorship, and/or publication of this article.

FUNDING

The author received no financial support for the research, authorship, and/or publication of this article.

ORCID iD

Nuchelle L. Chance, https://orcid.org/0000-0003-3806-5953

REFERENCES

Alexander-Lee M. L. (2014) *A qualitative study of African-American female administrators in the academy: Identification of characteristics that contribute to their advancement to senior level positions of authority* [Doctoral dissertation]. ProQuest Dissertations and Theses database. (UMI No. 3584503)

Allport G. (1954) *The nature of prejudice*. Addison-Wesley.

American Council on Education. (2017) *American college president study 2017*. https://www.acenet.edu/Research-Insights/Pages/American-College-President-Study.aspx

Assari S. (2017) Number of chronic medical conditions fully mediates the effects of race on mortality; 25-year follow-up of a nationally representative sample of Americans. *Journal of Racial and Ethnic Health Disparities*, 4(4), 623-631. Crossref

Banutu-Gomez M. B. (2004) Great leaders teach exemplary followership and serve as servant leaders. *American Academy of Business Journal*, 4(1/2), 143-153. http://www.journalbrc.com

Baxter-Nuamah M. (2015) *Through the looking glass: Barriers and coping mechanisms encountered by African American women presidents at predominately White institutions* [Doctoral dissertation]. ProQuest Dissertations and Theses database. (UMI No. 3702781)

Beaudan E. (2002) Leading in turbulent times. *Ivey Business Journal*, 66(5), 22-26. https://iveybusinessjournal.com/publication/leading-in-turbulent-times/

Becks-Moody G. (2004) *African American women administrators in higher education: Exploring the challenges and experiences at Louisiana public colleges and universities* [Unpublished doctoral dissertation]. Louisiana State University and Agricultural and Mechanical College, Baton Rouge, LA.

Beckwith A. L., Carter D. R., Peters T. (2016) The underrepresentation of African American women in executive leadership: What's getting in the way? *Journal of Business Studies Quarterly*, 7(4), 115-134.

Benjamin L. (1997) *Black women in the academy: Promises and perils*. University Press of Florida.

Boin A., Hart P. T. (2003) Public leadership in times of crisis: mission impossible? *Public Administration Review*, 63(5), 544-553. Crossref

Bower B. L., Wolverton M. (2009) *Answering the call: African American women in higher education leadership*. Stylus Publishing, LLC.

Bright D. A. (2010) Pioneering women: Black women as senior leaders in traditionally white community colleges [Doctoral dissertation]. ProQuest Dissertations and Theses database. (UMI Number: 3397642)

Brown L. (2016) An examination of African American leadership practices and upward mobility within the North Carolina community college system [Unpublished doctoral dissertation]. East Carolina University, Greenville, NC.

Burnett J. J. (1998) A strategic approach to managing crises. *Public Relations Review*, 24(4), 475-488. Crossref

Cho S., Crenshaw K. W., McCall L. (2013) Toward a field of intersectionality studies: Theory, application, and praxis. *Signs*, 38(4), 785-810. Crossref

Chun E., Evans A. (2016) *Diverse administrators in peril: The new indentured class in higher education*. Routledge.

Comas-Díaz L., Hall G. N., Neville H. A. (2019) Racial trauma: Theory, research, and healing: Introduction to the special issue. *American Psychologist*, 74(1), 1-5. Crossref

Crenshaw K. W. (1989) Demarginalizing the intersection of race and sex: A Black feminist critique of antidiscrimination doctrine, feminist theory, and antiracist politics. *University of Chicago Legal Forum*, 1989(1), 139-167. https://chicagounbound.uchicago.edu/uclf/vol1989/iss1/8/

Creswell J. W. (2013) *Qualitative inquiry and research design: Choosing among five approaches* (3rd ed.). Sage.

Croizet J., Claire T. (1998) Extending the concept of stereotype threat to social class: The intellectual underperformance of students from low socioeconomic backgrounds. *Personality and Social Psychology Bulletin*, 24(6), 588-594. Crossref

Dahlberg K. (2006) The essence of essences—the search for meaning structures in phenomenological analysis of lifeworld phenomena. *International Journal of Qualitative Studies on Health and Well-Being*, 1(1), 11-19. Crossref

Davis D. R. (2012) *A phenomenological study on the leadership development of African American women executives in academia and business* [Doctoral Dissertation]. ProQuest Dissertations and Theses database. (UMI Number 3553634)

Davis D. R., Maldonado C. (2015) Shattering the glass ceiling: The leadership development of African American women in higher education. *Advancing Women in Leadership*, 35, 48-64.

Dean D. R., Bracken S. J., Allen J. K. (2009) *Women in academic leadership: Professional strategies, personal choices*. Stylus Publishing, LLC.

Dickens D. D., Womack V. Y., Dimes T. (2019) Managing hypervisibility: An exploration of theory and research on identity shifting strategies in the workplace among Black women. *Journal of Vocational Behavior*, 113(August), 153-163. Crossref

Edwards J. (1997) *African-American women administrators in higher education: Adaptations between internal motivations and external expectations* [Unpublished Doctoral Dissertation]. University of Cincinnati, Cincinnati, OH.

Erskine S. E., Archibold E. E., Bilimoria D. (2020) Afro-diasporic women navigating the black ceiling: Individual, relational, and organizational strategies. *Business Horizons*, 64(1), 37-50. Crossref

Galloway B. (2016) *Shattering the concrete ceiling: Exploring the moderating effects of mass media messages as it relates to the perceived self-efficacy of African-American women* [Doctoral dissertation]. ProQuest Dissertations and Theses database. (UMI: 10127918)

Gasman M., Abiola U., Travers C. (2015) Diversity and senior leadership at elite institutions of higher education. *Journal of Diversity in Higher Education*, 8(1), 1-14. Crossref

Gaudiano P. (2019, December 2) Why Black women are better leaders. *Forbes*. https://www.forbes.com/sites/paologaudiano/2019/12/02/why-black-women-are-better-leaders/#432e123e259b

Goleman D. (2000) Leadership that gets results. *Harvard Business Review*, 78(2), 4-17. https://hbr.org/2000/03/leadership-that-gets-results

Grant C. M. (2012) Advancing our legacy: A Black feminist perspective on the significance of mentoring for African-American women in educational leadership. *International Journal of Qualitative Studies in Education*, 25(1), 101-117. Crossref

Gupta V. K., Bhawe N. M. (2007) The influence of proactive personality and stereotype threat on women's entrepreneurial intentions. *Journal of Leadership and Organizational Studies*, 13(4), 73-85. Crossref

Gutiérrez y Muhs G., Niemann Y. F., González C. G., Harris A. P. (2012) *Presumed incompetent: The intersections of race and class for women in academia*. University Press of Colorado.

Henley W. E. (1919) Invictus. In Sir Arthur Thomas Quiller-Couch (Ed.), *The Oxford book of English verse, 1250-1900* (Vol. 1, p. 1019). The Clarendon Press, Oxford. https://hdl.handle.net/2027/mdp.39015010922790

Hewlett S. A., Green T. (2015) *Black women ready to lead*. http://www.talentinnovation.org/_private/assets/BlackWomenReadyToLead_ExecSumm-CTI.pdf

Hill C., Miller K., Benson K., Handley G. (2016) *Barriers and bias: The status of women in leadership*. American Association of University Women. https://www.aauw.org/resources/research/barrier-bias/ Crossref.

Holmes S. L. (2003) Black female administrators speak out: Narratives on race and gender in higher education. *National Association of Student Affairs Professionals Journal*, 6(1), 45-65. https://eric.ed.gov/?id=EJ669365

Hughes D., Dodge M. A. (1997) African American women in the workplace: Relationships between job conditions, racial bias at work, and perceived job quality. *American Journal of Community Psychology*, 25(5), 581-599. Crossref

Inglehart R., Norris P., Ronald I. (2003) *Rising tide: Gender equality and cultural change around the world*. Cambridge University Press. Crossref.

Inzlicht M., Ben-Zeev T. (2000) A threatening intellectual environment: Why females are susceptible to experiencing problem-solving deficits in the presence of males. *Psychological Science*, 11(5), 365-371. Crossref

Jackson J. F. L., O'Callaghan E. M. (2009) *Barriers encountered by administrators of color in higher and postsecondary education*. ASHE Higher Education Report, 35(3), 1-95. Crossref

Jackson S., Harris S. (2007) African American female college and university presidents: Experiences and perceptions of barriers to the presidency. *Journal of Women in Educational Leadership*, 5(2), 119-137. https://bit.ly/2BwmXY4

Jean-Marie G. (2006) Welcoming the unwelcomed: A social justice imperative of African-American female leaders at historically Black colleges and universities. *Journal of Educational Foundations*, 20(1/2), 85-104. https://eric.ed.gov/?id=EJ751762

Jones C., Shorter-Gooden K. (2003) *Shifting: The double lives of Black women in America*. Harper Collins.

Jones T. B., Dawkins L. S., McClinton M. M., Glover M. H. (Eds.). (2012) *Pathways to higher education administration for African American women*. Stylus Publishing, LLC.

Kaba A. J. (2008) Race, gender and progress: Are Black American women the new model minority? *Journal of African American Studies*, 12(4), 309-335. Crossref

Kanter R. M. (1977) Some effects of proportions on group life: Skewed sex ratios and responses of token women. *American Journal of Sociology*, 82(5), 965-990. Crossref

Kelly B. T., Raines A., Brown R., French A., Stone J. (2019) Critical validation: Black women's retention at predominantly White institutions. *Journal of College Student Retention: Research, Theory & Practice*. Advance online publication. Crossref.

Kirschman S. (2009) Women at the top: What women university and college presidents say about effective leadership. *International Journal of Educational Advancement*, 9(3), 188-190. Crossref

Liao K., Wei M., Yin M. (2020) The misunderstood schema of the strong Black woman: Exploring its mental health consequences and coping responses among African American women. *Psychology of Women Quarterly*, 44(1), 84-104. Crossref

Lincoln Y. S., Guba E. G. (1985) *Naturalistic inquiry* (Vol. 75). Sage. Crossref.

Longman K. A., Madsen S. R. (Eds.). (2014) *Women and leadership in higher education*. Information Age Publishing.

Lord C. G., Saenz D. S. (1985) Memory deficits and memory surfeits: Differential cognitive consequences of tokenism for tokens and observers. *Journal of Personality and Social Psychology*, 49(4), 918-926. Crossref

Madsen S. R. (2008) *On becoming a woman leader: Learning from the experiences of university presidents* (Vol. 124). John Wiley.

Miller J. E., Groccia J. E. (Eds.). (2011) *To improve the academy: Resources for faculty, instructional, and organizational development* (Vol. 30). Jossey-Bass.

Moorosi P., Fuller K., Reilly E. (2018) Leadership and intersectionality: Constructions of successful leadership among Black women school principals in three different contexts. *Management in Education*, 32(4), 152-159. Crossref

Moustakas C. (1994) *Phenomenological research methods*. Sage. Crossref.

Murphy M. C., Steele C. M., Gross J. J. (2007) Signaling threat: How situational cues affect women in math, science, and engineering settings. *Psychological Science*, 18(10), 879-885. Crossref

Naderifar M., Goli H., Ghaljaie F. (2017) Snowball sampling: A purposeful method of sampling in qualitative research. *Strides in Development of Medical Education*, 14(3), 1-6. Crossref

Oltmann S. (2016, May) Qualitative interviews: A methodological discussion of the interviewer and respondent contexts. *Forum: Qualitative Social Research*, 17(2), 1-16. Crossref

Opedenakker R. (2006, September) Advantages and disadvantages of four interview techniques in qualitative research. *Forum: Qualitative Social Research*, 7(4), 1-13. Crossref

Parker L., Lynn M. (2002) What's race got to do with it? Critical race theory's conflicts with and connections to qualitative research methodology and epistemology. *Qualitative inquiry*, 8(1), 7-22. Crossref

Patterson C. A. (2006) *The glass ceiling effect: A perspective of African American women* [Doctoral Dissertation]. ProQuest Dissertations and Theses database. (UMI 3226231)

Pillai R., Meindl J. R. (1991, August) The effect of a crisis on the emergence of charismatic leadership: A laboratory study. *Academy of Management Proceedings*, 1991(1), 235-239. Crossref

Pulley M. L., Wakefield M. (2001) *Building resiliency: How to thrive in times of change*. Center for Creative Leadership.

Rein M. (2017) *From policy to practice*. Routledge. Crossref.

Rosette A. S., Livingston R. W. (2012) Failure is not an option for Black women: Effects of organizational performance on leaders with single versus dual-subordinate identities. *Journal of Experimental Social Psychology*, 48(5), 1162-1167. Crossref

Scott O. (2011) *Retention and advancement of African American women into senior leadership positions in high technology companies* [Doctoral dissertation]. Proquest Dissertations and Theses database. (UMI No. 1502566)

Sesko A. K., Biernat M. (2010) Prototypes of race and gender: The invisibility of Black women. *Journal of Experimental Social Psychology*, 46(2), 356–360. Crossref

Smith A. M. (2016) *Black girl magic: How Black women administrators navigate the intersection of race and gender in workspace silos at predominantly white institutions* [Doctoral dissertation]. Lousiana State University, Baton Rouge, LA. https://digitalcommons.lsu.edu/gradschool_dissertations/3470 Crossref.

Sobers S. T. (2014) *Can I get a witness?: The resilience of four Black women senior student affairs administrators at predominantly White institutions* [Doctoral dissertation]. ProQuest Dissertations and Theses database. (UMI No. 3625189)

Steele C. M. (1997) A threat in the air: How stereotypes shape intellectual identity and performance. *American Psychologist*, 52(6), 613. Crossref

Steele C. M., Aronson J. (1995) Stereotype threat and the intellectual test performance of African-Americans. *Journal of Personality and Social Psychology*, 69(5), 797-811. Crossref

Steele J., James J. B., Barnett R. (2002) Learning in a man's world: Examining the perceptions of undergraduate women in male-dominated academic areas. *Psychology of Women Quarterly*, 26(1), 46-50. Crossref

Stone J. (2002) Battling doubt by avoiding practice: The effect of stereotype threat on self-handicapping in white athletes. *Personality and Social Psychology Bulletin*, 28(12), 1667-1678. Crossref

The State of Women-Owned Businesses. (2018) https://ventureneer.com/wp-content/uploads/2018/08/2018-state-of-women-owned-businesses-report_FINAL.pdf

Thomas A. J., King C. T. (2007) Gendered racial socialization of African American mothers and daughters. *Family Journal*, 15(2), 137-142. Crossref

Trusteeship. (2002) Roadblocks on the road to diversity. *Trusteeship Association of Governing Boards of Universities and Colleges*, 10(3), 13-18. https://eric.ed.gov/?id=EJ649062

Vagle M. D. (2014) *Crafting phenomenological research* (1st ed.). Routledge.

Vagle M. D. (2018) *Crafting phenomenological research* (2nd ed.). Routledge. Crossref.

Valle M. (1999) Crisis, culture and charisma: The new leader's work in public organizations. *Public Personnel Management*, 28(2), 245-257. Crossref

Valverde L. A. (2003) *Leaders of color in higher education: Unrecognized triumphs in harsh institutions*. Rowman Altamira.

Vogt W. P., Johnson R. B. (2011) *Dictionary of statistics and methodology: A nontechnical guide for the social sciences* (4th ed.). Sage.

Walker G. N. (2016) *Missing in leadership: Mentoring African American women in higher education* [Doctoral Dissertation]. ProQuest Dissertations and Theses database. (UMI No. 10099584)

Wolverton M., Bower B. L., Hyle A. E. (2009) *Women at the top: What women university and college presidents say about effective leadership*. Stylus Publishing, LLC.

Woods-Giscombé C. L. (2010) Superwoman schema: African American women's views on stress, strength, and health. *Qualitative Health Research*, 20(5), 668-683. Crossref

AUTHOR BIOGRAPHY

Nuchelle L. Chance, PhD, is a social activist, educator, academic, scholar, mentor, advocate, leader and the list goes on. As a Black woman who has endured extreme adversity, her fortitude continues to push her to motivate and inspire. Being driven by the help and support that she received from those who had "made it" she continues to reach back for the next generation. Her living testament is the modified quote by Psychologist Carl Jung that "[You] are not what happened to you [or where you came from], [you] are what [you] choose to become." As someone who works in higher education and is all too aware of the racial and sexual disparities that exist in this industry, Dr. Chance is increasingly motivated to inspire young Black girls and women to strive for leadership development while promoting an advanced education. Her research interests are in Social Cognition, Sex and Gender Differences, Women's Studies, Race, Learning, Memory & Recall, Perceptions & Attitudes, Consciousness & Awareness, Leadership.

APPENDIX C

Aging With Intellectual Disabilities in Families: Navigating Ever-Changing Seas—A Theoretical Model

Henrietta Trip[1], Lisa Whitehead[1,2], Marie Crowe[1], Brigit Mirfin-Veitch[1,3], and Chris Daffue[4]

[1]University of Otago, Christchurch, New Zealand

[2]Edith Cowan University, Joondalup, WA, Australia

[3]Donald Beasley Institute, Dunedin, New Zealand

[4]Canterbury District Health Board, Christchurch, New Zealand

Source: The material in this appendix originally appeared in *Qualitative Health Research*, 29(11),1595–1610. https://doi.org/10.1177/1049732319845344. Copyright 2019, Sage Publications, Inc.

Corresponding author(s)

Henrietta Trip, Centre for Postgraduate Nursing Studies, University of Otago, P.O. Box 4345, Christchurch 8140, New Zealand. Email: henrietta.trip@otago.ac.nz

ABSTRACT

Life expectancy is increasing for people with intellectual disability, many of whom live with family. While there has been research about aging and future planning, there is limited evidence about the characteristics of the caregiving relationship. The aim of this study was to examine perspectives of caregiving for older people with intellectual disability and their family. A constructivist grounded theory approach was used, and 19 people with intellectual disability and 28 family members were interviewed. Caregiving was informed by transitions across the life course. Three interrelated concepts, *Riding the Waves, Shifting Sands—Changing Tides*, and *Uncovering Horizons* comprise the core components of the theoretical model—*Navigating Ever-Changing Seas*. This model informs complex, trans-generational relationships that impact decision-making for people with a long-term condition. Applications within health care indicate a need for systems to include individuals and their networks of care in policy, practice, research, and service delivery across the lifespan.

KEYWORDS

aging, decision-making, families, learning disability, reflexivity, grounded theory, health, communication, caregivers, caretaking, long-term condition, qualitative, New Zealand

BACKGROUND

In keeping with the general population, the longevity of people with intellectual disability has increased though life expectancy is lower and is dependent on the level of impairment or associated conditions (Coppus, 2013). In New Zealand, this is 18 years less than their nondisabled peers for males with intellectual disability (or 59.7 years of age), while for females, it is 23 years less (or 59.5 years); Ministry of Health [MOH], 2011). Despite lower life expectancy, it is estimated that 12% of people with intellectual disability in the Asia-Pacific region will be over 65 years of age by 2020 (Janicki, 2009). This population commonly receives lower levels of health screening and experiences higher rates of ill health than the general population (Reichard, Stolzle, & Fox, 2011). Health issues are often masked due to presenting overt behavior (Davis & Mohr, 2004), mental health needs, and polypharmacy (McCarron et al., 2011). Lower life expectancy correlates with higher morbidity rates for people with intellectual disability who have comorbid respiratory and neurological conditions (Leeder & Dominello, 2005; MOH, 2011) and who are at a higher risk for developing cardiac disease (MOH, 2011; van den Akker, Maaskant & van der Meijden, 2006). Health outcomes, however, have not improved in New Zealand for people with an intellectual disability despite accessing health services more frequently than previously. In addition, there are higher rates of chronic conditions, including kidney disease and cancer, lower rates for mammography and cervical screening, and reduced access to health-promotion activities. Dementia has a similar prevalence to the general population rate with the exception for those with Down syndrome who are at an increased risk of Alzheimer's disease (MOH, 2011).

The majority of people with intellectual disability reside with family, may be unknown to specialist services, and/or may be invisible to health and disability systems (Ryan, Taggart, Truesdale-Kennedy, & Slevin, 2014). The nature of care within families can impact an individual's ability to express their autonomy and participate in communities of choice (Parley, 2010), and those living with a parent as they age may be at risk when trying to access services as it often takes time to arrange appropriate alternative supports (Dodd, Guerin, Mulvany, Tyrrell, & Hillery, 2008). The roles of the carer and recipient present a number of challenges and mutual benefits in regard to household income, social isolation, a lack of informal supports, changes in traditional roles, and preferred care options (Argyle, 2001). The impact of this on the health of familial carers cannot be ignored as it may affect not only physical well-being but also the way in which roles and decision-making may evolve over time. Yamaki, Hsieh and Heller (2009) found middle aged and older female carers experienced "higher rates of arthritis, high blood pressure, obesity and activity limitations" compared with the general population (p. 429), which places them at greater risk for developing cardiovascular disease, stroke, and diabetes. It has also been identified that aging carers also experienced depression and anxiety (Taggart, Truesdale-Kennedy, Ryan, & McConkey, 2012). Hence, there may be either sudden or gradual changes in the caregiving relationship due to illness of family members. As a result, health and social connectedness may impact adversely the future life trajectory of the person with intellectual disability (Cuskelly, 2006).

The need for increased awareness of the realities faced by parents (Dillenburger & McKerr, 2009) and siblings caring for older adults with intellectual disabilities (Dew, Llewellyn, & Balandin, 2004) is evident given that this relationship "is one of the most durable influences on the development and quality of life" (Esbensen, Seltzer, & Wyngaarden Krauss, 2012, p. 287). Families in these roles constitute informal carers, and society relies on them to maintain this role in whatever capacity (Dillenburger & McKerr, 2009). In the United Kingdom, a third of carers are over 70 years of age (Department of Health, 2001), and in New Zealand, 69% of all informal carers are aged between 30 and 64 years of age with 12% above 65 years of age—63% of whom are female (Ministry of Social Development, 2008). Similarly, in Australia, those over 65 years of age comprise 10%, the majority of whom have a family member with a severe or profound intellectual disability (Llewellyn, Gething, Kendig, & Cant, 2003), and in Ireland, caregivers in this age group make up 32.7% (Barron, McConkey, & Mulvany, 2006). Critically, people living with a mild intellectual disability are likely to have fewer supports, be under represented in statistics, and may outlive their carers. The implications for appropriate future planning around aging with an intellectual disability, therefore, cannot be ignored (Kelly & Kelly, 2011).

Many families have had a lifelong career in caring for their family member, which exists long into middle adulthood (Gilbert, Lankshear, & Petersen, 2008). Families relinquish care for a number of reasons: level of disability and associated support needs (severe or profound 75%), challenging behavior (64.5%), physical and psychological health and well-being (Grey, Totsika, & Hastings, 2018), exhaustion, and/or the recognition of natural milestones suggesting that young adults should move out of home (Nankervis, Rosewarner, & Vassos, 2011). This relationship can be stressful, and when formal or informal supports are deemed insufficient, it impacts the family unit (Taggart et al., 2012). For example, access to information and respite services that have specific eligibility criteria (Gilbert et al., 2008) can be stressful when the ability of carers to balance their roles may be dependent on gaining such access. Moreover, for the individual with intellectual disability, life-stage transitioning and decision-making may only occur when a crisis arises in the family (Haley & Perkins, 2004) and the opportunity for them to develop new skills may be limited if alternative care is perceived as negative (Chadwick et al., 2013).

It is difficult to fully capture the intricacies of the familial context (Stoneman, 2005), and given the increased life expectancy, the acquired role of siblings, as informal carers, is more widely recognized (Arnold, Heller, & Kramer, 2012). Furthermore, as people with intellectual disability are more likely to be unemployed, socially isolated, less likely to have a partner or children, the caregiver role is more likely to default, to siblings (Ryan et al., 2014), particularly females who reside nearby (Burke, Taylor, Urbano, & Hodapp, 2012). However, the extent to which siblings are involved in conversations about the future or hold knowledge about disability service systems is limited (Heller & Kramer, 2009). Furthermore, 37% of family members may find themselves in a compound caregiving role, parenting an adult son, daughter, or sibling with intellectual disability as well as caring for parents or others (Perkins & Haley, 2010). While health and disability services are predominantly funded on the basis of standardized algorithms for measuring individual needs, the needs of others in the caregiving relationship are not always clear (Williams & Robinson, 2001a).

It is common to find that family carers have not undertaken specific future planning (O'Grady Reilly & Conliffe, 2002). However, while such planning does not guarantee access to relevant services, having a plan has been found to increase the probability of it occurring (Freedman, Wyngaarden Krauss, & Mailick Seltzer, 1997). Parents may be reluctant to explore the conversation about future planning with other family members due to the belief that the knowledge they possess is not transferable (Williams & Robinson, 2001b), a recognition of their own fragility or significance of altered roles (Taggart et al., 2012), the perceived suitability of accommodation options for their relative with intellectual disability (Llewellyn et al., 2003), their behavior and vulnerability (Williams & Robinson, 2001b), funding for appropriate caregiving support (Black & McKendrick, 2010), reluctance of the family member to move (Bowey & McGlaughlin, 2005), and service continuity (Cuskelly, 2006). Many familial carers have thought they would outlive their relative with intellectual disability, and that kin and services would take responsibility when needed (Taggart et al., 2012). In addition, caregiving roles sometimes contain a symbiotic dynamic, in which neither the relative nor the adult with intellectual disability would be able to continue living independently without the presence of each other (Foundation for People with Learning Disabilities, 2010).

Future planning has been explored with people who have an intellectual disability and/or their family. "What the future holds" enabled families to plan what is desirable for the future, while simultaneously ensuring that systems do not negate this when supporting transitions (O'Grady Reilly & Conliffe, 2002). "The future is now" is a peer support intervention, which was important for family members as "was the inclusion of individuals with developmental disabilities in the planning process" (Heller & Caldwell, 2006, p. 198). However, future planning should not be the sole responsibility of familial carers and should include funders of health and disability services (Janicki, 2009) who are sufficiently knowledgeable, sensitive, and flexible to allow appropriate responses to idiosyncratic situations within longstanding informal caregiving relationships (Black & McKendrick, 2010). While there is research about the nature of aging and future planning in this field, the complex experiences of caregiving, receiving, and decision-making within familial systems of care have received little attention. The aim of this study was to examine the nature and dynamics of caregiving and receiving for older people with intellectual disability and their family. Therefore, a qualitative approach was needed to explore this social phenomena from the perspectives of all parties in the caregiving relationship. This was informed through exploring their individual and collective perspectives about aging and future considerations.

DESIGN

From its roots in classical grounded theory (Glaser & Strauss, 1967), the epistemology of the constructivist paradigm within grounded theory necessitates a process of engagement in building a collective understanding of experiences (Charmaz, 2006, 2008 2014). This approach was used to explore the dynamic nature of the caregiving relationship between people with an intellectual and family members. The process was underpinned by axiology, which stems from the transformative paradigm of seeking what is ethical for populations considered to be vulnerable (Harris, Holmes & Mertens, 2009), and the ontology of relativism, which requires the researcher to critique their existing knowledge or assumptions while engaging with participants' realities and the constructs that inform them (Birks & Mills, 2011; Guba & Lincoln, 1994). The purpose of the former is to question and understand the contentions within disability research in regard to inclusion, access, equity and fairness across the lifespan (Harris et al., 2009). Constructivist grounded theory, therefore, required the first author to be cognizant of her own lenses and interactions in relation to others (Giles, King, & de Lacey, 2013): This is reflexivity, which enables the social and mutual construction of experiences (Charmaz, 2008) as understandings that are co-created inform the theoretical perspective about "*how* and sometimes *why* [emphasis in original] participants construct meanings and actions in specific situations" (Charmaz, 2006, p. 130). Constructivist grounded theory is not a linear process, and thus, the core features of theoretical sampling, memo writing, concurrent data collection, and constant comparative analysis were undertaken (Charmaz, 2006, 2014) (Figure 1).

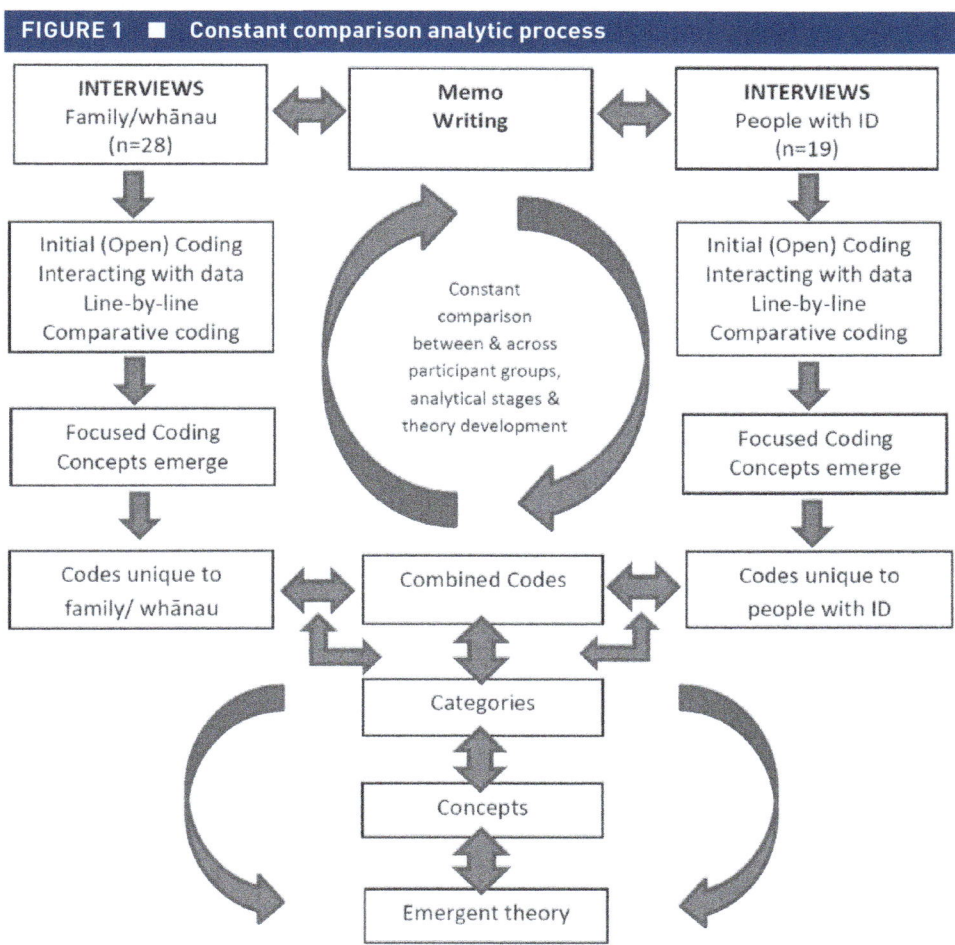

FIGURE 1 ■ Constant comparison analytic process

Recruitment and Participants

Using nonprobability sampling, the first author approached residential and vocational intellectual disability service providers to ascertain whether people accessing the service met the inclusion criteria. Information was also sent to primary health care settings in the South Island of New Zealand. Advertisements were placed in a religious publication, a carers newsletter, and public notices in local newspapers and on websites. Services discussed the proposed research with prospective participants before providing them with a Letter of Invitation, Information Sheet, and Expression of Interest Form. Snowball sampling was also used as a form of recruitment (Becker, Roberts, Morrison, & Silver, 2004).

Participants with intellectual disability were to be approximately 40 years of age or older, as recommended by Taggart et al. (2012); have a mild to moderate level of intellectual disability; have some form of expressive language; and who could consent or assent to an interview. They were required to have lived with, or to have been supported by, someone they identified as "family" for at least 5 years. Nineteen individuals with intellectual disability nominated 28 informants to participate in the study.

Data Collection

Semistructured open-ended questions guided the sharing of experiences (Charmaz, 2006) and allowed participants to place information into a relevant context to reduce the risk of misunderstandings (Gilbert et al., 2008). The interview guide was informed by the Family Life Interview, which identifies and locates the needs of the family in relation to the connections and conflicts that may exist between them and the wider community (Llewellyn et al., 2010). The Family Quality of Life (FQOL) questionnaire explores importance, opportunity, initiative, and stability across the domains of family life: health, finances, family relationships, support from other people, support from disability-related services, influences of values, careers and planning for careers, leisure and recreation, and community interaction (Werner et al., 2009). Questions included the following:

- How would you describe yourself as a person?
- Who is important to you? (Prompt: Tell me about your family/friends)
- What do you enjoy doing during the day/week in the community?
- What support/help do you get now? And/or provide within the family?
- What other caregiving responsibilities do you have or anticipate?
- Tell me about your health.
- What do you think about getting older?
- What might change in your body as you get older?
- Where would you like to be? What would you like to be doing in the future?
- What would be needed? How do you/your family make decisions?

Prior to the study, the first author discussed the draft questions with three individuals with intellectual disability (who were not eligible to participate), to gauge their understanding and interpretation (Northway, Howarth, & Evans, 2015). Demographic data for participants included age, ethnicity, gender and health status, and relationship between the person with intellectual disability and the nominated informant. Up to three face-to-face contacts were made by the first author with participants with intellectual disability to enable introductions, discuss the research, complete the consent process, and undertake the interview, which was digitally audio-recorded and transcribed. Interviews with participants with intellectual disability took between 30 and 139 minutes (mean 62 minutes) and for family members 30 and 150 minutes (mean 76 minutes). Six people with intellectual disability chose to be interviewed alone, seven with the nominated family member, and the remaining six with other supports. Eleven participants with intellectual disability nominated one person to be invited to contribute to the study, seven participants chose two, and one chose three family members. The range of relationships comprised mother, father, brother, sister, sister-in-law, friend, and aunt. One nominated sister declined to participate, and while a son with intellectual disability declined to participate, they nominated their mother. No reasons for either were received. Three participants with intellectual disability chose to review the transcribed interview with the first author, and family members were sent the transcript and invited to make further comment.

Data Analysis

Through constant comparative analysis, initial and focused coding requires the fracturing of data: This process explores inter-relationships between the data, enabling it to be reassembled as theory emerges (Mills, Bonner, & Francis, 2006a) while simultaneously ensuring that the emerging codes, categories, and their properties are grounded in the data (Charmaz, 2006, 2014). This is termed *theoretical sensitivity* (Birks & Mills, 2011) and safeguards reflexivity by separating out the influence of the researcher (Giles et al., 2013). Coding was undertaken by the first author and were named in the active tense ("gerunds"), which reflect both the social and psychological processes (Charmaz, 2006, 2011) and the dynamic nature of the code (Mills, Bonner, & Francis, 2006b), resulting in categories that evoke "crucial properties that make data meaningful and carry the analysis forward" (Charmaz, 2014, p. 247).

An example of a memo to capture reflexivity by the first author was as follows: *As a nurse with over 20 years experience in the specialist field of ID, I have knowledge of health & disability systems—some families struggle with. Not sharing this knowledge could impact interactions, interpretation and the co-construction of their experience . . . Separating out the roles of researcher and clinician presents both an ethical obligation and responsibility to reduce the likelihood of moral distress.* Memos also distilled both the historical, current, and prospective context offered by participants. This process also illustrates reflexivity in terms of channeling the researcher's lens to the "tacit knowledge and implicit meanings of participants" (Charmaz, 2015, p. 1615), and hence, memos were completed both during data collection and throughout data analysis. In regard to implicit meanings, for example, *the family is in a "holding pattern," members are getting on with their own lives amidst ongoing influences in which the outlook keeps changing (within and external). They have parallel yet disparate existences—intrinsic knowledge that the situation would change when Mother got sick or died. All parties capture aspirations of what they want for themselves, not previously heard by each other.* This was a response to interviewing a man with intellectual disability, his mother, and two sisters. The following memo relates to the experiences of several siblings and identifies that some perspectives were unique to participant groups: *Feel like a facilitator of transitions across and between lifespans—their own and others.* Participants with intellectual disability spoke of *being to others . . . waiting, wanting, anticipating, hoping things to be different with uncertainty of how to make happen a future for themselves.*

Data analysis involved initial coding, which were managed in Excel. As the constant comparative process evolved (which included reviewing the wider context in transcripts), the coded data from across participants were then printed so that focused coding could ensue, be visualized by the co-authors, and be developed conceptually as subsequent dimensions became evident. In constant comparative inquiry, there is no defining point at which theory is said to emerge. The process is the progression of evolving theoretical development until saturation has occurred, which ensures that grounded theory meets the social justice criteria of credibility, originality, resonance, and usefulness (Charmaz, 2006). Therefore, a concept must not be solely applicable to the context in which it arose; its utility is in its transferability (Morse, 2004). These core components of grounded theory underpinned the methodological approach undertaken in this study and were conducted in partnership with the researcher's supervisors (L.W. and M.C.) and the specialist advisors for the project who have clinical and research expertise in the field (B.M.-V. and C.D.).

Ethical Considerations

Ethical approval (URA/11/02/004) was received from the Upper South A Regional Ethics Committee, Ministry of Health, New Zealand. Historically, including people with intellectual disability in research was considered inappropriate (Polit & Beck, 2004); such gatekeeping by others excludes participation, and is often based on unsubstantiated assumptions on the need to protect the individual as well as potentially perceptions regarding overall capability (McDonald & Kidney, 2012; Morrisey, 2012; Ponterotto, 2013). Conversely, without external facilitation by others, the person's ability to access and participate in research would be hindered (Lennox et al., 2005), and the core lived experience would not be heard. Fundamentally, it is important to hear from the people themselves about issues that affect them to ensure transparency of reporting and equity of representation, and in turn, society learns about populations considered vulnerable (McDonald, Conroy, & Olick, 2016). As with the general population, people with intellectual disability must be "assumed to have capacity to consent, unless it is proven otherwise" (Dye, Hendy, Hare, & Burton, 2004, p. 145). Consent by proxy was used by one person with intellectual disability who was able to assent to participate but was unable to provide informed consent (Veenstra et al., 2010): This means that their legal guardian could consent to their participation having ascertained their understanding about the project even if the logistics of research process per se are unclear to them. All the remaining participants consented for themselves.

FINDINGS

The demographics of participants are summarized in the supplemental table and Table 1 namely, people with intellectual disability and their nominated family respectively. What follows is a presentation of each theoretical concept: Riding the Waves, Shifting Sands—Changing Tides,

TABLE 1 ■ Demographic Data—Family/Whanau (*n* = 28)		
Gender	Male	5
	Female	23
Age	Range (20–83 years)	
	<25 years	1
	25–40 years	2
	41–50 years	3
	51–60 years	2
	61–70 years	6
	>70 years	14
Ethnicity	NZ European	24
	Cook Island	1
	Other (Canadian, South African, Dutch)	3
Axis 1 Diagnosis	Phobia	1
	Depression	2
	Bipolar disorder	1
Highest Qualification	Nil	6
	Secondary school	8
	Certificate/diploma/trade	6
	University degree	6
	Other	2
Marital Status	Single	4
	Married	13
	Divorced	4
	Widowed	3
	De facto or separated	4

(Continued)

TABLE 1 ■ Demographic Data—Family/Whanau (n = 28) (Continued)		
Income	NZ Superannuation	17
	Student allowance	1
	Invalid's and disability benefit	2
	Wage/salary earner	6
	Self-employed	1
	Other	2
Length of Time Residing Together	All their life	15
	5–10 years	4
	11–20 years	3
	21–30 years	3
	N/A Other (Shared Care/SIL)	3
Relationship to Participant With Intellectual Disability	Friend	3
	Mother	11
	Father	3
	Sister (includes sister-in-law)	9
	Brother	1
	Aunt	1
Carer Support	Yes allocated (range 20–103 days/year)	14
	Not able to use	5
	Nil allocated	2
	Nonapplicable	3

Note: SIL = supported independent living.

and Uncovering Horizons. For each concept, links are provided between the inductive codes and categories of which each is comprised, together with evidence from the data. The theoretical model, *Navigating Ever-Changing Seas*, is then introduced and explained.

Demographics of Participants

Concept 1: Riding the waves. This concept comprises three categories: reciprocating relationships, emerging (in)dependence, and taking cognizance, which illustrate and represent the ebb and flow of relationships, focus on daily living, and is about getting on with life and simply taking things as they come. Riding the waves represents the challenges and opportunities of living alongside and being responsive to others over time (Table 2). Parents spoke about others not understanding their isolation, and commented "we were never invited out . . . my sisters thought he was spoiled." One sister, however, "thought that every family was just like us . . . it's hard to tell what life would have been like without her." Another example of the diversity was expressed by a mother who said this was her job—"I sort of do things myself and take everything in my stride. I used to get a lot of help when he was younger."

Reciprocating relationships denotes connections within the caregiving system of support evidenced by the roles, relationships, sense of duty, and expectations. Challenging the common expectations about who provides and who receives care, one sister reflected about her brother that "amazingly, it got to a place where he has become a caregiver for Mum." Conversely, he felt he had to co-ordinate the services involved with his mother as it was like a "train station—people coming and going." Another stated that while it could be trying at times, her flatmate, who has intellectual disability and mental health needs, is "a really good friend and you've always got company," thus illustrating the reciprocity of caregiving relationships. A number of mothers of people with intellectual disability spoke about the sense of duty, "I must do it" or "I've still got a child . . . who is dependent," and similarly, for a sibling, "I felt obligated that it's my duty as the eldest."

Emerging (in)dependence is reliant on the underlying context, and this changes over time. For example, while some participants identified aging as a way of moving toward independence, for others, increasing dependence with age was likely. While autonomy was valued, the level at which it was able to be exercised varied. "We really owe him right now otherwise she'd [Mum] be in a home" (sister). Growing up, one sister struggled with understanding why she "always had to keep an eye on him . . . it was always my job. [Other siblings] would not have a clue what he needs now." The aunt spoke about not having her own life due to her nephew's support needs

TABLE 2 ■ Riding the Waves

Code	Category	Concept
Conceptualizing family	Reciprocating Relationships	Riding the Waves
Continuing the duty		
Reflecting on roles		
Providing companionship		
Valuing autonomy	Emerging (In)dependence	
Acquiring skills		
Maintaining status quo		
Accommodating the disability	Taking Cognizance	
Conflicting perspectives		
Rationalizing the reality		
Reaching saturation		

whereas some parents said their son kept them young. Notwithstanding, many participants identified that their life had meaning and, for some family, the person with intellectual disability needed to learn new skills for the future despite the family maintaining the status quo.

Taking cognizance was seen to apply only to family members in this study. They weighed up and reflected on finding themselves accommodating the disability and rationalizing their reality. Siblings reflected on this in terms of communication, for example, "it is quite rewarding [living together] but sometimes it's terrible . . . when he doesn't have the words to why he's annoyed," and another identified the need to be patient, and contextualize the perceived challenge in terms of the disability to work out what was true and had meaning for her sister with intellectual disability. Accommodating the disability extended to the physical environment as one accepted that her sister-in-law does things at a slower pace. The code of reaching saturation was reflected by many family members in terms of recognizing their own limitations, as one friend said he gets tired with being available and feels terrible about feeling that way.

Concept 2: Shifting sands—Changing tides. This concept was informed by unknown and known realities about the past, present, and those still emerging (Table 3). While some ambivalence was noted, these realities are based on how participants were configuring aging or anticipating change. One elderly mother noted that "life would change very quickly [for her daughter] if I couldn't drive. . . ." Over the years, family members had seen significant changes in health and disability systems and were not enamored with what was available but resigned themselves to not speak up because "he's at least got a placement or somewhere to go in the day—so shut up!" These examples mirrored the perspectives of many participants about what the context of the older may be like in terms of service access and delivery, which informed considerations and decision-making about the future.

All participants with intellectual disability had specific ideas about configuring aging as defined by time, health, socialization, and mobility, which could be altered through a person's

TABLE 3 ■ Shifting Sands—Changing Tides		
Code	Category	Concept
Defining aging	Configuring ageing	Shifting Sands—Changing Tides
Recognizing altered function		
Dying is part of living		
Looming responsibilities	Anticipating change	
Limiting factors		
Feeling disillusioned		
Letting go—Enabling others		
Unknowing explorers		
Evolving expectations		

change in function and, therefore, result in potential changes in life circumstances. One person saw older people as those who "can't do much . . . Standing, walking and bending down [are harder] . . . slow in their thinking . . . you've got to yell—cos they're deaf . . . They are really slow." Another thought that people "start to get grumpy," and a third knew people with dementia who "forget where the toilet is . . . can't manage eating." One participant considered his own aging in comparison with what he could do when he was younger, namely, sitting unaided. When talking about getting older, several made the connection that dying is part of living in that it would be "really sad to be that old . . . To have a walking stick because they're dying or don't want to live." Others spoke specifically about being scared and "not looking forward to dying . . . I don't want to be put in a coffin [or] cremated. When I die I want to be buried" (Kate). Leslie added to this conversation about what happens when one dies, stating "it goes up there . . . Your soul [indicating skywards]. The body goes underground." For participants with intellectual disability and their family members, configuring aging made visible the likelihood that changes in the existing caregiving relationship were inevitable based on their individual and collective aging.

The category of anticipating change reflected a willingness to embrace looming responsibilities, intrinsic and extrinsic factors, and feeling disillusioned. Over time, beliefs within families had been presumed or expected and eventually became an accepted truth. Two mothers were adamant that responsibility should not fall to other offspring nor was this fair to the son or daughter with intellectual disability: "It's not their job . . . that's what really started me thinking about it [making a plan]." There were, however, assumptions about the availability of others to step up: "I'm pretty sure [daughter] would take care of him—she wouldn't put him anywhere" (mother), and for several siblings, this was a clear expectation. Three daughters felt this role was assumed and inevitable based on their gender, proximity, and the absence of other family members, and they wanted siblings to pitch in: "I do all the donkey work down here, she [sister] can have a turn." One brother was aware of his own aging and was concerned he would not outlive his sister who has Down syndrome.

Limiting factors, both intrinsic and extrinsic, impacted how the needs of the person with intellectual disability could continue to be met by the family. Six siblings and eight other family members, for example, expressed mistrust of health and disability services and were concerned about sustainability of such services in time to come. Two fathers reiterated, "Can you make any plans because things change all the time? You know it's very difficult. They get homes so far out, no transport . . . those kids miss out on a lot." Examples were given of "service fatigue" in terms of timeframes, who to contact, assessment for access, and then limited receipt of services. Changes in legislation for the funding and delivery of disability services were also noted as having had a negative impact on what was available. Despite this reticence, many carers acknowledged the importance of letting go and enabling others for change to occur, all the while feeling like unknowing explorers. Despite identifying the sense of looming responsibilities for themselves, half the family members voiced expectations that others step up to support the family member with intellectual disability: "Hopefully we've set a precedent for the others to follow" (sister-in-law) and "she's the mother of my granddaughter . . . I'm still mum to her . . . that's where he's [brother] going when I die" (sister). The intergenerational positioning regarding caregiving responsibility was seen to be instilled (by parents) and distilled (by siblings) for individuals, collective family, and service systems.

Concept 3: Uncovering horizons. Thinking beyond the present saw participants uncovering horizons. For some, this was daunting yet there was an inevitability of a future that held potential—for everyone. This concept was informed by the categories of entertaining possibilities, creating a good life, and mastering decisions (Table 4). These identified the facets of safeguarding and enabling the future to become a reality for all concerned. "My hope is that he would be able to live with other people . . . a small group of people" (sister).

Entertaining possibilities evoked anticipation for all participants as looking forward to changing circumstances would allow for individual development of identity. Mothers spoke about being cautious as to "whose life you are living" if one does not explore the future and, in preparing her daughter to move out, thought "I'm looking forward to starting my life . . . the ton of weight's already been lifted off my shoulders." Some participants with intellectual disability found it hard to identify things they would like to do in the future: Nine had clear goals including "going out more" or wanting to learn "how to spell, read, and use the phone," and four wanted to retire, which meant moving into aged care whereas others thought going on an overseas holiday would make retirement worthwhile.

While the opportunity to discuss changing life circumstances had been minimal within most families, 15 participants with intellectual disability spoke of preferred alternative living arrangements. For example, "whatever happens to mum and dad, I'll probably be staying with my sister for a while," or wanting one's own home: "I'd live there by myself . . . get people in to do the lawns and garden but I'll do the rest." Wherever they saw themselves, having an identity was a key goal be it a paid part-time job, spending time with friends at the library, or resuming art classes. Creating a good life was about keeping well and enjoying living: It was recognized that one is dependent on the other, and participants spoke about health and supports needed to achieve these goals.

TABLE 4 ■ Uncovering Horizons

Code	Category	Concept
Looking forward	Entertaining possibilities	Uncovering Horizons
Changing circumstances		
Having an identity		
Enjoying living	Creating a good life	
Keeping well		
Connecting with others	Mastering decisions	
Knowing the person		
Facilitating ownership		
Engaging the system		

In regard to the aforementioned, mastering decisions presented questions for individuals and their families about when it would be the right time to take the next step, whose interests would be at the forefront, and who should be included in the process. Connecting with others comprised extended family, neighbors, respite care, friends, church community, and even strangers:

> We didn't realize that all the people on the bus keep an eye on him [son] . . . he got off the bus one day and went the wrong way . . . the bus driver . . . came back because [passengers] said he's going the wrong way!

However, this category of mastering decisions also identified several concerns that families had about the lack of natural supports as well as staff turnover in services as they trusted them to know the person. For families, the code facilitating ownership linked perceptions about ability with the manner in which choices are made for, and with, people with intellectual disability. Family shared lessons learned about the ability of the individual and/or response around decision-making. For example, one family member was surprised when her brother suggested he go into respite care when he said, "I think it's good sister because you're going to have a break from me and I'm going to have a break from you." A mother explained about giving her daughter a choice, and while it took two days, she decided who was to stay with her when Mum was away. One set of parents admitted the family had a discussion about the future, which resulted in the father getting a slap across the face. "The next day he apologized and we had a chance to sit down and talk to him about what was going on." It transpired their son was upset as decisions were being made without him, and this acknowledgement enabled individuals and family, in turn, to consider engaging the system. Decision-making has been, and continues to be, a fluid, dynamic, and intermittent process across the lifespan. While family members were grateful for what they were already receiving, the majority found future planning daunting in terms of what it would require in terms of their readiness and engagement with complex changing service systems to meet the current and future needs of all family members.

Navigating Ever-Changing Seas: A Theoretical Model

The concepts of Riding the Waves, Shifting Sands—Changing Tides, and Uncovering Horizons are interpretive co-constructions of the participants' narrative experiences. In other words, as individual perspectives were given voice within and between systems, it allowed for the overlaying of all contributions, which ensured the simultaneous validity of both the individual and the collective experiences: A new meta-level of understanding commonalties thus emerged and allowed for the shared evolution of caregiving experiences. As a result, these three concepts represent dynamic, cyclical, and evolving trans-generational relationships, and illustrate the realities of individuals and their family who found themselves *Navigating Ever-Changing Seas* (Figure 2). The "sea" as a metaphor represents no definitive beginning or ending in understanding aging and future planning and in which "navigation" (decision-making and purpose) is ongoing, and the intrinsic and extrinsic factors that underpin participant perspectives are ever-changing. At the heart of this theoretical model is that decision-making in the frame of health and disability tends to shift, evolve, and devolve as an ongoing function of the dynamic and fluid intersections between relationships (personal, familial, and formal service

FIGURE 2 ■ Navigating ever-changing seas: A theoretical model

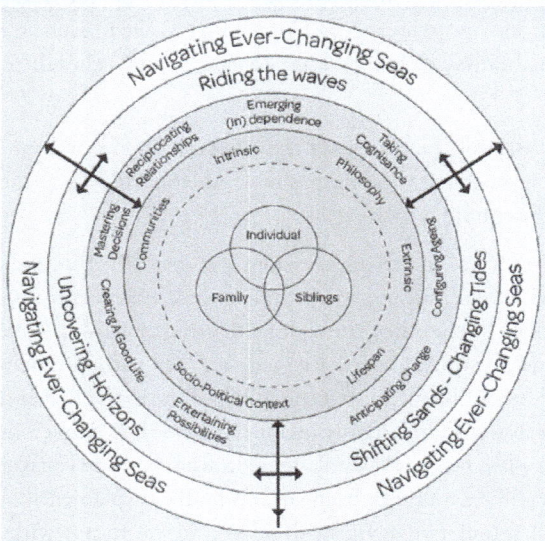

systems) and the perceptions and beliefs held by the very occupants of those systems with regard to caregiving and receiving across the lifespan.

The three circles in the center of the model signify the interrelationship of people with intellectual disability, those nominated as family (including siblings and subsequent generations). While each have their own unique qualities, the spheres of influence repeatedly wax and wane between and across each group. The broken line signifies the permeability between the parties in the caregiving relationship(s) with six factors influencing their individual and collective lives: health and disability philosophy, the socio-political and cultural context, communities of identity, intrinsic features, extrinsic elements and one's place within the lifespan. The impact of these factors is dependent on variables such as the setting, timing, and magnitude of the perceived or actual experience. While the properties of each concept are linked to the respective categories, the four-way omnidirectional arrows illustrate the flexibility of the static and dynamic factors within and between the concepts.

A number of inherent drivers were evident over the lifespan for families and the member with intellectual disability in respect to how perspectives about caregiving (as it pertained to aging) were and continue to be formed. The values intrinsic to the system of care are critical to this process, and simultaneously, extrinsic societal factors shaped the experience of caregiving and receiving for all parties that informed retrospective and prospective decision-making. Without exception, the influence of changing government policy in terms of funding for, and access to, alternative accommodation options and vocational services, significantly impacted how and why decisions were made by families over time. It also clearly influenced participant's perspectives about aging and future planning. The socio-political backdrop of disability philosophy over time, such as institutionalization and community living, provided a context for families and underpinned their approach to decision-making, and thus the theoretical model *Navigating Ever-Changing Seas.*

As with all models, encapsulating the identified properties (within a concept) implies that a finite number of elements exist, which follow a linear process, and are equally applicable for all participants. In this study, this was not always the case as evidenced by participants' experiences of caregiving and receiving as they pertained to perspectives of aging and future planning. Korzybski, cited by Bateson (1973), states "the map is not the territory" (p. 423). In other words, a map is a static entity and only provides an indication at a specific point in time of what has happened across the lifespan but not the lived, dynamic territory. Theoretical models cannot fully substitute for the individual's experience or map and, consequently, it is the territory (or variables in the model) that are the elements of driving and shaping change. Consequently, *Navigating Ever-Changing Seas* reflects the unspoken, yet evolving territory that intersects with the changing maps of others' lives. Maps, by subjective interpretation, are constantly being redrawn based on "differences [which] are the things that get onto the map" (Bateson, 1973, p. 426). Such differences can refer to how events are remembered, represented, and interpreted across the lifespan and the practicalities that inform how and why decisions are made. The former are characteristics unique to individuals, whereas the latter refers to the history and social context of participant groups (Shanahan & Profelli, 2002) — in this case people with intellectual disabilities, siblings, parent(s), and others denoted as family. The territory is what emerges from the differences between expectations of the map versus the experiences of participants (based on existing knowledge, perceptions, interpretations, and relationships), and thus, the map is continually in a state of flux. Having a map is important, but as the future is unknown, the territory or individual permutations intersecting the network of care are seen to demand and require continuous navigation.

DISCUSSION

While limited, the complexities of intergenerational caregiving have been explored from a life-course perspective and acknowledges that transitions in later life are largely influenced by individual, familial, and societal factors (Baumbusch, Mayer, Phinney, & Baumbusch, 2017; Esbensen et al., 2012). This study, however, identified the experiences of those in the caregiving relationship about negotiating and navigating decision-making, in regard to the future, and elicited what informed their respective perspectives.

People with intellectual disability and their family may not always be aware of the myriad of co-existing identities, roles, and life-stages, nor be conscious of what has informed their beliefs or position, or be able to articulate why these are important and which factors may help or impede them in moving forward in a preferred direction. *Navigating Ever-Changing Seas* illustrates a flexible platform from which families can explore their individual and collective maps to date and recognize the interchange of their respective territories through the concepts of *Riding the Waves, Shifting Sands—Changing Tides,* and *Uncovering Horizons.* The properties of the first concept denote an intrinsic awareness of potential demands, balanced against taking life as it comes by dealing with each challenge as and when it arises. The second delineates the recognition of differences between the current territory of one or other party in the system of care, and which prompts a need to identify and adjust one's perspective to accommodate these. Hence, through *Shifting Sands—Changing Tides*, there are constant opportunities for an unintentional yet self-determined emergence of either common or distinct territories; these find their expression in *Uncovering Horizons*. In so doing, new territories or perspectives emerge, which require re-visiting over time. Hence, *Navigating Ever-Changing Seas* provides a personal and an all-encompassing perspective through which the direction or construction of individual and family maps and/or territories may be reconfigured as people engage in caregiving relationships across the lifespan. The application of this model is crucial both developmentally and chronologically at each stage of decision-making at an actual or perceived transition throughout one's life; caregiver(s) and care recipient(s) can use this model as an external framework through which one identifies and communicates their current or desired future territory (life stage or direction). As demonstrated in this study, role-confusion and identity-confusion occur when it is not always clear as to who is the carer and who is the recipient. The model is, thus, beneficial to all parties within the caregiving system — including the family member with intellectual disability. There is a transactional and ever-changing context stemming from intrinsic and extrinsic influences, which can create opportunities for transitions and evolution to occur (Jokinen, Janicki, Hogan, & Force, 2012). Intrinsic influences refer to one's sense of support from others in the family (Resch et al., 2010) including personal resilience, hopes, and the bank of experiences, which inform the truths or map for each party. Extrinsic influences include philosophical shifts stemming from the prevailing socio-political context. These have an impact on the individual experience of intellectual disability in relation to one's family and/or community, as well as the availability and accessibility of services (Resch et al., 2010). Moreover, families have their own beliefs, culture, and ecology, which inform the way in which they interact and engage with each other, services, and, socio-politically, with the community at large (Skinner & Weisner, 2007).

It is proposed that, as a theoretical model, *Navigating Ever-Changing Seas* can be applied in the wider context of health care. It is a means of understanding past decision-making, anticipating possible future points of transition and is a framework from which one can be made aware and be guided through. In this study, it evolved from an exploration of perspectives about future planning from the lenses of the aging person with intellectual disability living with family. The experience of decision-making as informed by the three core concepts that comprise the model could be applied to an individual with a long-term condition and reflects elements nominated by Wackerbarth (1999). She examined decision-making for those caring for a person with dementia and identified styles that resonate here and include those who "take it one day at a time" (p. 308), recognize intrinsic factors, plan ahead, or require external support to do so. In their review, Devaney et al. (2009) unpacked health barriers to cancer screening and concluded women did not have the:

> . . . opportunity to tell their stories, they miss the fact that previous experiences that are apparently unrelated to cancer screening on the surface have a profound impact on whether or not disabled women will advocate for and/or choose to engage in preventive health care services . . . Their past experiences of such engagements were often

challenging and not always respectful of the particular expertise that lived experience as disabled women produces (p. 748).

Using this model with individuals and their families to unpack the nature of caregiving and decision-making could promote engagement with health and disability systems to enable future planning and, potentially, improve health care outcomes of all members in the system of care. The above two examples highlight the opportunity of the model to serve as a framework for examining and understanding decision-making in a range of long-term conditions and in which there are reciprocal perspectives of caregiving and receiving, for example, diabetes, mental health, and neurological conditions such as epilepsy.

LIMITATIONS

The majority of participants with intellectual disability chose to be interviewed at home, and therefore, it is not clear whether the presence of family impacted their being able to freely express themselves. Conversely, it may have facilitated communication by having someone who knew them well as families were respectful of the opportunity to be present and actively supported their family member with intellectual disability to participate as independently as possible. Access to precise diagnoses for intellectual disability was a further challenge. There is a presumption that those already accessing intellectual disability services must have had confirmed eligibility to government-funded services. Some individuals, however, self-identifying as having an intellectual disability, had attended special education but had not yet accessed adult disability services. A number of contacts were required to engage participants for the purposes of consent and interview, which may have served as both a limitation and a strength. The inclusion of people with intellectual disability in research is considered best practice, and as such, gate-keeping practices may be a limiting factor as autonomy is often linked with capacity to consent (Lai, Elliott, & Ouellette-Kuntz, 2006).

RECOMMENDATIONS

The recommendations pertain to aging and future planning in terms of how caregiving or receiving can enhance or limit the promotion of individual and collective autonomy and decision-making. They are relevant for (a) people with intellectual disability, their family and wider networks of care; (b) health and disability service systems and policy-makers; and (c) informing further research:

- a. Conversations about health and aging should include:
  - The subjective narrative of the person to give voice to their decision-making and meaningfully support them in their journey across the lifespan.
  - The collation of information about the person needs to include life history, their likes, dislikes, communication, and support needs.
  - Appropriate and regular education with regard to rights and responsibility, life skills, health literacy, and facilitative choice and access.

- Ongoing development of existing formal and informal networks of support.
- The development of regular re-visiting of inclusive advance-care plans with each party in the caregiving relationship.

b. Knowing the populations:
- A lifespan approach to the education and training of health, disability, and service system providers in regard to the health and aging needs of the population.
- Flexibility and co-ordination is needed between the disability and aged care sectors as existing resources from each may, in isolation, be insufficient for one or both parties to age in place. When responses to increasing care needs occur at the point of crisis, there is a risk of further increasing the vulnerability of individuals (Eley, Boyes, Young, & Hegney, 2009).
- Information management systems to identify the composition of families who have a member with an intellectual or other disability to inform system planning.

c. Further exploration and evaluation of *Navigating Ever-Changing Seas* in regard to its application to other populations and contexts.

CONCLUSION

This study provided a unique insight into the nature of caregiving and receiving for older people with intellectual disability and their family. When the former reside with the latter into their middle-adult years, this may pose a number of additional challenges and opportunities. While some families may be "criticized if they do not make plans for their future . . . [they may feel] unsupported by the system when they do take positive steps" (Grey, Griffith, Totsika, & Hastings, 2015, p. 55). The interpretive constructivist grounded theory approach enabled participant perspectives to be shared, and their accounts allowed a co-construction of their individual and collective realities across both time and with others. There was clear evidence of an enduring parallel process for participants with intellectual disability and their family in recognizing their multiple roles within the system of care as well as the unique features that shaped it. Hence, it is essential that caregiving is recognized as being both dynamic and reflexive rather than a linear process. *Navigating Ever-Changing Seas* defines the concepts that comprise the interconnecting realities of all participants on the journey of living with a long-term condition, aging, and planning for the future. Furthermore, it provides a flexible map by which the respective territories of the individual and collective outlooks can (and should) continue to be identified, acknowledged, developed, and shaped over time. Pivotally, this notion of perpetuating engagement needs to be considered as it applies not only to the study participants and their family (regardless of age and stage of life) but also to others in the health and disability sector.

Critically, *Navigating Ever-Changing Seas* is a theoretical model concerned with an interactive process of influences, which both enabled and disabled the engagement of people with intellectual disability and their family in conversations and/or processes about aging and planning for the future. It draws together three theoretical concepts *(Riding the Waves, Shifting*

Sands—Changing Tides, and *Uncovering Horizons)*, which together illustrate the ever-evolving inter-relationships between all parties in the caregiving system. Furthermore, it demonstrates that there exists a core set of elements that can identify and/or inform the knowledge and processing gaps that exist in the journey of living, dying, aging, and planning for the future. *Navigating Ever-Changing Seas* acknowledges the dynamic nature of interdependent, transgenerational relationships and the influences that permeate these relationships, perspectives, and experiences of decision-making across the lifespan.

DECLARATION OF CONFLICTING INTERESTS

The authors declared no potential conflicts of interest with respect to the research, authorship, and/or publication of this article.

FUNDING

The authors received no financial support for the research, authorship, and/or publication of this article.

ORCID iD

Henrietta Trip, https://orcid.org/0000-0001-5844-3400

REFERENCES

American Psychiatric Association. (2013). *Diagnostic and statistical manual of mental disorders* (5th ed.). Washington, DC: Author. Crossref.

Argyle E. (2001). Poverty, disability and the role of older carers. *Disability & Society*, 16, 585-595. Crossref Crossref.

Arnold C. K., Heller T., Kramer J. (2012). Support needs of siblings of people with developmental disabilities. *Intellectual and Developmental Disabilities*, 50, 373–382. Crossref PubMed.

Barron S., McConkey R., Mulvany F. (2006). Family carers of adult persons with intellectual disabilities on the island of Ireland. *Journal of Policy and Practice in Intellectual Disabilities*, 3, 87–94. Crossref

Bateson G. (1973). *Steps to an ecology of mind: Collected essays in anthropology, psychiatry, evolution, and epistemology.* San Francisco: Chandler. (Original work published 1972).

Baumbusch J., Mayer S., Phinney A., Baumbusch S. (2017). Aging together: Caring relations in families of adults with intellectual disabilities. *Gerontologist*, 57, 341–347. Crossref PubMed.

Becker H , Roberts G., Morrison J., Silver J. (2004). Recruiting people with disabilities as research participants: Challenges and strategies to address them. *Mental Retardation*, 42, 471–475. Crossref PubMed.

Birks M., Mills J. (2011). *Grounded theory. A practical guide.* London: Sage.

Black L. A., McKendrick V. (2010). *Careful plans report: A study of the aspirations of older carers of family members with a learning disability living in South Eastern Health and Social Care Trust; Lisburn Sector.* Lisburn, UK: Positive Futures. Retrieved from http://www.positive-futures.net/cmsfiles/downloads/research/Careful-Plans-Report-May-2010.pdf

Bowey L., McGlaughlin A. (2005). Adults with a learning disability living with elderly carers talk about planning for the future: Aspirations and concerns. *British Journal of Social Work*, 35, 1377–1392. Crossref

Burke M. M., Taylor J. L., Urbano R., Hodapp R. M. (2012). Predictors of future caregiving by adult siblings of individuals with intellectual and developmental disabilities. *American Journal of Intellectual and Developmental Disabilities*, 117, 33–47. Crossref PubMed. ISI.

Chadwick D. D., Mannan H., García-Iriarte E., McConkey R., O'Brien P., Finlay F., &#hillip1; Harrington G. (2013). Family voices: Life for family carers of people with intellectual disabilities in Ireland. *Journal of Applied Research in Intellectual Disabilities*, 26, 119–132. Crossref PubMed. ISI.

Charmaz K. (2006). *Constructing grounded theory. A practical guided through qualitative analysis.* Thousand Oaks, CA: Sage.

Charmaz K. (2008). Grounded theory. In Smith J. A. (Ed.), *Qualitative psychology: A practical guide to research methods.* (2nd ed., pp. 81–110). London: Sage. Crossref.

Charmaz K. (2011). Grounded theory methods in social justice research. In Denzin N. K., Lincoln Y. S. (Eds.), *The SAGE handbook of qualitative research* (4th ed., pp. 359–380). Thousand Oaks, CA: Sage.

Charmaz K. (2014). *Constructing grounded theory.* London: Sage.

Charmaz K. (2015). Teaching theory construction with initial grounded theory tools: A reflection on lessons and learning. *Qualitative Health Research*, 25, 1610–1622. Crossref PubMed. ISI.

Coppus A. M. (2013). People with intellectual disability: What do we know about adulthood and life expectancy? *Developmental Disabilities Research Reviews*, 18, 6–16. Crossref PubMed. ISI.

Cuskelly M. (2006). Parents of adults with an intellectual disability. *Family Matters*, 74, 20–25.

Davis R., Mohr C. (2004). The assessment and treatment of behavioural problems. *Australian Family Physician*, 33(8), 609–613. ISSN: 0300-8495. PubMed.

Department of Health. (2001). *Valuing people: A new strategy for learning disability for the 21st century: A white paper.* London: Author. Retrieved from https://www.gov.uk/government/uploads/system/uploads/attachment_data/file/250877/5086.pdf

Devaney J., Seto L., Barry N., Odette F., Muraca L., Fernando S., &#hillip1; Angus J. (2009). Navigating healthcare: Gateways to cancer screening. *Disability & Society*, 24, 739–751. Crossref

Dew A., Llewellyn G., Balandin S. (2004). Post-parental care: A new generation of sibling-carers. *Journal of Intellectual & Developmental Disability*, 29, 176–179. Crossref ISI.

Dillenburger K., McKerr L. (2009). "40 years is an awful long time": Parents caring for adult sons and daughters with disabilities. *Behavior and Social Sciences*, 18, 155–174. Crossref

Dodd P., Guerin S., Mulvany F., Tyrrell J., Hillery J. (2008). Assessment and characteristics of older adults with intellectual disabilities who are not accessing specialist intellectual disability services. *Journal of Applied Research in Intellectual Disabilities*, 22, 87–95. Crossref

Dye L., Hendy S., Hare D. J., Burton M. (2004). Capacity to consent to participate in research – A recontextualization. *British Journal of Learning Disabilities*, 32(3), 144–150. Crossref

Eley D. S., Boyes J., Young L., Hegney D. G. (2009). Accommodation needs for carers of and adults with intellectual disability in regional Australia: Their hopes for and perceptions of the future. *Rural and Remote Health*, 9, 1239–1251. Retrieved from http://www.rrh.org.au

Esbensen A. J., Seltzer M. M., Wyngaarden Krauss M. (2012). Life course perspectives in intellectual disability research: The case of family caregiving. In Burack J. A., Hodapp R. M., Iarocci G., E Zigler. (Eds.), *The Oxford handbook on intellectual disability and development* (pp. 380–391). New York: Oxford University Press.

Foundation for People with Learning Disabilities. (2010). *Mutual caring: Supporting mutual caring amongst older families that include a person with a learning disability*. London: Mental Health Foundation. Retrieved from https://www.mentalhealth.org.uk/sites/default/files/need_2_know_mutual_caring.pdf

Freedman R. I., Wyngaarden Krauss M., Mailick Seltzer M. (1997). Aging parents' residential plans for adult children with mental retardation. *Mental Retardation*, 35, 114–123. Crossref PubMed.

Gilbert A., Lankshear G., Petersen A. (2008). Older family-carers' views on the future accommodation needs of relatives who have an intellectual disability. *International Journal of Social Welfare*, 17, 54–64. Crossref

Giles T., King L., de Lacey S. (2013). The timing of the literature review in grounded theory research: An open mind versus an empty head. *Advances in Nursing Science*, 36, E29–E40. Crossref PubMed.

Glaser B. G., Strauss A. L. (1967). *The discovery of grounded theory. Strategies for qualitative research*. New Jersey, USA: Aldine Transaction, Division of Transaction Publishers, Rutgers-The State University.

Grey K. M., Griffith G. M., Totsika V., Hastings R. P. (2015). Families' experiences of seeking out-of-home accommodation for their adult child with an intellectual disability. *Journal of Policy and Practice in Intellectual Disabilities*, 12, 47–57. Crossref

Grey K. M., Totsika V., Hastings R. P. (2018). Physical and psychological health of family carers co-residing with an adult relative with an intellectual disability. *Journal of Applied Research in Intellectual Disabilities*, 2, 191–202. Crossref

Guba E. G., Lincoln Y. S. (1994). Competing paradigms in qualitative research. In Denzin N. K., Lincoln Y. S. (Eds.), *Handbook of qualitative research* (pp. 105–117). Thousand Oaks, CA: Sage.

Haley W. E., Perkins E. A. (2004). Current status and future directions in family caregiving and aging people with intellectual disabilities. *Journal of Policy and Practice in Intellectual Disabilities*, 1, 24–30. Crossref

Harris R., Holmes H. M., Mertens D. M. (2009). Research ethics in sign language communities. *Sign Language Studies*, 9(2), 104–131. Crossref

Heller T., Caldwell J. (2006). Supporting aging caregivers and adults with developmental disabilities in future planning. *Mental Retardation*, 44, 189–202. Crossref Crossref. PubMed.

Heller T., Kramer J. (2009). Involvement of adult siblings of persons with developmental disabilities in future planning. *Intellectual and Developmental Disabilities*, 47, 208–219. Crossref PubMed.

Janicki M. P. (2009). The aging dilemma: Is increasing longevity among people with intellectual disabilities creating a new population challenge in the Asia-Pacific region? *Journal of Policy and Practice in Intellectual Disabilities*, 6, 73–76. Crossref

Jokinen N. S., Janicki M. P., Hogan M., Force L. T. (2012). The middle years and beyond: Transitions and families of adults with down syndrome. *Journal on Developmental Disabilities*, 18(2), 59–69. Retrieved from http://oadd.org/wp-content/uploads/2012/01/41012_JoDD_18-2_59-69_Jokinen_et_al.pdf

Kelly F., Kelly C. (2011). *HRB statistics series 13. Annual report of the National Intellectual Disability Database Committee 2010*. Dublin, UK: Health Research Board. Retrieved from https://www.hrb.ie/

fileadmin/publications_files/NIDD_Committee_Annual_Report_2010_-_HRB_Statistics_Series_13.pdf

Lai R., Elliott D., Ouellette-Kuntz H. (2006). Attitudes of research ethics committee members toward individuals with intellectual disabilities: The need for more research. *Journal of Policy and Practice in Intellectual Disabilities*, 3, 114–118. Crossref

Leeder S. R., Dominello S. (2005). Health, equity and intellectual disability. *Journal of Applied Research in Intellectual Disability*, 18, 97–100. Crossref ISI.

Lennox N., Taylor M., Rey-Conde T., Bain C., Purdie D. M., Boyle F. (2005). Beating the barriers: Recruitment of people with intellectual disability to participate in research. *Journal of Intellectual Disability Research*, 49, 296–305. Crossref PubMed. ISI.

Llewellyn G., Gething L., Kendig H., Cant R. (2003). *Invisible carers facing an uncertain future: Report if a study conducted with funding from the National Health and Medical Research Council, 2000-2002.* Sydney: Faculty of Health Sciences, University of Sydney. Retrieved from http://sydney.edu.au/health-sciences/afdsrc/docs/invisible.pdf

Llewellyn G., Bundy A., Mayes R., McConnell D., Emerson R., Brentnall J. (2010). Development and psychometric properties of the family life interview. *Journal of Applied Research in Intellectual Disabilities*, 23, 52–62. Crossref Crossref.

McCarron M., Swinburne J., Burke E., McGlinchey E., Mulryan N., Andrews V., Foran S., McCallion P. (2011). *Growing older with an intellectual disability in Ireland 2011: First results from the intellectual disability supplement of the Irish longitudinal study on ageing.* Dublin: School of Nursing & Midwifery, Trinity College Dublin. Retrieved from https://www.tcd.ie/tcaid/assets/pdf/idstildareport2011.pdf

McDonald K. E., Conroy N. E., Olick R. S. (2016). Is it worth it? Benefits in research with adults with intellectual disability. *Intellectual and Developmental Disability*, 54, 440–453. Crossref PubMed.

McDonald K. E., Kidney C. A. (2012). What is right? Ethics in intellectual disabilities research. *Journal of Policy and Practice in Intellectual Disabilities*, 9, 27–39. Crossref ISI.

Mills J., Bonner A., Francis K. (2006a). Adopting a constructivist approach to grounded theory: Implications for research design. *International Journal of Nursing Practice*, 12, 8–13. Crossref PubMed.

Mills J., Bonner A., Francis K. (2006b). The development of constructivist grounded theory. *International Journal of Qualitative Methods*, 5, 25–35. Crossref

Ministry of Health. (2011). *Health indicators for New Zealanders with an intellectual disability.* Wellington, New Zealand: Author. Retrieved from http://www.moh.govt.nz

Ministry of Social Development. (2008). *The New Zealand carer's strategy and five-year action plan 2008.* Wellington, New Zealand: Author. Retrieved from http://www.msd.govt.nz

Morrisey B. (2012). Ethics and research among persons with disabilities in long-term care. *Qualitative Health Research*, 22, 1284–1297. Crossref PubMed. ISI.

Morse J. M. (2004). Constructing qualitatively derived theory: Concept construction and concept typologies. *Qualitative Health Research*, 14, 1387–1395. Crossref PubMed. ISI.

Nankervis K., Rosewarner A., Vassos M. (2011). Why do families relinquish care? An investigation of the factors that lead to relinquishment into out-of-home respite care. *Journal of Intellectual Disability Research*, 55, 422–433. Crossref PubMed. ISI.

Northway R., Howarth J., Evans L. (2015). Participatory research, people with intellectual disability and ethical approval: Making reasonable adjustments to enable participation. *Journal of Clinical Nursing*, 24, 573–581. Crossref PubMed. ISI.

O'Grady Reilly K., Conliffe C. (2002). Facilitating future planning for ageing adults with intellectual disabilities using a planning tool that incorporates quality of life domains. *Journal of Gerontological Social Work*, 37, 105–119. Crossref

Parley F. F. (2010). What does vulnerability mean? *British Journal of Learning Disabilities*, 39, 266–276. Crossref

Perkins E. A., Haley W. E. (2010). Compound caregiving: When lifelong caregivers undertake additional caregiving roles. *Rehabilitation Psychology*, 55, 409–417. Crossref PubMed. ISI.

Polit D. F., Beck C. T. (2004). *Nursing research: Principles and methods*. Philadelphia, PA: Lippincott Williams & Wilkins.

Ponterotto J. G. (2013). Qualitative research in multicultural psychology; Philosophical underpinnings, popular approaches, and ethical considerations. *Qualitative Psychology*, 1(Suppl.), 19–32. Crossref

Reichard A., Stolzle H., Fox M. H. (2011). Health disparities among adults with physical disabilities or cognitive limitations compared to individuals with no disabilities in the United States. *Disability and Health Journal*, 4, 59–67. Crossref PubMed. ISI.

Resch J. A., Mireles G., Benz M. R., Grenwelge C., Peterson R., Zhang D. (2010). Giving parents a voice: A qualitative study of the challenges experienced by parents of children with disabilities. *Rehabilitation Psychology*, 55, 139–150. Crossref PubMed. ISI.

Ryan A., Taggart L., Truesdale-Kennedy M., Slevin E. (2014). Issues in caregiving for older people with intellectual disabilities and their ageing family carers: A review and commentary. *International Journal of Older People Nursing*, 9, 217–226. Crossref PubMed.

Shanahan M. J., Profelli E. (2002). Integrating the life and life-span: Formulating research questions with dual points of entry. *Journal of Vocational Behavior*, 61, 398–406. Crossref ISI.

Skinner D., Weisner T. S. (2007). Sociocultural studies of families of children with intellectual disabilities. *Mental Retardation & Developmental Disabilities Research*, 13(4), 301–312. Crossref

Stoneman Z. (2005). Siblings of children with disabilities: Research themes. *Mental Retardation*, 43, 339–350. Crossref Crossref. PubMed.

Taggart L., Truesdale-Kennedy M., Ryan A., McConkey R. (2012). Examining the support needs of ageing family carers in developing future plans for a relative with an intellectual disability. *Journal of Intellectual Disabilities*, 16, 217–234. Crossref PubMed.

van den Akker M., Maaskant M. A., van der Meijden M. J. R. (2006). Cardiac disease in people with intellectual disability. *Journal of Intellectual Disability Research*, 50(7), 515–522. Crossref PubMed.

Veenstra M. Y., Walsh P. N., van Schrojenstein Lantman-de Valk H. M. J., Haveman M. J., Linehan C., Kerr M. P., &#hillip1; Moravec D. (2010). Sampling and ethical issues in a multicenter study on health of people with intellectual disabilities. *Journal of Clinical Epidemiology*, 63, 1091–1100. Crossref PubMed. ISI.

Wackerbarth S. (1999). Modeling a dynamic decision process: Supporting the decisions of caregivers of family members with dementia. *Qualitative Health Research*, 9, 294–314. Crossref ISI.

Werner S., Edwards M., Baum N., Brown I., Brown R.I., Isaacs B.J. (2009). Family quality of life among families with a member who has an intellectual disability: An exploratory examination of key domains and dimensions of the revised FQOL Survey. *Journal of Intellectual Disability Research*, 53, 501–511. Crossref Crossref.

Williams V., Robinson C. (2001a). More than one wavelength: Identifying, understanding and resolving conflicts of interest between people with intellectual disabilities and their family carers. *Journal of Applied Research in Intellectual Disabilities*, 14, 30–46. Crossref

Williams V., Robinson C. (2001b). 'He will finish up caring for me': People with learning disabilities and mutual care. *British Journal of Learning Disabilities*, 29, 56–62. Crossref

Yamaki K., Hsieh K., Heller T. (2009). Health profile of aging family caregivers supporting adults with intellectual and developmental disabilities at home. *Intellectual and Developmental Disabilities*, 47(6), 425–435. Crossref PubMed.

AUTHOR BIOGRAPHIES

Henrietta Trip is a registered nurse and senior lecturer with the Centre for Postgraduate Nursing Studies at the University of Otago, Christchurch, New Zealand. Her research interests are long-term conditions, healthcare accessibility, and vulnerable populations, particularly people with intellectual and other disabilities.

Lisa Whitehead is the associate dean research at the School of Nursing and Midwifery, Edith Cowan University, Australia, and an Honorary Professor of Nursing Research with the University of Otago, New Zealand. She has a particular interest in improving health outcomes for people living with chronic conditions, self-management interventions and working with families to support health outcomes within primary care and community nursing contexts.

Marie Crowe is a registered nurse and works across the Department of Psychological Medicine and the Centre for Postgraduate Nursing Studies with the University of Otago, New Zealand. She has extensive research experience and clinical expertise particularly in the areas of psychosocial interventions for mood disorders and long-term health conditions.

Brigit Mirfin-Veitch is the Director of the Donald Beasley Institute, Dunedin and a senior research fellow with the University of Otago, New Zealand. As a sociologist, she has a particular interest in understanding the lives of people with learning disability and seeks to initiate and achieve social change through research into physical health and mental wellbeing, deinstitutionalisation, parenting and the law.

Chris Daffue is a consultant clinical psychologist with the Specialist Mental Health Service, Canterbury District Health Board, New Zealand. He specialises in the field of intellectual disability and has a specific interest and expertise in developmental trajectories, ageing, ethics, risk management and systems theory.

APPENDIX D

An Ethnography—"British-Born Pakistani and Bangladeshi Young Men: Exploring Unstable Concepts of Muslim, Islamophobia and Racialization"

Mairtin Mac an Ghaill
Newman University, UK

Chris Haywood
Newcastle University, UK

Source: This article originally appeared in *Critical Sociology, 41*, 97–114. Copyright 2015, Sage Publications, Inc.

ABSTRACT

Much recent academic work on making sense of the changing public profile of the Muslim community in Britain operates within an explanatory framework that assumes a shift from ethnicity to religion and an accompanying shift from racialization to Islamophobia. A key limitation of this work, often grounded in media representations, is that it tends to be disconnected from contemporary lived social relations. In response, this paper critically engages with these debates, drawing upon qualitative research that explores a changing cultural condition that is inhabited by British born, working-class Pakistani and Bangladeshi young men. It is argued that this emergent cultural condition cannot conceptually be contained within a singular category of religion as the contours of the young men's cultural condition are embedded within a range of intensified and ambivalent rapidly shifting local, national and international geo-political processes. Therefore in contrast to recent theorizing and research on Muslim communities and identities, the young men in this study critically engage with the contextually-based local meanings of Muslim, Islamophobia and racialization to secure complex masculine subjectivities. Alongside this, the article highlights that young men recognize that Islamophobia, displacing a notion of racialization, is a danger for their community because of the attendant invisibility of the current impact of social class within conditions of socio-economic austerity, which for them is a central element of their social and cultural exclusions.

KEYWORDS

Britain, gender, Islamophobia, Muslim, racialization, class

INTRODUCTION

For young working-class men born in Britain of Pakistani and Bangladeshi heritage, much British political, media and academic commentary on Muslims serves to re-inscribe them as a major social problem (Richardson, 2004; Hussain, 2008). This is occurring at a time of the emergence of an assertive English nationalism involving a forging of a renewed British identity and a European-wide political questioning about state-led multiculturalism (Fekete, 2004; Ibrahim, 2005; Townsend, 2011). A range of discourses have been projected by government, media and popular culture about failed multi-culturalism, parallel communities and self-segregation (Phillips, 2006; Nagle, 2009; Kundnani, 2009). For McGhee (2008: 145):

> In national level debates . . . . Britain has entered an authoritarian and 'anti-multiculturalism' period in which multiple identities, loyalties and allegiances are both problematized and are deployed in order to facilitate 'our' primary identifications as British citizens who must accept British values above all else.

In response, this article argues for engagement with Pakistani and Bangladeshi young men's narratives that focus upon the reductive representations of Islam, the Muslim community and being a young Muslim man. At the same time, there is an urgent need to critically interrogate the assumed social separateness, cultural fixity and boundedness of religious, ethnic and national categories of difference that they claim are imputed to them. Within the context of the institutional regulatory production of these containing categories, it is important to highlight that identity formation is embedded within the temporal and spatial specificity of a community's diasporian history and the accompanying making of identity affiliations through diverse sources of nationhood, ethnicity, religion, culture and tradition (Bauman, 1996; Zaretsky, 1996).

In turn, these resources are highly classed, gendered, generationally and regionally specific within conditions of late modernity (Brah et al., 2000). Yet we continue to know little of the processes that constitute these positions. Therefore, a combination of materialist and post-colonial theoretical frameworks and young men's accounts provides an alternative representational space that critically explores debates about the racialization of religion, the central role that religion plays in the process of racialization, and Islamophobia as a contemporary form of the racialization of Muslims. The paper begins by outlining our methodological position and the search for an alternative representational space in response to much recent social and cultural theorizing on Muslim representation, identity formation and subjectivity that has disconnected from lived relations within institutions, specific local contexts and broader social and economic processes. This is followed by a discussion of the shifting racialized representations of young Muslim men, addressing the need to go beyond a singular category of religion in exploring their lives. A major focus of the paper is an exploration of their discussion of the instability of concepts such as Muslim, Islamophobia and racialization. Finally, we address the students' nuanced understanding of racialization that highlights the invisibility of the stratification of young Pakistani and Bangladeshi men as classed subjects.

RESEARCH METHODS: YOUNG MEN'S NARRATIVES

There is a tendency within the academy, government and media to over-generalize about the Muslim diaspora living in Europe and North America. For example, within a North American context the popular representation of the Muslim is often portrayed as Arab; within a British context the popular representation is often portrayed as South Asian (Haddad, 2004). In reality, the global Muslim diaspora is nationally and ethnically a highly diverse population. Feminist and post-colonial theorists have provided a sophisticated map of British Muslim young women in late modernity (Shain, 2003; Brah and Phoenix, 2004). This article draws upon this work in focusing on young Muslim men, as a generationally-specific gendered category that remains an under-researched field of inquiry.

As indicated above, this study is based upon Birmingham-born young men of Pakistan and Bangladesh heritage. It is suggested that 21 per cent (approximately 232,000 people) of the population resident in Birmingham Local Authority identified as Muslim (Birmingham City Council, 2013) compared to 4.8 per cent in the UK population (Office for National Statistics [ONS], 2012). This is the highest number of Muslims for a local authority in the UK. Furthermore, in terms of ethnicity, the electoral ward of Birmingham records 144,627 (13.5%) Pakistani, and 32,532 (3%) Bangladeshi within these communities. Within this context, such communities are highly diverse, and as a qualitative and explorative study, the paper does not seek inductive validity by suggesting that the participants represent the experiences of the broader Muslim male population of the area or the general population. Instead, as Crouch and McKenzie (2006: 493) argue:

> Rather than being systematically selected instances of specific categories of attitudes and responses, here respondents embody and represent meaningful experience-structure links. Put differently, our respondents are 'cases', or instances of states, rather than (just) individuals who are bearers of certain designated properties (or 'variables').

Our work with a younger generation of Pakistani and Bangladeshi young men, in Newcastle, London and Birmingham, makes clear their geographically-specific local experiences of growing up in a rapidly changing Britain (Popoviciu and Mac an Ghaill, 2004; Mac an Ghaill and Haywood, 2005). In other words, the young men in this Birmingham-based study inhabit specific lifestyles within a spatial context of diverse social trajectories among a changing Muslim diaspora in Britain. Therefore, it is the exploration of the young Muslim men's meaningful experiences that was a key objective of the research design.

Drawing upon our own ethnographic work, we set out to enable the research participants to inhabit an alternative representational space that provides insightful narratives about the complexity of inhabiting subject positions across public and private spaces. During a three year period, 2008–11, we have recorded the experiences of 48 Pakistani (30) and Bangladeshi (18) working-class young men, aged 16–21. Twenty-five of the young men's narratives are reported in this paper. The majority of the young men (38) (20 in this paper) attended local secondary schools, sixth-form colleges and further education colleges. However, as suggested in previous work, Bangladeshi and Pakistani young people's participation in education is highly fractured and non-linear (see Bradley and Devadason, 2008). For example, young men stagger their engagement on part-time courses over a number of years, often to accommodate responsibilities within the home and at work.

The interview groups contained a mix of Bangladeshi and Pakistani young men, as indicated by their names, who shared not only intimate friendships but were part of a broader social community that included attending the same youth and community organizations and colleges, sharing the same employers, and participating together in leisure activities. Furthermore, although they were diverse individuals, in terms of ethnicity, age, past experience and social status with different current experiences of being in education, work/training or unemployed, they held a shared critical reflexivity of ethnic majority assumptions of Muslim identities. The latter emerged as of central importance to the main themes of this paper about Islamophobia and the racialization of Muslims.

While carrying out empirical work with young people, we were introduced to two young men who were politically involved in the local area. In turn, they introduced us to other young people that subsequently led to further snowballing of other friends, family and community representatives (Patton, 1990). Access was greatly enabled by our being known for our social commitment to the local area, working with families in the local community. Group and life history interviews provided the framework through which to explore a range of critical incidents experienced by these young men.

The group interviews were carried out at local community centres and the life history interviews were carried out in a variety of places, including at youth and community organizations and local cafes. These interviews lasted around 45 to 90 minutes and provided insight into growing up, family, schooling, social life and local community. These interviews were supplemented by a range of other research strategies that included observations, informal conversations and interviews with parents and local community representatives (Alvesson and Skoldberg, 2000), as part of a wider critical ethnography on the impact of globally-inflected change upon the local formation of diasporic young men's subjectivity and identity (Appadurai, 1991; Harvey, 2003; Ansari, 2004).

The datasets from each of the methods was subject to thematic analysis (Braun and Clarke, 2006) that enabled us to explore 'the underlying ideas, constructions, and discourses that shape or inform the semantic content of the data' (Ussher et al., 2013: 902). The subsequent analysis was taken back to the young people themselves not simply as a form of 'face validity' but also as a way of exploring the practical and political implications of the findings. All interviews throughout the study were both anonymized and the research participants were given pseudonyms to protect their confidentiality (Wetherell, 1998).

SHIFTING RACIALIZED REPRESENTATIONS OF YOUNG MUSLIM MEN: 'FROM ETHNICITY TO RELIGION'— BEYOND A SINGULAR CATEGORY OF RELIGION

The young men, as post-colonial subjects, have an implicit or explicit understanding of earlier racialized representations of their grandparent and parent generations that do not make sense of contemporary social and spatial relations of their lives in Birmingham (Gilroy, 2004). Importantly, they note that state and public institutional figures have little understanding of their community, of inter-generational changes or, perhaps most significantly, the changing morphology of western urban sites, such as Birmingham, in which new identities, both minority and majority ethnic, are being manufactured (Bhattacharyya, 2008). In a group interview below, Abdul begins a discussion about the generational specific experiences of young men in relation to the racialization of their ethnicities:

> **Abdul**: A lot of people would have heard about how are grandparents/parents were treated really bad when they came from Pakistan. But it's different for the kids, for us. Like the stereotypes our parents had are more like what the Somalis, the Yemenis, or even the Poles, cos they've just arrived, with different language and all that.
> **MM**: So, what about your generation?
> **Abdul**: It's different for us because we're born here, so we're British and have a Pakistan heritage. And, anyway probably everything changed round here and everywhere after 9/11.
> **Azam**: It's changed and not changed, white kids will still call you 'Paki' in certain areas but it's also that we're seen as a terrorist or fundamentalist, those kinds of words, those stereotypes.
> **Majid**: When you start thinking about it, it's all mixed up. Like words like Asian, Pakistani, ethnics, what else, and worst of all the BME and all the rest. I don't know, they're not really about us are they? They're about older generations.
> **Shabbir**: Maybe not about them, just white people giving us labels.
> **Wasim**: There is no straight, no straight-forward stereotype of young Muslims because you get all the propaganda stuff about not joining the terrorists. Like you hear government people on telly after some terrorist stuff has taken place, they're saying that we need the most help, so as not to be persuaded to go off to Afghanistan and train to become a terrorist. But the main stereotype of us is that we are terrorists.
> **Yusuf**: Governments and police and even probably a lot of teachers they don't know nothing. They don't really know about us. About people who live around here. They don't even know anything about our white mates who live here and they're white. They talk as if we have just arrived in this country but even I can see in a few years this city has really changed and our parents say it's really changed. It's not just about us, the whole city has changed. Go and talk to the white kids and their parents and they will tell you. But government and people in charge they don't know this. They don't live here. [Group interview]

One of the experiences within these young men's narratives is the lack of identification with available representations and language (Sandhu, 2011). Current attempts by state institutions to contain them within the singular category of religion often oscillates between representations of the responsible, family-orientated hard-working, socially-passive Muslim father and shifting racialized representations that contradictorily position them as both potential terrorists and highly vulnerable to terrorist recruitment. Exploring the experiences of contemporary young Muslim men, we find complex identifications, affiliations, investments and positionings of a highly visible diasporic group, of whom we know little. More specifically, we know little about the complex processes of subjectivity and accompanying processes of subjectivication, inter-subjectivities and social biographies, complex investments/affiliations and the occupying of multiple and diverse identifications. This lack of social knowledge begins with the conceptual ambiguity and confusion of the deployment of the term Muslim in the social science literature, including 'the re-categorisation of various ethnic (Mirpuri, Bangladeshi, Pakistani) groups into religious (Muslim) ones' (Shain, 2011: 15). The young men discussed the suggested shift from ethnicity to religion as the primary official marker of their public (racial) identity. For example, Anthias and Yuval-Davis (1993: 55) have claimed that:

> Since the 'Rushdie Affair', the exclusion of minority religions from the national collectivity has started a process of racialization that especially relates to Muslims. People who used to be known for the place of origin, or even as 'people of colour' have become identified by their assumed religion. The racist stereotype of the 'Paki' has become the racist stereotype of the 'Muslim fundamentalist'.

For the young men, their social lives are marked by an intensified global surveillance, cultural pathologization and social and racial exclusion that is more complex than this suggested shifting classification (Said, 1978). Most importantly, as illustrated in the discussion below, notions of ethnicity, religion and cultural belonging are not clearly demarcated, and the separation of these categories is experienced contradictorily:

> **Amir**: You … I can't get my head around it. I can't even say it.
> **M.M**: Say what?
> **Amir**: You feel you're been watched all the time, here comes the Muslim. But you can't prepare or something for when it happens, or know how to react, cos it's different, it happens in different ways.
> **M.M**: Like how?
> **Amir**: Like Yusuf was saying the other day, the teachers, the police would look at you differently. Then again, different teachers will act out differently.
> **Kashif**: You can't separate these things like that. You can't split people up like that. It don't work that way. It's not like our parents are ethnic or Asian or Bangladeshi or Bengali or whatever and now younger people are just religious. These things are all mixed up for everyone.
> **Abdul**: Like I said to you the other day, when you said why go to the mosque to pray, you can pray anywhere. That's very true. But deep in being a Muslim is looking after your neighbour. So it's important to meet people, to check out they're OK.
> **Kashif**: So you can't choose between calling us ethnics or religious. That's stupid, makes no sense. [Group interview]

With the young men's ambivalence towards generationally specific ways of being Muslim men, based upon culturally infused religious identities and their rejection of masculinities underpinned by violence, identifications have involved the reconfiguration of the meaning of Muslim. From the above discussion, the notion of a singular homogeneous Muslim identity is not experienced by these young men. Furthermore, representational spaces such as those projected by the police or teachers, which are often based on particular religious and/or political differences, appear not to be connecting with their lived experiences:

> **Farhad**: Do you understand? In the past the word 'Paki' was the stereotype. Now people say Muslims are called terrorists but the real stereotype now is to be called a Muslim.
> **Kashif**: That's what's changed. In the past our parents were seen as good for being religious by white people, well like teachers and police and that, even the government. Now we are seen as bad because of our religion, like we are all extremists or something.
> **Sajid**: That is very true. It's like for these people, religion for them is like a big cage that they try and lock us up in. [Group interview]

These institutional representations are dependent upon the instantiation of such difference, which it can be argued can consolidate Muslim identities. For example, Qureshi (2004) found that a group of young Pakistani men in her research made their masculinities through the Othering of young white men. One of the characteristics of the young men in our research was that the process of Othering of whiteness was seen as a characteristic of an older form of Muslim identity; an identification to which these young men held a growing ambivalence. As a consequence, securing masculine subjectivities appears to be generationally more complex. Here we focus on the young men securing their masculine subjectivities through the unstable concepts of being a Muslim young man, Islamophobia and racialization.

THE INSTABILITY OF CONCEPTS: MUSLIM, ISLAMOPHOBIA AND RACIALIZATION

During the early 2000s, exploring the forging of ethnic and national identities among young Bangladeshi men and women, we found increasing diversity of masculine formation in relation to assumed ethno-religious identifications and social practices (Mac an Ghaill and Haywood, 2005). We need to hold onto a socio-historical perspective, in order to trace a range of contemporary fragmented male subjectivities, social trajectories, cultural belonging and contested meanings of the concepts of Muslim, Islamophobia and racialization within regional spaces. As suggested above, Pakistani and Bangladeshi young men are experiencing a specific cultural condition that conceptually cannot be contained within the singular identity category of religion. Their narratives serve to critique the dominant culturalist explanation that the state, including institutional sites, such as schooling and policing, ascribes to them (Faas, 2010). The contours of the young men's cultural condition are embedded within intensified and ambivalent rapidly shifting geo-political processes, involving developments in global economic restructuring and its impact on local and global labour markets, advanced technological systems and increased cultural exchange, a series of western-led wars on Muslim societies, shifting patterns of migration, new forms of racial exclusion, the restructuring of a new world order and the apparent reclamation of ethno/religious identities.

At the same time, young men in this study are subjectively experiencing such changes in terms of dynamic dissonances that are (re) constituting their remembering of the past, the living and doing of the present and their imagined futures. This process is demonstrated through the negotiation of the meanings attached to being Muslim:

> **Asif**: It's wrong to talk about the Muslim perspective and the Muslim community and Muslim young men and women act like this and that. There is no such thing. If you look at young people round here, they have, they take up really different styles, different ways. And, definitely you make friends cos you have things in common that are really different to other groups.
>
> **M.M**: Like what?
>
> **Asif**: Like what? Like everything. Obvious things, like whether you go to college or uni, or you're not working or those who join gangs, different interests, music, how you dress, where you go with your mates, everything.
>
> **Wasim**: You go up North or down to London and its really different. We always say it at the weddings. These people are not like us.
>
> **Yasin**: When you ask about the future, for young Muslim people, yeah everything is mixed together. When people are planning for the future, it's very different futures. Just even in our college, the future thinking is kind of linked to how you think about the past, and whether you want to get away from it or how much you know about the past in this country and Pakistan and everything that's happening now about all the talk about Muslims. But mostly about how you make the future good, same as any younger people.
>
> [Group interview]

In discussion with the young men, they explain that the increasing mobilization of the term Muslim as a collective self-referent, that is seen in the research literature as highly significant in terms of their changing self-definition, does not mean that a young generation of Pakistanis and Bangladeshis are becoming more religious (Samad, 1998). They also point out that the contemporary deployment of the term Muslim does not displace the terms Asian and Pakistani/Bangladeshi that have historically served to mark difference, but rather are contextually used across different sites. Importantly, regulatory mechanisms of power and control of a 'suspect community' are differentially experienced within institutionally specific contexts (Pentazis and Pemberton, 2009). Interestingly, the young men make a distinction between their own self-definition as Muslims embedded within a generationally-specific cultural politics and 'white people's' racialized use of the term (Pilkington and Johnson, 2003; Said, 1993):

Wasim: When you asked us were we proper Muslims, we all laughed and said, no. So, things around prayers, fasting and going to the mosque, no, not real Muslims for most of us, for younger people.

Imran: Groups can label themselves, like we label ourselves Muslim. But it's not the same as when white people use the label.

M.M: What do you mean?

Imran: It's hard to explain, we're both using the same word. But they use Muslim and they don't even know us, or they mean something bad. For us it's a definite good thing or just a normal thing.

M.M: And do you know what it means?

Imran: A good question. I think if I'm been honest, then no. I think a lot of the time, we don't know what Muslim means. Like we're saying here, it can mean lots of things.
[Group interview]

A key theme to which the students returned over the period of the research was how to make sense of the range of social and cultural exclusions that they experienced at a time of rapid change within the city. Historically, one of the major ways in which the concept of race and social change and the accompanying social and cultural exclusions has been problematized in the literature is through the use of the term racialization. Banton (1977) used the concept of racialization to refer to the use of the idea of race to structure people's perceptions of different populations. During the 1980s and 1990s the notion was used as a key signifier of racial meanings in a range of discourses (Reeves, 1983; Miles, 1993; Troyna, 1993). Small (1994: 32–3) adopts the 'racialization' problematic in order to unravel the relative influence of multiple factors (economics, politics, demography, culture, ideology and myth) in patterns of 'racialized relations'. As Solomos (1993: 1) argues, a main focus here is 'the growth of ideologies which have focused upon race as an important political symbol, the role of anti-racist and black political mobilisation and the impact of social and economic restructuring on racial and national identities in British society'. Changing processes of racialization are operationalized through the impact of changing race imagery in a range of institutional settings as well as processes of deracialization (Husband, 1982; Miles, 1989).

The usefulness of the concept is indicated by the fact that it has been adopted by theorists from a wide range of perspectives, including those from a race-relations problematic, as well as neo-Marxist and post-structuralist positions (Banton, 1977; Reeves, 1983; Miles, 1989; Smith, 1989; Solomos, 1993; Small, 1994; Holdaway, 1996). Theorists have deployed the concept in different ways in order to address the limits of conventional accounts of race and racism. From a materialist perspective, theorists have challenged the notion of distinct races as biologically given and pointed to the need to explore the conditions under which specific processes of racialization result in differential outcomes. This work has been particularly successful in examining the cumulative institutional effects of ascribing reified meanings to minorities, particularly South Asians and African-Caribbeans. As Green and Carter (1988: 23) have argued, processes of racialization in post-war Britain were 'structurally determined, politically organised and ideologically inflected . . . within the relations of domination and subordination'. Miles (1982) provided an early account of this with reference to post-war labour migration to Britain. Keith (1993: 239) has cogently captured a post-structuralist understanding of race and racialization, while not losing sight of relations of domination and subordination. Arguing that race is not an essential characteristic, he suggests that:

> The pervasive practices of racism, however, and the evolution of racial formations over time and space . . . guarantee some correspondence in the harsh reality of the day-to-day world between the ideological fictions of racial divisions between people and the empirical circumscription of specific groups in society. The generation of racial divisions in society is most easily grasped by use of the notion of racialization, which stresses both the reality of the group formation process as well as the social construction of differences between the racial collective identities so formed. The process of racialization is also of particular significance because it is one of the principal means through which subordination is produced and reproduced in an unjust society.

More recently, theorists have suggested that the concept of racialization is productive in capturing the contemporary structural positioning and subjective experiences of Muslims in Britain (Brah and Phoenix, 2004; Mac an Ghaill and Haywood, 2005). However, the last ten years has seen the term Islamophobia emerge as the dominant explanation of Muslim social and cultural exclusions.

Among the students various positions were taken up in relation to different understandings of the deployment of racialization and Islamophobia. For some students, the term Islamophobia was of key strategic importance in highlighting questions of cultural and religious discrimination that they felt earlier notions of racism and racialization did not capture (Halliday, 1999; Kundnani, 2002). Historically, this has been a central argument among sections of the Muslim community in Britain, highlighted in two main issues: their campaign for government recognition and financial support for Muslim schools and their mobilization against the publication of Salman Rushdie's book *The Satanic Verses* (see Asad, 1990; Al-Azmeh, 1993). In other words, anti-Islamophobia mobilization was a response to the under-theorization of the concept of racialization. In the recent past, within the context of anti-racist politics, the latter term remained locked within the reductionist black/white colour paradigm that underplayed key elements of South Asian and black lives, including religion, culture and migration. More specifically, this younger generation emphasize the role that religious identities and identity-making play in the process of racialization at a time of 'faith-hate' (McGhee, 2005: 92–117).

> **Tahir**: When people talked about racism in the past, they meant Black people, not us, not Muslims.
> **Raqib**: If you said we were getting racism at school, everyone would think of colour, but what about religion? And Islamophobia is like special to us. It explains about bad things happening to Muslim people, and our culture.
> **Iftikhar**: If you want to talk about racialization stuff today, it has to include what is really important to us and that is about our religion. [Group interview]

Other students addressed what they considered to be some of the limitations of the pervasiveness of the concept of Islamophobia. A key issue was the extent to which the concept served to disconnect the Muslim community from a wider anti-racist movement and the historical benefits of a broader understanding of racialization. For, example, they identified the effects of the shift from a politics of redistribution to a politics of recognition, and the accompanying limited understanding of processes of racialization within conditions of socio-economic austerity (Fraser, 1998) (explored further below). For others, there was much confusion about the meaning of Islamophobia, with some suggesting that it was a contemporary form of racialization (Commission on British Muslims and Islamophobia, 1997). Life history interviews in particular drew out the differing personal (dis)identifications associated with Islamophobia:

> **Tamim**: My father and his uncles were all involved in the anti-racist movement in the past. At that time, they would have big campaigns and demonstrations about things like unemployment and bad housing and crap schooling. As well as all the racist discrimination. It brought lots of different communities together. But now our community leaders, they couldn't get anyone to, or they wouldn't want to, get people to demonstrate about the recession and what it's doing to all people round here. [Life History Interview]
>
> **Yasin**: It's true. The only thing they will demonstrate about now is something they think is kind of very religious or offends our religion. [Life History Interview]
>
> **Asif**: Everyone is really confused about the talk of Islamophobia. Like you listen to racist groups and they say Islam is a threat to the British nation. But they seem to be confused, one minute talking about religion and then about nationality and the British state. [Life History Interview]
>
> **Shoaib**: I think it is best to see Islamophobia as a new way of been racist to Muslims. [Life History Interview]

In response to the suggested limitations of the concept of Islamophobia, for many young men there was a further limitation of the deployment of Islamophobia, which they perceived as circulating in the form of a universal and homogeneous category of exclusion. In contrast, they emphasized the significance of understanding how diverse international changes are mediated at a local (national and regional) level. More specifically, illustrating the demographic diversity within the Muslim faith, the young people emphasize the need to focus on Muslims' differentiated experiences of discrimination and how they differ historically and geographically across the interconnecting categories of generation, class, and gender (for example, see Tehranian, 2008, for discussion of contemporary American Muslims and Mandeville, 2009, for state responses to Muslims across Europe). Their argument resonates with a major limitation of an abstract notion of 'othering' in the academic literature, which has disconnected from empirical work in 'old' institutional sites, such as family life, schooling, and workplace, resulting in the figure of the Muslim male been represented as an over-generalized racial 'other' (Said, 1978; Mac an Ghaill and Haywood, 2007).

> **Naqeeb**: When it's used generally, it kind of means that people, western people, hate Muslims and have always hated them. But that's not true is it? [Life history interview]
>
> **Tamim**: You hear people saying this is Islamophobic and that is Islamophobic, like everything. It becomes meaningless. One word cannot mean all those things happening in all Muslim countries and everywhere.
>
> **Ali**: Lots of Muslim countries are going through loads of changes. And on the telly, in the papers, they talk in bad stereotyped ways about Afghanistan, Syria, Pakistan. But they talk bad about them in different ways. [Group interview]

Many of the young men argued for a complex and nuanced understanding of racialization that acknowledged the effect of the contemporary positioning of Muslims, in which they carry the anxieties of the wider society at a time of globally-inflected changes. These anxieties were seen to produce the specificity of current social and cultural exclusions experienced by Birmingham-based Muslims. They identified a series of issues that have a common theme of projecting Birmingham-based Pakistanis and Bangladeshis as marked by social separateness, cultural fixity and boundedness of religious identity. In short, they are projected as figures of 'anti-modernity' in a late modern urban space.

There is a long history that at a time of crisis in dominant public forms of Anglo-ethnicity, national identity and cultural belonging, racial minorities are forced to carry the burden of the national and ethnic majority's sense of moral disorder (Weeks, 1990; Mercer, 1992; McGhee, 2005). The young Muslim men contextualized the specificities of their highly contradictory masculine identity, as indicated above — represented as both potential terrorists and highly vulnerable to terrorist recruitment — emphasizing how dominant British responses combine internal doubt and external anxiety that are projected onto them. They suggested that the starting point for addressing issues of religious identity should not focus on their community but rather address the wider British society's shifting meanings of religion, faith and secularism and the assumed crisis in the role of Christianity in the making of national identity in a modern era (Woodhead, 2012). They felt that current debates on this issue assumed a highly reductionist dualism between the projected threatening significance of the emergence of a *global* Islamic identity and a disappearing *local* allegiance to Christianity. As a recent editorial in *The Guardian* newspaper (2012: 34) suggested in its commentary on the latest census results, we are a society that is:

> . . . . changing very rapidly, in profound and interesting ways, without any clear overall direction. . . . The most obvious sign of this transformation is the decline of notional Christianity and the rise of the 'no religion' category, or 'nones'. 'No religion', a kind of undogmatic secular humanism, is not the established religion, but it is the source of values for the people who have replaced the old establishment.

Interestingly, the instability of the religious categories held by ethnic majorities is recognized by young Muslim men:

> **Parvez**: I think people concentrate too much on Islam and Muslims when they talk about Islamophobia. I don't know, really. But maybe it's not so much Muslims are the real problem.
>
> **Waqar**: But maybe the real problem for British, for white British people is religion itself. I think if you studied it, you would see. Like for my grandparents when they came

here, Britain was still a Christian country, there was a lot more Christians about but you ask one of your white mates, he wouldn't know anything about religion or being a Christian. Even at Christmas, it's about shopping and drinking for them.

Imtiaz: It's true when you say it. I don't think they are thinking about baby Jesus. And for the old white people, you have to feel sorry for them, cos they see their churches empty and no young people. Then they see all these mosques full of people, everyone and the young kids all going off to pray. They must think, what's going on?

Furooq: It's not just going to church, that they're not doing. It's on a bigger scale. It's the whole culture has changed. You can hear those atheist guys. I think they're saying if you want to live in Britain today, you should be, have to be modern, you have to move with the times.

Yusuf: That is true, when you think of it. So, when they see all the young Muslim kids especially being religious, they think, these people aren't modern, these people aren't British.

Ali: And round here, lots of people are Mir, and a lot of them are religious, so maybe if they say Islamophobia is growing that's a real reason, a deeper reason, not just hating us because we are Muslim but because we are religious and they don't believe in religion any more.

Shoaib: It's pretty mixed up though, because the older white people round here probably think that young Muslims are like what they were when they were young, and for them Britain has lost this and it's a bad thing. [Group interview]

As illustrated above, in contrast to recent theorizing and research on Muslims, the young men in this study critically engage with the contextually-based local meanings of key unstable concepts, including Muslim, Islamophobia and racialization, through which they are securing complex masculine subjectivities in a 'post-secular' society' (McGhee, 2013). An important theme that emerges from this, as they highlight in the next section, is that Islamophobia displacing a notion of racialization is a danger for their community because of the attendant invisibility of the current impact of social class within conditions of socio-economic austerity. For them, class is a central element of their social and cultural exclusions.

THE INVISIBILITY OF THE STRATIFICATION OF YOUNG PAKISTANI AND BANGLADESHI MEN AS CLASSED SUBJECTS

In an earlier period, drawing upon sociology, class was the central analytical concept in researching minority ethnic young people's experiences. For example, Anthias and Yuval-Davis (1993: 65), in their critical re-reading of sociological work in the 1970s and 1980s, identify a range of materialist positions that link race to class: 'Rex's underclass thesis, migrant labour theories, racism as an ideology that is relatively autonomous of class, Gilroy's view that class formation is linked to race, and the dual labour market approaches'. This work was politically important in establishing commonalities of racism among Asians and African-Caribbeans and investigated their different institutionalized positioning, across institutional sites, within a multi-racist industrial-based Britain. It was especially significant in critiquing the dominant culturalist approach, with its focus on ethnic attributes. As Mercer and Prescott (1982: 102) argued: 'The most significant feature of the minority experience is not their ethnicity but their place in the class structure. Their relative powerlessness ensures that they remain in a subordinate position politically and culturally'. This class-based analytical work provided explanatory frameworks to make sense of the social and cultural reproduction of racially structured societies. More specifically, it illustrated the productiveness of deploying class analysis in highlighting how racism, which pervasively structured minority ethnic young people's social world, was mediated through the existing institutional frameworks that discriminated against (white) working-class youth *and* through the operation of race-specific mechanisms, such as gender-inflected racist stereotyping of Asian and African-Caribbean students (Mac an Ghaill, 1988; Mirza, 1992; Bourdieu and Passeron, 1977).

Presently, there is much evidence of the historical continuity of class-based structural constraints on working-class Pakistani and Bangladeshi men. Their collective profile includes highest levels of unemployment and over-representation in low-skilled employment, over-representation in prisons, over-representation in poor housing, high levels of poor health and lowest levels of social mobility (Eade and Garbin, 2002; ONS, 2006; Garner and Bhattacharyya, 2011; Barnard and Turner, 2011; Laird et al., 2007; Ahmad at al., 2003). More specifically, reading through the research literature, a main government and academic image of Pakistani and Bangladeshi students is that of underachievement, with Pakistani and Bangladeshi male students, in terms of ethnicity, faith group, class and gender, placed at the bottom of league tables on academic school performance (DfES, 2007). This is a significant shift from earlier representations of an assumed homogeneous Asian community of 'high achievers'. However, several researchers challenged this account, highlighting the complexity and variability of Asian students' school attainment with reference to class, gender and national group origins. For example, most importantly, middle-class Indian students' academic success served to mask the relatively low examination attainment among working-class Pakistani and Bangladeshi boys (Rattansi, 1992; Mac an Ghaill, 1994). More recently, Archer (2003) has made the argument about the continuing impact of socio-economic inequalities on the education of Muslim boys.

Young men in our study articulate a consciousness of the different social logics that are lived out by working- and middle-class people in the city of Birmingham. More particularly, they suggest a generationally-specific identification with local white working-class young people and a (local) place-affiliation around the increasing socio-economic divisions that circumscribe their collective social lives. It is difficult to capture the intense anger that they feel about the cultural demonization and polarization that they suggest all young people experience within the most deprived areas in the city. Of significance are the classed divisions within social minorities that contributes to (dis) identifications within and across ascribed ethnic boundaries:

Farooq: Lots of people talk about the us and them around religion and segregation and tension and everything. But no-one talks about, like in this city, people from around here, even our white mates, we'd never go to a posh area. They'd think we're aliens.

Shoaib: An' the posh areas have got posher and posher and the poor areas are getting really poor every day, more people out of work and kids leave schools and no jobs.

Javed: My uncle, he reckons that Asians, Bangladeshi people are really looked down upon much more now than before when he came here because they are poor. And that's the Asian middle-class people doing that. They're doing it as well.

Parvez: On telly, in the papers, everywhere, poor people are really hated. I think that it's worse for the poor whites. They have special labels for them, rich people have, like they call them chavs. They've made up a word, special word for them. I feel sorry for the white kids around here. No one looks after them, do you know what I mean? [Group interview]

These comments resonate with Farzana Shain's (2011) work. In response to dominant government and academic representations, she provides one of the most sustained critical explanations of contemporary Muslim boys' experiences in England, arguing for a more theoretically sophisticated approach that includes the development of a socio-economic dimension. She adopts a Gramscian analysis emphasizing the articulation of multiple structures of race, gender *and* class with socio-economic and political relations of domination and subordination (Gramsci, 1970). Shain maintains that:

> Gramsci's framework recognises that young people are located within material contexts that structure and limit the structure of possibilities for agency and action. This entails the recognition of the role of historical forces — in this case colonialism and imperialism — in shaping the class locations and settlements of Muslim communities in areas of England that have suffered most from economic decline. These settlement patterns have had a lasting legacy in terms of the types of schooling and educational and employment opportunities available. Pakistani and Bangladeshi communities find themselves located in some of the most materially deprived wards in the country. (2011: 50)

However, as the young men indicated, across government, media, education and popular culture there is an absence of class representation of Pakistani and Bangladeshi young men. Rather, the cumulative effect of the projected representations of social failure that circulates across different sites is, as argued above, to position them within the singular category of religion, i.e. exclusively as Muslims rather than bearers of any other identity. The invisibility of Pakistanis and Bangladeshis *as classed subjects* across the political spectrum is discursively achieved through two major explanatory frameworks: that of the underclass (the political right) and Islamophobia (the political left). Shain (2011: 7) identifies what have become iconic moments in revisiting a notion of under-class. She writes: 'The Gulf War in 1991, the Bradford riots in 1995, the [2011]summer disturbances, 9/11, the London bombings in 2005 and numerous failed bomb plots have all continued to fuel fears about extremist Muslims, and the discourse conflates the issue of violent Asians and Muslim gangs'. More specifically, she notes how European and British political commentators 'conflate educational underachievement, criminality and the Islamification of Europe through the notion of a Muslim underclass. These three issues form a dominant cultural narrative of a Muslim underclass that is responsible for its own marginality' (Shain, 2011: 9). The young men in our study share Shain's analysis that a major effect of this cultural narrative is that class inequalities are displaced, with different sectors of the working class ascribed specific forms of cultural deficit, as government and media discourses serve to blame individual subjects rather than address the structural causes of social and cultural exclusions (Munt, 2000; Bourdieu, 1986).

> **Parvez**: In poor areas like around here, why don't they give us jobs and good education? But no, if you're from this area and you go for a job, they'll tell you to get lost.
> **Abdul**: Somehow the ruling people have turned the world upside down. Nearly everything that Muslim kids are blamed for, the ones that go bad, it could all be sorted if you gave them proper education and jobs and got rid of all the discrimination against us.
> **Asif**: I think the bad thing now is that there is this big image and you can't move it. All the people in charge just see Muslims as one big problem as bombing the world or causing big trouble here.
> **M.M**: How does this affect people in the area?
> **Asif**: Most of these people are just ordinary people. There's a lot of poverty, unemployment and things, and nothing for the kids to do, they're just bored. They've nothing to do with the racist stereotypes about being radicals and all that. They wouldn't even know what any of that means round here. But like all the kids who came out from our year. How many of them got jobs, went to college or anything? My mother thinks there's much less opportunities for our generation. [Group Interview]

A second explanatory framework can be found in recent empirical work within schools that reinscribes the cultural invisibility of young Pakistani and Bangladeshi men as classed subjects by selectively drawing upon a limited range of signifiers, including *umma, hijab, jilbab,* the war on terror, etc. These signifiers, understood exclusively as religious phenomena, are located within an explanatory framework of Islamophobia, which is projected as a mechanism of entrapment in which it is assumed that young men's social practices can simply be read off as defensive strategies of religious survival.

In work using the notion of Islamophobia, subjectivity is under-theorized, reminiscent of early anti-racist accounts of the black and white dualism. One consequence of this is that state institutions are conceptualized as reflecting the possible identities that can be taken up and lived out. A further limitation of this position is that it is unable to realize the significant challenges of new social movements, which are to create theoretical frameworks that can accommodate a range of inequalities, such as those around ethnicity, class, gender, sexuality and disability (Mac an Ghaill and Haywood, 2012). In short, this position produces difficulties in articulating an inclusive account of multiple forms of social power (Anthias, 2008). It could be argued that the young people's narratives enable an understanding that challenges the view of Islamophobia as a monolithic force that can be read off from the assumed responses of individuals — the Muslim-'non-Muslim' dualism. Rather, within particular institutional sites, there are a range of contextually-based (racist) ideologies and discourses that may place subjects in subordinate positions. These racialized processes are temporally and spatially specific, and articulate in complex ways with other categories of social difference, including class.

CONCLUSION

The social and cultural uncertainties in contemporary England are creating a series of symbolic spaces where national anxieties and promises around race/ethnicity are being projected. Miller (2006) has discussed the emergence of fear as a key feature of the governability of national otherness. In the context of young Muslim men, one dynamic for such fear is the state's claim of an unsuccessful inclusion and identification with 'Britishness'. In previous historical moments, youth culture has been seen in opposition to parent cultures. At present, the institutional conflation of young people with radicalization and fundamentalism appeals to a potential hyperbolic re-instatement of ascribed parental values by young people. The narratives reported in this article suggest a more complex situation, where the older religious and political designations of being Muslim were reworked. At the same time, young Muslim men were concerned with the material basis of their social and economic location, through which cultural difference was being read. The fieldwork undertaken with these young men could be understood as a process, where they were given the opportunity to explore and discuss the contradictions and tensions that were circulating through their attempts to convey their identifications and subjectivities. One of the difficulties when listening to their narratives has been to resist representation of their identities though pre-existing popular and academic explanations. Rather, the focus here is on facilitating ways of understanding how *they* are participating in the production of ideas of being Muslim, racialization and Islamophobia.

Funding

This research received no specific grant from any funding agency in the public, commercial, or not-for-profit sectors.

REFERENCES

Ahmad F, Modood T and Lissenburgh S (2003) *South Asian Women and Employment in Britain: The Interaction of Gender and Ethnicity*. London: Policy Studies Institute.

Al-Azmeh A (1993) *Islams and Modernities*. London: Verso.

Alvesson M and Skoldberg K (2000) *Reflexive Methodology: New Vistas for Qualitative Research*. London: SAGE.

Ansari H (2004) *'The Infidel Within': Muslims in Britain since 1800*. London: C. Hurst and Co.

Anthias F (2008) Thinking through the lens of translocational positionality: An intersectionality frame for understanding identity and belonging. *Translocations: Migration and Social Change* 4(1):5–20.

Anthias F and Yuval-Davies N (1993) *Racialized Boundaries: Race, Nation, Gender, Colour and Class and the Anti-racist Struggle*. London: Routledge.

Appadurai A (1991) Global ethnoscapes: Notes and queries for a transnational anthropology. In Fox RG (ed.) *Recapturing Anthropology: Working in the Present*. Santa Fe, CA: School of American Research.

Archer L (2003) *'Race', Masculinity and Schooling: Muslim Boys and Education*. Berkshire: Open University Press.

Asad T (1990) Multiculturalism in the wake of the Rushdie affair. *Politics and Society* 18(4):455–80.

Banton M (1977) *The Idea of Race*. London: Tavistock.

Bauman Z (1996) From pilgrim to tourist: A short story of identity. In: Hall S and du gay P (eds) *Questions of Cultural Identity*. London: SAGE.

Barnard H and Turner C (2011) *Poverty and Ethnicity: A Review of Evidence*. York: Joseph Rowntree Foundation.

Bhattacharyya G (2008) State racism and Muslim men as a racialised threat. In: Bhattacharyya G, *Dangerous Brown Men: Exploiting Sex, Violence and Feminism in the War on Terror*. London: Zed Books.

Birmingham City Council (2013) Ethnic groups: Population and census. Available (accessed 7 February 2014) at: http://www.birmingham.gov.uk/cs/Satellite?c=Page&childpagename=Planning-and-Regeneration%2FPageLayout&cid=1223096353923&pagename=BCC%2FCommon%2FWrapper%2FWrapper

Blackmore J (2000) Warning signals or dangerous opportunities? Globalization, gender, and educational policy shifts. *Education Theory* 50:467–486.

Bourdieu P (1986) *Distinction: A Social Critique of Judgement*. London: Routledge.

Bourdieu P and Passeron JC (1977) *Reproduction*. London: SAGE.

Bradley H and Devadason R (2008) Fractured transitions: Young adults' pathways into contemporary labour markets. *Sociology* 42(1):119–135.

Brah A, Hickman MJ and Mac an Ghaill M (eds) (2000) *Global Futures: Migration, Environment and Globalization*. London: Macmillan.

Brah A and Phoenix A (2004) Ain't I a woman? Revisiting intersectionality. *Journal of International Women's Studies* 5(3):75–86.

Braun V and Clarke V (2006) Using thematic analysis in psychology. *Qualitative Research in Psychology* 3(2):77–101.

Cainkar L (2009) *Homeland Insecurity: The Arab American and Muslim American Experience after 9/11*. New York, NY: Russell Sage Foundation Publications.

Choudhurry T (2007) The role of Muslim identity politics in radicalisation (a study in progress). London: Department of Communities and Local Government.

Commission on British Muslims and Islamophobia (1997) *Islamophobia: A Challenge for Us All*. London: Runnymede Trust.

Crouch M and McKenzie H (2006) The logic of small samples in interview-based qualitative research. *Social Science Information* 45(4):483–499.

Department for Education and Skills (2007) *Gender and Education: The Evidence on Pupils in England Research Information*. London: Department for Education and Skills.

Eade J and Garbin D (2002) Changing narratives of violence, struggle and resistance: Bangladeshis and the competition for scarce resources, *Oxford Development Studies* 30(2):127–44.

Faas D (2010) *Negotiating Political Identities: Multi-ethnic Schools and Youth in Europe*. Farnham: Ashgate.

Fekete L (2004) Anti-Muslim racism and the European security state. *Race and Class* 43:95–103.

Fraser N (1998) From redistribution to recognition? Dilemmas of justice in a post-socialist age. In: A Phillips (ed.) *Feminism and Politics*. Oxford: Oxford University Press.

Garner S and Bhattacharyya G (2011) *Poverty, Ethnicity and Place*. York: Joseph Rowntree Foundation.

Gilroy P (2004) *After Empire: Melancholia or Convivial Culture*. London: Routledge.

Gramsci A (1970) *Selections from the Prison Notebooks*. London: Lawrence and Wishart.

Green M and Carter B (1988) 'Races' and 'race-makers': The politics of racialization. *Sage Race Relations Abstracts* 13:4–30.

The Guardian (2012) Diverging into diversity [editorial], 12 December, p. 34.

Haddad YY (2004) *Not Quite American? The Shaping of Arab and American Identity in the United States*. Waco, TX: Baylor University Press.

Hall S (1992) The question of cultural identity. In: Hall S, Held D and McGrew T (eds) *Modernity and Its Futures*. Cambridge: Polity.

Halliday F (1999) 'Islamophobia' reconsidered. *Ethnic and Racial Studies* 22(5):892–902.

Harvey D (2003) *The New Imperialism*. Oxford: Oxford University Press.

Holdaway S (1996) *The Racialization of British Policing*. London: Macmillan.

Husband C (1982) *'Race' in Britain: Community and Change*. London: Hutchinson.

Hussain S (2008) *Muslims on the Map*. London: Tauris Academic Studies.

Ibrahim M (2005) The securitization of migration: A racial discourse. *International Migration* 43:163–87.

Jamal A (2008) Civil liberties and the otherization of Arab and Muslim Americans. In: Jamal A and Naber N (eds) *Race and Arab Americans Before and After 9/11: From Invisible Citizens to Visible Subjects*. Syracuse, NY: Syracuse University Press.

Keith M (1993) *Race, Riots and Policing: Lore and Disorder in a Multi-racist Society*. London: UCL Press.

Kundnani A (2002) An unholy alliance? Racism, religion and communalism. *Race and Class* 44:71–80.

Kundnani A (2009) *Spooked! How Not to Prevent Violent Extremism*. London: Institute of Race Relations.

Laird LD, Amer MM, Barnett ED and Barnes LL (2007) Muslim patients and health disparities in the UK and the US. *Archives of Disease in Childhood* 92(10):922–26.

Mac an Ghaill M (1988) *Young, Gifted and Black: Teacher-Student Relations in the Schooling of Black Youth*. Milton Keynes: Open University Press.

Mac an Ghaill M (1994) *The Making of Men: Masculinities, Sexualities and Schooling*. Buckingham: Open University Press.

Mac an Ghaill M and Haywood C (2005) *Young Bangladeshi People's Experience of Transition to Adulthood*. York: Joseph Rowntree Foundation.

Mac an Ghaill M and Haywood C (2007) *Gender, Culture and Society: Contemporary Femininities and Masculinities*. London: Palgrave Macmillan.

Mac an Ghaill M and Haywood C (2012) Schooling, masculinity and class analysis: Towards an aesthetics of subjectivity. *British Journal of Sociology of Education* 32(5):729–44.

Mandeville P (2009) Muslim transnational identity and state responses in Europe and the UK after 9/11: Political community, ideology and authority. *Journal of Ethnic and Migration Studies* 35(3):491–506.

McGhee D (2005) *Intolerant Britain? Hate, Citizenship and Difference*. Berkshire: Open University Press.

McGhee D (2008) *The End of Multi-culturalism: Terrorism, Integration and Human Rights*. Berkshire: Open University Press.

McGhee D (2013) Responding to the post 9/11 challenges facing 'post-secular societies': Critical reflections on Habermas's dialogic solutions. *Ethnicities* 13(1):68–85.

Mercer K (1992) Just looking for trouble: Robert Mapplethorpe and fantasies. In: Segal L and McIntosh M (eds) *Sex Exposed: Sexuality and the Pornography Debate*. London: Virago.

Mercer N and Prescott W (1982) Perspectives on minority experience. In: *Minority Experience* (Open University Studies, Course E254, Block 3, Units 8 and 9). Milton Keynes: Open University Press.

Miles R (1982) *Racism and Labour Migration*. London: Routledge and Kegan Paul.

Miles R (1989) *Racism*. London: Routledge.

Miles R (1993) *Racism after Race Relations*. London: Routledge.

Miller B (2006) The globalization of fear. In: Conway D and Heynen N (eds) *Globalization's Dimensions: Forces of Discipline, Destruction and Resistance*. New York, NY: Routledge, 161–177.

Mills M and Keddie A (2010) Cultural reductionism and the media: polarising discourses around schools, violence and masculinity in an age of terror. *Oxford Review of Education* 36(4):427–44.

Mirza HS (1992) *Young, Female and Black*. London: Routledge.

Munt SR (ed.) (2000) *Cultural Studies and the Working Class: Subject to Change*. London: Cassell.

Nagle J (2009) *Multiculturalism's Double Bind: Creating Inclusivity, Cosmopolitanism and Difference*. Farnham: Ashgate.

Office for National Statistics (2006) *Religion-Labour Market*. London: Office for National Statistics.

Office for National Statistics (2012) 2011 Census: Religion (detailed), local authorities in England and Wales, Table QS210EW. Available (accessed 1 October 2013) at: http://www.ons.gov.uk

Patton M (1990) *Qualitative Evaluation and Research Methods*. Newbury Park, CA: SAGE.

Pentazis C and Pemberton S (2009) From the 'old' to the 'new' suspect community: Examining the impacts of recent UK counter-terrorist legislation. *British Journal of Criminology* 49:464–66.

Phillips D (2006) Parallel lives? Challenging discourses of British Muslim self-segregation. *Environment and Planning D: Society and Space* 24:25–40.

Phoenix A (2004) Neoliberalism and masculinity: Racialization and the contradictions of schooling for 11- to 14-year-olds. *Youth & Society* 36(2):227–246.

Pilkington HA and Johnson R (2003) Peripheral youth: Relations of identity and power in global/local context. *European Journal of Cultural Studies* 6(3):259–283.

Popoviciu L and Mac an Ghaill M (2004) Racisms, ethnicities and British nation-making. In: Devine F and Walters MC (eds) *Social Identities in Comparative Perspective*. London: Blackwell.

Qureshi K (2004) Respected and respectable: The centrality of 'performance' and 'audiences' in the (re) production and potential revision of gendered ethnicities. *Particip@tions* 1(2).

Rattansi A (1992) Changing the subject: Racism, culture and education. In: Donald J and Rattansi A (eds) *Race, Culture and Difference*. London: SAGE.

Reeves F (1983) *British Racial Discourse: A Study of Political Discourse about Race and Race-Related Matters*. Cambridge: Cambridge University Press.

Richardson JE (2004) *(Mis)representing Islam: The Racism and Rhetoric of British Broadcast Newspapers*. Amsterdam: John Benjamins.

Said EW (1978) *Orientalism*. London: Routledge & Kegan Paul.

Said EW (1993) *Culture and Imperialism*. London: Vintage.

Samad Y (1998) Media and Muslim identity: Intersections of generation and gender. *Innovation. European Journal of Social Studies* 11(4):425–38.

Sandhu S (2011) Stretch out and wait. *The Guardian, Saturday Review* 24 December, p. 15.

Shain F (2003) *The Schooling and Identity of Asian Girls*. Stoke on Trent: Trentham Books.

Shain F (2011) *The New Folk Devils: Muslim Boys and Education in England*. Stoke on Trent: Trentham Books.

Small S (1994) *Racialised Boundaries: The Black Experience in the U.S. and England in the 1980s*. London: Routledge.

Smith SJ (1989) *The Politics of 'Race' and Residence*. Cambridge: Policy Press.

Solomos J (1993) *Race and Racism in Britain*. 2nd Edition. Basingstoke: Macmillan.

Tehranian J (2008) *Whitewashed: America's Invisible Middle Eastern Minority*. New York, NY: New York University Press.

Townsend M (2011) Poll reveals surge of sympathy for far right. *The Observer*, 27 February, p. 1.

Troyna B (1993) *Racism and Education: Research Perspectives*. Buckingham: Open University Press.

UK Government (2009) *The United Kingdom's Strategy for Countering International Terrorism*. London: The Stationery Office.

Ussher JM, Sandoval M, Perz J, Wong WKT and Butow P (2013) The gendered construction and experience of difficulties and rewards in cancer care. *Qualitative Health Research* 23(7):900–15.

Weeks G (1990) The value of difference. In: J Rutherford (ed.) *Identity: Community, Culture and Difference*. London: Lawrence and Wishart.

Wetherell M (1998) Positioning and interpretative repertoires: Conversation analysis and post-structuralism in dialogue. *Discourse and Society* 9(3):387–412.

Woodhead L (2012) A British Christmas has lost faith in rituals, but not religion. *The Observer*, 23 December, p. 32.

Zaretsky E (1996) Identity theory, identity politics: Psychoanalysis, Marxism, poststructuralism. In: C Calhoun (ed.) *Social Theory and the Politics of Identity*. Oxford: Blackwell.

APPENDIX E

Learning from Error in Violence Prevention: A School Shooting as an Organizational Accident

Sarah Goodrum[1], Jessie Slepicka[2], William Woodward[1], and Beverly Kingston[1]

[1]University of Colorado Boulder, Boulder, CO, USA

[2]The Pennsylvania State University, State College, PA, USA

Source: The material in this appendix is reprinted from Goodrum, S., Slepicka, J., Woodward, W., & Kingston, B. (2022). Learning from error in violence prevention: A school shooting as an organizational accident. *Sociology of Education*, 95(4), 257–275. https://doi.org/10.1177/00380407221120431

Corresponding author(s)

Sarah Goodrum, Center for the Study and Prevention of Violence, Institute of Behavioral Science, University of Colorado Boulder, 1440 15th Street, Boulder, CO 80309, USA. Email: sarah.goodrum@colorado.edu

ABSTRACT

This article argues that the organizational structure and culture of schools may impede the prevention of violence in America's schools, specifically threat assessment and management for students of concern. The data come from a qualitative case study of a school shooting where two students died; the data include deposition testimony from 12 school officials and more than 4,000 pages of school and law enforcement records. The findings illustrate the way the school's organizational structure and culture shaped and hindered violence prevention practices. The tightly coupled guidelines for threat assessment created an institutional myth of safety and a false sense of security for the school and district, and the loosely coupled structure of the organization led educators to modify guidelines and make decisions about the student's behavior problems and discipline without consulting others. The school's culture of autonomy for staff and fresh start mentality for students created unintentional secrets about the history of the student's difficulties, which gave educators little context for understanding the problem behaviors they observed and inhibited the threat assessment team's ability to adequately evaluate and monitor those behaviors. Recommendations for building organizational structures and cultures that support violence prevention in schools are discussed.

KEYWORDS

school organization, school policy, violence in schools, at-risk students, tracking

School administrators, law enforcement officials, and federal agencies have increasingly taken active measures to prevent targeted acts of school violence in the United States. Over the past 20 years, more than half of middle and high schools in the U.S. have adopted an anonymous tip line (Planty et al. 2020), and the U.S. Secret Service has twice issued federal guidelines on threat assessment in schools (Fein et al. 2004; National Threat Assessment Center [NTAC] 2018). From 2014 to 2017, the National Institute of Justice (2020) awarded approximately $246 million in grants to support nearly 100 projects on school safety. Despite these prevention efforts, there were 57 active shooter incidents in U.S. schools from 2000 to 2018 (Blair and Schweit 2014; Federal Bureau of Investigation 2016, 2018, 2019). In 2020–2021, more school shootings with casualties occurred in the United States than in any other academic year since data collection began (Irwin et al. 2022); as of July 2022, 27 school shootings have resulted in injury or death in the United States this academic year ("School Shootings This Year" 2022). The investigations that follow these tragic events consistently identify "failures of foresight" to recognize and interrupt the attacker's path toward violence within schools and across communities (Erickson 2001; Fein et al. 2004; Goodrum et al. 2018, 2019; Goodrum, Woodward, and Thompson 2017; Marjory Stoneman Douglas High School Public Safety Commission [MSDHSPSC] 2019; NTAC 2019; Turner 1976; Virginia Tech Review Panel 2007). Recent reports on the Uvalde school shooting at Robb Elementary School, where the attacker killed 19 children and two teachers, show a similar trajectory (Burrows, Moody, and Guzman 2022; Condon 2022).

Studies from sociology and organizational psychology suggest these failures of foresight arise when an organization's structure creates a culture that inhibits employees from recognizing, evaluating, and addressing problems or concerns (Doyle 2010; Fox and Harding 2005; Vaughan 2016). In a detailed study of two school attacks, Newman and colleagues (2004) found that the loosely coupled structure of the schools discouraged staff from seeing and interpreting students' pain and rage as needing intervention. Building on this work, Fox and Harding (2005) concluded that the schools lacked the resources to help staff recognize and address students' social and mental health needs. In 2002, the U.S. Secret Service and Department of Education released the *Safe School Initiative*, a study of 37 school attacks (Vossekuil et al. 2002). The Initiative informed the development of threat assessment guidelines to help school staff identify and evaluate students of concern (Fein et al. 2004; NTAC 2018; Randazzo et al. 2006; Reeves and Brock 2018; Vossekuil et al. 2002).

Although school attacks are still rare in the United States, the number of school attacks with fatalities rose from 5 in 2009–10 to 27 in 2019–20 (Irwin et al. 2021), raising questions about our approach to violence prevention. Costa (2012) argues that when complex problems persist even after the introduction of straightforward solutions, we need to reexamine the organizational structure, culture, and beliefs shaping those problems and forestalling the solutions. Admittedly, the availability of firearms is a key societal factor that accounts for high homicide rates in the

United States compared to other Western countries (Wintemute 2015). Thus, individuals intent on using a firearm for criminal purposes are likely to find a way to obtain one (Alper and Glaze 2019; Thrush 2021). Acknowledging this reality, this article focuses on processes that can avert and prevent violence and that have been proven to save lives (Langman and Straub 2019). Using case study evidence from a high school attack where two students died, this research examines the role of the school's organizational structure on the evaluation and management of the attacker in the weeks and months leading up to his deadly rampage. This study builds on the literature in sociology, organizational theory, and violence prevention in general and the work of Newman and colleagues (2004), Fox and Harding (2005), and Vaughan (2016) in particular.

ORGANIZATIONAL ACCIDENTS

Tragic Errors

Sociologists and psychologists have argued that major organizational accidents, such as wrongful convictions, aviation disasters, and medical errors, are not the result of one mistake or one bad apple employee; instead, they are the result of a series of smaller mistakes that build on each other and compound to a tragic end (Dörner 1996; Doyle 2010; Vaughan 2016). In these cases, the structure of the organization fosters a culture that leads employees to let small problems go unaddressed, sometimes repeatedly (Reason 1998; Vaughan 2016). In the preface to the second edition of her book *The Challenger Launch Decision*, Vaughan (2016) described her and others' dismay to learn that the same organizational problems she identified in 1996 with NASA's *Challenger* disaster (1986) contributed to NASA's *Columbia* disaster (2003). We feel similar dismay to learn about another targeted school attack in the United States.

Research on targeted school attacks repeatedly finds that a "patchwork of information mini-systems" hindered school and university officials from identifying and discussing students' concerning behaviors (Erickson 2001; MSDHSPSC 2019; Newman et al. 2004; Virginia Tech Review Panel 2007; see Doyle 2010:124). Prior to their attacks, many attackers became disengaged from school, experienced difficulties with school or law enforcement, and were recognized as troubled (Vossekuil et al. 2002; see also NTAC 2019). Connecting these pieces of information together to heed the warning signs, however, remains challenging because the problem behavior often arises across different settings and with different personnel (Virginia Tech Review Panel 2007). The solution to connecting these pieces of information together appeared to be threat assessment and management procedures for students of concern.

In 2004, the U.S. Secret Service and Department of Education's federal guidelines on threat assessment and management sought to help schools evaluate the likelihood a concerning student would perpetrate an act of targeted violence (Fein et al. 2004; see also NTAC 2018). The guidelines created a framework for the threat assessment process, and they were meant to address the challenges that Newman, Fox, Harding, and others identified in a school's ability to address a student's behavioral and mental health issues. States, safety centers, and school districts across the country have used the guidelines to develop school-based threat assessment policies, protocols, and procedures. Organizational theorists, however, would note that formal guidelines rarely match actual work activity, creating an "institutional myth" (Meyer and Rowan 1977).

This case study examines the match between guidelines and activities in the threat assessment process for one student of concern and how that match influenced decision-making.

The Coupling Continuum

The level of match between an organization's formal bureaucratic guidelines and the staff's implementation of those guidelines is called coupling, and the level of match can range from loosely to tightly coupled (Meyer and Rowan 1978; Paino 2018). In a loosely coupled organization, the parts are minimally interdependent of each other for everyday functioning such that a problem in one part does not typically disrupt work in another part (Bidwell 1965; Fox and Harding 2005; Meyer and Rowan 1977, 1978; Paino 2018). In a tightly coupled organization, the match between policies and procedures is strong and is maintained through formal bureaucratic controls and leaders' close oversight (Bidwell 1965; Meyer and Rowan 1978; Paino 2018).

Schools are frequently characterized as the quintessential example of a loosely coupled system due to educators' autonomy over curriculum delivery and classroom management. Recently, however, researchers have provided a more nuanced explanation for the organizational structure of schools. Paino (2018) argues that schools have three levels of coupling (not just one):(1) micro-level (i.e., principal–teacher relationships), (2) meso-level (i.e., district–school relationships), and (3) macro-level (i.e., government policies–school relationships). In addition, decoupling describes the disconnect between bureaucratic rules and work activity, and recoupling describes the effort to reset an organization from loosely to tightly coupled so that bureaucratic rules align with work activity and uphold "institutional mythical" ideals (Hallett 2010). Other researchers have noted that one organization can support both loosely and tightly coupled structures, and all types of coupling have their positives and negatives.

Examples of the coupling continuum and the upsides and downsides of coupling emerge in all types of organizations, including schools. As an example of tight coupling, state and federal guidelines provide strict rules for schools on the frequency and reporting of fire drills, student attendance, and academic testing. These rules provide clear guideposts for action, but they can also hinder creativity and autonomy. Examples of loose coupling include teachers' freedom to manage their classrooms and student conduct with minimal oversight from administrators, which can benefit job satisfaction and limit communication (Bidwell 1965; Paino 2018). Sociologists have found that unintentional silos of information can arise when there is little need for communication across parts of a loosely coupled system (Doyle 2010; Fox and Harding 2005).

Structural Secrecy

Fox and Harding (2005) refer to the information lost within loosely coupled organizations as "structural secrecy" because critically important details about a person or case remain unknown to other decision makers (see also Newman et al. 2004; Vaughan 2016). In these organizations, the division of labor and hierarchical structure make communication less necessary and also more difficult. Interestingly, what starts as a highly efficient organizational structure can create bureaucratic and human obstacles to learning about and relaying information from one employee to another and from one office to another (Doyle 2010; Fox and Harding 2005; Newman et al. 2004; Vaughan 2016; Weber 1978). For example, schools have access to a plethora of student information (e.g., academic records, testing scores, family status, immunization records), but they do not always have information about students' behavioral, mental health, or criminal histories (Erickson 2001; Fox and Harding 2005; Goodrum et al. 2017; MSDHSPSC 2019; Vaughan 2016; Virginia Tech Review Panel 2007). The concerning behaviors addressed in a teacher's classroom or documented in a teacher's email to parents may not carry forward when that student moves from one classroom, grade level, or school to the next (MSDHPSC 2019; Virginia Tech Review Panel 2007).

The public health approach to violence prevention recommends that schools and communities work to "identify and assess youth from a very young age . . . [to deliver] effective mental health and educational service[s], and [facilitate] . . . cross-system communication among professionals charged with the care of children" (Office of the Child Advocate 2014:3; see also Kingston et al. 2018). This type of "cross-system communication," however, may prove difficult to operationalize in complex educational settings, where the organizational structure (e.g., procedures, policies, staffing, resources) does not include consistent or institutionalized support for violence prevention and intervention. In addition, existing procedures and policies may discourage staff from sharing information about students in crisis. Some research suggests that misinterpretations of the Family Educational Rights and Privacy Act (FERPA) can lead school officials to withhold information about students' concerning behavior from other staff or agencies (Chapman 2009; Goodrum et al. 2017). These structural realities can create gaps in violence prevention in schools, but we have yet to fully understand how these structural realities shape cultural norms and everyday practices for school safety.

Using the sociological and psychological literature on organizations to examine the evidence from a targeted school attack, this qualitative case study asks the following questions: (1) How was the school's organizational structure coupled? (2) How did the school's organizational structure influence staff communication and decision-making? (3) Did the school's organizational structure inhibit violence prevention? If so, how might staff develop strategies to overcome the structural order of schools, and between districts, to prevent violence and support troubled students? By illustrating the specific ways a school's organizational structure shapes communication and decisions about students of concern, we identify the path toward safer and more aware school systems.

DATA AND METHODS

Data Collection

Data for the study came from an investigative arbitration on the circumstances leading to a school attack where two students died (Goodrum et al. 2017, 2018, 2019). To date, the case remains one of only two known cases where a threat assessment was conducted with a student prior to their deadly attack (for another case, see MSDHPSC 2019). The investigative arbitration yielded numerous interviews and thousands of documents, including (1) deposition testimony from 12 school and district officials covering more than 2,500 transcript pages, (2) 27 PDF documents containing more than 4,000 pages of text from the sheriff's office's investigation, (3) 171 PDF documents containing more than 4,200 pages of text from the district, and (4) 64 exhibits produced and introduced during deposition testimony. The 12 school and district officials deposed included nine school staff (i.e., principal, two assistant principals, school psychologist, two teachers, counselor, school resource officer, campus security officer) and three district administrators. Nine of the deponents were male, three were female, and all were Caucasian.

The depositions offer detailed narrative accounts of the circumstances, interactions, and communications prior to the attack. Similar to qualitative interviews, the deposition testimony allowed participants to describe their perceptions and experiences in their own words. Each deposition took between two and eight hours. To emphasize the lessons learned instead of personal identities, all participants are identified by their job title and a number when more than one participant held the title, such as Assistant Principal 1, Assistant Principal 2, District Official 1, School Psychologist, and School Resource Officer. To avoid contributing to the subculture of violence, the pseudonym "JD" is used in place of the attacker's name.

The project data provide rich insight on the school shooting as an organizational accident for two reasons. First, other research on school violence consistently finds that people knew something was wrong with the attacker prior to their attack, but they did not know who to tell or how to intervene (Erickson 2001; MSDHSPSC 2019; Virginia Tech Review Panel 2007). By examining educators' decision-making process, we start to understand the organization's management of and response to a troubled student. Second, as the frontline workers often blamed for these tragic events, educators are intimately knowledgeable about students and schools and are best situated to reflect on and offer lessons learned on threat assessment and school safety. These staff provide detailed information on the context for school procedures and decision-making, which can inform the development of effective intervention strategies (Harding, Fox, and Mehta 2002; Yin 2014).

Case study method. The qualitative case study method provides a rich and meaningful investigation of the structural factors that influenced the situation and decision-making (Birkinshaw, Brannen, and Tung 2011; Bryman and Bell 2011; George and McKeown 1985; Gephart 2004; Mahoney 1999, 2000; Maxwell 2013). This method provides an in-depth, multifaceted, and contextualized examination of the phenomenon and detailed insight into an uncommon form of behavior, a targeted school attack (Crowe et al. 2011; Geis 1991; Harding et al. 2002; McCutcheon and Meredith 1993; Yin 2014).

As an extensively utilized research design in sociology, case studies allow researchers to build a knowledge base for how to evaluate abstract theoretical concepts and principles (e.g., coupling, structural secrecy) to inform professional practice and scientific understanding (Crowe et al. 2011; Flyvbjerg 2006; Gill and Stenlund 2006; Keen and Packwood 1995; McCutcheon and Meredith 1993; Yin 2014). More specifically, the case study provides knowledge that transcends the specific case to offer lessons learned for other cases (Mills, Durepos, and Wiebe 2010; Stake 1995, 2005). This approach is particularly useful when answering what, why, and how research questions (Crowe et al. 2011) and when trying to understand and prevent acts of targeted school violence (Harding et al. 2002). To set the stage for the findings, we provide some background information on the school, the student, and his family.

Case background. In the fall of 2013, an 18-year-old White male senior named JD threatened to kill his debate coach, yelling "I"m gonna kill that guy" in the parking lot of the high school after he was demoted from a leadership role in the school's debate club. Another teacher overheard JD's outburst and reported it to an assistant principal, who requested a threat assessment. The assistant principal and a school psychologist formed the high school's two-person threat assessment team, and they met with JD and his parents to ask him questions about his threat, risk behaviors, and support system. During the assessment, the team noted that "Mom reports 'deep seeded anger'" and that the student admitted he "had anger issues for a while" (School Psychologist). The team evaluated him as a low-level risk for violence. Shortly after the assessment and unbeknownst to the team, however, the student began keeping a diary on his tablet documenting his plan to perpetrate violence at the school during finals week.

The postattack investigation revealed that JD had a history of low-level behavior problems. In elementary school, he hit students with his lunch box, kicked a student in the stomach, and hit another student in the head. JD's student behavior records document his claims of being "picked on" (Exhibit 19); however, the investigation did not reveal specific instances of victimization but instead identified multiple instances where JD verbally and physically bullied classmates (Exhibit 24). In the months following the threat assessment, JD exhibited problem behaviors in several different settings and had an enraged outburst in a foreign language class. (For a detailed timeline of his behaviors, see Goodrum et al. 2017). Three months after his threat assessment and two days after his outburst, he entered the school with a shotgun and other weapons; he was looking for the debate coach, but he killed a classmate and himself instead.

The large suburban high school where this shooting happened included approximately 2,200 students and a little more than 100 full-time teachers. Approximately 80 percent of students identify as White, and 7 percent of students receive free or reduced-priced lunch. The debate coach described the school's culture as embracing "perfectionism," wishing that school staff and students could admit that "it's not perfect here . . . mistakes are made and [students] can learn from those mistakes. And we tell kids that all the time [but] I wonder how true it is [in this school]" (Debate Coach).

The attacker's parents may have sensed the school's culture of perfectionism. JD's parents were not part of the arbitration agreement or deposed in the case, but the evidence suggests they had a strained relationship with the school. For example, one teacher described JD's mother as nonresponsive to her emails about his profane language and inappropriate comments in class and said she arrived 75 minutes late to pick up her son from a cross-country event (Teacher 1). During a parent-teacher conference, this teacher said JD's father "sat down [with her] and . . . said something like, 'What horrible things do you have to say about my son, like every teacher in this place?'" (Teacher 1). During the threat assessment, JD's mother described him as having anger issues, and she requested but did not provide documentation to support an Individualized Education Plan for her son (School Psychologist). As is common in postattack investigations, we do not have detailed information from the attacker's parents, which may be a limitation of the project data (Fein et al. 2004; NTAC 2019).

Data Analysis

The deposition transcripts are the main data source for the study. To code the transcripts, we relied on Strauss's (1987) guidelines for qualitative data analysis and line-by-line coding. Each transcript was read several times and coded using themes from the literature on organizational theory (i.e., a deductive approach; Bradley, Curry, and Devers 2007). The codes included tight coupling, loose coupling, and structural secrecy. Coding was executed through a five-step process. First, for each code, the first and second authors conducted a line-by-line review of each deposition transcript. Second, when an excerpt illustrated a theme, the excerpt was highlighted and labeled with the code, using the qualitative data management software NVivo. This process allowed the coded text to be organized into electronic folders by code while retaining information about the deposed witness's job title (e.g., Teacher 1). When an excerpt addressed more than one theme, it was coded for all relevant themes with a note about the cross-listing. Third, once all transcripts were coded, all of the text excerpts within each code were reviewed to ensure correct placement and to identify subthemes. During this review, two new themes emerged: the fresh start mentality and autonomy. In the fourth step, all transcripts were reviewed and coded for the newly identified themes. Finally, to consider the possibility that educators' roles influenced their perceptions, we reviewed and compared the coded data by role (e.g., teacher vs. administrator). These comparisons reveal the competing interests (e.g., student privacy, school safety) shaping educators' decision-making. Here, we present the quotes and case details that most clearly illustrate the findings (Burnard et al. 2008). Additional project data from the school's records, law enforcement investigation, and deposition exhibits provide context for deposition testimony.

FINDINGS

Organizational theory provides a powerful tool for examining the circumstances leading to a tragic accident. Schools, like other organizations, fall on a coupling continuum from tight to loose and can use recoupling to tighten up decoupled components (Hallett 2010; Meyer and Rowan 1978; Paino 2018). Recoupling allows organizations to reestablish the connection between bureaucratic ideals and actual work activity, but these efforts can feel frustrating to staff (Hallett 2010). The findings presented here illustrate the ways the tightly and loosely coupled components of the school and district influenced the implementation of federal threat assessment guidelines, encouraged a culture of autonomous decision-making, and created structural secrets about the extent and seriousness of the student's troubles.

Tightly Coupled Guidelines for Threat Assessment

On paper, the district's threat assessment and management policies and procedures were tightly coupled to federal guidelines, offering clear steps for action with students of concern (Firestone 1984; Weick 1976). For example, in 2004, approximately nine years before the attack, the district started providing schools with information on threat assessment, and by 2008, the district had created "standardized [district] threat assessment protocols . . . [which] aligned with the recommended model from the U.S. Secret Service, the FBI, and Dr. Smith [a pseudonym]" (Exhibit 9). These standards included a two-hour threat assessment team training, a 51-slide threat assessment presentation, and a four-page threat assessment and action plan protocol (Exhibits 9, 4, and 35, respectively). The district's threat assessment protocol closely modeled the U.S. Secret Service's guidelines, which is noteworthy due to the state's tragic history with targeted attacks (Erickson 2001; Hamm 2021). In this context, the Secret Service's framework for threat assessment provided legitimacy for the district's safety practices, offering a powerful example of recoupling as a response to tragedy (Hallett 2010).

The tight match between the Secret Service's guidelines for threat assessment and the district's policies on threat assessment started to loosen with implementation, specifically in the district's oversight of the school-level threat assessment team and the team's investigation of the student (Goodrum et al. 2018, 2019). For the team, the district's Coordinator of Student Support Services explained:

> [T]here's a lot of [federal] documentation and guidance that says you need an established [threat assessment] team. . . . But [we do] not necessarily [think it needs to be] the exact same three or four people [for every threat assessment]. (District Official 1)

This district official did not expect schools to strictly follow federal guidelines for threat assessment teams, creating a small buffer between the bureaucratic rules and actual staff activities. In this case, the team included two staff, not three or four as recommended by federal guidelines (Fein et al. 2004). This represented the start of the decoupling between guidelines and action on threat assessment.

Other research from this case indicates that the implementation of the U.S. Secret Service's six principles and 11 questions for threat assessment also differed from guidelines such that not all of the principles or questions were addressed with the student of concern (Goodrum et al. 2018, 2019). The Coordinator of Student Support Services explained:

> [We] don't [spend] hours and hours in a training and making sure [staff] know exactly how to fill out every box [on the threat assessment protocol]. The point of the [district] training is: Can we help people get those big principles?

This district official's rational explanation for the purpose of the threat assessment training captures the ambivalence schools may feel when trying to balance an outside entity's formal guidelines with their informal cultural practices. Certainly, strict adherence to guidelines can create consistency in procedures, but it may also depersonalize interactions and escalate conflict (Meyer and Rowan 1977, 1978). As one example, strict zero-tolerance policies and exclusionary discipline practices to crack down on students' behavior problems have been shown to disproportionately target students of color (Porowski, O'Conner, and Passa 2014). Loosely applying guidelines for threat assessment, however, may leave unintentional, and even dangerous, gaps in the school's knowledge about and understanding of a student's potential for violence.

This district's reluctance to tightly couple threat assessment guidelines with staff activities is not unique. The field of implementation science consistently finds that the delivery of prevention programs proves challenging in school settings (Fixsen et al. 2005; Greenberg 2010; Mihalic and Irwin 2003). In fact, fewer than 50 percent of school-focused prevention programs rely on best-practice methods for implementation (Biglan et al. 2003; Gottfredson and Gottfredson 2002; Ringwalt et al. 2009; U.S. Department of Education 2011). Translating guidelines into practice proves difficult in busy school settings, where staff are underresourced and overburdened (Biglan et al. 2003; Gottfredson and Gottfredson 2002; Osher 2012; Ringwalt et al. 2009). The district's Coordinator for Student Support Services described principals' frustration with strict threat assessment guidelines:

> A principal [will say to me,] "Everybody [who is talking about a threat assessment] safety plan says, 'We need to have eye-to-eye supervision on this kid,' [but] I don't have the staff to do it." . . . [Or they'll say to me,] "We want . . . this kid [to meet] on a weekly basis with [the school] psychologist," but their schedule is so booked, it makes it difficult. . . . These principals want to know, "[Should] I implement the safety plan fully and take staff away from other pieces . . . or [should] I say, 'I can't have this kid in my building.'"

Schools simply lack the capacity and resources to implement violence prevention programs and practices with fidelity (Forman et al. 2009; Mihalic and Irwin 2003). Thus, providing strict mandates and close supervision may seem like a solution for an effective threat assessment process, but tight coupling is likely to falter if the school's organizational structure, staffing, and resources cannot support them. In this scenario, adopting the Secret Service's guidelines for threat assessment without the institutional support to manage, support, and monitor a student of concern creates an institutional myth of school safety (Edelman et al. 2011; Hallett 2010; Myer and Rowan 1978). Hallett (2010:42) explains, "myths are idealized cultural accounts, not necessarily something false . . . and [they] provide legitimacy" but often do not match workers' activity. In this case, the institutional myth of threat assessment provided a false sense of security that the right systems were in place to prevent a targeted school attack.

Loosely Coupled Components and Staff Autonomy

In practice, the school's organizational structure was loosely coupled. An organization or parts of an organization are loosely coupled when staff or entities function independent of one another (Weick 1976). Staff in such systems have the freedom to perform their duties with little oversight, and this autonomy promotes creativity and job satisfaction, but it can also inhibit communication (Eck and Goodwin 2010; Firestone 1984; Pinelle and Gutwin 2006; Scheid-Cook 1990; Weick 1976).

Teacher autonomy. As in other high schools across the country, teachers in this case had the authority to handle student behavior problems in their classrooms (Lortie 2002: Newman et al. 2004; Weick 1976). A foreign language teacher described how she handled JD's inappropriate behavior prior to his attack:

> [One day in class] we watched a little video about the celebrations [for the] Day of the Dead in Mexico. And [he] raised his hand, and I thought he had a question. And then he said, "So when can we start drinking tequila in here?" And several students said, "That is really disrespectful in Mrs. [Smith's] class." And . . . he said "F— you." So, I

walked over to his desk, and I said, "[Y]ou may not talk like that in class. I need that behavior to stop" . . . and then I e-mailed his mom. (Teacher 1)

When asked if she relayed this incident to the school's principal or assistant principal, she said:

I did not [report it to the principal or assistant principal] . . . [his behavior in my class] wasn't to the point where I needed to get an administrator involved. . . . [T]he [problems] were things like I would say, "[A]re you listening?" Because he was always talking [and] he was always on his iPad or tablet. And I had to redirect [him] on a pretty regular basis to get back in focus with the class. At least once every class period . . . which is not unusual with teenagers. . . . And he would say, "Yes, ma'am," in this really kind of arrogant voice and he did that every day. (Teacher 1)

Although disrespectful and arrogant, these low-level behavior problems did not warrant an administrator's involvement (see Durkheim [1895] 1966; Vaughan 2016). This teacher had the authority to handle this and other students' disruptive classroom behavior on her own and without input from others (see also Duke, Showers, and Imber 1980; Myers 1973). Hallett (2010) argues that this autonomy grants teachers status as professionals and a reassuring sense of order.

A teacher's ability to make these classroom decisions in busy school settings is both practical and efficient (see Weber 1978). For practical reasons, teachers try to address behavior problems quickly and reinforce classroom norms and values consistently. For efficiency reasons, teachers often need to handle these problems without consulting an administrator because a teacher who regularly involves administrators in student behavior problems may be viewed as ineffective, overwhelmed, or unskilled by both students and administrators. The school's division of labor supported and the principal reinforced this approach (see Weber 1978). The Principal explained:

Specifically, from [this teacher], no [she didn't need to report it]. She is very good with kids, and I think she has a good, strong relationship with her students and handles things in her classroom and is great about contacting parents and things like that. So, if she felt like it was resolved through conversations with the parents, and they were notified, [I would] not necessarily [expect to hear about it].

Thus, although not a formal school policy, the school's structure (e.g., division of labor, loose coupling) created a culture (e.g., norms) that encouraged teachers to handle low-level behavior problems without consulting an administrator (Becker 1953; McPherson 1972). These deeply engrained cultural norms created a small but significant gap in the school's knowledge about the student's pattern of troubling behavior, and these cultural norms represented the glue that connected the school's structure to staff's daily work activities.

The upside to localizing problems and solutions is that it empowers staff. Using local control, the system "can isolate its trouble spots and prevent trouble from spreading" to other parts of the school or system (Weick 1976:7). Localizing problems and solutions for students of concern, however, has two major downsides. The first downside to localization is that each teacher has to "negotiate separately" with the student to address and redirect the same behavior problem

(Weick 1976:7). As a result, one teacher's decision about a student's disruptive classroom behavior does not address the student's recurring difficulties, which may emerge in other classrooms. In this case, JD's difficulties included bullying classmates in International Relations class; talking about his genitals in a debate competition; showing a teacher and peers a picture of his gun, which he named the "Kurt Cobain"; telling a teacher, "[I have] always been someone's bitch . . . why wouldn't I make him my bitch after all that has been done to me?"; saying "teachers [are] out to get me" and "my peers have often pushed me"; and telling a classmate to "go cut yourself."

To address the bullying behavior, JD's International Relations teacher asked JD to stay after class; JD did not stay, which struck the teacher as "very unusual" (Teacher 2). Explaining that students rarely disregarded his requests to stay after class, he decided, "I needed to further investigate who the student [was] . . . [to figure out] what made him tick and . . . what his problem was . . . [to know] how to reach [him]" (Teacher 2).[1]

The teacher talked with other teachers in his department to figure out how to connect with the student and manage his classroom conduct; he developed a plan for JD. These independent negotiations, however, did not address JD's underlying issues (e.g., anger) or recurring behavior problems (e.g., threats, inappropriate comments; Weick 1976). This teacher resisted the "normalization of deviance" in his classroom, but his efforts did not come to the attention of the larger school organization (Vaughan 2016). When problems and solutions remain local, "it [can] be difficult for the loosely coupled system to repair the defective element" (Weick 1976:7). In the end, each teacher's separate, independently brokered negotiation did not solve the "real" problem underlying the student's disruptive behavior (e.g., anger, grievances).

The second downside to teachers' independent negotiations with troubled students is that school administrators never learn about the full extent of a student's behavior problems or boundary testing, making it difficult to see a pattern or escalation. In everyday practice, organizations support and even take for granted the routines that make work efficient. Sociologists, however, note that these routines can impede our ability to imagine an alternative approach (Edelman et al. 2011; Vaughan 2016). Thus, although educator autonomy is highly valued for classroom management, it may limit the ability of other school staff to learn about and effectively address a troubled student's warning signs. By the time JD yelled "I'm going to kill that guy" (referring to the debate coach who had demoted him) in his senior year of high school, the intervention provided by the school's threat assessment team ended up being "too little [and] too late" (Weick 1976:7). These examples shed light on the ways a school's loosely coupled organizational structure can foster a culture of autonomy for teachers, supporting independent decision-making about students of concern. These examples also reveal the way a student of concern may fall through the cracks between an organization's structure and educators' practices.

Administrator autonomy. Like teachers, school administrators have considerable autonomy (Eck and Goodwin 2010; Meyer and Rowan 1978). The principal and assistant principal in this case held discretion over what behavior problems to investigate, whether and how to discipline students, and whether to notify staff of student behavior problems. Administrators' autonomy originated in the school's organizational structure (e.g., procedures, task segregation, staff hierarchy) and was reinforced through cultural norms and beliefs. For example, the school's structure did not provide a clear or standardized process for sharing a student's threat assessment results or reasons for suspension with teachers (e.g., student database, email notifications). During a deposition, JD's International Relations teacher was asked, "[I]s that typical for you to not know whether or not a student in your class has been suspended?" He replied:

> Well, usually what happens is I'll get an e-mail with a form I can print out, and it will say, "This student has been suspended." It will not say why, but it will say the length of time they're suspended and how [they will need] to make up their assignments. (Teacher 2)

In a follow-up question, he was asked, "[D]o you believe that it would be useful and helpful for the teachers, such as yourself, to be told . . . why [a student was] suspended?" The teacher replied:

> You know, as teachers, I mean, we're kind of . . . on both sides of this issue. So, it's hard for me to really respond, I mean, because we all have different jobs. And so, as a teacher, I think sometimes we want to know why, but I also know there's, you know, [FERPA] rights involved and reasons why we can't. (Teacher 2)

This segregation of tasks across "different jobs" shaped perceptions of roles and responsibilities. In this case, task segregation fostered the view that teachers did not have the right to know about the problems leading to a student's discipline even when safety concerns arose (see Fox and Harding 2005; Weber 1978). In another study to come from this case, administrators and teachers noted their widespread confusion about the safety exception within the FERPA, creating a code of silence among staff (Goodrum et al. 2017).

The hierarchy of staff in the school also shaped expectations and norms about information sharing. The attacker's foreign language teacher was asked if she expected the assistant principal to ask her whether to suspend JD for his outburst in her class. She said, "I didn't expect to be asked. . . . I think that's [the administrator's] job . . . and I didn't have prior knowledge about [the student's] behavior" (Teacher 1).

An unintended consequence of the task segregation and staff hierarchy in bureaucratic organizations is that lower ranked staff may feel reluctant to question a supervisor's decision. In this case, the organization's policies became tightly coupled with cultural norms. The debate coach explained: "I wasn't really in a position to agree or disagree [with the assistant principal's decision to not suspend the student after he threated to kill me]. All I could do was accept it."

The blanket acceptance of administrators' decisions likely arises for two reasons. First, teachers may grant administrators a range of decision-making behaviors or "zone of acceptance" they are willing to accept (Kunz and Hoy 1976). The responsibility for student discipline in the school fell to administrators, and the responsibility for student management in classrooms fell to teachers. Second, teachers may hesitate to question an administrator's decision due to expectations of "reciprocal autonomy." Teachers may grant administrators autonomy over disciplinary actions in exchange for their own autonomy over classrooms (Duke et al. 1980).

Granting a zone of acceptance and reciprocal autonomy foster collegial relationships among school staff, but they also create a culture where staff cannot review or question each other's decisions. These powerful norms and beliefs about the sanctity of educators' autonomy elucidate the way an organization's loosely coupled structure gets embedded in a school's cultural fabric and daily activities. Edelman and colleagues (2011:890) note, "[C]ertain organizational structures become widely institutionalized and taken for granted as rational forms of organizational governance," making it difficult for workers to question and even imagine an alternative arrangement.

Structural Secrets about a Student of Concern

In loosely coupled systems, information fails to reach the right people (Doyle 2010; Vaughan 2016). Fox and Harding (2005:73) note, "as a whole, schools have access to a variety of information about students—information about [their] physical health, academic progress, disciplinary history, relationships with peers. . . . But since tasks are highly segregated in schools, that information is spread over multiple actors within the school." This task segregation creates unintentional "secrets" within an organization's structure. Fox and Harding (2005:85) continue, "we prize privacy [in schools]—and for good reason—but we do so occasionally at a high cost." The cost arises for two interrelated reasons. First, connecting the dots of concern about a student proves challenging when that concern is scattered across people, classrooms, and time periods. Second, knowing the context for a student's current behavior creates the opportunity for the staff encountering the student to provide compassionate understanding and effective intervention across the system.

Connecting the dots. The culture of autonomy represents one way that gaps arise between an organization's structure and staff decisions, and information silos represent another. Prior research on school attacks notes the silos of information that can emerge in school settings (Fox and Harding 2005; Newman et al. 2004). These findings highlight how those silos emerged and how they hindered the assessment and management of the student in this case. The foreign language teacher explained:

> Part of the problem . . . is that we're very compartmentalized. So, I might tell one of my coworkers in the [foreign language] department about [a student], but it wouldn't leave the [foreign language] department. I wouldn't walk over to math, you know, for instance. I didn't know about [the math teacher's] situation [with JD] at all. (Teacher 1)

Thus, this teacher's and others' concerns about JD remained in their respective departments. Despite exhibiting a series of warning signs in the months leading up to his deadly attack, no one understood the seriousness or totality of those warning signs. The debate coach, the attacker's intended target, explained:

> I was working in isolation in the fall of 2013 when all of this was happening [with JD]. It appears that [the foreign language teacher] was having problems with [him] and that [his junior year math teacher] had had some previous problems [with him] and [his senior year math teacher] had some issues. None of us knew this. None of the faculty that had direct interaction with the student was aware of [his behavior problems].

During the law enforcement investigation following the attack, school administrators learned that campus security officers had witnessed the student viewing photos of firearms on his laptop in the cafeteria. Campus security officers reported their observations to an assistant principal, but the assistant principal never relayed that information to the student's threat assessment team or the school's principal. The principal acknowledged:

> [An assistant principal] was told [that the student was seen looking at photos of guns online on his laptop in the school cafeteria in October] by a campus [security] supervisor.... [After the shooting] I just asked him why he never told anyone. Why didn't you let us know? Why didn't [the assistant principal who conducted the threat assessment] know? And he said he didn't think it was that bad.... I think [one assistant principal] knew some things about [the student] and [the other assistant principal] knew some things about [the student but] never did it all come together.

The assistant principal who conducted the threat assessment expressed frustration over not learning about campus security's observations: "I wish you would have told me [that the student had been seen viewing photos of guns on his laptop in the cafeteria] . . . you knew we had a threat assessment on [the student] . . . I would have liked to have known that."

Indeed, research on school shootings consistently finds that attackers exhibited warning signs among classmates, in classrooms, and at home, but these warning signs fell through the cracks in the systems for violence prevention (Goodrum et al. 2017; Langman and Straub 2019; MSDHSPSC 2019; Virginia Tech Review Panel 2007). The postattack investigation in the Marjory Stoneman Douglas case revealed that the attacker had 69 incidents of talking about weapons, engaging in concerning behavior, and threatening or engaging in violence in local law enforcement's records and 55 incidents of disciplinary referrals in the school district's records (MSDHSPSC 2019:234, 243).

Some might try to blame JD's teachers for not sounding the alarm sooner in this case, but this response would neglect the fact that the school's organizational structure lacked the procedures and cultural norms to support proactive communication about and interventions for students of concern. The school resource officer in this case lamented:

> [I wish] we had more information given to us about students . . . like an information vortex . . . where everything [is] brought together and where law enforcement is involved, the therapist outside of the school [is] involved. . . . [This] information needs to be shared with everybody. Everybody needs to be brought in.

The public health approach to school violence supports the idea of cross-agency communication for addressing the difficult challenges facing students and their families (Office of the Child Advocate 2014). To support this type of communication, schools need policies (e.g., Memorandum of Understanding), trusted partnerships (e.g., law enforcement, social services), and mechanisms (e.g., monthly meetings, emails) that can prove difficult to broker in under-resourced schools and communities.

Knowing the context. The second reason structural secrets hinder violence prevention in schools relates to context. When critical information about a student's concerning behavior remains unknown to teachers and other staff, they may misinterpret observed behavior problems as isolated incidents, not as evidence of a recurring or escalating problem. Context is critical to the way people perceive and process information, particularly unusual information. When we do not know the background or history of a student's concerning behavior (e.g., threats, anger, aggression, weapons use), it becomes easy to normalize, misinterpret, and dismiss moderately troubling interactions and communications.

In violence prevention, having general knowledge of the warning signs for violence proves helpful for identifying students of concern (Fein et al. 2004; NTAC 2019); having knowledge of a *specific student's history of warning signs* proves critical to understanding and interpreting that student's subsequent behavior and communications. The student's foreign language teacher recalled, "No, absolutely not [the assistant principal did not tell me that JD had been the subject of a threat assessment]. . . . No one in my department knew" (Teacher 1).

Without knowing of JD's threat assessment, teachers and other staff downplayed his angry outbursts as concerning but not alarming. When asked to explain the rationale for not informing teachers about JD's threat assessment results, the principal said:

[Teachers] would know that a student was suspended, though they may not know the reason why . . . but we have explicitly said multiple times in staff meetings [and] training that we've had with the staff around discipline, "if they ever have a question to come see an administrator [or] a counselor."

But school staff did not realize they had questions about the student's behavior until *after the shooting* because they had no context with which to interpret his problem behavior.

Without information on the big picture, observers can only see the smaller picture right in front of them (see Costa 2012). The debate coach in the case explained:

Not every student that screams and yells is going to turn violent; so, we can't . . . target every kid that raises their voice. But we've got to be able to talk among ourselves and figure out—When is this a concern? When is this justified?—to follow up about students and concerns.

This discussion and follow-up can prove critical when monitoring and supporting a threat-assessed student. The debate coach continued:

I was fumbling in the dark [in dealing with JD]. [And] I didn't know what to do, and I tried my best. I don't think anybody [on the school's staff] did anything illegal. [But] I think maybe some bad decisions were made, bad judgment calls [were made]. . . . I don't know that we could have done anything to [stop him], but we could have maybe tried harder.

Of course, "trying harder" remains admirable, particularly for school staff juggling multiple responsibilities, but it proves incredibly challenging within a system that lacks the organizational structure and cultural norms to support those efforts. Expecting or asking school staff to "try harder" can never compensate for a system ill-equipped to gather and share information about a student of concern.

In a loosely coupled organization, there are often reasonable explanations for the decision *not to share* information (Vaughan 2016). Identifying these reasonable explanations helps map the connection between organizational structures and cultural norms. The school's principal explained:

> [Behavioral and disciplinary problems were not shared with teachers prior to the shooting because] it just had been the practice . . . we wanted to make sure that kids weren't inappropriately judged by teachers, that they were given a fair shot whether they moved from, you know, one teacher to another from year to year, that if something happened in one classroom, it didn't necessarily mean that it was going to happen again. [We wanted to] give them a *fresh start* with a new teacher, that kind of thing, really just erring more on the side of protecting the kid, giving them a second chance.

The "fresh start mentality" means negative information about the student gets lost within the organization's structure, and as a result, any future negative information about the student is undervalued and misinterpreted (Fox and Harding 2005). When school staff do not have all the relevant information—whether it is mental health concerns, behavioral concerns, or medical history—they cannot effectively evaluate, intervene, and monitor students. The challenge remains, however, in what information should be provided to whom when safety concerns arise.

Tightly coupling (or recoupling) the way information about students of concern is shared through formal policies and strict oversight may create other problems (Hallett 2010). For example, sharing information about a student's threat assessment results could prejudice a teacher against the student so that benign behavior is misinterpreted as malicious; at the same time, those results could provide a teacher with insight that prompts a compassionate response and tailored intervention. The manner in which this type of sensitive information is treated (e.g., respectful vs. gossip) is shaped by the culture (i.e., norms and values) and climate (e.g., feelings) of the organization (Fein et al. 2004; Reason 1997; Vaughan 2016). Despite the district's tightly coupled threat assessment guidelines, the school's loosely coupled structure shaped cultural beliefs about what information could be shared and with whom, hindering the prevention of violence in this case.

CONCLUSION

Nearly 20 years ago, the U.S. Secret Service and U.S. Department of Education developed guidelines for threat assessment and management for students of concern, using findings from 37 school attacks (Fein et al. 2004). These guidelines have provided schools across the country with a framework for how to evaluate and handle students of concern (Fein et al. 2004; NTAC 2018), and several national organizations have supplemented these guidelines with best practices for threat assessment in K–12 settings (NASP School Safety and Crisis Response Committee 2021). The recent increase in school attacks in the United States (Irwin et al. 2021, 2022), however, raises questions about our approach to violence prevention in U.S. schools. How is it possible that school violence could be on the rise despite federal guidance and evidence-based practices for school safety?

One answer lies in the structure and culture of the organizations where these tragic accidents occur (Fox and Harding 2005; Newman et al. 2004). An "organizational accident" refers to a "complex event [where] small mistakes combine with each other and with latent conditions hidden in the system to produce [an] unexpected traged[y]" (Doyle 2010:145). In this study, the "small mistakes" related to the way the threat assessment team evaluated and managed the troubled student and the way teachers and administrators handled the student's concerning behavior in isolation. Calling educators' encounters "mistakes," however, misrepresents the fact that the school's organizational structure remained ill-equipped to support threat assessment. The latent conditions in the school system included the tightly coupled threat assessment guidelines, the loosely coupled organizational structure, and the culture of educator autonomy.

On paper, tightly coupling the U.S. Secret Service's federal guidelines for threat assessment to the school district's policies on threat assessment gave the appearance of compliance with national recommendations for safety, creating an institutional myth (i.e., symbolic and ceremonial legitimacy; Hallett 2010; Meyer and Rowan 1977, 1978). In practice, the school's loosely coupled structure created gaps between threat assessment guidelines and workers' activities. The distance between policy and practice is common, particularly in busy school settings where educators juggle competing concerns with limited resources (Osher 2012). In their study of more than 3,000 school-based prevention programs in the United States, Gottfredson and Gottfredson (2002) found that only 44 percent of evidenced-based programs met a standard for effective implementation. Increasing the bureaucratic controls over threat assessment in schools may sound like the obvious solution to violence prevention in this and other cases, but research suggests that increasing control does not necessarily yield safety improvements (Perrow 1984), particularly for complex issues like violence prevention (Costa 2012). In fact, rigid guidelines may produce unintended consequences, such as an increased use of threat assessment with some student groups but not others (e.g., along lines of race/ethnicity) or frustration and turmoil among staff (see Hallett 2010; Porowski et al. 2014).

When reflecting on the lessons learned in this case, the attacker's foreign language teacher said, "I think there should be a way that we know of every student in trouble in that school. . . . [I]t's a big school and there's a lot of kids. And I think the more of us that are watching after these sweet creatures . . . [the] better" (Teacher 2). Watching after concerning students remains challenging when schools and districts do not have the structural or cultural conditions to support the institutionalization of evidence-based violence prevention programs and procedures. How can schools and communities balance the tightly coupled procedures for threat assessment with personalized strategies for addressing students' concerning behaviors in underresourced school settings? The U.S. Secret Service, U.S. Department of Education, and others have argued that a positive school culture and climate is key to school safety (Goodrum et al. forthcoming; NTAC 2019; Vossekuil et al. 2002). *This emphasis on culture and climate, however, neglects the reality that in bureaucracies, the organizational structure shapes the culture and climate.* Thus, efforts to prevent violence in schools should start by improving the structure first and the culture and climate second. A school's organizational structure creates a strong force shaping the culture and workers' actions (see Weber 1978).

LIMITATIONS

A case study, like other methods of data collection, has its drawbacks (for a discussion, see Harding et al. 2002; Roth and Mehta 2002). To minimize the effect of these limitations on the project, we followed Roth and Mehta's (2002) suggestions by gathering data from multiple sources (e.g., law enforcement interviews, depositions, school records) and by investigating conflicting reports through an analysis of school records, deposition testimony, and the law enforcement investigation. Also, during data analysis, facts were confirmed through a triangulation of data using multiple deponents and official documents.

RECOMMENDATIONS

Sociobiologist Rebecca Costa (2012) has argued that difficult and persistent social problems, like school violence, require a comprehensive strategy whereby multiple solutions are implemented simultaneously within social institutions and the culture. The findings from this study suggest three recommendations for future safety efforts in schools.

Fortify the Structure

First, when existing solutions do not resolve the problem, conduct a gap analysis to consider whether the organizational structure has the capacity (e.g., resources, motivation) to effectively implement those solutions. The field of implementation science consistently finds that delivering evidence-based programs proves challenging in busy school settings, where staff remain underresourced and overworked (Greenberg 2010; Mihalic and Irwin 2003; Osher 2012). At the school level, a school's capacity to implement a new program can be measured and improved, which would likely benefit implementation and outcomes (Kingston et al. 2018).

At the societal level, research should seek to identify the common structural weaknesses in violence prevention efforts across U.S. schools. How many other schools have gaps between guidelines and practices in threat assessment and other violence prevention programs? Using this evidence, state and federal governments could explore ways to provide schools with the financial support and implementation assistance needed to help institutionalize best practices for violence prevention and threat assessment (Greenberg 2010). Finally, schools could use existing institutionalized procedures in the academic realm, such as the steps for building an Individualized Education Program (IEP) for students with learning needs, as a model for how to approach students with behavioral and mental health needs. An IEP-like plan for students with behavioral and mental health needs would provide educators with information about and guidance on how to best support these students in a consistent and compassionate manner, which would yield improved academic outcomes.

Leverage the Culture

Second, schools could consider leveraging the deeply valued culture of autonomy to empower educators to recognize and report the warning signs for violence, including threats, intense anger, weapons interest, bullying victimization, depression, and harassing others (NTAC 2019). Educator training on the warning signs for violence could include (a) an explanation of the difference between disrespectful adolescent behavior and the warning signs for violence, (b) the need to report warning signs to school administrators, (c) the purpose for and role of teachers in threat assessment, and (d) guidance on how to prevent discrimination and bias in reporting warning signs (NTAC 2019; Reeves and McCarthy 2021).

Share the Responsibility

Finally, as a society, we need to recognize that the prevention of violence is a social problem, not a school problem, and this social problem requires a comprehensive approach with multicomponent strategies (e.g., reduce access to firearms, educate bystanders on anonymous reporting, implement programs for violence prevention). To share the responsibility for addressing the warning signs for violence, communities should consider developing community-based threat assessment teams that work with school-based threat assessment teams to identify and manage individuals of concern. The public health approach to violence prevention supports a multidisciplinary perspective where community stakeholders (e.g., educators, law enforcement officials, social services professionals, and criminal justice officials) come together to define the problem, consider the factors influencing the problem, and create and implement strategies to address the problem (Centers for Disease Control and Prevention 2022). We can no longer expect school administrators, teachers, and school psychologists to address the problem of violence prevention on their own. The complexity of the school violence problem, the financial implications of the solutions, and the fear of an innovative comprehensive approach must not paralyze us (Costa 2012). We have the knowledge to build organizational structures and cultures of safety; it is time to translate that knowledge into institutionalized everyday practice.

ACKNOWLEDGMENTS

The authors are grateful to the parents of the victim in this case, who sought an investigative arbitration with the school district to learn lessons on how to prevent the type of violence that took their daughter. We are also indebted to the school and district officials who gave testimony, helping us to reflect on and improve violence prevention practices in schools.

FUNDING

The study was funded by a grant from the Denver Foundation.

ORCID iDs

Sarah Goodrum, https://orcid.org/0000-0002-9529-5563

Jessie Slepicka, https://orcid.org/0000-0002-9328-5716

NOTES

Research ethics Institutional review board approval was not required because the authors did not recruit or interview subjects. In addition, all parties in the case agreed to the public release of the project data to share lessons learned on violence prevention.

1. The sheriff's report noted, "[The teacher] wanted to know how to deal with [the student] because [he] was telling other kids they were stupid. [He] was concerned because [the student] is . . . being seen as a 'verbal bully'" (Exhibit 14).

REFERENCES

Alper Mariel, Glaze Lauren. 2019. *Source and Use of Firearms Involved in Crimes: Survey of Prison Inmates, 2016*. Washington, DC: U.S. Department of Justice, Office of Justice Programs, Bureau of Justice Statistics. https://bjs.ojp.gov/content/pub/pdf/suficspi16.pdf.

Becker Herbert. 1953. "The Teacher in the Authority System of the Public School." *The Journal of Educational Sociology* 27 (3): 128– 41.

Bidwell Charles E. 1965. "The School as Formal Organization." Pp. 972–1018 in *Handbook of Organizations*, edited by March J. G.. Chicago, IL: Rand McNally.

Biglan Anthony, Mrazek Patricia, Carnine Douglas, Flay Brian R.. 2003. "The Integration of Research and Practice in the Prevention of Youth Problem Behaviors." *American Psychologist* 58 (6-7): 433– 40. Crossref

Birkinshaw Julian, Brannen Mary Yoko, Tung Rosalie L.. 2011. "From a Distance and Generalizable to up Close and Grounded: Reclaiming a Place for Qualitative Methods in International Business Research." *Journal of International Business Studies* 42: 573– 81. Crossref.

Blair J. Pete, Schweit Katherine W.. 2014. *A Study of Active Shooter Incidents, 2000-2013*. Washington, DC: Texas State University and Federal Bureau of Investigation, U.S. Department of Justice.

Bradley Elizabeth H., Curry Leslie A., Devers Kelly J.. 2007. "Qualitative Data Analysis for Health Services Research: Developing Taxonomy, Themes, and Theory." *Health Services Research* 42 (4): 1758– 72. Crossref.

Bryman Alan, Bell Emily. 2011. *Business Research Methods*. 3rd ed. Oxford, UK: Oxford University Press.

Burnard Philip, Gill Paul, Stewart Kate, Treasure Elizabeth, Chadwick Barbara. 2008. "Analyzing and Presenting Qualitative Data." *British Dental Journal* 204 (8): 429– 32. Crossref. PubMed.

Burrows Dustin, Moody Joe, Guzman Eva. 2022. *Investigative Committee on the Robb Elementary Shooting, Interim Report 2022*. Austin, TX: House of Representatives. https://static.texastribune.org/media/files/d005cf551ad52eea13d8753ede93320c/Uvalde%20Robb%20Shooting%20Report%20-%20Texas%20House%20Committee.pdf?_ga=2.253815820.5600916.1658677320-1012249026.1658677320.

Centers for Disease Control and Prevention. 2022. *The Public Health Approach to Violence Prevention*. Atlanta, GA: Centers for Disease Control and Prevention. https://www.cdc.gov/violenceprevention/pdf/PH_App_Violence-a.pdf.

Chapman Katrina. 2009. "A Preventable Tragedy at Virginia Tech: Why Confusion Over FERPA's Provisions Prevents Schools from Addressing Student Violence." *Public Interest Law Journal* 18: 349– 85.

Condon Bernard. 2022. "Texas School Shooter Left Trail of Ominous Warning Signs." *Washington Post*, July 19. https://www.washingtonpost.com/national/texas-killer-earned-ominous-nickname-school-shooter/2022/07/18/24962b94-06e5-11ed-80b6-43f2bfcc6662_story.htmlhtmlfile/Shell/Open/Command.

Costa Rebecca. 2012. *The Watchman's Rattle: A Radical New Theory of Collapse*. Philadelphia, PA: Vanguard Press.

Crowe Sarah, Cresswell Kathrin, Robertson Ann, Huby Guro, Avery Anthony, Sheikh Aziz. 2011. "The Case Study Approach." *BMC Medical Research Methodology* 11 (1): 100– 108. Crossref. PubMed.

Dörner Dietrich. 1996. *The Logic of Failure: Recognizing and Avoiding Error in Complex Situations*. Cambridge, MA: Perseus Press.

Doyle James. 2010. "Learning from Error in American Criminal Justice." *The Journal of Criminal Law and Criminology* 100 (1): 109– 47.

Duke Daniel L., Showers Beverly K., Imber Michael. 1980. "Teachers and Shared Decision Making: The Costs and Benefits of Involvement." *Educational Administration Quarterly* 16 (1): 93– 106. Crossref. ISI.

Durkheim Emile. [1895] 1966. *The Rules of Sociological Method*. New York, NY: Free Press.

Eck James, Goodwin Bryan. 2010. "Autonomy for School Leaders." *School Administrator* 67 (1): 24– 27.

Edelman Lauren B., Krieger Linda H., Eliason Scott R., Albiston Catherin R., Mellema Virginia. 2011. "When Organizations Rule: Judicial Deference to Institutionalized Employment Structures." *American Journal of Sociology* 117 (3): 888– 954. Crossref. ISI.

Erickson William. 2001. *The Report of Governor Bill Owens' Columbine Review Commission*. Denver, CO: The State of Colorado.

Federal Bureau of Investigation. 2016. *Active Shooter Incidents in the United States in 2014 and 2015*. Washington, DC: U.S. Department of Justice.

Federal Bureau of Investigation. 2018. *Active Shooter Incidents in the United States in 2018*. Washington, DC: The Advanced Law Enforcement Rapid Response Training Center at Texas State University and U.S. Department of Justice.

Federal Bureau of Investigation. 2019. *Active Shooter Incidents in the United States in 2019*. Washington, DC: The Advanced Law Enforcement Rapid Response Training Center at Texas State University and U.S. Department of Justice.

Fein Robert, Vossekuil Bryan, Pollack William, Borum Randy, Modzeleski William, Reddy Marisa. 2004. *Threat Assessment in Schools: A Guide to Managing Threatening Situations and to Creating Safe School Climates*. Washington, DC: United States Secret Service and United States Department of Education.

Firestone William A. 1984. "The Study of Loose Coupling: Problems, Progress, and Prospects." Pp. 3– 30 in *Research in Sociology of Education and Socialization*. Vol. 5, ed ited Kerckhoff A.. Greenwich, CT: JAI Press.

Fixsen Dean L., Naoom Sandra F., Blasé Karen A., Wallace Frances. 2005. *Implementation Research: A Synthesis of the Literature*. Tampa: University of South Florida, National Implementation Research Network.

Flyvbjerg Bent. 2006. "Five Misunderstandings about Case-Study Research." *Qualitative Inquiry* 12 (3): 219– 45.

Forman Susan G., Olin S. Serene, Hoagwood Kimberly Eaton, Crowe Maura, Saka Nao. 2009. "Evidence-Based Interventions in Schools: Developers' Views of Implementation Barriers and Facilitators." *School Mental Health* 1: 26– 36. Crossref Crossref.

Fox Cybelle, Harding David J.. 2005. "School Shootings as Organizational Deviance." *Sociology of Education* 78 (1): 69– 97. Crossref. ISI.

Geis Gilbert. 1991. "The Case Study Method in Sociological Criminology." Pp. 200– 23 in *A Case for the Case Study*, edited by Feagin J. R., Orum A., Sjoberg G.. Chapel Hill: University of North Carolina Press.

George Alexander L., McKeown Timothy J.. 1985. "Case Studies and Theories of Organizational Decision Making." *Advances in Information Processing in Organizations* 2 (1): 21– 58.

Gephart Jr., P Robert. 2004. "Qualitative Research and *The Academy of Management Journal*." *The Academy of Management Journal* 47 (4): 454– 62.

Gill Peter Edward, Stenlund Max Allen. 2006. "Dealing with a Schoolyard Bully: A Case Study." *Journal of School Violence* 4: 47– 62.

Goodrum Sarah, Evans Mary K., Thompson Andrew J., Woodward William. 2019. "Learning from a Failure in Threat Assessment: Eleven Questions and Not Enough Answers." *Behavioral Sciences & the Law* 37 (4): 353– 71. Crossref Crossref. PubMed.

Goodrum Sarah, Kingston Beverly, Mattson Sabrina Arredondo, Argamaso Susanne, Witt Jody, Matthews Amanda. Forthcoming. *Balancing the Components of a Comprehensive School Safety Framework: Findings from NIJ's Comprehensive Safe School Initiative*. Washington, DC: U.S. Department of Justice, National Institute of Justice.

Goodrum Sarah, Thompson Andrew J., Ward Kyle C., Woodward William. 2018. "A Case Study on Threat Assessment: Learning Critical Lessons to Prevent School Violence." *Journal of Threat Assessment and Management* 5 (3): 121– 36. Crossref Crossref.

Goodrum Sarah, Woodward William, Thompson Andrew J.. 2017. "Sharing Information to Promote a Culture of Safety." *NASSP Bulletin* 101 (3): 215– 40. Crossref Crossref.

Gottfredson Denise C., Gottfredson Gary D.. 2002. "Quality of School-Based Prevention Programs: Results from a National Survey. *Journal of Research in Crime and Delinquency* 39: 3– 35. Crossref Crossref. ISI.

Greenberg Mark T. 2010. "School-Based Prevention: Current Status and Future Challenges." *Effective Education* 2 (1): 27– 52. Crossref.

Hallett Tim. 2010. "The Myth Incarnate: Recoupling Processes, Turmoil, and Inhabited Institutions in an Urban Elementary School." *American Sociological Review* 75 (1): 52– 74. Crossref. ISI.

Hamm Kevin. 2021. "Tracking Colorado's Mass Shootings: 52 Have Died in Nine Incidents Since 1993." *The Denver Post*, March 24. https://www.denverpost.com/2021/03/24/colorado-mass-shootings-incidents-list/.

Harding David J., Fox Cybelle, Mehta Jal D.. 2002. "Studying Rare Events through Qualitative Case Studies: Lessons from a Study of Rampage School Shootings." *Sociological Methods & Research* 31 (2): 174– 217. Crossref. ISI.

Irwin Veronique, Wang Ke, Cui Jiashan, Thompson Alexandra. 2022. *Report on Indicators of School Crime and Safety: 2021* (NCES 2022-092/NCJ 304625). Washington, DC: National Center for Education Statistics, U.S. Department of Education, and Bureau of Justice Statistics, Office of Justice Programs, U.S. Department of Justice. https://nces.ed.gov/pubsearch/pubsinfo.asp?pubid=2022092.

Irwin Veronique, Wang Ke, Cui Jiashan, Zhang Jizhi, Thompson Alexandra. 2021. *Report on Indicators of School Crime and Safety: 2020* (NCES 2021-092/NCJ 300772). Washington, DC: National Center for Education Statistics, U.S. Department of Education, and Bureau of Justice Statistics, Office of Justice Programs, U.S. Department of Justice. https://nces.ed.gov/pubsearch/pubsinfo.asp?pubid=2021092.

Keen Justin, Packwood T.. 1995. "Qualitative Research: Case Study Evaluation." *BMJ* 311: 444– 46. Crossref. PubMed.

Kingston Beverly, Mattson Sabrina Arredondo, Dymnicki Allison, Spier Elizabeth, Fitzgerald Monica, Shipman Kimberly, Goodrum Sarah, Woodward William, Witt Jody, Hill Karl G., Elliott Delbert. 2018. "Building Schools' Readiness to Implement a Comprehensive Approach to School Safety." *Clinical Child and Family Psychology Review* 21: 433– 49. Crossref.

Kunz Daniel W., Hoy Wayne K.. 1976. "Leadership Style of Principals and the Professional Zone of Acceptance of Teachers." *Educational Administration Quarterly* 12 (3): 49– 64. Crossref. ISI.

Langman Peter, Straub Frank. 2019. *A Comparison of Averted and Completed School Attacks from the Police Foundation's Averted School Violence Database*. Washington, DC: Office of Community Oriented Policing Services.

Lortie Dan C. 2002. *Schoolteacher: A Sociological Study*. 2nd ed. Chicago, IL: University of Chicago Press. Crossref.

Mahoney James. 1999. "Nominal, Ordinal, and Narrative Appraisal in Macrocausal Analysis." *American Journal of Sociology* 104 (4): 1154– 96. Crossref.

Mahoney James. 2000. "Strategies of Causal Inference in Small N Analysis." *Sociological Methods and Research* 28 (4): 387– 424. Crossref. ISI.

Marjory Stoneman Douglas High School Public Safety Commission. 2019. *Initial Report*. Tallahassee, FL: Governor's Office.

Maxwell Joseph A. 2013. *Qualitative Research Design: An Interactive Approach*. Thousand Oaks, CA: Sage Publications.

McCutcheon David, Meredith Jack. 1993. "Conducting Case Study Research in Operations Management." *Journal of Operations Management* 11: 239– 56. Crossref.

McPherson Gertrude H. 1972. *Small Town Teacher*. Cambridge, MA: Harvard University Press. Crossref.

Meyer John W., Rowan Brian. 1977. "Institutional Organizations: Formal Structure as Myth and Ceremony." *American Journal of Sociology* 83 (2): 340– 63. Crossref.

Meyer John W., Rowan Brian. 1978. "The Structure of Educational Organizations: Formal Structure as Myth and Ceremony." Pp. 78– 109 in *Environments and Organizations*. Vol. 80, edited by Meyer M.. San Francisco, CA: Jossy Bass.

Mihalic Sharon F., Irwin Katherine. 2003. "Blueprints for Violence Prevention: From Research to Real-World Settings – Factors Influencing the Successful Replication of Model Programs." *Youth Violence and Juvenile Justice* 1 (4): 307– 29. Crossref.

Mills Albert J., Durepos Gabrielle, Wiebe Elden, eds. 2010. *Encyclopedia of Case Study Research, Volumes I and II*. Thousand Oaks, CA: Sage Publications. Crossref.

Myers Donald A. 1973. *Teacher Power*. Lexington, MA: Lexington Books.

NASP School Safety and Crisis Response Committee. 2021. *Behavioral Threat Assessment and Management: Best Practice Considerations for K-12 Schools*. National Association of School Psychologists. https://www.nasponline.org/btam

National Institute of Justice. 2020. *A Comprehensive School Safety Framework: Report to the Committees on Appropriations*. Washington, DC: U.S. Department of Justice, Office of Justice Programs, National Institute of Justice. https://www.ojp.gov/pdffiles1/nij/255078.pdf.

National Threat Assessment Center. 2018. *Enhancing School Safety Using a Threat Assessment Model: An Operational Guide for Preventing Targeted School Violence*. Washington, DC: U.S. Secret Service, Department of Homeland Security.

National Threat Assessment Center. 2019. *Protecting America's Schools: A U.S. Secret Service Analysis of Targeted School Violence*. Washington, DC: U.S. Secret Service, Department of Homeland Security.

Newman Katherine S., Fox Cybelle, Roth Wendy, Mehta Jal, Harding David. 2004. *Rampage: The Social Roots of School Shootings*. New York, NY: Perseus Books.

Office of the Child Advocate. 2014. *Shooting at Sandy Hook Elementary School: Report of the Office of the Child Advocate*. Hartford, CT: State of Connecticut.

Osher David. 2012. "Commentary: Implementation in Busy Kitchens and Swampy Lowlands." *Social Policy Report* 26 (4): 23– 24.

Paino Maria. 2018. "From Policies to Principals: Tiered Influences on School-Level Coupling." *Social Forces* 96 (3): 1119– 54. Crossref.

Perrow Charles. 1984. *Normal Accidents: Living with High-Risk Technologies*. New York, NY: Basic Books.

Pinelle David, Gutwin Carl. 2006. "Loose Coupling and Healthcare Organizations: Deployment Strategies for Groupware." *Computer Supported Cooperative Work* 15 (5–6): 537– 72. Crossref.

Planty Michael, Banks Duren, Lindquist Christine, Cartwright Joel, Witwer Amanda. 2020. *Tip Lines for School Safety: A National Portrait of Tip Line Use*. Research Triangle Park, NC: RTI International.

Porowski Allan, O'Conner Rosemarie, Passa Aikaterini. 2014. *Disproportionality in School Discipline: An Assessment of Trends in Maryland, 2009–12* (REL 2014–017). Washington, DC: U.S. Department of Education, Institute of Education Sciences, National Center for Education Evaluation and Regional Assistance, Regional Educational Laboratory Mid-Atlantic. http://ies.ed.gov/ncee/edlabs

Randazzo Marisa, Borum Randy, Vossekuil Bryan, Fein Robert, Modzeleski William, Pollack William. 2006. "Threat Assessment in Schools: Empirical Support and Comparison with Other Approaches." Pp. 147– 56 in *Handbook of School Violence and School Safety: From Research to Practice*, edited by Jimerson S., Furlong M.. Mahwah, NJ: Lawrence Erlbaum.

Reason James. 1997. *Managing the Risks of Organizational Accidents*. Farnham, UK: Ashgate Publishing.

Reason James. 1998. "Achieving a Safe Culture: Theory and Practice." *Work & Stress* 12 (3): 293– 306. Crossref Crossref. ISI.

Reeves Melissa, Brock Stephen. 2018. "School Behavioral Threat Assessment and Management." *Contemporary School Psychology* 22 (2): 148– 62.

Reeves Melissa A., McCarthy Courtenay. 2021. *Upholding Student Civil Rights and Preventing Disproportionality in Behavioral Threat Assessment and Management*. Bethesda, MD: National Association of School Psychologists.

Ringwalt Chris, Vincus Amy A., Hanley Sean, Ennett Susan T., Bowling J. Michael, Rohrbach Louise Ann. 2009. "The Prevalence of Evidence-Based Drug Use Prevention Curricula in U.S. Middle Schools in 2005." *Prevention Science* 10: 33– 40. Crossref. PubMed. ISI.

Roth Wendy D., Mehta Jal D.. 2002. "The Rashomon Effect: Combining Positivist and Interpretivist Approaches in the Analysis of Contested Events." *Sociological Methods & Research* 31: 131–73. Crossref Crossref.

Scheid-Cook Teresa. 1990. "Ritual Conformity and Organizational Control: Loose Coupling or Professionalization?" *The Journal of Applied Behavioral Science* 26 (2): 183–99. Crossref.

"School Shootings This Year: How Many and Where." 2022. *Education Week*, January 5. https://www.edweek.org/leadership/school-shootings-this-year-how-many-and-where/2022/01.

Stake Robert E. 1995. *The Art of Case Study Research*. London: Sage Publications.

Stake Robert E. 2005. "Qualitative Case Studies." Pp. 443–66 in *Handbook of Qualitative Research*. 3rd ed., edited by Denzin N., Lincoln Y.. Thousand Oaks, CA: Sage Publications.

Strauss Anslem. 1987. *Qualitative Analysis for Social Scientists*. New York, NY: Cambridge University Press. Crossref.

Turner Barry A. 1976. "The Organizational and Interorganizational Development of Disasters." *Administrative Science Quarterly* 21: 378–97. Crossref. PubMed.

Thrush Glenn. 2021. "'Ghost Guns': Firearm Kits Bought Online Fuel Epidemic of Violence." *The New York Times*, November 20. https://www.nytimes.com/2021/11/14/us/ghost-guns-homemade-firearms.html.

U.S. Department of Education. 2011. *Prevalence and Implementation Fidelity of Research-Based Prevention Programs in Public Schools: Final Report*. Rockville, MD: U.S. Department of Education.

Vaughan Diane. 2016. *The Challenger Launch Decision: Risky Technology, Culture, and Deviance at NASA*. Enlarged 2nd ed. Chicago, IL: University of Chicago Press.

Virginia Tech Review Panel. 2007. "Mass Shootings at Virginia Tech: Report of the Review Panel." scholar.lib.vt.edu/prevail/docs/VTReviewPanelRe port.pdf.

Vossekuil Bryan, Fein Robert, Reddy Marisa, Borum Robert, Modzeleski William. 2002. *The Final Report and Findings of the Safe School Initiative: Implications for the Prevention of School Attacks in the U.S*. Washington, DC: U.S. Secret Service and Department of Education.

Weber Max. 1978. *Economy and Society*. Berkley and Los Angeles: University of California Press.

Weick Karl. 1976. "Educational Organizations as Loosely Coupled Systems." *Administrative Science Quarterly* 21 (1): 1–19. Crossref. ISI.

Wintemute Garen J. 2015. "The Epidemiology of Firearm Violence in the Twenty-First Century United States." *Annual Review of Public Health* 36: 5–19. Crossref. PubMed. ISI.

Yin Robert. 2014. *Case Study Research Design and Methods*. 5th ed. Thousand Oaks, CA: Sage Publications.

AUTHOR BIOGRAPHIES

Sarah Goodrum, PhD, is a senior research associate at the Center for the Study and Prevention of Violence at the University of Colorado Boulder. Her main fields of study include intimate partner violence, homicide victimization, and violence prevention. She is currently studying the relationship between organizational culture and violence prevention and the impact of training on threat assessment procedures.

Jessie Slepicka is a doctoral candidate in the Department of Sociology and Criminology at The Pennsylvania State University. His research interests include criminological theory, green criminology, comparative criminology, spatial criminology, and quantitative research methods.

William Woodward, MPA, is a research associate at the University of Colorado's Center for the Study and Prevention of Violence and is former Colorado State Director of Criminal Justice. He coauthored the Arapahoe High School shooting investigation study and the Colorado Attorney General's School Safety Guide. He presented a TEDx talk on preventing school shootings in 2016.

Beverly Kingston, PhD, is director and senior research associate at the Center for the Study and Prevention of Violence at the University of Colorado Boulder. Her main fields of interest are comprehensive public health approaches to violence prevention, school safety, neighborhood social processes, and implementation science. She currently leads several school and community initiatives and research studies focused on these topics.

GLOSSARY

The definitions in this glossary represent key terms as they are used and defined in this book. Many definitions exist for these terms, but the most workable definitions for us (and we hope for the reader) are those that reflect the content and references presented in this book. We group the terms by approach to inquiry (narrative research, phenomenology, grounded theory, ethnography, case study) and alphabetize them within the approach, and at the end of the glossary, we define additional general qualitative terms that cross all of the five different approaches.

NARRATIVE RESEARCH

arts-based study: This is a form of narrative inquiry in which creative literary forms of writing (e.g., poetry, nonfiction) and use of visuals (e.g., photos, photovoice, digital storytelling) are part of the research product or performance (Kim, 2015).

autobiographical study: This is a form of narrative study in which the researcher takes themselves as the subject of study and uses "the story of the researcher's self" (Kim, 2015, p. 121).

autoethnography: This form of narrative is written and recorded by the individuals who are the subject of the study (Ellis, 2004; Muncey, 2010). Muncey (2010) defines *autoethnography* as the idea of multiple layers of consciousness, the vulnerable self, the coherent self, critiquing the self in social contexts, the subversion of dominant discourses, and the evocative potential.

biographical study: This is the study of a single individual and their experiences as told to the researcher or as found in documents and archival materials (Denzin, 1989). We use the term to connote the broad genre of narrative writings that includes individual biographies, autobiographies, life histories, and oral histories.

digital storytelling: This refers to a short (e.g., 3-to-5 minute) visual narrative integrating any number of images of photos, artwork, and video with audio recordings of voice and music (Willox et al., 2012).

epiphanies: These are special events in an individual's life that represent turning points. They vary in their impact from minor to major epiphanies, and they may be positive or negative (Denzin, 1989).

historical contexts: These are the contexts in which the researcher presents the life of the participant. The context may be the participant's family, society, or the historical, social, or political trends of the participant's times (Denzin, 1989).

life course stages: These are stages in an individual's life or key events that become the focus for the biographer (Denzin, 1989).

life history: This is a form of biographical writing in which the researcher reports an extensive record of a person's life as told to the researcher (see Geiger, 1986). Thus, the individual being studied is alive, and life as lived in the present is influenced by personal, institutional, and social histories. The investigator may use different disciplinary perspectives (L. M. Smith, 1994), such as the exploration of an individual's life as representative of a culture, as in an anthropological life history.

lived experiences: This term is used in narrative studies to emphasize the importance of individual experiences in the collaborative storytelling.

narrative research: This is an approach to qualitative research that is both a product and a method. It is a study of stories or narrative or descriptions of a series of events that accounts for human experiences (Pinnegar & Daynes, 2007).

oral history: In this biographical approach, the researcher gathers personal recollections of events and their causes and effects from an individual or several individuals. This information may be collected through tape recordings or through written works of individuals who have died or are still living. It often is limited to the distinctly "modern" sphere and to accessible people (Plummer, 1983).

progressive-regressive method: This is an approach to writing a narrative in which the researcher begins with a key event in the participant's life and then works forward and backward from that event (Denzin, 1989).

restorying: This is an approach in narrative data analysis in which the researchers retell the stories of individual experiences, and the new story typically has a beginning, a middle, and an ending (Ollerenshaw & Creswell, 2002).

stories: These are aspects that surface during an interview in which the participant describes a situation, usually with a beginning, a middle, and an end, so that the researcher can capture a complete idea and integrate it, intact, into the qualitative narrative (Clandinin & Connelly, 2000; Czarniawska, 2004; Denzin, 1989; Riessman, 2008).

PHENOMENOLOGY

clusters of meaning: This is the third step in phenomenological data analysis, in which the researcher clusters the statements into themes or meaning units, removing overlapping and repetitive statements (Moustakas, 1994).

epoché (or bracketing): This is the first step in "phenomenological reduction," the process of data analysis in which the researcher sets aside, as far as is humanly possible, all preconceived experiences to best understand the experiences of participants in the study (Moustakas, 1994).

essential, invariant structure (or essence): This is the goal of the phenomenologist, to reduce the textural (*what*) and structural (*how*) meanings of experiences to a brief description that typifies the experiences of all the participants in a study. All individuals experience it; hence, it is invariant, and it is a reduction to the "essentials" of the experiences (Moustakas, 1994, van Manen, 2014).

hermeneutical phenomenology: A form of phenomenology in which research is oriented toward interpreting the "texts" of life (hermeneutical) and lived experiences (van Manen, 1990).

horizontalization: This is the second step in the phenomenological data analysis, in which the researcher lists every significant statement relevant to the topic and gives it equal value (Moustakas, 1994).

intentionality of consciousness: Being conscious of objects is always intentional. Thus, when perceiving a tree, "my intentional experience is a combination of the outward appearance of the tree and the tree as contained in my consciousness based on memory, image, and meaning" (Moustakas, 1994, p. 55).

lived experiences: This term is used in phenomenological studies to emphasize the importance of individual experiences of people as conscious human beings (Giorgi, 2009; Moustakas, 1994).

phenomenological data analysis: Several approaches to analyzing phenomenological data are represented in the literature. Moustakas (1994) reviews these approaches and then advances his own. We rely on the Moustakas modification that includes the researcher bringing personal experiences into the study, the recording of significant statements and meaning units, and the development of descriptions to arrive at the essence of the experiences. Giorgi (2009) advances a rigorous yet more open approach in his book.

phenomenological reflection: According to van Manen (2014), this involves two processes of bracketing (withdrawal) and reduction (constitution of meaning).

phenomenological research: This research approach describes the common meaning of experiences of a phenomenon (or topic or concept) for several individuals. In this type of qualitative study, the researcher reduces the experiences to a central meaning or the "essence" of the experience.

phenomenology of practice: Describes the "development and articulation of meaning-giving methods of phenomenology" that are based on what van Manen (2014, p. 212) considers to be the practical examples from the primary literature of phenomenology.

phenomenon: This is the central concept being examined by the phenomenologist. It is the concept being experienced by subjects in a study, which may include psychological concepts such as grief, anger, or love.

structural description: From the first three steps in phenomenological data analysis, the researcher writes a "structural" description of an experience, addressing *how* the phenomenon was experienced. It involves seeking all possible meanings, looking for divergent perspectives, and varying the frames of reference about the phenomenon or using imaginative variation (Moustakas, 1994).

textural description: Based on the first three steps in phenomenological data analysis, the researcher writes about *what* was experienced—a description of the meaning individuals have experienced (Moustakas, 1994).

transcendental (or descriptive, empirical, psychological) According to Moustakas (1994), Husserl espoused transcendental phenomenology, and it later became a guiding concept for Moustakas as well. In this approach, the researcher sets aside prejudgments regarding the phenomenon being investigated. Also, the researcher relies on intuition, imagination, and universal structures to obtain a picture of the experience, and the inquirer uses systematic methods of analysis as advanced by Moustakas (1994).

GROUNDED THEORY

axial coding: This step in the coding process follows open coding in grounded theory research. The researcher takes the categories of open coding, identifies one as a central phenomenon, and then returns to the database to identify (a) what caused this phenomenon to occur, (b) what strategies or actions actors employed in response to it, (c) what context (specific context) and intervening conditions (broad context) influenced the strategies, and (d) what consequences resulted from these strategies. The overall process is one of relating categories of information to the central phenomenon category (Corbin & Strauss, 2015; Strauss & Corbin, 1990, 1998).

category: This is a unit of information analyzed in grounded theory research. It comprises events, happenings, and instances of phenomenon (Strauss & Corbin, 1990) and given a short label. When researchers analyze grounded theory data, their analysis leads, initially, to the formation of several categories during the process called open coding. Then, in axial coding, the analyst interrelates the categories and forms a visual model (Corbin & Strauss, 2015).

causal conditions: In axial coding, these are the categories of conditions researchers identify in their data that cause or influence the central phenomenon to occur in a grounded theory study.

central phenomenon: This is an aspect of axial coding and the formation of the visual theory, model, or paradigm (Corbin & Strauss, 2015). In open coding, the researcher chooses a central category around which to develop the theory by examining their open coding categories and selecting one that holds the most conceptual interest, is most frequently discussed by participants in the study, and is most "saturated" with information. The researcher then places it at the center of their grounded theory model and labels it *central phenomenon*.

coding paradigm or logic diagram: In axial coding, the central phenomenon, causal conditions, context, intervening conditions, strategies, and consequences are portrayed in a visual diagram. This diagram is drawn with boxes and arrows indicating the process or flow of activities. It is helpful to view this diagram as more than axial coding; it is the theoretical model developed in a grounded theory study.

conditional context: In axial coding, this is the particular set of conditions that inform the strategies that occur in the grounded theory research context (Corbin & Strauss, 2015).

conditional or consequential matrix: This is a diagram, typically drawn late in a grounded theory study, that presents the conditions and consequences related to the phenomenon under study. It enables the researcher to both distinguish and link levels of conditions and consequences specified in the axial coding model (Corbin & Strauss, 2015; Strauss & Corbin, 1990). It is a step seldom seen in data analysis in reports of grounded theory studies.

consequences or outcomes of the central phenomenon: In axial coding, these are the actions taken by participants in the grounded theory study. These outcomes may be positive, negative, or neutral (Strauss & Corbin, 1990).

constant comparative: This was an early term (Conrad, 1978) in grounded theory research that referred to the researcher identifying incidents, events, and activities and constantly comparing them to an emerging category to develop and saturate the category.

constructivist grounded theory: This is a form of grounded theory squarely in the interpretive tradition of qualitative research. As such, it is less structured than traditional approaches to grounded theory. The constructivist approach incorporates the researcher's views; uncovers experiences with embedded, hidden networks, situations, and relationships; and makes visible hierarchies of power, communication, and opportunity (Charmaz, 2006, 2014).

dimensionalized: This is the smallest unit of information analyzed in grounded theory research. The researcher takes the properties and places them on a continuum or dimensionalizes them to see the extreme possibilities for the property. The dimensionalized information appears in the "open coding" analysis (Corbin & Strauss, 2015; Strauss & Corbin, 1990).

grounded theory research: This research approach involves generating or discovering a theory to explain a process or action, "grounding" the study in views of participants.

in vivo codes: In grounded theory research, the investigator uses the exact words of the interviewee to form the names for these codes or categories. The names are catchy and immediately draw the attention of the reader (Strauss & Corbin, 1990, p. 69).

intervening conditions: In axial coding, these are the broader conditions—broader than the context—within which the strategies occur. They might be social, economic, and political forces that influence the strategies in response to the central phenomenon of the grounded theory study (Strauss & Corbin, 1990).

memoing: This is the process in grounded theory research of the researcher writing down ideas about the evolving theory. The writing could be in the form of preliminary propositions (hypotheses), ideas about emerging codes or categories, or some aspects of the connection of categories as in axial coding. In general, these are written records of analysis that help with the formulation of theory (Strauss & Corbin, 1990).

open coding: This is the first step in the data analysis process for a grounded theorist. It involves taking data (e.g., interview transcriptions) and segmenting them into categories of information (Corbin & Strauss, 2015; Strauss & Corbin, 1990). We recommend that researchers try to develop a small number of categories, slowly reducing the number to approximately 30 codes that are then combined into major themes in the study.

properties: These are other units of information analyzed in grounded theory research. Each category in grounded theory research can be subdivided into properties that provide the broad dimensions for the category. Strauss and Corbin (1990) refer to them as "attributes or characteristics pertaining to a category" (p. 61). They appear in open coding analysis.

propositions: These are hypotheses, typically written in a directional form, that relate categories in a study. They are written from the axial coding model or paradigm and might, for example, suggest why a certain cause influences the central phenomenon that, in turn, influences the use of a specific strategy.

saturate, saturated, or saturation: In the development of categories and data analysis phase of grounded theory research, researchers seek to find as many incidents, events, or activities as possible to provide support for the categories. In this process, they come to a point at which the categories are saturated, and the inquirer no longer finds new information that adds to an understanding of the category or aspects of the central phenomenon.

selective coding: This is the final phase of coding the information in grounded theory research. The researcher takes the central phenomenon and systematically relates it to other categories, validating the relationships and filling in categories that need further refinement and development (Strauss & Corbin, 1990).

substantive-level theory: This is a low-level theory that is applicable to immediate situations. This theory evolves from the study of a phenomenon situated in "one particular situational context" (Strauss & Corbin, 1990, p. 174). Grounded theory researchers differentiate this form of theory from theories of greater abstraction and applicability, called midlevel theories, grand theories, or formal theories.

theoretical sampling: In data collection for grounded theory research, the investigator selects a sample of individuals to study based on their contribution to the development of the theory. Often, this process begins with a sample of individuals who are similar, and as the data collection proceeds and the categories emerge, the researcher turns to a heterogeneous sample to see under what sample conditions the categories hold true.

ETHNOGRAPHY

analysis of the culture-sharing group: In this step in ethnography, the ethnographer develops themes—cultural themes—in the data analysis. It is a process of reviewing all the data and segmenting them into a small set of common themes, well supported by evidence in the data (Wolcott, 1994).

complete observer: The ethnographer is neither seen nor noticed by the people under study.

complete participant: The ethnographer is fully engaged with the people under observation. This may help the ethnographer establish greater rapport with the people being observed (Angrosino, 2007).

critical ethnography: This type of ethnography examines cultural systems of power, prestige, privilege, and authority in society. Critical ethnographers study marginalized groups from different classes, races, and genders, with an aim of advocating for the needs of these participants (Madison, 2011; J. Thomas, 1993).

cultural behaviors: These are the focus of attention for the ethnographer as they attempt to understand what people do (Spradley, 1980).

cultural interpretation: The ethnographer makes an interpretation of the meaning of the culture-sharing group. The researcher derives this interpretation from literature, personal experiences, or theoretical perspectives. Often, the ethnographer identifies how the cultural group works (Wolcott, 1994).

cultural portrait: One key component of ethnographic research is composing a holistic view of the culture-sharing group or individual. The final product of an ethnography should be this larger portrait, or overview of the cultural scene, presented in all its complexity (Spradley, 1979).

culture: This term is an abstraction, something that one cannot study directly. From observing and participating in a culture-sharing group, an ethnographer can see "culture at work" and provide a description and interpretation of it (H. F. Wolcott, personal communication, October 10, 1996; Wolcott, 2010). It can be seen in behaviors, language, and artifacts (Spradley, 1980).

culture-sharing group: This is the unit of analysis for the ethnographer as they attempt to understand and interpret the behavior, language, and artifacts of people. The ethnographer typically focuses on an entire group—one that shares learned, acquired behaviors—to make explicit how the group "works." Some ethnographers will focus on part of the social-cultural system for analysis and engage in a micro-ethnography.

deception: This is an ethnographical fieldwork issue that has become less and less of a problem since the ethical standards were published in 1967 by the American Anthropological Association. It relates to the act of the researcher intentionally deceiving the informants to gain information. This deception may involve withholding important information about the purpose of the study or gathering information secretively.

description of the culture-sharing group: One of the first tasks for an ethnographer is to simply record a description of the culture-sharing group and incidents and activities that illustrate the culture (Wolcott, 1994). For example, a factual account may be rendered, pictures of the setting may be drawn, or events may be chronicled.

emic: This term refers to the type of information being reported and written into an ethnography when the researcher reports the views of the participants. When the researcher reports their own personal views, the term used is *etic* (Fetterman, 2019).

ethnographic research: This research approach involves the study of shared patterns over time among a culture-sharing group.

ethnography: This is the study of an intact cultural or social group (or an individual or individuals within the group) based primarily on observations and a prolonged period of time spent by the researcher in the field. The ethnographer listens and records the voices of informants with the intent of generating a cultural portrait (J. Thomas, 1993; Wolcott, 1987).

ethnographic fieldwork: In ethnographic data collection, the researcher conducts data gathering in the "field" by going to the site or sites where the culture-sharing group can be studied. Often, this involves the researcher's prolonged involvement in the field with varying degrees of immersion in activities, events, rituals, and settings of the cultural group (Sanjek, 1990).

etic: This term refers to the type of information being reported and written into an ethnography when the researcher reports their own personal views. Alternatively, when the researcher reports the views of the participants, the term used is *emic* (Fetterman, 2019).

holistic perspective: The ethnographer assumes this outlook in research to gain a comprehensive and complete picture of a social group. It might include the group's history, religion, politics, economy, and/or environment. In this way, the researcher places information about the group into a larger perspective or "contextualizes" the study (Fetterman, 2019).

key informants (or participants): These are individuals with whom the researcher begins in data collection because they are well informed, are accessible, and can provide leads about other information (Wolcott, 2008a).

language: This is the focus of attention for the ethnographer as they discern what people say (Spradley, 1980).

nonparticipant observation: The researcher is an outsider of the group under study, watching and taking field notes from a distance. They can record data without direct involvement with activity or people.

participant observation: The ethnographer gathers information in many ways, but the primary approach is to observe the culture-sharing group and become a participant in the cultural setting (Fetterman, 2019).

realist ethnography: A traditional approach to ethnography taken by cultural anthropologists, this approach involves the researcher as an "objective" observer, recording the facts and narrating the study with a dispassionate, omniscient stance (Van Maanen, 1988).

social structure: An ethnographer creates themes or concepts to represent the basic structure and function of the social-cultural system or group under study. It refers to the social structure or configuration of the group, such as the kinship or political structure of the social-cultural group. This structure might be illustrated by an organizational chart (Fetterman, 2019).

CASE STUDY

analysis of themes: Following description, the case study researcher analyzes the data for specific themes, aggregating information into large clusters of ideas and providing details that support the themes. Stake (1995) calls this analysis "development of issues" (p. 123).

assertions: This is the last step in the analysis, where the case study researcher makes sense of the data and provides an interpretation of the data couched in terms of personal views or in terms of theories or constructs in the literature.

bounded system: The case selected for study has boundaries, often bounded by time and place. It also has interrelated parts that form a whole. Hence, the proper case to be studied is both "bounded" and a "system" (Stake, 1995).

case: This is the unit of analysis in a case study. It involves the study of a specific case within a real-life, contemporary context or setting (Yin, 2017). The case might be an event, a process, a program, or several people (Stake, 1995). The case could be the focus of attention (intrinsic case study) or the issue and the case used to illustrate the case (Stake, 1995).

case description: This simply means stating the facts about the case as recorded by the investigator. This is the first step in analysis of data in a qualitative case study; Stake (1995) calls it narrative description (p. 123).

case study research: This research approach involves the study of a case within a real-life, contemporary context or setting (Yin, 2017)

case themes: These are one aspect of the major findings in a case study. In Stake's (1995) terms, these would be called categorical aggregations, the larger categories derived during case study data analysis and made up of multiple incidents that are aggregated.

collective case study: This type of case study consists of multiple cases. It might be either intrinsic or instrumental, but its defining feature is that the researcher examines several cases (e.g., multiple case studies; Stake, 1995).

context of the case: In analyzing and describing a case, the researcher sets the case within its setting. This setting may be broadly conceptualized (e.g., large historical, social, political issues) or narrowly conceptualized (e.g., the immediate family, the physical location, the time in which the study occurred; Stake, 1995).

cross-case analysis: This form of analysis applies to a collective case (Stake, 1995; Yin, 2017) in which the researcher examines more than one case. It involves examining themes across cases to discern themes that are common and different to all cases. It is an analysis step that typically follows within-case analysis when the researcher studies multiple cases.

direct interpretation: This is an aspect of interpretation in case study research where the researcher looks at a single instance and draws meaning from it without looking for multiple instances of it. It is a process of pulling the data apart and putting them back together in more meaningful ways (Stake, 1995).

embedded analysis: In this approach to data analysis, the researcher selects one analytic aspect of the case for presentation (Yin, 2017).

holistic analysis: In this approach to data analysis, the researcher examines the entire case (Yin, 2017) and presents description, themes, and interpretations or assertions related to the whole case.

instrumental case study: This is a type of case study with the focus on a specific issue rather than on the case itself. The case then becomes a vehicle to better understand the issue (Stake, 1995).

intrinsic case study: This is a type of case study with the focus of the study on the case because it holds intrinsic or unusual interest (Stake, 1995).

multisite case study: When sites are selected for the case, they might be at different geographical locations. This type of study is considered a multisite study. Alternatively, the case might be at a single location and considered a within-site study.

multiple sources of information: One aspect that characterizes good case study research is the use of many different sources of information to provide "depth" to the case. Yin (2017), for example, recommends that the researcher use as many as six different types of information in their case study.

naturalistic generalizations: In the interpretation of a case, an investigator undertakes a case study to make the case understandable. This understanding may be what the reader learns from the case or its application to other cases (Stake, 1995).

patterns: This is an aspect of data analysis in case study research where the researcher establishes patterns and looks for a correspondence between two or more categories to establish a small number of categories (Stake, 1995).

purposeful case sampling: This is a major issue in case study research, and the researcher needs to clearly specify the type of sampling strategy in selecting the case (or cases) and a rationale for it. It applies to both the selection of the case to study and the sampling of information used within the case.

within-case analysis: This type of analysis may apply to either a single case or multiple collective case studies. In within-case analysis, the researcher analyzes each case for themes. In the study of multiple cases, the researcher may compare the within-case themes across multiple cases in cross-case analysis.

within-site case study: When a site is selected for the case, it might be located at a single geographical location. This is considered a within-site study. Alternatively, the case might be different locations and considered to be multisite.

GENERAL QUALITATIVE TERMS

abstraction: This process involves transforming raw data from the individual instances in which it was generated to form broader and broader categories by creating, exploring, and using themes derived from the data (Richards & Morse, 2013).

approaches to inquiry: This is an approach to qualitative research that has a distinguished history in one of the social science disciplines and that has spawned books, journals, and distinct methodologies. These "approaches," as we call them, are known in other books as "strategies of inquiry" (Denzin & Lincoln, 1994) or "varieties" (Tesch, 1990). We refer to narrative research, phenomenology, grounded theory, ethnography, and case studies in this book as approaches to inquiry.

artifacts: This is the focus of attention for the qualitative researcher. Artifacts can take many forms and be used by researchers and participants in different ways. For example, in narrative research personal-family-social artifacts may help individuals tell their stories whereas in ethnographical research cultural artifacts can represent what people make and use, such as clothes and tools.

audit trail: This is a document that allows a researcher to retrace the process by which the researcher arrived at their final findings.

autobiography: This form of biographical writing is a firsthand account of a person's life that they have personally written or otherwise recorded (Angrosino, 1989).

axiological assumption: This philosophical assumption holds that all research is value laden and includes the value systems of the inquirer, the theory, the paradigm used, and the social and cultural norms for either the inquirer or the respondents (Guba & Lincoln, 1988; Mertens, 2019). Accordingly, the researcher admits and discusses these values in their research.

central question: A central question in a study is the broad, overarching question being addressed in the research study. It is the most general question that could be asked to address the research problem.

codebook: This document contains the record of the codes and categories for a study for the purpose of guiding consistent application of codes either by an individual researcher or across a research team.

coding: This is the process of aggregating the text or visual data into small categories of information, seeking evidence for the code from different databases being used in a study, and then assigning a label to the code.

collective reflexivity: This involves the engagement of a group in an active, ongoing process of critical reflection on how researchers co-construct knowledge based on their identities, experiences, subjectivities, ontologies, and epistemologies during the research team process (Poth et al., 2023).

concern for justice: This ethical principle refers to the "need to treat people fairly and equitably and concerns all who participate in the research" (Poth, 2021, p. 15). As researchers, this means we must carefully consider recruitment and justifications for sampling strategies, data collection methods as well as site selection and criteria guiding site choice.

concern for welfare: This ethical principle is about the "protection of participants by minimizing harm and maximining benefits of the research" (Poth, 2021, p. 15). This means that researchers must take all possible measures to protect the privacy and confidentiality of those involved in the research.

credibility According to Lincoln and Guba (1985), credibility is a measure of the truth value, that is, whether the study's findings are correct and accurate. It is dependent on the researcher's production and documentation of the document (Flick, 2018).

critical race theory: This is an interpretive lens used

in qualitative research that focuses attention on race and how racism is deeply embedded within the framework of American society (Parker & Lynn, 2002).

critical theory: This is an interpretive lens used in qualitative research in which a researcher examines the study of social institutions and their transformations through interpreting the meanings of social life; the historical problems of domination, alienation, and social struggles; and a critique of society and the envisioning of new possibilities (Fay, 1987; Madison, 2011; R. A. Morrow, 1994).

data management: This involves the practices and policies related to recording, sorting, auditing, archiving, analyzing, interpreting, sharing, and publishing data.

disability theories: Disability is focused on as a dimension of human difference and not as a defect. As a human difference, its meaning is derived from social construction (i.e., society's response to individuals), and it is simply one dimension of human difference.

embedded writing structures: These are often literary devices that help the researcher fulfill the focus of the qualitative approach.

encoding: This term means that the writer places certain features in their writing to help a reader know what to expect. These features not only help the reader but also aid the writer, who can then draw on the habits of thought and specialized knowledge of the reader (Richardson, 1990). Such features might be the overall organization, code words, images, and other "signposts" for the reader. As applied in this book, the features consist of terms and procedures of an approach that become part of the language of all facets of research design (e.g., purpose statement, research subquestions, methods).

epistemological assumption: This is a philosophical assumption for the qualitative researcher. It addresses the relationship between the researcher and that being studied as interrelated, not independent. To minimize the "distance" between researchers and those being researched, researchers spend time at the research site, and get to know the participants.

ethical reasoning: This involves making a decision in response to a moral dilemma based on a careful and thorough assessment of different options in light of the facts, circumstances, and ethical issues (Poth, 2021).

ethical review: A process intended to protect research participants by minimizing the harms or risks to which they are exposed during research activities. Often takes place within a community, an organization, or an institution.

evaluation: This term represents the various strategies used to assess and appraise the quality of a qualitative study.

feminist research approaches: Feminist research embraces many of the tenets of postmodern and poststructuralist critiques as a challenge to the injustices of current society. The goals of feminist research approaches center on establishing collaborative and nonexploitative relationships, to place the researcher within the study to avoid objectification, and to conduct transformative research.

foreshadowing: This term refers to the technique that writers use to portend the development of ideas (Hammersley & Atkinson, 1995). For example, the wording of the problem statement, purpose statement, and research subquestions foreshadows the methods—the data collection and data analysis—used in the study.

gatekeeper: This is a data collection term and refers to the individual the researcher must visit before entering a group or cultural site. To gain access, the researcher must receive this individual's approval.

informed consent: In research, this is the process of making a free and informed decision such as to participate in research. Individuals who provide informed consent must be legally competent and have enough decision-making capacity to consent to participating in the research.

intercoder agreement: This term means that researchers check for reliability of their coding among two or more coders in the data analysis process. It involves coding agreements by multiple coders when they assign and check their code segments.

interpretation: This term represents a phase in qualitative data analysis involving abstracting out beyond the codes and themes to the larger meaning of the data.

interview protocol: The interview protocol is a form in qualitative data collection in which the researcher states instructions and questions for an interview and records information provided by the interviewee. It consists of a header, the major substantive question (typically five to seven research subquestions phrased in a way that interviewees can answer) and closing instructions.

maximum variation sampling: This is a popular form of qualitative sampling. This sampling approach consists of determining in advance some criteria that differentiate the sites or participants and then selecting sites or participants that are quite different on the criteria.

methodological congruence: This describes the interconnectedness and interrelatedness of a study purpose, questions, and methods that appears cohesive rather than as fragmented parts (Morse & Richards, 2002; Richards & Morse, 2013).

methodological assumption: This philosophical assumption relates to how researchers go about qualitative procedures in a study. A qualitative inquirer relies on views of participants and discusses their views within the context in which they occur, to inductively develop ideas in a study from particulars to abstractions.

methods of data collection: This is a general term describing the ways in which researchers generate data. Common techniques for gathering qualitative data include observations, interviews, focus groups, questionnaires, records, documents, and social media data.

multifaceted experiences: This represents the diverse and varied experiences that individually and collectively influence what researchers bring to their inquiries, including, but not limited to, their personal histories, cultural assumptions, research traditions, views of themselves and others, and ethical and political issues.

observational protocol: This is a form used in qualitative data collection for guiding and recording observational data. It typically consists of two columns representing descriptive and reflective notes. The researcher records information from the observation on this form.

ontological assumption: This is a philosophical assumption about the nature of reality. It addresses this question: When is something real? The answer provided is that something is real in qualitative research when it is constructed in the minds of the actors involved in the situation (Guba & Lincoln, 1988). Thus, reality is not "out there," apart from the minds of actors.

overall writing structures: These are writing structures that provide the organizational framework for the reporting of research.

paradigm: This is the philosophical stance taken by the researcher that provides a basic set of beliefs that guides action (Guba, 1990). It defines, for its holder, "the nature of the world, the individual's place in it, and the range of possible relationships to that world" (Denzin & Lincoln, 1994, p. 107).

philosophical assumptions: These are stances taken by the researcher that provide direction for the study such as the researcher's view of reality (ontology), how the researcher knows reality (epistemology), the value-stance taken by the inquirer (axiology), and the procedures used in the study (methodology). These assumptions, in turn, are often applied in research through the theories (or, as we call them, interpretive frameworks).

postcolonial theory: This interpretive perspective intends to assess how knowledge production and theories of the past and the present have been shaped by ideas and power relations of imperialism, colonialism, neocolonialism, globalization, and racism.

postmodernism: This interpretive perspective is considered a family of theories and perspectives that have something in common (Slife & Williams, 1995). Postmodernists assert that knowledge claims must be set within the conditions of the world today and in the multiple perspectives of class, race, gender, and other group affiliations.

postpositivism: This interpretive perspective has the elements of being reductionistic, logical, empirical, cause-and-effect oriented, and deterministic based on a priori theories.

pragmatism: This interpretive lens focuses on the outcomes of the research—the actions, situations, and consequences of inquiry—rather than antecedent conditions. There is a concern with applications—"what works"—and solutions to problems. An important aspect of research is the problem being studied and the questions asked about this problem.

purpose statement: This is a statement typically found in an introduction to a qualitative study in which the author sets forth the major objective or intent of the study. It can be considered a "road map" to the entire study.

purposeful sampling: This is the primary sampling strategy used in qualitative research. It means that the inquirer selects individuals and sites for study because they can purposefully inform an understanding of the research problem and central phenomenon in the study.

qualitative data analysis software (QDAS): This is specialized software also called computer-assisted (or -aided) software with features supporting qualitative data analysis.

qualitative research: This is an inquiry process of understanding based on a distinct methodological approach to inquiry that explores a social or human problem. The researcher builds a complex, holistic picture; analyzes words; reports detailed views of participants; and conducts the study in a natural setting.

quality criteria: This involves the features we would expect to see in a "good" qualitative study. We acknowledge and describe some of the diverse perspectives within the qualitative community of these criteria in Chapter 10.

queer theory: This is an interpretive lens challenging the social and political constructions of sexualized and gender identity and how it is culturally and historically constituted, is linked to discourse, and overlaps gender and sexuality (Alexander, 2018; Watson, 2005).

reciprocity: This is an aspect of good data collection in which the author gives back to participants by providing rewards for their participation in the study. These rewards may be money or gifts or other forms of remuneration to cover their expenses such as parking, child care or transportation costs.

reflexivity: An active, ongoing process of engaging in critical reflection on how the researcher constructs knowledge from and during the research process. In writing a reflexive passage, the researcher discusses their experiences with the central phenomenon and then how these experiences may potentially shape the interpretation that the researcher provides. This passage can be written into a qualitative project in different places in the final report (e.g., methods, vignette, threaded throughout, at the end).

reliability: indicates that the qualitative researcher's approach is consistent across different researchers and among different projects using strategies such as intercoder reliability (Gibbs, 2018).

represent the data: This is a step in the data analysis process of packaging findings (codes, themes) into text, tabular, or figure form.

research design: We use this term to refer to the entire process of research, from conceptualizing a problem to writing the narrative, not simply the methods such as data collection, analysis, and report writing (Bogdan & Taylor, 1975).

research approaches: We use this term or methodologies to describe the procedures for research that span the steps from broad assumptions to detailed methods of data collection, analysis, and interpretation (Creswell & Creswell, 2023).

research ethics: The application of fundamental ethical principles to the planning and implementation of research. Researchers are often guided by three principles for conduct of ethical research: respect for persons, concern for welfare, and concern for justice, which require ongoing thought and judgment specific to each research project (Poth, 2021).

research focus: We use this term in reference to a general area of study interest such as a study objective or goal. This area of interest typically leads to the researcher narrowing the focus for the need of the study and the specific research problem.

research outcome: A research outcome in a study is the final product (e.g., individual stories,

research problem: A research problem typically introduces a qualitative study, and in this opening passage, the author advances the issue or concern that leads to a need to conduct the study. We discuss this problem as framed from a real-life perspective or a deficiency in the literature perspective.

research questions: These help researchers narrow the focus of their study and guide how qualitative researchers approach their study.

research strategies: These are called approaches in this book and we focus on five of them that have recognizable characteristics that guide researchers in their studies.

respect for persons: This ethical principle addresses the "treatment of persons and their data involved in the research process" (Poth, 2021, p. 15). This means we need to provide evidence in our study procedures of measures for respecting the privacy of participants and ensuring the consent process is clearly communicated, including the right of participants to withdraw from the study. Researchers should protect the interests of those who may be vulnerable.

rhetorical: This assumption means that the qualitative investigator uses terms and a narrative unique to the qualitative approach. The narrative is personal and literary (Creswell, 1994, 2009). For example, the researcher might use the first-person pronoun *I* instead of the impersonal third-person voice.

sample size: Sample size in qualitative research generally follows the guidelines to study a few individuals or sites, but to collect extensive detail about the individuals or sites studied.

social constructivism: In this interpretive framework, qualitative researchers seek understanding of the world in which they live and work. They develop subjective meanings of their experiences—meanings directed toward certain objects or things. These meanings are varied and multiple, leading the researcher to look for the complexity of views rather than narrow the meanings into a few categories or ideas. The goal of research, then, is to rely as much as possible on the participants' views of the situation. Often these subjective meanings are negotiated socially and historically.

social justice theories: These advocacy/participatory theories seek to bring about change or address social justice issues in our societies.

social science theories: These are the theoretical explanations that social scientists use to explain the world (Slife & Williams, 1995). They are based on empirical evidence that has accumulated in social science fields such as sociology, psychology, education, economics, urban studies, and communication.

subquestions: Subquestions are a form of research question in a qualitative study in which the researcher subdivides the central question into parts and examines these parts. These subquestions are often used in interview and observational protocols as the major topics.

themes: In qualitative research, themes are broad units of information that consist of several codes aggregated to form a common idea.

theories or theoretical orientations: They are found in literature and provide a general explanation as to what the researcher hopes to find in a study or a lens through which to view the needs of participants and communities in a study.

transformative framework: Researchers who use this interpretive framework advocate that knowledge is not neutral and it reflects the power and social relationships within society. Thus, the purpose of knowledge construction is to aid people to improve society (Mertens, 2003). These individuals include marginalized groups such as lesbian, gay, bisexual, transgender, and queer communities, and societies that need a more hopeful, positive psychology and resilience (Mertens, 2009, 2019).

triangulation: Researchers make use of multiple and different sources, methods, investigators, and theories to provide corroborating evidence for validating the accuracy of their study.

trustworthiness: This refers to the degree of confidence in the data and the methods used to collect them as well as the researcher's interpretations.

unit of analysis: This refers to the main subject or entity that the researcher intends to comment on, for example, an individual (and their experiences), a group of individuals, an organization or a society.

validity This refers in qualitative research to the checks for the accuracy of the findings by a qualitative researcher by employing certain procedures such as the strategies of triangulating data sources or conducting member checks (Creswell & Creswell, 2023).

validation strategies: These are procedures (e.g., member checking, triangulating data sources) that together are used by qualitative researchers to establish the accuracy of their findings and provide evidence to readers of this accuracy.

verisimilitude: This is a criterion for a good literary study, in which the writing seems "real" and "alive," transporting the reader directly into the world of the study (Richardson, 1994).

writing structures: These are common structures for guiding the writing process of a proposal or report. Each of the qualitative approaches has different yet common writing structures.

REFERENCES

Aanstocs, C. M. (1985). The structure of thinking in chess. In A. Giorgi (Ed.), *Phenomenology and psychological research* (pp. 86–117). Duquesne University Press.

Abrams, J. A., Tabaac, A., Jung, S., & Else-Quest, N. M. (2020). Considerations for employing intersectionality in qualitative health research. *Social Science & Medicine*, *258*, Article 113138. https://doi.org/10.10´6/j.socscimed.2020.113138

Adams, J., Braun, V., & McCreanor, T. (2014). "Aren't labels for pick.e jars, not people?" Negotiating identity and community in talk about "being gay." *American Journal of Men's Health*, *8*(6), 457–469. https://doi.org/10.1177/1557988313518800

Adler-Nissen, R., & Eggeling, K. A. (2022). Blended diplomacy: The entanglement and contestation of digital technologies in everyday diplomatic practice. *European Journal of International Relations*, *28*(3), 640–666. https://doi.org/10.1177/13540661221107837

Adolph, S., Kruchten, P., & Hall, W. (2012). Reconciling perspectives: A grounded theory of how people manage the process of software development. *Journal of Systems and Software*, *85*(6), 1269–1286. https://doi.org/10.1016/j.jss.2012.01.059

Agar, M. H. (1980). *The professional stranger: An informal introduction to ethnography*. Academic.

Agar, M. H. (1986). *Speaking of ethnography*. Sage.

Agar, M. H. (1996). *The professional stranger: An informal introduction to ethnography* (2nd ed.). Academic.

Agger, B. (1991). Critical theory, poststructuralism, postmodernism: Their sociological relevance. In W. R. Scott & J. Blake (Eds.), *Annual review of sociology* (Vol. 17, pp. 105–131). Annual Reviews.

Alexander, B. K. (2018). Queer/quare theory: Worldmaking and methodologies. In N. K. Denzin & Y. S. Lincoln (Eds.), *The SAGE handbook of qualitative research* (5th ed., pp. 275–308). Sage.

American Psychological Association. (2017). *Publication manual of the American Psychological Association* (6th ed.). Author.

American Psychological Association. (2020). *Publication manual of the American Psychological Association* (7th ed.). Author.

Anderson, R. A., Toles, M. P., Corazzini, K., McDaniel, R. R., & Colon-Emeric, C. (2014). Local interaction strategies and capacity for better care in nursing homes: A multiple case study. *BMC Health Services Research*, *14*, 244–261. https://doi.org/10.1186/1472-6963-14-244

Angen, M. J. (2000). Evaluating interpretive inquiry: Reviewing the validity debate and opening the dialogue. *Qualitative Health Research*, *10*(3), 378–395. https://doi.org/10.1177/104973230001000308

Angrosino, M. V. (2007). *Doing ethnographic and observational research*. Sage.

Annamma, S. A., Handy, T., Miller, A. L., & Jackson, E. (2020). Animating discipline disparities through debilitating practices: Girls of color and inequitable classroom interactions. *Teachers College Record*, *122*(5), 1–46. https://doi.org/10.1177/016146812012200512

Armstrong, D., Gosling, A., Weinman, J., & Marteau, T. (1997). The place of inter-rater reliability in qualitative research: An empirical study. *Sociology*, *31*(3), 597–606. https://doi.org/10.1177/0038038597031003015

Arur, A., & DeJaeghere. J. (2019). Decolonizing life skills education for girls in Brahmanical India: A Dalitbahujan perspective. *Gender and Education*, *31*(4), 490–507. https://doi.org/10.1080/09540253.2019.1594707

Asgeirsdottir, G. H., Sigurbjornsson, E., Traustadottir, R., Sigurdartottir, V.,

Gunnardottir, S., & Kelly, E. (2013). "To cherish each day as it comes": A qualitative study of spirituality among persons receiving palliative care. *Support Cancer Care*, *21*, 1445–1451. https://doi.org/10.1007/s00520-012-1690-6. Are we missing a name here in the author list?

Asmussen, K. J., & Creswell, J. W. (1995). Campus response to a student gunman. *Journal of Higher Education*, *66*(5), 575–591. https://doi.org/10.1080/00221546.1995.11774799

Atkinson, P. A. (2015). *For ethnography*. Sage.

Atkinson, P., & Hammersley, M. (1994). Ethnography and participant observation. In N. K. Denzin & Y. S. Lincoln (Eds.), *Handbook of qualitative research* (pp. 248–261). Sage.

Banfield, G. (2020). Critical realism for ethnography. In G. Noblit (Ed.), *The Oxford encyclopedia of qualitative research methods in education* (pp. 1034–1068). Oxford University Press. https://doi.org/10.1093/acrefore/9780190264093.013.543

Banks, M. (2014). Analysing images. In U. Flick (Ed.), *The SAGE handbook of qualitative data analysis* (pp. 394–408). Sage.

Barbour, R. S. (2000). The role of qualitative research in broadening the "evidence base" for clinical practice. *Journal of Evaluation in Clinical Practice*, *6*(2), 155–163. https://doi.org/10.1046/j.1365-2753.2000.00213.x

Bauer, W. M., & Gaskell, G. (Eds.). (2007). *Qualitative research with text, image and sound: A practical handbook for social research*. Sage.

Baxter, P., & Jack, S. (2008). Qualitative case study methodology: Study design and implementation for novice researchers. *The Qualitative Report*, *13*(2), 544–559. http://www.nova.edu/ssss/QR/QR13-4/baxter.pdf

Bazeley, P. (2002). The evolution of a project involving an integrated analysis of structured qualitative and quantitative data: From N3 to NVivo. *International Journal of Social Research Methodology*, *5*(3), 229–243. http://dx.doi.org/10.1080/13645570210146285

Bazeley, P. (2013). *Qualitative data analysis: Practical strategies*. Sage.

Bazeley, P. (2021). *Qualitative data analysis: Practical strategies*. (2nd ed.). Sage.

Beck, C. T. (2020). *Introduction to phenomenology*. Sage.

Berger, R. (2015). Now I see it, now I don't: Researcher's position and reflexivity in qualitative research. *Qualitative Research*, *15*(2), 219–234. https://doi.org/10.1177/1468794112468475

Bernard, H. R. (2017). *Research methods in anthropology: Qualitative and quantitative approaches* (6th ed.). Rowman & Littlefield.

Bernard, H. R., & Ryan, G. W. (2016). *Analyzing qualitative data: Systemic approaches* (2nd ed.). Sage.

Bettcher, T. A. (2015). Intersexuality, transgender, and transsexuality. In L. Disc & M. Hawkesworth (Ed.). *The Oxford handbook of feminist theory* (pp. 407–427). Oxford University Press.

Bidabadi, F. S., Yazdannik, A., & Zargham-Boroujeni, A. (2019). Patient's dignity in intensive care unit: A critical ethnography. *Nursing Ethics*, *26*(3), 738–752. https://doi.org/10.1177/0969733017720826

Birks, M., & Mills, J. (2023). *Grounded theory: A practical guide* (3rd ed.). Sage.

Bloland, H. G. (1995). Postmodernism and higher education. *Journal of Higher Education*, *66*(5), 521–559. https://doi.org/10.1080/00221546.1995.11774797

Bloomberg, L. D. (2022). *Completing your qualitative dissertation* (5th ed.). Sage

Bogdan, R. C., & Biklen, S. K. (1992). *Qualitative research for education: An introduction to theory and methods*. Allyn & Bacon.

Bogdan, R., & Taylor, S. (1975). *Introduction to qualitative research methods*. Wiley.

Bogdewic, S. P. (1999). Participant observation. In B. F. Crabtree & W. Miller (Eds.), *Doing qualitative research* (2nd ed., pp. 47–70). Sage

Borgatta, E. F., & Borgatta, M. L. (Eds.). (1992). *Encyclopedia of sociology* (Vol. 4). Macmillan.

Bradbury, H. (2015). *The SAGE handbook of action research*. Sage.

Braun, V., & Clarke, V. (2006). Using thematic analysis in psychology. *Qualitative Research in Psychology*, *3*(2), 77–101. https://doi.org/10.1191/1478088706qp063oa

Brimhall, A. C., & Engblom-Deglmann, M. L. (2011). Starting over: A tentative theory exploring the effects of past relationships on postbereavement remarried couples. *Family Process*, *50*(1), 47–62. https://doi.org/10.1111/j.1545-5300.2010.01345.x

Brinkmann, S. (2018). The interview. In N. K Denzin & Y. S. Lincoln (Eds.), *The SAGE handbook of qualitative research* (pp. 576–599). Sage.

Brinkmann, S., & Kvale, S. (2015). *InterViews: Learning the craft of qualitative research interviewing* (3rd ed.). Sage.

Brisolara, S. (2014). Feminist theory: Its domain and applications. In S. Brisolara, D. Seigart, & S. SenGupta (Eds.), *Feminist evaluation and research: Theory and practice* (pp. 3–41). Guilford.

Brisolara, S., Seigart, D., & SenGupta, S. (Eds.). (2014). *Feminist evaluation and research: Theory and practice*. Guilford.

Brown, J., Sorrell, J. H., McClaren, J., & Creswell, J. W. (2006). Waiting for a liver transplant. *Qualitative Health Research*, *16*(1), 119–136. https://doi.org/10.1177/1049732305284011

Bryant, A., & Charmaz, K. (2007a). Grounded theory in historical perspective: An epistemological account. In A. Bryant & K. Charmaz (Eds.), *The SAGE handbook of grounded theory* (pp. 31–57). Sage.

Bryant, A., & Charmaz, K. (Eds.). (2007b). *The SAGE handbook of grounded theory*. Sage.

Bryant, A., & Charmaz, K. (Eds.). (2019). *The SAGE handbook of current developments in grounded theory*. Sage.

Burr, V. (2015). *Social constructionism* (3rd ed.). Routledge.

Caine, V., Clandinin, D. J., & Lessard, S. (2022). *Narrative inquiry: Philosophical roots*. Sage.

Campbell, J. L., Quincy, C., Osserman, J., & Pederson, O. K. (2013). Coding in-depth semistructured interviews: Problems of unitization and intercoder reliability and agreement. *Sociological Methods & Research*, *42*(3), 294–320. https://doi.org/10.1177/0049124113500475

Carspecken, P. F., & Apple, M. (1992). Critical qualitative research: Theory, methodology, and practice. In M. L. LeCompte, W. L. Millroy, & J. Preissle (Eds.), *The handbook of qualitative research in education* (pp. 507–553). Academic.

Carter, K. (1993). The place of a story in the study of teaching and teacher education. *Educational Researcher*, *22*(1), 5–18. https://doi.org/10.3102/0013189X022001005

Chan, E. (2010). Living in the space between participant and researcher as a narrative inquirer: Examining ethnic identity of Chinese Canadian students as conflicting stories to live by. *The Journal of Educational Research*, *103*(2), 113–122. https://doi.org/10.1080/00220670903323792

Chance, N. L. (2022). Resilient leadership: A phenomenological exploration into how Black women in higher education leadership navigate cultural adversity. *Journal of Humanistic Psychology*, *62*(1), 44–78. https://doi.org/10.1177/00221678211003000

Chapman, T. K., & Crawford, J. (2023). Scholar activism in critical race theory in education. In M. Lynn and A. D. Dixson (Eds), *Handbook of critical race theory in education* (2nd ed., pp. 79–90). Routledge.

Charmaz, K. (2005). Grounded theory in the 21st century: Applications for advancing social justice studies. In N. K. Denzin & Y. S. Lincoln (Eds.), *The SAGE handbook of qualitative research* (3rd ed., pp. 507–536). Sage.

Charmaz, K. (2006). *Constructing grounded theory*. Sage.

Charmaz, K. (2014). *Constructing grounded theory* (2nd ed.). Sage.

Chase, S. (2005). Narrative inquiry: Multiple lenses, approaches, voices. In N. K. Denzin & Y. S. Lincoln (Eds.), *The SAGE handbook of qualitative research* (3rd ed., pp. 651–680). Sage.

Chase, S. (2018). Narrative inquiry: Toward theoretical and methodological maturity. In N. K. Denzin & Y. S. Lincoln (Eds.), *The SAGE handbook of qualitative research* (5th ed., pp. 546–560).

Cheek, J. (2004). At the margins? Discourse analysis and qualitative research. *Qualitative Health Research*, *14*(8), 1140–1150. https://doi.org/10.1177/1049732304266820

Chenitz, W. C., & Swanson, J. M. (1986). *From practice to grounded theory: Qualitative research in nursing*. Addison-Wesley.

Chepp, V. (2015). Black feminist theory and the politics of irreverence: The case of women's rap. *Feminist Theory*, *16*(2), 207-226. https://doi.org/10.1177/1464700115585705

Cherryholmes, C. H. (1992). Notes on pragmatism and scientific realism. *Educational Researcher*, *21*(6), 13-17. https://doi.org/10.3102/0013189X021006013

Chilisa, B. (2020). *Indigenous research methodologies* (2nd ed.). Sage.

Chilisa, B., & Mertens, D. M. (2021). Indigenous made in Africa evaluation frameworks: Addressing epistemic violence and contributing to social transformation. *American Journal of Evaluation*, *42*(2), 241-253.

Chilisa, B., & Phatshwane, K. (2022). Qualitative research within a postcolonial Indigenous paradigm. In U. Flick (Ed.), *The SAGE handbook of qualitative research design* (pp. 225-240). Sage.

Chipango, E. F. (2021). Constructing, understanding and interpreting energy poverty in Zimbabwe: A postmodern perspective. *Energy Research & Social Science*, *75*, Article 102026. https://doi.org/10.1016/j.erss.2021.102026

Chirgwin, S. K. (2015). Burdens too difficult to carry? A case study of three academically able Indigenous Australian masters students who had to withdraw. *International Journal of Qualitative Studies in Education*, *28*(5), 594-609. https://doi.org/10.1080/09518398.2014.916014

Christians, C. (2018). A history of qualitative inquiry in social and educational research. In N. K. Denzin & Y. S. Lincoln (Eds.), *The SAGE handbook of qualitative research* (5th ed., pp. 36-65). Sage.

Churchill, S. L., Plano Clark, V. L., Prochaska-Cue, M. K., Creswell, J. W., & Onta-Grzebik, L. (2007). How rural low-income families have fun: A grounded theory study. *Journal of Leisure Research*, *39*(2), 271-294. https://doi.org/10.1080/00222216.2007.11950108

Clandinin, D. J. (Ed.). (2007). *Handbook of narrative inquiry: Mapping a methodology*. Sage.

Clandinin, D. J. (2013). *Engaging in narrative inquiry*. Left Coast.

Clandinin, D. J. (2023). *Engaging in narrative inquiry* (2nd ed). Routledge.

Clandinin, D. J., & Caine, V. (2013). Narrative inquiry. In A. Trainor & E. Graue (Eds.), *Reviewing qualitative research in the social sciences* (pp. 188-202). Taylor & Francis/Routledge.

Clandinin, D. J., & Connelly, F. M. (2000). *Narrative inquiry: Experience and story in qualitative research*. Jossey-Bass.

Clandinin, D. J., Huber, J., Huber, M., Murphy, M. S., Murray Orr, A., Pearce, M., & Steeves, P. (2006). *Composing diverse identities: Narrative inquiries into the interwoven lives of children and teachers*. Routledge.

Clarke, A. E. (2005). *Situational analysis: Grounded theory after the postmodern turn*. Sage.

Clarke, A. E., Friese, C., & Washburn, R. (Eds.). (2015). *Situational analysis practice: Mapping research with grounded theory*. Routledge.

Clarke, A. E., Friese, C., & Washburn, R. (Eds.). (2017). *Situational analysis: Grounded theory after the interpretive turn* (2nd ed.). Sage.

Clifford, J., & Marcus, G. E. (Eds.). (1986). *Writing culture: The poetics and politics of ethnography*. University of California Press.

Colaizzi, P. F. (1978). Psychological research as the phenomenologist views it. In R. Vaile & M. King (Eds.), *Existential phenomenological alternatives for psychology* (pp. 48-71). Oxford University Press.

Collins, C. S., & Stockton, C. M. (2018). The central role of theory in qualitative research. *International Journal of Qualitative Methods*, *17*(1), 1-10. https://doi.org/10.1177/1609406918797475

Connelly, F. M., & Clandinin, D. J. (1990). Stories of experience and narrative inquiry. *Educational Researcher*, *19*(5), 2-14. https://doi.org/10.3102/0013189X019005002

Conrad, C. F. (1978). A grounded theory of academic change. *Sociology of Education*, *51*(2), 101-112. https://doi.org/10.2307/2112242

Corbin, J., & Strauss, A. (1990). Grounded theory research: Procedures, canons, and evaluative criteria. *Qualitative Sociology*, *13*(1), 3-21. https://doi.org/10.1007/BF00988593

Corbin, J., & Strauss, A. (2007). *Basics of qualitative research: Techniques and* procedures for developing grounded theory (3rd ed.). Sage.

Corbin, J., & Strauss, A. (2015). *Basics of qualitative research: Techniques and procedures for developing grounded theory* (4th ed.). Sage.

Cortazzi, M. (1993). *Narrative analysis*. Falmer.

Crabtree, B. F., & Miller, W. L. (2022). *Doing qualitative research* (3rd ed.). Sage.

Creamer, E. G. (2022). *Advancing grounded theory with mixed methods*. Routledge.

Creswell, J. W. (1994). *Research design: Qualitative and quantitative approaches*. Sage.

Creswell, J. W. (2009). *Research design: Qualitative, quantitative, and mixed methods approaches* (3rd ed.). Sage.

Creswell, J. W. (2013). *Qualitative inquiry & research design: Choosing among the five approaches* (3rd ed.). Sage.

Creswell, J. W. (2014). *Educational research: Planning, conducting, and evaluating quantitative and qualitative research* (5th ed.). Pearson.

Creswell, J. W. (2018). *Research design: Qualitative, quantitative, and mixed methods approaches* (5th ed.). Sage.

Creswell, J. W. (2021). *A concise introduction to mixed methods research* (2nd ed.). Sage.

Creswell, J. W., & Báez, J. (2021). *30 essential skills for the qualitative researcher* (2nd ed.). Sage.

Creswell, J. W., & Brown, M. L. (1992). How chairpersons enhance faculty research: A grounded theory study. *Review of Higher Education*, *16*(1), 41–62. https://doi.org/10.1353/rhe.1992.0002

Creswell, J. W., & Creswell, J. D. (2023). *Research design: Qualitative, quantitative, and mixed methods approaches* (6th ed.). Sage.

Creswell, J. W., & Guetterman, T. C. (2019). *Educational research: Planning, conducting, and evaluating quantitative and qualitative research* (6th ed.). Pearson.

Creswell, J. W., & Miller, D. L. (2000). Determining validity in qualitative inquiry. *Theory Into Practice*, *39*(3), 124–130. https://doi.org/10.1207/s15430421tip3903_2

Creswell, J. W., & Plano Clark, V. L. (2018). *Designing and conducting mixed methods research* (3rd ed.). Sage.

Critelli, F. M., Lewis, L. A., Yalim, A. C., & Ibraeva, J. (2021). Labor migration and its impact on families in Kyrgyzstan: A qualitative study. *Journal of International Migration and Integration*, *22*, 907–928. https://doi.org/10.1007/s12134-020-00781-2

Crotty, M. (1998). *The foundations of social research: Meaning and perspective in the research process*. Sage.

Cypress, B. (2019). Data analysis software in qualitative research: Preconceptions, expectations and adoption. *Dimensions of Critical Care Nursing*, *38*(4), 213–220. https://doi.org/10.1097/DCC.0000000000000363

Czarniawska, B. (2004). *Narratives in social science research*. Sage.

Daiute, C. (2014). *Narrative inquiry: A dynamic approach*. Sage.

Daiute, C., & Lightfoot, C. (Eds.). (2004). *Narrative analysis: Studying the development of individuals in society*. Sage.

Darcy, S., Collins, J., & Stronach, M. (2022). Entrepreneurs with disability: Australian insights through a social ecology lens. *Small Enterprise Research*, *30*(1), 24–48. https://doi.org/10.1080/13215906.2022.2092888

Davidson, J., & di Gregorio, S. (2011). Qualitative research, technology, and global change. In N. K. Denzin & M. D. Giardina (Eds.), *Qualitative inquiry and global crises* (pp. 79–96). Left Coast.

Deem, R. (2002). Talking to manager-academics: Methodological dilemmas and feminist research strategies. *Sociology*, *36*(4), 835–855. https://doi.org/10.1177/0038038502036004003

de Lauretis, T. (1991). Queer theory: Lesbian and gay sexualities. *Differences: A Journal of Feminist Cultural Studies*, *3*(2), iii–xviii.

Delgado, R., & Stefancic, J. (2023). *Critical race theory: An introduction* (4th ed.). New York University Press.

Denzin, N. K. (1989). *Interpretive biography*. Sage.

Denzin, N. K. (2001). *Interpretive interactionism* (2nd ed.). Sage.

Denzin, N. K., & Lincoln, Y. S. (Eds.). (1994). *Handbook of qualitative research*. Sage.

Denzin, N. K., & Lincoln, Y. S. (Eds.). (2000). Handbook of

qualitative research (2nd ed.). Sage.

Denzin, N. K., & Lincoln, Y. S. (Eds.). (2005). *The SAGE handbook of qualitative research* (3rd ed.). Sage.

Denzin, N. K., & Lincoln, Y. S. (2011a). Introduction: The discipline and practice of qualitative research. In N. K. Denzin & Y. S. Lincoln (Eds.), *The SAGE handbook of qualitative research* (4th ed., pp. 1–19). Sage.

Denzin, N. K., & Lincoln, Y. S. (Eds.). (2011b). *The SAGE handbook of qualitative research* (4th ed.). Sage.

Denzin, N. K., & Lincoln, Y. S. (2013). *Strategies of qualitative inquiry*. Sage.

Denzin, N. K., & Lincoln, Y. S. (2018a). Introduction: The discipline and practice of qualitative research. In N. K. Denzin & Y. S. Lincoln (Eds.), *The SAGE handbook of qualitative research* (5th ed., pp. 1–26). Sage.

Denzin, N. K., & Lincoln, Y. S. (Eds.). (2018b). *The SAGE handbook of qualitative research* (5th ed.). Sage.

Denzin, N. K., Lincoln, Y. S., Giardina, M. D., & Cannella, G. S. (Eds.). (2023). *The SAGE handbook of qualitative research* (6th ed.). Sage.

De Santis, D., Hopkins, B. D., & Majolino, C. (Eds.). (2021). *The Routledge handbook of phenomenology and phenomenological philosophy*. Routledge.

DeVault, M. L. (2018). Feminist qualitative research: Emerging lines of inquiry. In N. K. Denzin & Y. S. Lincoln (Eds.), *The SAGE handbook of qualitative research* (5th ed., pp. 176–194). Sage.

Dewey, J. (1938). *Experience and education*. Simon & Schuster.

Dey, I. (1993). *Qualitative data analysis: A user-friendly guide for social scientists*. Routledge.

Dey, I. (1995). Reducing fragmentation in qualitative research. In U. Keele (Ed.), *Computer-aided qualitative data analysis* (pp. 69–79). Sage.

Donnor, J., & Ladson-Billings, G. (2018). Critical race theory scholarship and the post-racial imaginary. In N. K. Denzin & Y. S. Lincoln (Eds.), *The SAGE handbook of qualitative research* (5th ed., pp. 195–213). Sage.

Dukes, S. (1984). Phenomenological methodology in the human sciences. *Journal of Religion and Health, 23*(3), 197–203. https://doi.org/10.1007/BF00990785

Edel, L. (1984). *Writing lives: Principia biographica*. Norton.

Edwards, L. V. (2006). Perceived social support and HIV/AIDS medication adherence among African American women. *Qualitative Health Research, 1*(5),, 679–691. https://doi.org/10.1177/1049732305281597

Eisner, E. W. (1991). *The enlightened eye: Qualitative inquiry and the enhancement of educational practice*. Macmillan.

Eisner, E. W. (2017). *The enlightened eye: Qualitative inquiry and the enhancement of educational practice*. Macmillan.

Elliott, J. (2005). *Using narrative in social research: Qualitative and quantitative approaches*. Sage.

Ellis, C. (1993). "There are survivors": Telling a story of sudden death. *The Sociological Quarterly, 34*(4), 711–730. https://doi.org/10.1111/j.1533-8525.1993.tb00114.x

Ellis, C. (2004). *The ethnographic it: A methodological novel about autoethnography*. AltaMira.

Ely, M., Anzul, M., Friedman, T., Garner, D., & Steinmetz, A. C. (1991). *Doing qualitative research: Circles within circles*. Falmer.

Emerson, R. M., Fretz, R. I., & Shaw, L. L. (2011). *Writing ethnographic fieldnotes* (2nd ed.). University of Chicago Press.

Erlandson, D. A., Harris, E. L., Skipper, B. L., & Allen, S. D. (1993). *Doing naturalistic inquiry: A guide to methods*. Sage.

Esposito, J., & Evans-Winters, V. (2021). *Introduction to intersectional qualitative research*. Sage.

Estrada, M. L., & Koolen, M. (2018). Audiovisual media annotation using qualitative data analysis software: A comparative analysis. *The Qualitative Report, 23*(13), 40–60. https://nsuworks.nova.edu/tqr/vol23/iss13/4

Evers, J. C. (2018). Current issues in qualitative data analysis software (QDAS): A user and developer perspective. *The Qualitative Report, 23*(13), 61–73. https://doi.org/10.46743/2160-3715/2018.3205

Evers, J., Caprioli, M. U., Nost, S., & Wiedemann, G. (2020). What is the REFI-QDA standard: Experimenting with the transfer of analyzed research projects between QDA software. *Qualitative Social Research*, *21*(2). https://www.qualitative-research.net/index.php/fqs/article/view/3439/4599

Ezeh, P. J. (2003). Participant observation. *Qualitative Research*, *3*(2), 191–205. https://doi.org/10.1177/14687941030032003

Fabricius, A. H. (2014). The transnational and the individual: A life-history narrative in a Danish university context. *Journal of Education for Teaching: International Research and Pedagogy*, *40*(3), 284–299. https://doi.org/10.1080/02607476.2014.903027

Fay, B. (1987). *Critical social science*. Cornell University Press.

Fetterman, D. M. (2010). *Ethnography: Step-by-step* (3rd ed.). Sage.

Fetterman, D. M. (2019). *Ethnography: Step-by-step* (4th ed.). Sage.

Fielding, N. G., Lee, R. M., & Blank, G. (Eds.). (2017). *The SAGE handbook of online research methods* (2nd ed.). Sage.

Fischer, C. T., & Wertz, F. J. (1979). An empirical phenomenology study of being criminally victimized. In A. Giorgi, R. Knowles, & D. Smith (Eds.), *Duquesne studies in phenomenological psychology* (Vol. 3, pp. 135–158). Duquesne University Press.

Flick, U. (Ed.). (2014). *The SAGE handbook of qualitative analysis*. Sage.

Flick, U. (Ed.). (2018). *The SAGE handbook of qualitative data collection*. Sage.

Flick, U. (2023). *An introduction to qualitative research* (7th ed.). Sage.

Flyvbjerg, B. (2006). Five misunderstandings about case-study research. *Qualitative Inquiry*, *12*(2), 219–245. https://doi.org/10.1177/1077800405284363

Foucault, M. (1972). *The archeology of knowledge and the discourse on language* (A. M. Sheridan Smith, Trans.). Harper.

Fox-Keller, E. (1985). *Reflections on gender and science*. Yale University Press.

Frankl, V. (1997). *Man's search for ultimate meaning*. Plenum.

Frelin, A. (2015). Relational underpinnings and professionality—A case study of a teacher's practices involving students with experiences of school failure. *School Psychology International*, *36*(6), 589–604. https://doi.org/10.1177/0143034315607412

Friese, S. (2019). *Qualitative data analysis with ATLAS.ti* (3rd ed.). Sage.

Friese, S. (2022). Role and impact of CAQDAS Software for designs in qualitative research. In U. Flick (Ed.), *The SAGE handbook of qualitative research design* (pp. 307–326). Sage.

Garcia, A. C., Standlee, A. I., Bechkoff, J., & Cui, Y. (2009). Ethnographic approaches to the Internet and computer-mediated communication. *Journal of Contemporary Ethnography*, *38*(1), 52–84. https://doi.org/10.1177/0891241607310839

García-Rapp, F. (2019). Trivial and normative? Online fieldwork within YouTube's beauty community. *Journal of Contemporary Ethnography*, *48*(5), 619–644. https://doi.org/10.1177/0891241618806974

Gee, J. P. (1991). A linguistic approach to narrative. *Journal of Narrative and Life History*, *1*(1), 15–39. https://doi.org/10.1075/jnlh.1.1.03ali

Geiger, S. N. G. (1986). Women's life histories: Method and content. *Signs: Journal of Women in Culture and Society*, *11*(2), 334–351. http://www.jstor.org/stable/3174056

Gergen, K. (1994). *Realities and relationships: Soundings in social construction*. Harvard University Press.

Gergen, K. J. (2023). *An invitation to social construction: Co-creating the future* (4th ed.). Sage.

Gibbs, G. R. (2014). Using software in qualitative analysis. In U. Flick (Ed.), *The SAGE handbook of qualitative data analysis* (pp. 277–294). Sage.

Gibbs, G. (2018). Analyzing qualitative data. In U. Flick (Ed.), *The SAGE qualitative research kit* (2nd ed.). Sage.

Gilbert, L. S., Jackson, K., & di Gregorio, S. (2014). Tools for analyzing qualitative data: The history and relevance of qualitative data analysis software. In J. M. Spector, M. D. Merrill, J. Elen, & M. J. Bishop (Eds.), *Handbook of research on educational communications and technology (4th ed., pp. 221–236). Springer Science+Business Media.

Gilgun, J. F. (2005). "Grab" and good science: Writing up the results of qualitative research. *Qualitative Health Research*, *15*(2), 256–262. https://doi.org/10.1177/1049732304268796

Giorgi, A. (Ed.). (1985). *Phenomenology and psychological research*. Duquesne University Press.

Giorgi, A. (1994). A phenomenological perspective on certain qualitative research methods. *Journal of Phenomenological Psychology*, *25*(2), 190–220. https://doi.org/10.1163/156916294X00034

Giorgi, A. (2009). *The descriptive phenomenological method in psychology: A modified Husserlian approach*. Duquesne University Press.

Glaser, B. G. (1978). *Theoretical sensitivity*. Sociology Press.

Glaser, B. G. (1992). *Basics of grounded theory analysis*. Sociology Press.

Glaser, B. G., & Strauss, A. L. (1965). *Awareness of dying*. Aldine.

Glaser, B. G., & Strauss, A. L. (1967). *The discovery of grounded theory*. Aldine.

Glaser, B. G., & Strauss, A. L. (1968). *Time for dying*. Aldine.

Glesne, C. (2016). *Becoming qualitative researchers: An introduction* (5th ed.). Pearson.

Glesne, C., & Peshkin, A. (1992). *Becoming qualitative researchers: An introduction*. Longman.

Goffman, A. (2014). *On the run: Fugitive life in an American city*. University of Chicago Press.

Goffman. E. (1989). On fieldwork. *Journal of Contemporary Ethnography*, *18*(2), 123–132.

Gomm, R., Hammersley, M., & Foster, P. (Eds.). (2000). *Case study method: Key issues, key texts*. Sage.

Goodrum, S., Slepicka, J., Woodward, W., & Kingston, B. (2022). Learning from error in violence prevention: A school shooting as an organizational accident. *Sociology of Education*, *95*(4), 257–275. https://doi.org/10.1177/00380407221120431

Gorski, P. C., & Pothini, S. G. (2018). *Future directions for case studies: Case studies on diversity and social justice in education*. Routledge.

Grande, S. (2000). American Indian identity and intellectualism: The quest for a new red pedagogy. *Qualitative Studies in Education*, *13*(4), 343–359.

Grbich, C. (2013). *Qualitative data analysis: An introduction* (2nd ed.). Sage.

Gready, P. (2013). The public life of narratives: Ethics, politics, methods. In M. Andrews, C. Squire, & M. Tamboukou (Eds.), *Doing narrative research* (2nd ed., pp. 240–254). Sage.

Grigsby, K. A., & Megel, M. E. (1995). Caring experiences of nurse educators. *Journal of Nursing Research*, *34*(9), 411–418. https://doi.org/10.3928/0148-4834-19951201-05

Guba, E. G. (1990). The alternative paradigm dialog. In E. G. Guba (Ed.), *The paradigm dialog* (pp. 17–30). Sage.

Guba, E. G., & Lincoln, Y. S. (1988). Do inquiry paradigms imply inquiry methodologies? In D. M. Fetterman (Ed.), *Qualitative approaches to evaluation in education* (pp. 89–115). Praeger.

Guba, E. G., & Lincoln, Y. S. (1989). *Fourth generation evaluation*. Sage.

Guell, C., & Ogilvie, D. (2015). Picturing commuting: Photovoice and seeking well-being in everyday travel. *Qualitative Research*, *15*(2), 201–218. https://doi.org/10.1177/1468794112468472

Guest, G., Namey, E. E., & Mitchell, M. L. (2013). *Collecting qualitative data: A field manual for applied research*. Sage.

Hacker, K. (2013). *Community-based participatory research*. Sage.

Hadley, G. (2019). Critical grounded theory. In A. Bryant & K. Charmaz (Eds.), *The SAGE handbook of current developments in grounded theory* (pp. 564–592). Sage.

Haenfler, R. (2004). Rethinking subcultural resistance: Core values of the straight edge movement. *Journal of Contemporary Ethnography*, *33*(4), 406–436. https://doi.org/10.1177/0891241603259809

Halfpenny, P., & Procter, R. (2015). *Innovations in digital research methods* (pp. 123–142). Sage.

Hamel, J., Dufour, S., & Fortin, D. (1993). *Case study methods*. Sage.

Hammersley, M., & Atkinson, P. (1995). *Ethnography: Principles in practice* (2nd ed.). Routledge.

Hammersley, M., & Atkinson, P. (2019). *Ethnography: Principles in practice* (4th ed.). Routledge.

Hammond, A., Priddis, H., Ormsby, S., & Dahlen, H. G. (2022). Improving women's experiences of perineal suturing: A pragmatic qualitative analysis of what is helpful and harmful. *Women and Birth*, *35*(6), e598–e606. https://doi.org/10.1016/j.wombi.2022.02.008

Harding, P. (2009). *Tinkers*. Bellevue Literary Press.

Harding, S. (1990). Feminism, science and the anti-enlightenment critiques. In L. J. Nicholson (Ed.), *Feminism/postmodernism*. Routledge.

Harding, S. (2012). Feminist standpoint. In S. N. Hesse-Biber (Ed.), *Handbook of feminist research: Theory and praxis* (2nd ed., pp. 46–64). Sage.

Harley, A. E., Buckworth, J., Katz, M. L., Willis, S. K., Odoms-Young, A., & Heaney, C. A. (2009). Developing long-term physical activity participation: A grounded theory study with African American women. *Health Education & Behavior*, *36*(1), 97–112. https://doi.org/10.1177/1090198107306434

Harper, W. (1981). The experience of leisure. *Leisure Sciences*, *4*(2), 113–126. https://doi.org/10.1080/01490408109512955

Harris, C. (1993). Whiteness as property. *Harvard Law Review*, *106*(8), 1701–1791. https://doi.org/10.2307/1341787

Hatch, J. A. (2002). *Doing qualitative research in education settings*. State University of New York Press.

Hayashi, P., Jr., Abib, G., & Hoppen, N. (2019). Validity in qualitative research: A processual approach. *The Qualitative Report*, *24*(1), 98–112.

Hays, D. G., & Singh, A. A. (2012). *Qualitative inquiry in clinical and educational settings*. Guilford.

Healey, G. K. (2014). Inuit family understandings of sexual health and relationships in Nunavut. *Canadian Journal of Public Health*, *105*(2), e133–e137. https://doi.org/10.17269/cjph.105.4189

Henderson, K. A. (2011). Post-positivism and the pragmatics of leisure research. *Leisure Sciences*, *33*(4), 341–346. https://doi.org/10.1080/01490400.2011.583166

Hesse-Biber, S. N. (2012). *Handbook of feminist research: Theory and praxis* (2nd ed.). Sage.

Hesse-Biber, S. N. (2016). *The practice of qualitative research* (3rd ed.). Sage

Hirani, S. A. A., & Wagner, J. (2022). Impact of COVID-19 on women who are refugees and mothering: A critical ethnographic study. *Global Qualitative Nursing Research*, *9*, 1–12. https://doi.org/10.1177/23333936221121335

Howe, K., & Eisenhardt, M. (1990). Standards for qualitative (and quantitative) research: A prolegomenon. *Educational Researcher*, *19*(4), 2–9. https://doi.org/10.3102/0013189X019004002

Hruschka, D., Schwartz, D., Cobb St. John, D., Picone-Decaro, E., Jenkins, R., & Carey, J. (2004). Reliability in coding open-ended data: Lessons learned from HIV behavioral research. *Field Methods*, *16*(3), 307–331. https://doi.org/10.1177/1525822X04266540

Huber, J., & Whelan, K. (1999). A marginal story as a place of possibility: Negotiating self on the professional knowledge landscape. *Teaching and Teacher Education*, *15*(4), 381–396. https://doi.org/10.1016/S0742-051X(98)00048-1

Huberman, A. M., & Miles, M. B. (1994). Data management and analysis methods. In N. K. Denzin & Y. S. Lincoln (Eds.), *Handbook of qualitative research* (pp. 428–444). Sage.

Huff, A. S. (2009). *Designing research for publication*. Sage.

Husserl, E. (1970). *The crisis of European sciences and transcendental phenomenology* (D. Carr, Trans.). Northwestern University Press.

Iphofen, R., & Tolich, M. (Eds.). (2018). *The SAGE handbook of qualitative research ethics*. Sage.

Ivankova, N. V. (2015). *Mixed methods applications in action research: From methods to community action*. Sage.

Jachyra, P., Atkinson, M., & Washiya, Y. (2015). "Who are you, and what are you doing here": Methodological considerations in ethnographic health and education research. *Ethnography and Education*, *10*(2), 242–261. https://doi.org/10.1080/17457823.2015.1018290

Jackson, K., & Bazeley, P. (2019). *Qualitative data analysis with NVivo* (3rd ed.) Sage.

Jacob, E. (1987). Qualitative research traditions: A review. *Review of Educational Research*, *57*(1), 1–50. https://doi.org/10.3102/00346543057001001

Janesick, V. J. (2016). *"Stretching" exercises for qualitative researchers* (4th ed.). Sage.

Job, J. M., Poth, C. A., Pei, J., Cassie, B., Brandell, D., & Macnab, J. (2013). Toward better collaboration in the education of students with fetal alcohol spectrum disorders: Integrating the voices of teachers, administrators, caregivers, and allied professionals. *Qualitative Research in Education*, *2*(1), 38–64. https://doi.org/10.4471/qre.2013.15

Job, J., Poth, C., Pei, J., Wyper, J., O'Riordan, T., & Taylor, L. (2014). Combining visual methods with focus groups: An innovative approach for capturing the multifaceted and complex work experiences of Fetal Alcohol Spectrum Disorder prevention specialists. *International Journal of Alcohol and Drug Research*, *3*(1), 71–80. https://doi.org/10.7895/ijadr.v3i1.129

Johnson, E. P., & Henderson, M. G. (Eds.). (2005). *Black queer studies*. Duke University Press.

Josselson, R., & Lieblich, A. (Eds.). (1993). *The narrative study of lives* (Vol. 1). Sage.

Jungnickel, K. (2014). Getting there . . . and back: How ethnographic commuting (by bicycle) shaped a study of Australian backyard technologists. *Qualitative Research*, *14*(6), 640–655. https://doi.org/10.1177/1468794113481792

Kemmis, S., & Wilkinson, M. (1998). Participatory action research and the study of practice. In B. Atweh, S. Kemmis, & P. Weeks (Eds.), *Action research in practice: Partnerships for social justice in education* (pp. 21–36). Routledge.

Kenny, M., & Fourie, R. (2014). Tracing the history of grounded theory methodology: From formation to fragmentation. *The Qualitative Report*, *19*(52), 1–9. http://www.nova.edu/ssss/QR/QR19/kenny103.pdf

Kidder, L. (1982). Face validity from multiple perspectives. In D. Brinberg & L. Kidder (Eds.), *New directions for methodology of social and behavioral science: Forms of validity in research* (pp. 41–57). Jossey-Bass.

Kim, J.-H. (2015). *Understanding narrative inquiry: The crafting and analysis of stories as research*. Sage.

Kincheloe, J. L. (2012). *Teachers as researchers: Qualitative inquiry as a path of empowerment*. Routledge. (Original work published 1991)

Knoblauch, H., Tuma, R., & Schnettler, B. (2014). Video analysis and videography. In U. Flick (Ed.), *The SAGE handbook of qualitative data analysis* (pp. 435–449). Sage.

Kroll, T., Barbour, R., & Harris, J. (2007). Using focus groups in disability research. *Qualitative Health Research*, *17*(5), 690–698. https://doi.org/10.1177/1049732307301488

Krueger, R. A., & Casey, M. A. (2014). *Focus groups: A practical guide for applied research* (5th ed.). Sage.

Kuckartz, U., & Rädiker, S. (2023). *Qualitative content analysis: Methods, practice and software* (2nd ed). Sage.

Kus, R. J. (1986). From grounded theory to clinical practice: Cases from gay studies research. In W. C. Chenitz & J. M. Swanson (Eds.), *From practice to grounded theory* (pp. 227–240). Addison-Wesley.

Labaree, R. V. (2002). The risk of "going observationalist": Negotiating the hidden dilemmas of being an insider participant observer. *Qualitative Research*, *2*(1), 97–122. https://doi.org/10.1177/146879410202001641

LaFrance, J., & Crazy Bull, C. (2009). Researching ourselves back to life: Taking control of the research agenda in Indian Country. In D. M. Mertens & P. E. Ginsburg (Eds.), *The handbook of social research ethics* (pp. 135–149). Sage.

Lancy, D. F. (1993). *Qualitative research in education: An introduction to the major traditions*. Longman.

Lather, P. (1991). *Getting smart: Feminist research and pedagogy with/in the postmodern*. Routledge.

Lather, P. (1993). Fertile obsession: Validity after poststructuralism. *Sociological Quarterly*, *34*(4), 673–693. https://doi.org/10.1111/j.1533-8525.1993.tb00112.x

Lauterbach, S. S. (1993). In another world: A phenomenological perspective and discovery of meaning in mothers' experience with death of a wished-for baby:

Doing phenomenology. In P. L. Munhall & C. O. Boyd (Eds.), *Nursing research: A qualitative perspective* (pp. 133–179). National League for Nursing Press.

Lavoie, M., & Caine, V. (2022). Contemplating framing: Unpacking the possibilities of printmaking in narrative inquiry. *International Review of Qualitative Research*, *15*(1), 42–61. https://doi.org/10.1177/19408447721991088

LeBlanc, A. M. (2017). Disruptive meaning-making: Qualitative data analysis software and postmodern pastiche. *Qualitative Inquiry*, *23*(10), 789–798. https://doi.org/10.1177/1077800417731087

LeCompte, M. D., & Goetz, J. P. (1982). Problems of reliability and validity in ethnographic research. *Review of Educational Research*, *52*(1), 31–60. https://doi.org/10.3102/00346543052001031

LeCompte, M. D., Millroy, W. L., & Preissle, J. (1992). *The handbook of qualitative research in education*. Academic.

LeCompte, M. D., & Schensul, J. J. (1999). *Designing and conducting ethnographic research: Ethnographer's toolkit*. (Vol. 1). AltaMira.

Leipert, B. D., & Reutter, L. (2005). Developing resilience: How women maintain their health in northern geographically isolated settings. *Qualitative Health Research*, *15*(1) 49–65. https://doi.org/10.1177/1049732304269671

Lempert, L. B. (2007). Asking questions of the data: Memo writing in the grounded theory tradition. In A. Bryant & K. Charmaz (Eds.), *The SAGE handbook of grounded theory* (pp. 245–264). Sage.

Levitt, H. M., Bamberger, M., Creswell, J. W., Frost, D. M., Josselson, R., & Suarez-Orozco, C. (2018). Journal article reporting standards for qualitative primary, qualitative meta-analytic, and mixed methods research in psychology: The APA publications and communications board task force report. *American Psychologist*, *73*(1), 26–46. http://dx.doi.org/10.1037/amp0000151

Levitt, H. M., Motulsky, S. L., Wertz, F. J., Morrow, S. L., & Ponterotto, J. G. (2017). Recommendations for designing and reviewing qualitative research in psychology: Promoting methodological integrity. *Qualitative Psychology*, *4*(1), 2–22. https://doi.org/10.1037/qup0000082

Lieberson, S. (2000). Small N's and big conclusions: An examination of the reasoning in comparative studies based on a small number of cases. In R. Gomm, M. Hammersley, & P. Foster (Eds.), *Case study method* (pp. 208–222). Sage.

Lieblich, A., Tuval-Mashiach, R., & Zilber, T. (1998). *Narrative research: Reading, analysis, and interpretation*. Sage.

Lincoln, Y. S. (1995). Emerging criteria for quality in qualitative and interpretive research. *Qualitative Inquiry*, *1*(3), 275–289. https://doi.org/10.1177/107780049500100301

Lincoln, Y. S. (2009). Ethical practices in qualitative research. In D. M. Mertens & P. E. Ginsberg (Eds.), *The handbook of social research ethics* (pp. 150–169). Sage.

Lincoln, Y. S., & Guba, E. G. (1985). *Naturalistic inquiry*. Sage.

Lincoln, Y. S., & Guba, E. G. (2000). Paradigmatic controversies, contradictions, and emerging confluences. In N. K. Denzin & Y. S. Lincoln (Eds.), *Handbook of qualitative research* (2nd ed.). Sage.

Lincoln, Y. S., Lynham, S. A., & Guga, E. G. (2011). Paradigmatic controversies, contradiction, and emerging confluences. In N. K. Denzin & Y. S. Lincoln (Eds.), *The SAGE handbook of qualitative research* (4th ed., pp. 97–128). Sage.

Lincoln, Y. S., Lynham, S. A., & Guba, E. G. (2018). Paradigmatic controversies, contradictions, and emerging confluences revisited. In N. K. Denzin & Y. S. Lincoln (Eds.), *The SAGE handbook of qualitative research* (5th ed., pp. 108–150). Sage.

Lofland, J. (1974). Styles of reporting qualitative field research. *American Sociologist*, *9*(3), 101–111. http://www.jstor.org/stable/27702128

Lomask, M. (1986). *The biographer's craft*. Harper & Row.

Lovern, L. L., & Locust, C. (2013). *Native American communities on health and disability: Borderland dialogues*. Palgrave Macmillan.

Luck, L., Jackson, D., & Usher, K. (2006). Case study: A bridge across the paradigms. *Nursing Inquiry*, *13*(2), 103–109. https://doi.org/10.1111/j.1440-1800.2006.00309.x

Lynn, M., & Dixson, A. D. (Eds.). (2023). *Handbook of critical race theory in education* (2nd ed.). Routledge.

Mac an Ghaill, M., & Haywood, C. (2015). British-born Pakistani and Bangladeshi young men: Exploring unstable concepts of Muslim, Islamophobia and racialization. *Critical Sociology*, *41*(1), 97–114. https://doi.org/10.1177/0896920513518947

MacKenzie, C. A., Christensen, J., & Turner, S. (2015). Advocating beyond the academy: Dilemmas of communicating relevant research results. *Qualitative Research*, *15*(1), 105–121. https://doi.org/10.1177/1468794113509261

Madison, D. S. (2005). *Critical ethnography: Method, ethics, and performance*. Sage.

Madison, D. S. (2012). *Critical ethnography: Method, ethics, and performance* (2nd ed.). Sage.

Madison, D. S. (2019). *Critical ethnography: Method, ethics, and performance* (3rd ed.). Sage.

Maeder, C. (2014). Analysing sounds. In U. Flick (Ed.), *The SAGE handbook of qualitative data analysis* (pp. 424–434). Sage.

Malecki, J. S., Rhodes, P., Ussher, J. M., & Boydell, K. (2022). A feminist phenomenological approach to the analysis of body maps: Childhood trauma and anorexia nervosa. *Health Care for Women International*. https://doi.org/10.1080/07399332.2022.2096026

Marion, J. S., & Crowder, J. W. (2013). *Visual research: A concise introduction to thinking visually*. Bloomsbury.

Marotzki, W., Holze, J., & Verstandig, D. (2014). Analysing virtual data. In U. Flick (Ed.), *The SAGE handbook of qualitative data analysis* (pp. 450–464). Sage.

Marshall, C., Rossman, G. B., & Blanco, G. L. (2021). *Designing qualitative research* (7th ed.). Sage.

Martin, J. (1990). Deconstructing organizational taboos: The suppression of gender conflict in organizations. *Organization Science*, *1*(4), 339–359. http://dx.doi.org/10.1287/orsc.1.4.339

Mavrogordato, M., & White, R. S. (2020). Leveraging policy implementation for social justice: How school leaders shape educational opportunity when implementing policy for English learners. *Education Administration Quarterly*, *56*(1), 3–45.

Maxwell, J. A. (2012). *A realist approach for qualitative research*. Sage.

Maxwell, J. A. (2013). *Qualitative research design: An interactive approach* (3rd ed.). Sage.

May, K. A. (1986). Writing and evaluating the grounded theory research report. In W. C. Chenitz & J. M. Swanson (Eds.), *From practice to grounded theory* (pp. 146–154). Addison-Wesley.

May, T., & Perry, B. (2017). *Reflexivity: The essential guide*. Sage.

McBride, K., Franks, C., Wade, V., King, V., Rigney, J., Burton, N., Dowling, A., Mitchell, J. A., Van Kessel, G., Howard, N., Paquet, C., Hiller, S., Nicholls, S. J., & Brown, A. (2022). Getting to the heart of the matter: A research partnership with Aboriginal women in South and Central Australia. *Critical Public Health*, *33*(3), 1–12. https://doi.org/10.1080/09581596.2022.2147417

McBride, R.-S. (2020). A literature review of the secondary school experiences of trans youth. *Journal of LGBT Youth*, *18*(2), 103–134. https://doi.org/10.1080/19361653.2020.1727815

McCracken, G. (1988). *The long interview*. Sage.

McVea, K., Harter, L., McEntarffer, R., & Creswell, J. W. (1999). Phenomenological study of student experiences with tobacco use at City High School. *High School Journal*, *82*(4), 209–222. https://www.jstor.org/stable/40364478

Mefteh, K. Y. (2022). Circumstances precipitating rural older adults for co-residential family care arrangements in Central Ethiopia. *Gerontology and Geriatric Medicine*, *8*, 1–11 https://doi.org/10.1177/23337214221113100

Mendoza Aviña, S., Morales, S., Delgado Bernal, D., & Alemán, E. (2023). Confronting our own complicity: Complexities and tensions of a critical race feminista praxis in higher education during the movement for Black lives. In M. Lynn & A. D. Dixson (Eds.), *Handbook of critical race theory in education* (2nd ed., pp. 296–307). Routledge.

Merleau-Ponty, M. (1962). *Phenomenology of perception* (C. Smith, Trans.). Routledge & Kegan Paul.

Merriam, S. (1988). *Case study research in education: A qualitative approach*. Jossey-Bass.

Merriam, S. B., & Tisdell, E. J. (2015). *Qualitative research: A guide to design and implementation* (4th ed.). Jossey-Bass.

Mertens, D. M. (2003). Mixed methods and the politics of human research: The transformative-emancipatory perspective. In A. Tashakkori & C. Teddlie (Eds.), *Handbook of mixed methods in social & behavioral research* (pp. 135–164). Sage.

Mertens, D. M. (2009). *Transformative research and evaluation*. Guilford.

Mertens, D. M. (2014). A transformative feminist stance: Inclusion of multiple dimensions of diversity with gender. In S. Brisolara, D. Siegart, & S. SenGupta (Eds.), *Feminist evaluation and research: Theory and practice* (pp. 95–112). Guilford.

Mertens, D. M. (2018). Ethics of qualitative data collection. In U. Flick (Ed.), *The SAGE handbook of qualitative data collection* (pp. 33–48). Sage. https://doi.org/10.4135/9781526416070

Mertens, D. M. (2019). *Research and evaluation in education and psychology: Integrating diversity with quantitative, qualitative, and mixed methods* (5th ed.). Sage.

Mertens, D. M. (2021). Transformative research methods to increase social impact for vulnerable groups and cultural minorities. *International Journal of Qualitative Methods*, *20*, 1–9. https://doi.org/10.1177/16094069211051563

Mertens, D. M., Cram, F., & Chilisa, B. (Eds.). (2013). *Indigenous pathways into social research*. Left Coast.

Mertens, D. M., & Ginsberg, P. E. (2009). *The handbook of social research ethics*. Sage.

Mertens, D. M., Sullivan, M., & Stace, H. (2011). Disability communities: Transformative research and social justice. In N. K. Denzin & Y. S. Lincoln (Eds.), *The SAGE handbook of qualitative research* (4th ed., pp. 227–242). Sage.

Mihas, P. (2021a). Memo writing strategies: Analyzing the parts and the whole. In C. Vanover, P. Mihas, & J. Saldaña (Eds.), *Analysing and interpreting qualitative research: After the interview* (pp. 243–258). Sage.

Mihas, P. (2021b). Section 4 reflection and analysic memoing strategie: Introduction. In C. Vanover, P. Mihas, & J. Saldaña (Eds.), *Analysing and interpreting qualitative research: After the interview* (pp. 223–226). Sage.

Mikos, L. (2014). Analysis of film. In U. Flick (Ed.), *The SAGE handbook of qualitative data analysis* (pp. 409–423). Sage.

Milani, R. M., & Borba, R. (2022). Queer(ing) methodologies. In U. Flick (Ed.), *The SAGE handbook of qualitative research design* (pp. 194–209). Sage.

Miles, M. B., & Huberman, A. M. (1994). *Qualitative data analysis: A sourcebook of new methods* (2nd ed.). Sage.

Miles, M. B., Huberman, A. M., & Saldaña, J. (2014). *Qualitative data analysis: A sourcebook of new methods* (3rd ed.). Sage.

Miles, M. B., Huberman, A. M., & Saldaña, J. (2019). *Qualitative data analysis: A sourcebook of new methods* (4th ed.). Sage.

Miller, D. W., Creswell, J. W., & Olander, L. S. (1998). Writing and retelling multiple ethnographic tales of a soup kitchen for the homeless. *Qualitative Inquiry*, *4*(4), 469–491. https://doi.org/10.1177/107780049800400404

Miller, R., Liu, K., & Ball, A. F. (2020). Critical counter-narrative as transformative methodology for educational equity. *Review of Research in Education*, *44*(1), 269–300. https://doi.org/10.3102/0091732X20908501

Miller, W. L., & Crabtree, B. F. (1992). Primary care research: A multimethod typology and qualitative road map. In B. F. Crabtree & W. L. Miller (Eds.), *Doing qualitative research* (pp. 3–28). Sage.

Millhauser, S. (2008). *Dangerous laughter*. Knopf.

Mills, A. J., Durepos, G., & Wiebe, E. (Eds.). (2010). *Encyclopedia of case study research*. Sage.

Morehead-Gee, A., Üsküp, D. K., Omokaro, U., Shoptaw, S., Harawa, N. T., & Heilemann, M. V. (2022). Relating "to her human side": A grounded theory analysis of cosmetologists' and aestheticians' relationships with clients in Black American beauty salons to inform sexual health interventions. *Culture, Health & Sexuality*, *25*(9), 1180–1197. https://doi.org/10.1080/13691058.2022.2141331

Morgan, D. L. (1997). *Focus groups as qualitative research* (2nd ed). Sage.

Morgan, D. (2019). *Basic and advanced focus groups*. Sage.

Morris, J. E., & Paris, L. F. (2022). Rethinking arts-based research methods in education: Enhanced participant engagement processes to increase research credibility and knowledge translation. *International Journal of Research & Method in Education*, *45*(1), 99–112. https://doi.org/10.1080/1743727X.2021.1926971

Morrow, R. A. (with Brown, D. D.). (1994). *Critical theory and methodology*. Sage.

Morrow, S. L., & Smith, M. L. (1995). Constructions of survival and coping by women who have survived childhood sexual abuse. *Journal of Counseling Psychology*, *42*(1), 24–33. https://doi.org/10.1037/0022-0167.42.1.24

Morse, J. M. (1994). Designing funded qualitative research. In N. K. Denzin & Y. S. Lincoln (Eds.), *Handbook of qualitative research* (pp. 220–235). Sage.

Morse, J. M., Bowers, B. J., Charmaz, K., Clarke, A. E., Cobin, J., & Poor, C. J. (with Stern, P. N.). (Eds.). (2021). *Developing grounded theory: The second generation revisited* (2nd ed.). Routledge.

Morse, J. M., Bowers, B. J., Clarke, A. E., Charmaz, K., Cobin, J., & Poor, C. J. (2021). The maturation of grounded theory. In J. M. Morse, B. J. Bowers, K. Charmaz, A. E. Clarke, J. Cobin, & C. J. Poor (with C. J. P. N. Stern) (Eds.), *Developing grounded theory: The second generation revisited* (2nd ed., pp. 3–22). Routledge.

Morse, J. M., & Field, P. A. (1995). *Qualitative research methods for health professionals* (2nd ed.). Sage.

Morse, J. M., & Richards, L. (2002). *README FIRST for a user's guide to qualitative methods*. Sage.

Morse, J. M., & Richards, L. (2013). *README FIRST for a user's guide to qualitative methods* (3rd ed). Sage.

Moss, P. (2007). Emergent methods in feminist research. In S. N. Hesse-Biber (Ed.), *Handbook of feminist research methods* (pp. 371–389). Sage.

Moustakas, C. (1994). *Phenomenological research methods*. Sage.

Muncey, T. (2010). *Creating autoethnographies*. Sage.

Munhall, P. L., & Oiler, C. J. (Eds.). (1986). *Nursing research: A qualitative perspective*. Appleton-Century-Crofts.

Murphy, J. P. (with Rorty, R.). (1990). *Pragmatism: From Peirce to Davidson*. Westview.

Natanson, M. (Ed.). (1973). *Phenomenology and the social sciences*. Northwestern University Press.

Navon, S., & Noy, C. (2022). Like, share, and remember: Facebook memorial pages as social capital resources. *Journal of Computer-Mediated Communication*, *28*(1), 1–12. https://doi.org/10.1093/jcmc/zmac021

Nelson, L. W. (1990). Code-switching in the oral life narratives of African-American women: Challenges to linguistic hegemony. *Journal of Education*, *172*(3), 142–155. http://www.jstor.org/stable/42742191

Nicholas, D. B., Lach, L., King, G., Scott, M., Boydell, K., Sawatzky, B., Reisman, J., Schippel, E., & Young, N. L. (2010). Contrasting Internet and face-to-face focus groups for children with chronic health conditions: Outcomes and participant experiences. *International Journal of Qualitative Methods*, *9*(1), 105–121. https://doi.org/10.1177/160940691000900102

Niedbalski, J., & Ślęzak, I. (2022). Encounters with CAQDAS: Advice for beginner users of computer software for qualitative research. *The Qualitative Report*, *27*(4), 1114–1132. https://doi.org/10.46743/2160-3715/2022.4770

Nieswiadomy, R. M. (1993). *Foundations of nursing research* (2nd ed.). Appleton & Lange.

Nunkoosing, K. (2005). The problems with interviews. *Qualitative Health Research*, *15*(5), 698–706. https://doi.org/10.1177/1049732304273903

Oiler, C. J. (1986). Phenomenology: The method. In P. L. Munhall & C. J. Oiler (Eds.), *Nursing research: A qualitative perspective* (pp. 69–82). Appleton-Century-Crofts.

O'leary, L. (2021). *The essential guide to doing your research project*. Sage.

Olesen, V. (2018). Feminist qualitative research in the millennium's first decade: Developments, challenges, prospects. In N. K. Denzin & Y. S. Lincoln (Eds.), *The SAGE handbook of qualitative* research (5th ed., pp. 151–175). Sage.

Ollerenshaw, J. A., & Creswell, J. W. (2002). Narrative research: A comparison of two restorying data analysis approaches. *Qualitative Inquiry*, *8*(3), 329–347. https://doi.org/10.1177/10778004008003008

Orkin, A., & Newbery, S. (2014). Marathon maternity oral history project: Exploring rural birthing through narrative methods. *Canadian Family Physician* [Médecin de famille canadien], *60*(1), 58–64.

Oswald, A. G. (2017). Improving outcomes with qualitative data analysis software: A reflective journey. *Qualitative Social Work*, *18*(3), 845–852. https://doi.org/10.1177/1473325017744860

Padilla, R. (2003). Clara: A phenomenology of disability. *The American Journal of Occupational Therapy*, *57*(4), 413–423. https://doi.org/10.5014/ajot.57.4.413

Paparo, S. A. (2022). Singing with awareness: A phenomenology of singers' experience with the Feldenkrais Method. *Research Studies in Music Education*, *44*(3), 541–553. https://doi.org/10.1177/1321103X211020642

Parker, L., & Lynn, M. (2002). What's race got to do with it? Critical race theory's conflicts with and connections to qualitative research methodology and epistemology. *Qualitative Inquiry*, *8*(1), 7–22. https://doi.org/10.1177/107780040200800102

Patton, M. Q. (1980). *Qualitative evaluation methods*. Sage.

Patton, M. Q. (1990). *Qualitative evaluation and research methods*. Sage.

Patton, M. Q. (2011). *Essentials of utilization-focused evaluation*. Sage.

Patton, M. Q. (2015). *Qualitative research and evaluation methods* (4th ed.). Sage.

Paulus, T. M., & Lester, J. N. (2020). Using software to support qualitative data analysis. In M R. M. Ward & S. Delamont (Eds.), *Handbook of qualitative research in education* (2nd ed., pp. 420–429). Edward Elgar.

Paulus, T. M., & Lester, J. N. (2021). *Doing qualitative research in a digital world*. Sage.

Paulus, T., Woods, M., Atkins, D., & Macklin, R. (2017). The discourse of QDAS: Reporting practices of ATLAS.ti and NVivo users with implications for best practices. *International Journal of Social Research Methodology*, *20*(1), 35–47. https://doi.org/10.1080/13645579.2015.1102454

Pauwels, L., & Mannay, D. (Eds.). (2019). *The SAGE handbook of visual research methods* (2nd ed.). Sage.

Pelias, R. J. (2011). Writing into position: Strategies for composition and evaluation. In N. K. Denzin & Y. S. Lincoln (Eds.), *The SAGE handbook of qualitative research* (4th ed., pp. 659–668). Sage.

Pereira, H. (2012). Rigour in phenomenological research: Reflections of a novice nurse researcher. *Nurse Researcher*, *19*(3), 16–19. https://doi.org/10.7748/nr2012.04.19.3.16.c9054

Phillips, D. C., & Burbules, N. C. (2000). *Postpositivism and educational research*. Rowman & Littlefield.

Pink, S. (2013). *Doing visual ethnography* (3rd ed.). Sage.

Pinnegar, S., & Daynes, J. G. (2007). Locating narrative inquiry historically: Thematics in the turn to narrative. In D. J. Clandinin (Ed.), *Handbook of narrative inquiry: Mapping a methodology* (pp. 3–34). Sage.

Plummer, K. (1983). *Documents of life: An introduction to the problems and literature of a humanistic method*. Allen & Unwin.

Plummer, K. (2011a). Critical humanism and queer theory: Living with the tensions. In N. K. Denzin & Y. S. Lincoln (Eds.), *The SAGE handbook of qualitative research* (4th ed., pp. 195–207). Sage.

Plummer, K. (2011b). Postscript 2011 to living with the contradictions: Moving on: Generations, cultures and methodological cosmopolitanism. In N. K. Denzin & Y. S. Lincoln (Eds.), *The SAGE handbook of qualitative research* (4th ed., pp. 208–211). Sage.

Polkinghorne, D. E. (1989). Phenomenological research methods. In R. S. Valle & S. Halling (Eds.), *Existential-phenomenological perspectives in psychology* (pp. 41–60). Plenum.

Polkinghorne, D. E. (1995). Narrative configuration in qualitative analysis. *Qualitative Studies in Education*, *8*(1), 5–23. https://doi.org/10.1080/0951839950080103

Poth, C. (2008). *Promoting evaluation use within dynamic organizations: A case study examining evaluator behavior* [Unpublished doctoral dissertation]. Queen's University, Kingston, Ontario.

Poth, C. (2019). Editorial—Rigorous and ethical qualitative data reuse: Potential perils and promising practices. *International Journal of Qualitative Methodology, 18.* https://doi.org/10.1177/1609406919868870

Poth, C. (2021). *Little quick fix: Research ethics.* Sage.

Poth, C., Creamer, E., & Cain, L. K. (2023). Promising practices for addressing unique ethical dilemmas arising from integration in mixed methods research. In R. Tierney, F. Rizvi, K. Ercikan, & G. Smith (Eds.), *International encyclopedia of education* (4th ed., pp. 522–530). Elsevier.

Prior, L. (2003). *Using documents in social research.* Sage.

Przybylski, L. (2020). *Hybrid ethnography: Online, offline, and in between.* Sage.

Quan-Haase, A., & Sloan, L. (Eds.). (2022). *The SAGE handbook of social media research methods* (2nd ed.). Sage.

Quayle, A. F., & Sonn, C. C. (2019). Amplifying the voices of Indigenous elders through community arts and narrative inquiry: Stories of oppression, psychosocial suffering, and survival. *American Journal of Community Psychology, 64*(1–2), 46–58. https://doi.org/10.1002/ajcp.12367

Ravitch, S. M., & Carl, N. M. (2020). *Qualitative research: Bridging the conceptual, theoretical, and methodological* (2nd ed.). Sage.

Ravitch, S. M., & Riggan, M. (2012). *Reason & rigor: How conceptual frameworks guide research.* Sage.

Reason, P., & Bradbury, H. (Eds.). (2006). *Handbook of action research.* Sage.

Rhoads, R. A. (1995). Whales tales, dog piles, and beer goggles: An ethnographic case study of fraternity life. *Anthropology and Education Quarterly, 26*(3), 306–323. http://www.jstor.org/stable/3195675

Richards, L. (2021). *Handling qualitative data: A practical guide* (4th ed.). Sage.

Richards, L., & Morse, J. M. (2013). *README FIRST for a user's guide to qualitative methods* (3rd ed.). Sage.

Richardson, L. (1990). *Writing strategies: Reaching diverse audiences.* Sage.

Richardson, L. (1994). Writing: A method of inquiry. In N. K. Denzin & Y. S. Lincoln (Eds.), *Handbook of qualitative research* (pp. 516–529). Sage.

Richardson, L. (2000). Evaluating ethnography. *Qualitative Inquiry, 6*(2), 253–255. https://doi.org/10.1177/107780040000600207

Richardson, L., & St. Pierre, E. A. (2005). Writing: A method of inquiry. In N. K. Denzin & Y. S. Lincoln (Eds.), The SAGE handbook of qualitative research (3rd ed., pp. 959–978). Sage.

Richardson, L., & St. Pierre, E. A. (2018). Writing: A method of inquiry. In N. K. Denzin & Y. S. Lincoln (Eds.), *The SAGE handbook of qualitative research* (5th ed., pp. 818–838). Sage.

Riessman, C. K. (1993). *Narrative analysis.* Sage.

Riessman, C. K. (2008). *Narrative methods for the human sciences.* Sage.

Rorty, R. (1983). *Consequences of pragmatism.* University of Minnesota Press.

Rorty, R. (1990). Pragmatism as anti-representationalism. In J. P. Murphy (Ed.), *Pragmatism: From Peirce to Davidson* (pp. 1–6). Westview.

Rose, G. (2016). *Visual methodologies: An introduction to research with visual materials* (4th ed.). Sage.

Roulston, K., deMarrais, K., & Lewis, J. B. (2003). Learning to interview in the social sciences. *Qualitative Inquiry, 9*(4), 643–668. https://doi.org/10.1177/1077800403252736

Rubin, H. J., & Rubin, I. S. (2012). *Qualitative interviewing: The art of hearing data* (3rd ed.). Sage.

Ruohotie-Lyhty, M. (2013). Struggling for a professional identity: Two newly qualified language teachers' identity narratives during the first years at work. *Teaching and Teacher Education, 30,* 120–129. https://doi.org/10.1016/j.tate.2012.11.002

Saldaña, J. (2011). *Fundamentals of qualitative research.* Oxford University Press.

Saldaña, J. (2021). *The coding manual for qualitative researchers* (4th ed.). Sage.

Salmona, M., Lieber, E., & Kaczynski, D. (2019). *Qualitative and mixed methods data analysis using Dedoose.* Sage.

Salmons, J. E. (2022). *Doing qualitative research online*. Sage.

Sampson, H. (2004). Navigating the waves: The usefulness of a pilot in qualitative research. *Qualitative Research*, *4*(3), 383–402. https://doi.org/10.1177/1468794104047236

Sandelowski, M. (2001). Real qualitative researchers do not count: The use of numbers in qualitative research. *Research in Nursing & Health*, *24*(3), 230–240. https://doi.org/10.1002/nur.1025

Sandelowski, M. (2010). What's in a name? Qualitative description revisited. *Research in Nursing & Health*, *33*(1), 77–84. https://doi.org/10.1002/nur.20362

Sanjek, R. (1990). *Fieldnotes: The makings of anthropology*. Cornell University Press.

Schildrick, M. (2020). Critical disability studies: Rethinking the conventions for the age of postmodernity. In N. Watson, A. Roulstone, & C. Thomas (Eds.), *Routledge handbook of disability studies* (2nd ed., pp. 32–44). Routledge.

Schwandt, T. A. (2015). *The SAGE dictionary of qualitative inquiry* (4th ed.). Sage.

Schwandt, T. A., & Gates, E. F. (2018). Case study methodology. In N. K. Denzin & Y. S. Lincoln (Eds.), *Handbook of qualitative research* (5th ed., pp. 341–358). Sage.

Shrum, W., & Scott, G. (2017). *Video ethnography in practice: Planning, shooting, and editing for social analysis*. Sage.

Silver, C., & Lewins, A. (2014). *Using software in qualitative research: A step-by-step guide* (2nd ed.). Sage.

Silverman, D. (2022). *Doing qualitative research: A practical handbook* (6th ed.). Sage.

Simmonds, S., Roux, C., & ter Avest, I. (2015). Blurring the boundaries between photovoice and narrative inquiry: A narrative-photovoice methodology for gender-based research. *International Journal of Qualitative Methods*, *14*(3), 33–49. https://doi.org/10.1177/160940691501400303

Slife, B. D., & Williams, R. N. (1995). *What's behind the research? Discovering hidden assumptions in the behavioral sciences*. Sage.

Smith, G. H. (2000). Protecting and respecting Indigenous knowledge. In M. Battiste (Ed.), *Reclaiming Indigenous voice and vision* (pp. 207–224). University of British Columbia Press.

Smith, J. A. (2017). Interpretive phenomenological analysis: Getting at lived experience. *The Journal of Positive Psychology*, *12*(3), 303–304. https://doi.org/10.1080/17439760.2016.1262622

Smith, J. A., Flowers, P., & Larkin, M. (2009). *Interpretative phenomenological analysis: Theory, method and research*. Sage.

Smith, J. A., Flowers, P., & Larkin, M. (2022). *Interpretative phenomenological analysis: Theory, method and research* (2nd ed.). Sage.

Smith, L. M. (1994). Biographical method. In N. K. Denzin & Y. S. Lincoln (Eds.), *Handbook of qualitative research* (pp. 286–305). Sage.

Smith, L. T. (2005). On tricky ground: Researching the native in the age of uncertainty. In N. K. Denzin & Y. S. Lincoln (Eds.), *The SAGE handbook of qualitative research* (3rd ed., pp. 85–108). Sage.

Smith, L. T. (2021). *Decolonizing methodologies: Research and Indigenous peoples* (3rd ed.). Bloomsbury.

Solorzano, D. G., & Yosso, T. J. (2002). Critical race methodology: Counter-storytelling as an analytical framework for education research. *Qualitative Inquiry*, *8*(1), 23–44. https://doi.org/10.1177/107780040200800103

Spiegelberg, H. (1982). *The phenomenological movement* (3rd ed.). Martinus Nijhoff.

Spindler, G., & Spindler, L. (1987). Teaching and learning how to do the ethnography of education. In G. Spindler & L. Spindler (Eds.), *Interpretive ethnography of education: At home and abroad* (pp. 17–33). Lawrence Erlbaum.

Spradley, J. P. (1979). *The ethnographic interview*. Holt, Rinehart & Winston.

Spradley, J. P. (1980). *Participant observation*. Holt, Rinehart & Winston.

Stake, R. E. (1995). *The art of case study research*. Sage.

Stake, R. E. (2005). Qualitative case studies. In N. K. Denzin & Y. S. Lincoln (Eds.), *The SAGE handbook of qualitative research* (3rd ed., pp. 443–466). Sage.

Stake, R. E. (2006). *Multiple case study analysis*. Guilford.

Stake, R. E. (2010). *Qualitative research: Studying how things work*. Guilford.

Stanfield, J. H., II (Ed.). (2011). *Rethinking race and ethnicity in research methods*. Left Coast.

Staples, A., Pugach, M. C., & Himes, D. J. (2005). Rethinking the technology integration challenge: Cases from three urban elementary schools. *Journal of Research on Technology in Education*, *37*(3), 285–311. https://doi.org/10.1080/15391523.2005.10782438

Stewart, A. J. (1994). Toward a feminist strategy for studying women's lives. In C. E. Franz & A. J. Stewart (Eds.), *Women creating lives: Identities, resilience and resistance* (pp. 11–35). Westview.

Stewart, D., & Mickunas, A. (1990). *Exploring phenomenology: A guide to the field and its literature* (2nd ed.). Ohio University Press.

Strauss, A. (1987). *Qualitative analysis for social scientists*. Cambridge University Press.

Strauss, A., & Corbin, J. (1990). *Basics of qualitative research: Grounded theory procedures and techniques*. Sage.

Strauss, A., & Corbin, J. (1998). *Basics of qualitative research: Techniques and procedures for developing grounded theory* (2nd ed.). Sage.

Stringer, E. T. (1993). Socially responsive educational research: Linking theory and practice. In D. J. Flinders & G. E. Mills (Eds.), *Theory and concept in qualitative research: Perspectives from the field* (pp. 141–162). Teachers College Press.

Strunk, W., & White, E. B. (2000). *The elements of style* (4th ed.). Pearson.

Suddick, K. M., Cross, V., Vuoskoski, P., Galvin, K. T., & Stew, G. (2020). The work of hermeneutic phenomenology. *International Journal of Qualitative Methods*, *19*, 1–14. https://doi.org/10.1177/1609406920947600

Sudnow, D. (1978). *Ways of the hand*. Knopf.

Suoninen, E., & Jokinen, A. (2005). Persuasion in social work interviewing. *Qualitative Social Work*, *4*(4). 469–487. https://doi.org/10.1177/1473325005058647

Swingewood, A. (1991). *A short history of sociological thought*. St. Martin's.

Sword, H. (2012). *Stylish academic writing*. Harvard University Press.

Tan, E., & Faircloth, B. (2023). One World: Refugee youth incubating epistemologies toward rightful presence with/in community-driven STEM. *Journal of Research in Science Teaching*, *60*(8), 1627–1656. https://doi.org/10.1002/tea.21846

Tashakkori, A., & Teddlie, C. (Eds.). (2003). *SAGE handbook of mixed methods in the social and behavioral sciences*. Sage.

Taylor, S. J., Bogdan, R., & DeVault, M. L. (2015). *Introduction to qualitative research methods: A guidebook and resource* (4th ed.). Wiley.

Tesch, R. (1988). *The contribution of a qualitative method: Phenomenological research* [Unpublished manuscript]. Qualitative Research Management.

Tesch, R. (1990). *Qualitative research: Analysis types and software tools*. Falmer.

Thomas, G. (2021). *How to do your case study* (3rd ed.). Sage.

Thomas, J. (1993). *Doing critical ethnography*. Sage.

Thomas, W. I., & Znaniecki, F. (1958). *The Polish peasant in Europe and America*. Dover. (Original work published 1918–1920).

Thornton, R., Nicholson, P., & Harms, L. (2020). Creating evidence: Findings from a grounded theory of memory-making in neonatal bereavement care in Australia. *Journal of Pediatric Nursing*, *53*, 29–35. https://doi.org/10.1016/j.pedn.2020.04.006

Tierney, W. G. (1995). (Re)presentation and voice. *Qualitative Inquiry*, *1*(4), 379–390. https://doi.org/10.1177/107780049500100401

Tiidenberg, K. (2018). Ethics in digital research. In U. Flick (Ed.), *The SAGE handbook of qualitative data collection* (2nd ed., pp. 466–479). Sage. https://doi.org/10.4135/9781526416070

Tracy, S. J. (2010). Qualitative quality: Eight "big-tent" criteria for excellent qualitative research. *Qualitative Inquiry*, *16*(10), 837–851. https://doi.org/10.1177/1077800410383121

Tracy, S. J., & Hinrichs, M. M. (2017). Big tent criteria for qualitative quality. In C. R. Scott & L. Lewis (Eds.), *The international encyclopedia of communication research methods* (pp. 1–10). Wiley. https://do

i.org/10.1002/9781118901731.iecrm0016

Travers, J. L., Schroeder, K., Norful, A. A., & Aliyu, S. (2020). The influence of empowered work environments on the psychological experiences of nursing assistants during COVID-19: A qualitative study. *BMC Nursing*, *19*, 98–110. https://doi.org/10.1186/s12912-020-00489-9

Trip, H., Whitehead, L., Crowe, M., Mirfin-Veitch, B., & Daffue, C. (2019). Aging with intellectual disabilities in families: Navigating ever-changing seas—A theoretical model. *Qualitative Health Research*, *29*(11), 1595–1610. https:/doi.org/10.1177/1049732319845344

Trujillo, N. (1992). Interpreting (the work and the talk of) baseball. *Western Journal of Communication*, *56*(4), 350–371. https://doi.org/10.1080/10570319209374423

Tuhiwai Smith, L. (2023). *Decolonizing methodologies* (3rd ed.). Bloomsbury Academic.

Tyson, L. (2023). *Critical theory today* (4th ed.). Routledge.

Urquhart, C. (2022). *Grounded theory for qualitative research* (2nd ed.). Sage.

Van der Hoorn, B. (2015). Playing projects: Identifying flow in the "lived experience." *International Journal of Project Management*, *33*(5), 1008–1021. http://dx.doi.org/10.1016/j.ijproman.2015.01.009

Van Hout, M. C., & Bingham, T. (2013). "Silk Road," the virtual drug marketplace: A single case study of user experiences. *International Journal of Drug Policy*, *23*(5), 385–391. https://doi.org/10.1016/j.drugpo.2013.01.005

Van Kaam, A. (1966). *Existential foundations of psychology*. Duquesne University Press.

Van Maanen, J. (1988). *Tales of the field: On writing ethnography*. University of Chicago Press.

Van Maanen, J. (2011). *Tales of the field: On writing ethnography* (2nd ed.). University of Chicago Press.

van Manen, M. (1990). *Researching lived experience: Human science for an action sensitive pedagogy*. State University of New York Press.

van Manen, M. (2006). Writing qualitatively, or the demands of writing. *Qualitative Health Research*, *16*(5), 713–722. https://doi.org/10.1177/1049732306286911

van Manen, M. (2014). *Phenomenology of practice: Meaning-giving methods in phenomenological research and writing*. Left Coast.

van Manen, M. (2023). *Phenomenology of practice: Meaning-giving methods in phenomenological research and writing* (2nd ed). Routledge.

Vanover, C., Mihas, P., & Saldaña, J. (Eds.). (2021). *Analysing and interpreting qualitative research: After the interview*. Sage.

Wallace, A. F. C. (1970). *Culture and personality* (2nd ed.). Random House.

Wallerstein, N., Duran, B., Oetzel, J. G., & Minkler, M. (2018). *Community-based participatory research for health: Advancing social and health equity* (3rd ed.). Sage.

Warren, C. A. B., & Xavia Karner, T. (2014). *Discovering qualitative methods: Ethnography, interviews, documents, and images* (3rd ed.). Oxford University Press.

Watson, K. (2005). Queer theory. *Group Analysis*, *38*(1), 67–81. https://doi.org/10.1177/0533316405049369

Watson, N., & Vehmas, S. (2020). *Routledge handbook of disability studies* (2nd ed.). Routledge.

Watts, I. E., & Erevelles, N. (2004). These deadly times: Reconceptualizing school violence by using critical race theory and disability studies. *American Educational Research Journal*, *41*(2), 271–299. https://www.jstor.org/stable/3699367

Weaver-Hightower, M. B. (2019). *How to write qualitative research*. Routledge.

Weiner-Levey, N., & Popper-Giveon, A. (2013). The absent, the hidden and the obscured: Reflections on "dark matter" in qualitative research. *Quality & Quantity*, *47*, 2177–2190. https://doi.org/10.1007/s11135-011-9650-7

Weis, L., & Fine, M. (2000). *Speed bumps: A student-friendly guide to qualitative research*. Teachers College Press.

Wertz, F. J. (2005). Phenomenological research methods for counseling psychology. *Journal of Counseling Psychology*, *52*(2), 167–177. https://doi.org/10.1037/0022-0167.52.2.167

Whittemore, R., Chase, S. K., & Mandle, C. L. (2001). Validity in qualitative research.

Qualitative Health Research, 11(4), 522–537. https://doi.org/10.1177/104973201129119299

Willis, P. (1977). *Learning to labour: How working class kids get working class jobs*. Saxon House.

Willox, A. C., Harper, S. L., & Edge, V. L. (2012). Storytelling in a digital age: Digital storytelling as an emerging narrative method for preserving and promoting Indigenous oral wisdom. *Qualitative Research, 13*(2), 127–147. https://doi.org/10.1177/1468794112446105

Winthrop, R. H. (1991). *Dictionary of concepts in cultural anthropology*. Greenwood.

Witteborn, S. (2012). Testimonio and spaces of risk: A forced migrant perspective. *Cultural Studies, 26*(4), 421–441. https://doi.org/10.1080/09502386.2011.587881

Wolcott, H. F. (1987). On ethnographic intent. In G. Spindler & L. Spindler (Eds.), *Interpretive ethnography of education: At home and abroad* (pp. 37–57). Lawrence Erlbaum.

Wolcott, H. F. (1990a). On seeking—and rejecting—validity in qualitative research. In E. W. Eisner & A. Peshkin (Eds.), *Qualitative inquiry in education: The continuing debate* (pp. 121–152). Teachers College Press.

Wolcott, H. F. (1990b). *Writing up qualitative research*. Sage.

Wolcott, H. F. (1992). Posturing in qualitative research. In M. D. LeCompte, W. L. Millroy, & J. Preissle (Eds.), *The handbook of qualitative research in education* (pp. 3–52). Academic.

Wolcott, H. F. (1994). *Transforming qualitative data: Description, analysis, and interpretation*. Sage.

Wolcott, H. F. (2008a). *Ethnography: A way of seeing* (2nd ed.). AltaMira.

Wolcott, H. F. (2008b). *Writing up qualitative research* (3rd ed.). Sage.

Wolcott, H. F. (2010). *Ethnography lessons: A primer*. Left Coast.

Yin, R. K. (2017). *Case study research and applications: Design and methods* (6th ed.). Sage.

Yussen, S. R., & Ozcan, N. M. (1997). The development of knowledge about narratives. *Issues in Educational Psychology: Contributions From Educational Psychology, 2*, 1–68.

INDEX

Abstraction, 19, 52, 56, 230, 237
Adams, J., 35, 39 (table)
Adler-Nissen, R., 114
Adolph, S., 195
Agar, M. H., 221
Agger, B., 3, 33
Alexander, B. K., 35
Aliyu, S., 67
AMRL cycle. *See* Anticipate-mitigate-respond-learn (AMRL) cycle
Analysis of the culture-sharing group, 111
Analysis of themes, 120
Anderson, R. A., 122
Angen, M. J., 286, 287 (table), 289
Annamma, S. A., 38 (table)
Anthias, F., 374, 381
Anticipate-mitigate-respond-learn (AMRL) cycle, 58, 59 (figure)
Approaches to inquiry, 2
Archer, L., 382
Artifacts, 80
Arts-based inquiry method, 195
Arts-based study, 82
Arur, A., 34, 39 (table)
Asgeirsdottir, G. H., 95
Asmussen, K. J., 122, 165, 169, 197, 231 (figure), 282, 321, 333–334
Assertions, 117, 120, 280
Atkinson, P., 107, 111, 113, 190
ATLAS.ti, 235
Audience, writing process, 262–263
Audiovisual materials, 221, 224
Audit trail, 222, 238
Authenticity, 291
Autobiographical study, 82
Autobiography, 52

Autoethnography, 82, 86, 183
Axial coding, 99, 100, 103, 245–246, 274, 276
Axiological assumptions, 22 (table), 23, 41–42 (table)
Ayers, W., 359

Baez, J., 58, 259
Banfield, G., 113
Bangladeshi young men. *See* Pakistani and Bangladeshi young men (British-born),
Banks, J. A., 347
Banks, M., 222
Banton, M., 377
Bay Street School, 350
Bazeley, P., 217, 218, 221, 222, 229, 232, 236, 296
Beck, C. T., 87, 88, 94
Bidabadi, F. S., 32, 38 (table)
Big net approach, 190
Biklen, S. K., 188
Bingham, T., 122
Biographical study, 81
Bird, G. W., 329, 329 (table)
Black women
  discrimination, 139, 272
  higher education leadership, 139, 149, 262
  leadership ambitions, 139, 272
  racial-gender leadership gap, 140, 273
Blanco, G. L., 6 (table)
Bloomberg, L. D., 54
Bogdan, R. C., 188
Borba, R., 35
Bounded system, 115
Bowers, B. J., 96, 97
Boydell, K., 38 (table), 67
Braun, V., 39 (table), 144, 250

Brimhall, A. C., 168
Brinkmann, S., 197, 198, 207
Brisolara, S., 31
Bromet, E. J., 329, 329 (table), 331
Brown, A., 105
Brown, J., 25, 28, 37 (table), 164
Brown, M. L., 182, 275
Bryant, A., 97
Buckworth, J., 105
Bullough, R. V., Jr., 347
Burbules, N. C., 26
Burr, V., 27
Burton, N., 105

Caine, V., 18, 78, 303
Campbell, J. L., 298
Carger, C., 348
Carl, N. M., 6 (table), 59, 223, 262
Carter, B., 377
Case description, 115, 117, 120
Case study research, 13, 76, 114, 320 (figure), 333–334, 391
  challenges and opportunities, 121–122
  data analysis and representation, 250–252, 251 (figure)
  data procedures, 125 (table)
  definition, 114–115
  embedded writing structure, 281–282
  evaluation, 312–314, 314 (figure)
  features, 116–117, 116 (figure)
  foundational considerations, 124 (table)
  origins, 115

505

Case study research (*Continued*)
  overall writing structure, 280–281
  procedures, 118–121, 119 (figure)
  purpose statement, 165
  qualitative studies, 147–149, 148 (table)
  research questions, 169
  research reporting, 126 (table)
  subquestions, 171
  types and variations, 117–118, 122–123
Case study research and applications: Design and methods (Yin), 13
Case themes, 115
Casey, M. A., 201
Category, 99
Causal conditions, 100, 246, 335
Central phenomenon, 103, 162–163
Central question, 166–169
Chan, E., 136, 137–138 (table), 159, 167, 170, 187, 241, 264, 269, 295, 346, 348
Chance, N. L., 136, 139, 140–141 (table), 165, 167, 170, 189, 196, 242, 262, 265, 270, 272, 294, 365
Chapman, T. K., 33
Charmaz, K., 12, 28, 97, 99, 101, 151, 246, 274, 276, 309, 310
Chase, S., 78, 81
Chenitz, W. C., 275
Cherryholmes, C. H., 30
Children's Aid Society (CAS), 355
Chilisa, B., 35, 188
Chipango, E. F., 29, 37 (table)
Churchill, S. L., 27, 37 (table)
Clandinin, D. J., 11, 30, 78, 82, 84, 85, 196, 238, 262, 267–270, 303, 334, 358
Clarke, A. E., 30, 96, 97
Clarke, V., 144, 250
Clifford, J., 260
Clusters of meaning, 93
Cochran-Smith, M., 347

Codebook, 225, 226 (table), 298–299
Coding
  axial, 99, 100, 103, 246, 274, 276
  case study, 251 (figure)
  definition, 215
  describing and classifying, 224–229, 225 (figure)
  ethnography, 249 (figure)
  grounded theory, 245 (figure)
  narrative study, 240 (figure)
  open, 100, 103, 245, 252, 275
  phenomenological study, 243 (figure)
Coding paradigm or logic diagram, 103
Colaizzi, P. F., 91, 242, 272
Collective case study, 118
Collective reflexivity, 57
Collins, J., 39 (table)
Colon-Emeric, C., 122
Complete observer, 111, 201
Complete participant, 111, 201
Computer-assisted qualitative data analysis, 297
Concern for justice, 58
Concern for welfare, 58
Conditional context, 103
Conditional or consequential matrix, 100
Conflicting stories, 137
Conle, C., 347
Connelly, F. M., 30, 82, 84, 85, 196, 238, 262, 267–270, 334, 358
Consent-to-participate form, 186 (figure)
Constant comparative, 100, 245
Constructivist grounded theory, 97, 101, 142
Context of the case, 120
Coping strategies, 331
Corazzini, K., 122
Corbin, J., 9 (table), 12, 27, 97, 99, 100, 101, 104, 189, 223, 245, 246, 257, 274, 307–308, 336
Cortazzi, M., 78, 84

Crabtree, B. F., 8
Craft, 198
Crawford, J., 33
Credibility, 285
Creswell, J. D., 26
Creswell, J. W., 6 (table), 25, 26, 37 (table), 58, 59, 66, 122, 158 (figure), 165, 169, 182, 188, 197, 231 (figure), 238, 259, 275, 282, 291, 321, 333–334
Critelli, F. M., 68
Critical ethnography, 107, 109
Critical race theory, 33–34, 38 (table), 42 (table)
Critical theory, 32–33, 38 (table), 42 (table)
Cross-case analysis, 120
Crotty, M., 27
Crouch, M., 371
Crowe, M., 141
Cultural anthropology, 217
Cultural behaviors, 111
Cultural interpretation, 108, 111
Cultural knowledge, 347
Cultural portrait, 108, 112, 128
Cultural system, 188
Culture-sharing group, 106, 108, 112, 149, 151, 190, 248, 336
Cummins, J., 347
Curriculum, 99, 346–349, 359
Czarniawska, B., 78, 84, 228, 260, 269

Daffue, C., 141
Dahlen, H. G., 38 (table)
Daiute, C., 78, 85, 180, 240, 334
Darcy, S., 39 (table)
Data analysis and representation
  case study, 250–252, 251 (figure)
  ethnography, 247–250, 249 (figure)
  grounded theory, 245–247, 245 (figure)
  layers, 238

Index **507**

narrative research, 238–241, 240 (figure)
phenomenology, 241–244, 243 (figure)
Data analysis spiral, 218 (figure)
  activities, strategies and outcomes, 219 (table)
  challenges, 218
  coding process, 224–229
  developing and assessing interpretations, 229–230
  ethical considerations, 220–221, 220 (table)
  managing and organizing, 221
  reading and memoing emergent ideas, 221–224
  representing and visualizing, 230–232
Data analysis strategies, 216–217, 216–217 (table)
Data collection
  access and rapport, 183–188
  activities, 176–177, 176 (figure), 178–179 (table)
  asynchronous, 193
  comparisons, 209–210
  data storage and security, 208
  ethical considerations, 177–180, 181 (table)
  ethical issues, 175
  fieldwork issues, 205–208
  forms, 192–203
  interviews types, 177
  positioning, 175
  purposeful sampling strategies, 188–192
  recording information procedures, 203–205
  site/individual, 180–183
  statistical inferences, 177
Data forms
  interviewing, 197–201
  observation, 201–203, 202 (figure)
  online, 194

qualitative research, 192–193, 193 (figure)
synchronous/asynchronous interviews, 192
Data-handling processes, 296
Data management, 221
Data storage systems, 208
Davidson, J., 234
Daynes, J. G., 86
Deception, 113, 177
Dedoose, 235
Deductive coding, 227
DeJaeghere, J., 34, 39 (table)
De Lauretis, T., 35
Denzin, N. K., 5, 8, 9 (table), 10 (table), 19, 26, 29, 30, 240, 257, 260, 269, 278, 304, 339
Description of the culture-sharing group, 111
Descriptive method approach, 11
DeVault, M. L., 32
Dewey, J., 78, 136, 348
Dialogic/performance analysis, 241
Digital files, 221
Digital storytelling, 82
Digital technologies, 193
Di Gregorio, S., 234
Dimensionalized, properties, 103, 245
Direct interpretation, 120, 251
Disability theories, 36, 39 (table), 42 (table)
Discourse analysis, 241
Discrimination, 139
Disruptions, 172
Documenting consent, 185–188
Document memos, 223
Dowling, A., 105
Dufour, S., 115
Dukes, S., 91, 192

Edel, L., 85, 304
Edwards, L. V., 192
Eggeling, K. A., 114
Eisenhardt, M., 300

Eisner, E. W., 286, 287 (table), 288
Elliott, J., 78
Ellis, C., 86, 163, 183, 269
Ely, M., 286
Embedded analysis, 119
Embedded writing structures, 265, 266–267 (table)
  case study, 280–281
  ethnography, 278–279
  grounded theory, 275–276
  narrative, 269–270
  phenomenology, 272–273
Embodied/voluptuous validation, 289
Emerson, R. M., 277
Emic, 108
Employee Assistance Program (EAP), 322–323
Encoding, 163, 263–264
Engblom-Deglmann, M. L., 168
Epiphanies, 84, 334
Epistemological assumptions, 22 (table), 23, 41–42 (table)
Epoché, 91, 243
Essential, invariant structure (or essence), 93–94
Ethical research principles, 177
Ethical reviews and approvals, 50, 58, 64, 183–184
Ethnic identity, 136, 159, 346–349, 358
Ethnographic fieldwork, 107, 111, 113
Ethnographic research, 12–13, 76, 106, 336–337
  challenges and opportunities, 112–113
  culture-sharing group, 149, 151, 182
  data analysis and representation, 247–250, 249 (figure)
  data collection, 197
  data procedures, 125 (table)
  definition, 106

embedded writing structure, 278–279
evaluation, 310–311, 312 (figure)
features, 107–108, 107 (figure)
file organization and visual model mapping, 249 (figure)
foundational considerations, 124 (table)
origins, 106–107
overall writing structure, 276–278
procedures, 109–112, 110 (figure)
purpose statement, 164
qualitative studies, 144–146, 145–146 (table)
research questions, 168
research reporting, 126 (table)
subquestions, 171
types and variations, 108–109, 113–114
Ethnography: A way of seeing (Wolcott), 13
Ethnography: Step-by-step (Fetterman), 12
Etic, 108
Evaluation of quality, 19, 20 (figure)
case study research, 312–314, 314 (figure)
ethnographic research, 310–311, 312 (figure)
grounded theory research, 307–310, 311(figure)
narrative research, 303–304, 305 (figure)
phenomenological research, 305–307, 307 (figure)
for qualitative research, 299–303, 300 (figure)
Evaluation standards, 314–316, 315 (table)
Evers, J. C., 208
Ezeh, P. J., 206

F4Analyse, 235
Fabricius, A. H., 87, 163

Faircloth, B., 114
Family Quality of Life questionnaire, 196
Feminist research approaches, 31
Feminist theories, 31–32, 38 (table), 42 (table)
Fetal alcohol spectrum disorders (FASD), 68, 225
Fetterman, D. M., 12, 107, 111, 113, 190, 250, 294
Feuerverger, G., 347
Fieldwork issues
  documents, audiovisual and social media materials, 207–208
  entry and organizational access, 205–206
  interpretive frameworks, 205
  interviewer and interviewee, 206–207
  participant observations, 206
File naming system, 221
Fine, M., 58, 207, 261
First-order narratives, 182
Fischer, C. T., 262
Flick, U., 303
Focus groups, 200–201
Foreshadowing, 270
Fortin, D., 115
Foucault, M., 97
Fourie, R., 97
Frankl, V., 25
Franks, C., 105
Frelin, A., 123, 252

García-Rapp, F., 113, 114, 248, 249 (figure)
Gatekeeper, 188, 202
Gee, J. P., 241
Gergen, K. J., 27, 180
Gibbs, G., 234
Gilbert, L. S., 234
Gilgun, J. F., 260
Giorgi, A., 90, 91, 242
Glaser, B. G., 97, 246
Glesne, C., 259
Goetz, J. P., 286, 287 (table)

Goodrum, S., 136, 147, 148 (table), 169, 171, 184, 188, 190, 197, 250, 263, 280, 292, 391
Grbich, C., 222, 224, 230, 232
Green, M., 377
Grounded theory research, 12, 76, 135, 149
  challenges and opportunities, 104
  data analysis and representation, 245–247, 245 (figure)
  data procedures, 125 (table)
  definition, 96
  embedded writing structure, 275–276
  evaluation, 307–310, 311 (figure)
  features, 98–99, 98 (figure)
  foundational considerations, 124 (table)
  individuals, 182
  origins, 97
  overall writing structure, 273–275
  procedural diagram, constant comparison analytic process, 247 (figure)
  procedures, 101–104, 102 (figure)
  purpose statement, 164
  qualitative studies, 141–144, 143 (table)
  research questions, 168
  research reporting, 126 (table)
  subquestions, 171
  types and variations, 99–101, 105–106
Guba, E. G., 27, 120, 229, 281, 286, 287 (table), 288, 293, 295, 333
Guell, C., 195
Guest, G., 192
Guetterman, T. C., 59, 188
Gunnardottir, S., 95

Hadley, G., 104
Haenfler, R., 164, 168, 195, 250

Hamel, J., 115
Hammersley, M., 107, 111, 113, 190
Hammond, A., 30, 38 (table)
Handy, T., 38 (table)
Harawa, N. T., 105
Harding, S., 31
Harley, A. E., 105, 183
Harms, L., 105
Harper, W., 272
Harter, L., 158 (figure)
Hatch, J. A., 6 (table)
Hayashi, P., Jr., 291
Haywood, C., 136, 144–145, 145–146 (table), 168, 171, 188, 190, 197, 250, 294
Healey, G. K., 25, 184
Heaney, C. A., 105
Heilemann, M. V., 105
Hermeneutical phenomenology, 90, 91
Hierarchical tree diagram, 230, 231 (figure)
Higher education leadership, 139, 149
Hiller, S., 105
Hirani, S. A. A., 114
Historical contexts, 83
Holistic analysis, 119
Holistic perspective, 112
Horizontalization, 93
Howard, N., 105
Howe, K., 300
Huber, J., 269
Huberman, A. M., 9 (table), 191 (table), 216–217, 216–217 (table), 227
Huff, A. S., 21
Husserl, E., 87
HyperRESEARCH, 235–236
HyperTRANSCRIBE, 235

Ibraeva, J., 68
Impression management, 202
In-depth interviews, 196
Indigenous communities, 188
Inductive–deductive logic process, 7
Informed consent, 64

Institutional review boards (IRBs), 180, 183, 184
Instrumental case study, 118
Intellectual disabilities, 141–142, 151, 159, 189, 246
Intentional analysis, 243
Intentionality of consciousness, 88
Interactional moments, 269
Intercoder agreement, 296
Interpretation, 19, 20 (figure)
Interpretive frameworks
  critical race theory, 33–34, 38 (table), 42 (table)
  critical theory, 32–33, 38 (table), 42 (table)
  disability theories, 36, 39 (table), 42 (table)
  feminist theories, 31–32, 38 (table), 42 (table)
  philosophical assumptions, research process, 18–19, 20 (figure), 25
  philosophical beliefs, 40–42, 41–42 (table)
  postcolonial theories, 34–35, 39 (table), 41 (table), 42 (table)
  postmodernism, 29–30, 37 (table), 41 (table)
  postpositivism, 26–27, 37 (table), 41 (table)
  practicing, common elements, 36, 40
  pragmatism, 30–31, 38 (table), 42 (table)
  queer theory, 35, 39 (table), 42 (table)
  social constructivism, 27–28, 37 (table), 41 (table)
  transformative frameworks, 28–29, 37 (table), 41 (table)
Intersectionality framework, 139
Intervening conditions, 100
Interviewer and interviewee, dynamics between, 206–207
Interviewing, 197–201

Interview protocol, 177, 200, 200 (figure), 203
Intrinsic case study, 118, 151
In vivo codes, 100
Iphofen, R., 59
IRBs. *See* Institutional review boards (IRBs)
Ironic validation, 288
Islamophobia, 369–372, 375–381, 384

Jackson, E., 38 (table)
Jackson, K., 236
Jackson, P., 359
Jacob, E., 8, 9 (table)
Job, J. M., 68, 225, 225 (figure), 226 (table)
Jokinen, A., 206
Jones, D. J., 329, 329 (table)
Journaling, 208
Jungnickel, K., 25

K–12 education, 206
Katz, M. L., 105
Keith, M., 378
Kelly, E., 95
Kenny, M., 97
Key informants (or participants), 111
Kidder, L., 288
Kim, J.-H., 269
Kincheloe, J. L., 33
King, V., 105
Kingston, B., 147, 391
Knoblauch, H., 222
Knowledge mobilization, 258
Kouritzin, S. G., 347
Kroll, T., 36
Krueger, R. A., 201
Kuckartz, U., 232
Kus, R. J., 275
Kvale, S., 197, 198, 207

Labaree, R. V., 206
Ladson-Billings, G., 347
Lancy, D. F., 8, 9 (table)
Language, 111
Lather, P., 31, 286, 287 (table), 288

Lauterbach, S. S., 96
Leadership development, 140
Lean coding, 224
LeCompte, M. D., 6 (table), 107, 111, 197, 286, 287 (table)
Lee, S. J., 348
Leipert, B. D., 164
Lester, J. N., 193, 215, 234
Letter of information, 184–185
Levitt, H. M., 257
Lewins, A., 295
Lewis, L. A., 68
LGBTQ₊ (lesbian, gay, bisexual, transgender, and queer) theory, 35
Li, G., 348
Lieberson, S., 118
Lieblich, A., 78
Life-based literary narrative, 137
Life course stages, 80
Life history, 81, 304, 379
Lightfoot, C., 78
Lincoln, Y. S., 5, 8, 9 (table), 10 (table), 19, 26, 27, 29, 59, 120, 229, 257, 281, 286, 287 (table), 288, 290, 293, 295, 301, 333
Line-by-line coding, 147
Linguistic analysis, 241
Lived experiences, 79, 88, 149, 304
Lofland, J., 311
Lomask, M., 270
Lynn, M., 34

Mac an Ghaill, M., 136, 144–145, 145–146 (table), 168, 171, 188, 190, 197, 250, 294
MacKenzie, C. A., 262
Madison, D. S., 107, 216–217, 216–217 (table)
Maeder, C., 222
Malecki, J. S., 32, 38 (table)
Marcus, G. E., 260
Marotzki, W., 222

Marshall, C., 6 (table), 10 (table), 190, 205, 230, 232
Martin, J., 228
Mavrogordato, M., 28, 37 (table)
Maximum variation sampling, 190
MAXQDA, 27, 236
Maxwell, J. A., 54
May, K. A., 273
May, T., 57
McBride, K., 105
McCaleb, S. P., 347
McClaren, J., 25, 37 (table)
McCreanor, T., 39 (table)
McDaniel, R. R., 122
McEntarffer, R., 158 (figure)
McGhee, D., 370
McKenzie, H., 371
McVea, K., 158 (figure)
Mefteh, K. Y., 96, 164
Member-checking, 139–140, 142, 220
Memoing process, 99, 102–103, 222, 223
Mercer, N., 382
Merriam, S. B., 115, 279, 282
Mertens, D. M., 10 (table), 26, 28, 35, 36, 180
Methodological assumptions, 22 (table), 23, 41–42 (table)
Methodological congruence, 54
Methods of data collection and analysis, 19, 20 (figure)
Mickunas, A., 88
Micro-ethnography, 338
Mihas, P., 222, 223
Mikos, L., 222
Milani, R. M., 35
Miles, M. B., 9 (table), 191 (table), 216–217, 216–217 (table), 221, 223, 227
Miles, R., 378
Miller, A. L., 38 (table)
Miller, D. L., 291
Miller, W. L., 8
Mirfin-Veitch, B., 141

Mitchell, J. A., 105, 329, 329 (table)
Morehead-Gee, A., 105
Morrow, R. A., 32, 33
Morrow, S. L., 276
Morse, J. M., 9 (table), 54, 96, 97, 166
Moustakas, C., 9 (table), 12, 88, 91, 93, 95, 139, 241, 242, 270, 272, 335
Multicultural education, 346
Multifaceted experiences, 19, 20 (figure)
Multiple sources of information, 115
Multisite case study, 115
Muncey, T., 82
Munhall, P. L., 9 (table)
Murphy, J. P., 30

Narrative methods for the human sciences (Riessman), 12
Narrative research, 11–12, 75
  challenges and opportunities, 85–86
  data analysis and representation, 238–241, 240 (figure)
  data procedures, 125 (table)
  defining features and guiding design questions, 137–138 (table)
  definition, 78
  embedded writing structure, 269–270
  evaluation, 303–305, 305 (figure)
  features, 79–80, 79 (figure)
  foundational considerations, 124 (table)
  immigrant student, 348
  origins, 78–79
  overall writing structure, 267–269
  procedures, 82–85, 83 (figure)
  purpose statement, 163

research questions, 167
research reporting, 126 (table)
subquestions, 170
template for coding, 240 (figure)
types and variations, 80–82, 86–87
Naturalistic generalizations, 120, 251
Navon, S., 67
Nelson, L. W., 167
Neonatal bereavement, 163
Nicholls, S. J., 105
Nicholson, P., 105
Niedbalski, J., 233
Nonparticipant observation, 111
Nonparticipant observer, 201
Norful, A. A., 67
Noy, C., 67
Nunkoosing, K., 207
NVivo, 236

Observational protocol, 203, 204 (figure), 205
Observations, 201–203, 202 (figure)
Odoms-Young, A., 105
Ogilvie, D., 195
Oiler, C. J., 9 (table)
Olesen, V., 31, 32
Ollerenshaw, J. A., 238
Omokaro, U., 105
One-on-one interviews, 200
Online data collection, 194
Online research ethics, 194 (figure)
Onta-Grzebik, L., 37 (table)
Ontological assumptions, 22 (table), 23, 41–42 (table)
Open coding, 100, 103, 245, 252, 275
Oral history, 81
Organizational psychology, 147
Organizational structure, 151
O'Riorcan, T., 68
Ormsby, S., 38 (table)
Overall writing structures, 265, 266–267 (table)

case study, 280–281
ethnography, 276–278
grounded theory research, 273–275
narrative research, 267–269
phenomenological research, 270–272
Ozcan, N. M., 238

Padilla, R., 167
Paparo, S. A., 96
Paquet, C., 105
Paradigms, 19
Paralogic validation, 288–289
Parker, L., 34
Participant as observer, 201
Participant observation, 106, 195, 201, 206
Patterns, 119
Patton, M. Q., 215, 221, 227, 229
Paulus, T. M., 193, 215, 234
Pei, J., 68
Pelias, R. J., 257, 260
Pereira, H., 91
Perry, B., 57
Phatshwane, K., 35
Phenomenological data analysis, 93
Phenomenological reflection, 90
Phenomenological research, 12, 76, 334–335, 365
challenges and opportunities, 94–95
data analysis and representation, 241–244, 243 (figure)
data procedures, 125 (table)
definition, 87
embedded writing structure, 272
evaluation, 305–307, 307 (figure)
features, 89–90, 89 (figure)
foundational considerations, 124 (table)
in-depth interviews, 196
origins, 87–88

overall writing structure, 270–272
participants, 182
procedures, 91–94, 92 (figure)
purpose statement, 164
qualitative studies, 139–141, 140–141 (table)
research questions, 167
research reporting, 126 (table)
subquestions, 170
types and variations, 90–91, 95–96
visual maps, 244 (figure)
Phenomenology of practice, 88
Phenomenon, 87
Phillips, D. C., 26
Philosophical assumptions, 17
axiological, 22 (table), 23
descriptions, 24–25
epistemological, 22 (table), 23
importance of philosophy, 21
and interpretive frameworks, research process, 18–19, 20 (figure), 25
methodological, 22 (table), 23
ontological, 22 (table), 23
overview, 17–18
in qualitative studies, 24
understanding of, 19
Philosophical perspectives, phenomenology, 88
Photo elicitation interviews, 195
St. Pierre, E. A., 286, 287 (table)
Piliriqatigiinniq, 25
Pinar, W. F., 359
Pinnegar, S., 86
Pitcher, G., 329, 329 (table), 330
Plano Clark, V. L., 37 (table), 67
Plummer, K., 35, 180, 304
Poland, S., 329, 329 (table), 330
Polkinghorne, D. E., 81, 91, 93, 196, 271, 304
Popper-Giveon, A., 293

Postcolonial theories, 34–35, 39 (table), 41 (table), 42 (table)
Postmodernism, 29–30, 37 (table), 41 (table)
Postpositivism, 26–27, 37 (table), 41 (table)
Post-secular society, 380
Poth, C., 3, 6 (table), 57, 58, 68, 184, 187
Power asymmetry, 207
Pragmatism, 30–31, 38 (table), 42 (table)
Prefigured coding scheme, 227
Prescott, W., 382
Priddis, H., 38 (table)
Principal Selection Committee, 202
Prochaska-Cue, M. K., 37 (table)
Progressive–regressive method, 269
Project memos, 223
Properties, 103, 245
Propositions, 99
Przybylski, L., 107
Purposeful case sampling, 119
Purposeful sampling, 175, 177
    participants, 189–190
    qualitative research, 188
    sample size, 192
    types, 190–191, 191 (table)
Purpose statement
    case study, 165
    definition, 155
    ethnographic research, 164
    grounded theory, 164
    narrative research, 163
    phenomenological research, 164
    qualitative research approaches, 162 (table)
    script, 161–162

QDA Miner, 235
Qualitative data analysis software (QDAS), 296, 299
    advantages and disadvantages, 233–234
    ATLAS.ti, 235
    Dedoose, 235
    definition, 215
    guidance for researchers, 234
    HyperRESEARCH, 235–236
    MAXQDA, 236
    NVivo, 236
    qualitative analysis tool, 232
    software programs, 215–216
    steps, 236–238
Qualitative data collection methods, 195–196
Qualitative research, 1, 299–303, 300 (figure), 319
    analysis strategies, 339–340
    characteristics, 5–8, 6 (table)
    complex account, 8
    complex reasoning, inductive/deductive logic, 7
    components, 159–161
    context-dependent, 7
    definition, 4–5
    emergent design, 7
    interpretive orientation, 338
    language use, 339
    multiple methods, 7
    natural setting, 5
    overview, 1–4
    participant samples, 339
    participants' perspectives/meanings, 7
    problem statement, 157–161, 158 (figure)
    reflexivity, 8
    report writing, 340
    researcher, key instrument, 5, 7
    research quality, 340
    study focus, 338
    study problem, purpose and questions, 156–157, 156 (figure)
    use, 48–49, 49 (figure)
Qualitative research approaches, 8–11, 9–10 (table), 75
    assessing, 76–77, 77 (figure)
    case study See Case study research
    ethnography See Ethnographic research
    grounded theory See Grounded theory research
    narrative See Narrative research
    overview, 75–76
    phenomenology See Phenomenological research
    research comparison, 123–128
    research focus, 76
    research outcome, 76
    research problem, 76
    research questions, 76
    unit of analysis, 76
Qualitative studies
    case study, 147–149, 148 (table)
    data analysis and representation, 239 (table)
    design ideas, 66–68
    differences, 149–152
    elements in phases, 56–57
    ethnographic study, 144–146, 145–146 (table)
    factors, 151–152
    features, 50–52, 51 (figure)
    foundational considerations, 150 (table)
    grounded theory, 135, 141–144, 143 (table)
    narrative study, 136–138, 137–138 (table)
    overview, 47–48
    phases in research process, 54–56, 55 (figure)
    phenomenological study, 139–141, 140–141 (table)
    preliminary considerations, 53–54
    process of, 53–57
    requirement, 49–50
    research ethics, 57–65
    research methods, 159
    writing proposal, structures, 68–70

Quality criteria, 285
Quayle, A. F., 87
Queer theory, 35, 39 (table), 42 (table)
Quirkos, 235
Qureshi, K., 375

Racial-gender leadership gap, 140, 273
Racialization, 144, 250, 370–375, 377–381
Rädiker, S., 232
Ravitch, S. M., 6 (table), 59, 223, 262
Realist ethnography, 109
Reciprocity 35, 40, 57, 62 (table), 72, 113, 175, 177, 179 (table), 188, 302, 312 (figure)
Recording information procedures, 203–205
Referential adequacy, 288
Reflexivity 5, 8, 14, 18, 29, 32, 35, 57, 72, 97, 101, 142, 143 (table), 175, 179 (table), 215, 220 (table), 257, 260, 290, 293, 302, 315 (table)
  collective, 57
  and representations, writing, 260–262
Reliability, intercoder agreement, 286, 296–299, 298 (figure)
Represent the data, 215
Research approaches, 75. *See also* Qualitative research approaches
Research design, 3
Research ethics
  AMRL cycle, 58, 59 (figure)
  analyzing data, 62 (table), 65
  beginning to conduct the study, 61 (table), 64
  collecting data, 61–62 (table), 64–65
  concern for justice, 58
  concern for welfare, 58
  ethical situations, 58–65, 60–63 (table)
  prior to conducting the study, 60 (table), 63–64
  publishing study, 63 (table), 65
  reporting data, 62–63 (table), 65
  respect for persons, 57–58
Research focus, 76
Research outcome, 76
Research problem, 76
Research quality assessment checklist, 50–52, 51 (figure)
Research questions, 76
  case study, 169
  central question, 166–169
  ethnography, 168
  grounded theory, 168
  narrative study, 167
  phenomenology, 167
  qualitative studies, 165
Research strategies, 19, 20 (figure)
Resilience, 140
Resilient leadership, 139
Respect for persons, 57–58
Responsive interviewing model, 198
Restorying, 81, 84
Retriggering, 327–328
Reutter, L., 164
Reynolds, W. M., 359
Rhetorical structure, 268
Rhizomatic validation, 289
Rhoads, R. A., 278
Rhodes, P., 38 (table), 67
Richards, L., 54, 208, 221, 229, 232, 294, 296, 297
Richardson, L., 260, 264, 279, 286, 287 (table), 290, 302
Riessman, C. K., 12, 78, 79, 81, 83, 238, 241, 268, 269, 303
Rigney, J., 105
Rigorous data collection procedures, 52
Roark, E. W., 322, 329, 329 (table)
Roark, M. L., 321, 322, 329, 329 (table)
Rodriguez, R., 347
Rolon-Dow, R., 348
Rorty, R., 30
Ross, V., 348
Rossman, G. B., 6 (table)
Roulston, K., 206
Rubin, H. J., 198
Rubin, I. S., 198
Ruohotie-Lyhty, M., 86
Rushdie, S., 378

The SAGE Handbook of Current Developments in Grounded Theory (Bryant & Charmaz), 97
The SAGE Handbook of Grounded Theory (Bryant & Charmaz), 97
Saldaña, J., 10 (table), 297
Salmona, M., 235
Salmons, J. E., 194 (figure)
Sample size, 192
Sampson, H., 199
Sanjek, R., 205
Sarroub, L. K., 347
Schensul, J. J., 6 (table), 107, 111, 197
School-based narrative inquiries, 358
School shooting, 147, 280–281, 391
Schroeder, K., 67
Schubert, W., 359
Schwandt, T. A., 27
Scott, G., 107
Second-order narratives, 182
Segment memos, 223
Selective coding, 99, 100, 103, 245–246
Self-reflection, 289
Self-study considerations, 182–183
Semi-structured interview, 196, 200
Shain, F., 383
Shildrick, M., 36
Shoptaw, S., 105
Shrum, W., 107
Sigurbjornsson, E., 95
Sigurdartottir, V., 95
Silver, C., 295
Silverman, D., 262, 300, 301

Slattery, P., 359
Slepicka, J., 147, 391
Ślęzak, I., 233
Slife, B. D., 9 (table)
Smith, J. A., 95
Smith, L. M., 269
Smith, M. L., 276
Smith-Hefner, N., 348
Social constructivism, 27–28, 37 (table), 41 (table)
Social justice theories, 26
Social-psychological theme, 333
Social science methodology development, 232
Social science publication, 302
Social science theories, 26
Social structure, 112
Sonn, C. C., 87
Sorrell, J. H., 25, 37 (table)
Sources of stress, 237
Spindler, G., 310
Spindler, L., 310
Spradley, J. P., 248
Stake, R. E., 115, 117, 118, 120, 147, 182, 251, 260, 280, 293, 295, 313, 333
Staples, A., 165
Stevick-Colaizzi-Keen method, 241
Stewart, A. J., 31
Stewart, D., 88
Stories, 79
Strauss, A., 9 (table), 12, 27, 97, 99, 100, 101, 104, 147, 189, 223, 245, 246, 257, 274, 307–308, 336
Stronach, M., 39 (table)
Structural description, 91, 93, 242
Structural form, 241
Student experiences, 346, 348
Subquestions, 166, 169–171
Substantive-level theory, 103, 151
Substantive validation, 289
Suddick, K. M., 244, 244 (figure)
Sudnow, D., 278
Suoninen, E., 206
Swanson, J. M., 275

Tan, E., 114
Taubman, P. M., 359
Taylor, L., 68
Tesch, R., 8, 91
Textural description, 91, 93
Thematic analysis, 11, 81, 137, 144, 229, 241, 250, 268
Themes, 215. *See also* Coding
Theoretical propositions, 336
Theoretical sampling, 100, 189
Theories or theoretical orientations, 19
Thomas, G., 13, 115, 121, 279, 313
Thomas, J., 30
Thornton, R., 105
Tierney, W. G., 262
Tisdell, E. J., 115
Toles, M. P., 122
Tolich, M., 59
Transana, 235
Transcendental phenomenology, 90–91
Transferability, 295
Transformative frameworks, 28–29, 37 (table), 41 (table)
Traustaddottir, R., 95
Travers, J. L., 67
Triangulation, 288
Trip, H., 136, 141, 143 (table), 151, 168, 171, 183, 187, 189, 246–247, 247 (figure), 293
Trujillo, N., 164
Trustworthiness, 286, 290
Tuhiwai Smith, L., 188

Unit of analysis, 76, 209
Unstructured interviews, 200
Usküp, D. K., 105
Ussher, J. M., 38 (table), 67

Valdes, G., 348
Validation, 285–286, 288
participants, 293–294
perspectives, 286–291, 287 (table)
readers/reviewer, 294–296
reliability, 296–299, 297 (figure)
researcher, 292–293
strategies, 291–296, 292 (figure)
Validity, 286
Van der Hoorn, B., 95, 195
Van Hout, M. C., 122
Van Kaam, A., 91
Van Kessel, G., 105
Van Maanen, J., 106–107, 109, 277
Van Manen, M., 12, 87, 88, 90, 91, 93, 94, 243, 271, 272, 304–306, 306 (figure)
Verisimilitude, 264
Violence prevention practices, 136, 147, 151, 391
Virtual focus groups, 194
Visual ethnography, 196
Visual model, 215, 335

Wade, V., 105
Wagner, J., 114
Walker, G., 329, 329 (table)
Wallace, A. F. C., 336
Weiner-Levey, N., 293
Weis, L., 58, 207, 261
Wertz, F. J., 262
Whelan, K., 269
White, R. S., 28, 37 (table)
Whitehead, L., 141
Whittemore, R., 286, 287 (table), 289
Williams, R. N., 9 (table)
Willis, P., 33
Willis, S. K., 105
Winthrop, R. H., 112
Within-case analysis, 120
Within-site case study, 115
Wolcott, H. F., 1, 8, 13, 107, 108, 111, 192, 201, 216–217, 216–217 (table), 247, 248, 277, 279, 286, 287 (table), 289, 337

Wong-Fillmore, L., 347, 352
Woodward, W., 147, 391
Writing structures, 75, 258
   audience, 262–263
   description, 257
   encoding, 263–264
   ethical considerations, 258–259, 258–259 (table)
   five approaches, 282–283
   general, 68–70
   quotes, 264–265
   reflexivity and representations, 260–262
   strategies, 259–265
   See also Embedded writing structures; Overall writing structures
Wyper, J., 68

Yalim, A. C., 68
Yazdannik, A., 38 (table)
Yin, R. K., 13, 27, 115, 117–119, 147, 197, 199, 251, 281, 312
Yussen, S. R., 238
Yuval-Davies, N., 374, 381

Zargham-Boroujeni, A., 38 (table)
Zelikoff, W. I., 329, 329 (table)
Zine, J., 347
Zoom videoconferencing software, 139, 200